Quattro Pro 2 Made Easy

Quattro Pro 2 Made Easy

Lisa Biow

Osborne **McGraw-Hill**
Berkeley New York St. Louis San Francisco
Auckland Bogotá Hamburg London Madrid
Mexico City Milan Montreal New Delhi Panama City
Paris São Paulo Singapore Sydney
Tokyo Toronto

Osborne **McGraw-Hill**
2600 Tenth Street
Berkeley, California 94710
U.S.A.

Osborne/McGraw-Hill offers software for sale. For information on software, translations, or book distributors outside of the U.S.A., please write to Osborne **McGraw-Hill** at the above address.

This book is printed on recycled paper.
This book was produced using Ventura Publisher Version 2.0.

Quattro Pro 2™ Made Easy

Copyright © 1990 by McGraw-Hill. All rights reserved. Printed in the United States of America. Except as permitted under the Copyright Act of 1976, no part of this publication may be reproduced or distributed in any form or by any means, or stored in a database or retrieval system, without the prior written permission of the publisher, with the exception that the program listings may be entered, stored, and executed in a computer system, but they may not be reproduced for publication.

1234567890 DOC 99876543210

ISBN 0-07-881656-4

Acquisitions Editor: Liz Fisher
Copy Editor: Barbara Conway
Word Processors: Lynda Higham, Judy Koplan, Stefany Otis
Composition: Bonnie Bozorg
Proofreaders: Julie Anjos, Jeff Green
Cover Design: Bay Graphics Design, Inc.
Production Supervisor: Kevin Shafer

Information has been obtained by Osborne McGraw-Hill from sources believed to be reliable. However, because of the possibility of human or mechanical error by our sources, Osborne McGraw-Hill, or others, Osborne McGraw-Hill does not guarantee the accuracy, adequacy, or completeness of any information and is not responsible for any errors or omissions or the results obtained from the use of such information.

CONTENTS AT A GLANCE

1	Getting Started	3
2	Entering Text and Numbers	29
3	Formulas	51
4	Rearranging the Spreadsheet	69
5	Formatting Your Spreadsheet	95
6	Printing Spreadsheets	123
7	Functions	155
8	More About Formulas	179
9	Advanced Editing and Formatting Commands	197
10	Dates and Times	217
11	Working with Windows	237
12	Customizing the Environment	261
13	Creating Graphs	275
14	Customizing Graphs	309
15	The Annotator	327
16	Designing and Building Databases	349
17	Sorting Your Database	367
18	Selecting Records from Your Database	375
19	Sensitivity Tables and Database Statistics	397

20	**Managing Your Files**	415
21	**The File Manager Utility**	431
22	**Combining, Extracting, and Linking Files**	449
23	**Introduction to Macros**	475
24	**Exchanging Data with Other Programs**	503
A	**New Features in Quattro Pro 2**	525
	Index	531

TABLE OF CONTENTS

Introduction   xxv
Why This Book Is for You   1

1   Getting Started **3**

A Few Basic Concepts   4
    What Is a Spreadsheet?   4
    What Is a Database?   5
    Graphics   7
Starting Up   7
The Quattro Pro Display   8
    The Spreadsheet Area   10
    The Input Line   10
    The Status Line   11
The Quattro Pro Keyboard   12
    Movement Keys   14
    Function Keys   15
The Quattro Pro Menu System   16
    The "Hold Everything" Keys   20
Getting Help   20
Using a Mouse in Quattro Pro   23
    Basic Mouse Techniques   23
    The Mouse Palette   24
    Mouse Practice   26
Leaving Quattro Pro   27

2   Entering Text and Numbers **29**

Entering Data   30
    Data Types   31
Changing Column Widths   34
    Menu Command Shortcuts   36
Label Alignment   36

　　　　Entering Numbers   39
　　　　Entering Dates   41
　　　　Editing Data   41
　　　　Saving and Retrieving Spreadsheets   45
　　　　　　Saving Your Spreadsheet for the First Time   45
　　　　　　Resaving Your Spreadsheet   47
　　　　　　Leaving Quattro Pro   48
　　　　　　Retrieving Files   48

3　Formulas **51**

　　　　Arithmetic Operators   52
　　　　Cell References   53
　　　　Automatic Recalculation   55
　　　　Pointing   58
　　　　Order of Calculation   59
　　　　Referencing Blocks of Cells   60
　　　　　　Designating Blocks   61
　　　　Common Mistakes in Formulas   62
　　　　　　Circular References   63
　　　　　　ERR Values   66
　　　　Building an Income Statement Model   67

4　Rearranging the Spreadsheet **69**

　　　　The Undo Feature   69
　　　　Inserting and Deleting Rows and Columns   71
　　　　　　Inserting Rows   71
　　　　　　Inserting Rows Within a Block   72
　　　　　　Deleting Rows   74
　　　　　　Inserting and Deleting Columns   75
　　　　Manipulating Blocks   75
　　　　　　Pointing Out Blocks in Commands   76
　　　　　　Copying Cells   80
　　　　　　Copying Formulas   84
　　　　　　Notes of Caution on Moving and Copying Blocks   87
　　　　　　Using the (END) Key to Define Large Blocks   88
　　　　　　Erasing a Block   90
　　　　Putting Blocks to Work on Your Spreadsheet   90

5　Formatting Your Spreadsheet **95**

　　　　Default Formats   96
　　　　Adjusting Column Widths   96
　　　　　　Changing the Width of Several Columns at Once   98

        Display Formats   99
            The Default Format Setting   99
            Quattro Pro's 10 Display Formats   101
            Changing the Spreadsheet's Numeric Format   103
            Changing the Numeric Format of a Block   105
            The Text (Show Formulas) Format   108
        Aligning Blocks of Data   110
            Aligning Labels   110
            Aligning Numeric Values   112
        More About Default Formats   113
            Hiding Zeros   114
            The Advantages of Default Formats   114
        Line Drawing and Shading   114
            Drawing Lines on the Spreadsheet   115
            Shading Cells   119

6 Printing Spreadsheets 123

        Selecting Printers   124
            Telling Quattro Pro About Your Printers   124
            Using a Serial Printer   125
            Switching Between Two Printers   126
            Other Options on the Options| Hardware | Printers
                Menu   126
            Saving Your Printer Specifications   127
        Standard Quattro Pro Reports   127
            Draft-Quality Versus High-Quality Printing   130
        Page Layout   132
            Adding Headers and Footers   132
            Setting Margins and Page Length   132
            Using Setup Strings   133
            Printing in Landscape Mode   135
            Saving Print Settings   136
            Other Layout Options   136
        Printing Large Spreadsheets   137
            Inserting Page Breaks   139
        Using Fonts   141
        Using Bitstream Fonts   142
            Applying Fonts for Sections of the Report   143
            Editing Fonts   143
            Using Different Fonts to Print LEARN1.WQ1   145
            Problems with Fonts   146
        The Screen Previewer   149

Special Print Options   153
    Printing Formulas   153
    Adding Bullets to a Report   153

7 Functions 155

Types of Functions   156
Function Syntax   157
The Functions Key   158
Basic Statistical Functions   159
    @SUM   159
    @COUNT   160
    @AVG   160
    @MAX AND @MIN   161
    Blank Cells and Labels in Statistical Functions   161
Functions for Dropping Decimal Places   162
    @ROUND   163
    @INT   166
    @IF   166
Complex Operators   168
@VLOOKUP and @HLOOKUP   170
String Functions   174
    @UPPER   175
    @PROPER   175
    @LENGTH   175
    @REPEAT   175
    @CHAR   176
Getting Help with Functions   176

8 More About Formulas 179

Absolute Versus Relative Cell Referencing   180
    Mixed Cell References   184
Using Named Blocks   185
    Naming a Block   187
    The Choices Key   188
    An Exercise in Naming Cells   188
    Changing and Deleting Block Names   190
    Naming Blocks Using Adjacent Labels   190
    Creating a Table of Block Names   191
Converting Formulas to Their Values   192

9 Advanced Editing and Formatting Commands 197

Searching and Replacing   198
    Conducting Simple Searches   198
    The Search Block   199
    The Search Direction   199
    Performing the Search   200
    The Other Search & Replace Options   201
Filling a Block with Values   204
Reformatting Text   206
Transposing Blocks   209
Hiding and Exposing Columns   211
Protecting Your Spreadsheet   213

10 Dates and Times 217

Working with Dates   218
    Date Arithmetic   220
    Date Functions   221
    Using Functions to Enter Dates   225
    Creating Month Headings   228
Working with Times   231
    The @NOW Function   232
    The @TIMEVALUE Function   234
    Time Arithmetic   234

11 Working with Windows 237

Customizing Individual Windows   238
    Using Titles   238
    Eliminating Column and Row Borders   243
    Splitting a Window in Two   243
    Synchronizing Panes   245
    Map View   246
Opening and Closing Windows   248
    Moving Among Windows   249
Rearranging and Resizing Windows   250
    Tiling and Stacking Windows   250
    Zooming Windows   252
    Moving and Resizing Windows   252
Experimenting with Multiple Windows   254
Saving and Retrieving Workspaces   256
Copying and Moving Data Between Windows   257

12 Customizing the Environment 261

Default Settings   261
    Telling Quattro Pro About Your Hardware   262
    Customizing Quattro Pro's Colors   263
    The International Settings   265
    Changing the Display Mode   267
    Defining Startup Settings   268
    Changing the Mouse Palette   269
    The "Other" Default Settings   269
    Recalculation Settings   270
    Updating the System Defaults   271
Creating Style Sheets   272
Menu Command Shortcuts   272

13 Creating Graphs 275

Choosing a Graph Type   275
    Line Graphs   276
    Bar Graphs   276
    Area Graphs   279
    Pie Graphs   280
    Column Graphs   280
    XY Graphs   281
    High-Low (Open-Close) Graphs   283
    Text Graphs   284
    Three-Dimensional Graph Types   285
    The Graphing Process   285
    Adding Text to Your Graph   287
    Hands-On Practice   289
    Shortcuts for Creating Graphs   292
    Naming and Restoring Graphs   297
    Resetting Series and Graphs   298
    Defining Pie Graphs and Column Graphs   298
    Defining XY Graphs   300
Printing Graphs   301
    Adjusting Print Speed and Quality   303
    Autoscaling Fonts   303
    Changing the Graph Print Layout   303
    Updating Graph Print Options   304
    "Printing" to Disk   305
    Graph Slide Shows   305
Inserting Graphs in a Spreadsheet   306

Printing an Inserted Graph   307

14 Customizing Graphs 309

Customizing Series   309
    Customizing Colors   310
    Altering Fill Patterns   310
    Relationship Between Series and
        Pie/Column Slices   310
    Changing Lines and Markers   311
    Changing the Width of Bars   312
    Labeling Points on a Graph   312
    Overriding the Graph Type   313
    Using a Second Y-Axis   314
    Resetting Graph Settings   315
    Updating Graph Settings   315
Customizing Pie and Column Graphs   316
    Changing the Label Format   316
    Eliminating Tick Marks   317
    Changing Pie or Column Fill Patterns   318
    Altering Colors   319
    Exploding Pie Slices   319
    Using a Second Series to Customize Pie
        and Column Graphs   319
Customizing the Axes   320
    Scaling Axes Manually   320
    Changing the Tick Marks   321
    Eliminating the Scaling Display   322
    Logarithmic Scaling   322
Customizing Graphs as a Whole   322
    Customizing Grid Lines   324
    Framing the Graph   324
    Changing the Background Color   325
    Displaying Graphs in Black and White   325
    Eliminating the Three-Dimensional Effect   326

15 The Annotator 327

The Annotator Environment   328
    The Annotator Screen   328
    The Toolbox   330
Adding Text and Lines to the Graph   332
    Hands-On Practice   334
Modifying Graph Elements   336

            Resizing Elements   337
            Changing Design Properties   337
            Modifying Several Elements at Once   338
            Modifying Non-Annotator Elements   339
    Fine-Tuning Text Elements   340
            Editing Text Elements   340
            Changing Text Design Properties   340
            Creating Text Graphs   341
    Drawing Curves   342
    Linking Elements to Points on the Graph   342
    Using the Clipboard   344
            Cutting and Pasting Graph Elements   344
            Creating and Using Clip Art Files   345
            Moving Elements Between Foreground and
                Background   347

16   Designing and Building Databases 349

    Database Terminology   350
    Designing a Database   351
            Field Content   351
            Values or Labels?   351
            Field Order and Length   352
            Field Names   352
            Cell Referencing in Databases   353
    Data Entry Commands   355
    Building a Sample Database   355
    Adding and Deleting Records   360
    Modifying Your Database   362
            Improving the ORDERS Database   363

17   Sorting Your Database 367

    The Sorting Process   368
    Sort Order   368
    Single-Key Sorts   369
    Multiple-Key Sorts   371
    Undoing a Sort   371
    Changing the Sort Rules   373

18   Selecting Records from Your Database 375

    Database Query Commands   375
            Preparing a Query   376
    Criteria Tables   377

Exact Matches   377
Using Wild Cards   378
Locating Records One at a Time   379
The Query Key   379
Hands-on Practice   379
Defining Complex Searches in a Criteria Table   381
Using Formulas in a Criteria Table   383
Complex Conditions in Logical Formulas   386
Using More Than One Complex Operator in a Condition   386
Putting Your Selections to Work   387
Extracting Records   387
Extracting Unique Records   388
Deleting Selected Records   391
Resetting the Query Settings   391
Database Statistical Functions   391
The @DCOUNT Function   392
The @DSUM Function   392
The @DAVG Function   393
The @DMAX and @DMIN Functions   393

19 Sensitivity Tables and Database Statistics   397

Sensitivity Tables   398
Setting Up a One-Variable Table   398
Setting Up a Two-Variable Table   402
Using [F8] to Recalculate Sensitivity Tables   404
Using Sensitivity Tables with Databases   405
Creating Frequency Distribution Tables   411

20 Managing Your Files   415

Using Different Directories   415
Loading Quattro Pro from Other Directories   416
Changing the Default Directory   417
Using Subdirectories   417
Manipulating File Lists   418
Displaying More Informative File Lists   418
Searching Through File Lists   419
Displaying More Specific File Lists   419
Shortcuts for Retrieving Files   420
Using Passwords   421
Managing Disk Space   422
Compressing Files   423

Managing Memory   424
    How Memory Is Utilized   424
    Determining How Much Memory Is Available   425
    Estimating How Much Memory You Need   426
    Running Out of Memory   426
    Recovering Memory   427
    Expanded Memory   428
Backing Up Files   429
Exiting to the Operating System   430

21 The File Manager Utility 431

The File Manager Window   432
The Control Pane   433
    Switching Drives or Directories   433
    Selecting Files to Display   434
    Opening a File   434
    Searching for a File   435
    Changing the Startup Directory   435
The File List Pane   436
    Sorting File Lists   438
Manipulating Files   438
    Selecting Files   440
    Opening Files   440
    Copying Files   441
    Copying a Group of Files to Multiple Disks   442
    Moving Files   442
    Deleting Files   443
    Duplicating Files   443
    Renaming Files   443
Displaying and Using Directory Trees   444
    Resizing the Directory Tree   445
Other File Manager Options   446
    Rereading the File List   447
    Making Directories   447
    Printing the Contents of a File Manager Window   447

22 Combining, Extracting, and Linking Files 449

Extracting Files   449
    Copying or Moving Versus Extracting Data   450
Combining Files   450
    The / Tools I Combine I Copy Command   452
    The / Tools I Combine I Add Command   452

　　　　　The / Tools I Combine I Subtract Command   453
　　　　　　　Hands-On Practice   453
　　　Linking Spreadsheets   457
　　　　　Creating Spreadsheet Links   459
　　　　　Hands-on Practice   462
　　　　　Opening Linked Spreadsheets   466
　　　　　Linking Spreadsheets Hierarchically   467
　　　　　Updating Spreadsheet Links   468
　　　　　Copying and Moving Link Formulas   470
　　　　　Graphing Linked Spreadsheets   471
　　　　　Linking Versus Combining Files   473

23 Introduction to Macros 475

　　　Creating Macros   476
　　　　　Recording Macros   476
　　　　　　A Macro for Date-Stamping a Spreadsheet   478
　　　Pasting Macros into the Spreadsheet   478
　　　　　Naming Macros   479
　　　　　Where to Store Your Macros   480
　　　Interpreting Macros   481
　　　Editing Macros   487
　　　Sample Database Macros   488
　　　Applications for Recorded Macros   493
　　　Introduction to the Macro Language   495
　　　Maintaining and Using Macros   495
　　　　　Documenting Your Macros   495
　　　　　Renaming and Deleting Macros   496
　　　　　Copying Macros to Another Spreadsheet   497
　　　　　Using Macro Libraries   497
　　　　　Changing the Macro Recording Method   499
　　　Playing Macros Automatically   501
　　　　　Startup Macros   501
　　　　　Autoloading Macros   501

24 Exchanging Data with Other Programs 503

　　　Exchanging Data with Lotus 1-2-3 and Symphony   504
　　　　　Trading Macros with Lotus 1-2-3   504
　　　　　Trading Data with Other Spreadsheet Programs   504
　　　　　The "Desktop Settings Are Removed" Message   505
　　　Trading Data with Paradox, dBASE, and Reflex   505
　　　　　Reading Paradox, Reflex, and dBASE Files   506
　　　　　Writing Paradox, Reflex, and dBASE Files   507

        Modifying the File Structure   508
        dBASE Memo Fields   509
        Potential Problems in Exchanging Data with
           Database Programs   510
        Linking to External Databases   511
   Exporting Data to Word Processing Software   513
   Exporting Data to Other Types of Software   514
   Importing Data into Quattro Pro   515
        Importing Delimited Files   516
   Parsing ASCII Text Files   517
        Creating Format Lines   519
        Editing Format Lines   521
        Defining Input and Output Blocks   523
        Initiating the Parse   524

A   New Features in Quattro Pro 2 525

Solve For   526
New Display Options   526
Paradox Access   527
Improved Laserjet Printing   527
Support for the Lotus 1-2-3 Release 2.2 File Format   527
Three-Dimensional Graph Types   528
Graph Buttons   528
Copying Graphs   529
Saving Graphs in Slide EPS and PCX Formats   529
Importing CGM Clip Art   530

Index 531

For Deborah

FOREWORD

Quattro Pro 2 Made Easy is the ideal book for the first-time spreadsheet user. Readers will find their skills building quickly as they follow author Lisa Biow in this tutorial approach to learning Quattro Pro 2. Here, in one easy-to-read and well organized volume, is an introduction to what Quattro Pro 2 is and what it can do.

After presenting a detailed explanation of the basic spreadsheet operations, Biow carefully leads you to an understanding of Quattro Pro 2's functions. By the time you have finished *Quattro Pro 2 Made Easy*, you will know how to build databases in Quattro Pro 2 and how to show off your work with Quattro Pro 2's outstanding graphics and printing capabilities. You will be able to take advantage of Quattro Pro 2's incredible speed. You will even be familiar with Quattro Pro 2's powerful macro language, which allows you to take time-saving shortcuts and to customize Quattro Pro 2.

In short, *Quattro Pro 2 Made Easy* teaches beginning spreadsheet users how to use Quattro Pro 2 quickly and efficiently.

Philippe Kahn
President
Borland International, Inc.

ACKNOWLEDGMENTS

This book would never have happened without considerable help from my friends. Thanks to my acquisitions editor Liz Fisher for talking me into this project and then valiantly juggling a tight production schedule, to associate editor Wendy Goss, for her patience with screen dump problems, and technical reviewers Sydney Drake and Clifford Krouse for their attention to detail and helpful suggestions.

Last but never least, thanks to my partner and friend Miriam Liskin for getting me into this business in the first place, teaching me much of what I know, reading every chapter, lending me her 386 and her VW bug, and showing up with cappuccinos when I needed them most. This book would truly never have happened without her.

INTRODUCTION

When it was introduced in 1989, Quattro Pro was heralded as one of the most exciting software packages ever. Version 2, released in the fall of 1990, added even more features to an already rich product.

Quattro Pro 2 is a combination spreadsheet, database, and graphics program that is both easy to use and extremely powerful. Given the range of its capabilities, Quattro Pro 2 can be used by almost anyone who needs to work with numbers, rapidly organize and access information, or speculate with different sets of data. Quattro Pro 2 is also extremely adaptable, providing a range of options for customizing the program to your own taste, informational needs, and style of working. And while newcomers to Quattro Pro 2 (and to spreadsheets in general) can learn to build functional worksheets in a matter of hours, experts will find that the program provides all the features, speed, and versatility they need.

ABOUT THIS BOOK

Quattro Pro 2's set of tools for entering, organizing, and extracting information include hundreds of commands, 113 special operators known as functions, and nineteen special function keys. Although this book does not cover all of these tools in depth, it introduces you to most of them. More important, it provides you with a thorough grounding in the basic concepts of spreadsheet organization and design; you can build on this foundation as you continue to explore Quattro Pro 2's more esoteric elements on your own.

This book presumes no experience with spreadsheets, graphics, or databases, although it does assume that you know how to turn your computer on, are familiar with the basic keyboard layout, and have a rudimentary knowledge of DOS (the disk operating system for IBM PCs and compatibles). If you are not familiar with DOS, you should read the appendix entitled "A DOS Primer" in your Quattro Pro 2 user's guide before installing or working with Quattro Pro 2.

While you don't need to know anything about Quattro Pro 2 to read this book, you can expect to know quite a bit by the time you finish. Most chapters alternate between explanations of new ideas and techniques, and instructions for trying them out yourself. In general, the discussion of each command and function not only covers what that tool does, but also how and when to apply it. The emphasis is on general concepts--how a spreadsheet works or the implications of Quattro Pro 2's way of linking different items of data through formulas, for example—as well as on specific techniques.

This book assumes that you will be working primarily with the regular Quattro Pro 2 menu tree, rather than with the alternate menu tree, which uses a command structure similar to that of Lotus 1-2-3.

HOW TO LEARN A NEW PROGRAM

If you are new to electronic spreadsheets, the good news is that they are not only extremely useful, they are also fun. Creating your own models, changing a few numbers and watching the effects ripple instantly through the data, and creating graphics can be dramatic and exciting. Because you can learn Quattro Pro 2's fundamentals quickly, the rewards are almost immediate.

Perhaps the most important assets you can bring to the learning process are a sense of adventure and a willingness to experiment. As mentioned, this book will walk you through most of the commands and techniques that Quattro Pro 2 offers, providing hands-on practice exercises wherever possible. You should use these exercises as a starting point, applying what you learn to data and situations of your own choosing. Often the best way to prove that you really understand a concept is to generalize from what you have read, putting a new tool to work in a different context. Try, when possible, to use real-life examples, drawn from your business area of study. The more you apply Quattro Pro 2 to the problems that concern you, the more you will appreciate Quattro Pro 2's potential and the more likely you will be to remember particular commands and techniques.

In drawing exercises from your business, however, be wary of letting your work in Quattro Pro 2 become too practical too soon. While you are learning Quattro Pro 2, your emphasis should remain on increasing your knowledge and confidence rather than on immediate productivity. If you need to put Quattro Pro 2 to immediate practical use, try to set aside some additional time to simply experiment without pressure of deadlines and without any goal other than increasing your mastery of the program.

As you follow the exercises in this book, you should also be aware that there is often more than one way to accomplish something in Quattro Pro 2. If the text dictates one method of doing something and you think of another, try it your own way. In some cases, you will discover that the particular commands or sequence of actions used in the text were chosen for some objective reason; in other cases, you will find that the choice was simply a matter of taste and that you are free to use whichever method feels most natural to you.

For those of you who are new to computers and are wary of rampant experimentation; no command or random set of characters that you type in Quattro Pro 2 can in any way harm your equipment. At worst, you can damage or erase part of your data, making it necessary to redo some work. Assuming you are working with practice data, such mishaps are hardly worth worrying about, and in any case potential damage can be minimized by frequently saving your work to disk and backing up your data files.

HOW THIS BOOK IS ORGANIZED

This book is organized into several groups of chapters that introduce you to and then explore each of Quattro Pro 2's major functional areas. Chapters 1 through 6 cover the basics of creating and using Quattro Pro 2 worksheets, including entering and editing data, saving and retrieving worksheets, manipulating blocks of data, rearranging and formatting worksheets, and printing reports. Chapters 7 through 12 build on that foundation, introducing more advanced concepts and techniques for manipulating your data, including the use of functions, as well as methods of customizing Quattro Pro 2 to your own work style.

Chapters 13 through 15 cover all the fundamentals of designing, displaying, printing, and customizing graphs. Chapters 16 through 19 cover everything you need to know about creating and using Quattro Pro 2 databases, and about sensitivity (or "what if") and statistical tables. Chapters 20 through 24 cover more advanced topics, including commands for combining worksheet files, file management techniques, macros (miniprograms that allow you to initiate an entire series of actions with a single keystroke), and importing and exporting data to and from other software packages.

Appendix A summarizes the new features that were added to Quattro Pro with version 2, including the four new three-dimensional graph types, a "solver" utility, new screen display options, improved integration with Paradox database management systems, and much more.

Depending on your needs and your schedule, you might work your way through this book in a matter of a few weeks, or you may decide to cover only a section at a time, postponing your study of graphs or databases until you have a need for those functions, for example. If you do decide to take a break before finishing the book, you should at least skim Chapter 20, which covers File Management. Although you may have a little trouble understanding all of it if you have not read the previous chapters, you can at least pick up the basic concepts and learn some important techniques that can greatly enhance your work.

CONVENTIONS USED IN THIS BOOK

The following terms and conventions are used throughout this book for consistency and ease of understanding:

- Special keyboard keys are printed in small capitals, as in (PGUP) or (HOME).
- Characters that you are supposed to type are displayed in boldface within numbered sequences.
- The word "type" means just type the characters indicated, while "enter" means type the characters indicated and then press the (ENTER) key.
- File names, block names, and cell references are always shown in uppercase, but entering them in lowercase will yield the same results.

WHY THIS BOOK IS FOR YOU

If you've heard a lot about the exciting features of Quattro Pro 2 and are anxious to find out what they are and how to use them effectively, this book is for you. You don't have to know anything about spreadsheets to use this book. The new ideas and concepts that form the basis of Quattro Pro 2 are clearly explained, coupled with step-by-step practical examples that show how they really work.

By using this book, you will rapidly learn the fundamentals of Quattro Pro 2 and be able to apply them to real life data. Your time will be well spent since minimal effort will give you immediate rewards. With this book as your guide, you will be able to create your own models and translate them into a variety of graphics that illustrate your results dramatically. If you want to quickly put Quattro Pro 2 to use as well as get the most from the program, *Quattro Pro 2 Made Easy* is the tool you need.

1

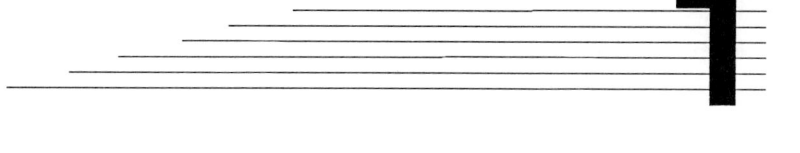

GETTING STARTED

A Few Basic Concepts
Starting Up
The Quattro Pro Display
The Quattro Pro Keyboard
The Quattro Pro Menu System
Getting Help
Leaving Quattro Pro

Quattro Pro 2 is a software package that combines three types of programs: spreadsheet, graphics, and database management. It is designed for organizing and manipulating data, particularly numeric data, and for translating that data into graphic form.

    This book acquaints you with both the basic techniques of using Quattro Pro and the essential concepts of spreadsheet, graph, and database design. By following the examples in the next six chapters, you will learn everything you need to know to build simple spreadsheets. From there you can delve into more advanced techniques, and then branch out into database management and into graphs.

A FEW BASIC CONCEPTS

Before you begin working with Quattro Pro, you need to understand what spreadsheets, databases, and graphs are and what you can do with them.

What Is a Spreadsheet?

A *spreadsheet* is a grid of rows and columns in which you enter, edit, and view data. A spreadsheet program, such as Quattro Pro, is like an electronic ledger pad—it presents you with a largely empty screen on which you can enter and manipulate numbers and text.

Spreadsheets can be employed for everything from the simplest expense reports to the most complex loan calculations or statistical analyses. Some of the more typical applications are budgets, income statements, profit and loss projections, portfolio analyses, schedules of accounts payable and receivable, production schedules, statistical analyses, loan analyses, and tax statements.

When you use a spreadsheet program, you generally begin by entering numbers and descriptive text; then you enter instructions that tell the program how to manipulate those numbers. For example, you might start a budget by entering a list of line items in one column, and then enter corresponding dollar amounts in the next column to the right. At the bottom of the numbers column, you would enter a set of instructions, known as a *formula,* directing the program to add all the numbers and display the result. A simple personal budget appears in Figure 1-1.

At this level the spreadsheet acts as little more than a glorified calculator. However, unlike a calculator, Quattro Pro offers the following capabilities:

- **Automatic recalculation** Once you have told the spreadsheet program what calculations to perform, you can "plug in" any set of numbers and the results are updated automatically. For example, as soon as you change the amount allocated for food in the budget shown in Figure 1-1, the total changes to reflect that modification. This capacity for automatic recalculation makes spreadsheets ideal for testing the effects of changing one or more items of data.

- **Ability to perform sophisticated calculations** While Quattro Pro can easily perform addition and subtraction, it also can handle over 100 other types of calculations, including financial, mathematical, and statistical calculations. Once you learn how to state the instructions to Quattro Pro, calculating loan payments on a car is about as difficult as 2 + 2.

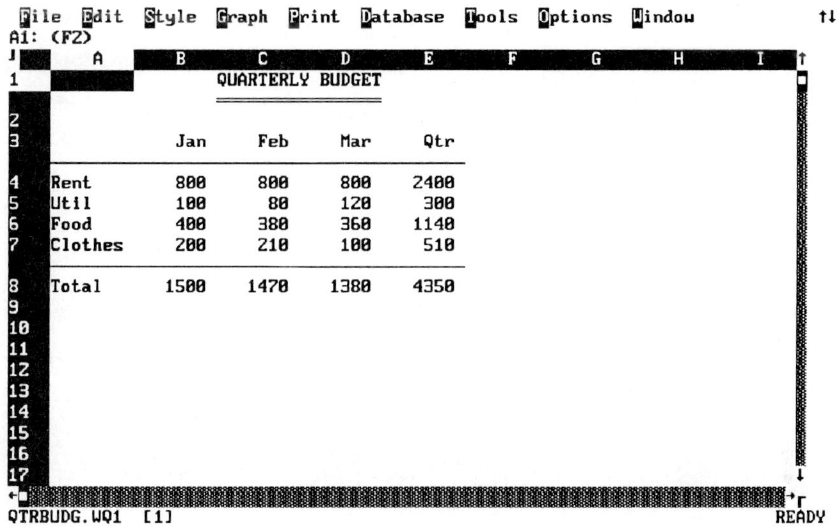

FIGURE 1-1. A simple budget

- **Ability to link spreadsheets**   In Quattro Pro, you can easily create spreadsheets that consolidate data entered in several other spreadsheet files. You might, for example, create separate files for each department, product line, or month in the year, and then design a single spreadsheet that calculates the totals for all departments, products, or months.

- **Macros**   As you work with any program, you inevitably find yourself repeating particular sequences of keystrokes. Quattro Pro allows you to create macros (which are like miniature programs) to automate such sequences. Using a macro is similar to speed-dialing on a telephone: You press one button and the machine responds as if you had pressed a series of buttons, one after another.

What Is a Database?

A *database* is any structured collection of data about people, organizations, or things. There are two characteristics that distinguish databases from other groups of data: how they are structured and how they are used. A database includes the same categories of information for every person, organization, or thing it contains. A phone book, for example, is a database of people and businesses that contains the names, addresses,

```
  File Edit Style Graph Print Database Tools Options Window           ↑↓
  B11: [W13] 'Barnes
         A            B           C       D       E              F
   1  PERSONNEL DATABASE, 1/1/91
   2
   3  FIRSTNAME    LASTNAME    HIRED    DEPT   POSITION          SALARY
   4  Marla        Cooper      10/01/86 FIN    Junior Accountant 24,000
   5  Dennis       Matthews    10/01/86 FIN    Accountant        28,000
   6  William      Weiss       11/15/86 MIS    Junior Programmer 19,500
   7  Alicia       Tower       03/04/87 MIS    Senior Programmer 30,500
   8  Timothy      Walker      03/21/87 MIS    Systems Analyst   38,000
   9  Richard      Curry       08/06/87 PER    Accounting Clerk  16,000
  10  Pat          Hernandez   11/12/87 MIS    Data Entry Clerk  15,000
  11  Carol        Barnes      01/04/88 FIN    Executive Secretary 22,000
  12  Thelma       Morgan      01/16/88 MIS    Junior Programmer 19,000
  13  John         Mcdermott   04/18/88 PER    Senior Accountant 40,000
  14  Lynne        Diamond     10/15/88 PER    Admin Asst        19,000
  15  Alan         Frank       02/03/89 FIN    Data Entry Clerk  16,000
  16  Martha       Walker      04/17/89 FIN    Accountant        32,000
  17  Lauren       Albert      11/05/89 MIS    Senior Programmer 26,000
  18  Anne         Mason       08/02/89 MIS    Data Entry Clerk  15,500
  19  Hector       Santiago    05/12/90 MIS    Admin Asst        20,500
  PERS.WK1    [1]                                                 READY
```

FIGURE 1-2. A personnel database

and phone numbers for a set of individuals or organizations. A customer list might include the name, contact person, address, phone, date of last order, and credit limit for each organization on the list. In the personnel database shown in Figure 1-2, the categories of information include first name, last name, date hired, department code, position, and salary.

In a Quattro Pro database, each column represents a single category of information, and the information for each person, organization, or thing in the database is located on a single row. You might not fill in every column of every row, but you leave space for every category of data.

Databases are also distinguished from other groups of data by the types of operations you perform on them. The operations you can perform on databases include the following:

- Sorting the data into a particular order

- Isolating data that meet particular criteria

- Generating summary information or statistics

These operations form the crux of *database management*—the process of organizing, manipulating, and extracting information from databases.

In Quattro Pro, a database is simply an area of a spreadsheet that you decide to treat as a database. When you work with a database, you use the same keys and many of the same commands that you would use when working with any other type of data on a spreadsheet. The only difference lies in the way you manipulate the data.

Graphics

Quattro Pro's third capability is displaying and printing graphs. Used properly, graphs are a succinct and engaging way to present information. They allow you to summarize a tremendous amount of data in a format that is easy to grasp.

Quattro Pro allows you to translate data from your spreadsheet or database into a graphic format quickly and easily. It offers 10 types of graphs: bar graphs (standard, stacked, and rotated), line graphs, column graphs, area charts, high-low graphs, XY graphs, pie charts, and text graphs.

While Quattro Pro makes it easy to create simple graphs, it also provides an extensive array of tools for customizing and embellishing graphs. The graph in Figure 1-3 shows that Quattro Pro's features rival those of any graphics program on the market. You can mix graph types, change the fill patterns and colors, alter the size and typefaces of titles, and add labels to particular points in the graph. Quattro Pro's Annotator feature also lets you add descriptive elements—such as arrows and lines, boxes, or floating text, and custom-drawn shapes or pictures.

STARTING UP

If you have not yet installed Quattro Pro, refer to Appendix A for instructions and install it now. The first step in starting Quattro Pro is to switch to the Quattro Pro directory, using the DOS change directory (CD) command. The form for this command is

CD \ *directory name*

For example, if Quattro Pro is stored in a directory called QPRO on drive C, you type **CD \QPRO** and press (ENTER).

The next step is to load the Quattro Pro program. To do this, type **Q** and press (ENTER).

Load Quattro Pro now so that you can follow the examples in the remainder of this chapter.

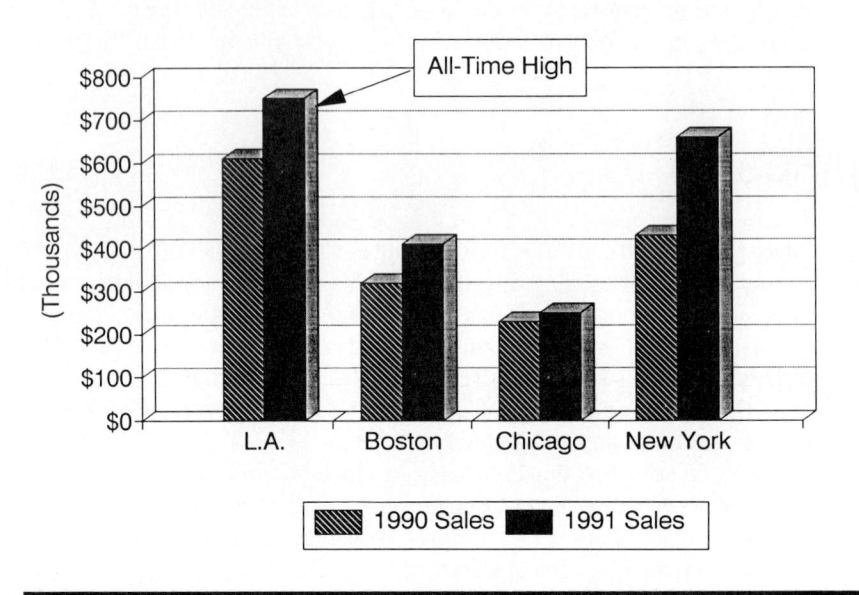

FIGURE 1-3. A presentation-quality graph

THE QUATTRO PRO DISPLAY

The Quattro Pro display consists of four sections, as shown in Figure 1-4.

- **The main menu bar** A list of nine options (File, Edit, Style, and so on) on the first line of the screen
- **The input line** The line immediately below the menu bar at the top of the screen
- **The spreadsheet area** The majority of the Quattro Pro display, bounded by a column of numbers along its left edge, a row of numbers across its top, and shaded bars at the right and bottom edges

Getting Started 9

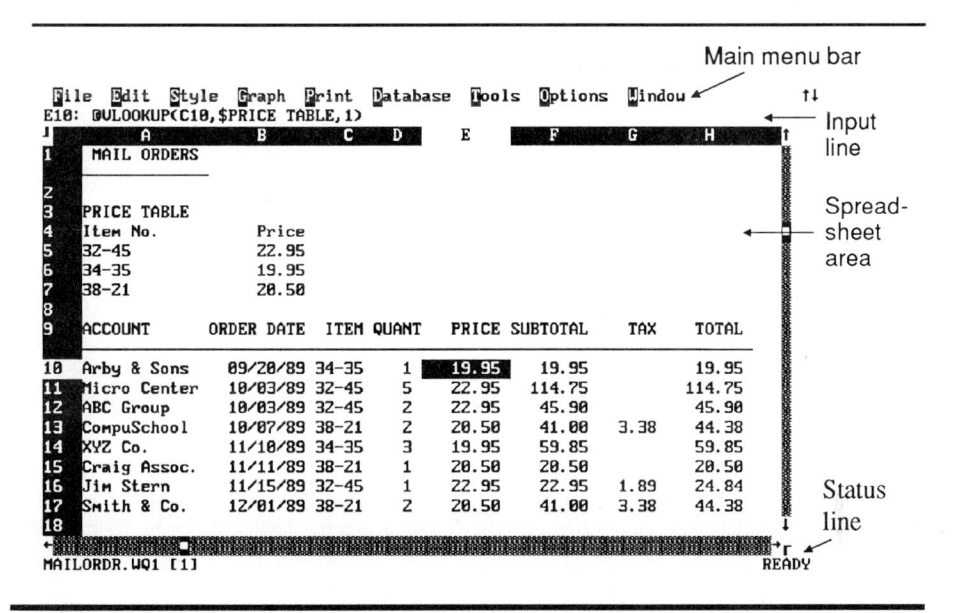

```
                                                            Main menu bar
        File Edit Style Graph Print Database Tools Options Window    ↑↓
        E10: @VLOOKUP(C10,$PRICE TABLE,1)                         ←───  Input
              A          B          C    D     E       F      G     H        line
         1   MAIL ORDERS
         2
         3   PRICE TABLE                                                  Spread-
         4   Item No.        Price                                    ←── sheet
         5   32-45           22.95                                        area
         6   34-35           19.95
         7   38-21           20.50
         8
         9   ACCOUNT     ORDER DATE  ITEM QUANT  PRICE SUBTOTAL  TAX  TOTAL
        10   Arby & Sons   09/20/89  34-35   1   19.95   19.95         19.95
        11   Micro Center  10/03/89  32-45   5   22.95  114.75        114.75
        12   ABC Group     10/03/89  32-45   2   22.95   45.90         45.90
        13   CompuSchool   10/07/89  38-21   2   20.50   41.00  3.38   44.38
        14   XYZ Co.       11/10/89  34-35   3   19.95   59.85         59.85
        15   Craig Assoc.  11/11/89  38-21   1   20.50   20.50         20.50
        16   Jim Stern     11/15/89  32-45   1   22.95   22.95  1.89   24.84
        17   Smith & Co.   12/01/89  38-21   2   20.50   41.00  3.38   44.38   Status
        18                                                                    line
        MAILORDR.WQ1 [1]                                            READY
```

FIGURE 1-4. Sections of the Quattro Pro display

- **The status line** The last line of the Quattro Pro display, immediately below the spreadsheet area

If you have installed a mouse and loaded your mouse software, a fifth section, known as the *mouse palette,* appears at the right edge of the screen.

The spreadsheet area, input line, and status line are discussed here. The menu bar and mouse palette are covered in the sections "The Quattro Pro Menu System" and "Using a Mouse in Quattro Pro."

Note If the menu bar at the top of your screen contains the options Worksheet, Range, Copy, Move, and others, Quattro Pro has been configured to use the Lotus 1-2-3 style menus rather than the regular Quattro Pro menus. To follow the examples in this book, you must change to the Quattro Pro menu tree by issuing the / **Worksheet | Global | Default | Files | Menu Tree** command and selecting QUATTRO.MU. You will find instructions for issuing commands later in this chapter. After using the / **Worksheet | Global | Default | Files | Menu Tree** command, be sure to issue the / **Options | Update** command to save the new menu tree setting.

The Spreadsheet Area

The spreadsheet area is the section in which you enter and view spreadsheet data. This area is actually a window onto a much larger spreadsheet surface. The entire surface of a Quattro Pro spreadsheet is 256 columns wide and 8192 rows long. (Columns are labeled A through Z, AA through AZ, BA through BZ, and so on up to IV.)

As you will see, you can move this window to view different sections of the spreadsheet. You can even split the spreadsheet area into sections and view two or more parts of the same spreadsheet or parts of different spreadsheets at the same time. The important thing to note is that what you see on the screen is only a small part of a large landscape: there may be more data beyond the borders of your display and there is definitely more room for data.

The spreadsheet area consists of individual *cells*—rectangles formed by the intersection of one row and one column. Every piece of data that you enter into a spreadsheet is placed in a single cell. Each cell is referred to by its column letter and row number. Cell A1, for example, is located in the upper-left corner of the spreadsheet. Three cells below cell A1 is cell A4; three cells to the right of cell A1 is cell D1. This letter and number combination is also known as the cell's *coordinates*.

The rectangular highlight that marks the currently selected cell is known as the *cell pointer*. When you first enter Quattro Pro, the cell pointer is positioned in cell A1, which is commonly referred to as the *home cell*. Whenever Quattro Pro is ready to accept data, the cell pointer is positioned in one and only one cell, which is referred to as the *current cell*. If you start entering data, the data will be placed in that cell as soon as you press (ENTER).

There are two ways to determine the address of the current cell. You can look at the top and left borders of the spreadsheet area, where the current cell's coordinates are displayed in reverse video or a contrasting color. For example, if the cell pointer is in cell G25, the letter "G" is highlighted on the upper border of the spreadsheet area, and the number 25 is highlighted on the left border, as shown in Figure 1-5. Quattro Pro also displays the coordinates of the current cell at the left side of the input line. If the cell contains data, the cell contents are displayed to the right of the cell address.

The Input Line

The information on the input line depends on the operation you are performing.

- When you enter data, the characters you type initially appear on the input line. They are transferred to the current cell when you press (ENTER) or one of the arrow keys.

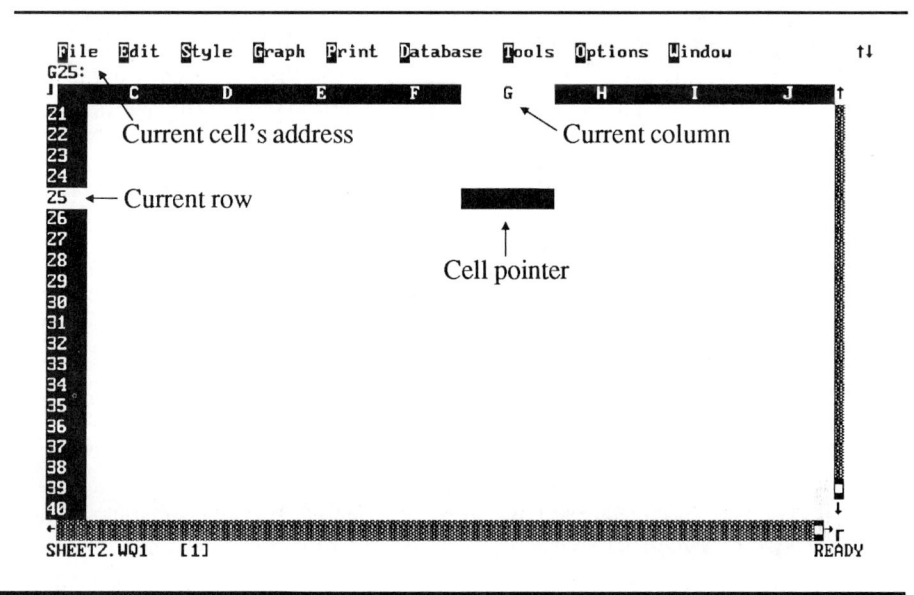

FIGURE 1-5. Determining the address of the current cell

- When you edit data, a copy of the contents of the current cell is displayed on the input line. You then modify the data on this line, and press (ENTER) or one of the arrow keys to transfer your changes back to the cell.

- When you issue a command, Quattro Pro often displays messages on the input line prompting you for more information. Your response appears on this same line.

- In all other cases, the input line displays the address and contents of the current cell.

The Status Line

The status line—the last line of the screen—is divided into left, middle, and right sections—and each displays information on the current working environment.

The information that appears on the left side of the status line depends on what you are doing.

- If you are simply moving around the spreadsheet, the left side of the status line contains the name of the spreadsheet and the spreadsheet number. (The number helps you determine where you are when you are working with several spreadsheets at once.)

- If you are editing previously entered data, the data currently stored in the cell appears on this line until you press (ENTER) to replace the old cell contents with the new.

- If you are using a menu, this line contains information about the currently highlighted menu option.

The middle of the status line displays information on the status of various keys. If (CAPS LOCK) is turned on, for example, the letters "CAP" appear here. If you press the (NUM LOCK) key, the letters "NUM" appear.

At the right side of the status line, Quattro Pro always displays a *mode indicator,* which specifies in which of 15 modes the program is currently operating. When you first enter Quattro Pro, the program is in Ready mode, meaning that it is ready to accept data. Quattro Pro's other modes include Help, when a help screen is displayed; Edit, when you are changing the contents of a cell; and Menu, when you activate the menu system.

THE QUATTRO PRO KEYBOARD

Quattro Pro assigns its own meanings to many of the nonalphanumeric keys (the keys other than numbers, letters, and punctuation) on your keyboard. Because there is a wide variety of microcomputer keyboards, it is impossible to specify exactly where these keys will be on your system. Figure 1-6 shows a typical keyboard layout. If you are not already familiar with your keyboard, take some time to locate each of the following keys:

(ENTER)	Sometimes labeled (RETURN)
(ESC)	The Escape key, often located in the upper-left corner of the keyboard or above the numeric keypad
(BREAK)	Generally shares a key with (SCROLL LOCK) or (PAUSE), in the upper-right section of the keyboard
(CTRL)	The Control key
(ALT)	The Alternate key

Getting Started 13

`BACKSPACE`	Located to the right of the number keys near the top of the keyboard
`CAPS LOCK`	The Capitals Lock key
`TAB`	Generally located to the left of the Q key
Function keys	Located either at the top or at the left edge of the keyboard, labeled `F1` through `F10` or `F12`
Numeric keypad	A set of number or cursor-movement keys, laid out like a calculator, located at the right side of keyboard
Directional keypad	Extra set of cursor-movement keys like those on the numeric keypad; only appears on newer keyboards; generally located to the right of the typewriter section of the keyboard and the left of the numeric keypad
`NUM LOCK`	The Number Lock key, usually located at the top of the numeric keypad at the right edge of the keyboard
`INS`	The Insert key; shares a key with the number 0 on the numeric keypad
`DEL`	The Delete key; shares a key with the decimal point on the numeric keypad

Don't worry about what these keys do for now. Just make sure you know where to find them.

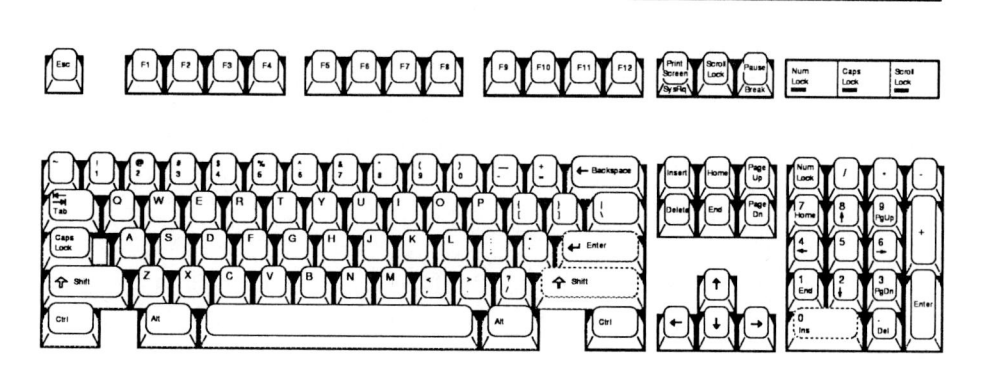

FIGURE 1-6. Common keyboard layout

Movement Keys

All computer keyboards include a numeric keypad at the right side of the keyboard. You can use this keypad either for cursor movement or, if you press (NUM LOCK), for entering numbers. The (NUM LOCK) key works like the (SHIFT LOCK) key on a typewriter. When it is off, the lower character printed on each key is active; when it is on, the upper characters (the numbers) are active. When Number Lock is off, pressing any of the arrow keys moves the *cursor* or cell pointer in the direction indicated by the arrow. Some keyboards contain a second set of arrow keys, so you can use that set for moving around on the screen and reserve the numeric keypad for numbers.

Several keys allow you to make large leaps on the spreadsheet—that is, move your display window an entire screen's worth of columns or rows at a time. In addition to the arrows, the numeric keypad contains four other cursor-movement keys: (HOME), (END), (PGUP), and (PGDN). Keyboards that have an extra set of arrow keys generally have a separate set of these keys as well.

The (HOME) key provides a shortcut to the top-left corner of the spreadsheet, immediately repositioning the cursor on cell A1. The (PGUP) key moves the spreadsheet display window up a screen, while maintaining the relative position of the cursor within the window. The (PGDN) key works similarly but in the opposite direction. Pressing this key causes the spreadsheet display to move down one screenful of rows, again maintaining the relative position of the cursor within the display.

Quattro Pro also provides keys for jumping sideways on the spreadsheet. (TAB) moves the display a screenful of columns to the right. Holding down one of the (SHIFT) keys and pressing (TAB) moves the display a screenful of columns to the left. (CTRL-RIGHT) (holding the (CTRL) key while tapping the (RIGHT ARROW) key) is the equivalent of (TAB), and (CTRL-LEFT) is the equivalent of (SHIFT-TAB).

(END), which occupies the same key as the number 1 on the numeric keypad, is always used in combination with another key. In combination with the arrow keys, it is used to move the cell pointer from one block of data on the spreadsheet to another. The (END-HOME) key combination (pressing (END) and then pressing (HOME)) moves the cell pointer to the lower-right corner of the spreadsheet. You will learn how to use the (END) key in Chapter 4, after you have entered more data.

If you haven't already tried the various movement keys, take a moment to do so now.

1. Try moving the cell pointer in all four directions using the arrow keys. Notice that the address on the input line changes to reflect the pointer's current position and that the row and column coordinates of the current cell are always highlighted on the screen borders. Make sure you move the cursor beyond the initial borders of the spreadsheet area—past column H and row 20—to see that your screen really is a movable window onto the spreadsheet.

2. If Number Lock is not already on, turn it on by pressing the (NUM LOCK) key. "NUM" appears on the status line of the display.

3. Press one of the arrow keys on the numeric keypad, and note that the number on that key appears on the input line near the upper-left corner of the screen. In addition, Quattro Pro changes the mode indicator from READY to VALUE because the program assumes that you are entering data into a cell. Press (ESC) to cancel the entry. If you have a second set of arrow keys on your keyboard, you can leave Number Lock on. Otherwise, press the (NUM LOCK) key again to return the numeric keypad to its orginal status.

4. Try the (PGUP), (PGDN), (TAB), and (SHIFT-TAB) keys. When you have wandered far from the upper-left corner of the spreadsheet, press (HOME) to return to cell A1.

Note that the (ESC) key was used in the previous exercise to cancel the entry of data into the spreadsheet. In Quattro Pro, (ESC) serves as a "hold everything" or "back up a step" key. The rule of thumb is that you can use (ESC) to interrupt any sequence of keystrokes that ends by pressing (ENTER), including the entry of data into a cell. Once you press (ENTER), Quattro Pro records the data in a cell or executes the command, and you need to take other steps to undo the action.

Function Keys

The function keys are labeled (F1) through (F10) or (F12), depending on your keyboard, and are located at either the top or the left side of the keyboard. Quattro Pro includes plastic templates to fit over or above the function keys as a memory aid.

Most of the function keys have different effects depending on whether you use them alone or in combination with other keys. For example, when pressed by itself, the (F2) key places Quattro Pro in Edit mode, allowing you to change the contents of the current cell. However, if you hold down the (SHIFT) key while pressing (F2), Quattro Pro enters Debug mode, which is used for locating errors in macros.

The function key templates are arranged to help you easily distinguish the various operations. The first row below the key name indicates the function key's meaning when pressed by itself. The second row indicates what (if anything) the function key does when pressed in combination with the (SHIFT) key. The third row indicates what (if anything) the key does when pressed in combination with the (ALT) key. The function key templates are coded by color as well as position: The words printed in black indicate what the keys do by themselves, the words in blue indicate what they do in combination with (SHIFT), and the words in green indicate what they do in combination with (ALT).

Most of the function keys are explained in this book as they become relevant in the learning process. The discussion here is limited to (F5), the GoTo key. When you press this key, Quattro Pro displays the prompt "Enter address to go to". To the right of this prompt, the coordinates of the current cell are displayed. These cell coordinates are the default—the setting that Quattro Pro assumes unless you specify otherwise. If you want to accept the default, press (ENTER); otherwise you can overwrite the default by typing in a setting of your choice. You will encounter similar default settings throughout your work with Quattro Pro. When you enter a cell address, Quattro Pro moves the cell pointer directly to the specified cell. If the specified cell is not already visible on the screen, Quattro Pro moves the spreadsheet area so that the cell appears in the upper-left corner.

Try the GoTo key now.

1. Press (F5), and when prompted for an address to go to, type any cell address and press (ENTER). (It does not matter whether you use capital or lowercase letters when you specify a cell address.)

2. Press (HOME) to return to cell A1.

A word of warning about (F10), Quattro Pro's Graph key: If you accidentally press (F10), the screen goes completely blank and then displays the error message "No series selected", unless you have already specified a group of values to graph. If you press this key accidentally, just press (ESC) to return to your spreadsheet.

THE QUATTRO PRO MENU SYSTEM

Much of your work in Quattro Pro will involve moving the cell pointer around on the spreadsheet, and entering and editing data. However, Quattro Pro also offers over 200 commands for such tasks as changing the spreadsheet environment; altering the appearance of data; printing, graphing, and saving your work; and retrieving spreadsheet files from disk. You issue these commands by choosing options from one or more menus and, in some cases, entering additional information as requested by the program.

The top line of the Quattro Pro screen always contains a menu bar. When you first enter the program, you see Quattro Pro's Main menu, which consists of the options File, Edit, Style, Graph, Print, Database, Tools, Options, and Window. This menu is your point of entry into the Quattro Pro menu system. Most options on this menu lead to other, more detailed menus, which in some cases lead to still more menus.

When you first enter Quattro Pro, the menu system is dormant. To activate the menus, you press either (F3) or, more commonly, the / (slash) key. (Use the slash that shares a key with the question mark character rather than the backslash, which shares a key with the vertical bar character.)

As soon as you press /, Quattro Pro highlights the first option on the menu, File. At this point, you still see only the main menu bar. If you select any of the options on this bar, Quattro Pro displays a pull-down menu, as shown in Figure 1-7. A *pull-down menu* is a menu that is pulled down over part of the screen when you select an option on a menu bar.

There are two methods of selecting menu options in Quattro Pro:

- **The pointing or point-and-shoot method**   Use the arrow keys to highlight the desired option, and then press (ENTER) to select it.

- **The typing method**   Type the highlighted letter within an option name.

Try activating the menu system now.

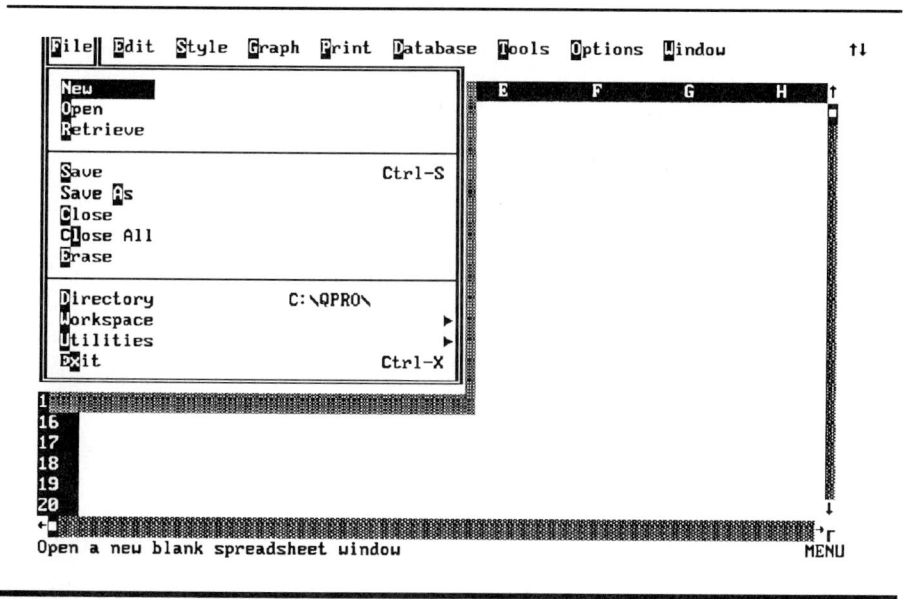

FIGURE 1-7.   Opening the File menu

1. Type /. Note that the File option on the menu bar is highlighted and that the mode indicator in the lower-right corner of the screen has changed from READY to MENU, indicating that Quattro Pro is now in Menu mode.

2. Press the (RIGHT ARROW) key to move through the options on the Main menu. Notice that the menu option on the last line of the screen changes as you move from one option to the next. Also notice that if you move past the last option on the menu bar (the Windows option), you cycle back to the first option.

3. Use the (RIGHT ARROW) or (LEFT ARROW) key to highlight the File option, and press (ENTER) to open the File menu. Your screen should now resemble Figure 1-7. Notice the triangles that appear to the right of some menu options. These indicate options that lead to other, more specific menus.

4. Press the (DOWN ARROW) key to move through the options. Again, note the menu option descriptions on the bottom line of the screen.

5. Again, try pressing the (RIGHT ARROW) key to move through the options on the Main menu bar. This time, because you have already opened one menu, you will see the menus associated with each option on the menu bar as you move right or left.

Now try issuing a command that directs Quattro Pro to display the current date and time (according to your computer's clock) on the status line at the bottom of the screen.

1. Press the (RIGHT ARROW) or (LEFT ARROW) key until the Options menu is open.

2. Press the (DOWN ARROW) key until the Other option is highlighted, and then press (ENTER).

3. Try the typing method to select an option: type **C** to select Clock. At this point, your screen should resemble Figure 1-8.

4. With the Standard option highlighted, press (ENTER).

5. When Quattro Pro returns you to the Options menu, type **Q** to select Quit. Quattro Pro will return to Ready mode. You should now see the date and time displayed on the bottom line of the screen. This date and time display lasts only for the current work session. Chapter 12 explains how to make such settings permanent.

In many cases, Quattro Pro deactivates the menu system and returns to Ready mode as soon as it has carried out your command. In other cases (including the previous

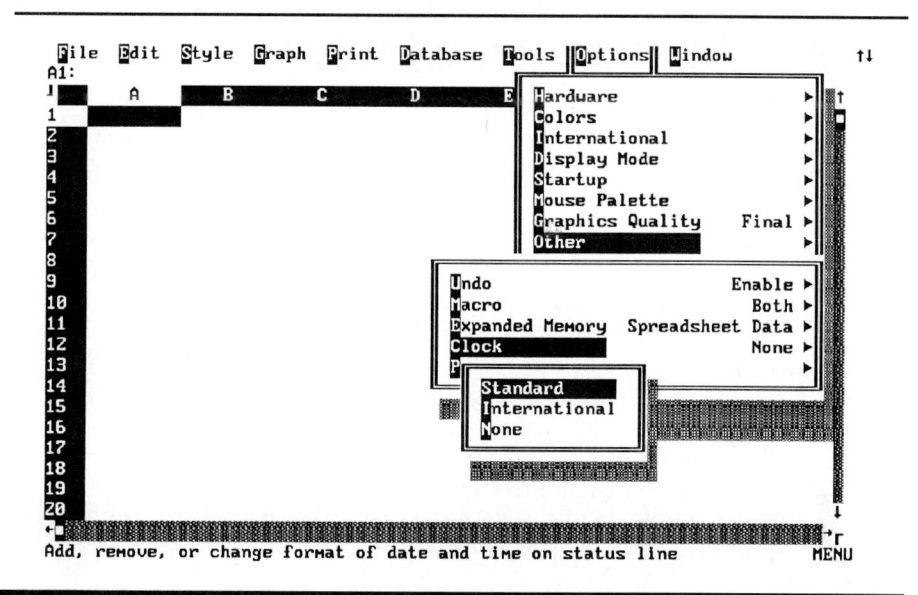

FIGURE 1-8. Issuing the / Options | Other | Clock | Standard command

exercise), it returns to the menu from which you made your selection or to the previous menu, on the assumption that you may want to make another selection. From there you can issue another command, or choose the Quit option or press (ESC) to return to the previous menu level (or to Ready mode if you are already on one of the Main menu bar's menus).

Quattro Pro commands are referred to by the sequence of menu selections required to execute them. The command that you just issued, for example, is the / Options | Other | Clock | Standard command. The general command for changing the clock display is simply the / Options | Other | Clock command. Because some menu options are two words long rather than one, commands are written with vertical bars separating one menu option from the next. The letter you type to select each menu option is printed in boldface. Quattro Pro menus are referred to by the option or, in some cases, the series of menu options, that you select to display that menu. For example, the menu displayed when you select the Other option from the Options menu is called the Other menu or perhaps the Options | Other menu. The menu displayed when you select Clock from the Other menu is called the Clock menu or the Options | Other | Clock menu.

The "Hold Everything" Keys

As you work with Quattro Pro, you undoubtedly will change your mind sometimes in the midst of a command sequence. Quattro Pro offers two means of backing out of a command. The (ESC) (Escape) key generally takes you back one step in the command sequence. For example, if you are on the Clock menu and decide not to continue with the / Options | Clock | Standard command, pressing (ESC) takes you back one menu level—from the Clock menu to the Other menu. If Quattro Pro was currently requesting additional information from you before executing a command, pressing (ESC) removes the default setting and then the information request from the input line and returns you to the previous menu.

You can undertake an even more dramatic escape from a command sequence with the (CTRL-BREAK) key combination. To use (CTRL-BREAK), hold down one of the (CTRL) keys and tap the (BREAK) key, which generally occupies the same key as (PAUSE) or (SCROLL LOCK) in the upper-right corner of the keyboard. (CTRL-BREAK) immediately returns you to Ready mode.

Take a moment now to try the (ESC) key.

1. Type / to activate the Main menu.

2. Type **S** to select Style, opening the Style menu.

3. Type **N** to select the Numeric Format option. Quattro Pro displays a Numeric Format menu with 11 options for defining the display of numbers on the spreadsheet.

4. Type **P** to select Percent. Quattro Pro displays a dialog box asking you to specify the number of decimal places, as shown in Figure 1-9.

5. Press (ESC) to erase the dialog box and return to the Numeric Format menu. Press (ESC) again to return to the Style menu. Press (ESC) a third time to deactivate the menu system and return to Ready mode.

GETTING HELP

When you use Quattro Pro, help is always available at the touch of the (F1) (Help) key. If you press (F1) while a menu is displayed on the screen, Quattro Pro displays a

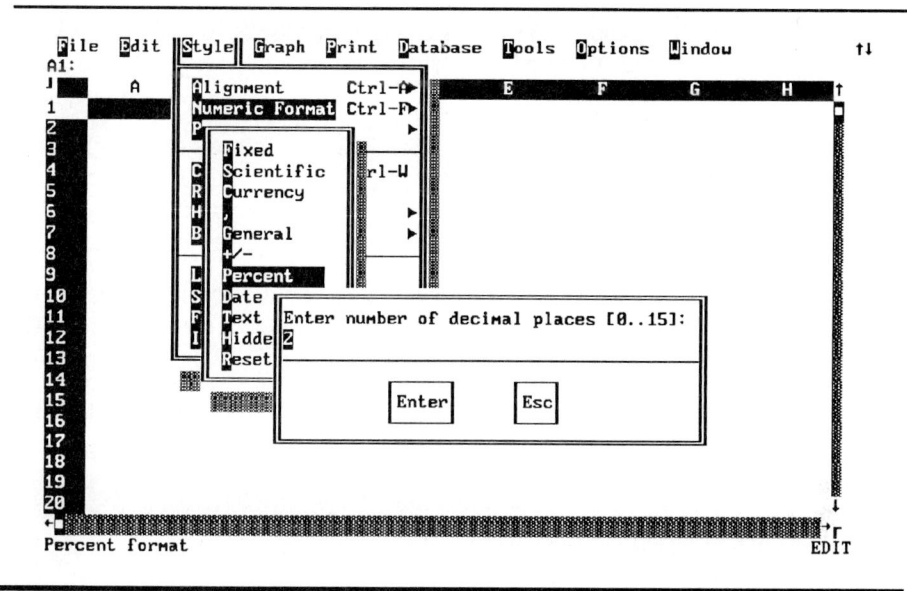

FIGURE 1-9. Issuing the / Style | Numeric Format | Percent command

screenful of information on the highlighted menu option. Otherwise it displays a Help Topics screen listing the main categories of information covered in the Help system.

A help screen contains a list of keywords on the current subject. (Keywords are displayed in boldface and marked with the / character.) To display information on one of the keyword topics, use the arrow keys to highlight the word, and then press (ENTER).

Most help screens also contain a list of related topics at the bottom of the screen. (The Quattro Pro documentation refers to these options as *control buttons*.) This list always includes an option for returning to the Help Topics screen, and usually an option for returning to the previous help topic you selected. As with the keywords, you can select one of these topics by highlighting the topic name and pressing (ENTER).

If you press (F1) while in the Help system, Quattro Pro displays a screen with information on using the Help system itself. If you press the (BACKSPACE) key, Quattro Pro redisplays the previous help screen. Pressing (ESC) or (CTRL-BREAK) deactivates the Help system and returns Quattro Pro to Ready mode.

Try out the Help key now.

1. Press (F1). You should immediately see the Help Topics screen shown in Figure 1-10. The cursor should be positioned on the keyword Help.

2. Press the (DOWN ARROW) or (RIGHT ARROW) key twice to move to the keyword Basics, and press (ENTER) to select it. Quattro Pro displays a screen labeled An Introduction to Quattro.

3. Press the (DOWN ARROW) or (RIGHT ARROW) key four times to highlight the keyword Starting and press (ENTER) to select it. You should now see a screen entitled Starting a Quattro Work Session. On this screen, the keywords are embedded in the text itself. When you first display the screen, the words "enter data" are higlighted.

4. Press the (DOWN ARROW) key eight times to move through all the keywords. Highlight the first control button at the bottom of the screen—Help Topics—and press (ENTER) to select it.

5. When Quattro Pro redisplays the Help Topics screen, leave the Help system by pressing (ESC).

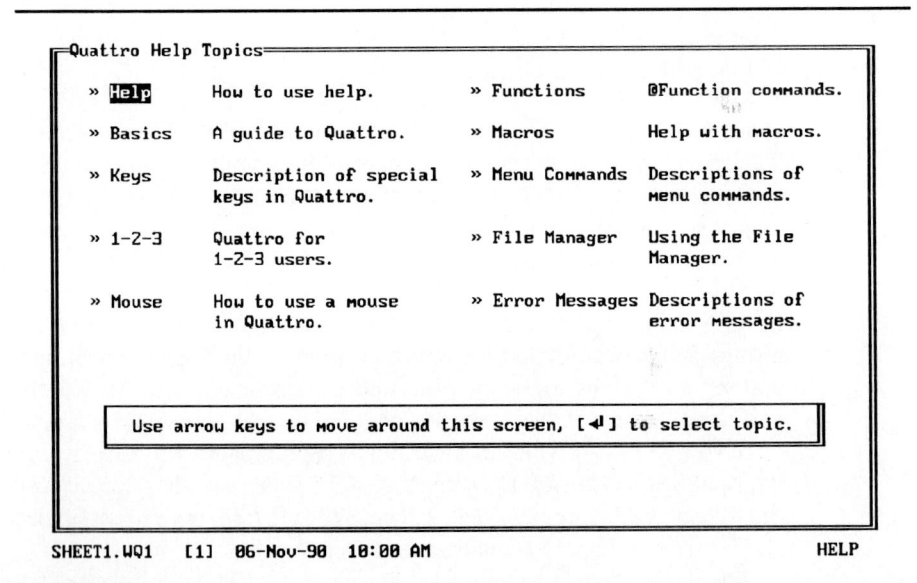

```
┌─Quattro Help Topics─────────────────────────────────────────────┐
│                                                                 │
│  » Help      How to use help.         » Functions    @Function commands. │
│                                                                 │
│  » Basics    A guide to Quattro.      » Macros       Help with macros.   │
│                                                                 │
│  » Keys      Description of special   » Menu Commands Descriptions of    │
│              keys in Quattro.                         menu commands.     │
│                                                                 │
│  » 1-2-3     Quattro for              » File Manager  Using the File     │
│              1-2-3 users.                             Manager.           │
│                                                                 │
│  » Mouse     How to use a mouse       » Error Messages Descriptions of   │
│              in Quattro.                              error messages.    │
│                                                                 │
│     ┌─────────────────────────────────────────────────────┐     │
│     │ Use arrow keys to move around this screen, [↵] to select topic. │
│     └─────────────────────────────────────────────────────┘     │
│                                                                 │
└─────────────────────────────────────────────────────────────────┘
SHEET1.WQ1   [1]   06-Nov-90   10:00 AM                     HELP
```

FIGURE 1-10. The Help Topics screen

USING A MOUSE IN QUATTRO PRO

A *mouse* is a hand-operated device for pointing to various objects or locations on your screen and making selections. Although you do not need a mouse to use Quattro Pro, it can be a very useful supplement to the keyboard. If you have a mouse, read on. Otherwise you may want to skip this section and move on to the section "Leaving Quattro Pro."

In Quattro Pro, you can use a mouse to

- Activate or deactivate the menu system and select menu options
- Move the cell pointer
- Point out a block of cells on the spreadsheet in preparation for moving, copying, deleting, or formatting data
- Accept or cancel cell entries or entries in a dialog box
- Scroll through lists of options
- Change the size of a column
- Resize or reposition windows
- Draw lines, boxes, and pictures to embellish graphs using the Annotator

If you have a mouse installed and your mouse software is loaded, a mouse pointer appears on your screen as soon as you load Quattro Pro. This pointer is initially displayed as a small highlighted rectangle. However, if you set your screen display to Graphics mode, the pointer changes to an arrow. (Graphics mode is only available on EGA or VGA monitors.)

Basic Mouse Techniques

If you have never used a mouse, there are a few terms that you need to know. *Point* means move the mouse until the mouse pointer is positioned on the desired object or spot on the screen. *Click* means press and release the left button on the mouse. *Drag* means hold down the left button while you move the mouse pointer on the screen. These three actions form the repertoire of mouse techniques you use in Quattro Pro.

To move the cell pointer with a mouse, simply point to the desired cell and click. The cell pointer jumps directly to the mouse pointer. Other techniques for moving around on the spreadsheet surface will be discussed shortly.

To activate the menu system, click on any option on the Main menu. Once you are in Menu mode, you can select menu options by clicking on them. If you want to move back a step, you can click on the (ESC) button. To leave the menu system, click on any cell in the spreadsheet area. Note that clicking on a cell when you are in Menu mode merely deactivates the menu system; it does not move the cell pointer to that cell. This allows you to leave the menu system without necessarily changing your position on the spreadsheet.

The Mouse Palette

When you load Quattro Pro with a mouse installed and mouse software loaded, you see a column of boxes, known as the *mouse palette*, at the right edge of the screen, as shown in Figure 1-11. The various panels in the mouse palette are referred to as *buttons*. These buttons allow you to duplicate the effects of various keys on your keyboard. You can use the / Options | Mouse Palette command (discussed in Chapter 12) to change the function of any of the buttons on the mouse palette except the Help icon (the question mark) and the End arrows.

At the top of the mouse palette are two adjacent arrows, one pointing up and the other pointing down. These two arrows are known as the *zoom icon*. If the current window occupies the entire screen, clicking on the zoom icon shrinks the window. Otherwise clicking on this icon expands the window so that it fills the screen.

Below the zoom icon is the Help icon (?), which is the mouse analogue for the (F1) (Help) key. Click on this symbol to activate the Quattro Pro Help system.

The next button on the mouse palette is labeled End and contains a set of four arrows. Clicking on one of these arrows has the same effect as pressing the analogous arrow key on your keyboard after pressing the (END) key.

The next three buttons replicate the functions of three single keys on your keyboard. Clicking on the Esc button has the same effect as pressing the (ESC) key. Clicking on the DY button is equivalent to pressing (ENTER). Clicking on the Del button is like pressing the (DEL) key.

You can use the @ button to display a list of Quattro Pro functions, which are operators used to perform specialized calculations. Clicking on this button is equivalent to pressing (ALT-F3).

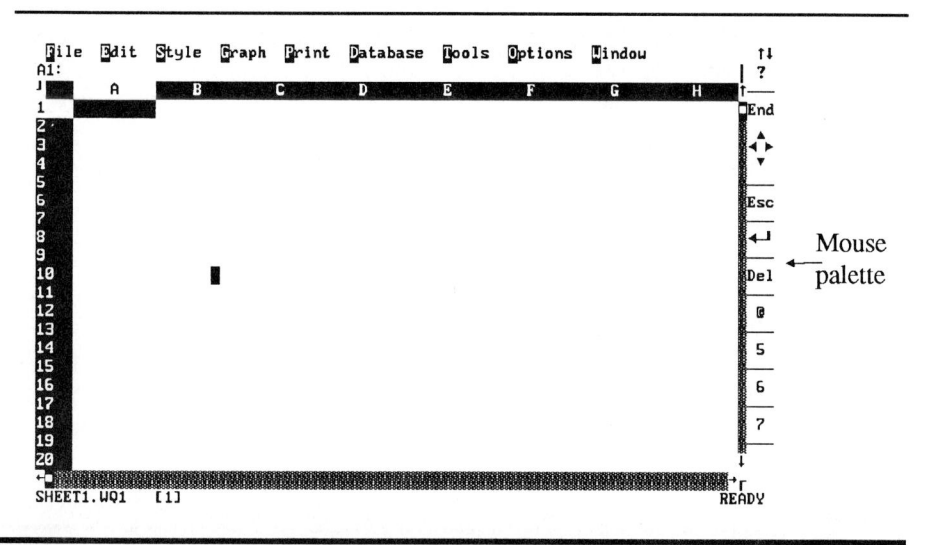

FIGURE 1-11. The mouse palette

    The last three buttons on the palette, labeled 5, 6, and 7, are assigned to macros. By default, they are assigned to the {BEEP} macro and cause Quattro Pro to beep if you click on them, but you can assign them to any macro you choose. (Macros are covered in Chapter 23.)

    In the lower-right corner of the spreadsheet is a *resize box* (displayed as ⌐) that can be used to change the size of the current spreadsheet window. To use it, just drag the icon—and with it the lower-right corner of the window—to a new spot on the screen. You can use the zoom icon to zoom the window back to full size.

    There are a few other mouse-related symbols on the screen aside from the mouse palette, as shown in Figure 1-12. At the upper-left corner of the spreadsheet is a close box, displayed as ⌐ . Clicking on this icon closes both the current spreadsheet file and the currently selected window.

    In the upper-right, lower-right, and lower-left corners of the spreadsheet window are scroll arrows that you can use to move the spreadsheet window across the entire surface of the spreadsheet. Clicking on the *scroll arrows* causes the window to scroll up or down a row at a time or left or right a column at a time.

    At the lower-right edge of each spreadsheet are *scroll bars* (shaded bars with small rectangles indicating the current position of the cell pointer). You can use these bars to move quickly through that section of the spreadsheet surface that currently contains data. Because they are only useful on fairly large spreadsheets, they are not covered until Chapter 9.

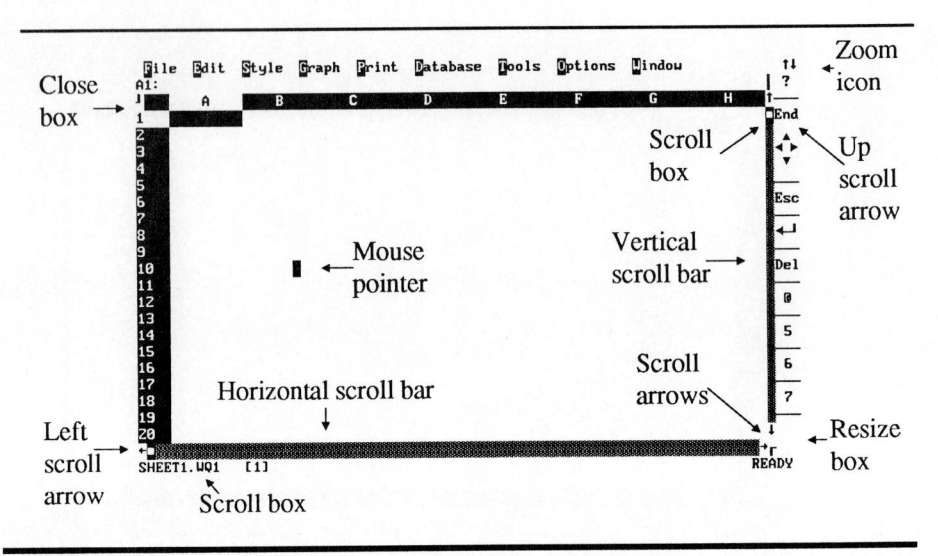

FIGURE 1-12. Other mouse icons

Mouse Practice

If you have a mouse installed and have already loaded your mouse software, take a moment to get acquainted with its basic operation in Quattro Pro.

1. Move the mouse pointer to a cell other than the current cell, and click the left mouse button to move the cell pointer.

2. Point to the downward-pointing arrow underneath the mouse palette (not the resize box, which looks like ⌐), and hold down the left mouse button for a few seconds. Note that the cell pointer initially remains in the same cell but the spreadsheet window itself moves. Eventually the cell pointer moves to new cells to remain within the current borders of the spreadsheet window.

3. Try scrolling the spreadsheet window to the right by pointing to the right scroll arrow and holding down the left mouse button.

4. Move the mouse pointer up to the menu bar at the top of the screen.

5. Point to the Options option and click to open the Options menu.

6. Point to the Startup option and click.

7. Point to the Menu Tree option and click.

8. Move the mouse pointer to any cell currently visible in the spreadsheet area and click. Note that Quattro Pro immediately closes all the open menus and returns to Ready mode. Also note that the cell pointer did not actually move to the cell you clicked on.

9. Click on the Help icon (the ? at the top of the mouse palette) to activate the Help system.

10. Click on the Basics keyword to display an Introduction to Quattro screen.

11. Click on the keyword Screen to display information on the Quattro Pro screen.

12. Click on the status line or any border of the Help window to leave the Help system and return to Ready mode.

This is only a quick introduction to using the mouse in Quattro Pro. Other applications for the mouse—entering and editing data, for example—are introduced in later chapters.

LEAVING QUATTRO PRO

The last operation covered in this chapter is the / File | Exit command. If you issue this command before entering any data, Quattro Pro immediately returns you to the operating system. If you have entered or changed data and have not yet saved your work, issue the / File | Exit command to have Quattro Pro display a dialog box that displays Lose changes and Exit? at the top, followed by the three options No, Yes, and Save and Exit. If you choose No, Quattro Pro simply returns you to the spreadsheet. If you select Yes, Quattro Pro discards any data you have entered or changed since the last time you saved your spreadsheet and returns you to the operating system. If you select Save and Exit, Quattro Pro saves the spreadsheet (asking you for a name if you just created the spreadsheet and otherwise using the previously assigned name) and then returns you to the operating system.

When you first install Quattro Pro, certain control keys known as *shortcuts* are assigned to some of most commonly used menu options. These key combinations allow you to execute a command by holding down (CTRL) and tapping the assigned letter.

The shortcut for the / File | Exit command is (CTRL-X). Using this key combination has exactly the same effect as choosing Exit from the File menu. In fact, when you open the File menu, the shortcut key combination is displayed next to the Exit option as a reminder. Other preassigned shortcuts are introduced in this book as relevant.

Try leaving Quattro Pro now, using either the menus or the `CTRL-X` shortcut to issue the / **File** | **Exit** command. Then, if you want to continue on to the next chapter, just enter **Q** to reload the program.

This chapter presented an overview of Quattro Pro's tools and capabilities. If this is your first exposure to spreadsheet or database software, the chapter may have covered more material than you can absorb at once. If so, don't worry and don't try to memorize the various keys and commands introduced so far. All you need at this point is a sense of the basic types of resources available with Quattro Pro. You will master the details easily once you begin putting these resources to work.

2

ENTERING TEXT AND NUMBERS

Entering Data
Changing Column Widths
Label Alignment
Entering Numbers
Entering Dates
Editing Data
Saving and Retrieving Spreadsheets

In this chapter you learn how to enter text, numbers, and dates. You also learn how to edit data, and how to save and retrieve your work. Much of your work in this and the following chapters will involve building and refining a sample spreadsheet. This spreadsheet is a model for projecting a company's income for 1992 and comparing it to actual income for 1991. Creating this typical financial model will acquaint you with the fundamentals you need to build any Quattro Pro spreadsheet.

Figure 2-1 shows the spreadsheet as it should look by the time you have completed this chapter. Illustrations of the spreadsheet-in-progress appear throughout the next three chapters to ensure that you are on the right track.

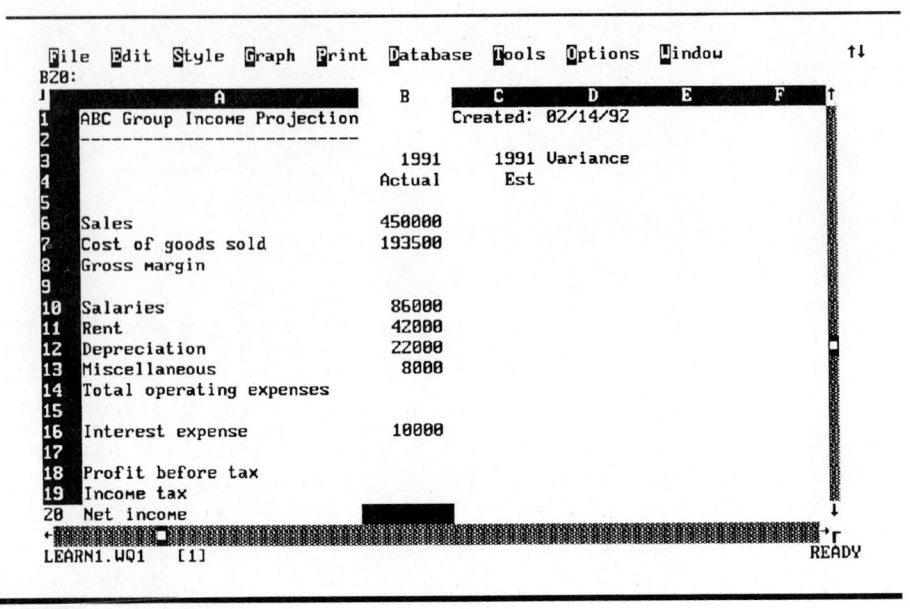

```
              File  Edit  Style  Graph  Print  Database  Tools  Options  Window        ↑↓
        B20:
                         A              B       C         D        E        F
         1  ABC Group Income Projection        Created: 02/14/92
         2  ---------------------------
         3                              1991    1991 Variance
         4                              Actual  Est
         5
         6  Sales                       450000
         7  Cost of goods sold          193500
         8  Gross margin
         9
        10  Salaries                     86000
        11  Rent                         42000
        12  Depreciation                 22000
        13  Miscellaneous                 8000
        14  Total operating expenses
        15
        16  Interest expense             10000
        17
        18  Profit before tax
        19  Income tax
        20  Net income
        LEARN1.WQ1   [1]                                                        READY
```

FIGURE 2-1. Chapter 2 spreadsheet

ENTERING DATA

Entering data into a cell entails three steps:

1. Move the cell pointer to the cell in which you want the data to appear.

2. Type the data. As you type, the characters appear on the input line at the top of the screen. If you make mistakes while you are typing, you can use the (BACKSPACE) key to erase characters to the left of the cursor, and then reenter them as necessary.

3. Press either the (ENTER) key or one of the cursor-movement keys to copy the data from the input line into the cell itself. If you press (ENTER), the cell pointer remains in the same cell. Using one of the cursor-movement keys to finish making the entry has the same effect as pressing (ENTER) and then pressing the cursor-movement key.

≡ Note ≡ If you are using a mouse, you will see [Enter] [Esc] displayed at the beginning of the input line whenever you enter or edit data. These characters represent mouse control buttons. Clicking on [Enter] is equivalent to pressing the (ENTER) key: It causes Quattro Pro to transfer the data on the input line to the current cell. Clicking on [Esc] is equivalent to pressing (ESC): It directs Quattro Pro to discard the contents of the input line, leaving the contents of the current cell unchanged.

If you notice a mistake after you have finished entering data into a cell, just pretend the cell is empty and enter the data again. As soon as you press (ENTER) or one of the arrow keys, the new data replaces the old. If you want to erase the cell contents altogether, simply move the cell pointer to the cell you want to erase and press the (DEL) key.

Data Types

You can enter two basic types of data into cells: values and labels.

- A *value* is anything that can be evaluated numerically, including numbers, dates, and mathematical formulas.

- A *label* is a string of characters generally used for descriptive text, such as report titles, column headings, or the names of line items on a financial report. Labels can consist of any combination of letters, numbers, and punctuation and can include up to 254 characters.

Quattro Pro decides what type of data you are entering as soon as you press your first key. If the first character you type is a letter, a punctuation mark, or a blank space, Quattro Pro decides that you are entering a label and changes the mode indicator to LABEL. If the first character is a digit or one of the symbols associated with values (such as a plus or minus sign), Quattro Pro assumes that you are entering a number, date, or formula, and changes the mode indicator to VALUE.

To start entering data into your spreadsheet,

1. If the cell pointer is anywhere other than A1, press the (HOME) key.
2. Type **Income Statement Projection**.
3. Press the (ENTER) key.

When you press (ENTER), the data is copied from the input line to the current cell and Quattro Pro returns to Ready mode. (Because the entire label does not fit into a single cell, some of the characters appear to spill into cells B1 and C1; the reason for this will be discussed shortly.) The characters that you typed still appear on the input line, only now they are preceded by the cell address, as shown in Figure 2-2. When

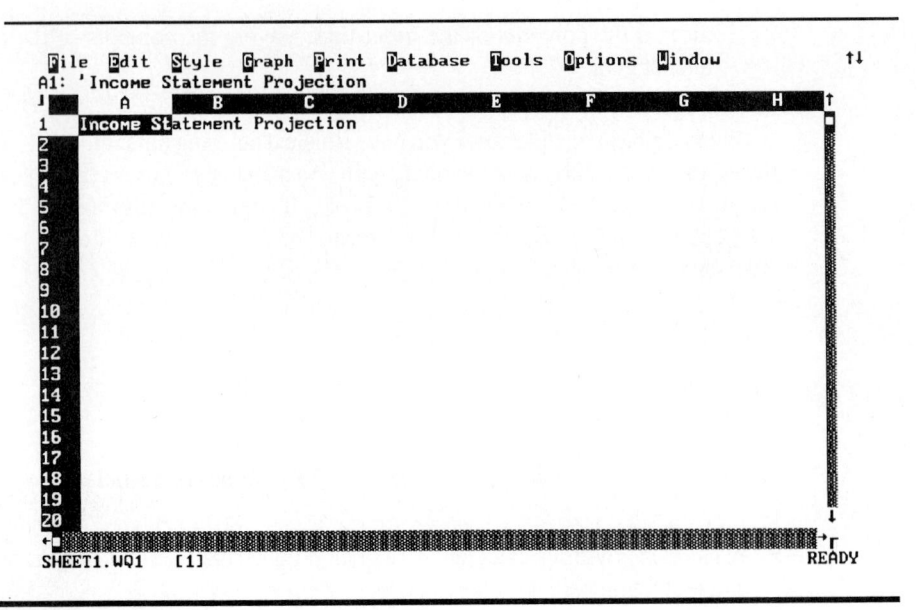

FIGURE 2-2. The spreadsheet title

you are not entering or changing data, the input line displays the address and contents of the current cell. (Ignore the apostrophe at the beginning of the data for now; it will be discussed soon.) If you move the cell pointer to an empty cell, you see only the current cell address on the input line. If you then move back to A1, the cell contents reappear.

Follow these steps to enter the rest of the labels in column A of the spreadsheet:

1. Press the (DOWN ARROW) key five times to move to A6.

2. Type **Sales**.

3. Rather than pressing (ENTER) this time, press (DOWN ARROW) both to enter the data into the cell and move the cell pointer down to A7.

4. Type **Cost of goods sold**.

5. Press (DOWN ARROW) once and, with the cell pointer in A8, type **Gross margin**.

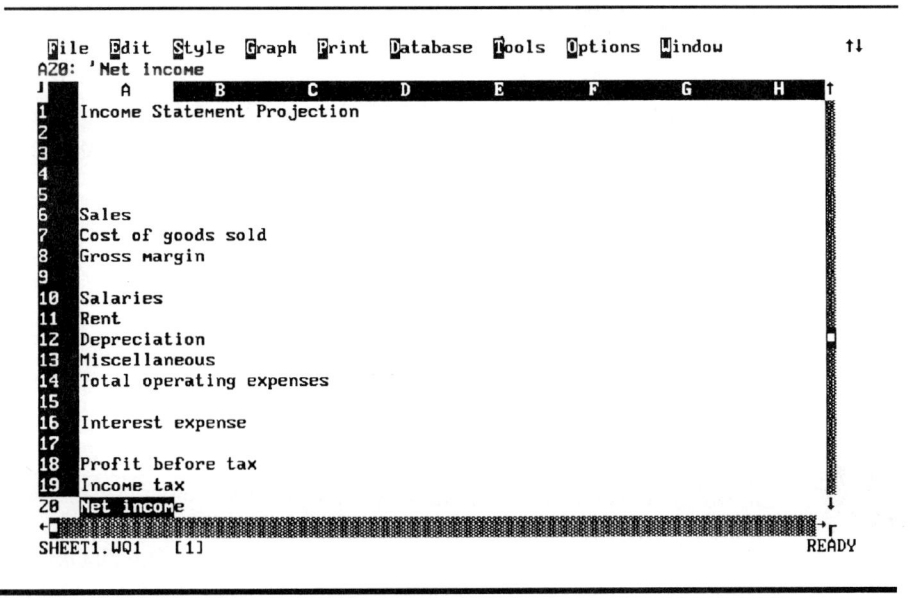

```
  File  Edit  Style  Graph  Print  Database  Tools  Options  Window        ↑↓
A20: 'Net income
J     A       B      C      D      E      F      G      H    ↑
1  Income Statement Projection
2
3
4
5
6  Sales
7  Cost of goods sold
8  Gross margin
9
10 Salaries
11 Rent
12 Depreciation
13 Miscellaneous
14 Total operating expenses
15
16 Interest expense
17
18 Profit before tax
19 Income tax
20 Net income                                                 ↓
                                                            →r
SHEET1.WQ1   [1]                                          READY
```

FIGURE 2-3. Spreadsheet with labels

6. Press (DOWN ARROW) twice and, with the cell pointer in A10, type **Salaries**.

7. Press (DOWN ARROW) once and, with the cell pointer in A11, type **Rent**.

8. Press (DOWN ARROW) and, with the cell pointer in A12, type **Depreciation**.

9. Press (DOWN ARROW) and, with the cell pointer in A13, type **Miscellaneous**.

10. Press (DOWN ARROW) and, in A14, type **Total operating expenses**.

11. Press (DOWN ARROW) twice and, in A16, type **Interest expense**.

12. Press (DOWN ARROW) twice and, in A18, type **Profit before tax**.

13. Press (DOWN ARROW) and, in A19, type **Income tax**.

14. Press (DOWN ARROW) one last time and, in A20, type **Net income**.

15. Press (ENTER).

Your spreadsheet should resemble the one shown in Figure 2-3.

CHANGING COLUMN WIDTHS

As you can see, the contents of several cells in column A spill into the next column to the right. (If the labels were even longer, they would spill into as many adjacent cells as necessary, provided those cells were blank.) This did not cause a problem at the time, but now enter data in column B and see what happens.

1. To move the cell pointer to B7, press the (F5) (GoTo) key and, when prompted for an address to go to, type **B7** and press (ENTER).

2. Type the number **193500**.

3. Press the (LEFT ARROW) key.

The new data is written over part of the data that was entered into A7, as shown in Figure 2-4. If you look at the input line, however, you will see that none of the data that you entered into A7 have actually been lost; Quattro Pro displays only as much data as fits within the cell's borders.

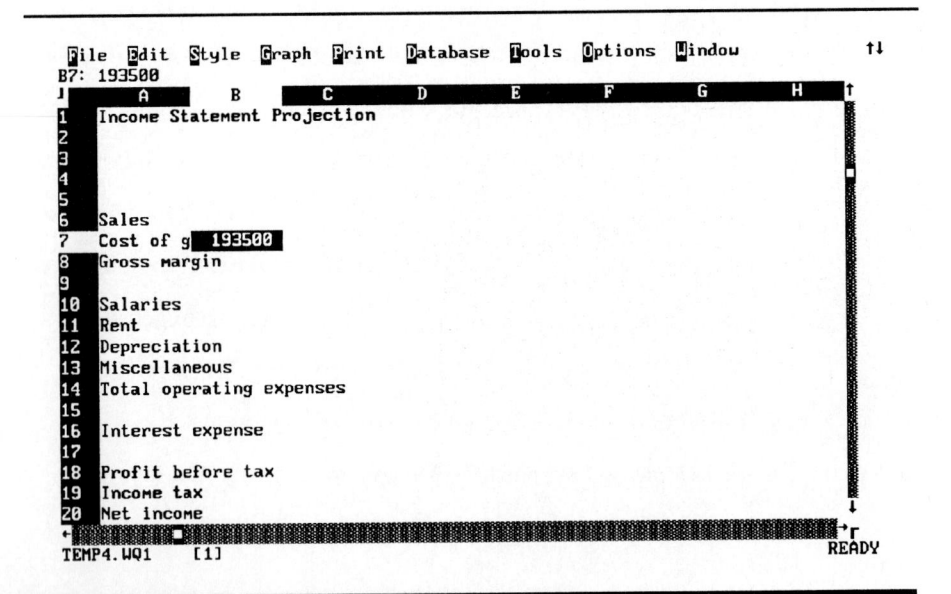

FIGURE 2-4. A label that overlaps a number

4. Move back to B7 and press the (DEL) key to delete the contents of the cell so that the "missing" piece of A7's data reappears on the spreadsheet.

This exercise illustrates one of the most important aspects of working with electronic spreadsheets: understanding the distinction between the way data are displayed on the spreadsheet and the way they are stored in your computer's memory. As far as your computer's memory is concerned, there is plenty of room in A7 for the label "Cost of goods sold" (or for any other label as long as it is under 255 characters). When you first entered this label, however, it appeared to occupy three different cells. This is because Quattro Pro allows the data to spill over into adjacent cells on the spreadsheet, as long as those cells do not contain data of their own. When you entered data in B7, part of "Cost of goods sold" appeared to be deleted, only to reappear when you erased B7. In reality, the data in A7 remained the same; only its image on the screen changed.

In general, the information displayed on the input line is a more accurate version of what is stored in a particular cell than what appears in the cell itself. This distinction between actual cell content and spreadsheet display, between the data's "appearance" and "reality," is important to keep in mind throughout your work with Quattro Pro.

You can widen a column using the / Style | Column Width command:

1. Press (HOME) to move to A1.

2. Type / to activate the Main menu.

3. Type **S** to select and pull down the Style menu.

4. Type **C** to select the Column option.

At this point Quattro Pro displays the prompt "Alter the width of the current column (1...254): 9" on the input line. The number 9 at the end of the prompt represents the current default setting for column widths. The prompt indicates that the width of a column can range from 1 to 254 characters. You can change the default width either by using (RIGHT ARROW) or (LEFT ARROW) to expand or shrink the column, or by simply typing in the desired width.

5. To accommodate the labels you have just entered, press (RIGHT ARROW) several times to widen the current column. Keep pressing until the label "Income Statement Projection" fits within the cell pointer and the column width indicated on the input line is 27 characters.

6. Press (ENTER) to lock in the new width.

Notice that the cell pointer immediately widens to reflect the change. The column width code [W27] now appears on the input line immediately after the coordinates of the current cell, indicating that the width of the column has been set to 27 characters.

If you are using a mouse, you can change the width of a column by clicking on the associated column letter on the top border of the spreadsheet area and dragging it to the left or right. If you wanted to narrow column C, for example, you would click on the letter and drag it to the left. Make sure that the mouse pointer is on or next to the column letter when you release the mouse button; otherwise Quattro Pro leaves the column width unchanged.

Menu Command Shortcuts

As you work with Quattro Pro, you will find that there are some commands you use at least once in almost every work session. Chapter 12 explains how to create command menu shortcuts for quickly selecting your favorite commands. These shortcuts allow you to execute a command just by holding down (CTRL) and pressing a letter key. When you first install Quattro Pro, several shortcuts are already assigned. If there is a shortcut for a particular menu option, Quattro Pro displays the assigned keys to the right of the command name on the menu. For example, when you open the Style menu, the shortcut keys assigned to the Alignment, Numeric Format, and Column Width options appear. Press (ESC) to close the Style menu.

Try using the / Style | Column Width shortcut now by holding down (CTRL) and tapping **W**. Quattro Pro responds by prompting you for a new column width, exactly as it would if you had typed **/SCW**. Cancel the command and return to Ready mode by holding down (CTRL) and pressing the (BREAK) key.

LABEL ALIGNMENT

As you enter labels you may notice an apostrophe on the input line at the beginning of each label. In Quattro Pro every label begins with a *label prefix character;* if you do not enter one, Quattro Pro automatically inserts the default alignment character—generally an apostrophe, indicating flush-left alignment. There are three label prefix characters in Quattro Pro:

Character	Effect
'	Align flush left
"	Align flush right
^	Center within cell

When you enter one of these three characters at the beginning of a label, Quattro Pro reads that character as a prefix rather than as part of the label text and aligns the text accordingly. It does not display the prefix character in the cell itself.

On the rare occasion when you want to enter a label that actually begins with one of the label prefix characters, you must type an additional label prefix character before the label itself. Quattro Pro reads this first character as a label prefix, and then reads and displays the second character as part of the label text.

To compare the three different label alignments, try this exercise:

1. Press (PGDN) to move to A21, and type **LABEL**.

2. Press (ENTER) and notice that the flush-left alignment character, an apostrophe, appears on the input line of the display.

3. Press (DOWN ARROW) to move to A22, and type ^**LABEL**. (The caret (^) character shares a key with the number 6 in the row of number keys on your keyboard.)

4. Press (DOWN ARROW) again to move to A23, and type "**LABEL**.

5. Press (DOWN ARROW).

Your screen should now contain the same label with three different alignments.

Label prefix characters not only determine the positioning of text within a cell, they also can indicate that the data being entered constitute a label. In particular, you can use label prefix characters when you are entering a label that begins with a number (see Figure 2-5). Because Quattro Pro determines the type of data you are entering from the first character you type, entering an alignment character before a number directs Quattro Pro to treat the data as a label rather than a value. To see how this works, follow these steps:

1. Use the (F5) (GoTo) key to move to B3, and type "**1991**.

2. Press (DOWN ARROW) to move to B4, and type "**Actual**.

3. Press (RIGHT ARROW) to move to C4, and type "**Est**.

4. Press (UP ARROW) to move to C3, and type "**1992**.

5. Press (RIGHT ARROW) to move to D3, and type "**Variance**.

6. Press (ENTER).

When you enter a column heading that consists entirely of numerals, it may not matter whether you enter it as a label (by including a label prefix character) or a value. However, when you enter a label that starts with numerals but also includes letters or punctuation, Quattro Pro beeps and displays an error message because you are trying

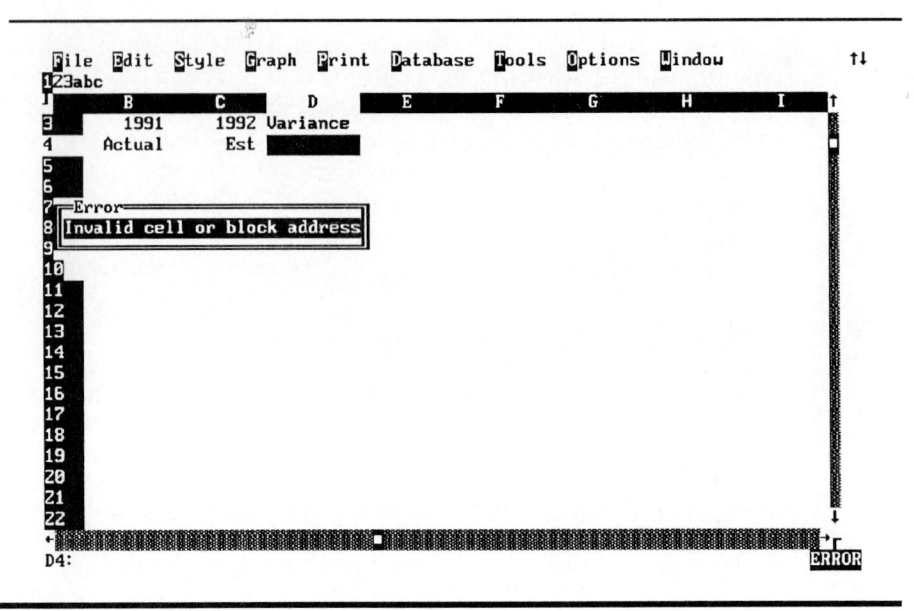

FIGURE 2-5. Entering a label with numbers

to include unacceptable characters in what it considers a value. You can clear the error message from the screen by pressing (ESC) or (ENTER).

Quattro Pro also uses two other label prefix characters. The vertical bar (|) is used as the prefix for printer command codes. This prefix character is covered in Chapter 6. The backslash (\) is used to repeat one or more characters across the width of a cell. When you enter a backslash as the first character in a cell, Quattro Pro replicates whatever character(s) you type after that across the entire cell. For example, if you were to enter \ABC in a cell that is 9 characters wide, Quattro Pro would display ABCABCABC in that cell. If you later changed the column width to 11 characters, you would see ABCABCABCAB displayed in the cell.

The \ prefix is particularly useful for drawing borders and underlines to improve the appearance of the spreadsheet. For example, you can fill an entire cell with dashes, as shown in Figure 2-6, by following these steps:

1. Move to A2 either by pressing (HOME) and then (DOWN ARROW) or by using the GoTo key.

2. Type \ followed by a hyphen (-).

3. Press (ENTER).

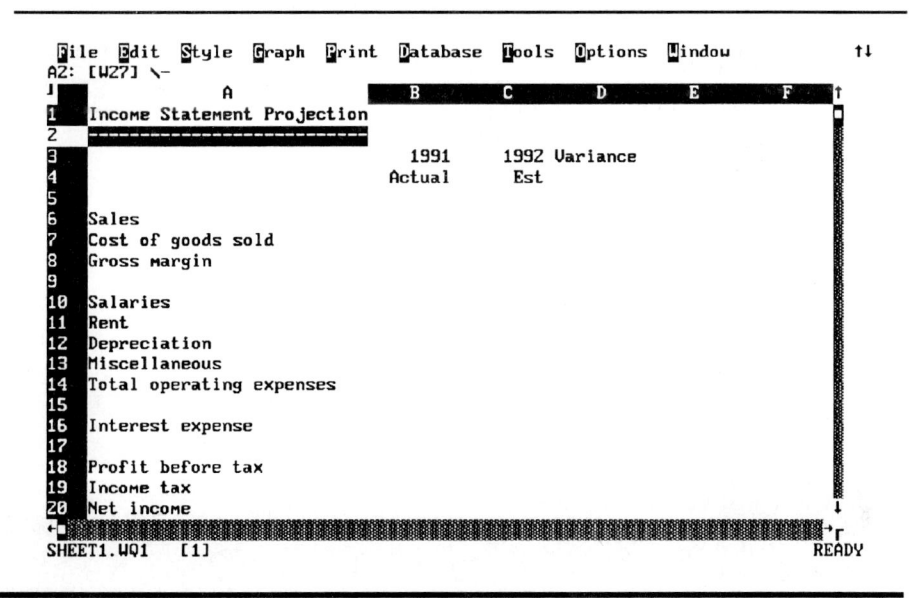

```
  File  Edit  Style  Graph  Print  Database  Tools  Options  Window              ↑↓
 A2: [W27] \-
  1              A                B         C         D         E        F
  1       Income Statement Projection
  2       ========================
  3                              1991      1992 Variance
  4                              Actual    Est
  5
  6       Sales
  7       Cost of goods sold
  8       Gross margin
  9
 10       Salaries
 11       Rent
 12       Depreciation
 13       Miscellaneous
 14       Total operating expenses
 15
 16       Interest expense
 17
 18       Profit before tax
 19       Income tax
 20       Net income

SHEET1.WQ1    [1]                                                          READY
```

FIGURE 2-6. Spreadsheet with column headings and dashes

A set of dashes should now appear underneath your spreadsheet title.

ENTERING NUMBERS

Although it is easy to enter numbers in Quattro Pro, you need to keep a few rules in mind. The only characters you can use when entering a number in Quattro Pro are numerals, plus or minus signs, percent signs, or a single decimal point; you cannot use dollar signs, parentheses, or commas. You will learn in Chapter 5 that you can display numbers with any of these symbols by changing the display format of the cell.

Like a label, a number can be up to 254 characters long. Unlike a label, however, numbers do not spill into adjacent cells if they do not fit within the borders of the current cell. Instead, they are displayed either in scientific (exponential) notation or as a row of asterisks, depending on the display format of the cell. (Numeric display formats are covered in Chapter 5). If you see a row of asterisks, be assured that the number is stored in its entirety—up to 16 digits—in Quattro Pro's memory; you only need to widen the cell to correct the display on the spreadsheet.

40 Quattro Pro 2 Made Easy

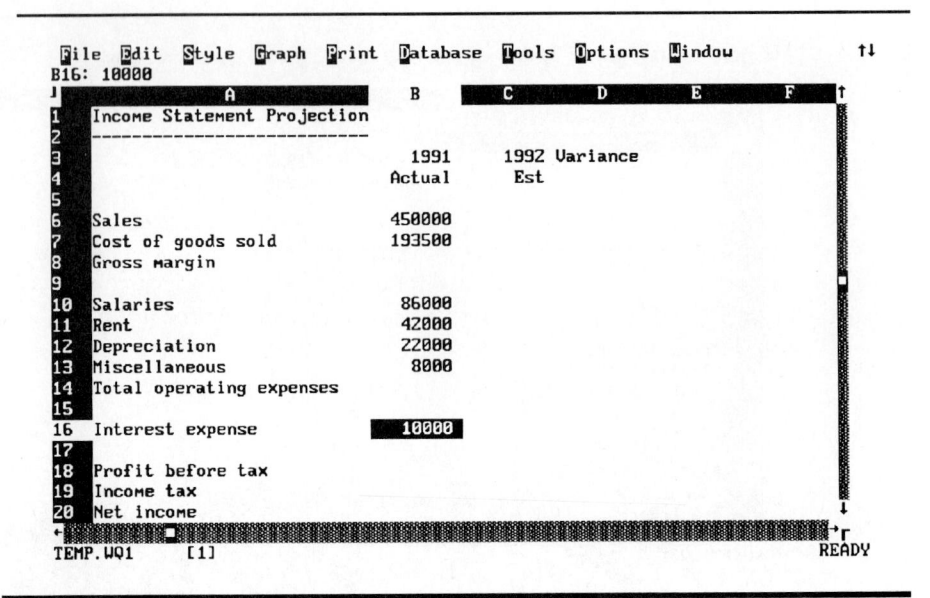

```
File  Edit  Style  Graph  Print  Database  Tools  Options  Window         ↑↓
B16: 10000
         A                    B         C        D         E        F
1   Income Statement Projection
2   ----------------------------
3                             1991      1992 Variance
4                             Actual    Est
5
6   Sales                     450000
7   Cost of goods sold        193500
8   Gross margin
9
10  Salaries                  86000
11  Rent                      42000
12  Depreciation              22000
13  Miscellaneous              8000
14  Total operating expenses
15
16  Interest expense          10000
17
18  Profit before tax
19  Income tax
20  Net income
TEMP.WQ1    [1]                                                        READY
```

FIGURE 2-7. Spreadsheet after entering numbers

To practice entering numbers in your spreadsheet,

1. Move to B6, and type **450000**.

2. Press (DOWN ARROW) to move to B7, and type **193500**.

3. Press (DOWN ARROW) three times to move to B10 and type **86000**.

4. Press (DOWN ARROW) and, in B11, type **42000**.

5. Press (DOWN ARROW) and, in B12, type **22000**.

6. Press (DOWN ARROW) and, in B13, type **8000.**

7. Press (DOWN ARROW) three times, and type **10000** in B16.

8. Press (ENTER).

Your spreadsheet should now look like the one shown in Figure 2-7.

ENTERING DATES

A date may be entered as a label or a value. To create a date label with the month, day, and year separated by slashes, you would enter **'08/06/91**. This method is fine if you plan to use the date merely as descriptive text. In other words, if you want your date to act as a label, you can enter it as a label. If you enter dates as values, however, you can use them to perform date arithmetic, such as adding a specified number of days to a date or calculating the number of days that has elapsed between two dates. You enter date values in Quattro Pro using a special date prefix: (CTRL-D). Just hold down (CTRL), type **D**, and then enter a date in one of several acceptable formats (see Chapter 10). For now, try using the familiar MM/DD/YY format:

1. Press the (F5) (GoTo) key to move to C1.
2. In C1, type the label **"Created:**.
3. Press (RIGHT ARROW) and, in D1, hold down (CTRL) and type **D**. Notice that Quattro Pro displays DATE in place of READY as the mode indicator at the bottom of the screen display.
4. Type today's date using the MM/DD/YY format.
5. Press (ENTER).

Your spreadsheet should now look like Figure 2-8. The information on the input line resembles the following:

D1: 33648

D1 refers to the coordinates of the current cell. The numeral (probably something other than 33648 on your spreadsheet) is the numeric equivalent of the date that you entered, calculated in terms of the number of days that have elapsed since the turn of the century.

EDITING DATA

When you enter data into cells, Quattro Pro gives you a limited number of options for correcting mistakes. If you make a typing error or have second thoughts about the data you have entered, you can either erase characters using the (BACKSPACE) key and then

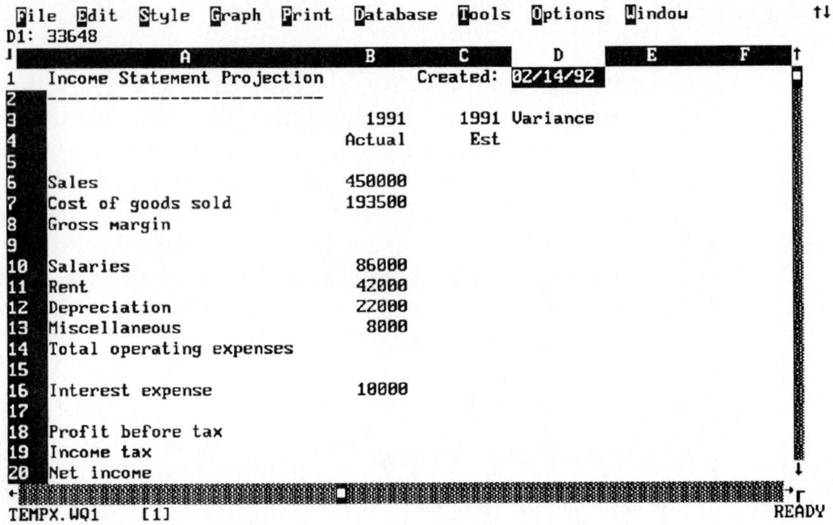

```
  File  Edit  Style  Graph  Print  Database  Tools  Options  Window                    ↑↓
  D1: 33648
         A                          B         C         D           E         F
   1  Income Statement Projection          Created:  02/14/92
   2  ------------------------------
   3                               1991      1991  Variance
   4                               Actual    Est
   5
   6  Sales                        450000
   7  Cost of goods sold           193500
   8  Gross margin
   9
  10  Salaries                     86000
  11  Rent                         42000
  12  Depreciation                 22000
  13  Miscellaneous                 8000
  14  Total operating expenses
  15
  16  Interest expense             10000
  17
  18  Profit before tax
  19  Income tax
  20  Net income
  TEMPX.WQ1    [1]                                                             READY
```

FIGURE 2-8. Entering a date value

reenter them, or press (ENTER) and then replace the entire contents of the cell by entering the data a second time.

If you want to edit the contents of a cell—that is, replace or delete existing characters or insert new ones—you must switch to Edit mode by pressing (F2), the Edit key. Once you press (F2), the mode indicator changes from READY to EDIT, and the cell contents appear on the input line. The editing cursor, which indicates your current position on the input line, is positioned immediately to the right of the cell's current data. Use the (LEFT ARROW) or (RIGHT ARROW) key to reposition the cursor and move through the cell's contents without erasing or overwriting any characters. Pressing (HOME) moves the cursor to the first character in the cell. Pressing (END) moves the cursor back to the right of the last character.

To erase characters you can use either (BACKSPACE) to move the cursor to the left, erasing as you go, or (DEL) to delete the character located immediately above the cursor. When you first enter Edit mode, Quattro Pro automatically switches to Insert mode, meaning that any characters you type are inserted into the data immediately to the left of the cursor. If you want to replace existing characters rather than insert new ones, you need to turn Insert mode off by pressing the (INS) key. When you do, the letters "OVR" appear in inverse video at the bottom-middle of the screen, indicating that you are now in Overwrite mode. To turn Overwrite mode off, simply press (INS) a second time. The changes that you make while in Edit mode are not recorded in the current

```
File  Edit  Style  Graph  Print  Database  Tools  Options  Window                    ↑↓
'ABC Group]ncome Statement Projection
            A                    B           C           D         E         F
 1   Income Statement Projection         Created: 02/14/92
 2   ----------------------------
 3                              1991      1991 Variance
 4                              Actual    Est
 5
 6   Sales                      450000
 7   Cost of goods sold         193500
 8   Gross margin
 9
10   Salaries                    86000
11   Rent                        42000
12   Depreciation                22000
13   Miscellaneous                8000
14   Total operating expenses
15
16   Interest expense            10000
17
18   Profit before tax
19   Income tax
20   Net income
A1: [W27] 'Income Statement Projection                                          EDIT
```

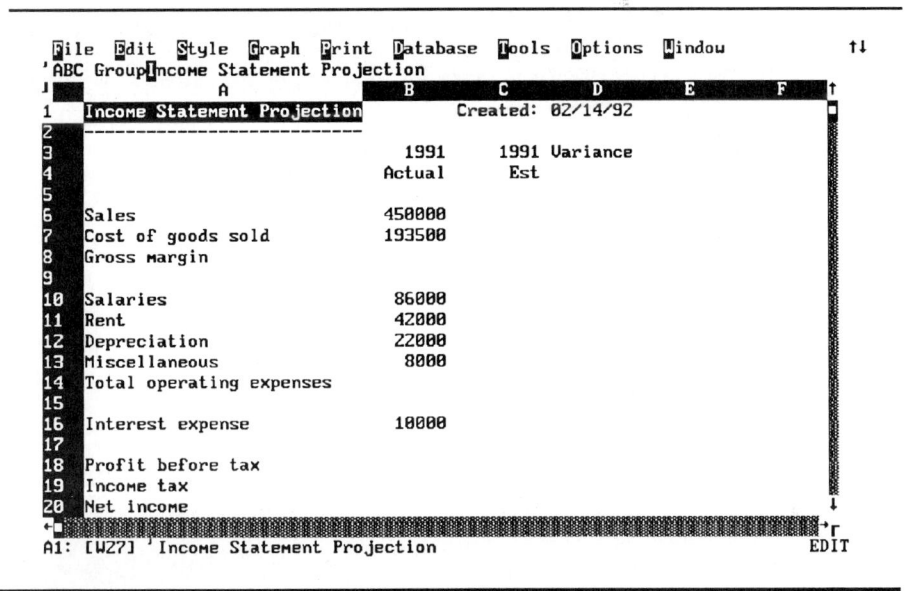

FIGURE 2-9. Editing the spreadsheet title

cell until you press (ENTER). Until then, if you press the (ESC) key, the changes are canceled and the cell contents are left as they were before you entered Edit.

Follow these steps to edit the title of your spreadsheet:

1. Press the (HOME) key to move to A1.

2. Press the (F2) (Edit) key.

3. Press (HOME) to move to the beginning of the text.

4. Tap the (RIGHT ARROW) key once to move the cursor to the right of the apostrophe (Quattro Pro's flush-left alignment character).

5. With the editing cursor positioned on the letter "I" of "Income," type **ABC Group**.

Your screen should now look like the one shown in Figure 2-9.

6. Press the spacebar to insert a space between "Group" and "Income."

7. Hold down the (RIGHT ARROW) key until the cursor reaches the "S" in "Statement." Use the (LEFT ARROW) key to move back if you overshoot your mark.

8. Press (DEL) 10 times to erase the word "Statement" and the extra space that follows.

9. Press (ENTER) to incorporate your changes into the cell and exit from Edit mode.

The title should now read "ABC Group Income Projection."

You have now seen the commonly used editing keys. A full list of editing keys appears in Table 2-1. You can also use a mouse to edit data. To enter Edit mode using a mouse, point to the cell you want to edit and click to move the cell pointer to that cell. Then point to the input line and click again to copy the cell's contents to that line. You can move the cursor by pointing to the desired spot and clicking. When you are done editing, click on the ↵ icon to enter your changes into the cell. If you prefer to discard your changes, click on Esc instead. Note that you can use any combination of keyboard keys and mouse commands when editing.

Key	Function
(ESC)	Erases the input line. If you press (ESC) again or press (ENTER) without entering any data, Quattro Pro discards any changes you made and returns to Ready mode.
(ENTER)	Copies the data as it appears on the input line into the current cell.
(LEFT ARROW)	Moves the cursor one character to the left.
(RIGHT ARROW)	Moves the cursor one character to the right.
(HOME)	Moves the cursor to the first character on the input line.
(END)	Moves the cursor to the last character on the input line.
(TAB) or (CTRL-RIGHT ARROW)	Moves the cursor five characters to the right.
(SHIFT-TAB) or (CRTL-LEFT ARROW)	Moves the cursor five characters to the left.
(BACKSPACE)	Deletes the character to the left of the cursor.
(INS)	Toggles between Insert mode and Overwrite mode.
(DEL)	Deletes the character immediately above the cursor.
(CTRL-\)	Deletes all characters from the cursor to the end of the input line.

TABLE 2-1. Editing Keys

SAVING AND RETRIEVING SPREADSHEETS

When you create a new spreadsheet, that spreadsheet exists only in the computer's memory until you save it to disk. A computer's memory is analogous to a blackboard—a temporary reading and writing surface that is wiped clean as soon as you leave the "classroom." If you want to retain the blackboard's contents beyond the current work session, you need to record them somewhere else.

Saving a spreadsheet essentially means copying the data currently in your computer's memory to a more permanent storage place—a disk file. When you save a Quattro Pro spreadsheet to disk, the resulting file contains not only the data you have entered but also formatting information, printing specifications, and graphs.

Once you have saved a spreadsheet to a disk file, you are free to erase the screen, load another spreadsheet into memory, or leave Quattro Pro without worrying about the contents of the spreadsheet. The next time you want to work with that spreadsheet, you can load Quattro Pro and *retrieve* the file—that is, copy the contents of the file from disk into memory, where you can again view and manipulate the data. There are good reasons for saving your work periodically throughout your work session, rather than waiting until you are done with a particular spreadsheet or ready to leave Quattro Pro. First, if you lose power or experience problems with your computer hardware, you could lose all your work. A good rule of thumb is that you should save your work before you reach the point where you would be miserable if you had to reenter the data. Second, it is fairly easy to wreck a spreadsheet. An ill-chosen command or an accidental deletion can reduce even a finely honed model to chaos. If you wreak havoc on your spreadsheet, you can discard the version currently in memory and retrieve the previous version from the disk file.

Saving Your Spreadsheet For the First Time

Quattro Pro has two commands for saving spreadsheets: / **File** l **Save** and / **File** l **Save As**. If you are saving a spreadsheet for the first time, these commands function identically. In both cases Quattro Pro displays a dialog box with the message "Enter save file name" at the top. Beneath this message, Quattro Pro displays the default data directory and a list of any spreadsheet files already stored in that directory, as shown in Figure 2-10.

Because you can have only one file in a particular directory with a particular name, selecting a file name from the list of existing files means choosing to replace that file with the spreadsheet currently in memory. In most cases you will opt to type in a new file name, creating a new file rather than overwriting an old one.

Save your spreadsheet under the name LEARN1.WQ1 on the drive and directory that Quattro Pro displayed when prompting you for a file name (probably C:\QPRO). You will use this file name to retrieve your spreadsheet from disk and load it into memory in future work sessions.

1. Type **/ F S** to issue the / File l Save command.

2. Type **LEARN1** and press (ENTER) (or click on the Enter button with a mouse).

The file name also appears in the lower-left corner of the screen. You can always tell whether the currently displayed spreadsheet has been saved to disk by looking in this spot. If the spreadsheet has not yet been saved, you will see the name SHEET1.WQ1, or possibly SHEET2.WQ1 or SHEET3.WQ1. These are temporary names that Quattro Pro assigns to a spreadsheet so that you can identify it in case you open multiple spreadsheet windows at once. Once you save the file to disk, Quattro Pro displays the name that you assigned to the file. If you want to store your spreadsheet somewhere other than the displayed default drive and directory, you must press (ESC) twice after issuing the / File l Save command—once to erase the file name and a second time to erase the default drive and directory. Then enter the drive letter,

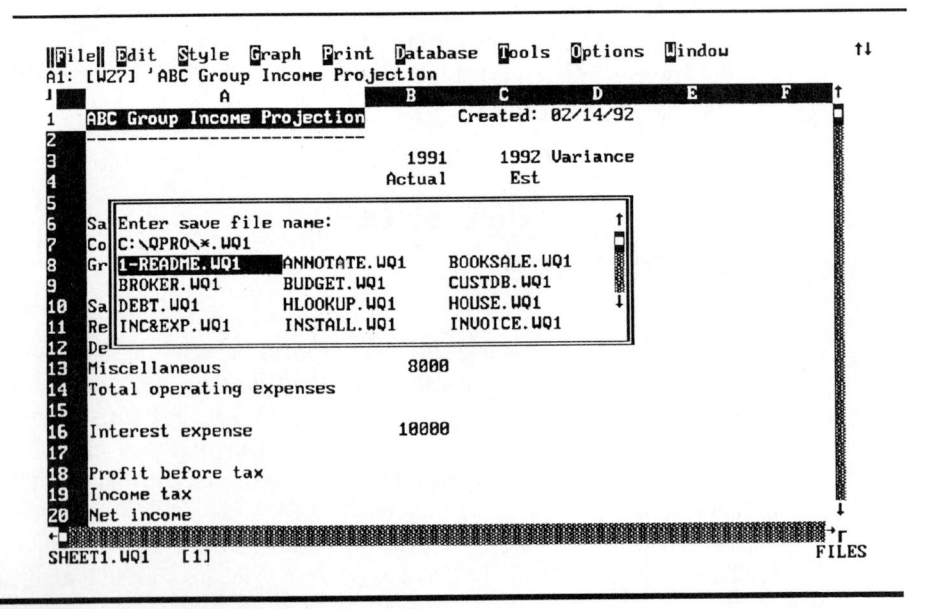

FIGURE 2-10. Saving a file

directory, and file name of your choice. For example, if you wanted to save LEARN1 to a directory called LESSONS on drive C, you would issue the /File | Save command, press (ESC) twice, and then enter **C:\LESSONS\LEARN1**.

Resaving Your Spreadsheet

The differences between the /File | Save and /File | Save As commands emerge when you save a file that you have previously saved to disk. In this case, if you want to save your data under the same name you would use the /File | Save command. Quattro Pro displays a dialog box like the one in Figure 2-11, warning you that there is already a file with that name in the current directory. At this point you have three choices. You can select Cancel to cancel the save operation and return to Ready mode. You can select Replace to confirm that you want to overwrite the existing file with this name. Lastly, you can select Backup to copy the old version of the file to a new file with the extension .BAK before overwriting. (If necessary, you can retrieve the backup file by specifying the BAK extension when you use the /File | Retrieve command.) Note that the /File | Save command has a preassigned shortcut of (CTRL-S). This makes it easy to save and resave your work throughout a long work session.

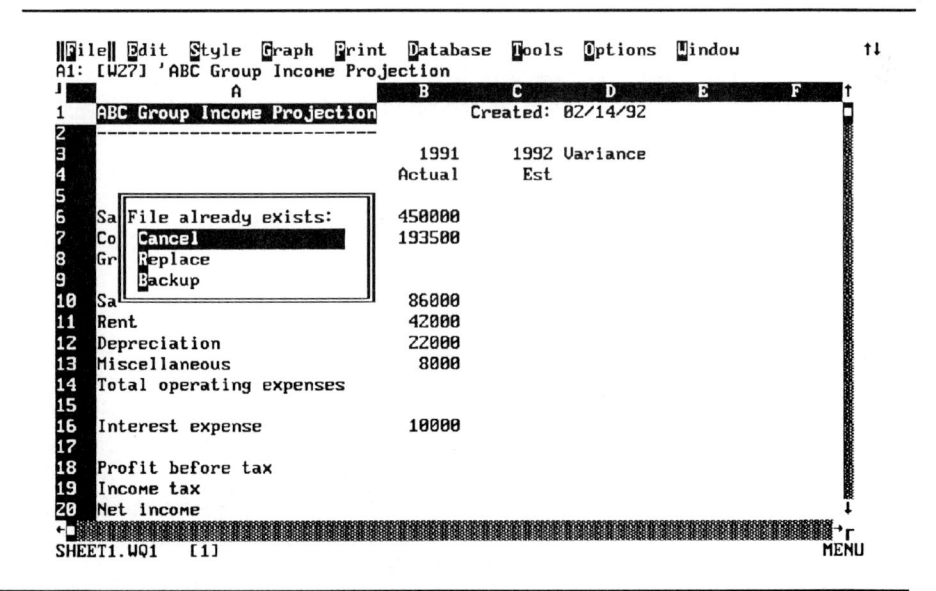

FIGURE 2-11. Resaving a file

Occasionally you will want to save the current version of your spreadsheet under a new name, leaving the old version intact. You might use last year's budget spreadsheet as the starting point for this year's model, for example. You could retrieve the old spreadsheet, update the figures, and then save it under a new name. To save a spreadsheet under a new name, use the / File | Save As command. Quattro Pro prompts you for a file name and displays the current name of the file. Just type in the new name and press (ENTER).

Note that saving a file under a new name means creating a new disk file, not renaming the old one. If you simply want to change a spreadsheet's name, it is more efficient to use Quattro Pro's File Manager utility or the DOS RENAME command.

Leaving Quattro Pro

The command to leave Quattro Pro is / File | Exit. If you have changed but not saved the current spreadsheet, Quattro Pro asks whether you want to lose your changes. Select No to cancel the operation and save your work. Select Yes to discard the latest version of your work.

Go ahead and issue the / File | Exit command now.

1. Type **/FX** to issue the / File | Exit command.

2. Once you see the operating system prompt, type **Q** to reload the program.

The preassigned shortcut for the / File | Exit command is (CTRL-X).

Retrieving Files

The command for retrieving files is / File | Retrieve. When you issue this command, Quattro Pro displays a list of all the files in the default data directory that have an extension beginning with "W." (WKQ is the extension assigned to files created in Quattro Pro's predecessor Quattro 1.0. WKS and WK1 are extensions that Lotus 1-2-3 assigns to spreadsheet files; you can use such files in Quattro Pro, just as you would Quattro Pro's own WKQ files.) Figure 2-12 shows an example of such a file list.

Files are listed alphabetically from left to right across each row, then left to right across the next row down, and so on. If Quattro Pro cannot fit all files in the default

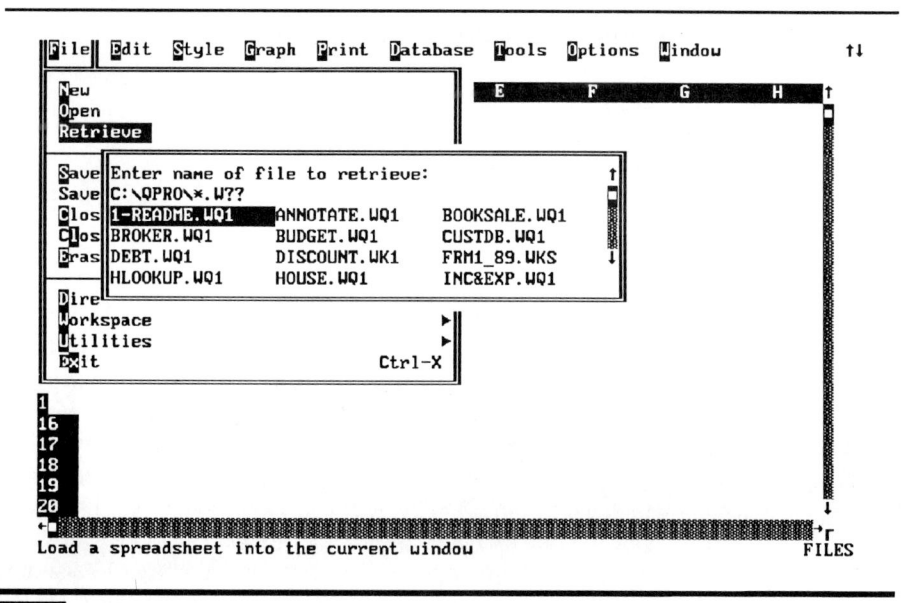

FIGURE 2-12. Retrieving a spreadsheet from disk

directory in the file name box, press (DOWN ARROW) or (PGDN) to view additional file names.

To select a file from the file list, highlight the desired file and press (ENTER), or point and click on the file name with a mouse. You can also type in the name of the file you wish to retrieve, which may be more efficient if you have a large number of files stored in the default directory.

If the spreadsheet file's extension is WQ1, you do not need to type it when entering the file name. If the file name extension starts with a letter other than W, however, the file does not appear in the file list and you must type in the entire file name, including the extension, in order to retrieve it. If you want to retrieve a file that is stored somewhere other than in the default data directory, press (ESC) twice to erase the default disk drive and directory, and then enter the drive and directory before the file name using the form

drive:\directory\filename

For example, to retrieve the LEARN1 spreadsheet from the QDATA directory on drive C, you would issue the / File | **R**etrieve command, press (ESC) twice, and then enter **C:\QDATA\LEARN1**.

To retrieve the spreadsheet file that you just saved,

1. Issue the / **F**ile | **R**etrieve command. Your file should appear in the file list as LEARN1.WQ1.

2. If the cursor is not already there, move it down to LEARN1.WQ1.

3. Press (ENTER) to select that file.

If you have been working with another spreadsheet and have not saved your work, when you issue the / **F**ile | **R**etrieve command, Quattro Pro displays a dialog box asking whether you want to lose your changes. Select Yes to discard the latest version of your work or No to cancel the command.

You will use the techniques covered in this chapter in all the work you do with Quattro Pro. If this is the first time you have created a worksheet or if you are at all uncertain about the techniques covered, you should practice what you have learned before moving on. In particular you should be comfortable moving around the worksheet and entering, editing, and deleting data. You should also understand the different types of data and how Quattro Pro distinguishes between them.

If you have any doubts, try experimenting with your own data. First save your spreadsheet. Issue the / **F**ile | **E**rase command, and then try entering your own numbers and text. If you get lost, you might also try recreating the worksheet from scratch using Figure 2-1, rather than the instructions in this chapter, as your guide.

3

FORMULAS

Arithmetic Operators
Cell References
Automatic Recalculation
Pointing
Order of Calculation
Referencing Blocks of Cells
Common Mistakes in Formulas
Building an Income Statement Model

Formulas are the heart of any spreadsheet. They determine what the spreadsheet does and how it links and processes a set of numbers. This chapter introduces you to using formulas. Once you have mastered these basics, you will have all the essential tools for building modest spreadsheets of your own. In later chapters you build on this base by learning to move and copy data, improve its appearance, print it, translate it into graphic form, and tackle more sophisticated calculations.

Briefly, a *formula* is a set of instructions for performing a calculation and displaying the result in a cell. The types of calculations you can perform in Quattro Pro range from the simple, such as adding a group of numbers, to the complex, like sophisticated statistical and trigonometric operations. You can create three types of formulas in Quattro Pro spreadsheets: *arithmetic, text, and logical*. In this chapter you learn to construct arithmetic formulas—the most common type of formula and the easiest to understand. Text and logical formulas are introduced in Chapters 7 and 17.

ARITHMETIC OPERATORS

Arithmetic formulas are made up of values (numbers or references to cells that contain numbers) and operators such as plus and minus signs. They are entered into cells in the same manner as values and labels: You move the cell pointer to the appropriate cell and start typing. Then you press (ENTER) or one of the cursor-movement keys to record the formula in the cell and return to Ready mode.

Formulas can be up to 240 characters long and can include numbers, cell references, arithmetic operators, and functions (specialized operators that are covered in Chapter 8). The simplest formulas contain only numbers and arithmetic operators, which are listed here:

Symbol	Operation
^	Exponentiation
+	Addition
-	Subtraction
*	Multiplication
/	Division

The easiest way to learn how to construct and enter formulas is to perform experiments on a blank spreadsheet. After practicing in this environment, you can retrieve LEARN1 (our sample spreadsheet from Chapter 2) and apply what you have learned. If LEARN1 is currently on your screen, save it with the / File | Save command, and then issue the / File | Erase command by typing /FE. This command removes the spreadsheet from memory and clears the spreadsheet area on the screen.

With the cell pointer at A1, type **1+1+1** and press (ENTER). The result of the calculation now appears in A1, while the input line still displays the formula, as shown in Figure 3-1.

You can try entering a few more formulas using different numbers and arithmetic operators. When you are done experimenting, make sure your spreadsheet again looks like Figure 3-1. Recall that you can erase a cell by highlighting it with the cell pointer and pressing (DEL).

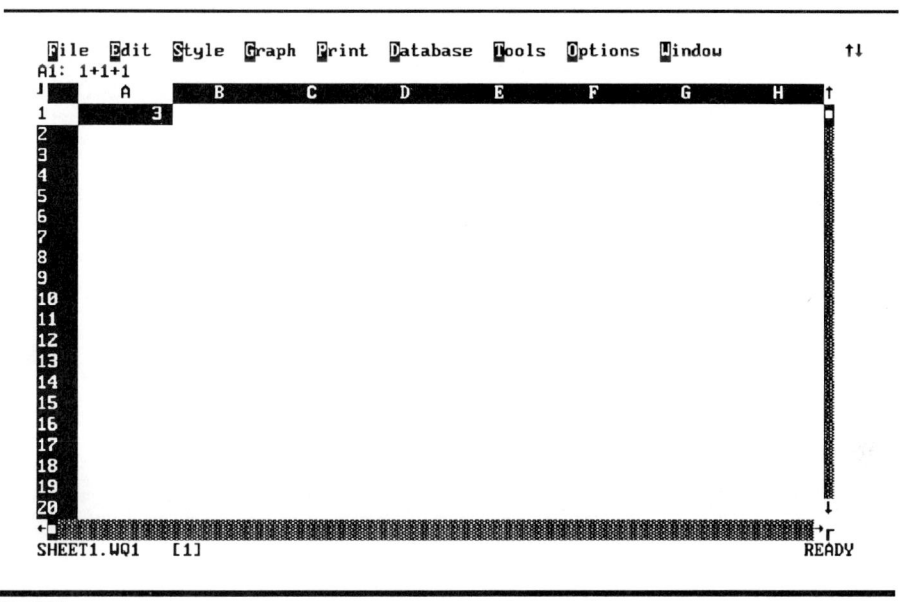

FIGURE 3-1. A simple formula

CELL REFERENCES

As you have seen, you can use formulas to perform arithmetic on numbers typed directly into the formula itself. However, to truly tap Quattro Pro's power, you need to create formulas that perform calculations on data contained in other cells. Rather than adding 2 and 4, for example, you might add the value in A1 to the value in A2. To see how this works, perform the following steps:

1. With the cell pointer still in A1, type **100**.

2. Press (DOWN ARROW) so that the cell pointer is in A2, and type **50**.

3. Press (DOWN ARROW) again, and in A3, type **+A1+A2**.

4. Press (ENTER).

Your spreadsheet should now look like Figure 3-2. When Quattro Pro evaluates a formula that contains a cell reference, it uses the current value of the referenced cell.

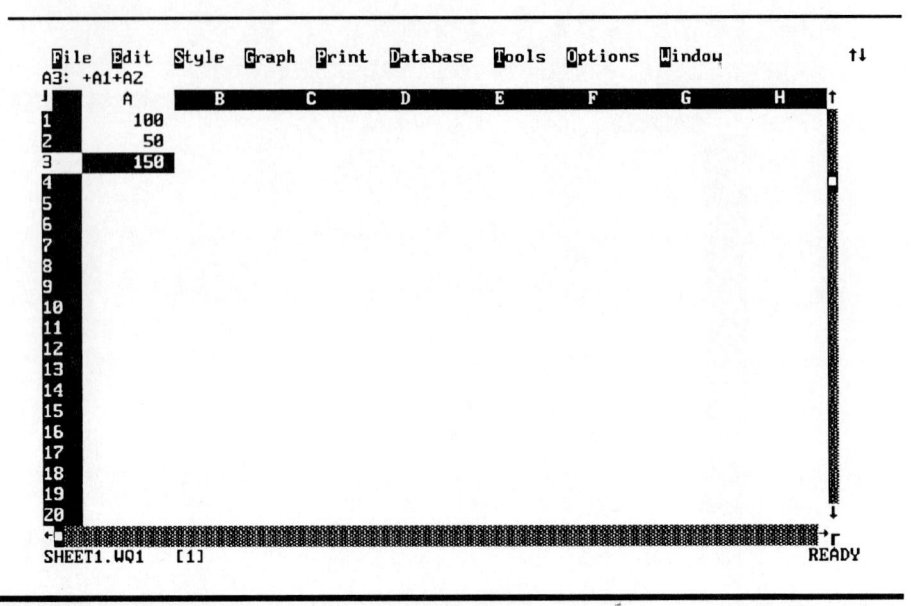

FIGURE 3-2. Referencing other cells

You can think of the formula in A3 as adding the number currently stored in A1 to the number currently stored in A2.

Notice that the first character entered in A3 is a plus sign. As you recall from Chapter 2, Quattro Pro determines the type of data that is being entered in a cell by looking at the first character. This means that if your formula starts with a cell reference, you must precede that reference with another character that indicates you are entering a value. Otherwise Quattro Pro will assume that you are entering a label. Try deleting the first plus sign to demonstrate the problem.

1. With the cell pointer still in A3, press the (F2) (Edit) key.

2. Press (HOME) to move to the first character in the cell—the plus sign—and press (DEL) to delete it.

3. Press (ENTER).

The input line now shows an apostrophe in the spot previously occupied by the plus sign. Once you delete the plus sign, Quattro Pro interprets the formula as a label rather than a value, inserts the default label alignment character, and displays the characters A1+A2 in the cell.

A formula can begin with any of the following characters:

0 1 2 3 4 5 6 7 8 9 . (+ - @ $ #

You will encounter the @ symbol later in this chapter and the last two symbols in later chapters; the other symbols should already be familiar. If you want to start a formula with a cell reference, you usually precede the cell reference with a plus sign or enclose the entire formula in parentheses.

To undo the "damage" you have just done,

1. Still in A3, press the (F2) (Edit) key again.
2. Press (HOME) to move to the first character on the input line, and press (DEL) to delete the apostrophe.
3. Type (.
4. Press (END) to move to the last character, type), and press (ENTER).

So far you have entered formulas that contain numbers and operators or cell references and operators. You can also combine numbers and cell references within one formula and reference cells that contain formulas of their own. Whenever Quattro Pro evaluates a formula that references another formula, it uses the referenced formula's current result in its calculations. To see this in action,

1. Press (DOWN ARROW) twice and, in A5, type +A1*3.
2. Press (DOWN ARROW) again and, in A6, type +A5*2.
3. Press (ENTER).

Your spreadsheet should now resemble Figure 3-3. The value of A6 depends on the value of A5, which in turn depends on the value of A1. At the moment, 100 (the value of A1) times 3 is 300 (the value of A5) times 2 is 600 (the value of A6).

AUTOMATIC RECALCULATION

In a sense, entering formulas that contain cell references is a means of "teaching" Quattro Pro how to perform a particular set of calculations. In an income statement spreadsheet, you must teach the program to calculate net income by subtracting the value in the total expenses cell from the value in the total revenue cell. The reason it is worth doing this is that you only have to teach Quattro Pro how to perform a particular calculation once. After you enter the formula, you can change the numbers at will. Quattro Pro remembers your instructions and automatically reexecutes them, generating a new result.

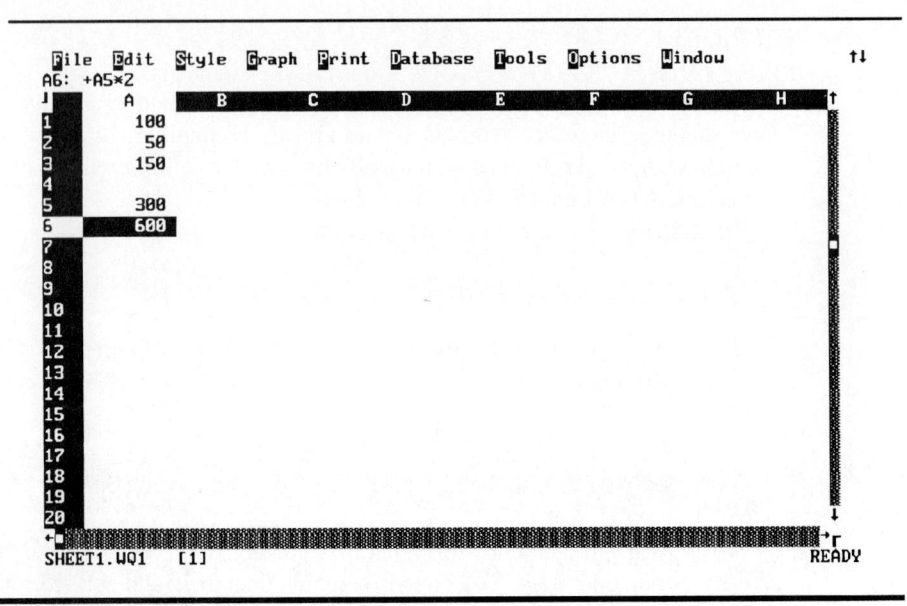

```
    File  Edit  Style  Graph  Print  Database  Tools  Options  Window              ↑↓
A6: +A5*2
      A         B        C        D        E        F        G        H
 1   100
 2    50
 3   150
 4
 5   300
 6   600
 7
 8
 9
10
11
12
13
14
15
16
17
18
19
20
SHEET1.WQ1  [1]                                                            READY
```

FIGURE 3-3. Referencing other formulas

This is known as *automatic recalculation*. It means that any time you change the value in a cell that is referenced by formulas in other cells, the results of those formulas are automatically and, in most cases, immediately recalculated. It is this feature that lets you use Quattro Pro to experiment with numbers, testing the effect of changing one or more items of data. What will happen to your net income, for example, if the cost of goods sold increases by 3%? What if total sales increases by 4%? Automatic recalculation also means that you can "recycle" your spreadsheets by using the same set of labels and formulas with a different set of numbers. For example, you might create a spreadsheet for your annual budget one year and then use it for the next five years, plugging in new sets of numbers and letting Quattro Pro do the rest.

While automatic recalculation is impressive even in the case of a single formula, the benefits are magnified when one cell is referenced directly or indirectly by several formulas across the spreadsheet. As you have already seen, you can construct a formula that references cells containing formulas of their own. When you do, the second formula "piggy backs" on the first, so that changes in cells referenced by the first formula are passed on to the second formula. Watch this in action:

1. Press (HOME) to move to A1.

2. Type **200**.

3. Keep your eyes on cells A3 through A6 while you press (ENTER). The values displayed in A3, A5, and A6 should immediately change to reflect the new value in that cell, and your spreadsheet should look like Figure 3-4.

The value of A6 changes even though its formula does not include any direct reference to the cell you changed. The formula in A6 refers *indirectly* to A1, by referring to A5, which in turn has a formula that refers to A1. Many real-life spreadsheets contain elaborate chains of references, with a formula in one cell referring to a formula in another, which refers to a formula in a third, and so on. A single change in data ripples through the entire spreadsheet, as dozens of formulas are recalculated.

Now that you have several numbers and formulas on your spreadsheet, you may have noticed that you cannot tell which numbers on the spreadsheet are the results of formulas and which are *constants*—numbers that you entered as numbers and that therefore have a set, unchanging value. The only way to determine whether a value is the product of a formula is to move to that cell and look at the input line. (In Chapter 5 you will learn how to display all the formulas on the spreadsheet as formulas.) The fact that numbers and numeric formulas look the same on the spreadsheet makes it all too easy to overwrite a formula accidentally. You will learn how to protect formulas from overwriting in Chapter 8.

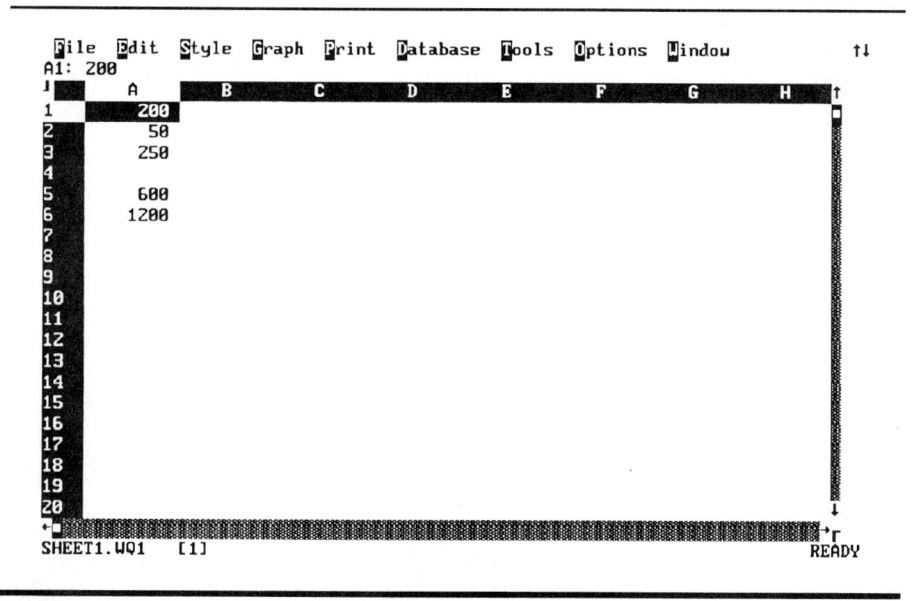

FIGURE 3-4. Automatic recalculation in action

POINTING

There are actually two ways to include cell references in a formula: typing cell coordinates, which you have already tried, and pointing to cells with the cell pointer. Although the typing method can be quite efficient if you know the exact address of the cells you want to reference, the pointing method is less likely to result in errors.

The cell-pointing method consists of three steps:

1. If you are at the beginning of the formula, enter a plus sign or opening parenthesis. If you are in the middle of a formula, enter any character that is allowable immediately before a cell address, such as an opening parenthesis, one of the arithmetic operators, or a comma.

2. Move to the cell that you want to reference. As soon as you move the cell pointer, Quattro Pro places you in Point mode, as indicated by the mode indicator at the bottom-right of the spreadsheet. This means that you can now move the cell pointer and that as you do, the address of the current cell appears at the end of your formula on the input line.

3. If you want to keep adding to the formula, type another operator. This locks the coordinates of the cell to which you were pointing into the formula and returns the cell pointer to the formula cell. You can then continue typing or point to another cell. When you are done entering the formula, press (ENTER) or one of the arrow keys. This writes the coordinates of the current cell into your formula, returns the cell pointer to the cell in which you are entering the formula, and records the entire formula in that cell.

To use the pointing method to enter the formula +A1+A3/A2 in A7, follow these steps:

1. Press (DOWN ARROW) until you reach A7, and type +.

2. Press (HOME) to move to A1. The instant you move the cell pointer, the mode indicator changes from VALUE to POINT, indicating that you are now in Point mode. Notice also that A1 now appears on the input line after the +.

3. Type another +. This locks in the address of the current cell and adds a second plus sign to the formula. Notice that the cell pointer has returned to A7.

4. Press (UP ARROW) four times to move to A3. As you move the cell pointer, the address of each cell you cross is displayed on the input line.

5. Type / to lock in the reference to A3 and add a / to your formula.

6. Press (HOME) again, and then press (DOWN ARROW) to move to A2.
7. Press (ENTER) to add the address A2 to your formula and to enter the entire formula into A7. The number 205 should now appear in A7 on your spreadsheet, as shown in Figure 3-5.

ORDER OF CALCULATION

Formulas that contain more than one operator are subject to strict rules governing the order of calculation. In some cases these rules cause Quattro Pro to evaluate a formula in a sequence other than the one you expected and to generate unintended results. The order of precedence among arithmetic operators is:

1. Exponentiation
2. A minus or plus sign occurring at the beginning of a formula
3. Multiplication and division
4. Addition and subtraction

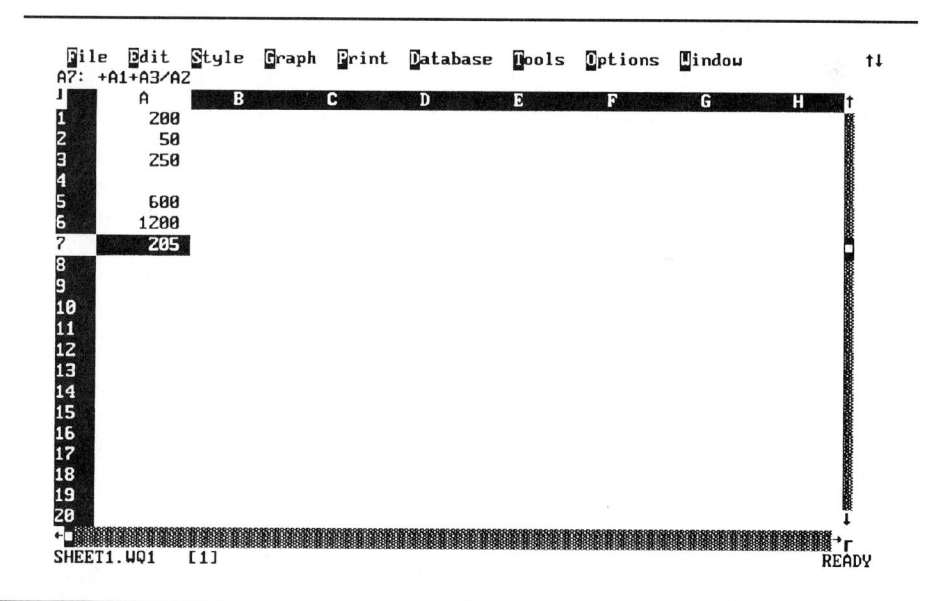

FIGURE 3-5. A formula using several operators

To illustrate the importance of precedence, consider the formula you just entered. You may have expected it to return 9 rather than 205. If Quattro Pro had read the formula from left to right, it would have added the value of A1 (200) plus the value of A3 (250) to get 450 and then divided that amount by the value of A2 (50) for a final result of 9. Instead, because division takes precedence over addition, Quattro Pro first divided A3 by A2 (250/50) and then added the value of A1 to the result (200+5).

If you want operations within a formula to be carried out in a sequence other than the one dictated by the rules of precedence, you need to use parentheses to group sets of numbers and operators. Any expression within a set of parentheses is evaluated first. If a formula contains nested sets of parentheses—sets of parentheses inside other sets of parentheses—the innermost set is evaluated first.

To edit your formula so it produces the expected result,

1. With the cell pointer still in A7, press (F2) (Edit).

2. Press (HOME) to move to the beginning of the cell, press (DEL) to erase the +, and type (.

3. Use (RIGHT ARROW) to move the editing cursor to the slash, and type).

4. Press (ENTER).

The formula should now read (A1+A3)/A2, and the result that appears in A7 should be 9. Technically you do not need to erase the plus sign at the beginning of the formula, but you may as well because once you add parentheses, the + only makes the formula harder to read.

REFERENCING BLOCKS OF CELLS

Adding numbers with the plus sign is fine when you want to add only two or three numbers at a time. It is less adequate when you want to add up an entire column or row of values. If you had a budget with 102 line items, you would not be happy typing +B2+B3+B4 and so on until you reached +B102. Fortunately there is a way to direct Quattro Pro to add up all the values that fall between two points on the spreadsheet.

Up to this point all the formulas you have created have referred to one or more individual cells. Formulas can also refer to a group of cells—known as a block—at one time. A *block* is any rectangular group of cells. It can range in size from a single cell to an entire worksheet, provided it forms an uninterrupted rectangular group. It can contain several cells within one row, several cells within one column, or cells in multiple rows and columns. Blocks are used in two situations: in formulas and in commands, particularly some of the commands on the Edit and Style menus. You will start learning about the latter in the next chapter.

All formulas that refer to blocks of cells contain functions, which are special operators used to perform specialized calculations beyond those performed by the arithmetic operators. The function used for totaling the values in a block of cells is called @SUM. Its form, for this purpose, is

@SUM(*first cell address..second cell address*)

with the cell addresses defining the block of cells that will be summed.

All Quattro Pro functions start with an @ sign. You type it by holding down (SHIFT) and typing **2**, located near the top of the keyboard.

Designating Blocks

As with other cell references, you have two choices when specifying a block in a formula: you can type in cell addresses or you can point to them. In Quattro Pro, cell blocks are generally designated by the addresses of their upper-left corners and lower-right corners. For example, a block that includes the rectangle of cells spanning rows 1 though 4 and columns B through E would be referred to as B1..E4. B7..B14 indicates a block of cells within column B, and F10..F10 indicates a single-cell block.

TYPING BLOCK COORDINATES   Quattro Pro is very precise in the way it displays block coordinates: the coordinates of the upper-left corner are always shown first, followed by two periods, and then the coordinates of the lower-right corner. However, when you specify a block, the rules are less strict. You are allowed to designate a block using the addresses of any two of its diagonally opposed corners. For example, you could refer to block B1..E4 as E4..B1, E1..B4, or B4..E1. You can also type in only one period between cell addresses, and Quattro Pro fills in the second period for you. For example, to add up the values in all the cells from B7 through B12, you can type **@SUM(B7.B12)**. As soon as you press (ENTER), the formula appears on the input line as @SUM(B7..B12).

To enter a formula that contains the @SUM function, follow these steps:

1. Move the cell pointer to C1, and type **1**.

2. Press (DOWN ARROW) to move to C2, and type **2**.

3. Press (DOWN ARROW) to move to C3, and type **3**.

4. Press (DOWN ARROW) to move to C4, and type **4**.

5. Press (DOWN ARROW) to move to C5, and type **@SUM(C1.C4)**.

6. Press (ENTER) to enter the formula. You should see a result of 10 displayed in C5.

You might think of the formula you just entered as "sum C1 through C4" because it adds up any values found within the specified block, including its starting and ending cells.

POINTING OUT BLOCK COORDINATES   To use the pointing method to enter a formula containing the @SUM function, you type **@SUM(** and then move the cursor to the first corner of the block. As soon as you move the cell pointer, Quattro Pro enters Point mode. You type a period to anchor the cell pointer, and then move the cell pointer to the diagonally opposite corner. (Usually you use @SUM to add values in a single row or single column, in which case the diagonally opposite corner is in the same row or column as the first corner.) As you move, the cell pointer expands. As soon as you have highlighted the entire group of cells you want to sum, you are ready to finish the formula. If you press (ENTER) at this point, Quattro Pro displays an error message because it "knows" the formula is not yet complete. Instead you must type in the closing parenthesis and press (ENTER) again to enter the completed formula into the cell.

Try reentering the previous formula using the pointing method:

1. In C5, press (DEL) to erase the formula.

2. Type **@SUM(**.

3. Press (UP ARROW) once, and type a period to anchor the cell pointer in cell C4. Quattro Pro displays a second cell reference on the input line, so the entry now reads @SUM(C4..C4.

4. Use the (UP ARROW) key to move to C1, expanding the cell pointer to encompass the block of cells C4..C1.

5. Type) and press (ENTER). Again, a result of 10 should appear in C5. Quattro Pro automatically reverses the order of the cell references, changing the formula to read @SUM(C1..C4) rather than @SUM(C4..C1).

COMMON MISTAKES IN FORMULAS

One of your first challenges in learning to build spreadsheets is learning to find and fix your mistakes. Table 3-1 lists the most common error messages you will receive when entering formulas, along with suggested solutions to the problems they indicate. Whenever Quattro Pro displays an error message, it also attempts to place the cursor

Error Message	Problem and Solution
Incomplete formula	Something is missing. Look for operators not followed by cell references or numbers.
Invalid cell or block address	You entered something that Quattro Pro is interpreting as a nonexistent cell address or block name. Look for typos or, if you are using named blocks (covered in Chapter 8), make sure you have named the blocks properly.
Invalid character	You entered a character that does not make sense in its current position. Look for extra commas or other inappropriate punctuation.
Missing operator	You omitted an operator between two values or cell references. Enter the missing operator.
Missing right parenthesis	You opened more sets of parentheses than you closed. Look for an extra left parenthesis or missing right parenthesis.
Syntax error	You made an error that does not fall into one of the above categories. Check for typos or syntactical mistakes.

TABLE 3-1. Common Error Messages When Entering Formulas

on or near the mistake on the input line. You should therefore start hunting for the problem at the cursor position. Remember that to clear the error message from the screen, you press either (ESC) or (ENTER).

The most frequent mistakes in formulas are typos, such as typing an equals sign when you mean a plus or inserting a space where it doesn't belong. The second most common mistake is forgetting to start the formula with a number or some symbol indicating that you are entering a value. (This includes omitting the @ in @SUM.) Some of these errors cause Quattro Pro to display an error message, but often it will simply return the wrong answer (sometimes displaying the formula itself rather than its result). When you enter formulas that refer to themselves or that attempt to divide a value by zero, Quattro Pro displays a different indication that you have a problem on your spreadsheet. These two types of errors are discussed next.

Circular References

A *circular cell reference* is a reference that refers to the formula cell itself. Here is an example:

1. Move to A8 and type **+A6+A7+A8**.
2. Press (ENTER).

At first the result, 1209, looks fine. Quattro Pro gets this result by adding the value of A6 (1200) to the value of A7, (9) and the value of A8 (which was initially 0).

3. Now try changing the value in A7 to 10—replacing the formula (+A1+A3)/A2).

The result has changed to 2419, as shown in Figure 3-6. As soon as you changed one of the numbers referenced in the formula, Quattro Pro recalculated the result. This time Quattro Pro has added 1200 plus 10 plus the previous value in A8 (1209). If you change the value in A6 or A7 again, Quattro Pro again reevaluates the formula, producing an even larger result.

One common breeding ground for circular references is formulas containing the @SUM function. Particularly if you use the typing method, it is easy to name the formula cell as one end of the block.

Quattro Pro does not prevent you from including circular references in formulas because some types of calculations, namely certain complex financial and engineering calculations, require them. However, Quattro Pro does warn you about such refer-

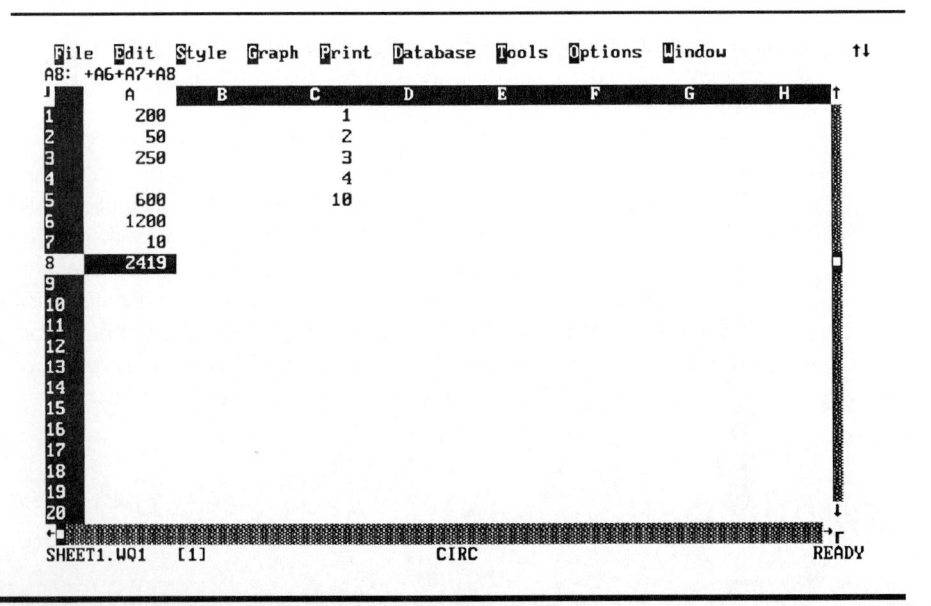

FIGURE 3-6. A circular formula

ences. Whenever your spreadsheet contains one or more circular references, you will see CIRC on the Status line at the bottom of the screen.

The most common circular references are found in formulas that refer directly to themselves—that is, they contain their own cell address—but these are not the only type. If a formula in A9 refers to a formula in A5 that refers to a formula in A1 that refers to A9, you have an indirect circular reference, with the same inherent problems as a direct one. These references can be much harder to find and correct because you must trace back the entire chain of references to look at all the cells that it refers to, and then at all the cells those cells refer to, and so on. In large, complex spreadsheets, this process can be difficult and time-consuming.

Fortunately, Quattro Pro provides a tool to assist in this process. If your spreadsheet contains a circular reference, Quattro Pro displays the address of the problematic formula on the Recalculation menu that is displayed when you issue the / Options | Recalculation command. If you issue the / Options | Recalculation command now, for example, you can see the address A8 on the Circular Cell line, as shown in Figure 3-7.

In cases where there is a chain of references involved—with one formula refering to a second formula referrring to a third formula that refers back to the first formula, for example—the Recalculation menu displays the address of only one link in the chain. It is up to you to find others. If you suspect there are a lot of circular references, you can use the map view discussed in Chapter 13 and look for every occurrence of the letter "C."

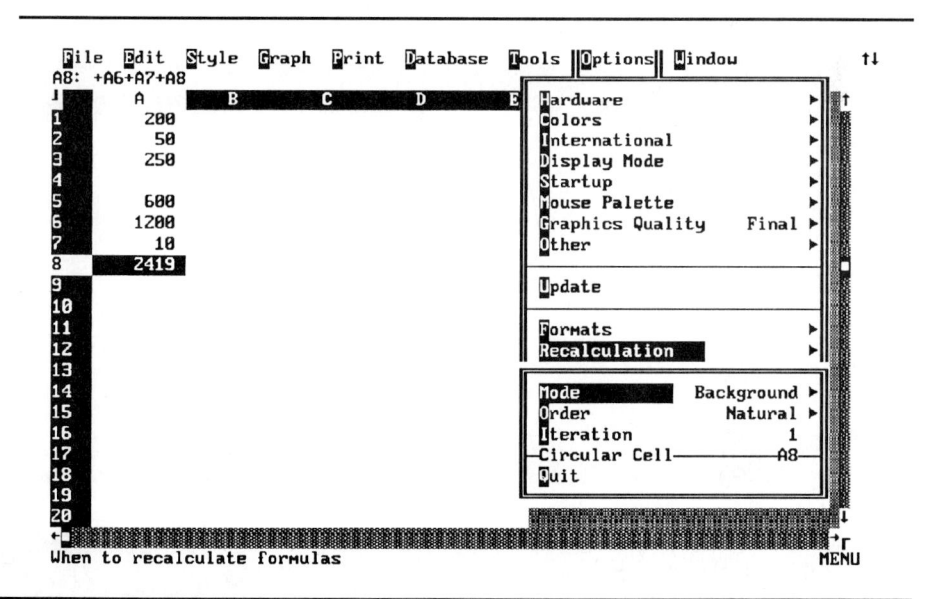

FIGURE 3-7. Using the Recalculation menu to find circular references

ERR Values

When you make certain types of mistakes in formulas, Quattro Pro displays ERR in the formula cell and, in most cases, in any formula cells that refer to that cell. These characters signify what is known as an *ERR value*. An ERR value does not indicate a syntactical error; there is nothing structurally wrong with the formula. Instead, it indicates some problem with one of the cells your formula references, a problem that Quattro Pro discovered when attempting to carry out the formula's calculations. Correcting the problem entails changing data in one of the referenced cells rather than editing the formula itself.

The most common cause of ERR values is an attempt to perform division by zero, by referencing a cell that either contains a zero or is blank. This exercise will illustrate this:

1. Move to C7 and type **+C5/C6**.

2. Press (ENTER). Your spreadsheet should now look like Figure 3-8.

3. Move to C6 and enter **100** to correct the problem.

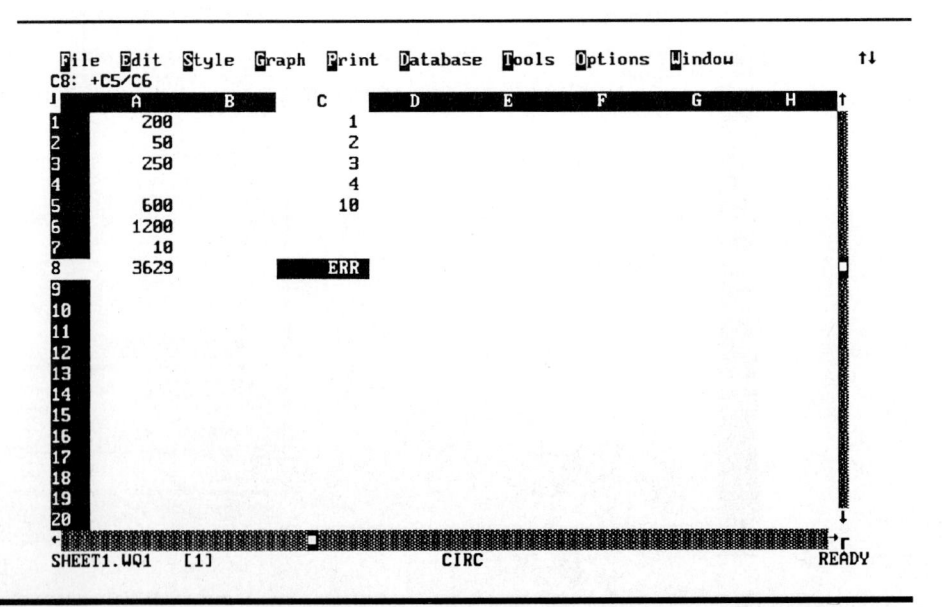

FIGURE 3-8. Attempting to divide by zero

Any formula that references an ERR value returns an ERR value itself. For example, 2 times ERR equals ERR. If you have a relatively complex spreadsheet with formulas that reference other formulas that reference other formulas, one attempt to divide by zero can produce multiple ERR values across the spreadsheet. To find the problem you should look at the last cell you changed, and then at all the formulas that reference that cell.

BUILDING AN INCOME STATEMENT MODEL

You can now add formulas to the LEARN1.WKQ spreadsheet that you started in Chapters 1 and 2.

1. Issue the / **File** | **Retrieve** command and select Yes when asked whether you want to lose your changes. Quattro Pro displays the LEARN1 spreadsheet on the screen.

2. Move to B8 and type (**B6-B7**).

3. Press (DOWN ARROW) six times and, in B14, type **@SUM(**.

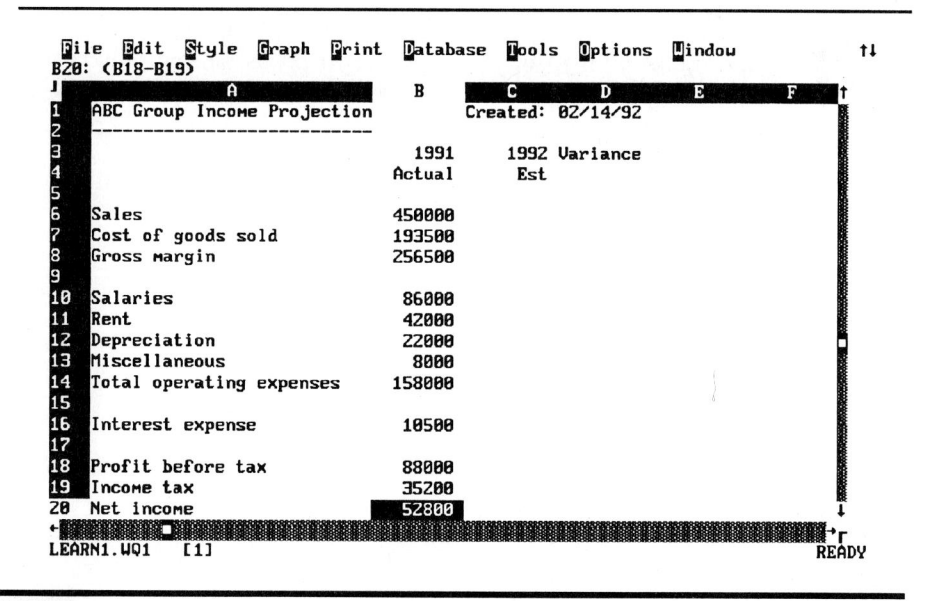

FIGURE 3-9. Adding formulas to LEARN1.WQ1

4. Press (UP ARROW) and type a period to anchor the cell pointer in B13.

5. Press (UP ARROW) three times and, in B10, type) and press (ENTER). The formula on the input line should now read @SUM(B10..B13) and the result should be 158000.

6. Press (DOWN ARROW) four times and, in B18, enter the formula (**B8-B14-B16**). The result should be 88500.

7. Press (DOWN ARROW) again and, in B19, type (**.4∗B18**).

8. Press (DOWN ARROW) and, in B20, type (**B18-B19**).

9. Press (ENTER). You have just created the model for an income statement: Revenue minus expenses equals profit before tax, and profit before tax less the tax (calculated as a percentage of profit before tax) equals net income. At this point, you can vary one or more of the variables on the spreadsheet (for example, Sales or Depreciation) and the effect of that change will ripple through the entire model.

10. Press (UP ARROW) four times to move to B16, and type **10500**.

11. Press (ENTER) while keeping your eye on cells B18 through B20. The spreadsheet should now look like the one shown in Figure 3-9.

When you ask what any particular spreadsheet "does," you are essentially asking how it links and processes a collection of numbers. You are, in other words, asking how its formulas work. And just as formulas are the heart of any spreadsheet, learning to construct formulas is central to the art of building spreadsheets. Your ability to obtain useful results from a spreadsheet depends on your ability to translate the relationships among the numbers pertinent to your business into formula format. The challenge is learning to translate what you already know—your business and your informational needs— into a form that Quattro Pro can use.

4

REARRANGING THE SPREADSHEET

The Undo Feature
Inserting and Deleting Rows and Columns
Manipulating Blocks
Putting Blocks to Work on Your Spreadsheet

This chapter introduces several commands for moving, copying, and deleting data. These commands are Quattro Pro's equivalents of scissors and paste—they are tools for "cutting and pasting" groups of data on the spreadsheet.

Because this chapter furnishes you with several tools that can wreak havoc on your spreadsheet, it also introduces Quattro Pro's Undo feature. This feature allows you to cancel the effect of all the cut and paste commands, and of many other operations.

THE UNDO FEATURE

Even the most experienced spreadsheet builders make mistakes. The more complex the spreadsheet, the more disastrous errors can be. Fortunately Quattro Pro has a special Undo feature that allows you to change your mind about many operations after the fact.

Two steps are involved in undoing an operation. The first is to turn on Quattro Pro's Undo feature by issuing the / Options | Other | Undo | Enable command. You then can issue another command, / Options | Update, to save that setting to disk, so that the Undo feature is automatically enabled every time you load Quattro Pro. This saves you the trouble of reissuing the / Options | Other | Undo | Enable command in every work session.

Once you have enabled Quattro Pro's protection feature, you use the / Edit | Undo command to undo a particular action. The operations you can undo with this command include:

- Entering data into a cell, editing data, and deleting a cell's contents
- Moving, copying, or erasing blocks of cells
- Inserting or deleting columns and rows
- Deleting graph names or block names
- Erasing the entire spreadsheet
- Retrieving files

The / Edit | Undo command always works on the last "undoable" operation, no matter how much time has elapsed since you performed it. For example, suppose you insert a row, move the cell pointer to another cell, activate the menus, start to issue a command, and then press (ESC). If you then issue the / Edit | Undo command, Quattro Pro removes the inserted row, because that was the most recent operation that / Edit | Undo can reverse. However, if you had entered data into a cell after inserting the row, / Edit | Undo would undo the data entry operation instead. If you issue the / Edit | Undo command when the Undo feature is not enabled, Quattro Pro displays the error message "Undo is not enabled. Cannot undo it."

The function key equivalent for / Edit | Undo is (ALT-F5). This key assignment is not technically a menu command shortcut because it does not involve the (CTRL) key and it cannot be changed. However, it works just like a shortcut.

As in the last chapter, you will experiment with new techniques on a blank practice spreadsheet first and later apply them to LEARN1. If you have LEARN1 on the screen, save it by issuing the / File | Save command, and then erase the screen with / File | Erase. If you have just reloaded Quattro Pro, you are ready to begin.

Start by enabling the Undo feature:

1. Issue the / Options | Other | Undo | Enable command.

2. Select the Update option from the Options menu to save that setting permanently.

3. Select **Q**uit to return to Ready mode.

Now you are ready to try / Edit | Undo.

1. In A1, type **111** and press (ENTER).
2. Issue the / Edit | Undo command.
3. Now undo the effect of the / Edit | Undo command itself. This time use (ALT-F5).
4. Delete the entry from A1 by pressing (DEL).
5. Press (ALT-F5) to undo that deletion.

INSERTING AND DELETING ROWS AND COLUMNS

The rest of this chapter covers commands for reorganizing and copying data on the spreadsheet. If you make a mistake and obtain a different result from that shown in the figures, use (ALT-F5) to undo your last command and try again.

Inserting Rows

At its simplest the / Edit | Insert | **R**ows command can be used to insert a single row immediately above the current cell. When you issue this command, Quattro Pro displays the prompt "Enter row insert block:" followed by a default block consisting of the current cell. For example, if you are positioned at D4 when you issue the / Edit | Insert | **R**ows command, Quattro Pro displays the message "Enter row insert block: D4..D4."

If you want to insert one row immediately above the current cell, you can simply press (ENTER). Try this now with some sample data.

1. Press (DOWN ARROW) and, in A2, type **222**.
2. Press (DOWN ARROW) and, in A3, enter **+A1+A2**.
3. Move to A2 and issue the / Edit | Insert | **R**ows command.
4. When Quattro Pro prompts you for a "row insert block," just press (ENTER) to insert a new row immediately above what was row 2.

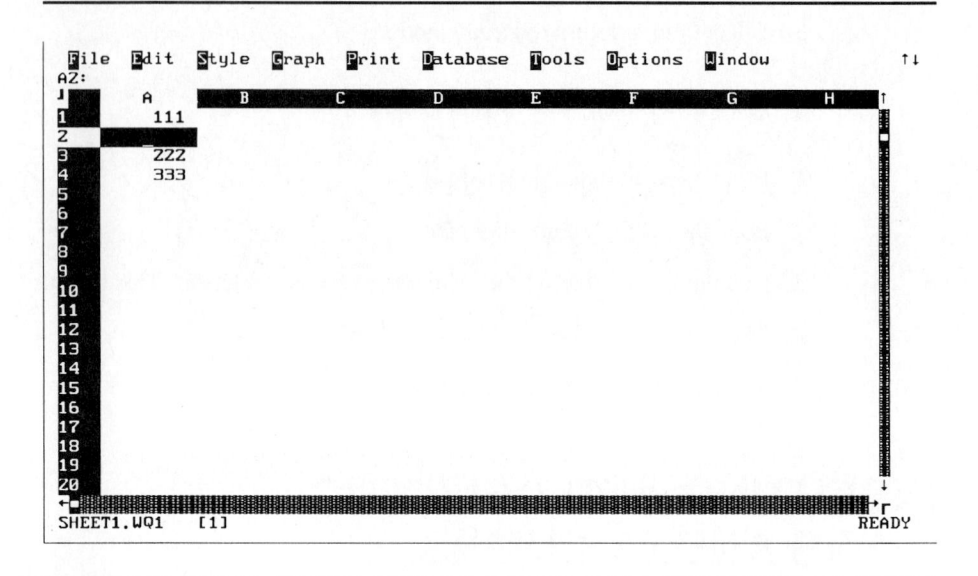

```
┌─────────────────────────────────────────────────────────────┐
│ File  Edit  Style  Graph  Print  Database  Tools  Options  Window    ↑↓│
│A2:                                                          │
│      A       B       C       D       E       F       G      H│
│ 1   111                                                     │
│ 2                                                           │
│ 3   222                                                     │
│ 4   333                                                     │
│ 5                                                           │
│ 6                                                           │
│ 7                                                           │
│ 8                                                           │
│ 9                                                           │
│10                                                           │
│11                                                           │
│12                                                           │
│13                                                           │
│14                                                           │
│15                                                           │
│16                                                           │
│17                                                           │
│18                                                           │
│19                                                           │
│20                                                           │
│SHEET1.WQ1    [1]                                      READY │
└─────────────────────────────────────────────────────────────┘
```

FIGURE 4-1. Inserting a row

Your spreadsheet should now look like Figure 4-1. Notice that the formula still returns the value 333, just as it did before the insertion. If you move to A4, you will notice that the formula now reads +A1+A3.

5. Press (ALT-F5) (Undo) to remove the inserted row.

Inserting Rows Within a Block

As you have seen, using the @SUM function rather than several plus signs to add a series of numbers can save you time and keystrokes. It has another advantage: When you sum a group of cells with the @SUM function, you can insert new cells in the block and they will automatically be included in the sum. Try this out next.

Now that you are familiar with the basics of data entry, you will no longer need as much detail in the instructions. *Enter,* from this point, will mean type the specified data and press (ENTER) (or one of the cursor movement keys) to enter data into a cell or complete a command. *Type* will mean type the specified characters without pressing (ENTER).

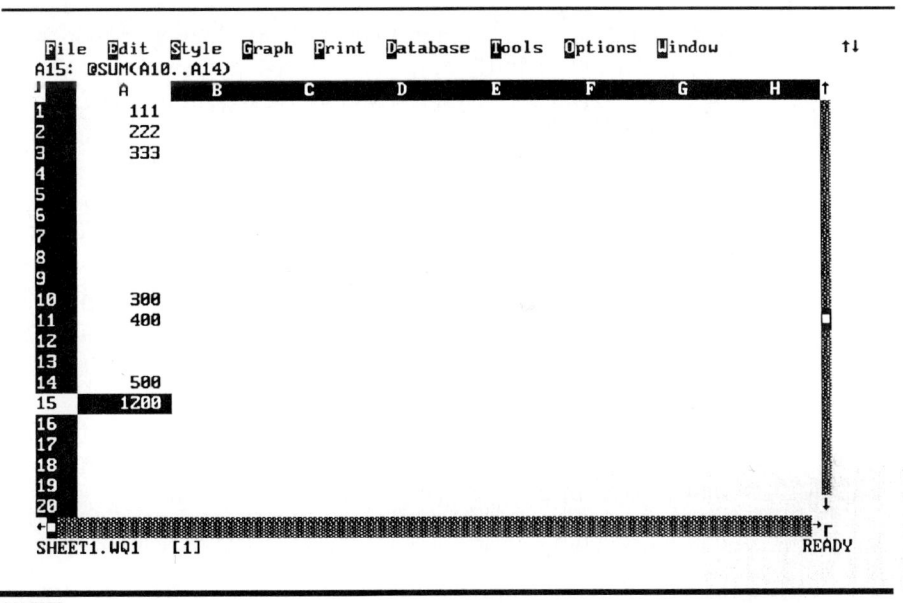

FIGURE 4-2. Inserted row's effect on a referenced block

1. Enter the following data:

   In A10 enter **300**
   In A11 enter **400**
   In A12 enter **500**
   In A13 enter **@SUM(A10.A12)**

2. This time use (CTRL-I), the shortcut for / Edit I Insert.

3. When Quattro Pro displays the Insert menu, select Rows by pressing (ENTER).

4. Now insert two rows at once. When Quattro Pro suggests A13..A13 as the "row insert block," move the cell pointer up one row to A12 and press (ENTER) to specify the block A13..A12. Note that Quattro Pro inserts new rows 12 and 13, pushing all the data in or below what was row 12 down two rows.

5. Move to A15 and notice that Quattro Pro has adjusted the formula to read @SUM(A10..A14). Your worksheet should now look like the one in Figure 4-2.

6. Enter **100** in A12 and A13 and note that these new numbers are automatically included in the total. If instead you had used the formula (+A10+A11+A12) and then inserted two new rows, you would have needed to edit the formula to include the new cells.

Quattro Pro has no way of discerning whether a cell located above or below a block's boundaries is related to the block. As a result, it only adjusts block references in formulas when you insert new rows within the borders of the original block. If you add rows above the uppermost row or below the lowermost row of a block reference, the scope of the block reference remains unchanged. To see this for yourself,

1. Move to A15, press (CTRL-I), and then press (ENTER).

2. Press (ENTER) again to insert a single row above what is now row 15 (above the formula cell but below the last cell in the @SUM block).

3. In the new cell A15, enter **200**. This entry has no effect on the figure in A16.

4. Move to A16 and notice that the formula still reads @SUM(A10..A14).

Deleting Rows

The **/ Edit | Delete | Rows** command operates like **/ Edit | Insert | Rows** in reverse. When you issue this command, Quattro Pro prompts you for a block of cells and deletes the rows specified within the block. It also automatically adjusts any formulas that reference cells relocated by the command. Try the following:

1. Move to A15 and type **/EDR**.

2. Press (ENTER) to accept the default of A15..A15 as the "block of rows to delete."

Whenever you delete a row, any data within that row is lost. If any of the cells within the row are referenced by formulas in other rows, those formulas return a value of ERR since they will, in effect, be referencing cells that no longer exist. For example, if you delete row 1, the formula in A3 changes to +ERR+A1, and Quattro Pro displays an ERR value in that cell.

If you delete rows that include cells that fall inside the boundaries of a block referenced by a formula, Quattro Pro simply adjusts the block coordinates as necessary. However, if you delete a row that contains one of the coordinate cells of a block (A10 or A14 in the current spreadsheet), any formula that references that block returns a value of ERR. To see this in action,

1. Move to A14, type **/EDR**, and press (ENTER) to delete row 14. ERR appears in A14, and the formula in that cell reads @SUM(ERR).

2. Press (ALT-F5) to undo the last command.

This is a particularly useful application for the Undo feature because once you delete a row containing a block corner cell, the block coordinates are entirely replaced by ERR. This makes it difficult to reconstruct the original formula even after you recognize the problem.

Inserting and Deleting Columns

The / Edit | Insert | Columns and / Edit | Delete | Columns commands work exactly like / Edit | Insert | Rows and / Edit | Delete | Rows, except that they operate on columns. Columns are always inserted to the left of the cell block that you specify.

Here's an exercise that involves inserting and deleting columns:

1. In any cell in column A, press (CTRL-I). Then select Columns.

2. When Quattro Pro prompts you for a "column insert block," move to column B and press (ENTER) to insert two columns to the left of column A. Look at C3 or C15 and notice that all cell references in the formulas have been adjusted to refer to column C.

3. Move back to column A and issue the / Edit | Delete | Columns command.

4. Again, move to column B, expanding the block to two columns, and press (ENTER) to delete what are now columns A and B. The two empty columns should disappear and your data should now be back in column A.

As with rows, when you delete columns you must be careful not to eliminate any cells referenced by formulas in other columns on the spreadsheet (including any cells used as block coordinates).

MANIPULATING BLOCKS

So far you have changed the position of data on your spreadsheet indirectly by inserting or deleting rows or columns. Quattro Pro also offers a command, / Edit | Move, that allows you to move a block of cells from one location to another. After learning this command, you will learn to copy blocks with / Edit | Copy and erase them with / Edit | Erase Block.

When you issue any block command, Quattro Pro prompts you for the block's coordinates and displays the current cell as the default. In most cases, Quattro Pro displays two addresses on the input line. If, for example, the cell pointer is positioned at D4 when you issue the command, Quattro Pro displays a message like

Source block of cells: D4..D4

or

Block to be modified: D4..D4

You now have several options for defining the block. If you want to accept the default (a block consisting only of the current cell), you can simply press (ENTER). Otherwise you can use either the typing or pointing method to define an alternative block. To use the typing method, simply type the address of one corner of the block, followed by one or two periods, and the address of the diagonally opposite corner. Then press (ENTER) or one of the cursor-movement keys. The pointing method, described next, takes a bit more getting used to.

Pointing Out Blocks in Commands

When you issue a block command, Quattro Pro assumes that you will be pointing to cells and enters Point mode immediately. It also assumes that you will use the current cell as one of the defining corners of your block. If the current cell is, in fact, located at one corner of the block you want to specify, you need only perform two steps to define the block:

1. Move to the opposite corner of the block. As you do, the cell pointer remains anchored at the first cell and the entire block of cells is highlighted.

2. When you reach the opposite corner, press (ENTER).

If the cell pointer is not already located in a corner of the desired block, you must take three steps:

1. Press (ESC) or (BACKSPACE) to unanchor the cell pointer from the current cell. When you do this, Quattro Pro erases the second corner of the default block from the input line.

2. Move to the cell you want to designate as the first corner of the block, and type a period to reanchor the cell pointer in this location.

3. Move to the diagonally opposite corner of the block and press (ENTER).

If you get lost while using this method, try looking at the number of addresses on the input line. If only one set of cell coordinates appears on the input line, Quattro Pro thinks you are still defining the first corner of the block. If you press one of the cursor-movement keys, the cell pointer moves in the specified direction and the address on the input line changes to reflect that position. When you reach one corner of the desired block, you must type a period to anchor the cell pointer there. Quattro Pro then displays a second address on the input line.

If you see two coordinates on the input line, Quattro Pro thinks that you have already finished defining your first corner and are now pointing to the second. If you press one of the cursor-movement keys now, the first address on the input line stays the same, the second address changes to reflect your current position, and the cell pointer expands to highlight all the cells in between those two addresses.

Start by moving the contents of block A13..A15 to C13..C15 using / Edit | Move. When you issue this command, Quattro Pro asks you for two pieces of information: the source block (the block of cells you want to move) and the destination (the spot that you want to move them to).

1. In A15, issue the / Edit | Move command. Quattro Pro displays the prompt "Source block of cells: A15..A15." Since A15 is one of the corners of the block that you want to move, you can immediately start moving to the other corner to highlight the entire source block.

2. Move to A13. Notice that as you move the cell pointer, Quattro Pro displays the current cell's address as the second address on the input line. It also illuminates the block of cells that would be specified if you chose the current cell as the second corner of the block. When you reach A13, A13 through A15 are highlighted.

3. Press (ENTER) to designate A15..A13 as the source block for this command. Quattro Pro displays the prompt "Destination for cells: A15." Now Quattro Pro is asking you to specify the upper-left corner of the area where you want to move the block. Because blocks always retain their shape when moved, you must specify a new location only for the upper-left corner; the rest of the block will "tag along" intact. A15, the cell in which you were positioned when you first issued the / Edit | Move command, is the address that Quattro Pro offers as a default. To specify a different location as the destination, you can either move to another cell or type the cell's address. Try the pointing method this time.

4. Move to C13 and press (ENTER). The cell block should now appear in rows C13 through C15. The total displayed in C15 is still correct, even though you have moved only part of the referenced block.

5. Move to C15. Look at the input line and notice that the formula in cell C15 reads @SUM(A10..C14). Your screen should now look like Figure 4-3.

Even though you have separated the cells specified in the formula, Quattro Pro has appropriately adjusted the cell references. Whenever you move cells that are referenced in a formula, Quattro Pro adjusts the references to fit the data's new location. Because Quattro Pro keeps track of blocks by keeping track of their upper-left and lower-right corners, moving one of those corner cells, in effect, changes the size of the block itself.

In the previous exercise, for example, moving C14 meant expanding the block referenced in C15. Quattro Pro adjusted the coordinates of that block to fit the new location of the corner cell C14. Because cell blocks must be rectangular, there is no way to keep C14 within the block without also including cells B10 through B14 and C10 through C12. If those additional cells contained values, or if you entered values in them now, those values would automatically be included in your total. If you move a cell that falls within the middle of a referenced block, Quattro Pro does not adjust the block references at all. For example, if you had moved only the value in A13 to column C, the formula in A15 would remain the same, and the value in C13 would be excluded from the total. (Remember, Quattro Pro only remembers a block's corners.)

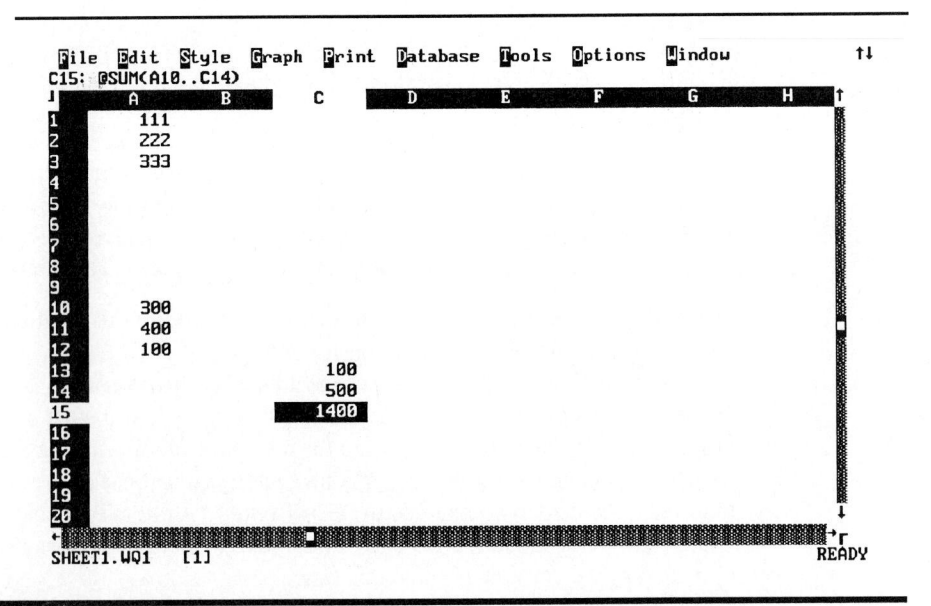

FIGURE 4-3. Effect of the move on the @SUM formula

If you move cells that are individually referenced by a formula, Quattro Pro adjusts the formula accordingly. For example, if you move the contents of A1 to C1, Quattro Pro changes the formula in A3 to read +C1+A2. No new cells would be included in the total.

Now try moving the same block of cells back to its original position. This time you will use the (CTRL-M) shortcut for / Edit | Move and will start in the destination cell rather than in one corner of the source block.

1. Move to A13 and press (CTRL-M). Quattro Pro displays the message "Source block of cells: A13..A13."

2. Press (ESC) to unanchor the cell pointer from A13. Only one address is now displayed on the input line; the second A13 has been erased. This means that you can now redefine the first corner of the source block.

3. Move to C13 and type a period to reanchor the cell pointer. The cell coordinate C13 should appear twice on the input line, indicating that you can now expand the highlight to the second corner of the block.

4. Move to C15 and press (ENTER) to specify a source block of C13..C15.

5. When Quattro Pro requests a destination for the block, press (ENTER) to accept the default of A13.

POINTING OUT BLOCKS IN ADVANCE Quattro Pro also allows you to point out the blocks of cells you want to manipulate before you issue a command. To move a block, for example, you can start by highlighting the source block; then issue the / Edit | Move command, and define the destination block by moving the cell pointer to one corner of the block. To point out a block in advance, you start by pressing (SHIFT-F7) (the Select function key combination). Quattro Pro displays EXT on the status line, indicating that it now expects you to extend the cell pointer to highlight the block. Next you move to the opposite corner of the block and issue the / Edit | Move command. Try this now.

1. In A13, press (SHIFT-F7). Notice that EXT appears on the status line.

2. Move to A10. The entire block of A10..A15 should now be highlighted.

3. Issue the / Edit | Move command. Quattro Pro automatically uses the predefined block of A10..A15 as the source block and asks you only for a destination.

4. Enter **B10** as the destination.

5. Press (ALT-F5) to undo the move.

POINTING OUT BLOCKS WITH A MOUSE You can also point out blocks with a mouse, before or during a command, by using either of the following methods:

Method 1

1. Click on one corner of the block.
2. Hold down the left button while you drag to the opposite corner. Quattro Pro highlights the block as you move the pointer.
3. Release the button.

Method 2

1. Click on one corner of the block.
2. Move the mouse pointer to the opposite corner of the block.
3. Hold down the right button on the mouse while you click the left button. Quattro Pro highlights the block.

If you are using a mouse, you might try these methods in some of the upcoming exercises, substituting either method whenever Quattro Pro prompts for a source block.

Copying Cells

/ Edit | Copy is one of the most useful commands in Quattro Pro's repertoire. At its simplest, it can be used to copy a block of cells, as is, from one location on the spreadsheet to another. As with / Edit | **M**ove, Quattro Pro asks for a source block and a destination. As soon as you specify the destination, Quattro Pro replicates the source block in the desired location. Try this now.

1. Press (HOME) and, in A1, issue the / Edit | Copy command.
2. When prompted for the source block, move to A3, and press (ENTER) to define the block A1..A3.
3. When prompted for the destination, type **B4** and press (ENTER). You have now copied the data in block A1..A3 to block B4..B6. Your screen should look like Figure 4-4.

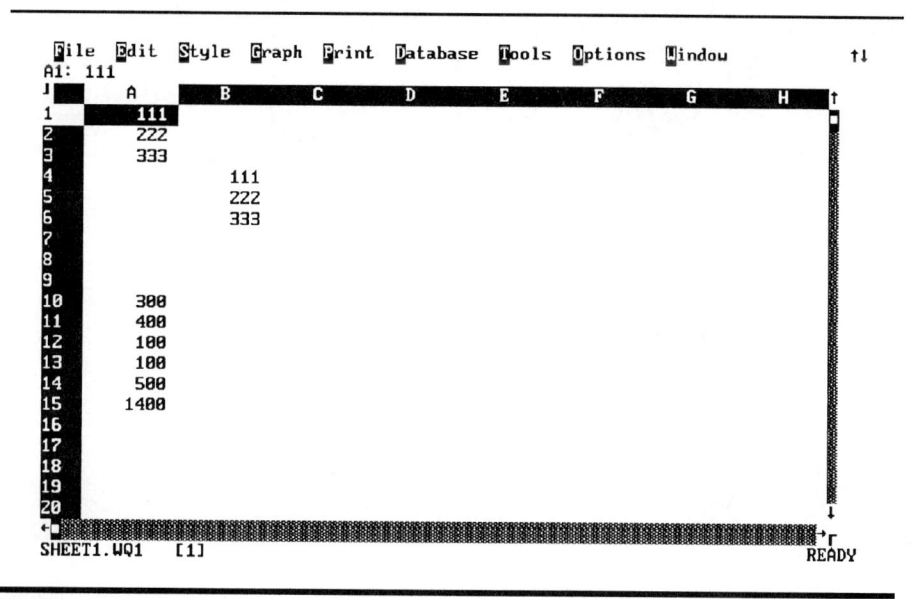

```
             File  Edit  Style  Graph  Print  Database  Tools  Options  Window              ↑↓
  A1: 111
  ↓      A        B        C        D        E        F        G        H   ↑
  1     111                                                                  □
  2     222
  3     333
  4              111
  5              222
  6              333
  7
  8
  9
  10    300
  11    400
  12    100
  13    100
  14    500
  15    1400
  16
  17
  18
  19
  20                                                                         ↓
  ←                                                                        →
  SHEET1.WQ1   [1]                                                       READY
```

FIGURE 4-4. The spreadsheet after copying a block

In this exercise, you simply replicated a block of cells in a new location, producing a second block that looks just like the original. You actually have four possible source block/destination block combinations with / Edit | Copy:

- Copying a block, consisting of one or more cells, to another block of the same size and shape
- Copying a single-cell block to a multiple-cell block
- Copying a row across several rows
- Copying a column across several columns

You have already tried the first of these combinations. Now try the others.

COPYING A SINGLE CELL ACROSS A BLOCK As you have seen, when you copy one block of cells to another block of the same dimensions, you specify two cell addresses for the source block and one address—the upper-left corner—for the destination. In all the other source block/destination block combinations, you specify two addresses for the source block and two for the destination. If you use the pointing method to designate the destination block, you always need to type a period to anchor the cell pointer at the first cell address before you can point to a second cell. Try this now.

```
      File  Edit  Style  Graph  Print  Database  Tools  Options  Window         ↑↓
A1: 111
        A         B         C         D         E         F         G         H
1     111       111       111       111       111       111
2     222
3     333
4               111
5               222
6               333
7
8
9
10    300
11    400
12    100
13    100
14    500
15    1400
16
17
18
19
20
SHEET1.WQ1  [1]                                                              READY
```

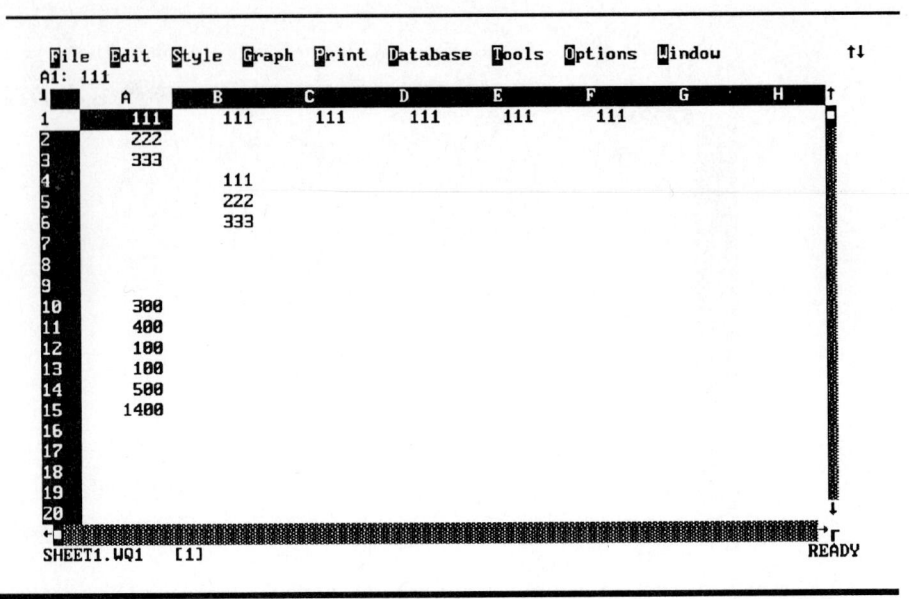

FIGURE 4-5. Effect of copying cell A1 across a multiple-cell block

1. In A1, press (CTRL-C), the shortcut for / Edit | Copy.

2. When prompted for the source block, press (ENTER) to accept the default A1..A1.

3. When prompted for a destination, type a period to anchor the cell pointer in A1.

4. Move to F1 and press (ENTER) to define a destination block of A1..F1. Your worksheet should now look like the one in Figure 4-5.

Here the source block (A1..A1) was included in the destination block (A1..F1). In effect, you have copied cell A1 over itself as well as over cells B1 through F1. Since this has no real effect on the content of A1, the only reason for including that cell in the destination block is to save yourself the trouble of moving to B1 before anchoring the cell pointer.

COPYING MULTIPLE-CELL BLOCKS ACROSS ROWS OR DOWN COLUMNS
In the last command, you copied a single cell across a block of cells by specifying two cell addresses for the destination rather than one. In certain circumstances, you can also copy a multiple-cell source block across a row or down a column using a similar method. To illustrate, try copying cells A1 and A2 across part of row 5.

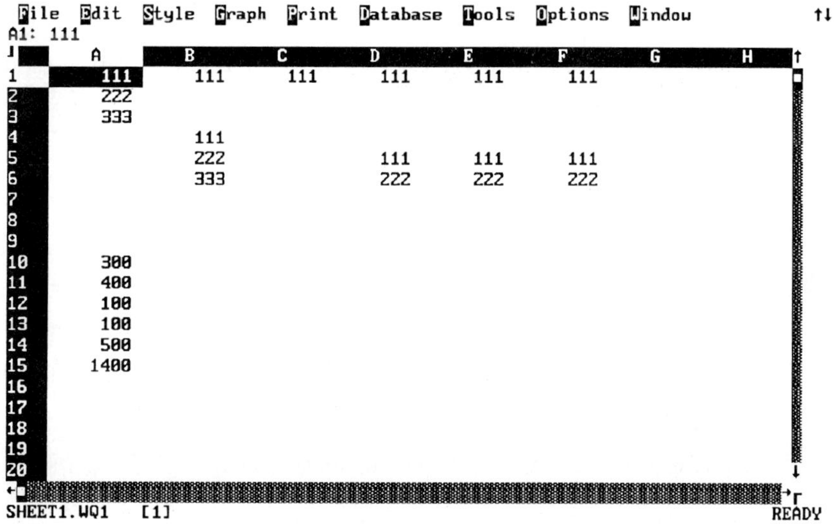

```
     File Edit Style Graph Print Database Tools Options Window          ↑↓
A1: 111
     A         B       C       D       E       F       G       H
 1   111      111     111     111     111     111
 2   222
 3   333
 4            111
 5            222                     111     111     111
 6            333                     222     222     222
 7
 8
 9
10   300
11   400
12   100
13   100
14   500
15  1400
16
17
18
19
20
SHEET1.WQ1   [1]                                                    READY
```

FIGURE 4-6. Copying a multiple-cell block across a row

1. In A1, press (CTRL-C).

2. When prompted for a source block, press (DOWN ARROW) to move to A2. Press (ENTER).

3. When prompted for a destination, type or point to the block D5..F5.

4. Press (ENTER). Your worksheet should now look like Figure 4-6.

You can use / Edit | Copy to replicate a multiple-cell block across a larger destination block in only a few situations. The source block has to consist of cells in a single row or a single column. When the source block falls within one column, you can only copy it across a row, creating adjacent duplicate columns. When the source block falls within one row, you can only copy it down a column, creating adjacent, duplicate rows.

> **Note** If you try to copy a block that spans multiple rows and columns across a larger block, Quattro Pro does not display an error message; instead, it simply replicates the source block once rather than many times.

Notice that both cells used to designate the destination block in the last command were within the top row of the block. This is actually quite consistent with the way you have specified destinations in previous commands. Most of the time, when you copy or move a block, you only specify an upper-left corner for the destination. Since the block maintains its shape when copied or transported, the rest of the block simply follows along. Similarly, when you copy a block across a row or down a column, you must specify only the top row or the left column. In effect, this is like specifying the upper-left corner for each one of a series of replications.

Copying Formulas

So far the / Edit | Copy command has been fairly straightforward and predictable. When you copy formulas, however, the outcome is less obvious.

When you copy a formula, Quattro Pro abandons the actual addresses of the referenced cells and remembers only their locations *relative to the formula cell*. Cell A3, for example, currently contains the formula (A1+A2). If you copy the contents of this cell to B3, Quattro Pro evaluates that formula as "add the contents of the cell located two cells above this one to the contents of the cell one cell above this one." Once the formula has been duplicated in B3, its cell references are adjusted to the new location. The formula +A1+A2 is therefore transformed into +B1+B2. Similarly, if you copy the formula in A15 to another cell, Quattro Pro adjusts the formula to fit the new location, in effect creating a new formula that totals the values in the five cells above it.

To see how this works, follow these steps:

1. Move to A15.

2. Issue the / Edit | Copy command.

3. When prompted for the source block, press (ENTER) to accept A15..A15.

4. When prompted for the destination, type a period to anchor the cell pointer. Then point to D15 and press (ENTER). Your spreadsheet should now look like the one in Figure 4-7.

5. Now look at the formulas in B15, C15, and D15. Notice that Quattro Pro has adjusted the formula to fit each of the columns: In each column, the formula cell adds up values in the five cells immediately above itself. If those cells had already contained numbers, these new formulas would have calculated their total. Instead, Quattro Pro shows zeros in cells B15..D15 because the cells that the formulas reference are currently empty.

6. Fill in all the cells in the block B10..D14 and watch Quattro Pro automatically add up the columns, as shown in Figure 4-8.

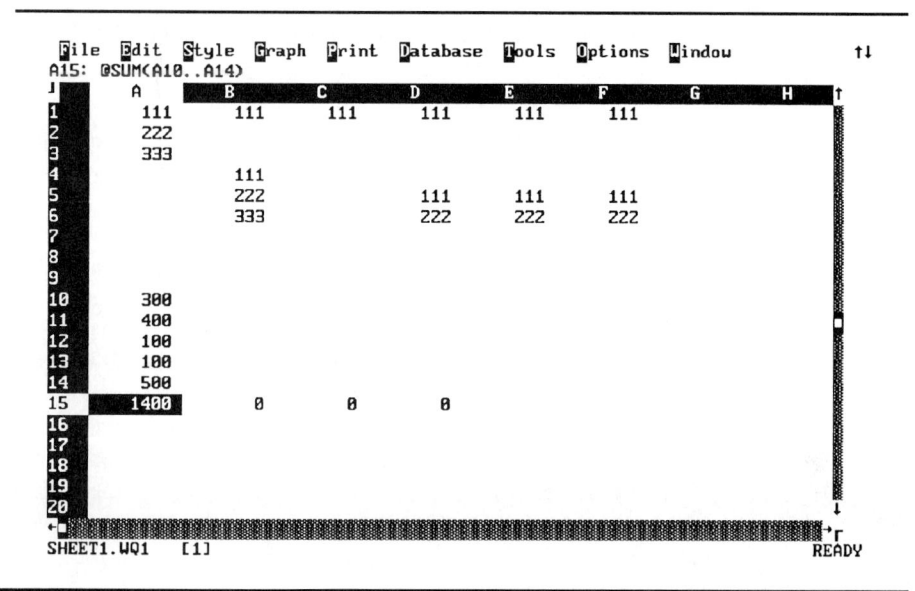

FIGURE 4-7. The spreadsheet after copying the @SUM formula

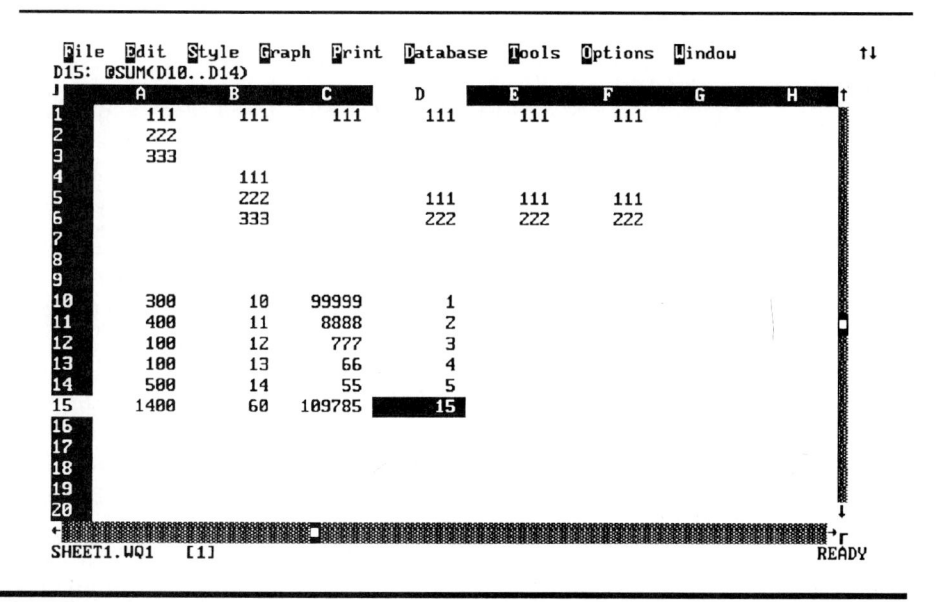

FIGURE 4-8. Filling in cells referenced by the new formulas

> **Note** Do not skip this step. Some of the exercises later in this chapter require data in the block B10..D14 in order to work properly.

Here is a review of what just happened. When you copied the formula, you created three new formulas, each of which replicates the general function of the formula in A15 (adding a column of five numbers) rather than its literal contents.

This method of handling cell references allows you to build typical spreadsheets quickly. Most business spreadsheets are structured as grids in which the same basic set of calculations is performed in several adjacent rows and columns. For example, Figure 4-9 shows a spreadsheet that calculates total monthly sales revenues in each of four sales regions. In this case a single formula— @SUM(B4..B7) —was entered in B8 to calculate total sales in January. This formula was then copied to C8 through G8 to calculate totals for the next five months. Next the formula @SUM(B4..G4) was entered in H4 to calculate sales revenue in the Northeast region over a six-month period. This formula was then copied to H4 through H7 to calculate six-month totals for the other regions, and to cell H8 to add the six monthly totals for all regions. Altogether, only two formulas were typed in the spreadsheet; the other nine were generated from those first two.

All the cell references you have entered in formulas are what are called *relative cell references*. As you have seen, whenever Quattro Pro replicates a relative cell reference, it "thinks" in terms of the referenced cell's position relative to the formula

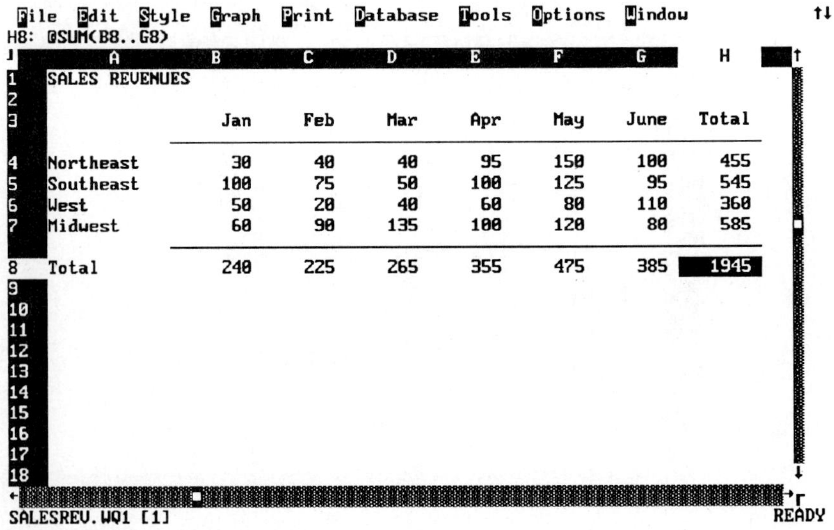

FIGURE 4-9. A spreadsheet built by copying formulas

cell, rather than in terms of a fixed location on the spreadsheet. Sometimes you want Quattro Pro to treat your cell references differently when you copy a formula and leave some or all of your cell references as is, no matter where you copy them. In such cases you can make the cell references absolute rather than relative. *Absolute cell references* do not change when copied; they always refer to exactly the same location. Absolute cell referencing is covered in Chapter 8.

Keep in mind that if you change the original formula, you need to reissue the / Edit I Copy command if you want the copies to change accordingly. This may seem strange because once you get used to Quattro Pro's automatic recalculation of formulas, you may expect Quattro Pro to reexecute other operations as well. However, unlike commands, formulas are actually stored in the spreadsheet. Quattro Pro can recalculate formulas because they are retained in your computer's memory. In contrast, when you issue a command, Quattro Pro may request information, but it discards your answers as soon as the operation is complete. With / Edit I Copy, once you have finished copying a formula to several other cells, Quattro Pro "forgets" about the entire operation; there is no longer any link, in the spreadsheet or in memory, between the original formula and its replicates.

Notes of Caution on Moving And Copying Blocks

When you move a block of cells, be careful not to overwrite any cells that are referenced by formulas. If you do, the cell reference is replaced with ERR and the formula yields a result of ERR on your worksheet. For example, if you moved a cell over A2, the formula in A3 would change to (A1+ERR) and would evaluate to ERR.

You can experience similar problems if you overwrite cells in a block that is referenced by a formula. In this case only the block's corners are at issue. If you overwrite cells in the middle of a referenced block, the formula is simply recalculated with the new values. However, if you overwrite a corner, or coordinate, cell of a block, Quattro Pro responds as if you had overwritten any cell references within a formula, replacing the block reference with the value ERR and evaluating the formula as ERR on the worksheet. Execute the following steps to see how this problem occurs:

1. Move to A1 and issue the / Edit I **Move** command.

2. Accept the default source block of A1..A1 and, when prompted for a destination, move to A10 and press (ENTER).

3. Move to A15 and note that the formula in that cell now reads @SUM(ERR).

4. Press (ALT-F5) (Undo) to undo the damage.

If any other formulas on the worksheet referenced A15, they too would have been changed to ERR. As explained in Chapter 3, an ERR value in one cell can, like any other change in value, ripple through your entire worksheet.

Overwriting cells with / Edit | Copy does not produce the same problems. For this reason, you should be all the more careful about copying one block of cells over another one. Quattro Pro does not produce warnings or generate ERR values, so it is easy to damage your worksheet by copying something to the wrong location.

You can also experience problems with / Edit | Copy if you copy a formula to a location that requires Quattro Pro to reference a cell off the edge of the worksheet. For example, if you enter a formula in column D that refers to a cell in column C and then attempt to copy that formula to column A, Quattro Pro tries to adjust the formula so that it refers to the column that is to the left of column A. Since there is no column to the left of A, Quattro Pro "wraps around" to the other edge of the worksheet, referencing a cell in column IV, the rightmost column on the worksheet. Because no error message is displayed in this case, this unintended result can easily go undetected.

On the other hand, if you try to copy or move a block of cells to a destination too close to the borders of the worksheet to accommodate the block, Quattro Pro displays the error message "Out of worksheet boundary." For example, you would see this error message if you tried to copy or move block A1..A3 to the destination A8192 (the lower-left corner of the worksheet).

Using the (END) Key to Define Large Blocks

The (END) key is a direction key that is particularly useful for pointing out blocks. When used to move around the spreadsheet, (END) is always used in conjunction with one of the arrow keys or with (HOME). With (END) key combinations, you press the (END) key first, release it, and then press the other key. This is in contrast to other key combinations, such as control keys, that require you to hold down (CTRL) while tapping the second key.

If the current cell contains data, the (END)-arrow key combination moves the cell pointer in the direction of the arrow key to the next cell immediately before or after an empty cell. If the current cell is empty, it moves the cell pointer in the specified direction to the next cell that contains data. This is less complicated than it sounds: You are essentially just moving the cell pointer from one block of data to the next.

You might also find it helpful to keep two rules in mind. The (END)-arrow key combinations always:

- Moves the cell pointer to an edge—either the edge of a block of cells (the boundary between a cell that contains data and one that is empty) or the edge of the spreadsheet itself

- Moves the cell pointer to a filled cell (that is, a cell that contains data) if there is such a cell in the indicated direction

There is one last (END) key combination: (END-HOME). This key combination always moves the cell pointer to the lower-right corner of that section of the spreadsheet that contains data. This corner cell is the intersection of the rightmost column that currently contains data, and the lowest row that currently contains data. This cell may or may not contain data itself. In your current spreadsheet, for example, (END-HOME) would move the cell pointer to F15. Even though F15 is empty, Quattro Pro considers it the lower-right corner of the spreadsheet.

This exercise demonstrates how the (END) key combinations work:

1. Press (HOME) to move to A1.
2. Press (END-DOWN ARROW) to move directly to A3, the last cell before a blank cell as you move downward.
3. Press (END-DOWN ARROW) again. This time the cell pointer moves immediately to A10 (the next cell, moving downward, that contains data).
4. Press (END-DOWN ARROW) to move to A15, the next filled-in cell above a blank cell.
5. Press (END-DOWN ARROW) one last time. Because no cells below A15 contain data, the cell pointer has now moved to cell A8192, the lower-left corner of the worksheet.
6. Press (END-UP ARROW) to move back to A15, the first cell as you move upward that contains data.
7. Press (END-RIGHT ARROW) to move to D15, the last filled-in cell in this block.
8. Press (END-UP ARROW) to move to D10.
9. Press (HOME) to move back to A1. This time try moving sideways by pressing (END) and then (RIGHT ARROW) to move to F1.
10. Press (END-RIGHT ARROW) again to move to IV1, the last column in the worksheet.
11. Press (HOME) to return to A1.

12. Press (END-HOME) to move the cell pointer to the lower-right corner of the filled-in section of the spreadsheet area: F15.

Erasing a Block

The / Edit I Erase Block command erases all data in a specified block of cells, as if you had moved the cell pointer to every cell in the block and pressed (DEL). The preasssigned shortcut for / Edit I Erase Block is (CTRL-E).

Keep in mind that Quattro Pro does not make you confirm your intention before erasing a large block. If you do erase cells by accident, be sure to issue the / Edit I Undo command immediately, before you perform another "undoable" operation.

To practice using / Edit I Erase, follow these steps:

1. Use the (F5) (GoTo) key to move to A10.
2. This time try defining the block in advance using the (END) key.
3. Press (SHIFT-F7) (Select).
4. Press (END-RIGHT ARROW) to extend the block to A10..D10.
5. Press (END-DOWN ARROW) to extend the block to A10..D15.
6. Issue the / Edit I Erase Block command. Quattro Pro erases all the data in the predefined block.
7. Press (ALT-F5) (Undo) to undo the last command.

Caution You must be careful not to erase cells that are referenced as the denominator in a division formula elsewhere on the spreadsheet. For example, if any cell on the worksheet contained the formula (B3/B4) and you erased a block that included B4, the formula would evaluate to ERR because you cannot divide by zero (a blank cell is read as the equivalent of zero).

PUTTING BLOCKS TO WORK ON YOUR SPREADSHEET

Now that you have learned the mechanics of cutting and pasting data, try putting this knowledge to work on your sample worksheet. The following instructions tell you only the operations to perform. You can choose between menu selections and command shortcuts, pointing and typing methods. To refresh your memory, the command shortcuts for commands covered in this chapter are

(CTRL-I)	/ Edit I Insert
(CTRL-M)	/ Edit I Move
(CTRL-C)	/ Edit I Copy
(CTRL-E)	/ Edit I Erase Block
(ALT-F5)	/ Edit I Undo

You also learned the (SHIFT-F7) (Select) key combination, which is used for predefining blocks.

1. Issue the / File I Retrieve command and select Yes when asked whether you want to lose your changes. When prompted for the name of a file to retrieve, either move the cursor to LEARN1.WKQ or type LEARN1. Press (ENTER).

Suppose you have decided that the spreadsheet would look less crowded with an extra row before the column headings, and that the word "Variance" would look better down one cell.

2. Move to row 3 and issue the / Edit I Insert I Row command. Press (ENTER) to accept the default row insert block.

3. Move to D4 and issue the / Edit I Move command. Specify a source block of D4..D4 and a destination of D5.

Follow the next few steps to insert a row within the block specified in the Total operating expenses formula and add another expense category.

4. Move to B13 and issue the / Edit I Insert I Row command.

5. Press (ENTER) when Quattro Pro displays the prompt "Enter row insert block: B13..B13" to insert a row between Rent and Depreciation.

6. In B13, enter **15500**.

7. In A13, enter **Utilities**.

8. Move to B16 and notice that the formula has been adjusted to include the new line item. The total displayed in cell B16 should be 173500.

Now you want to copy the data in column B to column C, on the assumption that most of the ABC group's revenues and expenses will be the same in 1992 as they were in 1991.

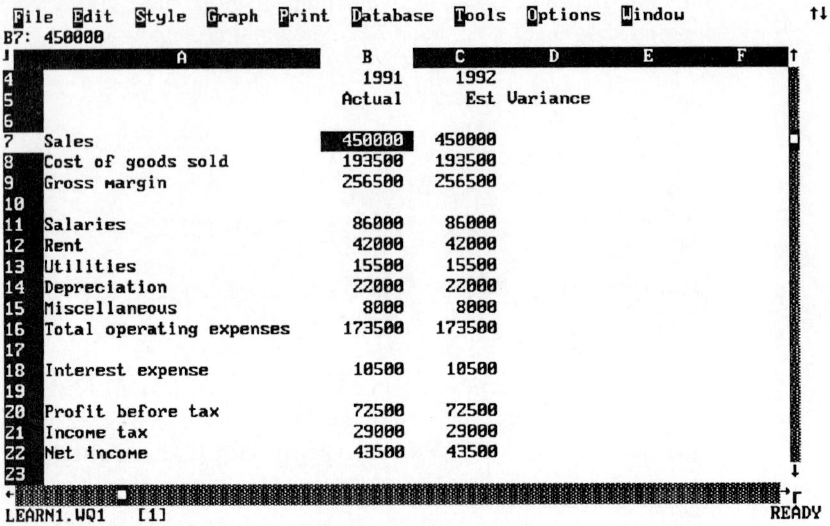

```
   File  Edit  Style  Graph  Print  Database  Tools  Options  Window         ↑↓
B7: 450000
                              A                  B        C      D      E    F
                                               1991     1992
                                               Actual   Est    Variance
   7  Sales                                   450000   450000
   8  Cost of goods sold                      193500   193500
   9  Gross margin                            256500   256500
  10
  11  Salaries                                 86000    86000
  12  Rent                                     42000    42000
  13  Utilities                                15500    15500
  14  Depreciation                             22000    22000
  15  Miscellaneous                             8000     8000
  16  Total operating expenses                173500   173500
  17
  18  Interest expense                         10500    10500
  19
  20  Profit before tax                        72500    72500
  21  Income tax                               29000    29000
  22  Net income                               43500    43500
  23
LEARN1.WQ1    [1]                                                          READY
```

FIGURE 4-10. LEARN1 after copying B7..B22 to column C

9. Use / Edit I Copy to copy cells B7 through B22 (the source block) to cell C7 (the destination). Your worksheet should now look like Figure 4-10.

Assume that some of your revenue and expense items are likely to increase by 5% in 1992. You can make this adjustment by entering a formula for calculating the 5% increase in one cell in column C and then copying that formula to several other cells in the column.

10. Move to C7 and enter the formula **(B7*1.05).**

11. Use / Edit I Copy to copy C7 to cells C8, C11..C13, and C15. There is no shortcut for doing this; you need to issue the command three times, defining C7..C7 as the source block each time and C8, C11..C13, and C15 as the various destinations. Leave Depreciation and Interest expense at the same levels as the previous year. Your spreadsheet should now look like Figure 4-11.

Use / Edit I Copy to fill column D with a set of formulas that calculate the variance between 1991's actual figures and the estimates for 1992.

12. Move to D7 and enter **(C7-B7).**

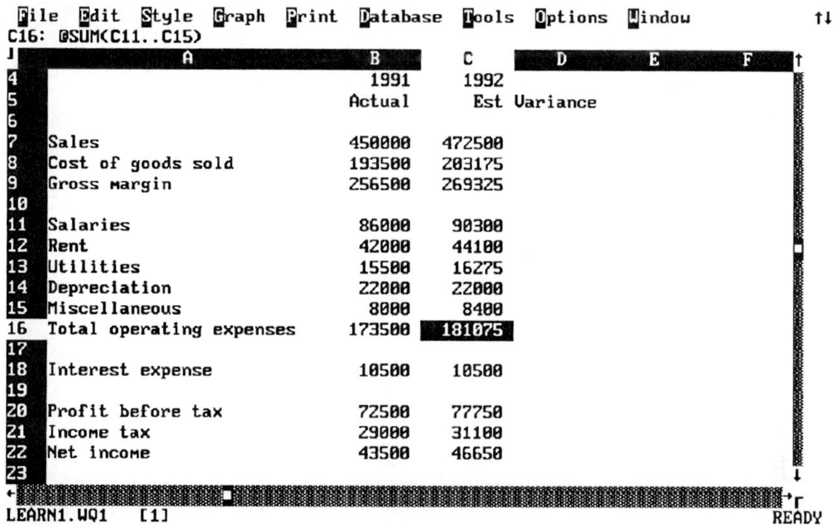

Rearranging the Spreadsheet   93

```
File  Edit  Style  Graph  Print  Database  Tools  Options  Window         ↑↓
C16: @SUM(C11..C15)
```

	A	B	C	D
4		1991	1992	
5		Actual	Est	Variance
6				
7	Sales	450000	472500	
8	Cost of goods sold	193500	203175	
9	Gross margin	256500	269325	
10				
11	Salaries	86000	90300	
12	Rent	42000	44100	
13	Utilities	15500	16275	
14	Depreciation	22000	22000	
15	Miscellaneous	8000	8400	
16	Total operating expenses	173500	181075	
17				
18	Interest expense	10500	10500	
19				
20	Profit before tax	72500	77750	
21	Income tax	29000	31100	
22	Net income	43500	46650	
23				

LEARN1.WQ1 [1]   READY

FIGURE 4-11.   Projecting revenue and expense increases in 1992

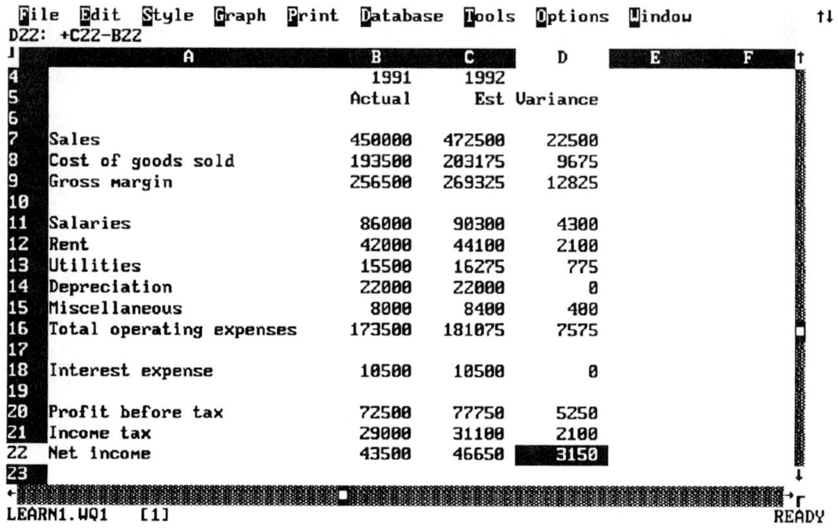

```
File  Edit  Style  Graph  Print  Database  Tools  Options  Window         ↑↓
D22: +C22-B22
```

	A	B	C	D
4		1991	1992	
5		Actual	Est	Variance
6				
7	Sales	450000	472500	22500
8	Cost of goods sold	193500	203175	9675
9	Gross margin	256500	269325	12825
10				
11	Salaries	86000	90300	4300
12	Rent	42000	44100	2100
13	Utilities	15500	16275	775
14	Depreciation	22000	22000	0
15	Miscellaneous	8000	8400	400
16	Total operating expenses	173500	181075	7575
17				
18	Interest expense	10500	10500	0
19				
20	Profit before tax	72500	77750	5250
21	Income tax	29000	31100	2100
22	Net income	43500	46650	3150
23				

LEARN1.WQ1 [1]   READY

FIGURE 4-12.   LEARN1 after constructing the Variance column

13. Use / Edit I Copy to copy this formula to the destination block D7..D22. Note that zeros now appear in cells D10, D17, and D19, because the formulas generated in those cells by the / Edit I Copy command—(C10-B10), (C17-B17), and (C19-B19)—reference cells that are blank.

14. Delete the contents of cells D10, D17, and D19 using the (DEL) key. (Be careful not to delete the zeros in D14 and D18; they are legitimate results.)

Finally, erase the block of cells used to test different label alignments in Chapter 2, and then save your work.

15. Use / Edit I Erase Block to erase cells A23 through A25.

16. Use the (F5) (GoTo) key to move the cell pointer to A4 (so that all the numeric values are visible on the screen), and compare your spreadsheet to Figure 4-12. Make any corrections that are necessary to achieve a total of 3150 in D22.

17. Issue the / File I Save command and, when prompted to Cancel, Replace, or Back Up, choose the Replace option.

LEARN1 is beginning to resemble the kind of spreadsheet you might use in your business. In subsequent chapters, you will enhance its appearance, print it, and improve its design, but even at this point it is a viable and realistic model.

This chapter has introduced some concepts—specifically the concept of relative cell referencing—that are often difficult for beginners. If you are not yet comfortable with this concept, take more time to experiment with copying formulas. You might also want to practice pointing out blocks and moving around with the (END) key. Much of your work in subsequent chapters draws and builds on the ideas and procedures introduced in this one. The better you understand the basics of block operations now, the easier it will be to master the complexities later.

5

FORMATTING YOUR SPREADSHEET

Default Formats
Adjusting Column Widths
Display Formats
Aligning Blocks of Data
More About Default Formats
Line Drawing and Shading

The layout and appearance of your spreadsheet often can be as important as the data it contains. Proper formatting can transform a mass of numbers and text into a storehouse of readable, usable information. Even if you intend to be the sole user of a spreadsheet, careful design can make your work easier to understand when you return to it next month or next year. If you expect others to read the spreadsheet, its appearance is even more important.

This chapter covers most of Quattro Pro's formatting commands—commands that let you change the appearance of your spreadsheet without altering the data itself. You learn to change the width of columns and the alignment of labels. You also learn to change the display format of numbers—add dollar signs, commas, and percent signs, control the number of decimal places, and so on. Lastly, you learn to draw lines and boxes and add shading to selected cells.

DEFAULT FORMATS

Column widths, label alignment, and the display format of numeric values can all be defined on two levels: the spreadsheet level and the level of individual cells. For example, every spreadsheet has a default column width. This width is used for all columns on the spreadsheet that you do not otherwise format with one of Quattro Pro's column width commands. Similarly, every spreadsheet has a default label alignment (usually flush left) that is used for every new label you enter. If you want particular labels aligned differently, you must type an alignment prefix character or issue a label alignment command. Each spreadsheet also has a default format for displaying numeric values. This format determines the appearance of every numeric value that you have not explicitly given a different format.

As mentioned, Quattro Pro allows you to change the alignment of labels, width of columns, and display of numbers on two levels. You can either assign a new format to a particular set of cells (or in the case of label alignment, enter a label alignment prefix in an individual cell) or you can change the default setting for the spreadsheet as a whole.

In most cases it is most efficient, in terms of both keystrokes and the size of the spreadsheet file, to use the spreadsheet default settings to format the majority of the spreadsheet. For example, if you want most of the columns on your spreadsheet to be 13 characters wide, but you want column A to be 30 characters wide, it is best to change the default column width to 13 and then change the width of column A (the exception to the general rule) to 30. The commands for altering the spreadsheet defaults are located on the Options | Formats menu. The commands for formatting sections of the spreadsheet are located on the Style menu. Table 5-1 lists both sets of commands.

ADJUSTING COLUMN WIDTHS

The default column width is initially nine characters. You can change this setting with / **Options** | **Formats** | **Global Width**. When you issue this command, Quattro Pro asks you to "set the default column width to a new value" and displays the current setting. You can either enter a new column width or use the [RIGHT ARROW] and [LEFT ARROW] keys to adjust the columns manually.

Try applying this command to the LEARN1.WQ1 spreadsheet.

1. If you do not currently have LEARN1.WQ1 on your screen, retrieve it using / **File** | **Retrieve**.

Changing Spreadsheet Format	Changing Cell Format
Column Width / Options I Format I Global Width	/ Style I Column Width / Style I Block Widths
Numeric Format / Options I Format I Numeric Format	/ Style I Numeric Format
Label Alignment / Options I Format I Align Labels	/ Style I Alignment

TABLE 5-1. Formatting Commands

2. Issue the / **Options** I **Formats** I **Global Width** command.

3. Press (RIGHT ARROW) four times, widening columns B, C, D, E, and all columns to the right to 13 characters.

4. Press (ENTER).

5. Press (ESC) twice to return to Ready mode.

Note that columns B, C, D, and E widen from 9 to 13 characters, while the width of column A remains unchanged. The cells in column A all contain a column width code that overrides the global column width setting. This code is an instruction to display the column as 27 characters wide, regardless of the global column width setting.

If you change the width to the default column width using either / **Style** I **Column Width** or / **Style** I **Block Widths**, Quattro Pro simply changes the column width code to that width. It does not remove the code. This allows you to reset the global width again without changing the width of any individually formatted columns. The only way to eliminate column width codes is by issuing the / **Style** I **Reset Width** or / **Style** I **Block Widths** I **Reset** command. / **Style** I **Reset Width** affects the current column. / **Style** I **Block Widths** I **Reset** affects all the columns in a specified block.

Try resetting column A to the current global width of 13 characters using the / **Style** I **Reset Width** command. Move to any cell in column A and type /**SR**. The column width code [W27] no longer appears on the input line as you move through cells in column A.

Changing the Width
Of Several Columns at Once

As you saw in Chapter 2, you can change the width of a single column by using the / Style | Column Width command. Quattro Pro also offers commands for adjusting the width of several columns simultaneously.

/ Style | Block Widths | Set Width adjusts the widths of all columns in a specified block. When you issue this command, Quattro Pro asks you for a block of columns. Type or point to a block that includes all the columns that you want to change. Quattro Pro asks you to specify a column width of 0 to 254 characters. Type in the desired width, or use the arrow keys to adjust the width manually. As soon as you press (ENTER), Quattro Pro changes every column in the block to the specified width.

Quattro Pro offers another command—/ Style | Block Widths | Auto Width—that allows you to widen one or more columns to fit the width of the existing entries. When you issue this command, Quattro Pro asks for the number of extra spaces between columns. You can enter any number from 0 through 40. Quattro Pro adds the number you specify to the width of the column's longest entry to calculate the column's new width. Next, Quattro Pro asks you to specify the block of columns. This time the row coordinates of the specified block actually make a difference, unlike in the / Style | Block Widths | Set Width command. If you specify a block containing just one row, Quattro Pro looks only at entries in that row and the rows below when calculating the column width. If you specify a multiple-cell block, Quattro Pro considers the entries within that block in its calculation.

Try the / Style | Block Width | Auto Width command now to adjust the width of column A.

1. Move to A7, and issue the / Style | Block Widths | Auto Width command.

2. When Quattro Pro asks for the number of characters between columns, press (ENTER) to accept the default of one character.

3. When asked for a block of columns, press (DOWN ARROW) twice to expand the block to A9. Press (ENTER).

Quattro Pro changes the column width to 19 characters—the exact width of the longest entry in the specified block ("Cost of goods sold" in A8) plus the one extra character you specified. Now, specify a column block consisting of the first cell in the column.

1. Press (HOME) to move to A1.

2. Issue the / Style | Block Widths | Auto Width command.

3. Enter **0** as the number of characters between columns.

4. Press (ENTER) to accept the default column block of A1..A1.

Because you specified a single-cell block, Quattro Pro looks at all of the entries in or below that cell—which, in this case, means all of the entries in the entire column. Quattro Pro then widens the column to match the width of the longest entries in that block—the entries in A1 and A2.

There is one other characteristic of / Style | Block Widths | Auto Width you should know about. If the longest entry in the block of cells you are formatting is a numeric value, Quattro Pro makes the column one character wider than it would if the value were a label. For example, if the longest entry in the block is 999 and you specify one character between columns, Quattro Pro makes the column five characters wide.

This is consistent with Quattro Pro's treatment of values in general. Quattro Pro always leaves at least one blank space at the left edge of any cell containing a numeric value. Whenever the number of digits in the value is the same as the column width, Quattro Pro either rounds the number or displays a series of asterisks. This prevents numbers in one column from running into numbers in adjacent columns. The blank space ensures that you can always tell where one number ends and the next begins.

DISPLAY FORMATS

Quattro Pro's display formats determine how values are displayed on the spreadsheet. As you learned in Chapter 2, the only characters you can use when entering numbers are the digits, plus sign, minus sign, and decimal point. Fortunately, Quattro Pro gives you far more flexibility in displaying numbers, offering a variety of options for formatting numeric data on your spreadsheet. Changing the display format of a cell has no effect on the data itself; it affects the data's form but not its content. As far as calculations are concerned, 0.5 is equivalent to 50%, and 25.00 is equivalent to 25.

The Default Format Setting

Every Quattro Pro spreadsheet has a default format for displaying values. Most of the time, this default is the General format, which approximates the way Quattro Pro actually stores values. These are the characteristics of the General format:

- Only those decimal places that affect the value of a number are displayed.

- Any trailing zeros to the right of a decimal point are dropped.

- Percentages are displayed as decimals, even if you enter a percent sign.

- Decimals are always preceded by a zero to the left of the decimal point (so that you see 0.14 rather than .14, for example).

- If the value is too long to fit within a cell, Quattro Pro displays as much of it as possible. If the portion to the left of the decimal point fits within the cell, Quattro Pro displays that portion, a decimal point, and as many decimal places as possible. Otherwise Quattro Pro displays the value in exponential notation.

Whenever Quattro Pro truncates a value to display it in the specified format or to fit it within a cell, it rounds the number. If the digit to be rounded off is 5 or higher, Quattro Pro rounds up; otherwise it rounds down. For example, if you enter the value 12345.678 in a cell that is nine characters wide in General format, Quattro Pro displays 12345.68 in the cell.

None of the values used in your sample spreadsheet so far have included decimal places or percent signs, so you may have thought that Quattro Pro displays numbers as you type them. Take a moment now to enter values in a different format and watch Quattro Pro change them to General format as soon as you press (ENTER).

1. Move to A21, and enter **350000.00**. Notice that Quattro Pro drops the decimal point and two zeros from the value both in the cell display and on the input line. The zeros are dropped because they do not affect the value.

2. Move down one cell and enter **45%** in A22. Notice that Quattro Pro stores and displays the number as 0.45.

3. Move down one cell and enter **.999** in A23. This time Quattro Pro automatically adds a leading zero, displaying the value as 0.999. Notice also that the decimal points in cells A21, A22, and A23 do not line up, making the values somewhat difficult to compare.

4. Issue the / Edit | Erase command and specify A21..A23.

As mentioned, the General format is similar to the way Quattro Pro actually stores numbers: in most cases what you see in the cell is the same as what appears on the input line. This is not true of Quattro Pro's other display formats. You will see shortly that when you use anything other than the General format, you enter the data in one form, but Quattro Pro may store it in a second form and display it in a third.

Quattro Pro's 10 Display Formats

Quattro Pro supplies 10 display formats for values. Depending on your data, you may choose to display all spreadsheet values in one format or to mix and match formats within the same spreadsheet. Table 5-2 illustrates 6 of the 10 formats.

Format	Decimals	Value	Display	Code
General	NA	9876.543	9876.543	(G)
	NA	-9876.543	-9876.543	(G)
Fixed	0	9876.543	9877	(F0)
	2	9876.543	9876.54	(F2)
	4	-9876.543	-9876.5430	(F4)
, (comma)	2	9876.543	9,876.54	(,2)
	0	9876.543	9,877	(,0)
	2	-9876.543	(9,876.54)	(,2)
Currency	2	9876.543	$9,876.54	(,2)
	0	9876.543	$9,877	(,0)
	2	-9876.543	($9,876.54)	(,2)
Percent	1	.123	12.3%	(P1)
	2	.123	12.30%	(P2)
	0	1.23	123%	(P0)
Scientific	0	10	1E+01	(S0)
	2	100	1E+02	(S2)
	1	333	3.33E+02	(S1)

TABLE 5-2. Display Formats for Values

FIXED FORMAT Displays values with the number of decimal places you specify, regardless of whether you typed in more or fewer decimal places when entering the value.

SCIENTIFIC FORMAT Displays values in scientific (also known as exponential) notation. In scientific notation, values are expressed as the product of two numbers, one of which is a number between 1 and 10 and the other of which is a power of 10. For example, when displayed in scientific notation, the number 1420 appears as 1.42E+3. The letter E in this format represents "10 to the power of," so the entire expression can be read as 1.42 times 10 to the power of 3, or 1.42×1000. Values can also be expressed with negative exponents. The number 0.00123, for example, can be expressed in scientific notation as 1.23E-3, meaning 1.23 times 10 to the power of -3, or $1.23 \times .001$.

CURRENCY FORMAT Displays values preceded by a currency symbol. The default symbol is $, but you can designate a different symbol with the Default International Currency command. The Currency format also inserts commas every three digits as you move left from the decimal point. Negative numbers are displayed in parentheses.

,(COMMA) FORMAT Like the Currency format, comma format inserts commas every three digits as you move left from the decimal point and displays negative numbers in parentheses.

GENERAL FORMAT Already discussed in detail. Most of the time this format displays numbers as entered, with the following exceptions: It displays only those decimal places that affect the value of the number; it drops decimal places as necessary to accommodate the column width or, if that is insufficient, displays the value in scientific notation.

+/- FORMAT Translates numbers into bar graphs, displaying plus signs for positive numbers, minus signs for negative numbers, and periods for zeros. The number of plus signs or minus signs displayed is equal to the value entered in the cell. 5 for example, would be displayed as +++++; -3 would be displayed as ---. Only as many pluses or minuses as fit in the cell are displayed. For this reason, this format is useful only for numbers less than or equal to the number of characters that can fit within the cell.

PERCENT FORMAT   Displays values as percentages, in effect multiplying the value by 100 and following it with a percent sign. The value 0.75, for example, is displayed as 75% in Percent format.

FIVE DATE FORMATS AND FOUR TIME FORMATS   These are considered numeric formats because Quattro Pro stores both dates and times as numbers. To select one of these formats, choose Date from the Numeric Format menu. If you want to choose a time format, choose Time from the resulting submenu. Date and Time formats are discussed in detail in Chapter 10.

TEXT (SHOW FORMULAS) FORMAT   Displays all formulas as entered rather than displaying the results of their calculations. This format is extremely useful when you are searching for potential problems or errors in your spreadsheet's logic, or examining the spreadsheet's structure.

HIDDEN FORMAT   Conceals data so that a cell actually containing data appears to be empty. This is the only Quattro Pro display format that affects labels as well as values; both text entries and values disappear from the spreadsheet. You can "unhide" cells by assigning them any other display formats or by using the Reset option discussed later. The Hidden format is particularly useful for hiding comments or confidential information from particular readers before you print the spreadsheet. It does not really hide anything from users who will be viewing the spreadsheet on screen because, even in Hidden format, you can display a cell's contents on the input line by moving the cell pointer to that cell.

Changing the Spreadsheet's Numeric Format

You can alter the numeric format of a cell in two ways: You can define a format for a block of cells with / Style | Numeric Format, or you can change the default format for the entire spreadsheet with / Options | Formats | Numeric Format. When you issue either command, Quattro Pro displays a menu with the 10 numeric formats. The Style | Numeric Format menu also contains a Reset option for changing the display format back to the spreadsheet default. If you select the Fixed, Percent, Comma, or Currency format, Quattro Pro will ask you to specify the number of decimal places next. In the case of / Options | Formats | Numeric Format, Quattro Pro then executes the command immediately, changing the spreadsheet's values to the specified format. If you use the / Style | Numeric Format command, Quattro Pro asks you for a block to modify, and then executes the command.

Try changing the default format for LEARN1.WQ1 to the comma format with 0 decimal places.

1. Issue the / Options | Formats | Numeric Format command.

2. Type **,** to select the comma format.

3. When prompted for the number of decimal places, enter **0**.

4. Press (ESC) twice or type **Q** (for Quit) twice to return to Ready mode. Your spreadsheet should now look like Figure 5-1.

5. Save the spreadsheet in its current form by pressing (CTRL-S) and choosing Replace.

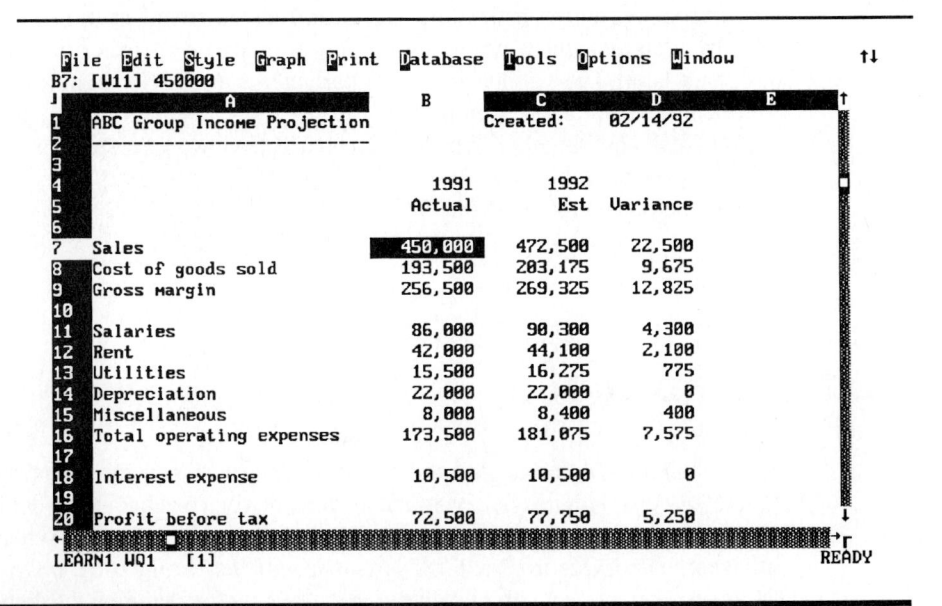

```
File  Edit  Style  Graph  Print  Database  Tools  Options  Window          ↑↓
B7: [W11] 450000
        A                    B         C          D          E
1   ABC Group Income Projection    Created:   02/14/92
2   ------------------------
3
4                            1991      1992
5                            Actual    Est       Variance
6
7   Sales                    450,000   472,500   22,500
8   Cost of goods sold       193,500   203,175    9,675
9   Gross margin             256,500   269,325   12,825
10
11  Salaries                  86,000    90,300    4,300
12  Rent                      42,000    44,100    2,100
13  Utilities                 15,500    16,275      775
14  Depreciation              22,000    22,000        0
15  Miscellaneous              8,000     8,400      400
16  Total operating expenses 173,500   181,075    7,575
17
18  Interest expense          10,500    10,500        0
19
20  Profit before tax         72,500    77,750    5,250

LEARN1.WQ1  [1]                                              READY
```

FIGURE 5-1. The , (comma) format

Changing the Numeric Format of a Block

The / Style I Numeric Format command changes the appearance of values within a specified block of cells. When you issue this command, you actually are applying numeric formats to particular cells rather than to the values those cells contain. If you format a cell and then change its contents, the new data will be displayed in whatever format you designated for that cell.

Quattro Pro "remembers" the format of a cell, regardless of changes in cell contents, by inserting numeric format codes in cells that are formatted with the / Style I Numeric Format command. Even if you delete the contents of a formatted cell, with either the (DEL) key or / Edit I Erase, the formatting code remains intact and affects the appearance of any data that you enter later.

You can always change a cell's format code by reformatting it, but the only way to get rid of the code altogether is with / Style I Numeric Format I Reset. Once you remove a cell's numeric format code with this command, the cell's format reverts to the numeric format of the spreadsheet as a whole. Table 5-2 shows most of the numeric format codes. The formats that do not appear on that table are

+/-	Represented by the code (+).
Text	Represented by the code (T).
Date	Both Date and Time formats are represented by the code (D) followed by the option number of the specific format, enclosed in parentheses. For example, (D2) represents Date format 2.
Hidden	Represented by the code (H).

When you issue the / Style I Numeric Format command, Quattro Pro displays the Numeric Formats menu. Once you select a format, Quattro Pro usually asks for the number of decimal places you want to display. Lastly, Quattro Pro asks you to specify the block to be formatted. The shortcut for the / Style I Numeric Format command is (CTRL-F).

Try applying the command to data on the LEARN1 spreadsheet.

1. Move to C7 and type **/SN** to display the Style I Numeric Format menu.

2. Type C to select the Currency option.

3. When prompted for a number of decimal places, accept the default of 2 by pressing (ENTER).

4. When given the "Block to be modified" prompt, specify C7..C22, using either the typing or pointing method.

Some of the cells in column C are filled with asterisks because they contain values that are too large to fit within the column at its current width. You can correct the problem by widening the column.

1. Press (CTRL-W), the shortcut for the / Style | Column Width command, and press (RIGHT ARROW) to widen the column and reveal all the numbers in Currency format.

2. Press (ESC) to cancel the command and return the column to its previous width of 11 characters.

3. Issue the / Style | Numeric Format | Currency command again.

4. When prompted for the number of decimal places, type **0** and press (ENTER).

5. When prompted for the block to be modified, specify C7..C22 again.

6. Try a different format on column D by moving to D7, pressing (CTRL-F), and typing **F** to select the Fixed format option.

7. Specify three decimal places and designate a block of D7..D22. Your spreadsheet should now look like the one shown in Figure 5-2.

Try other formats on a single cell. Notice the different display codes that appear on the input line as you change from one format to another.

1. Still in D7, issue the / Style | Numeric Format | **P**ercent command.

2. Specify zero decimal places and accept the default block D7..D7.

3. Issue the / Style | Numeric Format | **H**idden command.

4. Accept the default block of D7..D7 by pressing (ENTER). The contents of the cell still appear on the input line even though the cell appears empty.

Whenever you relocate cells with / **E**dit | **M**ove, the format moves along with the cell. Whenever you copy cells, the format is copied too, determining the display of all the cell's duplicates. However, if you insert columns or rows in a block that has been formatted, the new cells will not be formatted automatically. In such cases you can

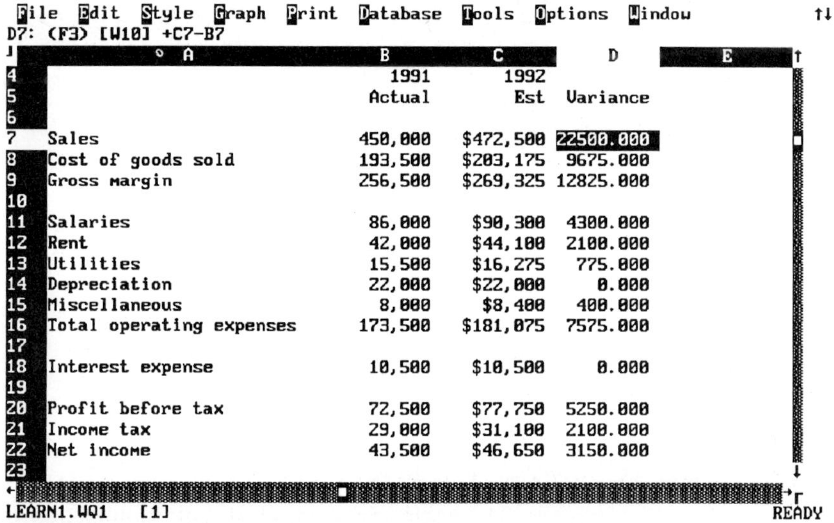

Formatting Your Spreadsheet 107

```
File  Edit  Style  Graph  Print  Database  Tools  Options  Window          ↑↓
D7: (F3) [W10] +C7-B7
         A                    B          C          D           E
  4                         1991       1992
  5                        Actual       Est    Variance
  6
  7   Sales                450,000   $472,500  22500.000
  8   Cost of goods sold   193,500   $203,175   9675.000
  9   Gross margin         256,500   $269,325  12825.000
 10
 11   Salaries              86,000    $90,300   4300.000
 12   Rent                  42,000    $44,100   2100.000
 13   Utilities             15,500    $16,275    775.000
 14   Depreciation          22,000    $22,000      0.000
 15   Miscellaneous          8,000     $8,400    400.000
 16   Total operating expenses 173,500 $181,075  7575.000
 17
 18   Interest expense      10,500    $10,500      0.000
 19
 20   Profit before tax     72,500    $77,750   5250.000
 21   Income tax            29,000    $31,100   2100.000
 22   Net income            43,500    $46,650   3150.000
 23
LEARN1.WQ1   [1]                                              READY
```

FIGURE 5-2.   Trying different numeric formats

often save yourself several steps by immediately copying an adjacent row or column into the newly inserted row or column—just to copy the formatting codes. You can then either erase or replace the data itself.

Try copying a formatted cell with the / Edit I Copy command.

1. Move to B23 and press (DEL) if the cell contains any data.

2. Issue the / Edit I Copy command.

3. Accept the default source block B23..B23 by pressing (ENTER) and specify a destination block of C23.

4. Move to C23 and look at the input line. Even though B23 contains no data, Quattro Pro has copied its numeric format code to the destination cell. If you had *moved* B23 to C23, the numeric format code would similarly have appeared in the cell's new location.

Now that you have formatted most of the values on your spreadsheet, see what happens if you change the numeric format for the spreadsheet as a whole, using the / Options I Formats I Numeric Format command.

1. Press (HOME) to move back to A1.
2. Issue the / **Options** | **Formats** | **Numeric Format** | **Fixed** command.
3. Enter **0** as the number of decimal places.
4. Press (ESC) twice to return to Ready mode.

The only values that change are those in column B. The other values retain their appearance because they contain formatting codes that override the default format.

The Text (Show Formulas) Format

Spreadsheet programs typically show the results of formulas on the spreadsheet surface rather than displaying the formulas themselves. Although this is exactly what you want most of the time, it can make it difficult to find errors or decipher an unfamiliar spreadsheet. To examine a formula or even to determine whether a particular cell contains a formula, you generally need to move the cell pointer to the cell in question and examine the input line.

The Text (Show Formulas) format is designed to remedy this problem by exposing all the formulas within a block of cells. Whenever you display cells in Text format, the literal contents of each cell appears on the spreadsheet itself, just as they would appear on the input line if you pointed to that cell. Try the Text format now.

1. Issue the / **Style** | **Numeric Format** | **Text** command.
2. When prompted for a block, enter **B1..D22**. As you can see, not every formula fits neatly within its cell. When you use this display format, you must usually widen columns to see the formulas in their entirety.
3. Issue the / **Style** | **Block Widths** | **Auto Width** command, press (ENTER) to accept the default of one extra space between columns, and specify a column block of B1..D1. Because the formulas are displayed with flush-left alignment, the data in the columns do not line up well at these widths, but you can see all the formulas. Your spreadsheet should now resemble Figure 5-3.

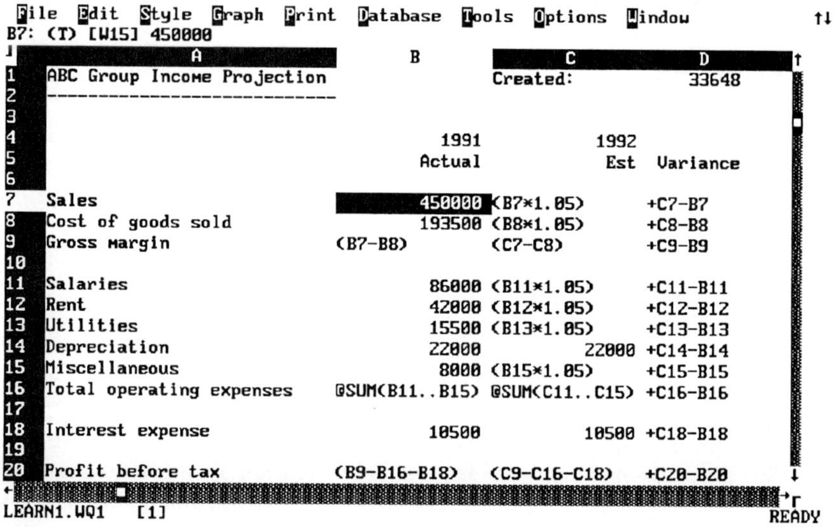

Formatting Your Spreadsheet 109

```
File  Edit  Style  Graph  Print  Database  Tools  Options  Window           ↑↓
B7: (T) [W15] 450000
            A                    B              C              D
 1  ABC Group Income Projection              Created:         33648
 2  ------------------------------
 3
 4                              1991           1992
 5                              Actual         Est       Variance
 6
 7  Sales                       450000 (B7*1.05)          +C7-B7
 8  Cost of goods sold          193500 (B8*1.05)          +C8-B8
 9  Gross margin               (B7-B8)         (C7-C8)    +C9-B9
10
11  Salaries                    86000 (B11*1.05)         +C11-B11
12  Rent                        42000 (B12*1.05)         +C12-B12
13  Utilities                   15500 (B13*1.05)         +C13-B13
14  Depreciation                22000          22000     +C14-B14
15  Miscellaneous                8000 (B15*1.05)         +C15-B15
16  Total operating expenses   @SUM(B11..B15) @SUM(C11..C15) +C16-B16
17
18  Interest expense            10500          10500     +C18-B18
19
20  Profit before tax          (B9-B16-B18)   (C9-C16-C18) +C20-B20
LEARN1.WQ1    [1]                                          READY
```

FIGURE 5-3. The Text (Show Formulas) format

One problem with the Text format is that it is just like any other numeric format. This means that if you use the / **Options** | **Numeric Format** | **Text** format command, the only cells that are affected are those that do not already have numeric formatting codes. However, if you use the / **Style** | **Numeric Format** | **Text** format command, the Text format codes replace any numeric format codes already in the specified block, making it difficult to restore the spreadsheet to its previous appearance.

You can circumvent these problems by saving the spreadsheet and then using the / **Style** | **Numeric Format** | **Text** command. When you are done viewing your spreadsheet in this form, discard the new format and retrieve the previous version of your spreadsheet from disk. In this case, you can retrieve the version of the spreadsheet saved immediately after issuing the / **Options** | **Formats** | **Numeric Format** | **,** (comma) **Financial** command.

1. Issue the / **File** | **Retrieve** command and select Yes when asked whether you want to lose your changes.

2. Select LEARN1.WQ1 from the file list.

ALIGNING BLOCKS OF DATA

Quattro Pro allows you to change the alignment of labels and numeric values, including dates. However, it aligns the two types of data somewhat differently.

Aligning Labels

As you learned in Chapter 2, when you enter labels they assume the label alignment of the spreadsheet as a whole unless you type in a different alignment character. In most spreadsheets the default alignment for labels is flush left, so if you enter a label that does not begin with an alignment character, Quattro Pro automatically inserts an apostrophe (the character that specifies left alignment). If you want to assign a different alignment, you can start the label with a quotation mark (for flush-right alignment) or a caret (for centered alignment). You can change the default label alignment for a spreadsheet with / Options | Formats | Label Alignment. You can change the alignment of blocks of labels using / Style | Alignment.

When you issue the / Options | Formats | Label Alignment command, Quattro Pro displays a menu with the choices Left, Right, and Center. When you issue the / Style | Alignment command, you will see a menu with the same three choices, plus a fourth choice, General, which will be discussed under "Aligning Numeric Values." The shortcut for the / Style | Alignment command is CTRL-A.

In some ways, aligning labels is just like assigning numeric formats. You can either change the spreadsheet default or you can format a block of cells. However, there are also important differences. First, label alignment characters are not really formatting codes. Rather, they are part of the labels themselves. If you delete a label, the label alignment character is deleted as well. This is quite different from numeric formatting codes that are stored in particular cells and remain in those cells even if you delete the cells' data.

Second, you cannot enter a label *without* a label alignment character; either you enter one or Quattro Pro does it for you. This means that you will not see any visible change on the spreadsheet when you issue the / Options | Formats | Align command. In effect, changing the default alignment only affects those labels that you enter in the future. It tells Quattro Pro which alignment character to include in any label that does not already start with such a character.

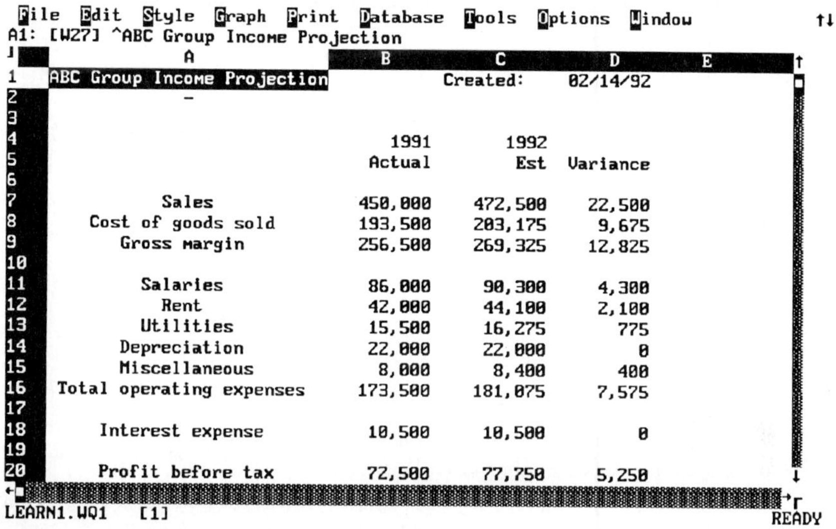

Formatting Your Spreadsheet 111

```
File  Edit  Style  Graph  Print  Database  Tools  Options  Window            ↑↓
A1: [W27] ^ABC Group Income Projection
         A                    B           C          D         E
 1  ABC Group Income Projection       Created:    02/14/92
 2
 3
 4                            1991        1992
 5                          Actual        Est    Variance
 6
 7              Sales      450,000     472,500     22,500
 8    Cost of goods sold   193,500     203,175      9,675
 9       Gross margin      256,500     269,325     12,825
10
11           Salaries       86,000      90,300      4,300
12               Rent       42,000      44,100      2,100
13          Utilities       15,500      16,275        775
14       Depreciation       22,000      22,000          0
15      Miscellaneous        8,000       8,400        400
16  Total operating expenses 173,500    181,075      7,575
17
18   Interest expense        10,500      10,500          0
19
20   Profit before tax       72,500      77,750      5,250
LEARN1.WQ1  [1]                                               READY
```

FIGURE 5-4. Centering a column of labels

To see the / Style | Alignment command in action, follow these steps:

1. Issue the / Style | Alignment command.

2. Select the Center option from the Alignment submenu and, when prompted for a block to align, designate A1..A22. Your spreadsheet should now look like the one shown in Figure 5-4.

3. Watch the input line as you move the cell pointer down column A. Note that Quattro Pro has inserted the ^ alignment character at the beginning of each label in the block. Even cell A2 has been affected: The \ prefix has been replaced with the ^.

4. Move to A5, type **TEST**, and press (ENTER). Even though this cell is located within the block that you designated for the / Style | Alignment command, the label's alignment is derived from the default alignment setting of flush left.

5. Press (DEL) to erase the data in A5.

6. Issue the /Style | Alignment command again, and return column A's labels to their previous state by left-aligning block A1..A22.

7. Move to A2 and press (DEL) to erase the contents of the cell.

8. Move to C1. Issue the /Style | Alignment command again. Select Right, and then press (ENTER) to accept the default block of C1..C1. This moves the word "Created:" closer to the date in cell D1, which looks a little better, especially when you print the spreadsheet.

Aligning Numeric Values

While / Options | Formats | Label Alignment affects labels only, / Style | Alignment affects numeric values as well. In practice, you will probably apply the / Style | Alignment command to blocks of numeric values that have exactly the same number of digits. Otherwise the numbers will be difficult to read.

Quattro Pro aligns labels and numeric values somewhat differently. When you modify a block of cells with / Style | Alignment, Quattro Pro changes the alignment character at the beginning of every cell within the block. As mentioned, these alignment characters are not formatting codes. They are part of the labels themselves and have no existence separate from those particular labels.

At the same time, / Style | Alignment also stores a hidden alignment code in each cell of the specified block. These codes have no effect on any new labels you enter. The alignment of new labels is always determined by the default label alignment setting for the spreadsheet (unless you enter a label alignment character). However, these hidden alignment codes will affect numeric values you enter later. Like numeric format codes, they are independent of the data currently stored in the cell. If you enter a numeric value into a cell that was left-aligned with /Style | Alignment, the new value is automatically left- aligned.

The only way you can eliminate these hidden alignment codes is by issuing / Style | Alignment | General. This command is analogous to / Style | Numeric Format | General: it restores all the cells in the specified block to the spreadsheet's default format. Since the default alignment for numeric values is always right-aligned, it effectively right- aligns all values within the block. The labels in the block are aligned according to any default label alignment setting for the spreadsheet.

Note: In some cases, you may be tempted to left-align or center numbers so that they are not too close to data in the next column to the right. Often a better solution to this problem is to insert a narrow, empty column in the middle. For example, in Figure 5-5 a three-character-wide column was inserted between the QUANT column (column C) and the COLOR column (column E) just to create a little breathing room between the two sets of data.

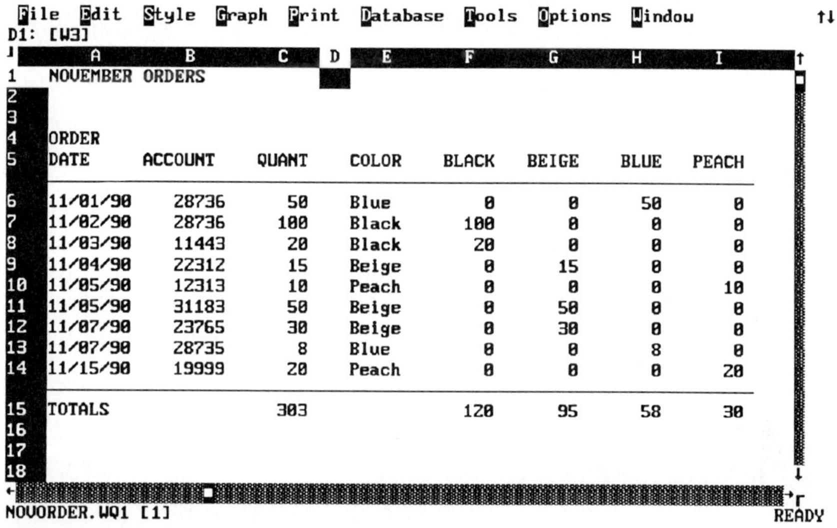

```
    File  Edit  Style  Graph  Print  Database  Tools  Options  Window        ↑↓
D1: [W3]
         A           B          C      D    E         F       G       H       I
   1  NOVEMBER ORDERS
   2
   3
   4  ORDER
   5  DATE        ACCOUNT    QUANT        COLOR     BLACK   BEIGE   BLUE   PEACH
   6  11/01/90    28736        50         Blue        0       0      50      0
   7  11/02/90    28736       100         Black     100       0       0      0
   8  11/03/90    11443        20         Black      20       0       0      0
   9  11/04/90    22312        15         Beige       0      15       0      0
  10  11/05/90    12313        10         Peach       0       0       0     10
  11  11/05/90    31183        50         Beige       0      50       0      0
  12  11/07/90    23765        30         Beige       0      30       0      0
  13  11/07/90    28735         8         Blue        0       0       8      0
  14  11/15/90    19999        20         Peach       0       0       0     20
  15  TOTALS                  303                   120      95      58     30
  16
  17
  18
NOVORDER.WQ1 [1]                                                            READY
```

FIGURE 5-5. Using a blank column to create space between columns

MORE ABOUT DEFAULT FORMATS

As you have seen, Quattro Pro has default settings for several spreadsheet attributes: numeric format, label alignment, and column width. Formatting a block of cells—with / Style | Numeric Format, / Style | Alignment, or / Style | Column Width—amounts to overriding the default format for one of those attributes within a specified section of the spreadsheet. Quattro Pro also allows you to change the default settings themselves, specifying formats for every cell on the spreadsheet that does not contain a formatting code to the contrary. The numeric format, for example, determines the appearance of values within every cell that does not contain a display code. The alignment default determines which label prefix Quattro Pro inserts in the beginning of a label when you do not enter one yourself. The column width default determines the width of every cell that does not contain a column width code.

Whenever you change the label alignment, display, or column width default settings and then save your file, the current default settings are stored with the spreadsheet. When you retrieve the spreadsheet later, those settings are retrieved. Though this feature is extremely useful, it can sometimes be confusing. Quattro Pro has no codes to indicate the default settings for a particular spreadsheet, so you have only two ways to determine what those settings are. First, you can open the Options | Formats menu and look at the settings displayed at the right side of the menu. Second, you can enter data in unformatted cells and watch what happens.

Hiding Zeros

The Options | Formats menu contains one option (not counting Quit) you have not seen yet: the Hide Zeros option. This option allows you to conceal all the zero values on your spreadsheet. Some people prefer this default format for most spreadsheets, particularly when generating formal reports.

The Advantages Of Default Formats

If you want to use a numeric format, label alignment, or column width other than the current system default for most of your spreadsheet, it is generally a good idea to use a default setting. Even when you want to use more than one format, you should set a default for the format you want to use most and format the exceptions with block formatting commands. Default settings have three advantages over block formatting commands:

- They require fewer keystrokes.
- They save memory and disk space.
- They are generally more efficient if you decide to change formats later.

LINE DRAWING AND SHADING

The / Style | Line Drawing and / Style | Shading commands allow you to add solid lines or boxes and shading to your spreadsheet. You can use these attributes to highlight elements of the spreadsheet, making it more visually appealing and easier to read. You can also use lines and shading to group elements on a spreadsheet, shading the totals on a spreadsheet, for example, or drawing a box around a lookup table.

Lines and shading differ from the other formatting tools discussed in this chapter. You always apply lines and shading to a particular cell or blocks of cells. There are no spreadsheet-wide or system-wide default settings. There are also no line or shading codes stored in the cells.

Drawing Lines On the Spreadsheet

The / Style | Line Drawing command lets you underline or draw boxes around spreadsheet titles, column headings, or other text, or to separate columns or rows for emphasis. You can even use this command to add a grid of horizontal and vertical lines to your spreadsheet, which can often make your data easier to read, particularly when printed.

When you issue the / Style | Line Drawing command, Quattro Pro prompts for the block you want to draw lines around. Once you specify a block, Quattro Pro displays a Placement menu that you use to specify where you want the lines drawn, relative to the specified block. The options on the Placement menu are as follows:

Option	Effect
All	Draws a box around the specified block, and draws vertical and horizontal lines between all cells in the block, producing a grid
Outside	Draws a box around the block
Top	Draws a horizontal line above the block
Bottom	Draws a horizontal line below the block
Left	Draws a vertical line along the left edge of the block
Right	Draws a vertical line along the right edge of the block
Inside	Draws vertical and horizontal lines between all cells in the block, producing a grid
Horizontal	Draws horizontal lines between each row in the block
Vertical	Draws vertical lines between each column in the specified block
Quit	Returns to Ready mode

Quattro Pro also displays a Line Types menu with the options Single, Double, Thick, and None. Select Single to draw a single line, Double to draw a double line, Thick to draw a thick band, and None to remove lines previously drawn around the specified block.

When Quattro Pro is done executing the command, it returns you to the Placement menu and automatically highlights the last Placement option you selected. As you will see in a moment, this makes it easy for you to experiment with different line types around the same block of cells. If you want to draw lines around a different block, press (ESC). Quattro Pro displays the prompt "Enter block to draw lines" on the input line and displays the block you last specified. You then can type or point to a new block and press (ENTER). If you are done drawing lines, simply select Quit from the Placement menu.

If you have a color monitor, you can change the color of lines with / Options I Colors I Spreadsheet I Drawn Lines.

Try adding lines to LEARN1.WQ1:

1. Move to B5 and issue the / Style I Line Drawing command.

2. When prompted for a "block to draw lines," press (RIGHT ARROW) twice to specify a block of B5..D5. Press (ENTER).

3. When Quattro Pro displays the Placement menu, type **B** to select Bottom.

4. When Quattro Pro displays the Line Types menu, type **D** to select Double.

5. When Quattro Pro redisplays the Placement menu, select Bottom again, and this time type **T** to select Thick from the Line Types menu—just to see what thick lines look like. The new line is superimposed on top of the previous one.

6. When Quattro Pro redisplays the Placement menu, select Bottom a third time, and then select Single from the Line Types menu.

7. When the Placement menu reappears, press (ESC) to move back one step. You will see the prompt "Enter block to draw lines" on the input line. Enter the block coordinates **B22..D22**.

8. Select Top from the Placement menu.

9. Select Single from the Line Types menu.

10. When Quattro Pro redisplays the Placement menu, select Quit. Your spreadsheet should look like Figure 5-6.

The first line you inserted is between rows—it pushes rows 6 through 19 down on the screen and causes row 20 to disappear off the bottom. The fact that lines are drawn in between cells has another implication. Suppose you decide you don't like the last line you drew (the line between rows 21 and 22). Because the line is not stored in any particular cell, you cannot use (DEL) to erase it. / Edit I Erase does not work either. Even the / Edit I Undo command is powerless in this context. If you delete a row, Quattro Pro erases lines drawn immediately above it. You could delete row 22 and

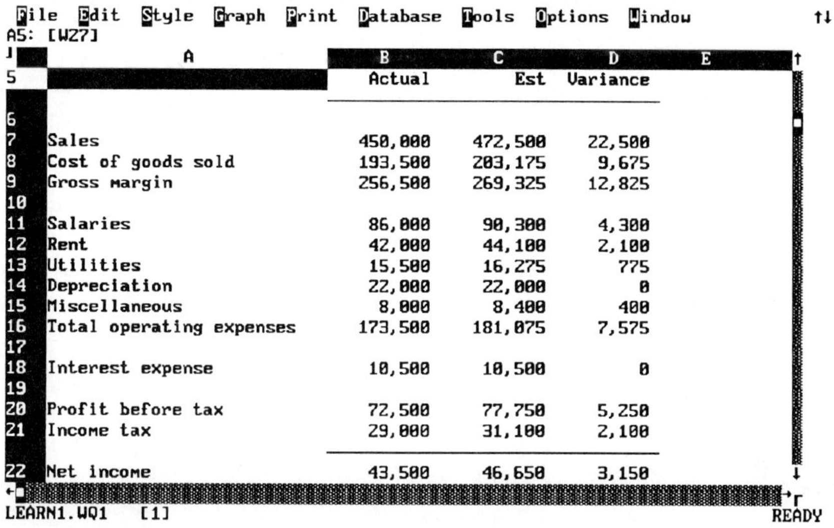

```
File  Edit  Style  Graph  Print  Database  Tools  Options  Window          ↑↓
A5: [W27]
             A                    B          C         D        E
   5                           Actual      Est    Variance

   7  Sales                    450,000   472,500    22,500
   8  Cost of goods sold       193,500   203,175     9,675
   9  Gross margin             256,500   269,325    12,825
  10
  11  Salaries                  86,000    90,300     4,300
  12  Rent                      42,000    44,100     2,100
  13  Utilities                 15,500    16,275       775
  14  Depreciation              22,000    22,000         0
  15  Miscellaneous              8,000     8,400       400
  16  Total operating expenses 173,500   181,075     7,575
  17
  18  Interest expense          10,500    10,500         0
  19
  20  Profit before tax         72,500    77,750     5,250
  21  Income tax                29,000    31,100     2,100

  22  Net income                43,500    46,650     3,150

LEARN1.WQ1   [1]                                              READY
```

FIGURE 5-6. LEARN1.WQ1 with single lines

then reenter all your formulas, but this is a lot of extra work. Fortunately, there is a much easier way: You can reissue the / Style I Line Drawing command, specify the same block and placement you chose last time, and choose a line type of None.

1. Issue the / **Style** I **Line Drawing** command.

2. Specify a block of B22..D22.

3. Select Top from the Placement menu.

4. Select None from the Line Types menu.

5. When Quattro Pro redisplays the Placement menu, select Quit.

6. Issue the / **File** I **Save** command, and select Replace from the submenu.

This is an attractive but judicious use of line drawing. You will print this version of the spreadsheet in the next chapter. Now try being a little more adventurous. Start by drawing a box around the spreadsheet title.

1. Press (HOME) to move to A1, and Issue the / Style | Line Drawing command.

2. Press (ENTER) to accept the default block of A1..A1.

3. Select Outside from the Placement menu.

4. Select Single from the Line Types menu.

5. When Quattro Pro redisplays the Placement menu, select Quit. The right edge of the box obscures the last character of the label in A1, because Quattro Pro does not have room to display both the left edge of the box and the label characters within the column's current display width. You can solve the problem by widening the column by one character.

6. Issue the / Style | Column Width command, press (RIGHT ARROW) once, and press (ENTER).

Next add a grid of lines to the spreadsheet. This time, practice defining the block before issuing the block command.

1. Move to A7 and press (SHIFT-F7) (Select). Then move to D22 and press (ENTER).

2. Issue the / Style | Line Drawing command again. Quattro Pro does not prompt you for a block this time because you predefined one.

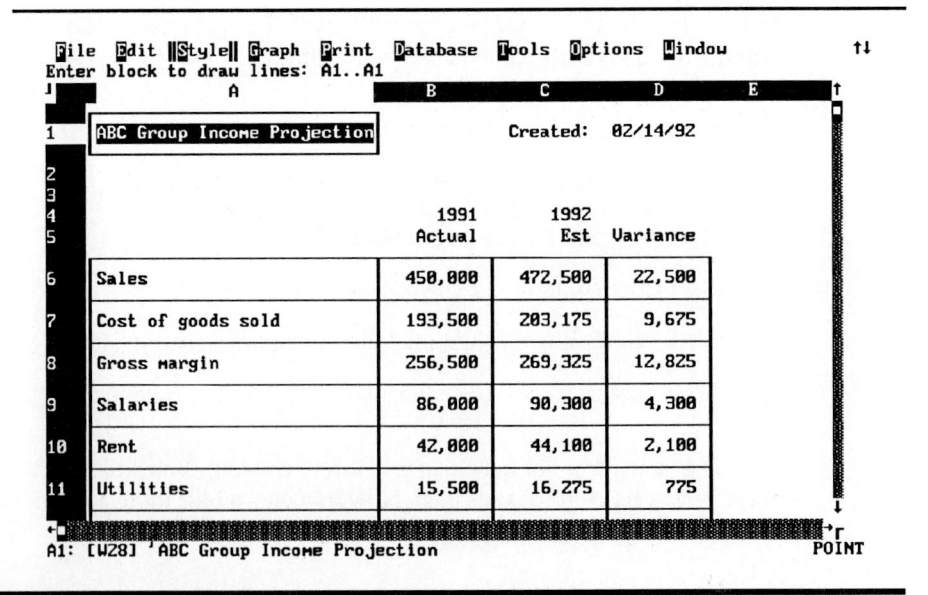

FIGURE 5-7. LEARN1.WQ1 with a grid of lines

| ABC Group Income Projection | | Created: | 02/14/92 |

	1991 Actual	1992 Est	Variance
Sales	450,000	472,500	22,500
Cost of goods sold	193,500	203,175	9,675
Gross margin	256,500	269,325	12,825
Salaries	86,000	90,300	4,300
Rent	42,000	44,100	2,100
Utilities	15,500	16,275	775
Depreciation	22,000	22,000	0
Miscellaneous	8,000	8,400	400
Total operating expenses	173,500	181,075	7,575
Interest expense	10,500	10,500	0
Profit before tax	72,500	77,750	5,250
Income tax	29,000	31,100	2,100
Net income	43,500	46,650	3,150

FIGURE 5-8. LEARN1.WQ1 printed with a grid of lines

3. Select All from the Placement menu.

4. Select Single from the Line Types menu.

5. Select Quit from the Placement menu.

If you like, you can use / **Edit** I **D**elete I **R**ows to delete row 6, then row 9, then row 15, and then row 16. Figure 5-7 shows the resulting spreadsheet, and Figure 5-8 shows it printed on a Hewlett Packard LaserJet Series II. If you like this version, save it with / **File** I **Save As**, and assign it any name other than LEARN1.

Shading Cells

Shading can be an effective means of highlighting data on the spreadsheet. In the following exercise, you will add shading to the totals at the bottom of LEARN1.WQ1,

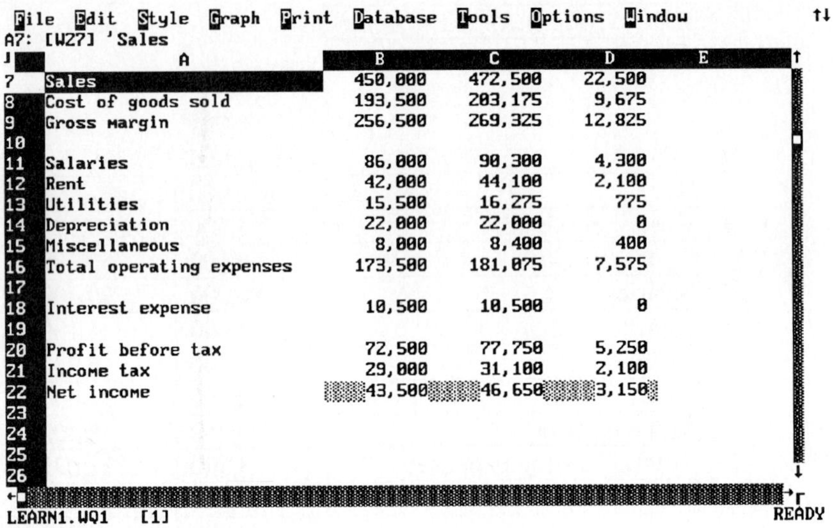

120   Quattro Pro 2 Made Easy

FIGURE 5-9.   Shading the totals on LEARN1.WQ1

as shown in Figure 5-9. You might also use shading to set off one set of cells from another; for example, you can apply gray shading to a lookup table to distinguish it from other sections of the spreadsheet.

When used sparingly, shading also enhances the appearance of printed reports, particularly if you have a high-resolution printer and direct Quattro Pro to print in final-quality mode. Figure 5-10 shows LEARN1.WQ1 printed on a Hewlett-Packard LaserJet Series II after black shading has been applied to A1 and grey shading to B22..D22.

To shade a block of cells, issue the / Style I Shading command. Quattro Pro displays a Shading menu with the options None, Grey, and Black. Next Quattro Pro prompts you for a block to shade. Once you specify the block, Quattro Pro adds the shading and returns to Ready mode.

1. Issue the / **File** I **Retrieve** command and select LEARN1.WQ1 from the file list. The previous version of the spreadsheet (before you added the grid) reappears on the screen.

2. Move to B22 and issue the / **Style** I **Shading** command.

3. When Quattro Pro displays the shading menu, select Grey.

	1991 Actual	1992 Est	Variance
ABC Group Income Projection		Created:	02/14/92

	1991 Actual	1992 Est	Variance
Sales	450,000	472,500	22,500
Cost of goods sold	193,500	203,175	9,675
Gross margin	256,500	269,325	12,825
Salaries	86,000	90,300	4,300
Rent	42,000	44,100	2,100
Utilities	15,500	16,275	775
Depreciation	22,000	22,000	0
Miscellaneous	8,000	8,400	400
Total operating expenses	173,500	181,075	7,575
Interest expense	10,500	10,500	0
Profit before tax	72,500	77,750	5,250
Income tax	29,000	31,100	2,100
Net income	43,500	46,650	3,150

FIGURE 5-10. Printed spreadsheet with black and gray shading

4. When prompted for a block to shade, press (RIGHT ARROW) twice and press (ENTER) to specify B22..D22.

5. Save the spreadsheet by pressing (CTRL-S). Select Replace.

Your spreadsheet should now resemble Figure 5-10.

Even if you delete the contents of a cell with the (DEL) key or / Edit | Erase, the shading remains. If you want to erase the shading as well, you must reissue the / Style | Shading command, include that cell in the shading block, and select None as the type of shading.

On the screen, shading is most effective if you have a color monitor. On monochrome monitors, the effect is subtle, and on some monitors there is no obvious difference between gray and black shading. You can change the color or appearance of shading with the / Options I Colors I Spreadsheet I Shading option. (On monochrome screens, you can make the shading bold, inverse, or underlined.) See Chapter 11 for more details on changing screen colors.

When you print the spreadsheet, lines and shading generally look best if you print in final-quality mode. There are, however, a few potential pitfalls, which are covered in Chapter 6.

Gray shading only appears in the background of the cell, in between the characters. This means that if the cell is completely full—that is, if the number of characters displayed in the cell is the same as the width of the column—you will not see any of the dotted shading pattern.

In this chapter, you have moved from creating the structure of the spreadsheet to making it readable, understandable, and easy to use. As you will see in the following chapter, Quattro Pro prints spreadsheets in the format that appears on the screen. In this sense, formatting your spreadsheet is also a crucial first step in the process of printing Quattro Pro reports.

As you master Quattro Pro's formatting tools, it is easy to get carried away with the possibilities. Few, if any, spreadsheets really merit hours of formatting, unless you are simply experimenting for fun. In addition, too much embellishment can be worse than none at all. The point of line drawing and shading is to highlight specific items, guiding the viewer's eye and helping focus his or her attention. Highlighting half the spreadsheet is counterproductive since it makes the screen or report visually overwhelming and difficult to read.

Restraint is the first rule of formatting. The second rule is to save formatting for last, when possible. If you worry about your spreadsheet's appearance prematurely, your efforts may be wasted, particularly if you later rearrange data, add or delete rows, and make other modifications to the structure. Instead, start with the essentials—entering the numbers, labels, and formulas; making sure that the formulas work as intended; and then saving your work to disk. Then work on the aesthetics. Here too, sequence is important. Begin by deleting rows and columns and adjusting column widths. Then format the numbers, adjust column widths if necessary, align the data, and add lines and shading if desired.

6

PRINTING SPREADSHEETS

Selecting Printers
Standard Quattro Pro Reports
Page Layout
Printing Large Spreadsheets
Using Fonts
The Screen Previewer
Special Print Options

Printing spreadsheets in Quattro Pro can range from an extremely simple to a fairly sophisticated operation, depending on how customized or elaborate you want your output to be. At the easy end of the spectrum, you can create a printed copy of all or part of your spreadsheet by simply defining the block to be printed, aligning your printer, and directing Quattro Pro to print. At the more complex end, you can add headers and footers, specify unusual page lengths and widths, define borders to be displayed on each printed page, add page numbers, choose special fonts for all or parts of the spreadsheet (including fonts to produce bold, underlined, italicized, compressed, or enlarged print), and insert page breaks at specific places in the spreadsheet. In other words, you can produce attractive, visually interesting, and professional reports working only with Quattro Pro.

This chapter introduces all the Quattro Pro print options (except for those related to printing graphs, which are covered in Chapter 13).

SELECTING PRINTERS

When you install Quattro Pro, you are prompted for information on your graphics printer—the printer you intend to use for printing both graphs and high-quality reports. If you do not plan to print graphs or use special fonts and line drawing, you do not need to specify a graphics printer at all; you can skip this section and move directly to the "Standard Quattro Pro Reports" section.

If you are using a daisy wheel printer, you have no choice in this matter. Your printer does not appear in Quattro Pro's list of supported printer models and you are limited to printing in draft mode without any of the desktop publishing extras. You can only print graphs and high-quality spreadsheets in Quattro Pro using a dot matrix, laser, or inkjet printer. Even if you do plan to print graphs or high-quality reports, you need to supply Quattro Pro with additional printer information only if one of the following is true:

- You did not already tell Quattro Pro about your printer during installation or have changed your mind about what printer you want to use

- You plan to use more than one printer to print graphs or high-quality reports

- Your printer is connected to a port other than the first parallel port on your computer

If none of these is true, skip directly to "Standard Quattro Pro Reports."

Telling Quattro Pro About Your Printers

To supply Quattro Pro with information on printers, you issue the / Options | Hardware | Printers command. In response, Quattro Pro displays the Printers menu. The printer you specified during during installation (if any) is considered to be the 1st Printer. Figure 6-1 shows the submenu displayed when you select either the 1st Printer or 2nd Printer option.

To specify a new printer, select the option Type of printer. Quattro Pro pops up a list of printer manufacturers. Once you select the appropriate manufacturer from the list, Quattro Pro displays a list of printer models produced by that manufacturer. Select

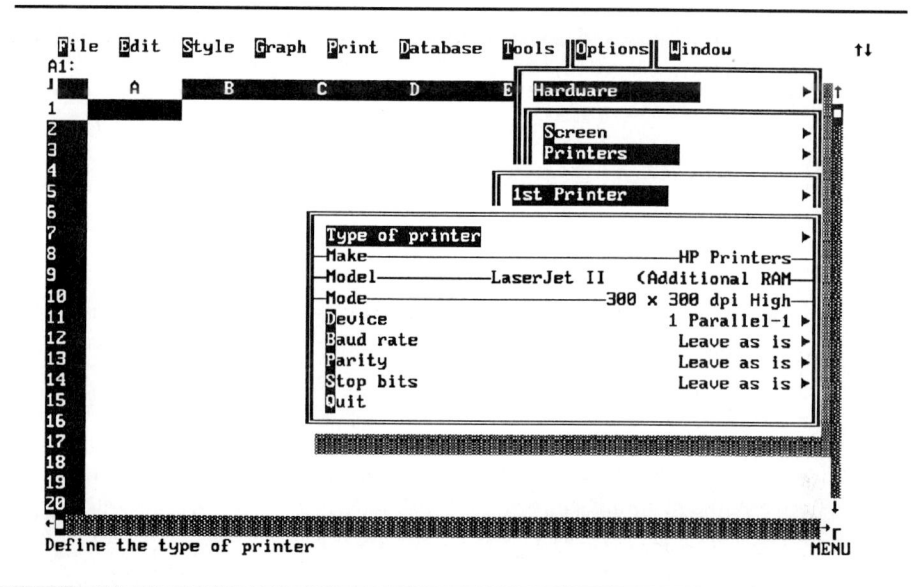

FIGURE 6-1. The Options | Hardware | Printers | 1st Printer menu

a printer model, and Quattro Pro displays a Mode submenu. For most printers you are given a choice between low-, medium-, and high-resolution printing. These settings determine how many dots per inch Quattro Pro will print. The smaller the number of dots, the faster the output and the poorer the print quality. If you are installing a PostScript printer, the Mode submenu includes the options Normal and Use Patterns. These options apply only to graphs and are discussed in Chapter 13.

Next Quattro Pro returns you to the 1st Printer or 2nd Printer submenu. If your printer is connected to anything other than your computer's first parallel port, select the Device option and specify a different output port.

Using a Serial Printer

You should only use the Baud rate, Parity, and Stop bits options on the 1st Printer and 2nd Printer menus if you have chosen a serial port as your output device. These three settings regulate the flow of information from your computer to your printer. If your printer is connected to a serial port, you can initialize the printer (that is, define the baud rate, parity, and stop bits) either from DOS or from Quattro Pro. If you initialize it from DOS, leave the Baud rate, Parity, and Stop bits options set to Leave as is (the default setting). Otherwise enter the appropriate values, as specified in your printer manual.

Switching Between Two Printers

If you plan to use two different printers to print graphs or high-quality spreadsheets, use the 2nd Printer option to tell Quattro Pro about the second device. Once you have defined a second printer, be sure to select the desired printer, using the Default Printer option on the Printers menu, before attempting to print a spreadsheet or graph. By default, this option is set to 1st Printer. If you want to send output to the printer you have specified as your 2nd Printer, select Default Printer, and then pick 2nd Printer from the resulting submenu.

Other Options on the Options | Hardware | Printers Menu

The four other options on the Options I Hardware I Printers menu (referred to from here on as simply the Printers menu) are Plotter Speed, Fonts, Auto LF, and Single Sheet.

PLOTTER SPEED This option applies only to printing graphs and is discussed in Chapter 13.

FONTS This option leads to a submenu with two more options: LaserJet Fonts and Autoscale Fonts. If you have a LaserJet printer and plan to use font cartridges, you must use the Laserjet Fonts option to tell Quattro Pro about them. Use the Left Cartridge and Right Cartridge options to specify which font cartridges you are using. If your laser printer has only one cartridge slot, choose either the Left Cartridge or Right Cartridge option. Once you have specified a font cartridge, its fonts appear in the fonts list when you edit fonts (as described under "Editing Fonts"). The Autoscale Fonts option applies only to printing graphs and is covered in Chapter 13.

AUTO LF (AUTOMATIC LINE FEED) Use this option on the Printers menu to specify whether your printer automatically inserts a carriage return and line feed at the end of each line. The default setting is No. If your reports appear double-spaced, you may need to change it to Yes. Before you try this, however, try printing a very small print block—a few columns wide and a few rows long. If it is not double-spaced, the problem is probably caused by a right margin setting that is too high for your printer.

SINGLE SHEET This option specifies whether you are hand feeding sheets of paper to your printer, one at a time. The default setting is No. If you change it to Yes, Quattro Pro pauses between pages of a multiple-page report to give you a chance to insert the next page.

Saving Your Printer Specifications

Like many other settings accessed through Quattro Pro's Options menu, printer definition settings last only as long as the current work session, unless you explicitly save them with the Update option on the Options menu. Be aware that when you select Update, Quattro Pro saves all the settings that you have changed in this work session, not just the printer settings. For example, if you have changed screen colors or any of the startup options (enabling the Undo feature, for example), those settings are saved as well. These other default settings are covered in Chapter 11.

If you have changed any of the Printers settings, press (ESC) or type **Q** for Quit until you are back on the Options menu (look for Hardware at the top of menu). Then select the Update option to save your changes and select Quit or press (ESC) to return to Ready mode.

STANDARD QUATTRO PRO REPORTS

The standard Quattro Pro report settings assume that you will be printing at 10 characters per inch (cpi) on 8 1/2-by-11-inch paper and that you want 4-character margins (almost 1/2 inch) at the left and right sides of the page and 2-line margins (1/3 inch) at the top and bottom. To produce a printout with these specifications and without extra embellishments follow these steps:

1. Specify the block to print by selecting Block from the Print menu. The menu disappears temporarily, and Quattro Pro prompts you for a block.

2. Select the print destination using the Destination option on the Print menu. Choose Printer to print simple draft-quality reports, without any desktop publishing features. Select Graphics Printer if you want to employ special fonts, or if you have used line drawing and shading in your spreadsheet and want it to look its best. You should also select Graphics Printer if you want to print in landscape mode and your printer does not have a built-in landscape font that you can access with a setup string.

   The Screen Preview option allows you to display high-quality reports on screen—with all the fonts, lines, and shading that will appear in the printed report. This option is discussed later in this chapter.

   The File option is used for sending draft-quality reports to a text file. You can print the reports later from DOS or perhaps import them into a word processing document. The Binary File option is the high-quality equivalent of the File option. Both of these options are covered in Chapter 22.

3. Adjust the printer by making sure it is at the top of a new page and then selecting the Adjust Printer option and choosing Align. The Align option sets the line and page counts to zero and informs Quattro Pro that you are at the top of a page. If you skip this step, Quattro Pro may insert page breaks at the wrong points. If you are using a laser or inkjet printer, make sure the Form Feed light on the printer control panel is off, indicating that the printer has finished the last print job. Otherwise press the On Line button to take the printer off line, press the Form Feed button to eject the page, and then press On Line again.

   If you are using a dot matrix printer, use the Form Feed option on Quattro Pro's Adjust Printer submenu rather than your printer's control panel to eject pages from the printer. If you align your printer properly when you first start printing, the Form Feed option always brings you to the top of the next page. You should also use the Skip Line option on the Adjust Printer menu rather than hand-rolling the paper, so that Quattro Pro can keep track of where you are on the page.

Note If you are using a Hewlett-Packard LaserJet or DeskJet printer, you must change the page length setting to 60 for Quattro Pro to eject the page properly. See the section "Setting Margins and Page Length" for details.

4. Select the Spreadsheet Print option from the Print menu to initiate printing. If your printer is not turned on and on line when you issue the / **Print** I **Spreadsheet Print** command, Quattro Pro displays a box with the message "Printer I/O errors" and the choices Abort and Continue. Choose Abort to cancel printing or fix the problem, and then choose Continue.

   Once printing starts, you can interrupt it before the report is finished by pressing (CTRL-BREAK). If your printer has a large buffer (section of memory that stores characters as they are sent from your computer), it may take a while for printing to stop. Pressing (CTRL-BREAK) again won't make it stop any faster.

5. If you are printing in draft-quality mode, use the Form Feed option on the Adjust Printer menu to advance the printer to the top of the next page.
6. Choose Quit or press (ESC) to return to Ready mode.

You can perform the first three steps—defining the print block, selecting the destination, and aligning the printer—in any order you like, as long as you perform them all before you initiate printing. Quattro Pro remembers your print block and destination settings, so you don't need to redefine them every time you print. When you issue the / **File** | **Save** or / **File** | **Save As** command, Quattro Pro saves the Block setting along with any print layout settings you have defined. The Destination setting lasts only as long as the current work session.

Try producing a draft quality printout of LEARN1.WQ1, as follows:

1. If you do not have the LEARN1 spreadsheet on your screen, retrieve it now using / **File** | **Retrieve**.
2. Type /**P** to display the Print menu. Take a moment to browse through the menu options, keeping your eye on the menu option descriptions displayed on the status line.
3. Select the Block option to define the block to be printed.
4. Press (HOME) and type a period to anchor the cell pointer in cell A1. Press (END-HOME) to expand the print block to A1.D22, and then press (ENTER).
5. If you are using a dot matrix or daisy wheel printer with a tractor feed, set your printer to the top of a page and turn the printer on.
6. Select the Adjust Printer option on the Print menu and then the Align option on the Adjust Printer submenu.
7. If the Destination option is set to anything other than Printer (that is, if you see anything other than the word Printer to the right of the word destination on the Print menu), select Destination. Quattro Pro displays the Destination menu. Select Printer. Quattro Pro will automatically return you to the Print menu.
8. Select Spreadsheet Print to start printing.
9. When the report stops printing, select the Adjust Printer option again and then select the Form Feed option to eject the printed page.
10. Select Quit to return to Ready mode.

You have just printed Quattro Pro's standard report. If this format is adequate for your needs, you can simply use the previous command sequence whenever you want to print all or part of your spreadsheet.

> **Note:** If you have drawn lines around the outside of your print block using / Style | Line Drawing, be sure to include an extra row at the bottom and an extra column at the right in your print block. Otherwise the right and bottom edge of the box will be omitted from your printout. If you use the (END-HOME) key combination to point out the print block, Quattro Pro automatically includes these extra cells in the block.

Draft-Quality Versus High-Quality Printing

When you print in draft-quality mode (that is, when the print destination is Printer), Quattro Pro uses your printer's own built-in character sets. When you print in high-quality mode (by choosing Graphics Printer as the destination), Quattro Pro sends instructions to the printer telling it how to construct each character. Draft-quality printing is considerably faster than high-quality printing. For this reason, you may want to reserve high-quality printing for reports that you intend to show others. If you are using a dot matrix printer, high-quality output generally looks more polished. If you are using a laser or inkjet printer, high-quality printing does not always look better than draft-quality, but it does offer some features that are not available in draft mode. There are three main areas of difference between draft-quality and high-quality printing: the appearance of lines/boxes and shading, the use of fonts, and landscape printing.

If you add lines to your spreadsheet with / Style | Line Drawing or shade cells with / Style | Shading, you obtain noticeably different results when printing in the different modes. When you print in draft-quality mode, Quattro Pro uses standard keyboard characters rather than graphics characters to produce any lines or boxes in your spreadsheet. Lines are printed as dashes rather than as solid lines, and the corners of boxes are printed with plus signs. Quattro Pro also uses a rather "quick and dirty" approach to printing shaded cells when you use draft-quality mode: shading appears only between sets of characters rather than as a continuous background of dots. To obtain better-looking lines and shading, you must print in high-quality mode. Figure 6-2 shows two printouts of a spreadsheet with lines and shading—one printed in draft-quality and the other in high-quality mode. Both reports were printed on a Hewlett-Packard LaserJet Series II.

Figure 6-2 also illustrates the other main difference between draft-quality and high-quality printing: the use of fonts. A *font* is a set of type with a particular style, typeface, and point size. When you print in draft-quality mode, Quattro Pro always uses your printer's default font for the entire spreadsheet. When you print in high-quality mode, Quattro Pro automatically uses one of its own special fonts. It also

```
ABC Group Income Projection              Created:  02/14/92


                              1991       1992
                            Actual        Est    Variance
                            --------------------------------

Sales                      450,000    472,500     22,500
Cost of goods sold         193,500    203,175      9,675
Gross margin               256,500    269,325     12,825

Salaries                    86,000     90,300      4,300
Rent                        42,000     44,100      2,100
Utilities                   15,500     16,275        775
Depreciation                22,000     22,000          0
Miscellaneous                8,000      8,400        400
Total operating expenses   173,500    181,075      7,575

Interest expense            10,500     10,500          0

Profit before tax           72,500     77,750      5,250
Income tax                  29,000     31,100      2,100
Net income                  43,500     46,650      3,150
```

ABC Group Income Projection   Created: 02/14/92

	1991 Actual	1991 Est	Variance
Sales	450,000	472,500	22,500
Cost of goods sold	193,500	203,175	9,675
Gross margin	256,500	269,325	12,825
Salaries	86,000	90,300	4,300
Rent	42,000	44,100	2,100
Utilities	15,500	16,275	775
Depreciation	22,000	22,000	0
Miscellaneous	8,000	8,400	400
Total operating expenses	173,500	181,075	7,575
Interest expense	10,500	10,500	0
Profit before tax	72,500	77,750	5,250
Income tax	29,000	31,100	2,100
Net income	43,500	46,650	3,150

FIGURE 6-2. LEARN1.WQ1 printed in draft-quality mode and high-quality mode

allows you to switch to another font, and to choose different fonts for different sections of the spreadsheet. All these options are discussed later under "Using Fonts."

PAGE LAYOUT

In many cases, Quattro Pro's standard layout is perfectly adequate for quick and simple reports. Eventually, you will want to deviate from that standard—change margins to center the report on the page or to accommodate a paper size other than 8 1/2 by 11 inches; add headers and footers, particularly in cases where the report is too long to fit on one page; print horizontally rather than vertically; or send your printer special commands for compressed print. The options for all of these operations are found on the Print | Layout menu.

Adding Headers and Footers

Headers and footers are single lines of text that appear at the top and bottom, respectively, of every page of the report. (Do not confuse the Header option with the Headings option on the Print menu. The Headings option is described under "Printing Large Spreadsheets.") Quattro Pro provides three special characters for use in headers and footers: |, @, and #. The | character is used to designate the position of text within headers and footers. Quattro Pro's headers and footers are divided into three sections: left, center, and right. The | character functions like a tab marker. Text that is not preceded by this character is printed in the left section of the header or footer; text preceded by a single | is printed in the center; text preceded by || is printed in the right section. The @ symbol is used to print the current date within headers and footers. The # symbol is used to print the current page number. Whenever you include page numbers in a header or footer, you must be careful to select the Align option on the Adjust Printer menu every time you print; otherwise page numbering will start from the last page number you printed rather than from page 1.

Setting Margins And Page Length

Quattro Pro's initial defaults for margins and page length are as follows:

Top margin	Two lines (approximately 1/2 inch) plus three lines for a header, whether you define a header or not. If you define a header, it is printed on the third line from the top of the page and is followed by two blank lines.
Bottom margin	Two lines (approximately 1/2 inch) plus three lines for a footer, whether or not you actually define a footer. If you define a footer, it is printed on the third line from the bottom of the page and is preceded by two blank lines.
Left margin	Four characters (just under 1/2 inch).
Right margin	76 characters (leaves a little less than 1/2 inch between the right edge and the edge of the page).
Page length	66 lines (62 available for text, including the 6 reserved for the header and footer).

You can change any or all of these defaults by choosing options from the Margins submenu. (Select Layout on the Print menu and then Margins on the Page menu.) You might want to change margins or page length when

- Your report is only slightly too long or too wide to fit on one page with the default settings.

- You are printing on paper that is larger or smaller than 8 1/2 by 11 inches or you are printing in landscape mode.

- You are using condensed or expanded print. The default margin settings assume you are printing at 10 cpi; if you are not, you need to adjust the right margin accordingly.

- You are using a Hewlett-Packard LaserJet or DeskJet printer, in which case you should change the Page Length setting to 60 to match the default form length setting of the printer itself.

In each of these cases, you may need to experiment a bit before finding the ideal settings. If you are printing a large spreadsheet, try several of these settings on a small block until you are satisfied with its appearance.

Using Setup Strings

Setup strings are codes that are sent to the printer to invoke special functions such as condensed or expanded printing. Setup strings only work in draft quality mode. If the print Destination setting is Graphics Printer rather than Printer, you must use fonts to determine print size and orientation; Quattro Pro ignores any setup strings you define.

The printer codes for different print options vary, depending on the type of printer you are using. Appendix E of your *Quattro Pro User's Guide* contains a list of commonly used printer codes for a variety of printers. If your printer is not included in that list, you must find the appropriate codes in your printer manual and then translate them into the form that Quattro Pro requires.

Printer codes generally consist of either a *control character* (a character pressed in combination with the CTRL key) or an *escape sequence* (a series of characters beginning with ESC). You cannot enter either control characters or ESC directly into a setup string. Instead, you need to enter \ followed by the three-digit decimal ASCII code for that character.

Most printer manuals contain the decimal ASCII codes for different printer commands. If your manual does not, you can look up the codes for particular keys, key combinations, and special characters in the ASCII table in Appendix G of the *Quattro Pro User's Guide*. When the decimal ASCII code is only two digits long, it should be preceded by a zero in the setup string. If your printer code contains letters, you can simply type them in your setup string as is rather than using their ASCII equivalent.

For example, the code for compressed print on most Epson and IBM graphics printers is CTRL-O or ASCII code 15. Therefore, the appropriate Quattro Pro setup string for this print option would be \015. The code for printing in double-strike mode on these same printers is ESC-G. Since the ASCII code for ESC is 27, the Quattro Pro setup string for this print option would be \027G. Capitalization *does* matter in setup strings.

You can specify multiple printer commands in one setup string; just enter the command codes one after the other, with a slash at the beginning of each code. For example, to send your Epson FX printer the codes for near-letter-quality mode (code \027x1) and elite pitch (code \027M), you would enter **\027x1\027M** as your setup string. Do not include any spaces between command codes.

Quattro Pro offers two methods of sending setup strings to your printer:

- You can use the Setup String option on the Print I Layout menu. This is the simplest way to define a setup string for the whole print block.

- You can enter a setup string in the first cell of a blank row within your print block. This is known as an *embedded setup string*. Embedded setup strings allow you to define different print options for different sections of the spreadsheet. You can use boldface for the title and then switch back to regular type, or print a footnote to the spreadsheet in condensed print.

When you embed a setup string, you must precede the printer code itself with || (two vertical bars) to let Quattro Pro know that the subsequent characters should be read as a setup string rather than as text. Usually the best way to embed a setup string is to insert a new row and then enter the setup string in the first column of that row that falls within the print block. Whenever Quattro Pro encounters an embedded setup string, it sends the code to your printer and then ignores the rest of that row. It does not print a blank line.

If you want to return to normal printing after using a setup string, you have two options. You can specify a new setup string with the printer code for undoing the print mode initiated by the last setup string. Alternatively, you can just turn your printer off and then on again to return to normal printing.

Printing in Landscape Mode

By default, Quattro Pro prints spreadsheets in portrait mode— that is, vertically on the page. When printing wide spreadsheets, you may prefer to print in landscape mode so that the data is printed horizontally.

There are three ways to print in landscape mode (not all of which can be used on all printers):

- If you have a late-model laser or inkjet printer, you can obtain landscape printing in draft mode using setup strings.

- If you are printing in high-quality mode, you can change the Orientation setting on the Print | Layout menu from Portrait to Landscape.

- If you are using a LaserJet or PostScript printer in high-quality mode, you can select a LaserJet or PostScript landscape font (see the discussion of fonts later in this chapter).

Regardless of which method you use, you need to adjust the margins for landscape printing. Change the page length to 7.5 inches (45 lines at 6 lines per inch) on Hewlett-Packard LaserJet and inkjet printers, 8.5 inches (51 lines at 6 lines per inch) on all others. If you are printing at 10 characters per inch, try a left margin of 1/2 inch (5 characters at 10 characters per inch) and a right margin of 10 inches (100 characters at 10 characters per inch).

Even if you change the Break Pages setting on the Layout menu to No, Quattro Pro breaks pages when printing in landscape mode. If you are using a tractor-fed dot matrix printer, there still is no way to print continuously across the page breaks. Instead, you must print individual pages and literally cut and paste them.

Saving Print Settings

Whenever you issue the / File | Save or / File | Save As command, Quattro Pro saves your print settings along with your data—just as it saves your numeric format and global column width defaults. If you neglect to save your spreadsheet after changing print settings, Quattro Pro asks whether you want to lose your changes when you issue a / File | Exit, / File | Erase, or / File | Retrieve command, even if you have not changed any data on the spreadsheet. The settings saved include

- The print block
- The Left Heading and Right Heading settings (if any)
- All the settings on the Print | Layout menu (including the Header and Footer settings)
- Current font definitions (created with the / Style | Fonts | Edit Fonts command)

When you retrieve the spreadsheet, those settings are automatically reinstated, even if you have defined different print settings for another spreadsheet in the current work session.

When you start printing reports regularly, you may find that you use certain settings for almost all your reports. If, for example, you always use high-quality print and a specific set of page layout options, you may want to save these settings as defaults for all future spreadsheets. You can do this using the Update option on the Print | Layout menu. The settings saved will include all the settings on the Layout menu except the Header and Footer settings, plus the Destination setting on the Print menu.

Other Layout Options

The Layout menu has four other options that allow you to control report printing: Break Pages, Dimensions, Orientation, and Reset.

By default, Quattro Pro issues a page eject command to your printer whenever it reaches the bottom of the page. If you prefer not to have any page breaks in your report, select the Break Pages option on the Layout menu and change the setting from Yes to

No. You might want to do this when printing a very wide spreadsheet in landscape mode or when "printing" to a disk file.

The Dimensions setting determines what unit of measurement Quattro Pro uses to define page margins. By default, this is set to Lines/Characters. If you are printing in high-quality mode and are using proportional fonts or mixing several fonts in one report, you may find it easier to specify margins in inches or centimeters. As discussed under "Using Fonts," proportional fonts use different amounts of space for different characters, making characters difficult for measuring portions of the page.

The Orientation setting determines which direction your report is printed in. By default, Quattro Pro prints in portrait mode. If you are printing in high-quality mode and select Landscape, the report is printed horizontally across the page.

You can use the Reset setting to restore some or all of the print options to their default settings. When you select this option, Quattro Pro displays a submenu with the options All, Print Block, Headings, and Layout. The All option clears the print block setting, clears any headings, and restores the Destination and all the layout options to the last set of defaults saved with the Update option on the Layout menu. Print Block erases the Print Block setting. Headings clears the settings from the Top and Left Heading options. Layout returns all options on the Layout menu and submenus (except for Header and Footer) to their default settings.

PRINTING LARGE SPREADSHEETS

If you define a print block that is too large to fit on a single page, Quattro Pro automatically splits the output across as many pages as required. Unfortunately the output is often difficult to decipher because only the first page includes all the column and row headings needed to identify the values. Figure 6-3, for example, shows a draft-quality printout of a six-month income statement. Notice that the line items on the second page of this report are impossible to identify.

The **/ Print | Headings** command solves this problem. When you select Headings from the Print menu, Quattro Pro displays a submenu with the options Left Heading and Top Heading. Use the Left Heading option to define a block of cells (generally row headings) to be printed at the left side of every page of the printout. This option is useful when you are printing spreadsheets that are too wide to fit on one page. Be sure to exclude all the cells in the Left Heading block from the print block; otherwise they will be printed twice.

Use the Top Heading option to define a block of cells (generally column headings) to be printed at the top of every page, immediately below the report header. Again, be sure to exclude cells in the heading from the print block itself. You can use both the Top Heading and Left Heading options on the same report; just be sure that the Top Heading and Left Heading blocks do not overlap.

```
                        ABC GROUP INCOME STATEMENT
                            FIRST HALF OF 1991


    Income Tax Rate:                  25%
    Monthly Growth Factor            1.004


                              Jan      Feb     March    1st Qtr    April
                             ------------------------------------------

    Sales                   37,500   37,650   37,801   112,951   37,952
    Cost of goods sold      16,125   16,190   16,254    48,569   16,319
    Gross margin            53,625   53,840   54,055   161,519   54,271

    Salaries                 7,166    7,195    7,223    21,584    7,252
    Rent                     3,500    3,514    3,528    10,542    3,542
    Utilities                1,291    1,296    1,301     3,889    1,307
    Depreciation             1,833    1,840    1,848     5,521    1,855
    Miscellaneous              666      669      671     2,006      674
    Total operating expenses 14,456  14,514   14,572    43,542   14,630

    Interest expense           875      879      882     2,636      886

    Profit before tax       38,294   38,447   38,601   115,342   38,755
    Income tax               9,574    9,612    9,650    28,836    9,689
    Net income              28,721   28,835   28,951    86,507   29,067



                     May      June    2nd Qtr  YTD Total
                    ---------------------------------

                   38,104   38,256   114,311   454,524
                   16,385   16,450    49,154   195,445
                   54,488   54,706   163,465   649,969

                    7,281    7,310    21,844    86,857
                    3,556    3,571    10,669    42,422
                    1,312    1,317     3,935    15,648
                    1,863    1,870     5,588    22,217
                      677      679     2,030     8,072
                   14,689   14,747    44,066   175,216

                      889      893     2,667    10,606

                   38,910   39,066   116,732   464,148
                    9,728    9,767    29,183   116,037
                   29,183   29,300    87,549   348,111
```

FIGURE 6-3. Printout of a wide spreadsheet

To appreciate the Headings options, you need to make your spreadsheet large enough to require additional pages of printed output. Do this now, and then define a header, footer, and left heading, and print the report.

1. Move to B4 and issue the / Edit | Copy command. Press (END-HOME) to expand the source block to B4..D22. Press (ENTER), and then enter a destination of **E4**. The spreadsheet is now seven columns wide.
2. Change the label in E4 to **"1993** and the label in F4 to **"1994**.
3. Issue the / **Print** | **Layout** | **Header** command, and enter a header of

    @ | ABC GROUP INCOME PROJECTION | Page #
4. Select Footer and enter **Prepared by** followed by your name.
5. Press (ESC) to return to the Print menu.
6. Select Headings on the Print menu. Then select the Left Heading option and, when the prompt "Enter block to use as left heading" appears, enter **A7..A22**.
7. Move to B3. Select the Block option on the Print menu. Type a period, and then press (END-HOME) to expand the block to B3..G22. Press (ENTER).
8. Select the Adjust Printer option and select Align to let Quattro Pro know the printer is at the top of page 1.
9. Select the Spreadsheet Print option to start printing.
10. When the report has stopped printing, select the Adjust Printer option and then select Form Feed. Your report should resemble the one shown in Figure 6-4.

There are, of course, other methods of printing reports that are too large for one page. Many people simply cut and paste printout pages so they can see the spreadsheet in one continuous piece. Some try, whenever possible, to design spreadsheets in small, discrete sections that can fit neatly on one printed page. You can also print in landscape mode—in effect rotating the spreadsheet 90 degrees and printing it broadside. In some cases you can squeeze a moderately wide report on one page with this method.

A few other Quattro Pro features are also useful for printing long reports. Compressed print and narrow margins can sometimes make the difference between a single- and multiple-page report. Quattro Pro also allows you to insert page breaks wherever you like within a report or to print without any page breaks at all.

Inserting Page Breaks

Unless you set page breaks, Quattro Pro automatically breaks the page whenever necessary, as determined by the page-length setting. You can also insert your own page breaks to separate multiple-page reports into coherent, readable sections.

```
02-Mar-92              ABC GROUP INCOME PROJECTION                 Page 1


                            1991        1992              1993
                            Actual      Est    Variance   Actual
                            ----------------------------------------

Sales                       450,000    472,500   22,500   450,000
Cost of goods sold          193,500    203,175    9,675   193,500
Gross margin                256,500    269,325   12,825   256,500

Salaries                     86,000     90,300    4,300    86,000
Rent                         42,000     44,100    2,100    42,000
Utilities                    15,500     16,275      775    15,500
Depreciation                 22,000     22,000        0    22,000
Miscellaneous                 8,000      8,400      400     8,000
Total operating expenses    173,500    181,075    7,575   173,500

Interest expense             10,500     10,500        0    10,500

Profit before tax            72,500     77,750    5,250    72,500
Income tax                   29,000     31,100    2,100    29,000
Net income                   43,500     46,650    3,150    43,500



02-Mar-92              ABC GROUP INCOME PROJECTION


                                        1994
                                        Est    Variance
                                       -----------------

Sales                                  472,500   22,500
Cost of goods sold                     203,175    9,675
Gross margin                           269,325   12,825

Salaries                                90,300    4,300
Rent                                    44,100    2,100
Utilities                               16,275      775
Depreciation                            22,000        0
Miscellaneous                            8,400      400
Total operating expenses               181,075    7,575

Interest expense                        10,500        0

Profit before tax                       77,750    5,250
Income tax                              31,100    2,100
Net income                              46,650    3,150
```

FIGURE 6-4. Printing a large spreadsheet with a left heading

The code for a hard page break (a break inserted whether or not the printer has reached the bottom of a page) is a vertical bar followed by two colons:

|::

Like setup strings, page break codes should be entered in the first column of your print block. Any data to the right of the code is ignored during printing.

Often the easiest way to insert a page break is to move the cell pointer to the first column of your print block within the row where you want to break the page and then issue the / Style | Insert Break command. Quattro Pro inserts a blank row immediately above the current cell and enters the page break code in the cell immediately above the current cell. (If you want to get rid of the page break later, just delete the row.) You must move to column A before issuing the command to obtain the proper results.

You can also enter a page break code manually. Remember to enter the code within the first column of your print block. If you do not have any blank or unnecessary rows on your spreadsheet where you want the page break to occur, use / **Edit** | **Insert** | **Row** to insert a row for this purpose.

The vertical bar character is like an alignment character—it is an instruction to Quattro Pro rather than a character to be displayed on the spreadsheet surface. When you enter the code—manually or with / Style | Insert Break—you will see the entire code on the input line, but only :: is displayed on the spreadsheet itself.

Note that Quattro Pro respects your page break codes even if you change the Page Breaks setting on the Print | Layout menu to No. If you decide you do not want those page breaks, you must delete the page break codes from the spreadsheet itself.

USING FONTS

When you print in draft-quality mode, Quattro Pro always uses your printer's default font. When you print in high-quality mode, Quattro Pro lets you select from three types of fonts:

- **Hershey fonts** A set of basic fonts that can be produced in all available sizes on almost any screen and most printers, without special preparation. Quattro Pro comes with eight Hershey fonts: Roman, Roman Light, Sans Serif, Sans Serif Light, Script, Monospace, Old English, and Eurostyle.

- **Bitstream fonts** A set of clearer and more attractive fonts. To use these fonts Quattro Pro must build a font file for each combination of typeface, style, and point size you use. Quattro Pro comes with three Bitstream typefaces: Dutch (similar to Times Roman), Swiss (similar to Helvetica), and Courier. Quattro Pro also supports other Bitstream fonts that you can purchase separately (refer to the *Quattro Pro User's Guide* for instructions on installing them).

- **Printer-specific fonts** Special fonts used only by PostScript or LaserJet printers.

Using Bitstream Fonts

When you print in high-quality mode, Quattro Pro uses Bitstream fonts by default (unless you have set the Graphics Quality option to Draft, as explained shortly). Before it can use these fonts, Quattro Pro needs to build a font file to specify exactly where each dot that makes up each character should be placed on the page.

Quattro Pro builds a font file every time you use a Bitstream typeface utilizing a combination of output device, print resolution, typeface, point size, and style that you haven't used before. For example, when you use a 12-point bold Bitstream Dutch typeface for the first time on your Epson printer at high resolution, Quattro Pro builds a font file. While it is building the new font file, Quattro Pro displays a "Now building font" message. The next time you use this font on your Epson, Quattro Pro uses the same file. However, if you use the same font on a different printer, with the Screen Previewer, or at a different level of resolution, or if you edit the font and turn italics on, Quattro Pro must build a new font file. Note that you need room in memory to create a Bitstream font. If you do not have enough space available, Quattro Pro briefly displays the message "Build Error: Not enough memory for that operation."

Every time Quattro Pro builds a font, it stores it on disk. If you work with fonts extensively, it is easy to fill up a megabyte or more with font files. Quattro Pro assigns all font files an extension of FON and stores them in a subdirectory of your Quattro Pro program directory called FONTS. The size of a font file can range from about 1000 bytes to 20,000 bytes or more, depending on the typeface, font, and point size. This is another reason to use fonts judiciously.

During installation, Quattro Pro asks two questions about fonts: whether you want to prebuild fonts to save time later, and whether you are willing to wait for font building during high quality printing. Unless you have disk space to burn, it is preferable to build fonts only as you need them. The answer to the second question—whether you are willing to wait for font building—determines the initial setting from the Options | Graphics Quality option. When this option is set to No, Quattro Pro uses only those fonts it has already built whenever you print a spreadsheet in high-quality mode. If Quattro Pro has not already built one of the Bitstream fonts used in the print block, it substitutes a similar Hershey font. If the Options | Graphics Quality option is set to Final, you see a Building Font message on the screen for a few moments before the Now Printing message whenever you use a new Bitstream font.

If you have a LaserJet printer, you may want to use LaserJet fonts rather than Bitstream fonts to avoid waiting for font building and to save disk space (see the upcoming section "Printer-Specific Fonts"). Otherwise, if appearance is important, the Bitstream fonts are generally worth waiting for—they are much more attractive than the faster-printing Hershey fonts. However, if you find the Hershey fonts adequate for your needs, issue the / Options | Graphics Quality | Draft command to change the Graphics Quality setting to draft mode.

For more information on fonts, see Appendix F of the *Quattro Pro User's Guide*.

Applying Fonts to Sections Of the Report

You can use up to eight fonts in any spreadsheet report. Quattro Pro uses the font defined as Font 1 as the default font for the spreadsheet whenever you specify high-quality printing. Font 1 is initially defined as Bitstream Dutch 12 point Black, although you can change that setting using the Edit Fonts option.

To apply a different font to a block of cells on the spreadsheet, issue the / Style I Font command. Then select the desired font from the Font submenu and specify the block to which you want that font applied.

Whenever you apply a font other than Font 1 to a section of your spreadsheet, Quattro Pro stores a font code in each cell of the specified block. If you apply Font 2 to a cell, for example, you will see the font code [F2] on the input line whenever you move the cell pointer to that cell. To get rid of a font code, you simply assign Font 1 to the cell.

Quattro Pro records only the font number in the cell, not a specific font. If you edit a font, any changes you make affect cells that already have that font code, as well as cells to which you apply the font afterward.

Editing Fonts

The set of default fonts for new spreadsheets is shown on the Print I Fonts menus. You can change any of the eight fonts by selecting the Edit Fonts option on that menu (thereby issuing the / Style I Font I Edit Fonts command). Quattro Pro displays an Edit Fonts menu with the same set of fonts. When you select a font from this menu, Quattro Pro displays a submenu with the following options:

- **Typeface**   The typeface determines the shape of individual characters. When you select the Typeface option, Quattro Pro displays a submenu with the 11 typefaces supplied with Quattro Pro. If you are using either a LaserJet or PostScript printer, the submenu includes additional printer-specific fonts, as described shortly.

- **Point Size**   The range of point sizes is from 6- to 72-point. The larger the number, the bigger the characters.

- **Style** When you select the Style option, Quattro Pro displays a menu with the options Underlined, Bold, Italic, Reset, and Quit. Select any one of these options to change the respective setting from Off to On (or back to Off again). Use the Reset option if you want to turn Underlined, Italic, and Bold off all at once.

- **Color** When you select the Color option, Quattro Pro displays a submenu of 16 colors—in case you are directing your output to a color printer. If you are not using a color printer, Quattro Pro simply ignores your choice.

- **Quit** The Quit option returns you to the Edit Fonts menu. Any changes you just made are reflected on this menu. Select another font to edit, or select Quit to return to the Fonts menu.

As mentioned, Quattro Pro uses Font 1 as the default font for the spreadsheet. If you plan to use a particular font for the majority of your spreadsheet, you should designate it as Font 1. This saves some space in memory. It can also help prevent some of the spacing problems discussed under "Problems with Fonts."

PRINTER-SPECIFIC FONTS If you are using a LaserJet or PostScript printer, additional fonts specific to your printer appear at the bottom of the Typeface submenu, underneath the Bitstream and Hershey fonts. If you are using font cartridges with a LaserJet printer, use / **Options** | **Hardware** | **Printers** | **Fonts** | **LaserJet Fonts** to tell Quattro Pro about them. Those additional fonts then are included in the Typeface submenu.

Do not attempt to change the attributes of the LaserJet fonts. Just select the one that most closely matches what you want—if you want to print in italics, select an Italic font; if you want to print in boldface, select a Bold font. If you attempt to modify the typeface, point size, or style, Quattro Pro either displays an error message or just ignores your changes.

SAVING YOUR FONTS When you edit fonts and then save the spreadsheet, your font changes are saved to disk along with other print settings and your spreadsheet data. However, those changes apply only to the current spreadsheet. If you create another spreadsheet, Quattro Pro displays its usual set of fonts when you issue the / **Style** | **Font** command.

There is no direct way to specify default fonts for future spreadsheets. If you find that you use the same set of fonts repeatedly, consider creating a style sheet with those fonts, as described in Chapter 11.

Using Different Fonts To Print LEARN1.WQ1

The following exercise requires a graphics printer—that is, a printer capable of producing graphics images. If you only have a daisy wheel printer, you will not be able to generate a "high-quality" printout in Quattro Pro.

1. If you have not already specified a graphics printer as Printer 1, do so now. (See the instructions under "Selecting Printers" at the beginning of this chapter.)
2. Discard the large spreadsheet you built in the previous exercise and retrieve LEARN1 by typing **/FR**, answering Yes when asked whether you want to lose your changes, and selecting LEARN1.WQ1 from the files list.
3. Make sure that the Options I Graphics Quality option is set to Final rather than Draft Select Quit to return to Ready mode.
4. Issue the **/ Print I Block** command. Press (HOME) if the cell pointer is not already in A1. Then press (END-HOME) to extend the block to A1..D22, and press (ENTER).
5. Issue the **/ Print I Destination I Graphics Printer** command.
6. Select Adjust Printer and then Align.
7. Select Spreadsheet Print to initiate printing.

Now try editing fonts and applying different fonts to the spreadsheet.

1. Issue the **/ Style I Font I Edit Fonts** command.
2. Select Font 1 and change the Typeface to Bitstream Swiss. Press (ESC) or select Quit to return to the Edit Fonts submenu.
3. Select Font 5 and change Point Size to 14. Select Style and change the Bold option to On. Press (ESC) three times to return to the Fonts submenu.
4. Select Font 5 and, when prompted for a block, enter **A1**.
5. Issue the **/ Print I Spreadsheet Print** command.
6. When the printing stops, issue the **/ Print I Adjust Printer I Align** command. Then press (ESC) to return to Ready mode. Your printout should resemble Figure 6-5.

ABC Group Income Projection Created: 02/14/92

	1991 Actual	1992 Est	Variance
Sales	450,000	472,500	22,500
Cost of goods sold	193,500	203,175	9,675
Gross margin	256,500	269,325	12,825
Salaries	86,000	90,300	4,300
Rent	42,000	44,100	2,100
Utilities	15,500	16,275	775
Depreciation	22,000	22,000	0
Miscellaneous	8,000	8,400	400
Total operating expenses	173,500	181,075	7,575
Interest expense	10,500	10,500	0
Profit before tax	72,500	77,750	5,250
Income tax	29,000	31,100	2,100
Net income	43,500	46,650	3,150

FIGURE 6-5. LEARN1.WQ1 printed in two Bitstream Swiss fonts

7. If you like the results, save your spreadsheet by pressing CTRL-S and selecting Replace. Your new selection of fonts and the current print destination is saved to disk.

Problems with Fonts

As you have seen, column widths are measured in numbers of characters in Quattro Pro. This means that the size of the columns depends on the size of the characters themselves. Quattro Pro measures columns in terms of the point size of Font 1, the default font for the spreadsheet. The larger the point size of this font, the wider the columns and the taller the rows.

Most Bitstream fonts are *proportional fonts,* meaning that different amounts of space are allocated to different characters. An "i" takes up less space in a proportional font than does an "m" or a "w." (Numbers are always given the same amount of space, so that they line up properly within columns.) Determining how wide to make a particular column is quite difficult, because each cell in the column will contain different sets of characters, each of which occupies a different amount of space.

Quattro Pro handles this problem by using the character 5 as a kind of yardstick for measuring column widths. It treats the amount of space a 5 occupies in a particular font as the average amount of space occupied per character. Column widths are calculated by multiplying the space allocated to the number 5 in Font 1 by the width assigned to that column on the spreadsheet. While this method is as good as any, it is far from infallible. If a particular cell happens to be filled with characters that take up more space than the character 5 occupies in Font 1, some of the characters may be truncated. You can solve the problem by widening the column or, if that adds too much space between columns, by narrowing the column and allowing the text to spill over into the column to the right.

You may also encounter problems lining up text within a column if your column contains labels that start with blank spaces. Again, this is something you need to fix manually, preferably using the Screen Previewer rather than wasting a lot of paper.

Quattro Pro's line drawing feature may also present difficulties when you are printing in proportional fonts or in fonts other than Font 1, because Quattro Pro matches the line to the calculated cell width. In other words, if you draw a line under a cell, that line is the number of characters specified in the spreadsheet column width times the amount of space occupied by the character 5 in Font 1. Even if you draw a line under a cell that is completely filled with characters and printed in Font 1, the line may be longer or shorter than the text—the characters in the cell may occupy, on average, more or less space than the character 5.

Sometimes you can fix the problem by adjusting the column width. If you are drawing lines around a cell (or cells) printed with a very large font, try including an extra cell to the right in the block you draw lines around, if possible.

If you have considerable trouble aligning lines with data, you might try substituting dashes entered into the spreadsheet for lines drawn with / Style | Line Drawing. You can also try using an underlined font. Figure 6-6, for example, shows a high-quality printout of LEARN1.WQ1 after the lines underneath the three column headings were eliminated and underlined fonts were applied to A1 and B5..D5.

When you print a spreadsheet with shaded cells, the width of the shading depends on the width of the cell (which in turn depends on the column width setting multiplied by the amount of space a 5 occupies in Font 1.) You may therefore need to widen or narrow columns slightly to adjust the size of shaded areas on your printout.

ABC Group Income Projection   Created: 02/14/92

	1991 Actual	1992 Est	Variance
Sales	450,000	472,500	22,500
Cost of goods sold	193,500	203,175	9,675
Gross margin	256,500	269,325	12,825
Salaries	86,000	90,300	4,300
Rent	42,000	44,100	2,100
Utilities	15,500	16,275	775
Depreciation	22,000	22,000	0
Miscellaneous	8,000	8,400	400
Total operating expenses	173,500	181,075	7,575
Interest expense	10,500	10,500	0
Profit before tax	72,500	77,750	5,250
Income tax	29,000	31,100	2,100
Net income	43,500	46,650	3,150

FIGURE 6-6.   LEARN1.WQ1 with underlined fonts

While Quattro Pro uses Font 1 to determine the width of each column, it uses the size of the largest font on any given row of the print block to determine the size of that line on the printed page. As a result, Quattro Pro may print fewer lines than the number specified in the Page Length setting.

A line in which the largest font is 30 points takes up about twice as much space vertically on the page as a line in which the largest font is 14 points.

There are no exact rules for preventing or fixing the potential pitfalls in using fonts, but here are some guidelines:

- Define the font you will use for most of the spreadsheet as Font 1 or, if you are having problems with a column, try making the font used for the data in that column Font 1. In either case, avoid defining a very large or very small font as Font 1.

- Use the Screen Preview option before printing, and be sure to zoom in on any sections of the spreadsheet that use large fonts. For fine-tuning, use the Ruler option to add a grid of one-inch squares to the display. This can be particularly useful when you are trying to adjust margins and page length. (In this case change the Printer | Dimensions setting from Characters/Lines to Inches so that the layout settings will appear in inches as well.)

- Whenever characters do not fit in a cell, try widening the column. If the label is exactly the same width as the column and the cell to its right is empty, you might also try making the column narrower and allowing at least one of the characters in the label to spill over into the adjacent column. Then Quattro Pro will use some of that additional cell's space to print the label.

THE SCREEN PREVIEWER

The Screen Preview option allows you to view your report as it will look when printed in high-quality mode. This option only works if you have a graphics adaptor for your monitor. The Screen Previewer can save you a tremendous amount of time and paper, particularly if you are using a variety of fonts in your report. It can help you see how the data will be laid out and where the pages will break. If you are combining several fonts in one report, the Screen Previewer can give you a sense of how the fonts will look together and help you make adjustments if necessary. It can also help you find and correct the types of problems described in the previous section, such as data not lining up properly in columns.

Note If you have selected a LaserJet or PostScript font, the Screen Previewer substitutes a similar Hershey or Bitstream font.

To preview a report, change the Destination setting to Screen Preview and then "print" the report to your screen using the Spreadsheet Print option. Quattro Pro displays a screen like the one in Figure 6-7, showing the first page of your report. At the top of the screen is a menu bar with the following nine options:

- **Help**   Displays a help screen with information on the Screen Previewer. Like other Quattro Pro help screens, this screen includes buttons at the bottom for displaying more detailed information on particular topics.

- **Quit**   Returns you to the regular spreadsheet display and the Print menu.

- **Color**   Allows you to alter the colors used to display your report on the screen. There are four predefined sets of colors. If you type C repeatedly, Quattro Pro displays each in turn.

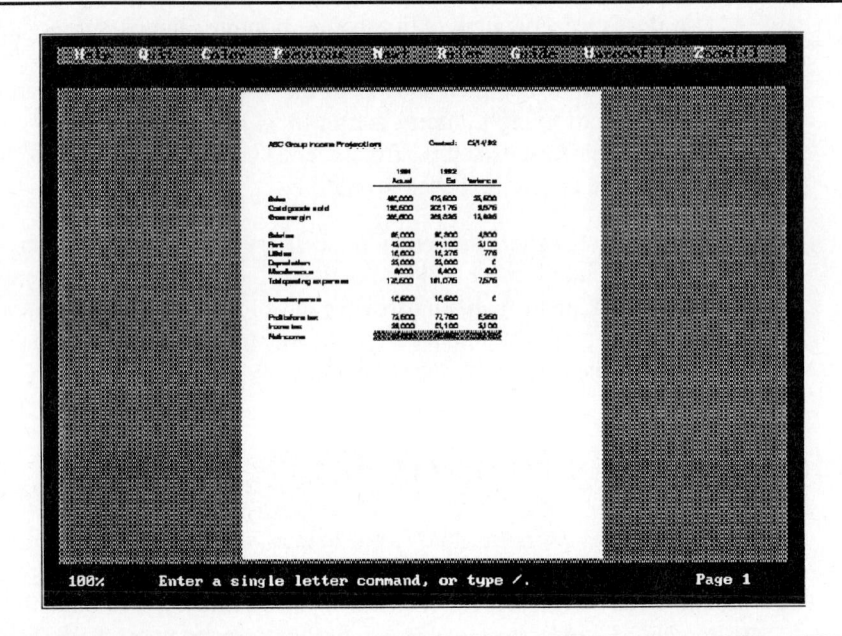

FIGURE 6-7. LEARN1.WQ1 in the Screen Previewer

- **Previous**   Displays the previous page of your report.
- **Next**   Displays the next page of your report.
- **Ruler**   Displays a one-inch grid over the previewed report to assist you in making exact modifications to the page layout. The left edge represents the left edge of the page, and each square of the grid is one square inch of the printed page. Select Ruler again to toggle the grid display off.
- **Guide**   Displays a miniature page in the upper-right corner of the screen when the display is zoomed to 200% or 400%. This page guide includes a box around the zoomed area—that is, around the area currently shown on the rest of the Screen Previewer screen. This box is known as the *zoom box*. To view a different section of your report, move the zoom box using the arrow keys or a mouse; then press (ENTER) to redraw the screen. To remove the page guide from the screen, press (DEL). To restore it, press (INS).

  The Guide option is a toggle: Pressing it once turns the Guide display off; pressing it again turns it on (assuming the image is zoomed to at least 200%).

- **Unzoom[-]**   Reverses the effects of the Zoom option, showing you more of the current page at once but with less detail.

- **Zoom[+]**   Allows you to zoom in on a portion of the page currently on screen and view sections of your report in greater detail. There are three levels of Zoom:

  100 % displays the whole page
  200% displays half a page at twice the size
  400% shows one-eighth of a page at four times the size

  When you first enter the Screen Previewer, you are at a Zoom level of 100%. The current level of Zoom (if any) is displayed on the status line at the bottom of the screen.

You can select options from the Screen Previewer menu either by pressing the first letter of the option name or by typing / (the slash character), using the (RIGHT ARROW) and (LEFT ARROW) keys to highlight the desired option, and pressing (ENTER).

You can also use your keys to perform some of the same operations and to move the zoomed display. The keys that you can use in the Screen Previewer are shown in Table 6-1.

Every time you print a report to the screen, Quattro Pro increases the page count (as reflected in the lower-right corner of the screen). You may want to reset the starting page number (by selecting Adjust Printer and then Align) before you select

Key	Description
(ESC)	Exits the Screen Previewer.
(F1)	Displays a help screen on the Screen Previewer.
(PGUP)	Displays the previous page.
(PGDN)	Displays the next page.
Arrow keys	Scroll the zoomed display in the direction of the arrow.
(HOME)	Displays the top of the zoomed page.
(END)	Displays the bottom of the zoomed page.
(ENTER)	Redisplays the area in the zoom box shown in the page guide.
(DEL)	Removes the page guide from the screen.
(INS)	Redisplays the page guide.

TABLE 6-1.   The Screen Previewer Commmand Keys

Spreadsheet Print, particularly if you are previewing multiple-page reports. If your report includes page numbers, be sure to reset the page count before you print the report.

If you have a graphics adaptor, take a few minutes to experiment with the Screen Previewer now.

SPECIAL PRINT OPTIONS

There are two last print options that you may want to use on occasion. / **Print** | **Format** | **Cell-Formulas** allows you to print the contents of your spreadsheet as stored rather than as displayed. Bullet characters allow you to create bulleted lists—to distinguish and highlight each item in a series.

Printing Formulas

Sometimes you may want to print a list of the literal contents of your spreadsheet, including the formulas, display format codes, and column widths. / **Print** | **Format** | **Cells-Formulas** generates such a list, printing exactly what you would see on the input line if you pointed to each cell in the print block in turn. This print option can be extremely useful when you are auditing a spreadsheet to make sure that it is performing as intended. When you print in Cells-Formulas format, Quattro Pro ignores all other print options you have defined (headers, footers, and so on).

	Bullet Number	Description
☐	0	Box
■	1	Filled box
☑	2	Checked box
✓	3	Check
❏	4	Shadowed box
☑	5	Shadowed checked box
●	6	Filled circle

FIGURE 6-8. The seven Quattro PRO bullet styles

Adding Bullets
To a Report

Bullet characters are another design element you can use to dress up high-quality printed reports. Figure 6-8 shows the seven bullet characters you can use when printing Quattro Pro spreadsheets or graphs. To add bullets to a spreadsheet, enter the following characters in the cell where you want the bullet to appear:

\bullet #\

where # is the number of the desired bullet character, as shown in Figure 6-8. For example, if you want to use a checked box (bullet character 2), you would enter **\bullet 2**. You can enter this bullet command either in a cell by itself or before or after label text. If the bullet command is the first set of characters in a cell, you must preface it with a label alignment command. For example, you can enter

'\bullet 4\ Enter current month's totals

to print a shadowed box at the left edge of a column followed by two blank spaces and then the words "Enter current month's totals." If you omit the alignment character, Quattro Pro interprets the \ character as an alignment character and attempts to repeat the entry as many times as fit within the column width.

Note that bullet characters work only in high-quality print mode. In draft-quality mode Quattro Pro simply prints the bullet command as text—that is, it prints the characters \bullet 4\ or \bullet 5\ rather than the desired bullet character.

In this chapter, you learned to print Quattro Pro spreadsheets, producing output that ranges from the simplest draft-quality printouts to elaborate, highly customized reports. Try not to get overwhelmed by the myriad of options at this point. At its simplest, printing in Quattro Pro is extremely easy, and simple may be perfectly adequate for now. On the other hand, if you are thrilled at all the desktop publishing possibilities, you may want to experiment before moving on to other chapters—to get a sense of all the printing tools available.

7

FUNCTIONS

Types of Functions
Function Syntax
The Functions Key
Basic Statistical Functions
Functions for Dropping Decimal Places
Complex Operators
@VLOOKUP and @HLOOKUP
String Functions
Getting Help with Functions

Functions are specialized operators that perform specific, often complex calculations. They allow you to manipulate values and text in ways that are difficult or impossible with traditional arithmetic operators. You have already tried the most commonly used function, @SUM. Quattro Pro furnishes an additional 112 of these tools to assist you in your work.

This chapter introduces you to functions in general and then covers a few of the more commonly used functions in detail. Additional functions are introduced in later chapters as they become relevant. Because Quattro Pro has so many functions and not all of them will be relevant to your work, only the general-purpose functions are covered in this chapter. For the details about all of Quattro Pro's functions, see the *Quattro Pro @Functions and Macros* manual.

TYPES OF FUNCTIONS

Quattro Pro functions can be classified into the following groups:

- *Mathematical functions*   Used to perform mathematical calculations, such as finding the square root or natural logarithm of a number. This group includes functions for rounding and for generating random numbers. It also includes several trigonometric functions.

- *Statistical functions*   Used to calculate statistics about a block of cells on a spreadsheet. @SUM falls in this category, along with functions that count the number of values in a block of cells and calculate the average, minimum, maximum, variance, and standard deviation.

- *Financial functions*   Used primarily for investment calculations, such as determining loan and mortgage payments or the value of long-term investments. They include functions for performing present- and future-value analyses and for applying different methods of depreciation.

- *Logical functions*   Allow you to build decision-making capabilities into your spreadsheet by displaying different values or by performing different calculations depending on the value of a cell. These functions generally involve evaluating some kind of condition and taking different actions depending on whether the condition is true or false.

- *String functions*   Allow you to manipulate text. String functions can be used to perform operations such as extracting part of a long string of a text or converting all the characters in a label to uppercase.

- *Lookup functions*   Grouped with "miscellaneous functions" in the Quattro Pro manuals, these functions are used to look up a specified number or group of characters in a separate table or list of values.

- *Date and time functions*   Used to enter and perform calculations on dates and times. They include functions for inserting the current date and time.

- *Database statistical functions*   Grouped with "statistical functions" in the Quattro Pro manuals, these functions are used to perform statistical calculations on values in a database—for example, counting all the records in which a particular field has a particular value, or determining the average value in a field.

- *System functions*   Grouped with "miscellaneous functions" in the Quattro Pro manuals, these include functions that return information about the Quattro Pro environment, including the currently selected menu item, the Quattro Pro version number, and the amount of available memory.

- *Miscellaneous functions*   Include functions that allow you to enter the special values ERR and NA into a spreadsheet. This group also includes several functions that return information about the status of a cell or of the spreadsheet as a whole.

FUNCTION SYNTAX

When you use a function in a formula, you type an @ character followed by the function name. In most cases the function name is followed by a set of parentheses containing the function's arguments, which is the raw data on which a function operates—the input you specify when you enter a function formula. For example, in the formula @SUM(A1..A5), the block A1..A5 is the argument; it is the portion of the expression on which Quattro Pro performs the calculation. This combination of function name, starting parentheses, arguments list, and ending parentheses in a formula is called a *function statement*. Sometimes function statements are formulas in themselves. While all function statements can stand alone as formulas in themelves, they are sometimes part of longer formulas.

A few Quattro Pro functions do not require arguments, many functions require only one argument, and others require several arguments in a specific order. Whenever functions require more than one argument, the arguments must be separated by commas. Therefore, the general syntax for using Quattro Pro functions is

@function(argument1,argument2,...)

In general, functions that require arguments also require that each argument evaluates to a particular data type—text, numbers, or blocks, as outlined here:

- When a character string argument is required, you can generally substitute any combination of sets of characters enclosed in quotation marks, cell references, values, operators, and functions that evaluate to a string of text.

- When a function requires a numeric argument, you can usually use any combination of cell references, numbers, operators, and functions that evaluate to a single numeric value.

- When a function requires a block as an argument, you can enter block coordinates, a single cell address, a block name, or a combination of the above.

Using one function as the argument for another function is referred to as *nesting functions*. You can nest as many functions as you like, provided each function has its own matching set of parentheses and the entire expression does not exceed 240 characters. This maximum length refers to the formula's length when all the formula's block names are translated into cell references.

You should, however, be wary of nesting too many functions in a single formula. The more functions you use, the more difficult it is to debug the formula if it generates either a Syntax Error or an unintended result. Instead, you should try breaking down complex formulas into components that contain only one or two functions each. You can then have the statement in one cell refer to the statement in another.

THE FUNCTIONS KEY

Quattro Pro's Functions key, (ALT-F3), can make it easier to construct function statements, particularly if you forget the function's exact name. To use it, hold down the (ALT) key and press (F3). Quattro Pro responds by displaying a menu of functions. You can use the arrow keys, (PGDN), and (PGUP) to scroll through the options. Once you find the desired function, highlight it and press (ENTER) to insert the function name and an opening parentheses into your formula.

Try using the Functions key to construct an @SUM function statement.

1. If you have anything other than a blank spreadsheet currently on your screen, save your spreadsheet and issue the / File | Erase command.

2. Enter **1** in A1 and **2** in A2.

3. Move to A3 and press (ALT-F3).

4. Press (PGDN) until you see the SUM function. Press (DOWN ARROW) until that function name is highlighted, and press (ENTER). @SUM(now appears on the input line.

5. Move to A1 and type a period.

6. Move to A2, type), and press (ENTER) to finish entering the function statement @SUM(A1..A2) in A3.

You can also press the Functions key after you have started entering a formula. For example, if you want to multiply the sum of A1..A2 by 3, you start by typing **3***, and then use ¢ALT-F3£ to start adding the function statement.

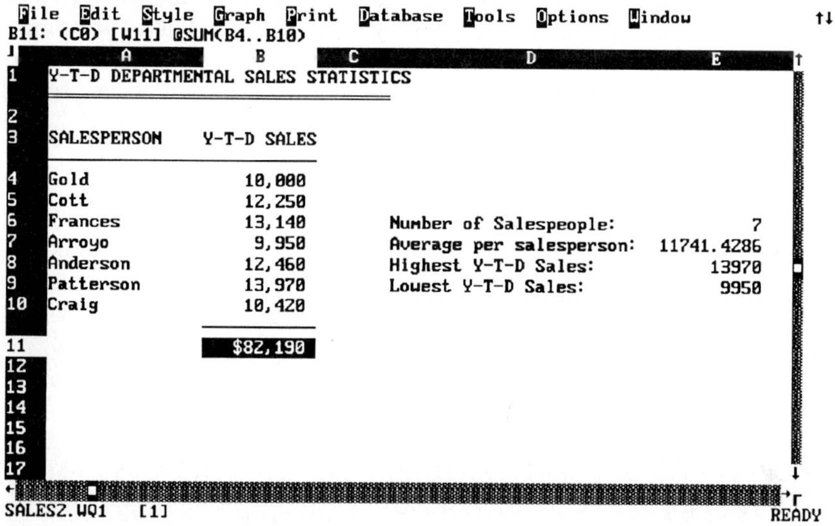

```
  File Edit Style Graph Print Database Tools Options Window         ↑↓
B11: (C0) [W11] @SUM(B4..B10)
        A           B           C           D           E
 1   Y-T-D DEPARTMENTAL SALES STATISTICS
 2
 3   SALESPERSON    Y-T-D SALES
 4   Gold           10,000
 5   Cott           12,250
 6   Frances        13,140      Number of Salespeople:              7
 7   Arroyo          9,950      Average per salesperson:     11741.4286
 8   Anderson       12,460      Highest Y-T-D Sales:              13970
 9   Patterson      13,970      Lowest Y-T-D Sales:                9950
10   Craig          10,420
11                  $82,190
12
13
14
15
16
17
SALES2.WQ1  [1]                                                READY
```

FIGURE 7-1. Spreadsheet illustrating statistical functions

BASIC STATISTICAL FUNCTIONS

Quattro Pro offers several functions for performing aggregation and counting operations on a group of values. These functions can be applied to any list of numbers, cell references, and block references. The simple statistical functions require only one argument, but you can include as many as you like, separated with commas. Usually the argument is a single block of cells. Figure 7-1 shows a spreadsheet illustrating the use of @SUM, @COUNT, @AVG, @MAX, and @MIN.

@SUM

The general syntax for the @SUM function is

@SUM(*List*)

where *List* is any series of cell references, block references, or expressions that evaluate to numbers. You have already used @SUM to calculate the total of a series of values within a column. You can also use @SUM to total the values in a single row, in a block consisting of several rows and columns, or in several blocks or cells. Here is a chart illustrating some of the possibilities:

Function Statement	Evaluates To
@SUM(A1,A3,B14)	The sum of the values in A1, A3, and B14
@SUM(A1..D2,B12)	The sum of the values in A1..D2, plus the value in B12
@SUM(*BlockName*)	The sum of the values in a named block (assigning names to blocks is covered in Chapter 8)
@SUM(A1,14)	The sum of the value in A1 plus the number 14

@COUNT

Quattro Pro's @COUNT function calculates the number of cells in a list of cells or blocks. Its syntax is

@COUNT(*List*)

where *List* consists of cell references, block coordinates, numbers, character strings, or other functions. For example, in Figure 7-1 the function statement in E6 is @COUNT(B4..B10). This function counts the number of nonblank cells in B4..B10. Because all the cells in this block contain data, the function returns a value of 7. The type of data a cell contains is irrelevant.

@AVG

The @AVG function calculates the average value within a group, dividing the sum of the values by the number of values. Its syntax is

@AVG(*List*)

where *List* is any series of cell references, block references, or expressions that evaluate to numbers. In Figure 7-1 cell E7 contains the formula @AVG(B4..B10). The result of 11741.4286 is generated by dividing the sum of all the values in the argument (82190) by the number of values in the argument (7).

@MAX AND @MIN

Quattro Pro's @MAX function evaluates to the highest value within a group of values; the @MIN function evaluates to the lowest of the group. The syntaxes for these functions are

@MAX(*List*)

and

@MIN(*List*)

where *List* is a series of expressions that evaluate to numbers. Cells E8 and E9 in Figure 7-1 contain examples of these functions. E8 contains the function statement @MAX(B4..B10) and evaluates to 13970, the highest number in the block B4..B10. The function in E9, @MIN(B4..B10), returns the value 9950, the lowest number in the block.

Blank Cells and Labels
In Statistical Functions

One potential problem is common to many of the statistical functions—a problem related to the ways Quattro Pro evaluates labels and blank cells included in the function arguments. Quattro Pro treats any labels included in the arguments for a statistical function as zeros, whether they are named individually or included in a block. For example, if the formula in cell B11 was changed from @SUM(B4..B10) to @SUM(B3..B11), Quattro Pro would treat the label in B3 as a zero. In the case of the @SUM function, this has no effect on the result. In other functions, however, including an unintended zero can skew the result.

For example, if you include a label in the argument for an @AVG function, the result generally is lower than you intended because Quattro Pro treats that label as a zero for the purpose of the calculation.

You can encounter similar problems with the @MIN function. Whenever you include labels in the argument for an @MIN function, the function returns a value of zero (unless the argument happens to include negative numbers).

Similar issues arise if your argument list includes blank cells. Quattro Pro ignores any blank cells that occur within any blocks you specify as arguments for a statistical function. However, if you specify blank cells as arguments in themselves, Quattro Pro treats them as zeros for the purposes of the calculation. For example, if cell A3 happens to be blank, Quattro Pro ignores it when performing a statistical calculation on (A1..A5), but treats it as a zero if you use an argument such as (A1,A3,A5).

When using the @AVG function, there are potential problems in both directions. You should avoid accidentally naming any blank cells (including the cells used in block references) in your argument or they will skew the result. If you use a block as your argument, you should also be careful not to leave any cells within the block blank when you actually want them be treated as zeros in the calculation. If you prefer not to see the zeros on your spreadsheet, you can use the Hide Zeros format.

A TRICK FOR KEEPING NEW ROWS IN AN @SUM BLOCK In the case of the @SUM function, you can actually turn the fact that Quattro Pro treats labels as zeros to your advantage. As discussed in Chapter 3, one of the benefits of using the @SUM function to add up the values in a block (as opposed to using a formula with multiple plus signs) is that Quattro Pro automatically includes any new rows or columns you insert within the block's current borders.

There is a potential pitfall here, however. If you accidentally insert a row above the first row in the block or below the last row, Quattro Pro does not expand the block to accomodate the new row. Similarly, if you have an @SUM formula that adds a row of values and then insert a column to the left of the first column or to the right of the last, Quattro Pro does not include the new cell in your calculation.

One way to solve this problem is to deliberately include labels in the referenced block when you enter the formula. In Figure 7-2, for example, a row of dashes was entered immediately above and below the line items in a budget. The formulas at the bottom of each column sum all the values in the block extending from the first row of dashes to the second row of dashes. The formula in B11, for example, is @SUM(B5..B10). Because Quattro Pro ignores labels in @SUM calculations, these dashes have no effect on the result. However, they do prevent a user from accidentally entering new rows outside the block's borders. As long as new rows are entered between the rows of dashes, they automatically are included in the @SUM results.

FUNCTIONS FOR DROPPING DECIMAL PLACES

Frequently you will enter a formula that returns more decimal places than you want to see on your spreadsheet. You have three ways to solve this problem:

- You can use a display format that limits the number of decimal places displayed
- You can use the @ROUND function to round the result

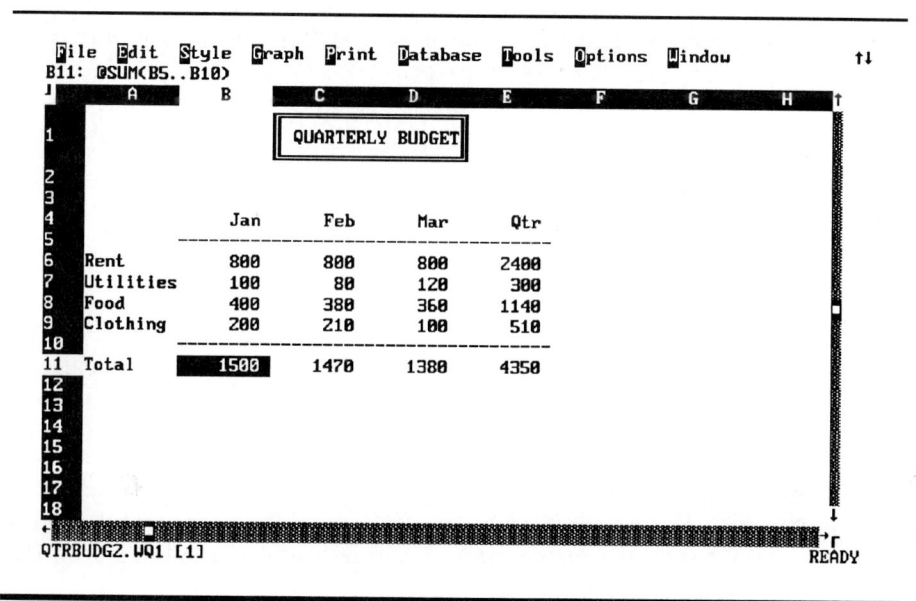

FIGURE 7-2. Including labels in an @SUM block

- In cases where you want no decimal places, you can use the @INT function, which returns the integer portion of a numeric value

These three solutions generate different values (even if they sometimes look the same on the spreadsheet) and can therefore have different impacts on your spreadsheet's calculations.

@ROUND

Quattro Pro's @ROUND function rounds values to a specified number of decimal places. The syntax for this function is

@ROUND(*Value,n*)

where *Value* is any combination of numbers, cell references, and operators that evaluates to a number, and *n* is a number between −1 and 15 that specifies the number of significant digits you want to include in the result. Here are some examples of the @ROUND function and its results:

Function Statement	Result
@ROUND(1562.637,2)	1562.64
@ROUND(1562.637,1)	1562.6
@ROUND(1562.637,0)	1563
@ROUND(1562.637,-1)	1560

In the first three examples, the second argument in the @ROUND function statement specifies the number of decimals to include in the result. In the last example, the -1 argument directs Quattro Pro to not only round off all the decimal places, but also to round the digit one place to the left of the decimal point. To generalize, when the second argument in an @ROUND statement is positive, it indicates the number of significant digits to the right of the decimal point you want included in the result. If the second argument is negative, it indicates the number of significant digits you want to the left of the decimal.

It is also important to keep in mind the difference between displaying a series of numbers without decimal places and eliminating decimal places with @ROUND. These alternatives produce results that are identical in appearance but different in

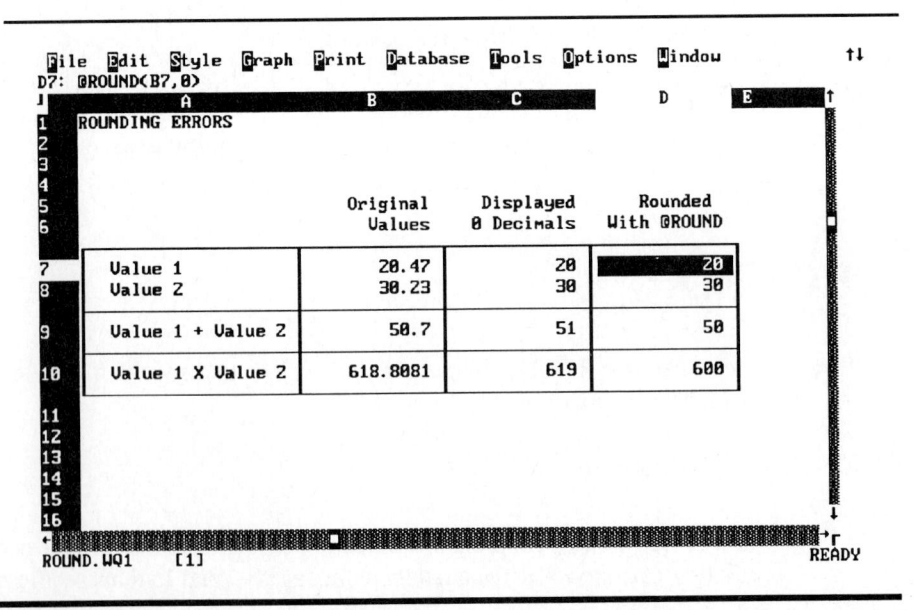

FIGURE 7-3. Spreadsheet illustrating rounding errrors

```
     File Edit Style Graph Print Database Tools Options Window              ↑↓
     A1: 'THE @INT AND @ROUND FUNCTIONS
              A                   B                   C                D
     1   THE @INT AND @ROUND FUNCTIONS
     2
     3
     4           Original      Displayed with     Displayed with
     5           Numbers       @INT Function      @ROUND Function
     6           --------      --------------     ---------------
     7            142.54            142                 143
     8            352.462           352                 352
     9           3939.1           3939                3939
    10           4434.182         4434                4434
    11
    12
    ...
    20
     INTROUND.WQ1 [1]                                                   READY
```

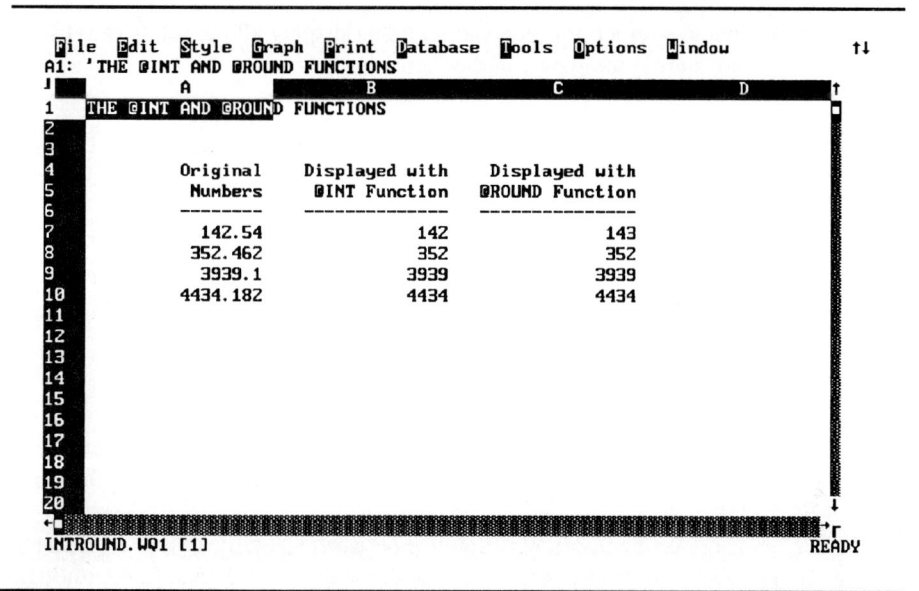

FIGURE 7-4. The effects of the @INT and @ROUND functions

value, and because they are different in value, they produce different results when used in formulas, as shown in Figure 7-3.

In general, displaying values with zero decimal places preserves a greater degree of mathematical accuracy than actually eliminating decimal places with @ROUND, because the numbers are still stored and used in calculations with all their digits. However, this method can also generate the appearance of rounding errors. In Figure 7-3, for example, displaying value 1 (20.47), value 2 (30.23), and their sum with zero decimal places creates the appearance of an error because the sum (50.7) is rounded to 51. You could solve this problem by rounding the two numbers and then adding the results, as shown in column D. This generates a result of 50, which *looks* correct, even though it is, strictly speaking, less accurate. You have, in this case, a choice between greater mathematical accuracy (the total of 50.7 is, in fact, closer to 51 than it is to 50) and the appearance of mathematical correctness (20 + 30 = 50).

The problem is magnified when you multiply rather than add two values, as shown in cell C10 of the same figure. In this case, the result appears to be off by 19 (with 20 times 30 apparently equaling 619). Again, you can make the result look correct by rounding the two values and then multiplying the results, which yields the 600 shown in cell D10.

The choice between rounding numbers and simply displaying them without decimals depends, in most cases, on your data and the needs of your audience. If approximate values are good enough, rounded numbers may be less confusing. If accuracy is important, you should either display all the digits or omit them but note the apparent discrepancy in the numbers.

@INT

The @INT function is used to truncate numbers to integers. Its syntax is

@INT(*Value*)

where *Value* is any combination of numbers, cell references, and operators that evaluates to a number. The @INT function returns the number represented by *Value* stripped of its decimal places. The function @INT(4623.7231), for example, returns 4623.

There is an important difference between using the @INT function and rounding a number to zero decimal places with the @ROUND function, although they sometimes produce identical results. The @INT function simply drops any digits to the right of the decimal point, regardless of their value. The @ROUND function, in contrast, evaluates the digit to the right of the decimal point (when rounding to zero decimal places) and rounds to the next integer if that digit is 5 or greater. As shown in Figure 7-4, at times, the two functions yield the same result, but at others they do not.

@IF

The @IF function allows you to add decision-making capabilities to your spreadsheet—to return different values depending on the value in one or more other cells. The syntax of the @IF function is

@IF(*Condition*, *Display if true*, *Display if false*)

When Quattro Pro encounters an @IF function, it begins by evaluating its first argument. If the first argument is true, Quattro Pro displays the result of the second argument; otherwise it displays the result of the third argument. The @IF function's first argument, *Condition*, therefore must be a *logical expression*—something that can be evaluated as either true or false. In a spreadsheet, logical expressions generally either make a comparison between two values, labels, or formulas, or test the contents of a particular cell.

The most commonly used syntax for conditions is

X Operator Y

where *X* and *Y* are expressions (consisting of numbers, character strings, cell references, arithmetic operators, and functions) that evaluate to numbers or text, and *Operator* performs some kind of comparison between those expressions. You can use six *comparison operators* to construct conditions:

=	Equal to
>	Greater than
<	Less than
>=	Greater than or equal to
<=	Less than or equal to
<>	Not equal to

Here are some examples of valid conditions:

A1 > 15
C2 <= D3
B14 <> "San Francisco"

Notice that the expression "San Francisco" is enclosed in quotation marks. Whenever you specify a set of characters that you want treated as text in a condition, you need to enclose it in quotes.

Now that you know the basic rules for the @IF function, let's explore a few applications. Figure 7-5 shows a spreadsheet for calculating sales commissions. The commission rate on each sale depends on the gross sales amount: The rate for a gross sale greater than or equal to $5000 is 14%; the rate for all other sales is 12%. For the first sale, B4 contains the sales amount and C4 contains the formula

@IF(B4>=5000,B4*0.14,B4*0.12)

The function is evaluated as follows:

1. Quattro Pro determines whether the function's first argument is true or false for the value in B4.

2. If the value in B4 is greater than or equal to 5000, Quattro Pro displays the result of the function's second argument, multiplying the value in B4 by 0.14. If B4 is

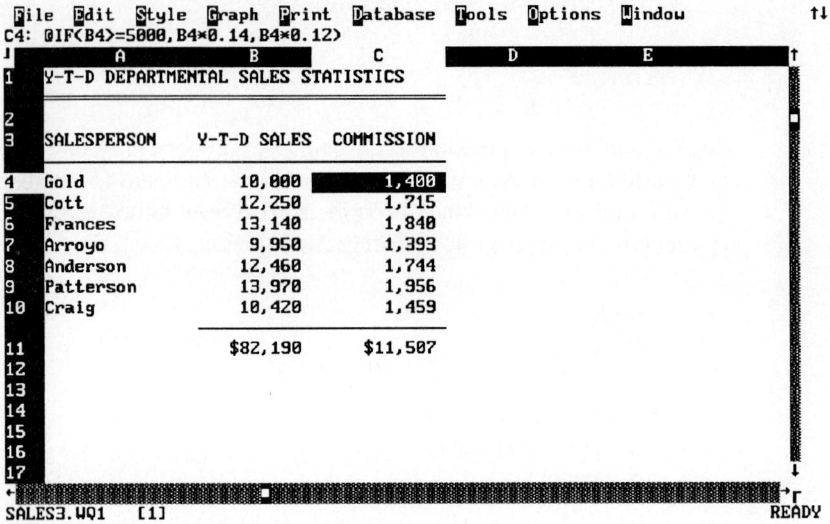

```
File  Edit  Style  Graph  Print  Database  Tools  Options  Window
C4: @IF(B4)=5000,B4*0.14,B4*0.12)
              A              B              C              D              E
1      Y-T-D DEPARTMENTAL SALES STATISTICS
2
3      SALESPERSON    Y-T-D SALES    COMMISSION
4      Gold              10,000         1,400
5      Cott              12,250         1,715
6      Frances           13,140         1,840
7      Arroyo             9,950         1,393
8      Anderson          12,460         1,744
9      Patterson         13,970         1,956
10     Craig             10,420         1,459

11                      $82,190        $11,507

SALES3.WQ1   [1]                                                    READY
```

FIGURE 7-5. Using @IF to calculate sales commissions

less than 5000 (the condition is false), Quattro Pro displays the result of the function's third argument, multiplying the value in B4 by 0.12.

COMPLEX OPERATORS

In some cases you need to create more elaborate conditions than you can manage with the basic comparison operators. Quattro Pro provides three complex logical oper-ators for this purpose: #AND#, #OR#, and #NOT. #AND# and #OR# are used to combine two or more conditions into a single complex condition. When two conditions are combined with the #AND# operator, the result is true only if both parts are true. For example, the condition

A4>0 #AND# A4<10

is true if A4 contains a value that is both greater than 0 and less than 10.

When two conditions are combined with the #OR# operator, the resulting condition is considered true if either condition is true. The expression

A4=C3 #OR# A4>100

is true if the value in A4 equals the value in C3 or the value in A4 is greater than 100.

The last complex operator, #NOT#, provides an alternative means of creating negative conditional tests. Unlike the other two complex operators, #NOT# is used as a preface to a single simple or complex condition, rather than as a means of combining two conditions. When a condition is preceded by #NOT#, the resulting condition is considered true if the initial condition (before it was prefaced by #NOT#) is false. For example, the condition

#NOT# A1=A2

is true if the value in A1 does not equal the value in A2.

#NOT# is a convenient tool for negating a long or complicated condition. Rather than reentering the entire condition in modified form, you can enter **#NOT#(** at the beginning of the condition and add a closing parentheses at the end. The result is a new condition that is exactly the opposite of the old one.

Applications for these tools are as limitless as the applications for the @IF function itself. In a database of mail orders, for example, you might use an @IF formula to selectively apply sales tax. Assuming that you apply sales tax only if the customer lives in California or Washington, and that the order amount is in column B and the state is in column D, you could calculate the sales tax for the order in row 5 with the formula

@IF(D5="CA" #OR# D5 = "WA",B5*.07,0)

Figure 7-6 illustrates the use of the #OR# operator in a check register spreadsheet. The formula

@IF(E6>0 #OR# F6>0,G5+E6-F6," ")

was entered in G6 and then copied down column G. The resulting formulas determine whether an amount has been posted in either the Deposit or Check column. If a value appears in either column, the new balance (G5+E6+F6) is displayed; otherwise a blank is displayed in the balance column. This allows you to copy a formula to rows that are

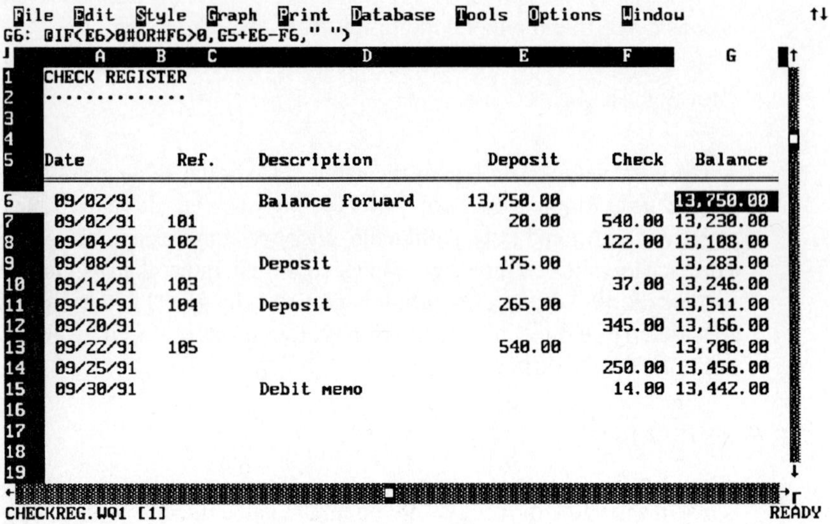

```
File Edit Style Graph Print Database Tools Options Window
G6: @IF(E6>0#OR#F6>0,G5+E6-F6," ")
        A         B       C          D              E           F         G
1   CHECK REGISTER
2   ..............
3
4
5   Date          Ref.     Description    Deposit      Check     Balance
6   09/02/91               Balance forward 13,750.00             13,750.00
7   09/02/91      101                         20.00    540.00    13,230.00
8   09/04/91      102                                  122.00    13,108.00
9   09/08/91               Deposit          175.00               13,283.00
10  09/14/91      103                                   37.00    13,246.00
11  09/16/91      104      Deposit          265.00               13,511.00
12  09/20/91                                           345.00    13,166.00
13  09/22/91      105                       540.00               13,706.00
14  09/25/91                                           250.00    13,456.00
15  09/30/91               Debit memo                   14.00    13,442.00
16
17
18
19
CHECKREG.WQ1 [1]                                                    READY
```

FIGURE 7-6. A check register using the @IF function

not yet used without displaying values in column G. Note that the formula in G5 is evaluated as 0 + 13750 + 0 because Quattro Pro treats the label in G5 as a zero for the purpose of the calculation.

@VLOOKUP AND @HLOOKUP

@VLOOKUP and @HLOOKUP are two of the most useful functions in Quattro Pro's repertoire. Both allow you to look up specified values in tables located elsewhere on your spreadsheet. For example, they can be used to look up rates in a tax table, locate prices in an inventory price list, or pull commission rates from a commission rates table. Because @VLOOKUP and @HLOOKUP work similarly, we will cover the former in detail and then extrapolate to the latter. The syntax for @VLOOKUP is

@VLOOKUP(*Lookup Value,Table Block,Offset*)

where *Lookup Value* is a number, numeric expression, character string, or cell reference that you want Quattro Pro to look up; *Table Block* is the block containing

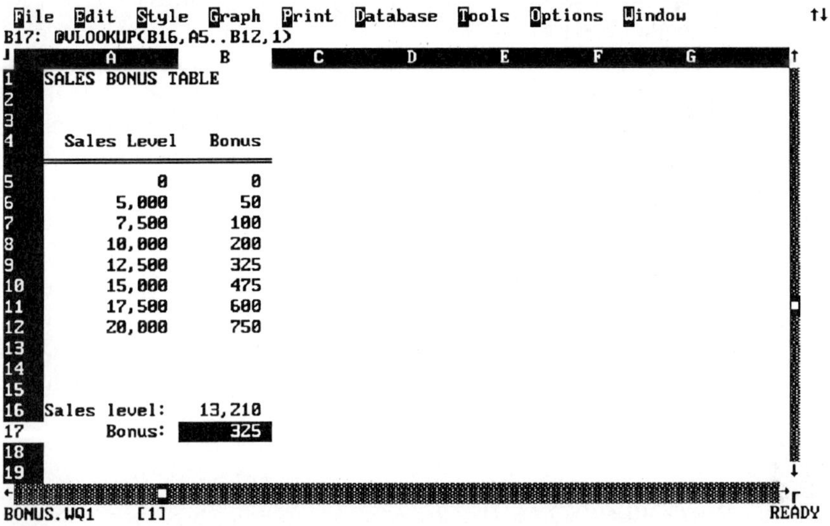

FIGURE 7-7. Looking up bonuses with @VLOOKUP

the lookup table; and *Offset* is the column that Quattro Pro uses to locate the value to return. An *Offset* of 2, for example, directs Quattro Pro to return the value located two cells to the right of that cell within the table block in which Quattro Pro found the lookup value.

When performing numeric lookups, Quattro Pro always begins at the top of the table and looks down the table's leftmost column until it finds a number greater than or equal to the lookup value. If the number it finds is equal to the lookup value, Quattro Pro returns the offset value in that row. Otherwise, Quattro Pro returns the offset value in the previous row.

In the spreadsheet shown in Figure 7-7, B17 contains the following formula:

@VLOOKUP(B16,A5..B12,1)

Quattro Pro handles this function statement by looking down the first column of the lookup table (A5 through A12) until it finds a value greater than or equal to the value in B16. Since B16 contains the value 13,210, Quattro Pro stops when it reaches A10, which contains the value 15,000. If this were an exact match (if B16 contained the value 15,000), Quattro Pro would simply return the value one cell to the right. Because it is not an exact match, Quattro Pro goes back to the previous row to the nearest match that is lower than the lookup value (12,500) and returns the value located one cell to the right of that cell.

Given Quattro Pro's method of executing numeric lookups, all values in the first column of your lookup block must be in order from the lowest to the highest. The first column should also include the lowest possible lookup value, because Quattro Pro returns the value ERR when you specify a lookup value lower than the first value in the table. If you specify a lookup value greater than the last number in the leftmost column, Quattro Pro returns the value corresponding to the last and highest number in the column.

Quattro Pro handles text lookups somewhat differently, beginning its search at the top of the leftmost column of the table, but stopping its search only when it finds an exact match. In the spreadsheet shown in Figure 7-8, the @VLOOKUP function is used to find the costs and prices of inventory items by looking up their part numbers on an inventory table. (The part numbers have been entered as labels because they include dashes.) The formula in C17,

@VLOOKUP(C16,A6..D12,2)

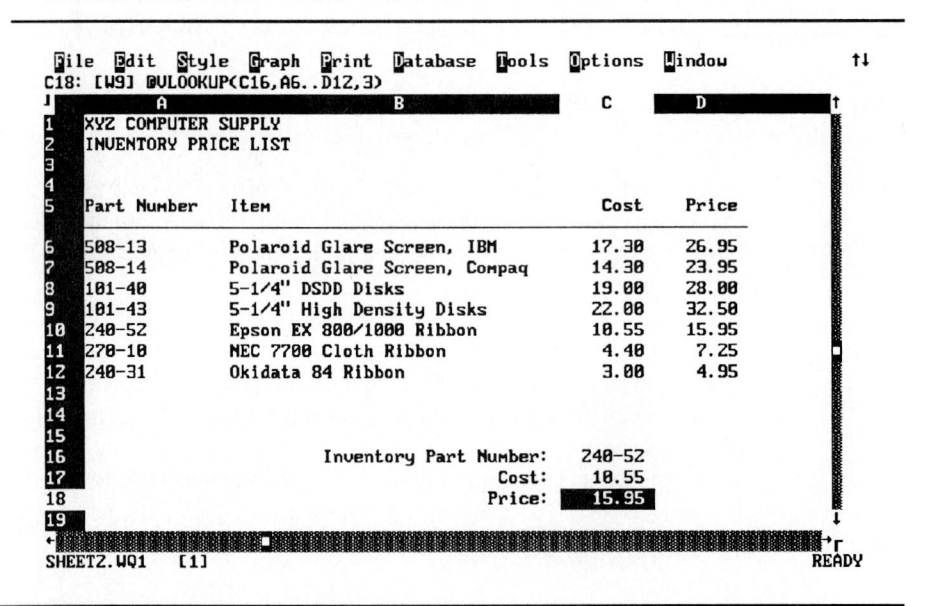

FIGURE 7-8. Finding a character string in a lookup table

directs Quattro Pro to find the set of characters in C16 (240-52) in the first column of the lookup table and then return the value located two cells to the right (offset 2). The formula in C18,

@VLOOKUP(C16,A6..D12,3)

directs Quattro Pro to find the same set of characters in the lookup table and then return the value located three cells to the right (offset 3). In both cases, because Quattro Pro is looking for an exact match for the specified part number (and will stop as soon as it finds one), the order of items within the table is inconsequential. What is important is that you do not have duplicate entries for any single lookup value and that the value can be found within the lookup table. If Quattro Pro cannot find the lookup value in the table, it returns an ERR value.

The @HLOOKUP function works exactly like @VLOOKUP except that the lookup table is arranged horizontally rather than vertically: Quattro Pro searches for the lookup value within the top row of the lookup table rather than the leftmost column. The offset value is interpreted as the number of rows below the top row in which to locate the return value. In Figure 7-9, the formula in B12 is

@HLOOKUP(B11,A4..E5,1)

This formula directs Quattro Pro to look up the current value of B11 in the table contained within the block A4..E5 and return whatever value is located one cell below the cell in which it finds the lookup value.

In the foregoing examples, @VLOOKUP and @HLOOKUP were used to cross-reference single values or labels. In most real spreadsheets, however, lookup functions are used to look up each cell within an entire column or row of values. In these cases, you would generally enter a lookup function in one cell—using absolute cell references to designate the lookup table—and then replicate it across a row or column using / Edit | Copy. Absolute cell references are covered in Chapter 8.

As mentioned, it also is possible to link spreadsheets so that values in one spreadsheet can be based on values in another (see Chapter 21). The ability to link spreadsheets allows you to store commonly used lookup tables (a tax table perhaps, or a product code list) in one spreadsheet and use lookup functions to refer to that table from other spreadsheets.

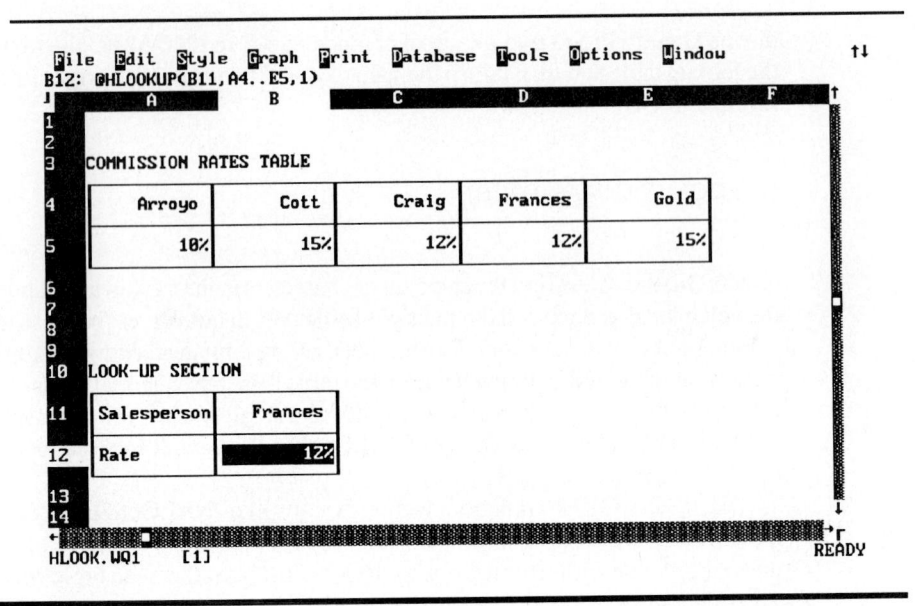

FIGURE 7-9. Looking up commission rates with @HLOOKUP

STRING FUNCTIONS

Quattro Pro offers several functions for manipulating text. Many of these functions are used primarily in complex macro operations, and most of them typically are used in database applications.

As mentioned in Chapter 3, Quattro Pro handles three types of formulas: numeric, text, and logical. The simplest text formula is *concatenation*, which means combining two character strings. The operator used for concatenation is the ampersand (&).

You can specify arbitrary character strings as well as cell references in text formulas, just as you can include numbers or cell references in numeric formulas. Whenever you designate a character string within a formula, however, you need to enclose the string in quotation marks to let Quattro Pro know that you are referring to an arbitrary set of characters, rather than a cell, block, or function.

Concatenation is commonly used to combine a column of first and last names, or cities and states, for printing on a report. In such cases, you would generally create a new column with formulas concatenating the labels in two or more other columns.

The ampersand is the only simple operator designed for use with character data. All other text formulas involve the use of string (text) functions. Some of the simplest are @UPPER, @PROPER, @LENGTH, @REPEAT, and @CHAR.

@UPPER

The @UPPER function changes text so that all letters are in uppercase. The syntax for the @UPPER function is

@UPPER(String)

where *String* is a character string, cell reference, or combination of the two. For example, if D14 contains the label "New York," the formula would return NEW YORK.

The @UPPER function (and the @PROPER function discussed next) can be useful when several people have entered data in different formats.

@PROPER

The @PROPER function modifies text so that the first letter of each word is uppercase and the remaining letters are lowercase. For example, if A12 contains the label "ABCDE," the function statement @PROPER(A12) would return Abcde.

@LENGTH

The @LENGTH function returns the number of characters in a label or other character string. Its syntax is

@LENGTH(String)

where *String* is a cell address, a character string enclosed in quotes, or a text formula such as A1&A2.

@REPEAT

The @REPEAT function repeats whatever character you specify as many times as you wish across a given row. The syntax is

@REPEAT(String,# of Repetitions)

@REPEAT is often used for replicating a character string across a row or column to create decorative borders or underlining.

You can use @REPEAT in combination with @LENGTH to generate a character string that is exactly the same length as the text located in another cell. This is extremely useful for underlining.

@CHAR

The @CHAR function returns the character that corresponds to a specified ASCII code. ASCII is a standard system used for representing all the characters on your keyboard, plus some additional graphics characters. You would generally use the CHAR function to display a character that you cannot simply type on your keyboard—such as the • character, which has the ASCII code 14 or the ♪ character, which has the ASCII code 7.

The syntax for @CHAR is

@CHAR(*Code*)

where *Code* is a number between 1 and 255 representing the ASCII code for a character. You can create underlines by combining @CHAR with @REPEAT in the same formula, as in

@REPEAT(@CHAR(7),27)

GETTING HELP WITH FUNCTIONS

As you work with Quattro Pro, you will undoubtedly find applications for the functions introduced in this chapter, and you will probably start exploring other functions on your own. For a quick tour of Quattro Pro's functions or a quick reminder of a particular function's syntax, you may find it easiest to refer to Quattro Pro's Help system.

There are two ways to look up functions in the Help system. You can press [F1] from Ready mode, and select Functions from the Help Topics list to display the Function Topics screen. If you are in the middle of entering a formula, you can press [ALT-F3] to display the Functions List, and then press [F1] to immediately display the

Function Index. When you select a function from the Function Index, Quattro Pro displays a help screen on the type of function you selected, with the syntax and a one-sentence description of each function in the group.

This chapter has introduced you to only the most commonly used, general-purpose functions. There are about 100 functions not even mentioned here. Although several other functions are introduced in later chapters, most of the more specialized functions are not discussed at all. Once you begin to develop your own spreadsheets, take time to experiment with those groups of functions that are most relevent to your work.

8

MORE ABOUT FORMULAS

Absolute Versus Relative Cell Referencing
Using Named Blocks
Converting Formulas to their Values

This chapter covers three more advanced topics in formulas: using absolute references, using named blocks, and converting formulas to their current values. Both absolute references and converting formulas to values allow you to exercise more control over your formulas—either by keeping them from changing when copied or by keeping them from responding to changes in other sections of the spreadsheet. In a sense named blocks also offer you more control over your spreadsheet by making your formulas easier to enter and to read.

ABSOLUTE VERSUS RELATIVE CELL REFERENCING

As you may recall, when you copy formulas Quattro Pro generally "thinks" of the formula's cell references in terms of their position relative to the formula cell itself. For example, if you copy the formula (B1-B2) from B3 to E11, Quattro Pro translates the source formula into "subtract the value one cell above this one from the cell two cells above this one." When copied to E11, this formula becomes (E9-E10).

In some cases you may want some of the cell references in a formula to stay the same when copied rather than letting Quattro Pro adjust those references to fit the formula's location. For example, in the LEARN1 spreadsheet you multiplied several 1991 revenue and expense figures by 1.05 to arrive at the 1992 projections. Suppose, however, that you put the estimated rate of increase in a cell by itself and then referenced that cell in calculating the 1992 figures, as shown in Figure 8-1. This allows you to play "what if " more easily with your data—to experiment with different rates by simply changing the value in a single cell (B5) rather than recreating all the formulas in column C. However, if you entered the formula +B11+(B11*B5) in C11 and then copied that formula down the column, the new formulas would be wrong.

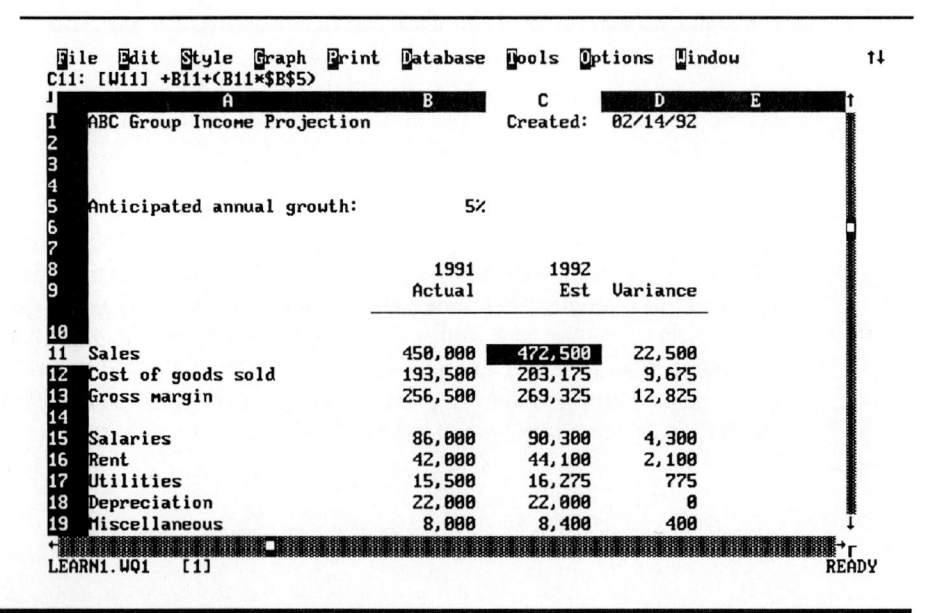

FIGURE 8-1. Using absolute references to reference a growth rate

For example, the formula in C12 would be +B12+(B12*B6) rather than +B12+(B12*B5); the formula in C13 would be +B13+(B13*B7) rather than +B13+(B13*B5). To keep the reference to cell B5 unchanged when copied, you must make that cell reference absolute by attaching it to one particular cell on the spreadsheet.

Relative and absolute cell referencing can be compared to two sets of directions: "Go to the corner, turn left, walk past three houses, turn right, and enter the fourth" and "Go to the Smiths' house." The first set of directions is entirely relative to your current position—where it leads depends on where you are at the moment. The second set of directions is independent of your current position—it will always lead you to the same spot (the Smith's house) regardless of your current location.

To make a cell reference absolute, you simply enter dollar signs ($) before its column and row coordinates. As you will see shortly, you can also create *mixed cell references*, in which one coordinate is absolute and the other relative. There are two ways to make a cell reference absolute: You can type the dollar signs while entering or editing a formula, or you can use (F4), the Abs key. To use the Abs key when you are entering a formula, just type in a cell reference and then press (F4). To use the Abs key when editing a formula, press (F4) while the cursor is on or immediately after the cell reference you want to change. As soon as you press (F4), Quattro Pro immediately inserts dollar signs before both coordinates of the appropriate cell reference, making the entire reference absolute. If you press (F4) repeatedly, Quattro Pro cycles through the following possibilities:

Option	Example
Both coordinates absolute	B5
Row coordinate absolute	B$5
Column coordinate absolute	$B5
Both coordinates relative	B5

Generally you should use absolute references when you want several formulas in a single row or column to refer to the same cell. Returning to the previous example, the reference to the increase rate in B5 should be absolute to keep it from changing when you copy the formula to other rows. Leave the reference to B11 relative, however, because you want this reference to change when copied (becoming B12 in row 12, B13 in row 13, and so on). The appropriate formula for B11, therefore, is +B11+(B11*B5).

You also should use absolute cell references when you refer to lookup tables with the @VLOOKUP or @HLOOKUP functions. Generally you want the reference to the lookup table block—which is a group of cells outside the main body of the spreadsheet—to stay the same when copied. This requires designating both corners

```
      File  Edit  Style  Graph  Print  Database  Tools  Options  Window          ↑↓
C4:  @VLOOKUP(B4,$F$4..$G$11,1)
           A            B           C        D       E         F         G
 1   DEPARTMENTAL SALES BONUSES                            BONUS TABLE
 2
 3   Salesperson   Y-T-D Sales    Bonus                     Level      Bonus
 4   Gold            10,000        200                          0          0
 5   Cott            12,250        200                      5,000         50
 6   Frances         13,140        325                      7,500        100
 7   Arroyo           9,950        100                     10,000        200
 8   Anderson        12,460        200                     12,500        325
 9   Patterson       13,970        325                     15,000        475
10   Craig           10,420        200                     17,500        600
11                  ------        -----                    20,000        750
12   Total           82,190       1,550
13
...
BONUS2.WQ1   [1]                                                         READY
```

FIGURE 8-2. Using absolute references to reference a lookup table

of the block as absolute. In the spreadsheet shown in Figure 8-2, for example, the formula

@VLOOKUP(B4,F4..G11,1)

was entered in C4 and then copied down column C. This formula directs Quattro Pro to look up values in column B in the bonus lookup table. Because the references to the lookup table's corner cells (F4 and G11) are absolute, they stay the same when the formula is copied down the column. The reference to B4 (the value to be looked up) is left relative so that it always refers to the cell immediately to the left of the formula cell when copied.

Another rule of thumb is that you should use relative references when referring to a cell in the same row as the formula cell if you intend to copy the formula down a column, or in the same column as the formula cell if you intend to copy the formula across a row.

Take a moment to experiment with relative and absolute cell references.

1. Unless your spreadsheet area is already blank, save your work and then issue the / File | Erase command.

2. Issue the /Options | Formats | Numeric Format | Fixed command. Press (ENTER) to accept the default setting of two decimal places.

3. Select Global Width from the Options | Formats menu and enter **15**.

4. Type **Q** (for Quit) twice to return to Ready mode.

5. Enter the following data:

   In A1, enter **Sales Commissions Spreadsheet**
   In A3, enter **Commission rate**
   In B3, enter **.15**
   In A6, enter **Invoice amount**
   In A7, enter **200**
   In A8, enter **150**
   In A9, enter **250**
   In A10, enter **100**
   In A11, enter **275**
   In B6, enter **"Commission**

Now try entering a formula to calculate the commission on each sale. First see what happens if you enter a formula using all relative references in B7, and then copy that formula down the column.

1. Move to B7 and enter **+A7*B3**.

2. Issue the / Edit | Copy command. Press (ENTER) to accept the default source block of B7..B7, and specify a destination block of B7..B11. Your spreadsheet should now look like the one in Figure 8-3.

The reference to B3 is relative, so it changes when copied, becoming B4 when the formula is copied to B8, B5 when copied to B9, and so on. The result is a series of useless formulas. The number 0 appears in B8, B9, and B10 because the formulas in those cells multiply the value to their left by a blank cell (B4, B5, and B6, respectively). Multiplying a value by a label is the equivalent of multiplying by zero and therefore always returns 0. The number 8250 appears in B11 because the formula in that cell multiplies the cell to the left (275) by the value in B7 (30).

Now make absolute the reference to B3 (the cell containing the commission rate) in B7's formula. You could do this by typing $ before both coordinates (B and 7), but try using the Abs key, (F4), instead.

1. Still in B7, press the Edit key (F2).

2. Press (F4) (Abs). A $ is immediately inserted before both cell coordinates, so that the formula now reads +A7*B3.

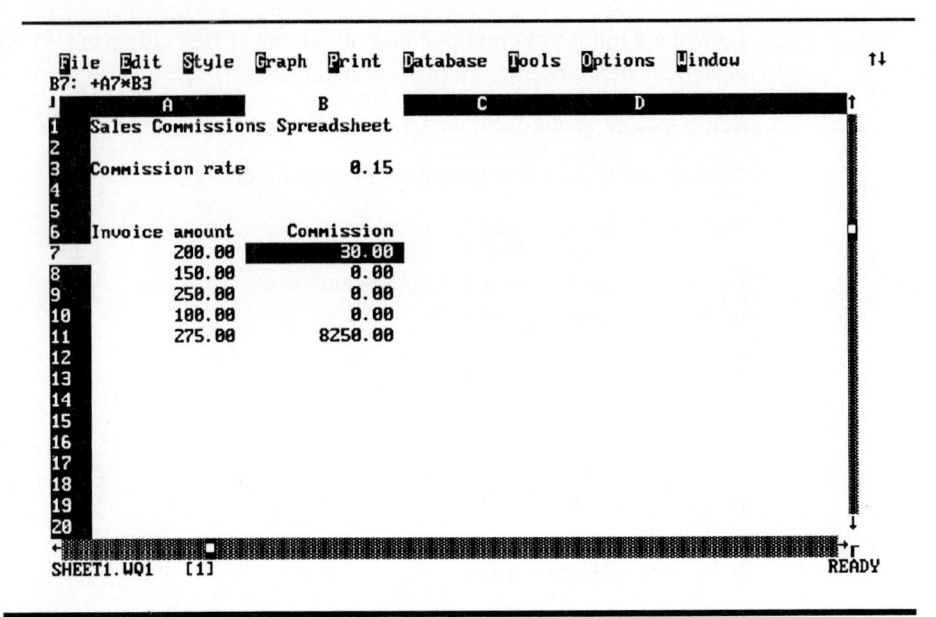

```
File Edit Style Graph Print Database Tools Options Window
B7: +A7*B3
       A              B              C              D
1  Sales Commissions Spreadsheet
2
3  Commission rate        0.15
4
5
6  Invoice amount    Commission
7         200.00         30.00
8         150.00          0.00
9         250.00          0.00
10        100.00          0.00
11        275.00       8250.00
12
...
SHEET1.WQ1  [1]                                          READY
```

FIGURE 8-3. Problems in copying relative cell references

3. Press (F4) (Abs) four more times to cycle through all the options, stopping when both cell coordinates are again absolute. Press (ENTER).

4. Issue the / Edit | Copy command a second time. Accept the default source block of B7..B7, and specify a destination of B7..B11. Your spreadsheet should now look like the one shown in Figure 8-4.

This time the first cell reference in the formula (A7) changes to reference whatever cell is located immediately to the left as you copy it down the block, while the second cell reference (B3) remains stable.

Mixed Cell References

As mentioned, you also can make one cell coordinate absolute while leaving the other relative. When you copy formulas containing such mixed references, the absolute coordinate remains the same, while the relative one changes in relation to the location of the formula on the spreadsheet. This can be useful in some cases where you want to copy a formula across more than one row or down more than one column.

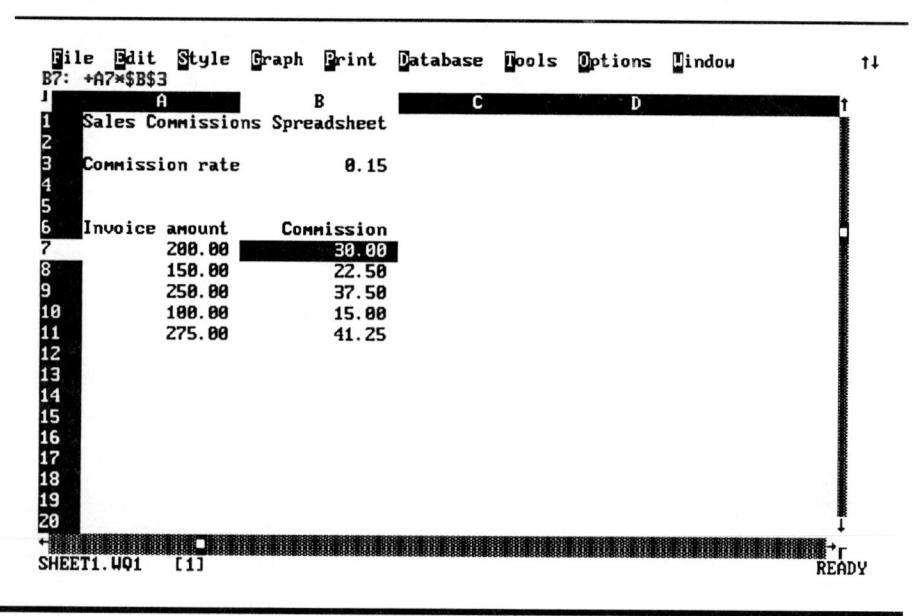

```
     File  Edit  Style  Graph  Print  Database  Tools  Options  Window              ↑↓
B7: +A7*$B$3
           A              B              C              D
1    Sales Commissions Spreadsheet
2
3    Commission rate      0.15
4
5
6    Invoice amount    Commission
7         200.00          30.00
8         150.00          22.50
9         250.00          37.50
10        100.00          15.00
11        275.00          41.25
12
...
20
SHEET1.WQ1  [1]                                                              READY
```

FIGURE 8-4. Spreadsheet after copying formulas with absolute references

USING NAMED BLOCKS

So far you have designated blocks by using the coordinates of their corner cells. Quattro Pro also allows you to assign names to blocks of cells and to refer to those blocks—in formulas, functions, and commands—by name rather than by coordinates. You might want to do this for the following reasons:

- Using block names can make formulas more understandable. For example, if you name a block of cells containing a tax rate lookup table TAX TABLE, you can enter lookup formulas by this name rather than by less informative coordinates.

- Block names are easier to remember than block coordinates. In most cases a name like FEB EXPENSE comes to mind more quickly than the coordinates G17..G29, particularly when the block you are referencing is located some distance from your current location on the spreadsheet.

- You can make use of (F3), the Choices key, to reference named blocks in formulas or commands. Quattro Pro's Choices key displays a menu of all the named blocks on the current spreadsheet. You can select block names from this list for use in formulas or commands by moving the cursor to the name and pressing (ENTER).

- You can use the Choices key to move quickly to different sections of the spreadsheet—pressing (F5) (GoTo) and then (F3) (Choices) and selecting a block name from the list. Quattro Pro moves the cell pointer to the upper-left corner of the specified block.

- Using block names increases accuracy. If you make a mistake when you enter block coordinates, Quattro Pro has no way of catching your error. If you specify a nonexistent block name in a command or formula, however, Quattro Pro immediately displays an error message.

- When you name a block, Quattro Pro not only allows you to use the block name in new formulas, but it also adjusts all formulas that currently reference that block. For example, if your spreadsheet already contains formulas that reference the block D4..G12 when you assign that block a name, Quattro Pro displays the block name on the input line (in place of the block coordinates) whenever you move the cell pointer to one of those formulas. If you delete the block name later, the formulas revert to referencing the block coordinates. If you edit a formula that references a named block, Quattro Pro displays the block's coordinates (rather than its name) on the input line until you press (ENTER). This allows you to change one or more of the block coordinates.

Quattro Pro also makes appropriate adjustments in the coordinates of a named block when you insert or delete rows within the block's borders or if you move the entire block. As with any block, you must be careful not to overwrite the corner cells of named blocks with / Edit | Move. Even if you refer to a block by name, Quattro Pro still identifies it by its corner cells. When you refer to a named block, Quattro Pro substitutes the appropriate block coordinates and proceeds from there. If you overwrite those coordinates, Quattro Pro "loses its place" and returns ERR values in those cells and in any formulas that reference them. You also need to beware of moving one of the block's corner cells without moving the other. If you do, Quattro Pro expands the block to include all cells between the corner cells.

As with other cell references, you must precede block names at the beginning of formulas with a parenthesis or arithmetic operator to inform Quattro Pro that you are entering a value rather than a label. This is true even when you pull the block name from the Choices list.

When you refer to a block by name you can place a dollar sign before the block name (by either typing $ or pressing (F4)) to make all the block coordinates absolute. If for some reason you want to employ mixed references or to have one corner absolute and the other relative, you must reference the block by coordinates rather than by name.

Unfortunately you cannot type $ and then pop up a Choices list using F3. If you try, Quattro Pro displays the error message "Invalid cell or block address." Also, if you type a plus sign (or other arithmetic operator), select a name from the Choices list, and then press F4 (Abs), Quattro Pro simply beeps. Use one of the following three methods to refer to a block by name:

- Type $ followed by the block name.

- If you are at the beginning of the formula, type (or + or another arithmetic operator. Then press F3 (Choices) and select the block name from the list. Press F2 (Edit) to switch to Edit mode, and then press the LEFT ARROW key until the cursor is on the first letter of the block name. Type $.

- Type (or + or another arithmetic operator. Then press F3 (Choices) and select the block name from the list. Press ENTER to enter the formula into the cell, and then press F2 (Edit). Instead of the block name, the block coordinates appear on the input line. Press F4 (Abs).

Naming a Block

The simplest way to create a named block is to issue the / Edit | Names | Create command. Quattro Pro then prompts you for a "name to create/modify."

Block names can be up to 15 characters long and can include any character, including blank spaces and punctuation marks. The name should always start with either a letter or a number; beginning with punctuation marks can cause problems. You should also be careful not to create a block name that looks like a cell reference. For example, if you name a block A1, Quattro Pro assumes you are referring to the cell A1 whenever you reference the block in formulas or commands.

If you assign the same name to more than one block at the same time, Quattro Pro simply assigns that name to the new block and removes it from the old one. Although it is possible to assign more than one name to the same block, it is not recommended. If you assign two names to one block and then assign one of those names to a different block, Quattro Pro automatically assigns the other block name to this new block as well, which may not be what you intended. If you highlight a formula that references that block, Quattro Pro displays only one of the names (the most recently assigned one) on the input line. It is permissible to create a named block that includes another named block.

The Choices Key

The Choices key, (F3), has different functions in different contexts. If you press this key while in Ready mode, Quattro Pro activates the menu bar, as if you had typed a slash (/). If you are in the midst of entering a formula or issuing a command, (F3) (Choices) displays a list of all the named blocks on the current spreadsheet. If you are entering a formula, pressing (F3) displays the last operator you entered at the top of the list. If you are issuing a command, it displays the current command prompt. For example, if you are copying a block, the prompt "Source block of cells" or "Destination for cells" appears. The second item on the Choices list is the address of the current cell. It is followed by the list of block names. Once the Choices list is on screen, pressing (F3) zooms the list so that is occupies the entire screen.

If the list of block names is too long to fit in the Choices box, you can use the (UP ARROW), (DOWN ARROW), (PGUP), or (PGDN) key to scroll through the list. To see the coordinates of the blocks, type a plus sign (+). Quattro Pro displays each block name on a separate line, followed by the associated block coordinates. Type a minus sign (-) to remove the coordinates from the display.

If you are using a mouse, just click on the desired block name in the Choices list to select it. You can move quickly through a long Choices list by dragging the scroll box on the scroll bar at the right edge of the list.

An Exercise in Naming Cells

To name a single-cell block on your current spreadsheet, follow these steps:

1. Move to B3 and issue the / Edit | Names | Create command. When prompted for "name to create/modify," enter **COMMISSION RATE**. Accept the default block coordinates of B3..B3.

2. Move through the formulas in column C and note that they now all reference $COMMISSION RATE rather than B3.

3. Move to B7 and type /ENC. This time enter **COMMISSIONS** as the name to create/modify. Press (END-DOWN ARROW) to expand the block to B7..B11, and then press (ENTER).

4. Move to B12 and enter "------ to draw a row of dashes under the commissions list.

5. Move to B13 and type **@SUM(**. Press (F3) to display a list of currently named blocks. Note that the mode indicator changes to NAMES, indicating that Quattro Pro is expecting you to select a block name from the list.

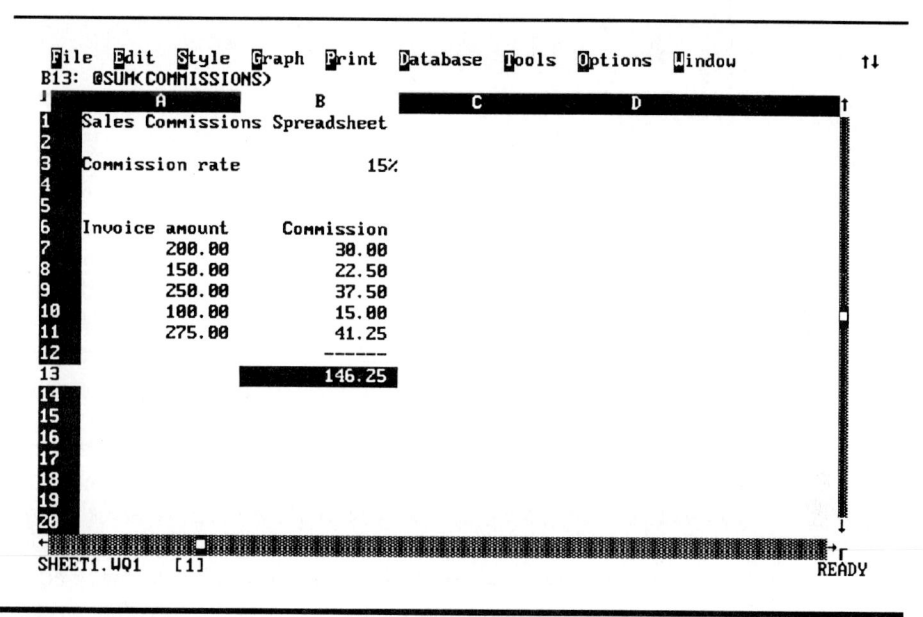

FIGURE 8-5. Using a block name in a formula

6. Type + to expand the menu to include the block coordinates on the Choices list.

7. Select COMMISSIONS from the list, inserting that block name into your formula.

8. Type) and press (ENTER) to finish entering the formula @SUM(COMMISSIONS) into your spreadsheet.

9. Issue the / Style | Numeric Format | Percent command. Enter **0** as the number of decimal places. When prompted for a block to modify, press (F3) and select COMMISSION RATE from the list of block names. Your spreadsheet should now look like Figure 8-5.

10. Press (HOME) to move to A1. Press (F5) and, when prompted for an address to go to, press (F3). Select COMMISSIONS from the list to move directly to the upper-left corner of that block.

As you can see, even on a small and simple spreadsheet, block names can make your formulas more readable. They also make it easier to reference blocks when entering formulas or issuing commands. These advantages are magnified on larger, more complex spreadsheets. The judicious use of block names is an excellent tool for clarifying your formulas and increasing your efficiency.

Changing and Deleting Block Names

Once you have created a block name, you can change the block to which the name refers. To change a named block, you simply issue the / Edit | Names | Create command again, pick that block name from the Named Blocks menu, and designate a different set of coordinates for the name. There is no direct method of changing the name assigned to a particular block, however. If you decide to change a block name, you should delete the current name for the block first and then create a new name for the block with the same coordinates. (If you create the new name first and then delete the old one, Quattro Pro may lose the block coordinates.)

You can delete a block name by issuing the / Edit | Names | Delete command and selecting the name you want to delete from the menu of block names. You can delete all the block names on a worksheet by issuing the / Edit | Names | Reset command. Be extremely careful with this command, however, since there is no way to retrieve your block names once you have deleted them. If you delete one or all of your block names accidentally, use / Edit | Undo immediately to restore them.

Naming Blocks Using Adjacent Labels

The / Edit | Names | Labels command uses the labels in a specified block of the spreadsheet to name a set of cells adjacent to that block. The specified block must fall within a single row or a single column.

When you issue the / Edit | Names | Labels command, Quattro Pro displays a submenu containing four options: Right, Left, Up, and Down. The option you choose determines which cells will be named by the command. If you choose Down, Quattro Pro assigns the names to the cells located below the block of labels you specify. If you choose Right, it assigns names to the cells located to the right of that block.

Once you have chosen an option from the Labels submenu, Quattro Pro prompts for a block of labels. If the block you specify contains labels that are longer than the 15-character limit for block names, Quattro Pro simply drops the extra characters. If the specified block contains values, they are ignored rather than used as names for the adjacent cells. Quattro Pro also ignores any blank cells in the block, which allows you to use this command with a block of labels that includes empty rows or columns.

In certain situations, / Edit | Names | Labels can be an efficient way to assign names to an entire set of single-cell blocks. It is often used to label a set of cells with a group of adjacent column or row headings. It can also be used to name single-cell blocks using text already entered in an adjacent cell on the spreadsheet. The / Edit | Names | Labels command can be particularly useful in working with databases and in naming macros. You might also use it to assign names to the first value in each column of a wide spreadsheet so that you can easily jump to a particular column using (F5) (GoTo).

Try inserting a new column at the left edge of the spreadsheet, entering invoice numbers, and then using those invoice numbers as block names for the invoice amounts in the adjacent column.

1. Press (HOME) to move to A1.
2. Issue the / Edit | Insert | Columns command. Press (ENTER) when prompted for a column insert block.
3. Press (CTRL-M), specify a source block of B1..C3, and accept the default destination of A1.
4. Enter the following data:
   In A7, enter **Inv. 111**
   In A8, enter **Inv. 112**
   In A9, enter **Inv. 113**
   In A10, enter **Inv. 114**
   In A11, enter **Inv. 115**
5. Issue the / Edit | Names | Labels command. Select Right from the submenu. Press (END-UP ARROW) to expand the label block to A11.A7 and press (ENTER). You have named all the cells in the block B11.. B7. You can prove this by examining the formulas in C7 through C11 and noting that they now refer to cells in column B by name rather than by address, as shown on the input line in Figure 8-6.

Creating a Table Of Block Names

The / Edit | Names | Make Table command creates a table of all the current named blocks on the spreadsheet, including both the names of the blocks and their coordinates. The table looks almost exactly like the expanded menu displayed with the Choices key. It is useful primarily when you are documenting the spreadsheet by printing its formulas or when there are too many named blocks to fit within the Choices window simultaneously. When you issue the / Edit | Names | Make Table command, Quattro Pro prompts you for a block in which to place the table. You need only specify the upper-left corner of this destination block.

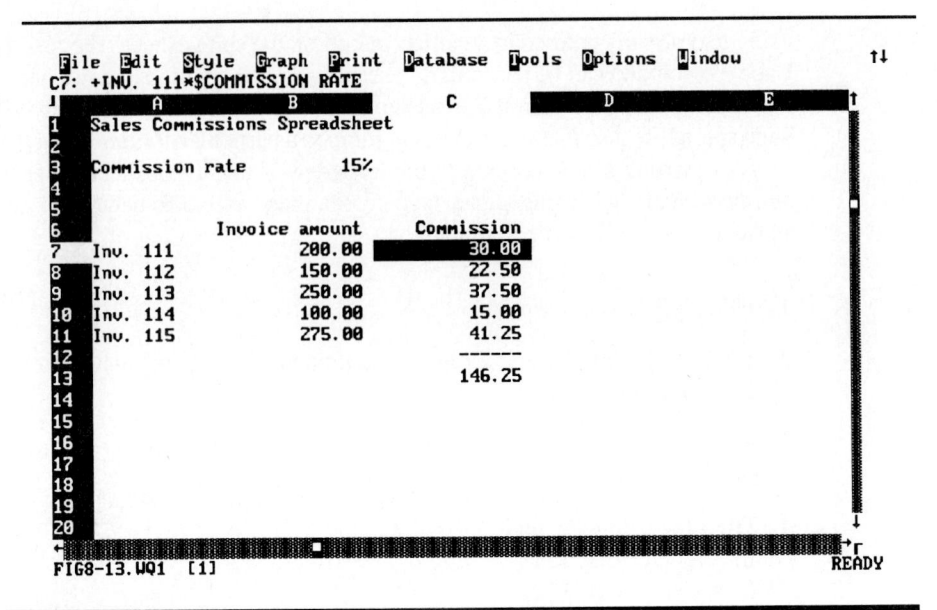

```
    File  Edit  Style  Graph  Print  Database  Tools  Options  Window          ↑↓
C7: +INV. 111*$COMMISSION RATE
         A              B              C              D              E
 1  Sales Commissions Spreadsheet
 2
 3  Commission rate         15%
 4
 5
 6                    Invoice amount      Commission
 7   Inv. 111             200.00             30.00
 8   Inv. 112             150.00             22.50
 9   Inv. 113             250.00             37.50
10   Inv. 114             100.00             15.00
11   Inv. 115             275.00             41.25
12                                          ------
13                                          146.25
14
15
16
17
18
19
20
FIG8-13.WQ1  [1]                                                         READY
```

FIGURE 8-6. Cell references after naming blocks with / Edit I Names I Labels

The table created with / Edit I Names I Make Table is not updated if you add, delete, or change any named blocks. If you make such modifications, be careful to reissue the / Edit I Names I Create Table command.

Try creating a table of block names.

1. Move to A15 and issue the / Edit I Names I Make Table command.

2. Accept the default block of A15..A15. You spreadsheet should now look like Figure 8-7.

CONVERTING FORMULAS TO THEIR VALUES

Occasionally you will want a formula to stop acting like one; that is, you will want it to return the same result regardless of changes in other cells on the spreadsheet. Quattro Pro provides the / Edit I Values command for effectively freezing formulas. This command can be used to replace a block of formulas with their current results, transforming them into the numeric values or text currently displayed on the

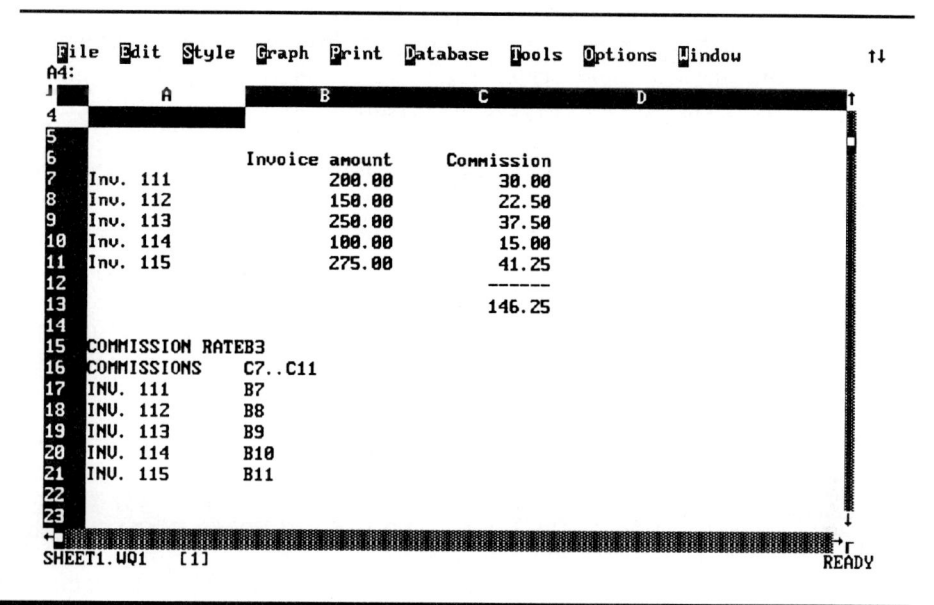

```
     File  Edit  Style  Graph  Print  Database  Tools  Options  Window         ↑↓
   A4:
   J          A              B                 C             D
   4
   5
   6                   Invoice amount      Commission
   7    Inv. 111            200.00            30.00
   8    Inv. 112            150.00            22.50
   9    Inv. 113            250.00            37.50
   10   Inv. 114            100.00            15.00
   11   Inv. 115            275.00            41.25
   12                                        ------
   13                                        146.25
   14
   15   COMMISSION RATEB3
   16   COMMISSIONS       C7..C11
   17   INV. 111          B7
   18   INV. 112          B8
   19   INV. 113          B9
   20   INV. 114          B10
   21   INV. 115          B11
   22
   23
   SHEET1.WQ1    [1]                                                       READY
```

FIGURE 8-7. A table of named blocks

spreadsheet. For example, / Edit | Values would change the formula (1+2) to the value 3; it would replace the formula (A1-A2) with whatever value that formula returns at the time you issue the command.

There are two reasons to use / Edit | Values. First, as mentioned, you can use it to prevent a cell from responding to changes in other cells. You might also want to use formulas to derive data initially, but then keep the results of those calculations stable. For example, you might create a budget for next year using formulas based on the current year's revenues and expenses. Once the budget has been approved, however, you want it to remain unchanged as you update figures for the current fiscal year.

You can use / Edit | Values to copy the results of some formulas to a separate section of the spreadsheet—for either printing or graphing purposes. Suppose you want to print a summary version of the LEARN1 spreadsheet, omitting the individual line items that make up the total operating expenses. You can use / Edit | Values to copy the data to a different section of the spreadsheet, and then delete the rows containing figures for Salaries, Rent, and so on. If you deleted these rows after simply copying the data with / Edit | Copy, the formulas in the Total operating expenses row (and all formulas that refer to cells in that row) would evaluate to ERR, because they would be attempting to sum the values in nonexistent cells. If you use / Edit | Values, however, the Total operating expenses row fills with numbers rather than formulas and therefore is immune to changes elsewhere on the spreadsheet.

The second reason for using / Edit I Values is that values take up less space than formulas in memory and on disk. If you no longer need your formulas to respond to changes in data, you can save space, particularly in large spreadsheets, by converting all formulas to their values.

/ Edit I Values works exactly like / Edit I Copy, except it transforms the source block as it copies by replacing formulas with their current results. When you issue the / Edit I Values command, Quattro Pro asks for a source block and then a destination. Unless you plan to make duplicated copies of the source block, you need only specify the upper-left corner of the destination.

Although you can use / Edit I Values to create a duplicate copy of the source block in another spot on the spreadsheet, more often you will copy the source block over itself by using the block's upper-left corner as the destination.

Try the / Edit I Values command now.

1. Move to C7 and issue the / Edit I Values command. Press (END-DOWN ARROW) to expand the source block to C7..C11 and press (ENTER). Specify a destination of D7.

2. Move through the cells in D7..D11 and notice that Quattro Pro displays numbers rather than formulas on the input line.

3. Move to D6, and enter the label **Commission at 15%**.

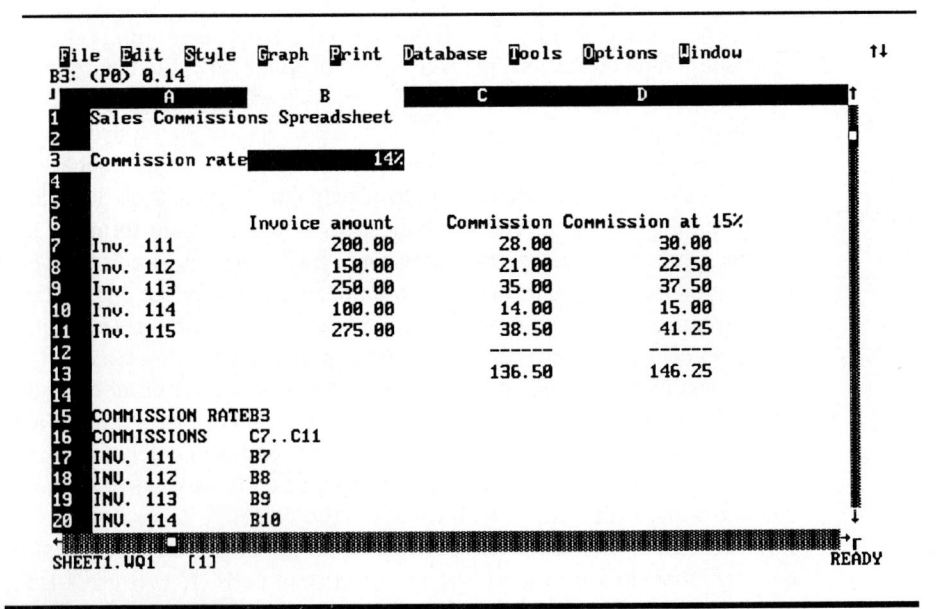

```
File Edit Style Graph Print Database Tools Options Window              ↑↓
B3: (P0) 0.14
            A                B              C              D
 1  Sales Commissions Spreadsheet
 2
 3  Commission rate         14%
 4
 5
 6                     Invoice amount   Commission Commission at 15%
 7  Inv. 111                 200.00         28.00          30.00
 8  Inv. 112                 150.00         21.00          22.50
 9  Inv. 113                 250.00         35.00          37.50
10  Inv. 114                 100.00         14.00          15.00
11  Inv. 115                 275.00         38.50          41.25
12                                         ------         ------
13                                          136.50         146.25
14
15  COMMISSION RATEB3
16  COMMISSIONS       C7..C11
17  INV. 111          B7
18  INV. 112          B8
19  INV. 113          B9
20  INV. 114          B10
SHEET1.WQ1    [1]                                               READY
```

FIGURE 8-8. Changing the commission rate after / Edit I Values

4. Change the value in C3 to 0.14. Your spreadsheet should now look like Figure 8-8. The change in commission rate had no effect on the values in column D, because those cells contain numeric constants rather than formulas.

Quattro Pro has a shortcut for changing individual cells to their values. Rather than using the / Edit I Values command and designating the same single cell as the source block and destination, you can simply press (F9), the Calc key, while you are either entering or editing the cell's data.

1. Move to C7 and press (F2) (Edit). The formula on the input line changes from +B7*$COMMISSION RATE to +B7*$B$3. As mentioned, Quattro Pro translates block names to coordinates when you edit a formula so you can change the coordinates individually if desired.

2. Before pressing (ENTER), press (F9) (Calc). The data on the input line changes immediately to 28, the formula's current value.

3. Press (ENTER) to enter the number 28 in the cell. You still can see the number 28 on the input line, indicating that the value in this cell is a constant rather than a formula.

4. Press (ALT-F5) (Undo) to undo the last operation, changing the value in C7 back to a formula.

5. Save the spreadsheet so you can use it in the next chapter by issuing the / File I Save command and entering the name **COMMISS**.

This chapter has introduced several techniques that allow you to manipulate formulas more easily. Absolute references allow you to copy formulas without necessarily adjusting all the references to fit their new locations. Named blocks make the formulas easier to read, offering a simple and rather elegant means of clarifying and documenting the spreadsheet's logic. Thanks to the Choices key, (F3), named blocks also make it easier for you to enter formulas and to move around on the spreadsheet. This chapter also introduced / Edit I Values—a tool for converting formulas to their results.

9

ADVANCED EDITING AND FORMATTING COMMANDS

Searching and Replacing
Filling a Block with Values
Reformatting Text
Transposing Blocks
Hiding and Exposing Columns
Protecting Your Spreadsheet

This chapter introduces a range of more advanced and specialized tools for changing the layout of data on the spreadsheet. It covers all the commands on the Edit and Style menus that you have not already learned. These include a command for replacing one set of characters with another (/ **Edit** | **Search & Replace**), for filling a block with sequential values (/ **Edit** | **Fill**), for word-wrapping text within a block (/ **Tools** | **R**eformat), for transposing (turning sideways) blocks of data (/ **Edit** | **Trans**pose), and for temporarily hiding one or more columns (/ **Style** | **Hide Columns**). You will use most of these commands only occasionally, but when you do need them, they are extremely useful.

This chapter also introduces Quattro Pro's protection feature, with which you can prevent inadvertent changes to your spreadsheet. This feature is invaluable, particularly if you create spreadsheets to be used by others.

SEARCHING AND REPLACING

Quattro Pro's / Edit | Search & Replace command allows you to search for a specified set of characters and replace them with a different set. When you issue the / Edit | Search & Replace command, Quattro Pro displays a menu of Search & Replace settings. This menu consists of three sections. The options in the first section—Block, Search String, and Replace string—define the basic settings that you will change or at least examine every time you perform a search. The middle section of the menu contains more specialized options that allow you to control the manner in which Quattro Pro will conduct the search. The bottom section contains two options—Next and Previous—that allow you to initiate the search. This section also contains a Quit option, with which you can return to Ready mode.

Conducting Simple Searches

You must supply Quattro Pro with at least two pieces of information before initiating a search:

- A sequence of characters to look for (the search string)

- A sequence of characters to replace them with (the replace string)

Although Quattro Pro allows you to conduct a search and replace operation without defining a replace string, you should do so with care. Whenever you initiate a search while the replace string is empty, Quattro Pro replaces each occurrence of the search string with nothing—in effect, deleting it from the spreadsheet. Occasionally you may want to perform a search operation rather than a search and replace, using the Search & Replace option to view or individually edit occurrences of the search string rather than to replace them automatically. In such cases you should either enter a replace string that is identical to the search string or consider searching for a condition, as described in the discussion of the Look In setting.

The maximum length for both the search string and replace string is 254 characters. Be careful not to include any unintended blank spaces when defining both the search and replace strings; Quattro Pro treats these blanks as characters just like any other.

The Search Block

The Block setting directs Quattro Pro to look for the search string within a particular section of the spreadsheet. If you do not define a block, Quattro Pro searches the entire spreadsheet, starting from the current position of the cell pointer. Even if you have a small spreadsheet, defining a search block can prevent you from changing more data than you intend.

Once you have entered a setting for the search block, it is easy to change but impossible to delete. To eliminate the block settings, use the Options Reset option, which wipes out all Search & Replace settings.

The Search Direction

When it performs a search, Quattro Pro eventually finds every occurrence of the search string within the search block or, if no block was specified, the spreadsheet. There are three factors that determine the order in which Quattro Pro will find these occurrences:

- The current position of the cell pointer
- The option you choose to initiate the search (Next or Previous)
- The Direction setting

Quattro Pro always starts the search from the current position of the cell pointer or, if the cell pointer is outside the search block, from one corner of the search block. If you want Quattro Pro to find occurrences of the search string in a particular order, move the cell pointer to the desired starting point before you initiate the search.

If you initiate the search with the Next option, Quattro Pro searches forward (moving down and right) from the current position of the cell pointer or the upper-left corner of the search block (if the cell pointer is outside that block). If you use the Previous option to start the search, Quattro Pro starts from the current position of the cell pointer or the lower-right corner of the search block (if the cell pointer is outside that block).

The Direction setting determines whether Quattro Pro searches by row or by column. If you select Row (the default), Quattro Pro searches from left to right in the first row of the specified block, then moves to the next row, and so on. If you select Column, Quattro Pro searches from top to bottom in the leftmost column, then moves to the next column.

Performing the Search

If Quattro Pro does not find your search string within the specified block, it displays the error message Not found. At this point you can press (ESC) or (ENTER) to return to Ready mode. Otherwise Quattro Pro stops when it finds the first occurrence of the search string and moves the cell pointer to the cell in which the occurrence was found so you can see the cell contents on the input line. Quattro Pro then displays a menu with the following five options:

Yes	Replaces an occurrence of the search string with the replace string, finds the next occurrence, and redisplays this menu.
No	Does not replace an occurrence of the search string, but finds the next occurrence (if any) and redisplays this menu.
All	Replaces with the replace string all occurrences of the search string found within the search block or, if no block has been specified, within the spreadsheet—without redisplaying this menu.
Edit	Does not replace an occurrence of the search string but allows editing of the cell in which the occurrence was found. When you select this option, Quattro Pro displays the contents of the cell on the input line and immediately places you in Edit mode. As soon as you press (ENTER) or a cursor-movement key other than (LEFT ARROW) or (RIGHT ARROW), Quattro Pro accepts your changes and looks for the next occurrence of the search string.
Quit	Cancels the operation without performing any more replacements, and returns to Ready mode.

Try using / Edit l Search & Replace to change "Inv." to "Invoice" in column A of your current spreadsheet.

1. Press (HOME) to move to A1.

2. Issue the / Edit l Search & Replace command.

3. Select Block and specify A7..A11.

4. Select Search String and enter **Inv.** (including the period at the end).

5. Select Replace String and enter the word **Invoice**.
6. Select Next to initiate the search. Quattro Pro stops at "Inv." in A7.
7. Select Yes to replace this first occurrence of the search string with the replace string and continue the search.
8. When Quattro Pro locates another occurrence of the search string, select No to leave this occurrence as is and continue searching.
9. When Quattro Pro finds the third occurrence of the search string, select Edit. Change "Inv." to "INV." and press (ENTER) to continue the search.
10. When Quattro Pro stops at the next occurrence of the search string, select All, directing Quattro Pro to replace all the remaining occurrences of the search string without waiting for your confirmation.
11. When Quattro Pro returns to Ready mode, press (HOME) to return to A1, and then use the (CTRL-N) shortcut to repeat the search. This time select All when Quattro Pro finds the first occurrence of the string, replacing the occurrences you did not change last time. Note that Quattro Pro considers "INV." a match even though the case does not match the case of the search string. Your spreadsheet should now look like Figure 9-1.

The Other Search & Replace Options

There are several other options on the Search & Replace menu that you can use to refine a search and replace operation.

LOOK IN   The Look In setting determines what data Quattro Pro looks at in its search. The Formula and Value settings offer different instructions on dealing with formulas in the search. The default setting—Formula—directs Quattro Pro to look for the search string within the formulas themselves. In contrast, if you select Value, Quattro Pro looks at the current values of formulas—that is, it examines the characters that appear on the spreadsheet rather than at the formulas on which they are based. Both settings tell Quattro Pro to look at labels and numbers as well as formulas when conducting the search.

The third choice for the Look In setting—the Conditions option—directs Quattro Pro to treat the search string as a condition. When entering the search string, either start with the address of the current cell or with a question mark to designate all cells (in which case Quattro Pro substitutes the address of the current cell as soon as you press (ENTER)). For example, if you want Quattro Pro to consider only cells that have a

```
    File  Edit  Style  Graph  Print  Database  Tools  Options  Window         ↑↓
    A7: 'Invoice 111
              A                B              C           D
     1   Sales Commissions Spreadsheet
     2
     3   Commission rate             14%
     4
     5
     6                      Invoice amount   Commission Commission at 15%
     7   Invoice 111           200.00          28.00        30.00
     8   Invoice 112           150.00          21.00        22.50
     9   Invoice 113           250.00          35.00        37.50
    10   Invoice 114           100.00          14.00        15.00
    11   Invoice 115           275.00          38.50        41.25
    12                                        ------       ------
    13                                        136.50       146.25
    14
    15   COMMISSION RATEB3
    16   COMMISSIONS     C7..C11
    17   INV. 111        B7
    18   INV. 112        B8
    19   INV. 113        B9
    20   INV. 114        B10
    COMMISS.WQ1   [1]                                              READY
```

FIGURE 9-1. COMMISS.WQ1 after the search and replace operation

value of 200 or more, select Look In and change the setting to Condition. Then select Search String and enter a formula such as **C1>=200** (assuming the cell pointer is in C1) or **?>=200**. If the search string you enter is not a valid condition, Quattro Pro beeps, displays an error message, and changes the Look In setting to Formula.

Setting the Look In option to Condition allows you to peform a simple search rather than a search and replace. Quattro Pro behaves differently when it searches for a condition; it simply moves the cell pointer to the first cell it finds that matches your criterion and then stops. It does not display a menu of replacement options. If you want to change the contents of the cell, you must do so manually. To look for other cells that match your criterion, you must press (CTRL-N) to initiate another search with the same Search & Replace settings.

This option is particularly useful in searching for numbers, because it allows you to specify ranges of values as well as exact numbers. You can also use it to search for text, but be sure to enclose character strings in quotation marks when entering the search string. Also be aware that Quattro Pro only considers cells that contain the characters you specify and nothing more. It ignores any differences in capitalization. When searching for a condition, Quattro Pro looks at the results of formulas rather than their actual contents.

MATCH   This setting determines whether the search string must match the entire entry in a cell or just part of it. The default setting is Part, which means that Quattro

Pro considers any cell that includes the search string to be a match. If you change the setting to Whole, Quattro Pro only considers a cell a match if its entire contents match the search string.

CASE SENSITIVE   By default, Quattro Pro ignores the case of the search string and considers any string containing the same characters, regardless of case, to be a match. If you want it to look for exact matches, change the Case Sensitive setting to Exact Case.

OPTIONS RESET   This option restores the default settings for all the Search & Replace options, including removing any settings you have defined for the Block, Search String, and Replace String options.

Try another search and replace operation to try out some of these options.

1. Press (HOME).

2. Issue the / Edit | Search & Replace | Options Reset command, restoring all the Search & Replace options to their default settings.

3. Select Search String and enter **Commission**.

4. Select Replace String and enter **COMMISSION**.

5. Select Next to initiate the search.

6. Keep selecting Yes until Quattro Pro has finished searching and replacing. When Quattro Pro stops at C7 because of the block name COMMISSION in that cell's formula, select Quit. If you were to continue, Quattro Pro would find and replace this block name in all the formulas in cells C7..C11 and C15. This would have no real effect on the spreadsheet because the case of block names does not affect formulas and Quattro Pro always displays block names in uppercase.

7. Press (HOME) to return to A1.

8. Type **/ESL** and change the Look In setting to Values.

9. Change the Replace String to "Commission." Although the search string and replace string are now identical, a search and replace based on these strings still changes the spreadsheet because Quattro Pro finds all occurrences of "commission," regardless of case, and replaces them with "Commission."

10. Select Next to initiate the search.

11. Keep selecting Yes until Quattro Pro has finished searching and replacing. Quattro Pro finds all occurrences of "Commission" in the spreadsheet's labels because the Case Sensitive setting is still No. However, Quattro Pro does not stop at the

formulas this time because you have directed it to look at the values (and labels) displayed on the spreadsheet rather than at the actual contents of the formula cells. Also notice that the block name COMMISSIONS in the table of block names now appears as CommissionS because Quattro Pro performed a replacement on all but the last letter.

In both of the previous search and replace exercises, you searched for letters. You can also use the Search & Replace command to find and replace numeric digits—either within labels or within numeric values. Defining a search string may seem inappropriate since the word "string" refers to text rather than numeric data, but there is a reason for this option name. Whenever it conducts a search, Quattro Pro treats all cell entries like text, ignoring the meaning of the characters and looking only for an apparent match. This means that if you specify a search string of "100," Quattro Pro finds and replaces the "100" in the value 100,000. It also finds and replaces the "100" in the label "Invoice 1001." If this is not what you intend, you should be careful to replace occurrences of the search string one at a time rather than selecting the All option and having Quattro Pro replace the occurrences without your verification.

FILLING A BLOCK WITH VALUES

The / Edit | Fill command fills a block of cells with a sequence of values. It can be used to assign invoice numbers, account numbers, loan repayment dates—any series that is separated by even intervals. As discussed in Chapter 16, this command is also useful for numbering records in a database so that you can return records to their original order after sorting.

When you issue the / Edit | Fill command, Quattro Pro prompts you for a block to be filled. In most cases this block consists of cells within a single row or a single column. If you designate a block with multiple rows and columns, Quattro Pro fills each column from top to bottom before moving on to the next column to the right (see Block 2 on the spreadsheet shown in Figure 9-2).

Once you define the block, Quattro Pro requests three values:

- **Start value**   The value to be placed in the first cell of the block. All values in the series increase or decrease from this starting point.

- **Step value**   The interval between each value in the series.

- **Stop value**   The last value in the series, unless Quattro Pro reaches the last cell in the specified block before it reaches this value. Quattro Pro stops when it reaches this value or fills in each cell in the specified block, whichever comes first.

Advanced Editing and Formatting Commands 205

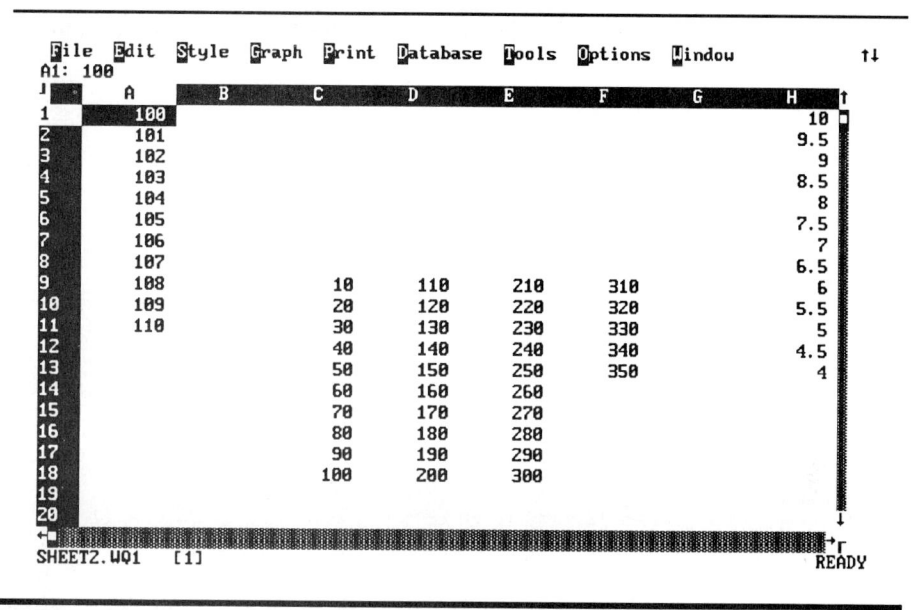

```
File Edit Style Graph Print Database Tools Options Window         ↑↓
A1: 100
      A        B        C        D        E        F        G        H
 1    100                                                             10
 2    101                                                            9.5
 3    102                                                              9
 4    103                                                            8.5
 5    104                                                              8
 6    105                                                            7.5
 7    106                                                              7
 8    107                                                            6.5
 9    108               10       110      210      310                 6
10    109               20       120      220      320               5.5
11    110               30       130      230      330                 5
12                      40       140      240      340               4.5
13                      50       150      250      350                 4
14                      60       160      260
15                      70       170      270
16                      80       180      280
17                      90       190      290
18                     100       200      300
19
20

SHEET2.WQ1   [1]                                                  READY
```

FIGURE 9-2. Blocks of values created with //Edit | Fill

You can use / Edit | Fill to create a decreasing series by entering a negative Step value and a Stop value that is lower than the Start value. Step values can also be decimals (0.5 or 1.5, for example) rather than whole numbers.

Figure 9-2 shows three blocks of data created with / Edit | Fill. Block 1 was created by specifying the block A1..A11, a Start value of 100 and a Step value of 1, and accepting the default of 8191 for the Stop value. Quattro Pro uses 8191 as the default stop value because there are 8192 rows on the spreadsheet. If you specify a block consisting of one entire column and use the default Start value of 0, the default Step value of 1 and the default Stop value of 8191, Quattro Pro completely fills the column.

Block 2 was created by specifying the block C9..F18, a Start value of 10, a Step value of 10, and a Stop value of 350. The right corner of the block—F18—is blank because Quattro Pro stops generating numbers in the series when it reaches the last cell in the block or the Stop value, whichever comes first. In this case, it reached the Stop value of 350 before it filled in the entire block.

Block 3 was created by specifying the block H1..H13, a Start value of 10, a Step value of -0.5, and a Stop value of 0. A descending series is created because the Step value is negative. Note that the Stop value is lower than the Start value.

In all three examples, simple numbers were used as the Start, Step, and Stop values. You can also use formulas, including cell references and functions, for one or all of these values. If you do this, the formulas are evaluated and their end values are used as the basis for the command.

Use / Edit | Fill to recreate the invoice numbers in column A, as follows:

1. Move to A6, type the label **Invoice number**, and press the (DOWN ARROW) key.
2. Issue the / Edit | Fill command.
3. Specify a destination of A7..A11.
4. Specify a Start value of 111 and a Step value of 1. Accept 8191 as the Stop value.
5. Issue the / Style | Numeric Format command. Specify the Fixed format with zero decimal places, and enter **A7..A11** as the block to be modified.
6. Issue the / Style | Alignment command. Select Center and specify a block of A7..A11. Your spreadsheet should now look like Figure 9-3.

REFORMATTING TEXT

Many spreadsheets, particularly those you plan to share with others, can benefit from comments, footnotes, and explanations. The / **Tools** | **R**eformat command facilitates inclusion of such descriptive text by breaking up long blocks of text into smaller blocks

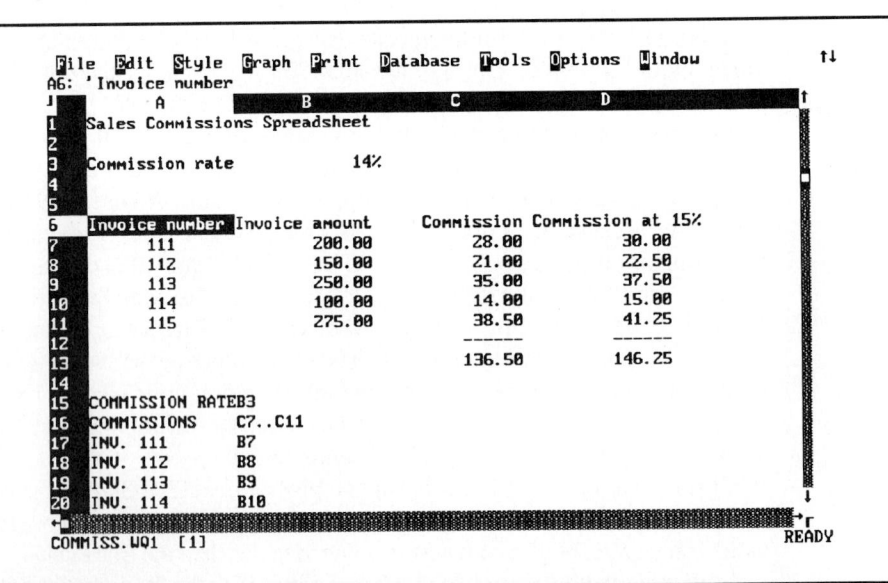

FIGURE 9-3. Invoice numbers created with / Edit | Fill

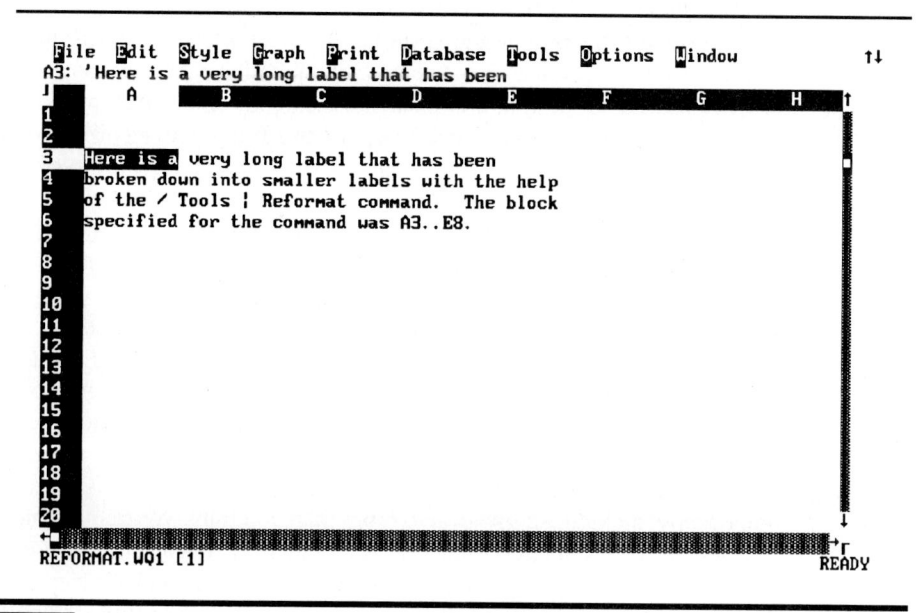

FIGURE 9-4. An example of reformatted text

distributed neatly across several cells. The command performs a type of rudimentary word processing on one or more adjacent labels, word-wrapping text at a specified margin. Figure 9-4 shows a block of text that was entered as a single label in A3 and then reformatted over the block A3..E6 with / Tools I Reformat.

When you issue the / Tools I Reformat command, Quattro Pro prompts for a "block to be modified." You may find this prompt slightly confusing because Quattro Pro is actually asking you where you want the text to go, not where it is at the moment. The block that you specify determines the margins that Quattro Pro uses to break the text into rows. For example, if you specify the block A1..D4, Quattro Pro displays as much data as fits within the margins of cells A1 through A4 on the first line (without breaking a word), as much of the remaining data as possible on the second line (cells B1 through B4), as much of the remainder as possible on the third line (in row C), and so on. The text in Figure 9-4 was entered in A3 and then reformatted over the block A3..E6. It is important to note, however, that even though / Tools I Reformat displays the data over the entire width of the designated block, the data itself is broken down into consecutive cells within the same column (A3, A4, A5, and A6 in Figure 9-4). The text appears in more than one column on the spreadsheet because it spills into adjacent cells to the right, just as do any labels that do not fit within their cells. If the adjacent cells to the right contain data, that data obscures part of the reformatted text.

It is possible to specify either a single row or a multirow block as the "block to be modified" by this command, but using a block with several rows is advisable unless the text you are reformatting is located beneath all other data on your spreadsheet. When you reformat text over one row, Quattro Pro automatically inserts new cells within your spreadsheet to accommodate the reformatted text. However, it only inserts cells within the columns designated in the "block to be modified" by the Reformat command. As a result, all the data in the specified columns is moved down on the spreadsheet, while data in adjacent columns remains in the same location. The result is a lopsided spreadsheet.

You can avoid this problem by reformatting the text over a block of cells. Make sure you have enough room for the reformatted text, inserting additional rows if necessary. You also must specify a block large enough to accommodate the text; otherwise Quattro Pro displays an error message and reformats only part of the label. Use (ALT-F5) to undo the damage and try again, using a larger reformat block. If possible, you should guess high when estimating how much space the reformatted text will occupy, including a row or two more than you think you actually need.

There is one set of circumstances under which / **Tools** I **Reformat** does not always work properly. If you try to reformat a long label within a block located above cells that contain formulas, Quattro Pro often displays a "Reformat block is full" message even if there is, in fact, room for the text within the specified block. To circumvent this problem, enter and reformat the text in an unused section of the spreadsheet and then move the reformatted data to the desired location.

Try using the / **Tools** I **Reformat** command.

1. Move to A24 and enter the following text. (As you type, the text wraps to another row on the input line when you fill a row. Don't worry if it wraps to the next row in the middle of a word.)

   This spreadsheet allows you to compare commissions at a rate you specify to commissions at a rate of 15%. To use it, highlight cell B7, type in a new rate, and press (ENTER).

   If you make a mistake, use (BACKSPACE) to erase characters and then retype them. If you notice the mistake later, press (F2) (Edit) and edit as usual. You cannot use (UP ARROW) or (DOWN ARROW) to move through the text. Even though the text appears on more than one line, Quattro Pro treats it as a single character string. The only way to back up through the text, unless you have a mouse, is with (LEFT ARROW).

2. After you have pressed (ENTER), issue the / **Tools** I **Reformat** command. To be safe, specify a block of A24..D24.

Advanced Editing and Formatting Commands 209

```
 File  Edit  Style  Graph  Print  Database  Tools  Options  Window         ↑↓
A4: 'This spreadsheet allows you to compare commissions at a rate
         A            B            C            D
 1  Sales Commissions Spreadsheet
 2
 3
 4  This spreadsheet allows you to compare commissions at a rate
 5  you specify to commissions at a rate of 15%.  To use it,
 6  highlight cell B7, type in a new rate, and press ENTER.
 7
 8
 9  Commission rate              14%
10
11
12  Invoice number Invoice amount   Commission Commission at 15%
13        111            200.00       28.00         30.00
14        112            150.00       21.00         22.50
15        113            250.00       35.00         37.50
16        114            100.00       14.00         15.00
17        115            275.00       38.50         41.25
18                                   ------        ------
19                                   136.50        146.25
20
COMMISS.WQ1  [1]                                            READY
```

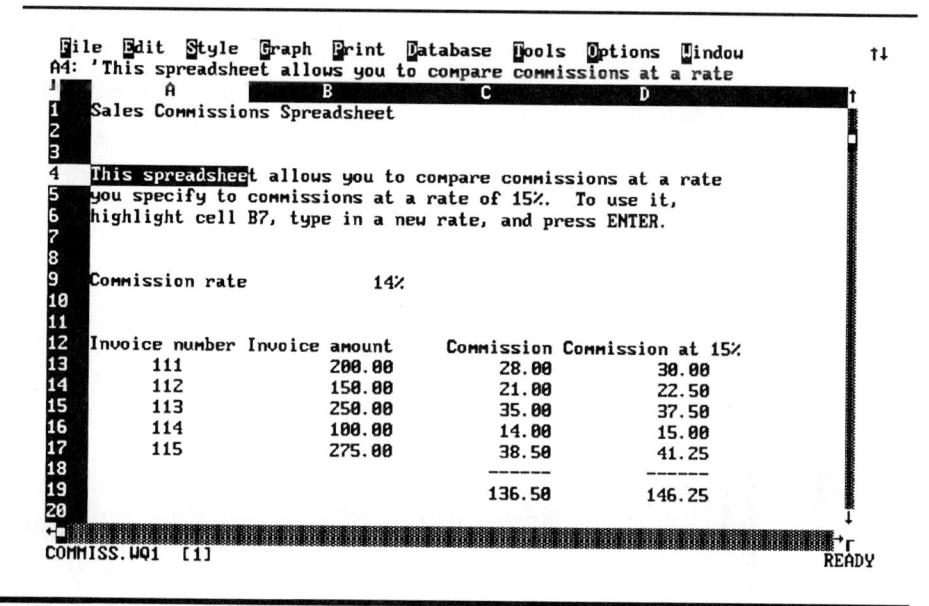

FIGURE 9-5. Reformatted text on COMMISS.WQ1

3. Look at the input line as you move from A24 to A25 to A26, and notice that the text has been distributed across these three cells. If you move to column B, you will see that none of the text is actually contained within that column, even though it appears that way.

4. Move to A3, issue the /Edit | Insert | Row command, press (DOWN ARROW) five times to expand the block to A3..A8, and press (ENTER) to insert six new rows above the commission rate.

5. Issue the / Edit | Move command. Specify a source block of A24..A26 and a destination of A4. Your spreadsheet should look like Figure 9-5.

TRANSPOSING BLOCKS

The /Edit | Transpose command is a specialized form of /Edit | Copy that allows you to rotate a block 90 degrees as you copy it. As you do this, the rows in the original block become columns in the new block; columns in the original become rows in the new. Figure 9-6 shows a spreadsheet in which the labels in row 4 have been transposed to column A. Quattro Pro does not erase the original block, so you can look at the block in its new form before erasing the original. Note that the spreadsheet in Figure

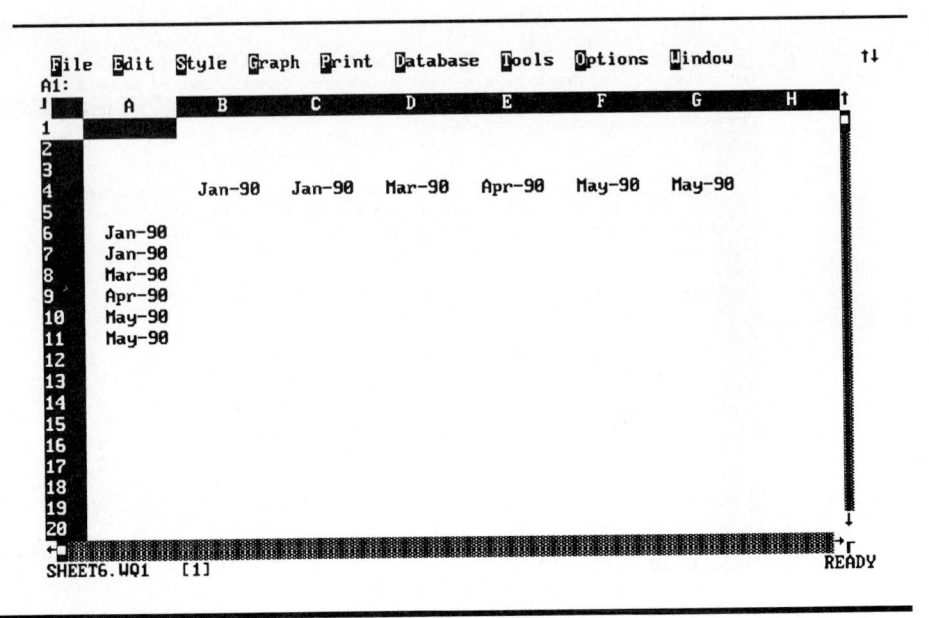

FIGURE 9-6. A row of labels transposed to a column

9-6 could have been constructed by using the block A6..A11 as the source block and transposing the data to row 4.

Try turning the block A12..D17 on its side using / Edit | Transpose. Start by erasing the table of block names to make room for the transposed block, so that you can see both the original and the transposed block at the same time.

1. Press (CTRL-E) and specify a block of A21..B27.

2. Move to A12 and issue the / Edit | Transpose command.

3. When prompted for a source block, press (END-DOWN ARROW) and then (RIGHT ARROW) to expand the block to A12..B17. When prompted for a destination, enter A22. Your spreadsheet should now resemble Figure 9-7.

4. Press (ALT-F5) to undo the effects of / Edit | Transpose.

In the examples you have seen so far, the source block and destination block do not overlap. Although it is possible to overlap the two blocks, you should avoid doing so unless you are transposing a single column or row. Otherwise, only the top row or leftmost column are transposed. If you are transposing a rectangular block, you

```
      File Edit Style Graph Print Database Tools Options Window          ↑↓
      A12: 'Invoice number
                A                B              C           D
      8
      9   Commission rate        14%
      10
      11
      12  Invoice number Invoice amount  Commission Commission at 15%
      13       111             200.00        28.00       30.00
      14       112             150.00        21.00       22.50
      15       113             250.00        35.00       37.50
      16       114             100.00        14.00       15.00
      17       115             275.00        38.50       41.25
      18                                     ------      ------
      19                                     136.50      146.25
      20
      21
      22  Invoice number          111           112         113
      23  Invoice amount       200.00        150.00      250.00
      24
      25
      26
      27
      COMMISS.WQ1  [1]                                          READY
```

FIGURE 9-7. Transposing two columns on COMMISS.WQ1

generally are better off transposing the block to a different location, deleting the original block, and then moving the new one to its desired location.

≡ Caution ≡ The / Edit | Transpose command is designed for transposing blocks of labels and numeric constants rather than formulas. If you transpose a block that contains formulas with relative cell references, those references are not adjusted properly. For example, if you transpose the block A12..D17, the formulas that compute the commissions reference the cells in the column to the left of the formula cells rather than to cells in the row above.

HIDING AND EXPOSING COLUMNS

Quattro Pro's / Style | Hide Column | Hide command can be used to conceal temporarily one or more columns on the spreadsheet. You can use this command to view only summary data— such as subtotals and totals—rather than all the detail. It allows you to customize the spreadsheet—to display different levels of detail at different times or for different viewers. There is no analogous command for hiding rows.

When Quattro Pro executes the /Style | Hide Column | Hide command, all columns to the right of the hidden column are moved to the left so that no gaps remain between columns. You can always tell that a column has been hidden, however, because this column's letter is skipped.

When you first issue the / Style | Hide Column | Hide command, Quattro Pro displays the prompt "Hide columns from view," and offers the current cell's coordinates as the default setting for the command. If you accept this default, Quattro Pro hides the current column. If you want to hide a different column, you can either type the coordinates of any cell in that column or move to that column and press (ENTER). To hide more than one column, designate a block spanning multiple columns.

To hide column D from view, follow these steps:

1. Move to any cell in column D, and issue the /Style | Hide Column | Hide command.

2. Press (ENTER) to accept the default cell. Your spreadsheet should now look like Figure 9-8. Notice that none of the text at the top of the spreadsheet is hidden because it is actually stored in column A (even though some of it initially appeared to spill over into column D).

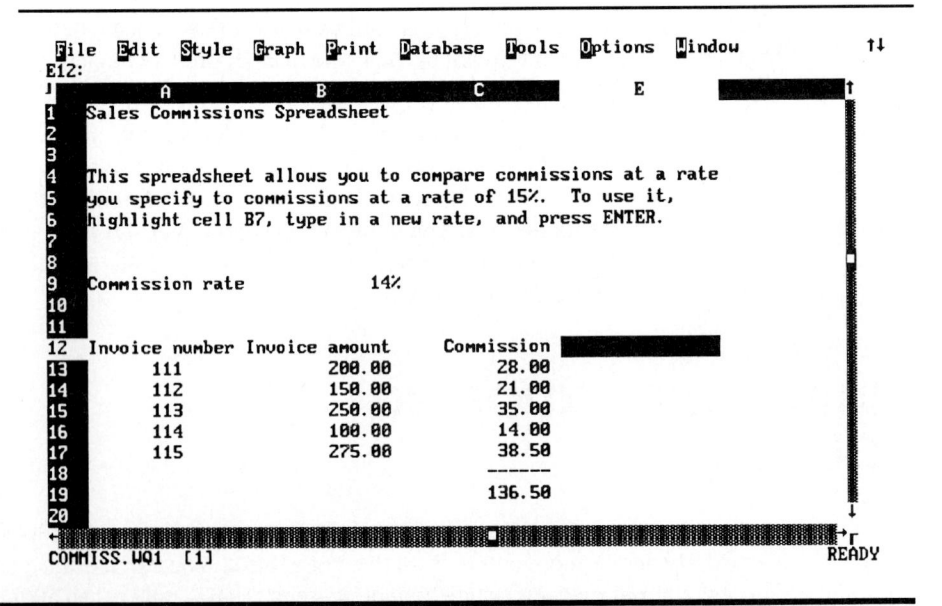

FIGURE 9-8. COMMISS.WQ1 after hiding column D

The / Style | Hide Column | Expose command undoes the effects of / Style | Hide Column | Hide. As soon as you issue this command, the previously hidden columns reappear on the screen, with asterisks displayed immediately to the right of their column coordinates on the top border of the spreadsheet area. At this point Quattro Pro displays the prompt "Expose hidden columns:" and offers the current column as a default. As with / Style | Hide Column | Hide, you can either move to the column you want to expose and press (ENTER), or designate a block if you want to expose more than one adjacent column.

To expose the column you have just hidden, follow these steps:

1. Issue the / Style | Hide Column | Expose Column command. Note the asterisk to the right of the D in the column headings at the top of the spreadsheet area.

2. Move to any cell in column D and press (ENTER).

You may choose to enter data with all columns exposed, but then conceal all but the subtotals and totals when printing a particular report.

The most common application for / Style | Hide Columns is in printing. You might print with hidden columns to squeeze a wide worksheet on a single page by simply eliminating unessential columns. You might also hide columns when printing to limit the information displayed on particular reports—either to conceal confidential information from a particular audience or to create summary reports for people who want to see only the big picture.

When you start to define a print block for a worksheet containing hidden columns, the columns immediately pop into view. Quattro Pro displays these columns not because they actually appear on your report but to remind you that they exist in case you want to expose them before printing.

Quattro Pro also temporarily redisplays hidden columns during operations such as / Edit | Move and / Edit | Copy so that you can place or access data within those columns. As soon as the operation is complete, the hidden columns disappear from view again.

PROTECTING YOUR SPREADSHEET

One of the side effects of Quattro Pro's flexibility is that it can take only a second to wreak havoc with a spreadsheet. One wrong move and half the values on your screen can change to ERR. In many cases you can undo the damage with the Undo key, but only if you notice it before you perform another "undoable" operation. For this reason Quattro Pro offers you the option of protecting all or part of your spreadsheet from modification. Once a particular cell has been protected, it cannot be edited, overwritten, or deleted. You also cannot delete a row or column that contains protected cells.

You frequently will construct a spreadsheet in one or two work sessions and thereafter modify it only slightly. Once you know the spreadsheet works and are pleased with its appearance, you generally will change only a few items of data while leaving the basic structure of the spreadsheet intact. You may want to protect every cell on the spreadsheet except those few that you want to be able to change easily. You will find this particularly useful when other people are using the spreadsheet. By protecting every cell that normally will not be changed, you can guard the spreadsheet's infrastructure against accidental modification.

Two factors determine whether a cell is modifiable:

- Whether Quattro Pro's protection feature has been enabled on the current spreadsheet

- Whether the cell itself has been designated as unprotected

When you first enable Quattro Pro's protection feature with / **Options** | **Protection** | **Enable**, every cell on the spreadsheet is immediately protected. At this point, if you move the cell pointer around the spreadsheet, you will notice the code PR (for protected) on the input line when you highlight any cell. If you try to change the contents of a cell, Quattro Pro beeps and displays an error message.

If you save a spreadsheet after enabling protection, Quattro Pro saves the protection setting with the spreadsheet—so the protection feature automatically is enabled the next time you retrieve the file. To turn off protection you can simply issue the / **Options** | **Protection** | **Disable** command. When you do, the protection codes are no longer displayed on the input line and you are again allowed to change any cell on the spreadsheet.

Once you have enabled protection, you generally will want to unprotect selected cells or blocks while leaving the rest of the spreadsheet (particularly its formulas) protected. You might think of the process of enabling protection as akin to placing a plastic covering over the entire spreadsheet—a covering that allows you to see all the cells but not "touch" them directly. In this analogy, unprotecting cells is like peeling back sections of that covering, exposing those sections of the spreadsheet that you want to be able to change.

The command for unprotecting cells is / **Style** | **Protection** | **Unprotect**. Quattro Pro displays unprotected cells in a different color or, on monochrome screens, in bolder text to distinguish them from the other cells on the spreadsheet. It also displays a U on the input line when you point to any cell that has been marked unprotected with this command. When you mark a cell as unprotected, this setting stays with the cell even if you later disable protection with / **Options** | **Protection** | **Disable**. Once you reenable the protection feature, the cell remains unprotected. This allows you to disable temporarily the protection feature to make adjustments in the structure of your spreadsheet, and then enable it again without having to unprotect the same set of cells. If you save your file after unprotecting cells, their unprotected status is saved along with the spreadsheet.

If you change your mind and decide to reprotect a set of cells that you previously unprotected, you can do so using / **Style** I **Protection** I **Protect**. When you reprotect a cell, the unprotected marker (the U at the beginning of the input line) is replaced by a protected marker (PR) again. Keep in mind that / **Style** I **Protection** I **Protect** cannot protect a cell if the protection feature is not currently enabled. It is used solely for removing the unprotected code from a set of cells that were previously unprotected with / **Style** I **Protection** I **Unprotect**. Those cells revert to the protection status of the spreadsheet as a whole. In this sense, it is similar to a reset command—it removes a code from a block of cells so they revert to the default setting for the spreadsheet.

Try this exercise to see Quattro Pro's various protection commands in action.

1. Issue the / **Options** I **Protection** I **Enable** command. Select Quit to return to Ready mode.

2. Move around the spreadsheet and note that every cell that does not contain a display format code has a PR immediately after the cell address on the input line.

3. Try to change or delete any cell on the spreadsheet that contains data and note the error message. Press (ENTER) to clear the message from the screen.

4. Move to B9 and issue the / **Style** I **Protection** I **Unprotect** command. Accept the default block of B9..B9. The code U now appears immediately after the display code on the input line.

5. Type a new value for B9 and press (ENTER). You can now change the content of this cell because it has been explicitly unprotected. Note that the change affects all the values in column B even though they remain protected. Protected formulas still respond to changes in other cells, they just cannot be changed directly.

6. Save the spreadsheet again by issuing the / **File** I **Save** command and selecting Replace.

Protecting valuable spreadsheets from carelessness is a simple and yet extremely worthwhile procedure. An unprotected spreadsheet can unravel in seconds, particularly in the hands of an inexperienced user. Even when you are the only person using a particular spreadsheet, protection can prevent you from accidentally overwriting formulas or critical items of data. In most cases it is far easier to guard against such mishaps than to correct them later.

10

DATES AND TIMES

Working with Dates
Working with Times

In Chapter 2 you learned to enter dates using the (CTRL-D) prefix. This chapter covers how to enter times, use date and time functions, perform date and time calculations, and change date and time display formats.

Quattro Pro stores dates and times as numbers. This allows it to perform date and time arithmetic—manipulate those values in the same way it would any other numeric values. Some of the more common uses for date and time arithmetic on spreadsheets include the following:

- Determining the amount of time elapsed between two dates; for example, to calculate how many days have passed since the invoice date on an accounts receivable aging spreadsheet, or how long it has been since a customer placed an order.

- Calculating a series of dates spaced at regular intervals, such as a loan repayment schedule.

- Determining the amount of time elapsed between two points in time; for example, to evaluate timecards in payroll calculations.

218   Quattro Pro 2 Made Easy

- Calculating a future date or time; for example, to establish dates for project management time lines, or determine renewal dates in a subscription database.

- Sorting records in a database into date or time order; for example, to list customers in order by first or last order date.

WORKING WITH DATES

As discussed in Chapter 2, you cannot simply type a date into the spreadsheet. If you enter **1/1/90**, Quattro Pro thinks you are trying to divide 1 by 1 by 90. You must use the (CTRL-D) prefix to let Quattro Pro know that you intend to enter a date. When you press (CTRL-D), you can enter a date in one of the following five formats:

Format	Example
DD-MMM-YY	01-Mar-91
DD-MMM	01-Mar
MMM-YY	Mar-91
MM/DD/YY	03/01/91
MM/DD	03/01

If you use a different format—03-01-91 for example—Quattro Pro beeps to let you know there is a problem and then ignores the (CTRL-D) prefix. Quattro Pro treats the entry of 03-01-90 as 3 minus 1 minus 90.

Caution You must be careful when entering dates using a format that omits the day or year. If you enter dates using the DD-MMM or MM/DD format, Quattro Pro assumes you are entering dates for the current year. If you enter a date using the MMM-YY format, Quattro Pro assumes you mean the first day of the month.

When you enter a date using (CTRL-D), the date appears in the format in which you entered it. If you look at the input line, however, you see that it is stored as a number. This *date serial number* indicates the number of days that have elapsed since December 31, 1899.

To practice entering a date on your spreadsheet, perform the following steps:

1. Save any data you currently have on screen, and then issue the / File | Erase command so you can start with a clean slate.

2. In A1, press (CTRL-D).

3. Enter **6/1/91**.

The input line should now read 33390.

> **Note:** Quattro Pro provides a special tool—the / **Database** | **Data Entry** | **Dates Only** command—that facilitates entry of a group of dates. This command allows you to specify a block of cells as "dates-only" cells. When you enter data into one of these cells using any one of the five Quattro Pro Date formats, Quattro Pro automatically acts as if you had pressed (CTRL-D) first.

USING DATE FORMATS As you have seen, the (CTRL-D) prefix directs Quattro Pro to translate the characters you type into a date serial number while displaying that number in Date format. Quattro Pro also allows you to apply a Date format to a number already on the spreadsheet. This is extremely useful when you perform date calculations. If you add a number to a date, for example, the result is a date serial value displayed as a simple number. If you want the number to look like a date, you must use / **Style** | **Numeric Format** | **Date**. Quattro Pro displays a submenu with the same five Date formats you can use when entering dates with (CTRL-D). You might also use / **Style** | **Numeric Format** | **Date** to change a date from one format to another.

> **Note:** Both the Long International (option 4) and Short International (option 5) settings on the **Style** | **Numeric Format** menu can be changed with the / **Options** | **International** | **Date** command discussed in Chapter 11. The forms for options 4 and 5 in the previous table are Quattro Pro's initial default settings.

Formatting a number as a date is slightly different from entering a date with (CTRL-D). When you use / **Style** | **Numeric Format**, Quattro Pro inserts a date format code in the cell. This format code, like any other numeric format code, remains in the cell even if you delete the data and affects any numeric values (including new dates) you subsequently enter in that cell. You can change the display code by reissuing / **Style** | **Numeric Format** and choosing a nondate format. The only way to eliminate these codes altogether is with / **Style** | **Numeric Format** | **Reset**.

Experiment now with all of Quattro Pro's date formats.

1. Issue the / **Options** | **Formats** | **Global Width** command, and then specify a new column width of 12. Return to Ready mode by typing **Q** twice.

2. In A2, try all five date formats by issuing the / **Style** | **Numeric Format** | **Date** command five times and selecting a different Date format each time. Accept the default block, and be sure to end with the first option on the date format menu (the DD-MMM-YY format).

3. Press (DEL) to delete the date. Note that the format code (D1) still appears on the input line.

4. Enter the number **12345**. Quattro Pro formats the number as a date, displaying 18-Oct-33 in the cell.

5. Press CTRL-D and enter **1/1/91**. Quattro Pro translates these characters into the date serial number 33239, formats that number as a date, and then displays 01-Jan-91.

Date Arithmetic

The basic unit for all Quattro Pro date calculations is a single day. If you subtract one date from another date, Quattro Pro returns the number of days between those two dates. If you add a number to a date, Quattro Pro returns the date that occurs the specified number of days later.

Try performing some simple date arithmetic now.

1. Move to A3 and enter today's date using the MM/DD/YY format.

2. Move to A4 and enter **+A3+70** to calculate the date 10 weeks from today. To display the result of this calculation as a date, you need to assign it a Date format.

3. Issue the / **Style** I **Numeric Format** I **Date** I **4** command, and accept the default block of A4..A4.

4. Move to A5 and enter **+A4-A3** to calculate the number of days elapsed between two dates. If the current date occurs after 1/1/91, the resulting number is positive; otherwise it is negative.

This type of simple date arithmetic has numerous applications on spreadsheets. Figure 10-1 shows a spreadsheet designed to calculate discounts allowed for rapid payment of invoices. The policy of this business is that a 2% discount is applied to all invoices paid within 10 days of their invoice date. The formula

@IF(D5<>0#AND#D5-C5<=10,B5*0.02,0)

was entered in E4 and copied down column E to perform the necessary calculations. This formula determines whether the payment date (D4) is both greater than 0 (not blank) and no more than 10 days after the invoice date (C4). If both conditions are true, the formula multiplies the invoice amount (B4) by 0.02; otherwise it returns zero.

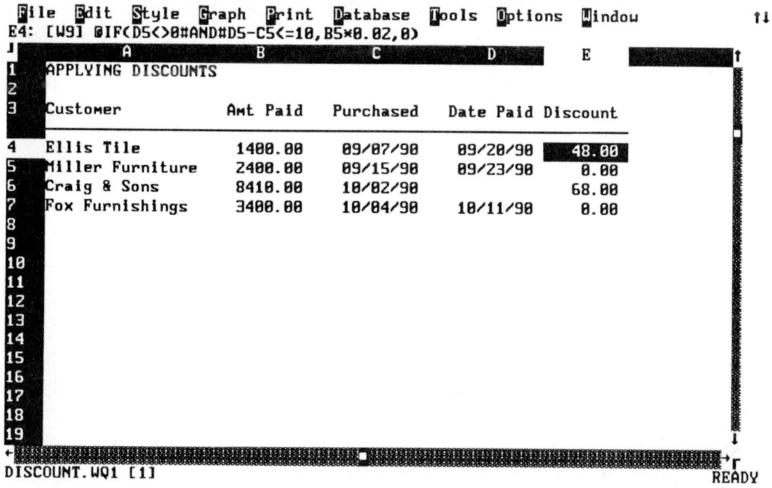

```
   File  Edit  Style  Graph  Print  Database  Tools  Options  Window        ↑↓
E4: [W9] @IF(D5<>0#AND#D5-C5<=10,B5*0.02,0)
```

	A	B	C	D	E
1	APPLYING DISCOUNTS				
2					
3	Customer	Amt Paid	Purchased	Date Paid	Discount
4	Ellis Tile	1400.00	09/07/90	09/20/90	48.00
5	Miller Furniture	2400.00	09/15/90	09/23/90	0.00
6	Craig & Sons	8410.00	10/02/90		68.00
7	Fox Furnishings	3400.00	10/04/90	10/11/90	0.00

```
DISCOUNT.WQ1 [1]                                                          READY
```

FIGURE 10-1. Using date arithmetic to calculate discounts

Date Functions

You have now performed a few simple date calculations. You can perform more sophisticated operations on dates by using one or more of Quattro Pro's date-related functions.

EXTRACTING PART OF A DATE The @DAY, @TIME, and @YEAR functions isolate an element of a date, extracting the numeric value of the day, month, or year. In each of these functions, the argument must be a number between 1 (corresponding to January 1, 1900) and 73050 (corresponding to December 31, 2099). Quattro Pro ignores decimal fractions.

The @DAY(*DateTimeNumber*) function returns the day of the month of the date specified by the argument. *DateTimeNumber* is used throughout this chapter to represent any date serial number, regardless of whether it is actually displayed as a date on the spreadsheet. This can be any numeric value between 0 and 73050. The function statement @DAY(33634), for example, yields the value 31, because 33634 is the serial value for Jan 31, 1992. The @MONTH(*DateTimeNumber*) function returns a number between 1 and 12 that corresponds to the month of the date specified in the argument. The @YEAR(*DateTimeNumber*) function returns a number between 0 (the year 1900) and 199 (the year 2099) corresponding to the year of the date specified in the argument.

To see how these functions work,

1. Move to B1 and enter **@DAY(A3)**.

2. In B2, enter **@MONTH(A3)**.

3. In B3, enter **@YEAR(A3)**.

Quattro Pro returns the current day, month, and year. You can use these three functions in several situations. Suppose your fiscal year extends from July 1 of one year to June 30 of the next. After entering a series of order dates in column C, you could enter the formula

@IF(MONTH(C3)>6,1990,1991)

in D1 and copy it down column D to return the fiscal year that corresponds to each order date in column C.

Figure 10-2 shows a similar use of date arithmetic. Column B contains the last order date for a group of customers. The formula

@IF(@YEAR(B6)<91,"Inactive","Active")

was entered in C6 and then copied down the column to indicate which of the customer accounts are active or inactive.

The values returned by the @DAY, @MONTH, and @YEAR functions sometimes supply information in a form slightly different from what you intended—returning two digits when you want four or the number of a month when you want its name. Following are a few tricks to get the information in the form you need. You can generate a four-digit year rather than a two-digit year from the @YEAR function using the following formula:

@YEAR(*DateTimeNumber*)+1900

As described in the next sections, you can use @DAY and @MONTH in combination with other functions to display the names of days and months.

Dates and Times 223

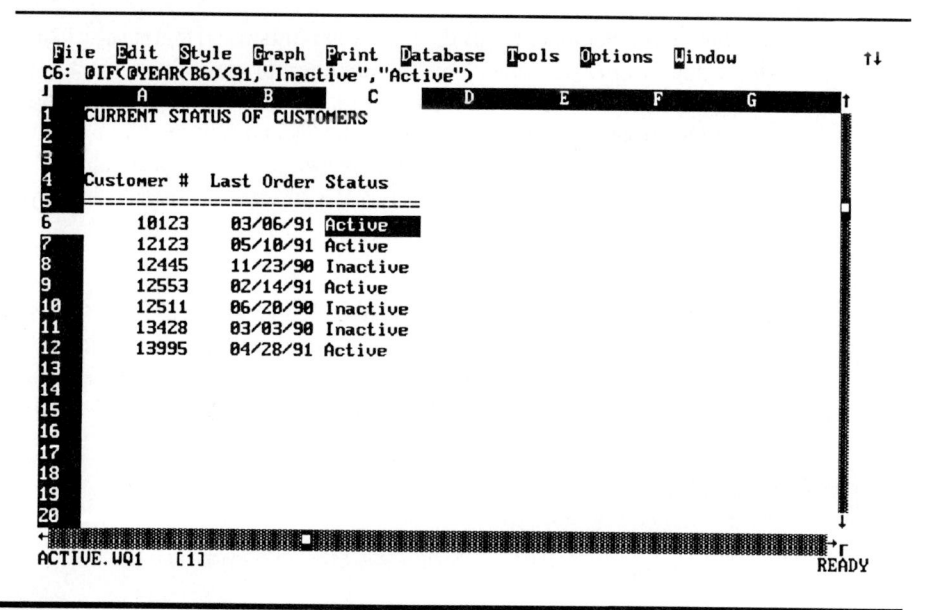

```
File Edit Style Graph Print Database Tools Options Window          ↑↓
C6: @IF(@YEAR(B6)<91,"Inactive","Active")
        A              B          C         D      E      F      G
 1  CURRENT STATUS OF CUSTOMERS
 2
 3
 4  Customer #   Last Order  Status
 5  =====================================
 6      10123      03/06/91  Active
 7      12123      05/10/91  Active
 8      12445      11/23/90  Inactive
 9      12553      02/14/91  Active
10      12511      06/20/90  Inactive
11      13428      03/03/90  Inactive
12      13995      04/28/91  Active
13
14
15
16
17
18
19
20
ACTIVE.WQ1  [1]                                                 READY
```

FIGURE 10-2. Using @YEAR to determine the status of customer accounts

USING THE @MOD FUNCTION TO DETERMINE THE DAY OF THE WEEK

The @MOD function is an arithmetic function that returns the remainder, or modulus, of a division. The syntax for the formula is

@MOD(*Dividend,Divisor*)

where *Dividend* is the numeric value you are dividing, and *Divisor* is the number you are dividing the *Dividend* by. Both arguments can by any expression that evaluates to a number, including cell references and function statements as well as numeric constants. For example, the formula @MOD(5,2) returns 1 because 5 divided by 2 equals 2 with a remainder of 1.

To determine the day of the week for a current date, enter a function statement with the form

@MOD(*DateTimeNumber,7*)

This function statement returns the remainder (modulus) that results from dividing the date value *DateTimeNumber* by the number of days in a week. A result of 1 corresponds to Sunday, 2 to Monday, and so on. A result of 0 corresponds to Saturday because Saturday is the seventh day of the week and 7 divided by 7 leaves a remainder of 0. (This works out neatly only because Quattro Pro's base date of December 31, 1899, happens to have been a Sunday.) If you want to display the day of the week rather than a number, you must use the function described next.

DISPLAYING THE NAMES OF MONTHS AND DAYS OF THE WEEK

Figure 10-3 illustrates the use of lookup tables for displaying the name of the month and the name of the day corresponding to a particular date. The formulas use the following block names:

- DATE is the name assigned to C3, which contains the date to be looked up.

- MONTHS is the name assigned to the block A8..B19, which contains the months lookup table.

- DAYS is the name assigned to the block D8..E14, which contains the days lookup table.

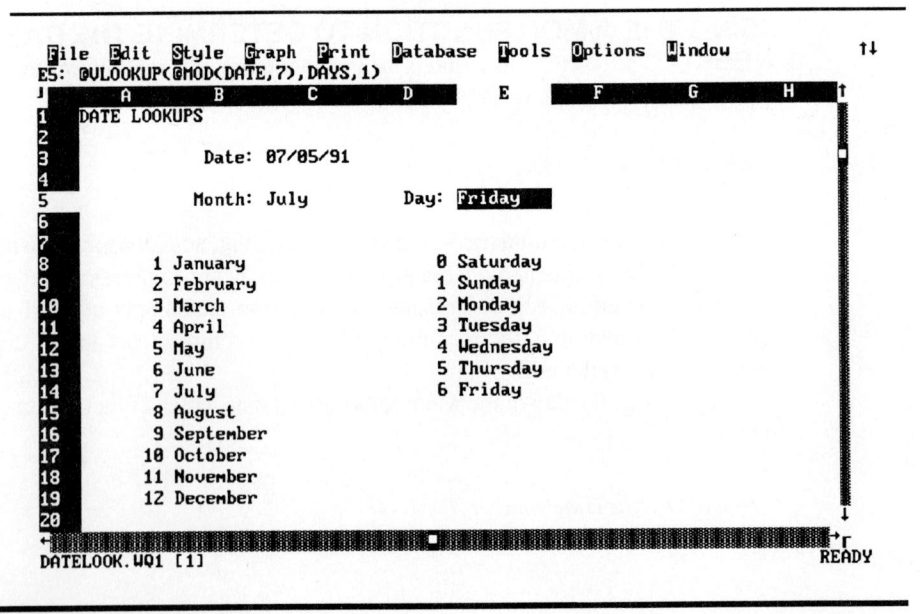

```
File Edit Style Graph Print Database Tools Options Window
E5: @VLOOKUP(@MOD(DATE,7),DAYS,1)
          A         B         C         D         E         F         G         H
  1  DATE LOOKUPS
  2
  3              Date:  07/05/91
  4
  5              Month: July           Day:  Friday
  6
  7
  8              1 January             0 Saturday
  9              2 February            1 Sunday
 10              3 March               2 Monday
 11              4 April               3 Tuesday
 12              5 May                 4 Wednesday
 13              6 June                5 Thursday
 14              7 July                6 Friday
 15              8 August
 16              9 September
 17             10 October
 18             11 November
 19             12 December
 20
DATELOOK.WQ1 [1]                                                    READY
```

FIGURE 10-3. Looking up the names of months and days of the week

The formula in C5, which returns the name of the month, is

@VLOOKUP(@MONTH(DATE),MONTHS,1)

It works by looking up the month portion of the cell named DATE (C3) in the lookup table DAYS. When it finds that number, it returns the label in the cell one column to the right (an offset of one).

The formula in E5, which returns the day of the week, is

@VLOOKUP(@MOD(DATE,7),DAYS,1)

This formula looks up a number representing the day of the week (the modulus produced by dividing the date by 7) in the lookup table DAYS and returns the value one column to the right.

Using Functions To Enter Dates

Although you will enter most dates using the (CTRL-D) prefix, Quattro Pro also provides three functions for entering dates: @TODAY, @DATE, and @DATEVALUE.

THE @TODAY FUNCTION The @TODAY function returns the numeric value of the current date. It does not require any arguments, but rather draws the date directly from the computer's system clock.

Figure 10-4 shows a spreadsheet calculating a schedule of accounts receivable. The formula in cell D5 (which was copied down column D) is

@IF(@TODAY-B5)<=30,C5,0)

If the number of days elapsed between today and the date in column B is less than or equal to 30, the function returns the value in C5; otherwise it returns 0. The formula in E5 is slightly more complex because it must determine whether the number of days between today and the due date is both greater than 30 and less than or equal to 60. The exact formula is

@IF(@TODAY-B5>30 #AND# @TODAY-B5<=60,C5,0)

Similarly the formula in F5 is

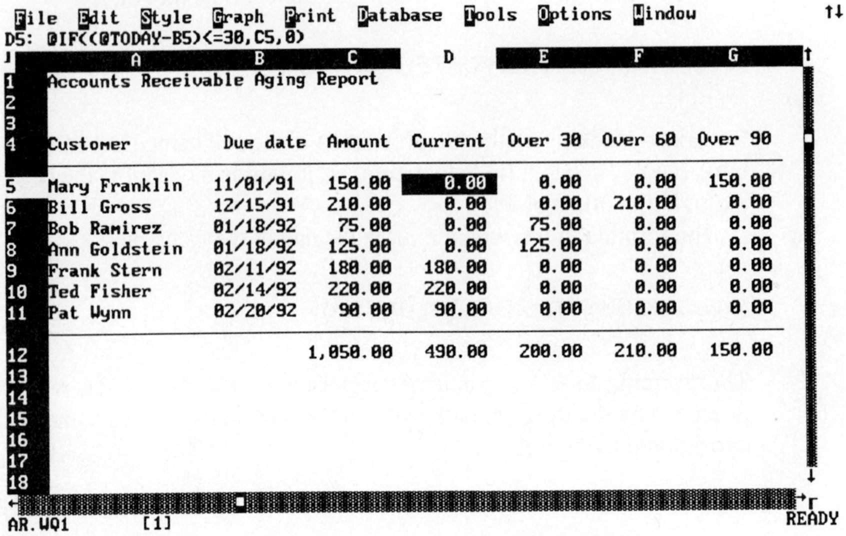

```
      File  Edit  Style  Graph  Print  Database  Tools  Options  Window              ↑↓
D5:   @IF((@TODAY-B5)<=30,C5,0)
             A            B         C        D         E         F         G
  1  Accounts Receivable Aging Report
  2
  3
  4  Customer        Due date   Amount   Current   Over 30   Over 60   Over 90
  5  Mary Franklin   11/01/91   150.00     0.00      0.00      0.00    150.00
  6  Bill Gross      12/15/91   210.00     0.00      0.00    210.00      0.00
  7  Bob Ramirez     01/18/92    75.00     0.00     75.00      0.00      0.00
  8  Ann Goldstein   01/18/92   125.00     0.00    125.00      0.00      0.00
  9  Frank Stern     02/11/92   180.00   180.00      0.00      0.00      0.00
 10  Ted Fisher      02/14/92   220.00   220.00      0.00      0.00      0.00
 11  Pat Wynn        02/20/92    90.00    90.00      0.00      0.00      0.00
 12                           1,050.00   490.00    200.00    210.00    150.00
 13
 14
 15
 16
 17
 18
AR.WQ1    [1]                                                                READY
```

FIGURE 10-4. A schedule of accounts receivable

@IF(@TODAY-B5)>60 #AND# @TODAY-B5<=90,C5,0)

The formula in G5 is

@IF(@TODAY-B5)>90,C5,0)

THE @DATE FUNCTION   The syntax for the @DATE function is

@DATE(*Year,Month,Day*)

where *Year* is a numeric value between 0 and 199 (representing the years 1900 through 2099), Month is a numeric value between 1 and 12, and Day is a numeric value between 1 and 31. This function returns a serial number corresponding to the date specified with the three arguments. The @DATE function generates an ERR message

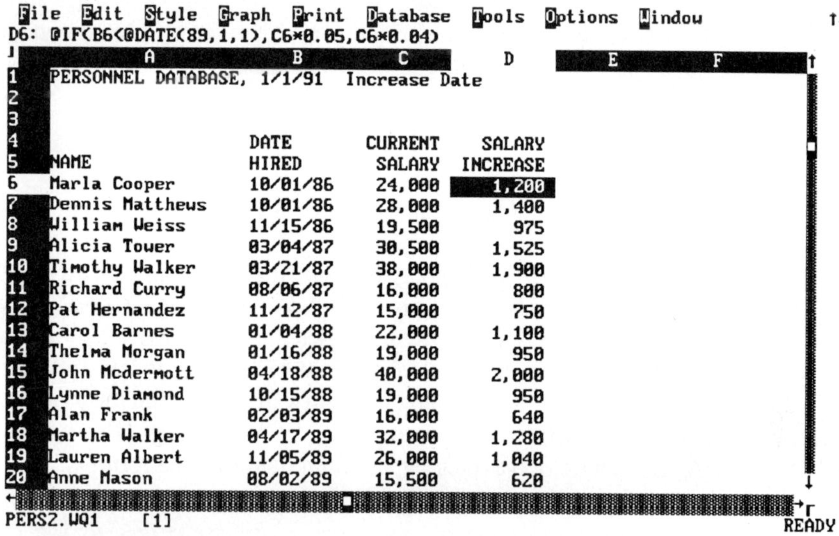

Dates and Times 227

```
File  Edit  Style  Graph  Print  Database  Tools  Options  Window
D6: @IF(B6<@DATE(89,1,1),C6*0.05,C6*0.04)
        A              B         C         D        E       F
 1  PERSONNEL DATABASE, 1/1/91   Increase Date
 2
 3
 4                     DATE      CURRENT   SALARY
 5  NAME               HIRED     SALARY    INCREASE
 6  Marla Cooper       10/01/86  24,000    1,200
 7  Dennis Matthews    10/01/86  28,000    1,400
 8  William Weiss      11/15/86  19,500      975
 9  Alicia Tower       03/04/87  30,500    1,525
10  Timothy Walker     03/21/87  38,000    1,900
11  Richard Curry      08/06/87  16,000      800
12  Pat Hernandez      11/12/87  15,000      750
13  Carol Barnes       01/04/88  22,000    1,100
14  Thelma Morgan      01/16/88  19,000      950
15  John Mcdermott     04/18/88  40,000    2,000
16  Lynne Diamond      10/15/88  19,000      950
17  Alan Frank         02/03/89  16,000      640
18  Martha Walker      04/17/89  32,000    1,280
19  Lauren Albert      11/05/89  26,000    1,040
20  Anne Mason         08/02/89  15,500      620
PERS2.WQ1    [1]                                           READY
```

FIGURE 10-5. Using @DATE to calculate a salary increase

if you use an invalid number for one of your arguments, specifying 15 for *Month*, for example.

@DATE is often used to maintain compatibility with Lotus 1-2-3. You can also use this function to express a particular date value within a formula. Figure 10-5 shows a personnel database in which the formulas in column D calculate a salary increase based on the date each employee was hired. Employees hired prior to 1/1/89 receive a 5% increase, while employees hired after that date receive a 4% increase. To accomplish this, the formula

@IF(B6<@DATE(89,1,1),C6*0.05,C6*0.04)

was entered in D6 and copied down the column.

The @DATE function is particularly useful when you are constructing a date on the basis of a year (and possibly a month and day) entered elsewhere on the spreadsheet. For example, if you want to display the first day of a year that was entered in another cell, you can use a formula such as @DATE(C1,1,1). You will see a spreadsheet illustrating this use of @DATE later in this chapter.

THE @DATEVALUE FUNCTION The @DATEVALUE function converts a character string that looks like a date into a date serial number that Quattro Pro can use in calculations. The syntax for the function is

@DATEVALUE(*DateString*)

where *DateString* is a string value—either a character string enclosed in quotation marks or a cell reference to a label on the spreadsheet—that was entered in any one of Quattro Pro's five Date display formats. If *DateString* is in an invalid format, the function evaluates to ERR. Quattro Pro also returns a value of ERR if you specify an invalid date or neglect to enclose a character string in quotes.

The most common application for @DATEVALUE is transforming date data that was either imported as text from other software or was entered as a label by someone unfamiliar with Quattro Pro date manipulation. You can also use it as you do the @DATE function—to express a particular date within a formula.

TRYING OUT @TODAY, @DATE, AND @DATEVALUE Take a moment now to try @TODAY, @DATE, and @DATEVALUE yourself.

1. Move to C1 and enter **@TODAY**. The result of this formula is displayed as a number rather than a date.

2. Issue the / **Style** I **Numeric Format** I **Date** I **1** command and press (ENTER) to accept the default block of C1..C1. Today's date should now appear in C1.

3. Move to C2 and enter the formula day of your birthdate. Quattro Pro displays the number of days that have elapsed since you were born.

4. Move to C3 and enter the formula **@DATEVALUE("1/1/91")**.

5. In C4, enter the label **"5/1/91**.

6. In C5, enter the formula **@DATEVALUE(C4)**. Like @TODAY, the @DATE and @DATEVALUE functions return date serial numbers, which must be explicity formatted to look like dates.

7. Issue the / **Style** I **Numeric Format** I **Date** I **1** command and specify a block of C3..C5. This has no noticeable effect on cell C4 because that cell contains a label.

Your spreadsheet should now resemble the one shown in Figure 10-6.

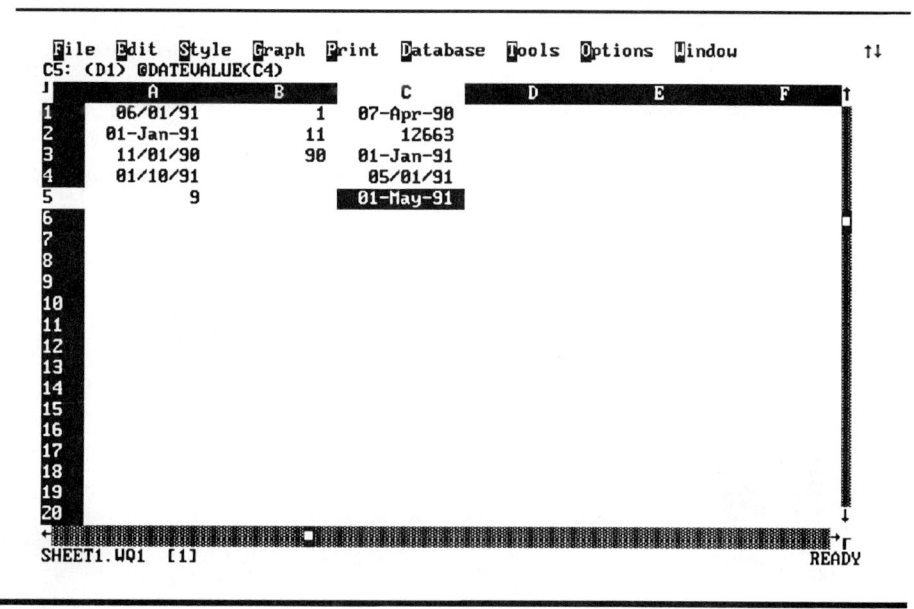

```
File Edit Style Graph Print Database Tools Options Window          ↑↓
C5: (D1) @DATEVALUE(C4)
         A           B            C           D           E           F
 1    06/01/91        1       07-Apr-90
 2    01-Jan-91      11          12663
 3    11/01/90       90       01-Jan-91
 4    01/10/91                05/01/91
 5            9               01-May-91
 6
 ...
SHEET1.WQ1  [1]                                                  READY
```

FIGURE 10-6. Results of entering date formulas and functions

Creating Month Headings

One common application for @DATEVALUE or @DATE is in creating monthly column or row headings for a spreadsheet. To do this, you use the / Edit | Fill command and use @DATEVALUE or @DATE to specify the Start and Stop values.

1. Start with a clean spreadsheet by issuing the / File | Erase command.

2. Issue the / Edit | Fill command, and specify a destination of A1..L1.

3. Enter a Start value of **@DATEVALUE("1/15/91")**.

4. Enter a Step value of **30**.

5. Enter a Stop value of **@DATEVALUE("12/31/91")**.

6. Issue the / Style | Numeric Format | Date | 3 command, and specify A1..L1 as the block to be modified. Your spreadsheet should now have a row of month headings.

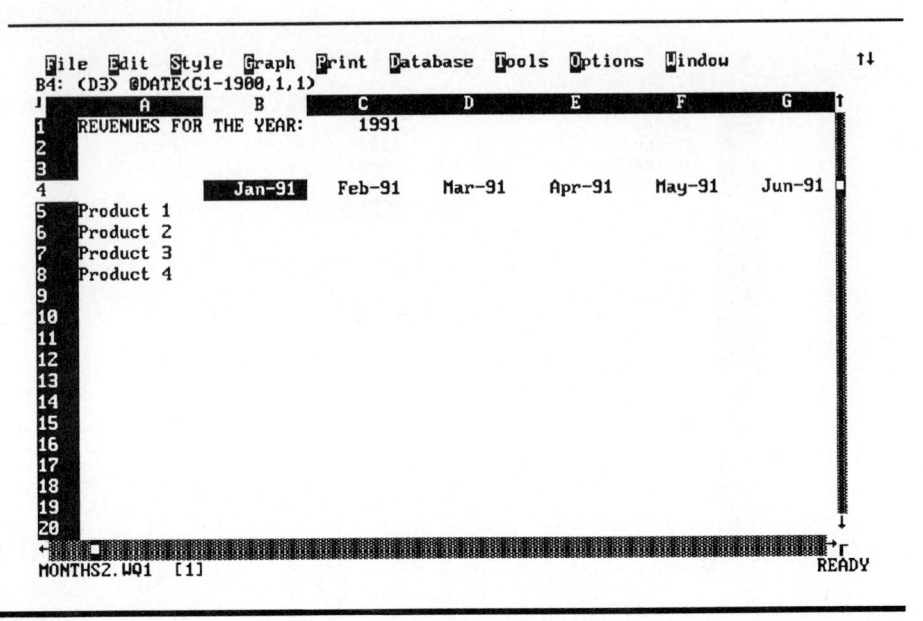

```
File  Edit  Style  Graph  Print  Database  Tools  Options  Window            ↑↓
B4: (D3) @DATE(C1-1900,1,1)
         A          B         C         D         E         F         G
  1  REVENUES FOR THE YEAR:   1991
  2
  3
  4                         Jan-91    Feb-91    Mar-91    Apr-91    May-91    Jun-91
  5  Product 1
  6  Product 2
  7  Product 3
  8  Product 4
  9
 10
 11
 12
 13
 14
 15
 16
 17
 18
 19
 20
MONTHS2.WQ1  [1]                                                            READY
```

FIGURE 10-7. Calculating dates for column headings

You could achieve the exact same result using a Start value of @DATE(91,1,15) and a Stop value of @DATE(91,12,31); the choice of functions is up to you.

Note that January 15 rather than January 1 was used as the Start value. This circumvents potential problems caused by the varying lengths of the months. The actual dates in this series are not all on the fifteenth day, but they do fall within consecutive months, resulting in the desired series of column headings.

You might want the column headings to change relative to other values on the spreadsheet. This makes it easy for you to recycle your spreadsheet year after year simply by changing a single value. For example, in Figure 10-7, the formula @DATE(C1-1900,1,1) is used to display the column heading in B4. The formula subtracts 1900 from the year in C1 to produce the two-digit year required by the @DATE function. The formulas in the other cells in row 4 are the same except for the second argument (the month), which increases by 1 in each column. The formula in D4, for example, is @DATE(C1-1900,2,1). The entire row of column headings was formatted with Date format number 3.

To update this spreadsheet for future years, you need only change the number in C1. Quattro Pro automatically recalculates the formulas in row 4, displaying appropriate column headings for the specified year.

WORKING WITH TIMES

Quattro Pro measures, stores, and represents time as a fraction of a day. For example, the time 12:00 noon is represented as 0.5 since it is half way through any given 24-hour period (Quattro Pro starts counting at midnight). Similarly 6:00 AM is represented as 0.25 and 6:00 PM is represented as 0.75.

As with dates, Quattro Pro stores times as numbers so it can easily perform calculations with the data. By treating times as numbers, Quattro Pro can use those values in arithmetic formulas and functions.

Quattro Pro has no equivalent to the CTRL-D key combination for entering times. Generally, times are entered using the @TIME function and then formatted with one of Quattro Pro's four time display formats. Entering times in a spreadsheet involves two steps:

- Entering data with the @TIME function

- Formatting the value with a Time display format

The order in which you perform these steps does not matter. You can even omit the second step if you don't mind your times appearing as decimals on the spreadsheet. The syntax of the @TIME function is

@TIME(*Hours,Minutes,Seconds*)

where *Hours*, *Minutes*, and *Seconds* specify the time you want to enter in the spreadsheet. Hours must be an integer between 0 and 23, and Minutes and Seconds must be integers between 0 and 59. Arguments higher or lower than these integers return a value of ERR.

The command for formatting a block with a Time display format is / **Style** I **Numeric Format** I **Date** I **Time**. Once you issue this command, Quattro Pro displays a menu with the four Time display formats:

Format	Code	Form	Example
1	D6	HH:MM:SS AM/PM	1:17:35 PM
2	D7	HH:MM AM/PM	1:17 PM
3 (Long International)	D8	HH:MM:SS (24-Hour)	13:17:35
4 (Short International)	D9	HH:MM (24-Hour)	13:17

Notice that the display format codes for the Time formats all begin with D. Quattro Pro treats the entire Time format submenu as a continuation of the Date format menu: the code for Time format 1 is D6, for Time format 2 is D7, and so on.

To enter times into your spreadsheet, follow these steps:

1. Press (PGDN), move to A21, and enter the time 2:24 AM by typing **@TIME(2,24,0)** and pressing the (DOWN ARROW) key. This time is stored as the numeric value 0.10.

2. In A22 enter the time 7:12 PM by typing @TIME(19,12,0) and pressing (ENTER). When you enter times that occur after noon, you must convert the time to a 24-hour clock for purposes of using the @TIME function. 1:00 PM is entered as 13 hours, 4:00 PM is entered as 16 hours, and so on. The time 7:12 PM is translated into 19 hours and 12 minutes for the @TIME function's arguments.

3. Issue the / Options | Formats | Global Width command and enter **12**. Press **Q** or (ESC) twice to return to Ready mode.

4. Still in A22, try all the various Time display formats by issuing / Style | **N**umeric Format | **D**ate | **T**ime four times, choosing a different time format each time.

The @NOW Function

The @NOW function allows you to insert the value of the current date and time into your spreadsheet. Like @TODAY, @NOW does not require any user input. Instead, it draws all the data it needs from your computer's clock and returns a combined date/time value. The integer portion of the result represents the current date, and the decimal portion represents the current time.

Once you have calculated the value of @NOW, you must choose whether to display it as a date or as a time; there is no combined Date/Time display format. If, for example, you display the value 33483.5 (the value of @NOW at noon on September 2, 1991) with Date format 4, you will see 9/2/91. If you display the same number with Time format 3, you will see 12:00:00. If you want to display both the date and the time value of @NOW, you should enter the function twice on the spreadsheet and use two different formats.

Quattro Pro updates the value of the @NOW function every time the spreadsheet is recalculated. If you are in automatic recalculation mode, Quattro Pro updates every time you enter or edit data on the spreadsheet. If you are in manual recalculation mode, Quattro Pro updates every time you press (F9) to recalculate the spreadsheet.

Sometimes you may want to freeze the value of @NOW, so it is calculated upon entry but never updated. Suppose you want to use the @NOW function to "stamp" your spreadsheet with the date and time you created it. You can enter the @NOW function as soon as you finish building the spreadsheet. Then you either use the / Edit I Values command or edit the cell and press (F9) (Calc) to replace the function itself with its current numeric value.

Try the @NOW function now.

1. Enter **@NOW** in B21 and B22.

2. Replace the function in B22 with its current value by pressing (F2) (Edit) with the cell pointer in that cell and then pressing (F9) (Calc). The value on the input line changes from a function to a number.

3. Press (ENTER). The values displayed in B21 and B22 are already slightly different due to the time that elapsed while you moved the cell pointer from one cell to the other and edited data.

4. In B23, enter 123. The value of cell B21 changes as soon as you press (ENTER). This is because any time you enter or edit data anywhere on the spreadsheet, Quattro Pro recalculates the @NOW function.

5. Press the Edit key and then (ENTER) several times; the value of B21 is updated with each edit.

6. Move to cell B22, issue the / Style I Numeric Format I Date command, pick any Date format, and accept the default block B22..B22.

7. Move to B21 and issue the / Style I Numeric Format I Date I Time command. Pick any Time format, and accept the default block B21..B21.

Just as there is no format for displaying a combined date/time value, there is no function for entering one. If you want to enter a specific time on a specific date on a spreadsheet, you must use a combination of date and time functions. For example, you can use the formula

@DATE(91,9,2)+@TIME(12,0,0)

to enter the date/time serial value for noon on September 2, 1991. Then you can add or subtract other dates, other times, or combined date/times.

The @TIMEVALUE Function

The @TIMEVALUE function is the time equivalent of @DATEVALUE: It allows you to transform labels that look like times into the numeric form that Quattro Pro requires for performing time calculations. The syntax for the function is

@TIMEVALUE(*TimeString*)

where *TimeString* is either a character string enclosed in quotation marks or a label containing data in any of Quattro Pro's four Time formats. Omitting quotes (in the case of character strings) or using an invalid format generates a value of ERR. Like @DATEVALUE, this function is useful primarily for transforming data imported from other software into a form that Quattro Pro can use. You can also use it to express a specific time within a formula.

Try the @TIMEVALUE function now.

1. Enter the label **'12:28:53** in C21.

2. Move to D21 and enter **@TIMEVALUE(C21)**.

The result should be 0.52005787. If you change the display format for cell D21 to Time format 1, it would be displayed as 12:28:53 PM.

Time Arithmetic

When you want to add or subtract a specific number of days from a date in Quattro Pro, you can specify the number of days as an integer. The formula @DATE(91,3,4)+14 calculates the serial date value of the date 14 days after 3/4/91. Performing calculations on time, however, is a bit more complicated because there is no simple way to determine the decimal equivalent of a time. If you are adding 12 hours to a time, you can quickly determine that 12 hours is half of the 24-hour period and add 0.5 to the time value. For most other time intervals, however, you will use the @TIME function. For example, to determine what time it will be 45 minutes after 7:34 AM, you can enter the formula

@TIME(7,34,0)+@TIME(0,45,0)

Similarly you can use the formula

@TIME(14,51,0)-@TIME(3,30,0)

to calculate the time value three and one half hours before 2:51 PM. This is quite different from date arithmetic: You would never add two date values together, although you might add a number of days to a date to calculate the date x number of days in the future. If you subtract one date value from another, the result is the number of days between the two dates, not another date value.

There are several applications for time calculations in spreadsheets. For example, Figure 10-8 shows a model for calculating payroll. The formula in F5,

((C5-B5)+(E5-D5))*24

was copied down column F to calculate the amount of time worked by each employee on a given day. The formula calculates the time that has passed between the first time out (C5) and the first time in (B5), plus the amount of elapsed time between the second time out (E5) and the second time in (D5). The result of this calculation is a decimal,

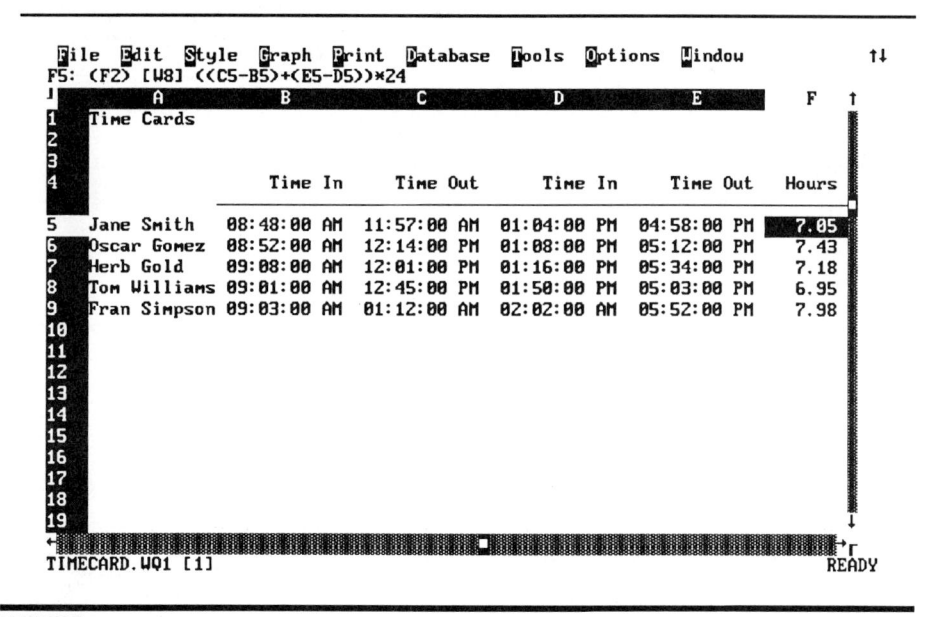

FIGURE 10-8. Calculating payroll

0.29, which represents some fraction of the 24-hour period. This result is then multiplied by 24 to convert the decimal into a quantity of hours.

The decimal portion of the formula's result represents a fraction of an hour, not a number of minutes. The value 7.05 (F5) represents 7.05 hours (7 hours and 3 minutes) rather than 7 hours and 5 minutes. You can then multiply this result by the employee's hourly wage to determine his wages due for the day. If you want the amount of time worked to be represented in hours and minutes, you can use the formula ((C5-B5)+(E5-D5)) and format the result with the Time format. The result is 07:03.

This chapter has introduced you to Quattro Pro's Date and Time display formats and functions. It has also presented ideas and illustrations on how you might employ date and time calculations on your own spreadsheets.

11

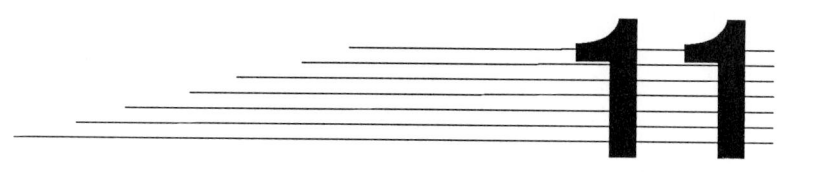

WORKING WITH WINDOWS

Customizing Individual Windows
Opening and Closing Windows
Rearranging and Resizing Windows
Experimenting with Multiple Windows
Saving and Retrieving Workspaces
Copying and Moving Data Between Windows

There are two types of windows in Quattro Pro: spreadsheet windows and File Manager windows. You have been working with spreadsheet windows since you first loaded Quattro Pro, although you learn more about them in this chapter. File Manager windows are covered in Chapter 21.

A spreadsheet *window* is a grid of rows and columns usually bordered by column letters at the top and row numbers at the side, within which you can create or retrieve a single spreadsheet. So far you have worked with one spreadsheet window at a time. Sometimes you have worked with several different spreadsheets within that window, building one file, saving it, retrieving another, and so on, but you have always worked with a single window.

Quattro Pro gives you several options for customizing the appearance and operation of individual spreadsheet windows—for example, allowing you to split the window in two or freezing selected rows or columns at the edges of the window. It also allows you to open up to 32 different windows at once, to display them in a variety of configurations, and to move or copy data between windows. This chapter introduces you to all these window options, starting with commands for customizing individual windows and then covering commands for opening and displaying several windows at once.

CUSTOMIZING INDIVIDUAL WINDOWS

All commands for customizing individual windows can be found on the Window | Options menu. The first five options on this menu—Horizontal, Vertical, Sync, Unsync, and Clear pertain to dividing a window into sections so you can view two parts of a spreadsheet at once. The last three options on the menu are as follows:

Locked Titles	Locks a row or column (or both) of labels as a set of titles at the left and/or top edges of the window. Once these titles are locked, they stay on screen even as you scroll through other data.
Row & Col Borders	Allows you to erase the row and column borders at the left and top edges of the spreadsheet area.
Map View	Displays an overview of the spreadsheet, with different codes indicating the position of labels, numbers, formulas, circular formulas, and linking formulas (formulas that refer to data in another spreadsheet).

Most of these commands are useful primarily when you are working with medium to large spreadsheets.

Using Titles

Most spreadsheets contain sets of labels—usually near the top or left edge of the spreadsheet—that identify the contents of individual rows and columns. Because most spreadsheets are too large to fit on a single screen, these column and row headings scroll off screen as soon as you move beyond the current borders of the spreadsheet area. This makes it difficult to identify individual items of data.

The / Window | Options | Locked Titles command solves this problem by allowing you to lock specific rows or columns at the left or top edge of the spreadsheet area.

Once a set of rows or columns have been locked, they remain in their current positions, regardless of how far you move the cell pointer.

When you issue the / **Window** | **Options** | **Locked Titles** command, Quattro Pro displays a submenu with the options Horizontal, Vertical, Both, and Clear. The Horizontal option locks all rows above the current position of the cell pointer. The Vertical option locks all columns to the left of the cell pointer. The Both option locks all rows above and columns to the left of the cell pointer.

Before issuing the / **Window** | **Options** | **Locked Titles** command, you should always move the cell pointer to the top (for Horizontal titles) or the left (for Vertical titles) of that section of the spreadsheet that you want to remain unlocked. If you are planning to use both horizontal and vertical titles, position the cell pointer in the upper-left corner of that section.

Once you lock part of a spreadsheet, you can no longer access the locked cells with any of the directional arrow keys or the (HOME) key. You can only move the cell pointer to one of those cells by using the (F5) (GoTo) key. When you move the cell pointer to a locked cell, Quattro Pro displays duplicate copies of that cell. This duplicate set of title cells is like a temporary blackboard on which you can write changes to the locked section of the spreadsheet. Any changes you make to these duplicate cells appear in the original, still-locked cells as soon as you press (ENTER).

You can remove the duplicate cells from the screen by moving the cell pointer past the current borders of the screen display. If you lock both horizontal and vertical titles and then go to a cell in the upper-left corner of the spreadsheet, four copies of the specified cell appear on your screen, but only one is changeable. As soon as you edit that one cell, your changes are reflected in all of the copies.

If you save a spreadsheet that has locked titles, the titles are saved along with the data and are restored the next time you retrieve the file. The command for eliminating titles is / **Window** | **Options** | **Locked Titles** | **Clear**.

Before you can experiment with / **Window** | **Options** | **Locked Titles** or the various commands for splitting windows, you must construct a fairly large spreadsheet, as described in the next few exercises. This process gives you a chance to practice several of the commands and techniques introduced in Chapter 9. It also introduces you to the @STRING function. This function is used to convert a numeric value to a character string, usually so it can be joined with another character string. The syntax for the @STRING function is

@STRING(*Value,Decimal places*)

where *Value* is a numeric value (usually a reference to a cell containing a number or numeric formula) and *Decimal places* is a numeric expression specifying the number of decimal places you want included in the resulting character string. If you specify a number of decimal places that is less than the number of meaningful decimals in the value itself, Quattro Pro rounds the value as necessary.

Start by entering data in two adjacent columns and then combining them in a single column.

1. If you have anything other than a blank spreadsheet on your screen, save your data and then issue the / File I Erase command.

2. In A4, enter the label **Item No.**.

3. Issue the / Edit I Copy command. Press (ENTER) to accept the default source block of A4..A4. Enter a destination block of **A4..A60**.

4. Issue the / Edit I Fill command. Enter a destination block of **B4..B60**, a Start value of **1**, a Step value of **1**, and a Stop value of **100**.

5. Move to C4 and enter the formula

   +A4&" "&@STRING(B4,0)

   Recall that & is the operator used for concatenating character strings.

6. Issue the / Edit I Copy command. Press (ENTER) to accept the default source block of C4..C4. Then specify a destination block of C4..C60.

Now convert the formulas in cell C to values so that you can delete columns A and B without generating ERR values.

1. Issue the / Edit I Values command. Specify a source block of C4..C60 and a destination of C4.

2. Delete columns A and B by issuing the / Edit I Columns command and specifying a block of A4..B4.

3. Use the / Style I Column Width command to widen column A to 14 characters.

Next add a spreadsheet title and column headings.

1. In A1, enter the label **Sample Spreadsheet**.

2. Issue the / Edit I Fill command. Enter a destination block of **B3..M3**, a Start value of **@DATE(88,1,15)**, a Step value of **30**, and a Stop value of **@DATE(88,12,31)**.

3. Issue the / Style I Numeric Format command. Type **D** to select Date and then 3 to select Date format. Again, specify the block B3..M3.

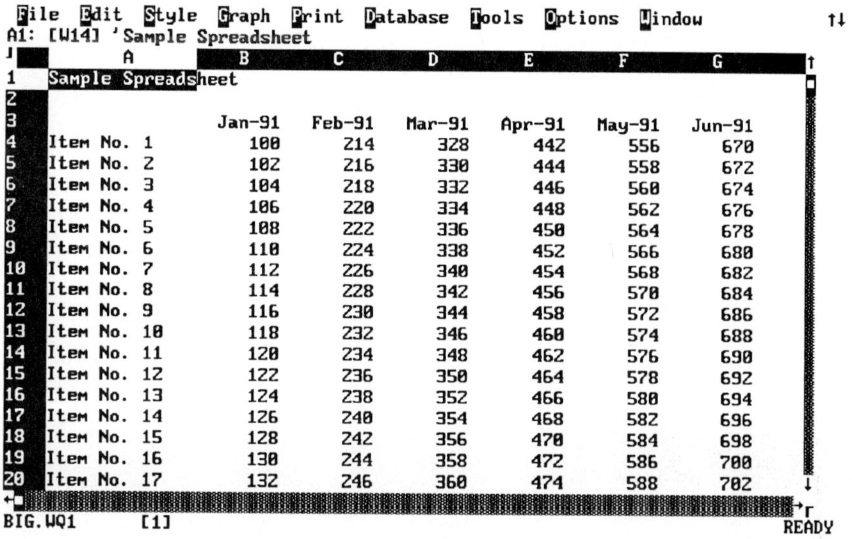

Working with Windows   241

```
File Edit Style Graph Print Database Tools Options Window          ↑↓
A1: [W14] 'Sample Spreadsheet
           A          B       C       D       E       F       G
  1  Sample Spreadsheet
  2
  3                  Jan-91  Feb-91  Mar-91  Apr-91  May-91  Jun-91
  4  Item No. 1      100     214     328     442     556     670
  5  Item No. 2      102     216     330     444     558     672
  6  Item No. 3      104     218     332     446     560     674
  7  Item No. 4      106     220     334     448     562     676
  8  Item No. 5      108     222     336     450     564     678
  9  Item No. 6      110     224     338     452     566     680
 10  Item No. 7      112     226     340     454     568     682
 11  Item No. 8      114     228     342     456     570     684
 12  Item No. 9      116     230     344     458     572     686
 13  Item No. 10     118     232     346     460     574     688
 14  Item No. 11     120     234     348     462     576     690
 15  Item No. 12     122     236     350     464     578     692
 16  Item No. 13     124     238     352     466     580     694
 17  Item No. 14     126     240     354     468     582     696
 18  Item No. 15     128     242     356     470     584     698
 19  Item No. 16     130     244     358     472     586     700
 20  Item No. 17     132     246     360     474     588     702
BIG.WQ1       [1]                                              READY
```

FIGURE 11-1.   The BIG.WQ1 spreadsheet

Lastly, fill in some numbers and formulas.

1. Issue the **/ Edit I Fill** command one last time. Enter the block **B4..M60**, a Start value of **100**, a Step value of **2**, and a Stop value of **2000**.

2. Move to A62 and enter the label **TOTALS**.

3. Move to B62 and enter the formula **@SUM(B4..B60)**.

4. Issue the **/ Edit I Copy** command. Specify a source block of B62..B62 and a destination of B62..M62. Your spreadsheet should now look like the one shown in Figure 11-1.

Now that you have enough data, lock the upper-left corner of the spreadsheet with the **/ Window I Options I Locked Titles** command.

1. Move to B4 and issue the / **W**indow | **O**ptions | **L**ocked Titles command.

2. Choose the Both option from the Titles submenu.

3. Try moving the cell pointer up and to the left, and note that column A and rows 1, 2, and 3 are now inaccessible.

4. Press the (RIGHT ARROW) key until you reach column G, and then keep moving, keeping your eye on the left side of the spreadsheet. Note that column A remains locked as columns B, C, D, and so on scroll off the screen.

5. Press (HOME), and note that this key now takes the cell pointer to B4 rather than A1.

6. Press the (DOWN ARROW) key until rows begin to scroll off the top of the screen. Note that rows 1, 2, and 3 remain locked at the top of the spreadsheet display.

7. Press (F5) (GoTo) and enter **A1** as the address to go to. Your screen should now resemble Figure 11-2.

8. Change the contents of A1 to **SAMPLE SPREADSHEET**.

9. Press (PGDN), (TAB), and (HOME) to clear the duplicate titles from the screen.

10. Issue the / **W**indow | **O**ptions | **L**ocked Titles | **C**lear command.

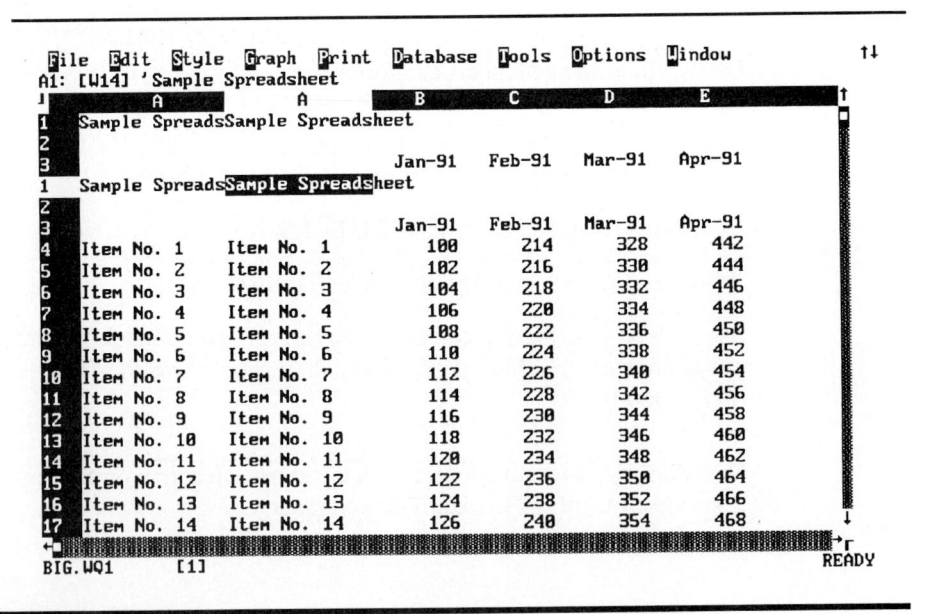

FIGURE 11-2. Going to a locked cell in BIG.WQ1

11. Press (HOME) again. This time the cell pointer is moved to A1 because that corner of the spreadsheet is now unlocked.

Eliminating Column And Row Borders

By default, all spreadsheet windows include column letters at the top edge of the window and row numbers at the left edge. Occasionally you will want to erase these borders from the screen. For example, if you create a data entry form (as discussed in Chapter 16), the user can only move the cursor into particular cells, and those cells probably are clearly labeled on the spreadsheet surface. The row and column headings thus are unnecessary and even potentially confusing.

The command for hiding the row and column borders in a spreadsheet window is / Window l Options l Row & Col Borders l Hide. To redisplay the borders, use / Window l Options l Row & Col Borders l Display.

Splitting a Window in Two

Both the / Window l Options l Vertical and / Window l Options l Horizontal commands split a single spreadsheet window in two, enabling you to view two different sections of the spreadsheet simultaneously. The two resulting window sections, known as panes, can be arranged either side by side (vertical panes) or one on top of the other (horizontal panes). Figure 11-3 shows LEARN1.WKQ split horizontally on the screen.

Splitting a window is particularly useful when you want to make changes in one set of cells and watch the effects of the changes on a distant section of the spreadsheet. A split window can also allow you to make changes in two different parts of the spreadsheet, without having to move back and forth over large distances.

Before you split a window, you must move to the spot where you want the division to occur. Then issue the appropriate / Window l Options command. / Window l Options l Horizontal splits the screen horizontally, immediately above the current position of the cell pointer. / Window l Options l Vertical splits the screen vertically, immediately to the left of the current position of the cell pointer. The preassigned shortcut for / Windows l Options l Vertical is (CTRL-V).

As soon as you issue one of the window-splitting commands, Quattro Pro erases the Windows menu and divides the screen into panes. If you split the window horizontally, you will see a second column border just below the cell pointer, as in Figure 11-3. If you split it vertically, you will see a second row border on the screen,

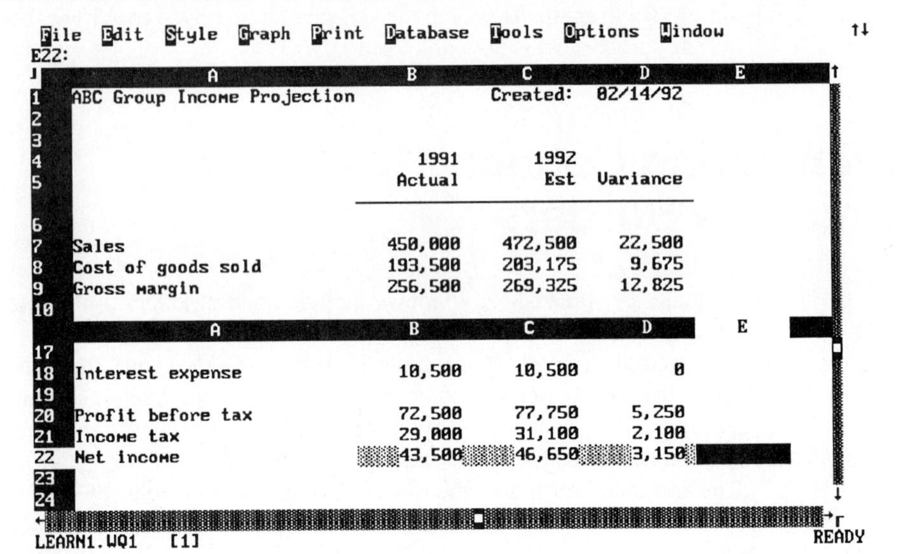

FIGURE 11-3. A window split horizontally

just to the right of the cell pointer. You can move from one pane to the other by pressing [F6], the Pane key. If you are using a mouse, just click the pane you want to select. If you save your spreadsheet while you have two panes open, the panes are saved and reappear the next time you retrieve the spreadsheet.

Many commands that alter the screen display—including / Window | Options | Titles, all commands related to columns, and all the / Options | Formats commands—affect only the pane that currently houses the cell pointer. For example, if you change the default numeric format while the cell pointer is in the bottom pane, the appearance of cells in the upper pane remains unchanged.

When you close the second pane with / Window | Options | Clear, the only changes in column widths, window titles, and global formats that remain in effect are those that you made while the cell pointer was in the top or left pane. Column widths, global formats, or window titles established while the cell pointer was in the bottom or right pane are lost as soon as you close that pane.

All other changes that you make to the spreadsheet—including changes in data and changes made with any options on the Style menu other than those related to column widths—affect both panes and remain in effect when you close the second pane.

Synchronizing Panes

When you open a second pane, the two panes are automatically synchronized, so they scroll together as you move the cell pointer. This allows you to scan two ends of the same set of columns or rows. With synchronized panes you can, for example, watch how changes at the top of your spreadsheet affect the bottom line, or how revisions in January sales figures affect year-to-date totals 10 columns to the right. As long as the panes are in sync, the second pane "keeps up" with the pane in which you are moving the cell pointer. In some cases, particularly when you are working on two separate, unrelated sections of the spreadsheet, you want the panes to be unsynchronized. The command for unsynchronizing panes is / **W**indow | **O**ptions | **U**nsync.

To create and use a horizontal pane on your sample spreadsheet, follow these steps:

1. Move to A11 and issue the / **W**indow | **O**ptions | **H**orizontal command. Quattro Pro immediately divides the screen at row 11, so that rows 1 through 10 appear in the top pane and rows 11 through 20 appear in the bottom pane, as shown in Figure 11-4.

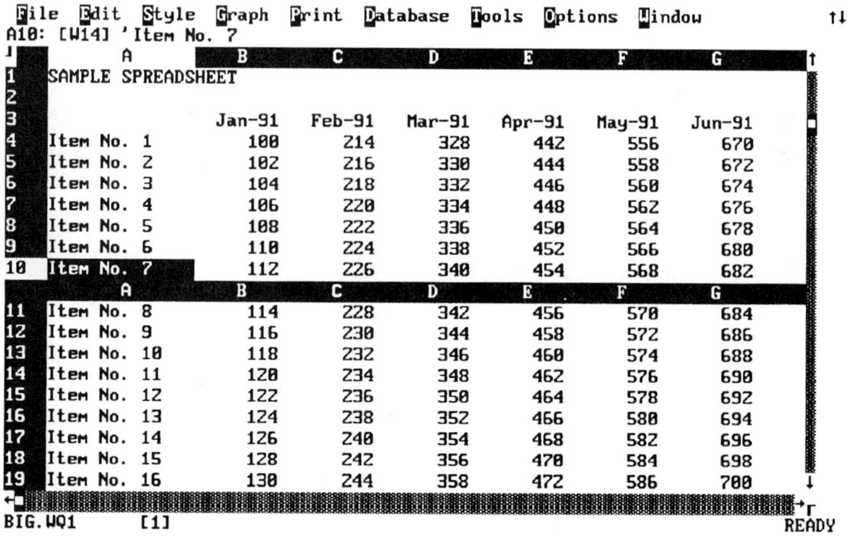

FIGURE 11-4. BIG.WQ1 split horizontally

2. Press (TAB) to move one screen to the right. Notice that columns H through O now appear in both panes. Press (HOME), and note that columns A through G now appear in both panes. Because the panes are synchronized, the bottom pane scrolls along with the top one.

3. Issue the /Window | Options | Unsync command. Press (TAB) again and note that different sets of columns now appear in the two panes. Because the panes have been unsynchronized, the bottom spreadsheet is no longer affected by scrolling in the top pane. Press (HOME) to return to A1. Type /**WOS** to resynchronize the panes.

4. Press (F6) (Pane) to move to the bottom pane.

5. In column A, issue the /Style | Column Width command, and change the column width to 12. Notice that the width of column A in the top pane is unchanged.

6. Press (PGDN) five times so that the last rows are visible in the bottom pane.

7. Press (F6) to move back to the top pane. Keeping your eye on B62 in the bottom pane, change the value in B4 of the top pane to 500. Press (ALT-F5) to undo the change and watch the total in B62 revert to 8892.

8. Issue the /Window | Options | Clear command.

Map View

Quattro Pro's Map View affords a kind of aerial view of your work. You can survey a large section of a spreadsheet and detect the type of data in each cell without seeing any of the details.

When you activate Map View, Quattro Pro narrows all columns to a single character and displays a code in each cell indicating the type of data the cell contains. The data type codes it uses are as follows:

Code	Type of Entry
l	Label
n	Number (or date)
+	Formula
-	Link formula
c	Circular formula
g	Inserted graph

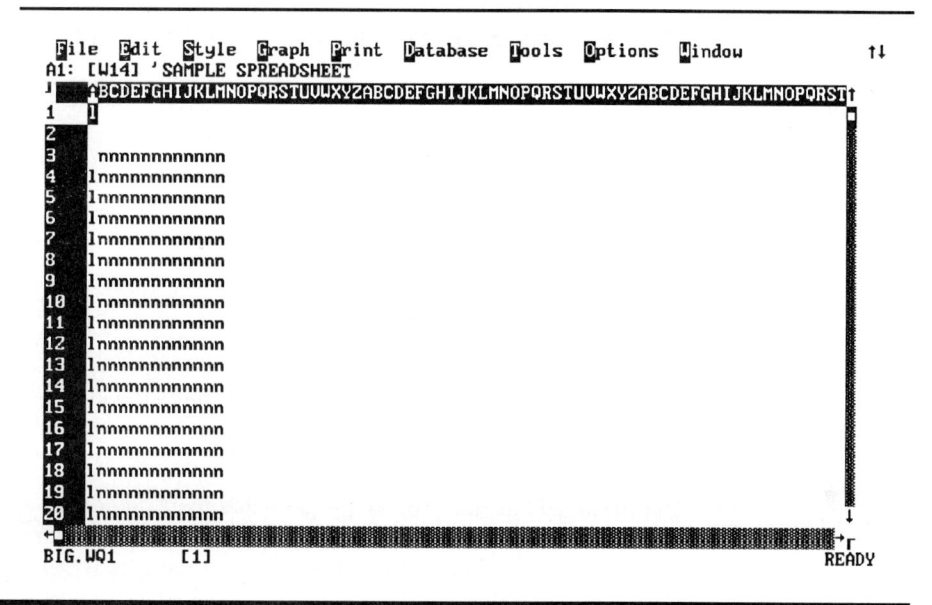

FIGURE 11-5. BIG.WQ1 in Map View

The command for changing to Map View is / **Window** I **Options** I **Map View** I **Yes**. The command for changing back to the regular spreadsheet display is / **Window** I **Options** I **Map View** I **No**.

Figure 11-5 shows BIG.WQ1 in Map View. This view indicates that the first column of the spreadsheet contains labels and the next 12 columns contain numbers.

If your spreadsheet is not too large, you may find it helpful to split the spreadsheet window and display a Map View of the data in one pane and a regular spreadsheet view in the other.

You can also use Map View in conjunction with / **Edit** I **Search & Replace** to locate particular types of data by searching for Map View data type codes. For example, if you want to find circular references, you can switch to map mode and specify a search string of "C". Make sure the **Edit** I **Search & Replace** I **Look-In** setting is Values rather than Formula or Condition. When you issue the / **Edit** I **Search & Replace** command while in Map View, Quattro Pro does not let you edit or replace occurrences of the search string. It simply stops on the first cell that matches the search string.

OPENING AND CLOSING WINDOWS

Quattro Pro allows you to open 32 windows at once. The following are some reasons you might want to open more than one window:

- To refer to one spreadsheet when creating or modifying another
- To copy or move data from one spreadsheet to another
- To do several things at once, by switching from one spreadsheet to another without constantly loading and unloading files from memory

When you first load Quattro Pro, the program automatically opens a spreadsheet window. To open additional windows, use either / **File** | **New** or / **File** | **Open**. / **File** | **New** creates a new spreadsheet in another window, without closing the current window. When you issue this command, Quattro Pro displays a second spreadsheet window that completely overlays the first one. The screen looks almost identical to the way it looks when only one window is open. You can tell that you are in the second window only by looking at the window number displayed in brackets on that status line, just to the right of the spreadsheet name.

The / **File** | **Open** command retrieves an existing spreadsheet from disk into another window—as if you issued the / **File** | **New** command and then immediately issued the / **File** | **Retrieve** command. When you issue this command, Quattro Pro prompts you for a file name and displays the same list of files it displays when you issue the / **File** | **Retrieve** command. As soon as you select a file, Quattro Pro opens a new window and displays the selected spreadsheet within it. The screen looks almost exactly as it does when you retrieve a file into the first window, except the window indicator on the status line is [2] instead of [1]. Quattro Pro does not allow you to open the same spreadsheet in two different windows.

When you plan to open several windows at once, keep in mind that Quattro Pro opens one window as soon as you load the program and fills it with a blank spreadsheet temporarily named SHEET1.WQ1. Unless you want to build a new spreadsheet in window 1, you should start by retrieving a spreadsheet into that window. Then use / **File** | **Open** to open additional spreadsheets in other windows.

You have used / **File** | **Retrieve** and / **File** | **Erase** many times in window 1. They work exactly the same way in other windows. Once you have opened a window, you can use / **File** | **Retrieve** to retrieve an existing spreadsheet into it, replacing any spreadsheet that was already there. You use / **File** | **Erase** to remove the spreadsheet in the currently selected window from memory and from the screen, and replace it with a blank screen.

Keep in mind that / **File** | **Erase** does not close the current window, any more than the / **File** | **Retrieve** command opens one. To close a window, you issue the / **File** | **Close** command or, if you are using a mouse, click the close box in the window's upper-left corner. If you attempt to close a window without saving your latest changes to the spreadsheet in that window, Quattro Pro displays a warning.

The command for closing all open windows is / **File** | **Close All**. Whenever you close the last open window—either with / **File** | **Close** or with / **File** | **Close All**—Quattro Pro displays a mostly blank screen with a menu bar containing only the File option at the top and the message "Press / to activate the menu" at the bottom. At this point you should type / and then press (ENTER) or **F** to open an abbreviated version of the File menu. This abbreviated menu contains only five options: Open, New, Workspace, Utilities, and Exit. Select Open or New to open a spreadsheet window, select Workspace to open a set of windows (as described later in this chapter), select Utilities to open a File Manager window (as described in Chapter 21), or select Exit to leave Quattro Pro. As soon as you open a window, Quattro Pro displays the full menu bar, and you can proceed as usual.

Moving Among Windows

Although you can have up to 32 windows open at any point, you can only work in one of those windows at a time. The window that contains the cell pointer is the *active window*. By default, any command that you issue applies to the active window.

When you first open a window, it is activated automatically. You can activate a window that is already open in any one of these ways:

- Press (SHIFT-F6), the Next Window key.

- Issue the / **Window** | **Pick** command or its shortcut (ALT-0). Quattro Pro displays a list of currently open spreadsheets and the windows in which they are displayed. If you have a File Manager window open, it is represented by a drive letter and possibly a directory. Highlight the desired window and press (ENTER) to select it, or type the first letter of the spreadsheet name. You can also display a list of windows by pressing (SHIFT-F5), the Pick Window key.

- Hold down the (ALT) key and press the number of the window that you want to select. To select window 3, for example, you would press (ALT-3).

- If you are using a mouse and have arranged the windows so that at least part of several windows are visible, you can simply click on any portion of the desired window.

REARRANGING AND RESIZING WINDOWS

When you first open multiple windows, Quattro Pro arranges them one on top of the other—rather like a neat stack of papers. Although you can shuffle through these window "pages" using (SHIFT-F6) (Next window), only the window currently on the top of the stack is visible. Quattro Pro allows you to change this arrangement and even provides commands for rearranging groups of windows in one of two common configurations: tiled and stacked. You can also shrink, expand, and reposition individual windows at will.

Tiling and Stacking Windows

Both the / **W**indow | **S**tack command and the / **W**indow | **T**ile command rearrange all the currently open windows. When you issue the / **W**indow | **S**tack command, Quattro

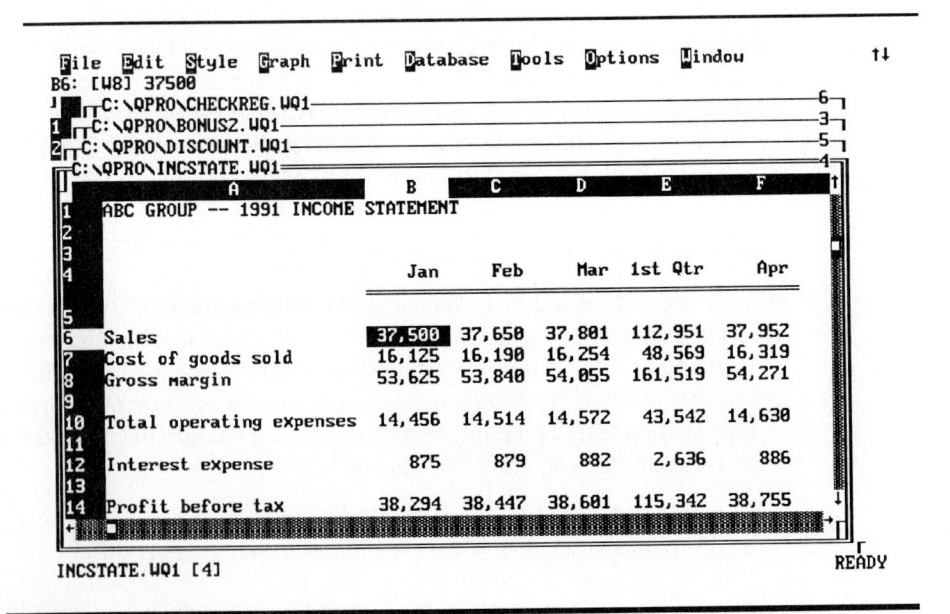

FIGURE 11-6. Stacked windows

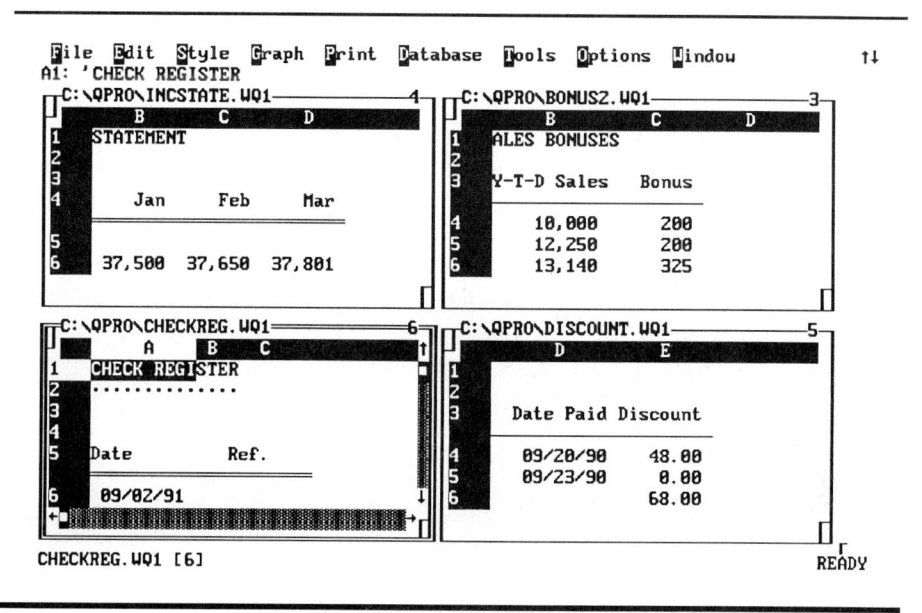

FIGURE 11-7. Tiled windows

Pro arranges the open windows in layers—the current window occupies most of the screen but the top edge of the other windows are visible above it. The resulting screen resembles a three-dimensional stack of papers, as shown in Figure 11-6. You can use any of the usual methods to activate one of the windows: (SHIFT-F6), (ALT-0), (ALT-#) ((ALT) plus a window number), / **Window** I **Pick**, or clicking with the mouse.

The / **Window** I **Tile** command splits the entire spreadsheet area into sections—one for each open spreadsheet. Figure 11-7 shows a screen with four tiled windows.

The maximum number of windows you can display with / **Window** I **Tile** is 32—the same as the maximum number of spreadsheets you can open. Although tiling 32 spreadsheets does not allow you to see much of any one spreadsheet, it works well as a window directory from which you can select windows to view in more detail (see the next section, "Zooming Windows"). If you have an EGA or VGA screen, you will find 43-line and 50-line display modes particularly useful when you are viewing several windows at once, because they allow you to see twice as much data. When you tile windows, all the open windows are visible on screen at once. However, as always, only one of those windows is active at any point. The active window is the one with the double borders.

The preassigned menu command shortcut for / **Window** I **Tile** is (CTRL-T).

Zooming Windows

To zoom means to expand a window temporarily until it occupies the entire area between the input line and the status bar. Zooming is particularly useful when you have several small windows on the screen and want to focus on one of them.

To zoom the active window, issue the / Window | Zoom command or press (ALT-F6) (the Zoom Window key). If you are using a mouse, click the zoom icon, which is the two arrows just above the mouse palette in the upper-right corner of the screen. Whenever you zoom a window, Quattro Pro remembers the size and position of all windows currently on the screen. As soon as you reissue the / Window | Zoom command (or press (ALF-F6) again), Quattro Pro restores the previous window configuration.

Moving and Resizing Windows

Although the window configurations produced by / Window | Tile or / Window | Stack are adequate in most situations, sometimes you may prefer a customized arrangement. You might want one window to occupy two thirds of the screen and another to occupy one third. You may want to arrange two windows one above the other rather than side by side. You may want to open a dozen windows but dedicate most of the screen to only two of those windows, selecting and zooming other windows only as needed. In all these cases, you must move and resize the windows individually.

To rearrange or resize windows, use the / Window | Move/Size command. Quattro Pro displays a small box with the word "MOVE" in the upper-left corner of the active spreadsheet, and erases the cell pointer and scroll bars at the right and bottom edges of the window, as shown in Figure 11-8. At the bottom of the screen you see the message "Press arrows to move, shift+arrows to resize." To move the active window, use (LEFT ARROW), (RIGHT ARROW), (UP ARROW), and (DOWN ARROW). Then press (ENTER).

Once you issue the / Window | Move/Size command, you can either use the (SCROLL LOCK) key or type a period to toggle back and forth between Move and Size mode. Quattro Pro indicates which mode you are in by displaying MOVE or SIZE in the upper-left corner of the window. If you are in Move mode, the arrow keys move the active window around on the screen. In Size mode, the arrow keys change the shape of the active window. To shrink the window, you can press either (UP ARROW) to move the bottom border up or (LEFT ARROW) to move the right border to the left. To expand the window, press (DOWN ARROW) to move the bottom border down or (RIGHT ARROW) to move the right border further to the right. You can also resize the active window while in Move mode by holding down (SHIFT) while pressing the arrow keys.

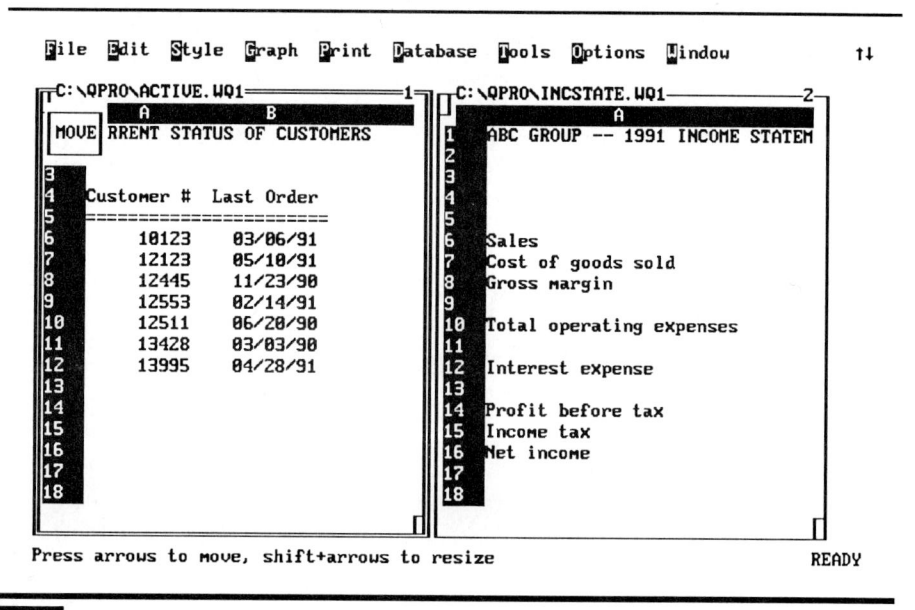

```
   File  Edit  Style  Graph  Print  Database  Tools  Options  Window                          ↑↓
   ┌─C:\QPRO\ACTIVE.WQ1══════════════1─┐┌─C:\QPRO\INCSTATE.WQ1──────────2─┐
   │      A            B               ││          A                      │
   │ MOVE RRENT STATUS OF CUSTOMERS    ││ 1  ABC GROUP -- 1991 INCOME STATEM
   │ 2                                 ││ 2                               │
   │ 3                                 ││ 3                               │
   │ 4  Customer #   Last Order        ││ 4                               │
   │ 5  ====================           ││ 5                               │
   │ 6      10123    03/06/91          ││ 6  Sales                        │
   │ 7      12123    05/10/91          ││ 7  Cost of goods sold           │
   │ 8      12445    11/23/90          ││ 8  Gross margin                 │
   │ 9      12553    02/14/91          ││ 9                               │
   │10      12511    06/20/90          ││10  Total operating expenses     │
   │11      13428    03/03/90          ││11                               │
   │12      13995    04/28/91          ││12  Interest expense             │
   │13                                 ││13                               │
   │14                                 ││14  Profit before tax            │
   │15                                 ││15  Income tax                   │
   │16                                 ││16  Net income                   │
   │17                                 ││17                               │
   │18                                 ││18                               │
   └───────────────────────────────────┘└─────────────────────────────────┘
   Press arrows to move, shift+arrows to resize                      READY
```

FIGURE 11-8. Moving a window

To move a window using the mouse, drag any of its borders until the window reaches the desired location. To resize a window, drag the resize box in the bottom right corner of the window. (The resize box looks like ⌐.) The window frame changes size as you drag.

Once you start resizing a window, all the data in that window disappears temporarily. The data reappears as soon as you press (ENTER). Quattro Pro also provides several single-key commands for rearranging the workspace once you are in Move/Size mode. The following keys both move and reposition the active window:

Key	Effect
T (top)	Moves the active window to the top half of the screen
B (bottom)	Moves the active window to the bottom half of the screen
L (left)	Moves the active window to the left half of the screen
R (right)	Moves the active window to the right half of the screen
Z (zoom)	Expands the active window until it fills the screen

As soon as you press one of these keys, Quattro Pro performs the operation and immediately returns to Ready mode. If you want to make further adjustments in your window configuration, you must reissue the / **W**indow | **M**ove/Size command.

When you save a spreadsheet with the / File | Save or / File | Save As command, Quattro Pro saves the current shape and location of the window in which the spreadsheet is displayed. The next time you retrieve the spreadsheet, it assumes that same shape and position. If you want to save a particular configuration of windows including the spreadsheets they contain, and their sizes and positions, you can use the / File | Workspace command described under "Saving and Retrieving Workspaces."

EXPERIMENTING WITH MULTIPLE WINDOWS

In the following exercise, you open two windows (in addition to the one that is already open), practice activating them, and then arrange them in several different configurations on the screen.

1. Press (HOME) to move to A1.
2. Issue the / File | Open command. When prompted for a file name, enter or select **LEARN1**. LEARN1.WQ1 appears on the screen, completely overlaying BIG.WQ1, and the window indicator [2] appears on the status line. Press (HOME) if the cell pointer is anywhere other than cell A1.
3. Issue the / File | Open command again, and this time enter **COMMISS**. Now you should see COMMISS.WQ1 on the screen and the window indicator [3] on the status line. Again, press (HOME) if the cell pointer is anywhere other than A1.
4. Press (SHIFT-F6) (Next Window) to activate the next window. Because you were looking at the last window you opened, Quattro Pro displays the first window you opened, which contains BIG.WQ1.
5. Press (SHIFT-F6) (Next Window) again to activate window number 2. LEARN1 should now appear on the screen.
6. Now try stacking the windows by issuing the **Window | Stack** command. The tops of the second and third windows should now be visible just below the input line at the top of the screen. Note the appearance of the window numbers at the right edge of the screen.
7. Activate LEARN1.WQ1 by pressing (ALT-2). Note that it is now difficult to see the other windows.

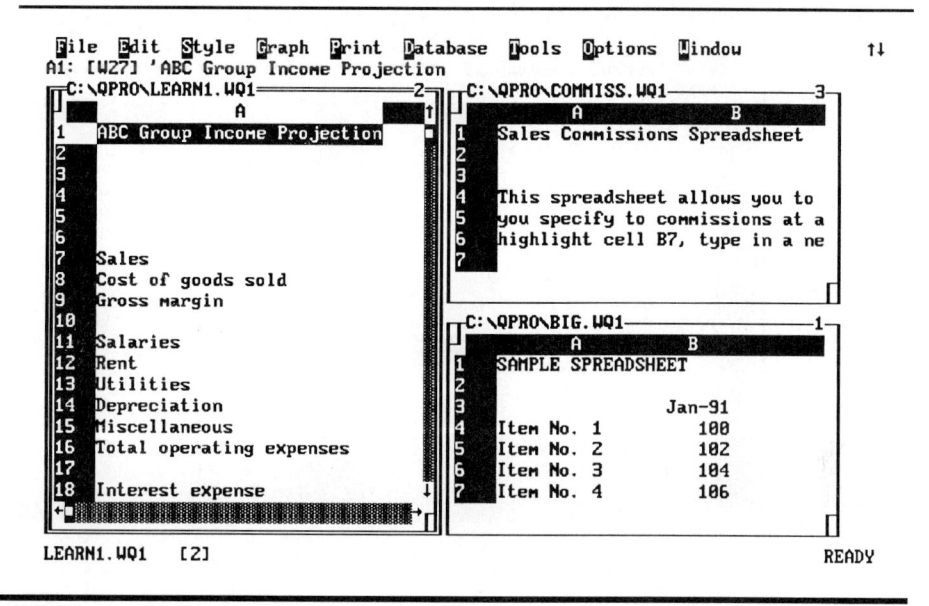

```
File  Edit  Style  Graph  Print  Database  Tools  Options  Window                    ↑↓
A1: [W27] 'ABC Group Income Projection
┌─C:\QPRO\LEARN1.WQ1════════════2═┐ ┌─C:\QPRO\COMMISS.WQ1═══════════3─┐
│         A                      ↑│ │        A              B         │
│1   ABC Group Income Projection  │ │1  Sales Commissions Spreadsheet │
│2                                │ │2                                │
│3                                │ │3                                │
│4                                │ │4  This spreadsheet allows you to│
│5                                │ │5  you specify to commissions at a│
│6                                │ │6  highlight cell B7, type in a ne│
│7   Sales                        │ │7                                │
│8   Cost of goods sold           │ └─────────────────────────────────┘
│9   Gross margin                 │ ┌─C:\QPRO\BIG.WQ1═══════════════1─┐
│10                               │ │        A              B         │
│11  Salaries                     │ │1  SAMPLE SPREADSHEET            │
│12  Rent                         │ │2                                │
│13  Utilities                    │ │3                      Jan-91    │
│14  Depreciation                 │ │4  Item No. 1          100       │
│15  Miscellaneous                │ │5  Item No. 2          102       │
│16  Total operating expenses     │ │6  Item No. 3          104       │
│17                               │ │7  Item No. 4          106       │
│18  Interest expense            ↓│ │                                 │
└─────────────────────────────────┘ └─────────────────────────────────┘
LEARN1.WQ1   [2]                                                    READY
```

FIGURE 11-9.   Tiling the three practice spreadsheets

8. Tile the three windows by issuing the **Window | Tile** command. Your spreadsheet should now look like Figure 11-9. Window 2 appears on the left side because it was the active window when you issued the command.

Now try moving window 3 (COMMISS.WQ1) to the lower-left corner so it overlaps window 2 and expanding BIG.WQ1 to fill the right side of the screen.

1. Press (ALT-3) to activate window 3.

2. Issue the **/ Window | Move/Size** command. The move box should appear in the upper-left corner of the window.

3. Press (LEFT ARROW) until window 3 reaches the left edge of the screen. Then press (DOWN ARROW) until it reaches the lower-left corner. Press (ENTER).

4. Press (ALT-1) to activate window 1.

5. Expand the window to fill the entire right half of the screen by pressing **R**. Your spreadsheet should now resemble Figure 11-10.

256 Quattro Pro 2 Made Easy

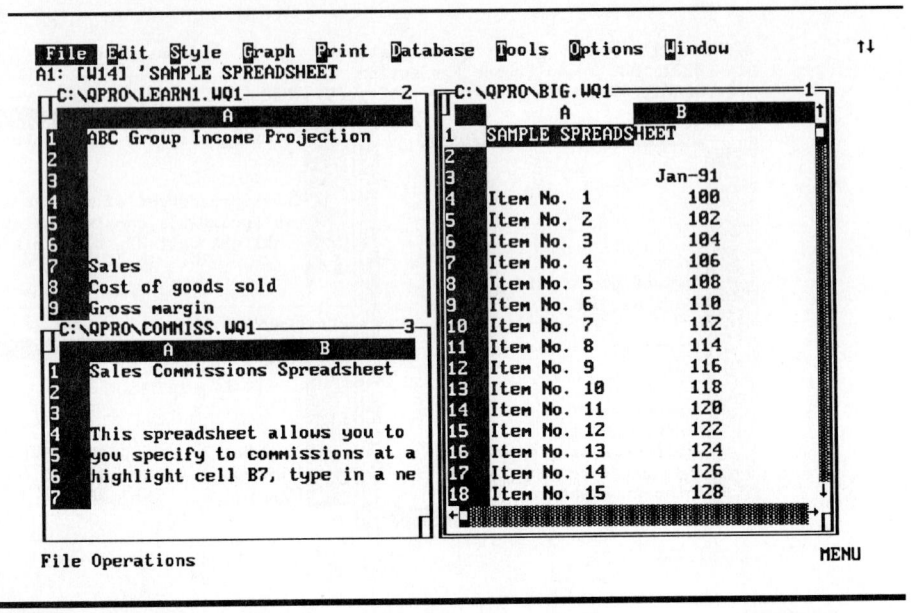

FIGURE 11-10. Rearranging the three windows

Lastly, try zooming the current window.

1. Issue the / **Window** I **Zoom** command. BIG.WQ1 should now fill the screen.

2. Issue the / **Window** I **Zoom** command again. Quattro Pro restores the previous window configuration.

SAVING AND RETRIEVING WORKSPACES

Once you have opened, sized, and positioned a set of windows, you may want to save the arrangement so that you can reuse it in the future. Using the / **File** I **Workspace** I **Save** command, you can create a special workspace file that contains all the details of the current window configuration, including the following:

- Size of each window
- Position of each window
- Name of the file displayed in each window

When you issue the / **File** I **Workspace** I **Save** command, Quattro Pro prompts you for a workspace file name. Do not specify an extension; Quattro Pro automatically assigns the WSP extension. Once you have saved a workspace, you can restore it at any time using the / **File** I **Workspace** I **Restore** command.

Keep in mind that workspace files do not contain any spreadsheet data—they contain only the names of spreadsheets displayed in the windows that were open when you issued the / **File** I **Workspace** I **Save** command. This has two implications. First, you still need to save your spreadsheets individually using / **File** I **Save** or / **File** I **Save As**. Second, you need not worry about retrieving outmoded versions of your spreadsheets when you issue the / **File** I **Workspace** I **Retrieve** command, even if you changed the spreadsheets after saving the workspace as a whole. Whenever you restore a workspace, Quattro Pro closes any open windows, reopens the workspace windows, and then fills those windows with the latest versions of your spreadsheets.

Try saving and restoring your current workspace.

1. Issue the / **File** I **Workspace** I **Save** command. When prompted for a name, enter **TEST**.

2. Issue the / **File** I **Close All** command.

3. Type / and press (ENTER) to open the abbreviated File menu, and select Workspace.

4. Because there are no windows open at the moment to save to a workspace file, Quattro Pro simply assumes that you want to restore rather than save a workspace and immediately displays a workspace file list. Select TEST from the file list.

COPYING AND MOVING DATA BETWEEN WINDOWS

Quattro Pro allows you to copy and move data between any two open windows. The steps involved are the same as when you move or copy data within a single window: Issue the / **Edit** I **Copy** or / **Edit** I **Move** command, specify a source block, and then specify a destination. The only difference is that either the source or the destination is in another unselected window.

When specifying cells in the second, nonactive window, you have a familiar choice between typing cell coordinates or pointing out cells on the spreadsheet itself. To use the typing method, type the name of the spreadsheet, enclosed in square brackets, followed by the cell or block coordinates. For example, to copy the block B10..B15 from XYZ.WQ1 into the active window, you would enter a source block of [XYZ]B10..B15. To copy cell A1 to cell B3 of the XYZ.WQ1 spreadsheet, you would enter a destination of [XYZ]B3. When specifying the file name, you must include the extension only if it is something other than WQ1.

To use the pointing method, press (SHIFT-F6) (Next Window) as soon as you are prompted for the source block or destination. Then point to the cell or block and press (ENTER). Quattro Pro immediately returns the cell pointer to the spreadsheet from which you issued the command.

Before you can move or copy data from one spreadsheet to another, you must open both spreadsheets. If you specify a source block or destination in an unopened spreadsheet, Quattro Pro simply displays an error message.

When you move cells from one window to another, you must be careful not to create links between two spreadsheets accidentally. For now, whenever you move blocks of cells, be sure to keep formulas and the cells they reference together. This means that you should avoid moving a formula without also moving all the cells that it references. You should also refrain from moving cells without also moving any formulas in which they are referenced. Otherwise you will have formulas in one spreadsheet that refer to (and are therefore affected by) cells in another spreadsheet. Such formulas are easy to identify because they contain the name of a spreadsheet in brackets. For example, the formula

+A1*[XYZ]B15

multiplies the value of cell A1 in the current spreadsheet by the value of B15 in a spreadsheet called XYZ.WQ1. You can also ferret out linking formulas using the Map View discussed earlier in this chapter.

There is nothing technically wrong with linking spreadsheets. It is a useful means of distributing and consolidating data across several spreadsheet files. For example, you might design an income statement spreadsheet that draws the data for individual revenue or expense items from separate, more detailed spreadsheets. However, you should know all the implications of linking spreadsheets before you attempt this. The subject is covered in Chapter 22.

You don't have to worry about accidentally linking spreadsheets when you copy (rather than move) data from one window to another. Even if you copy a formula that contains absolute references, Quattro Pro assumes that you want to refer to the specified cell on the current spreadsheet rather than on the spreadsheet from which you copied the formula. Nonetheless, you should always check formulas after copying them to a new window. It is extremely easy to make mistakes such as copying a formula to column A that refers to the cell to its left (in which case Quattro Pro adjusts the formula to refer to the last column on the spreadsheet).

Try opening an empty window and copying cells from the COMMISS.WQ1 spreadsheet into the new, blank spreadsheet.

1. Issue the / File I New command.

2. Move to A9 and issue the / Edit I Copy command.

3. When prompted for a source block, press (ALT-0) to display a list of open windows. Select the window that contains COMMISS.WQ1. Quattro Pro temporarily brings that spreadsheet to the foreground so that you can see the data you are working with. The directory path and file name of the COMMISS.WQ1 spreadsheet now appear on the input line as part of the default source block setting.

4. Press (ESC) to unanchor the cell pointer, move to A9 of the COMMISS spreadsheet, and type a period. Press (END-HOME) to expand the block to D19 and press (ENTER). Quattro Pro will redisplay the new, empty window.

5. When prompted for a destination, press (ENTER) to accept the default of A9. The columns are too narrow to display all the data, and the numbers are displayed in General format. Quattro Pro does not copy any of the global formats when you copy data from one window to another (although it does copy numeric formats and label alignment characters, just as it does when you copy data within a single window).

6. Issue the / Options I Formats I Global Width command, and enter a new column width of **15**.

7. Select the Numeric Format option from the Options I Formats menu and specify the Fixed format with two decimal places. Type **QQ** to return to Ready mode.

8. Save the spreadsheet under any name you like.

9. Issue the File I Close All command to close all the open windows. Because you have changed the size and position of windows 1, 2, and 3, Quattro Pro pauses before closing those windows and asks whether you want to lose your changes. Select the Yes option in each case.

You must copy the data to the same cells they occupied on COMMISS.WQ1, because the formulas in column D contain an absolute reference to cell B9. If you want to eliminate some of the blank rows at the top of the spreadsheet, you can use / Edit I Delete I Rows after copying the data.

This chapter introduced you to a wealth of new tools for manipulating the Quattro Pro environment. You will find the commands for locking titles and splitting a window into panes indispensable as soon as you start building spreadsheets that contain too much data to display in a single window. Map View and the removal of row and column borders are more specialized tools—rarely used but extremely helpful when they are.

12

CUSTOMIZING THE ENVIRONMENT

Default Settings
Creating Style Sheets
Menu Command Shortcuts

This chapter explains how to change Quattro Pro's default settings for individual spreadsheets, the entire work session, and future work sessions. It also covers two other techniques for customizing the environment: style sheets and menu command shortcuts.

DEFAULT SETTINGS

Quattro Pro has default settings for everything from the extension it assigns to spreadsheet files to the colors used on the help screens. You can modify these default settings using various / Options commands.

Although some of these commands are fairly esoteric, others are immediately applicable to your work.

Default settings can be divided into two groups:

- **Spreadsheet defaults** Established with selected / Options | Formats, / Options | Recalculation, / Options | Protection, and / Options | Colors | Conditional commands. These settings are stored in the spreadsheet file along with your data and placed in effect each time you retrieve that spreadsheet from disk. Spreadsheet defaults have no effect on future spreadsheets: as soon as you create a new spreadsheet, Quattro Pro reinstates the system defaults.

> **Note** The Quattro Pro documentation refers to spreadsheet defaults as global option settings.

- **Work session defaults** Established with any of the other Options menu commands or submenus—that is, through any of the first eight options on the Options menu. (The Options | Colors | Conditional settings are the one exception to this rule; they are specific to the current spreadsheet.) Work session defaults remain in effect throughout the current work session, unless you explicitly change them. They are not saved when you issue the / File | Save or / File | Save As command. You can, however, make them into permanent system defaults by issuing the / Options | Update command.

> **Note** The Quattro Pro documentation refers to the work session settings as system defaults. In this book, the term "system defaults" applies to the settings that are placed in effect when you start a Quattro Pro work session. This category includes work session settings that you have saved with the / Options | Update command, and which therefore affect future work sessions.

Telling Quattro Pro About Your Hardware

The / Options | Hardware menu contains only two options: Screen and Printers. The Screen option is discussed shortly. The / Options | Printer commands are discussed in Chapter 6. The other three items on the menu—Normal Memory, EMS, and Coprocessor—are for display only; they cannot be changed. The Normal Memory line indicates the amount of standard memory currently available. The EMS setting indicates the amount of currently available expanded memory (if any). The Coprocessor setting indicates the type of math coprocessor (if any) installed in your computer.

The Options | Hardware | Screen options allow you to fine-tune the settings for your screen display. In most cases Quattro Pro automatically detects the type of video display card you are using and loads a special driver file that tells Quattro Pro how to display data on your screen. If you are using an unusual video display card or more than one monitor, you may need to find-tune some of the settings yourself. The options on the Options | Hardware | Screen menu are as follows:

- **Screen Type** Lets you specify a second screen that you intend to use for displaying graphs. When you choose this option, Quattro Pro displays a menu of screen types; select the appropriate type.

- **Resolution** Lets you change the resolution used for displaying graphs. The default setting is the highest resolution available for your screen type. You may need to choose a lower resolution if you are using an external projection system to display graphs.

- **Aspect Ratio** Lets you change the way that Quattro Pro displays circles, so that the circle appears perfectly round when you draw pie charts. Use this option if your pie charts appear elongated. Quattro Pro displays a circle in the middle of the screen. Use the (UP ARROW) and (DOWN ARROW) keys to adjust the height of the circle until it appears round.

- **CGA Snow Suppression** Lets you alleviate problems with flickering that sometimes occur on CGA screens.

Customizing Quattro Pro's Colors

The / Options | Colors commands allow you to alter the colors used for menus, various sections of the spreadsheet, and the Help screens. They also include an option for defining *conditional colors*, which are used to highlight cells that fulfill particular conditions, such as falling below a particular numeric range. You can use the / Options | Colors commands with a color or monochrome monitor. With monochrome, your choices are limited to Normal, Bold, Inverse, Underlined, and Empty, but these options are enough to make substantial alterations in the spreadsheet's appearance.

With color monitors, your choices expand to dozens of color combinations. After you select an item to define, such as spreadsheet labels or menu explanations, Quattro Pro displays a box full of colors. Each row of this box represents a different background shade. The diamonds in the box represent various foreground shades. Select colors by moving the rotating cursor to the desired set of colors and pressing (ENTER).

The options for customizing menu, spreadsheet, help system, and File Manager colors are fairly self-explanatory.

USING COLORS TO EMPHASIZE DATA ON A SPREADSHEET

Quattro Pro offers several commands that allow you to distinguish or highlight particular entries on a spreadsheet. You can use the / Options | Colors | Spreadsheet | Labels command to define colors for labels. Similarly, you can use the / Options | Colors | Spreadsheet | Unprotected option to highlight those cells that are unprotected on a spreadsheet on which the protection feature has been enabled).

The Conditional Colors menu contains options that allow you to designate colors for cells that fulfill particular conditions. For example, you can define a color for cells that return a value of ERR, so those cells are more noticeable on the spreadsheet. You can also define a range of values that you consider "normal" (using the Smallest Normal Value and Greatest Normal Value options) and then specify different sets of colors for normal, below-normal, and above-normal values. You can define a Smallest Normal Value without defining a Greatest Normal Value and vice versa. For example, Figure 12-1 shows a spreadsheet after setting the Greatest Normal Value to 35000, leaving the Smallest Normal Value at the default setting of NA (Not Applicable) and changing the Above Normal Color setting to Bold.

Note ≡ Conditional color settings do not take effect until you select the On/Off option on the / Options | Colors Conditional menu and change the setting from Disable to Enable. This allows you to define conditional colors but then turn them off temporarily without losing your settings.

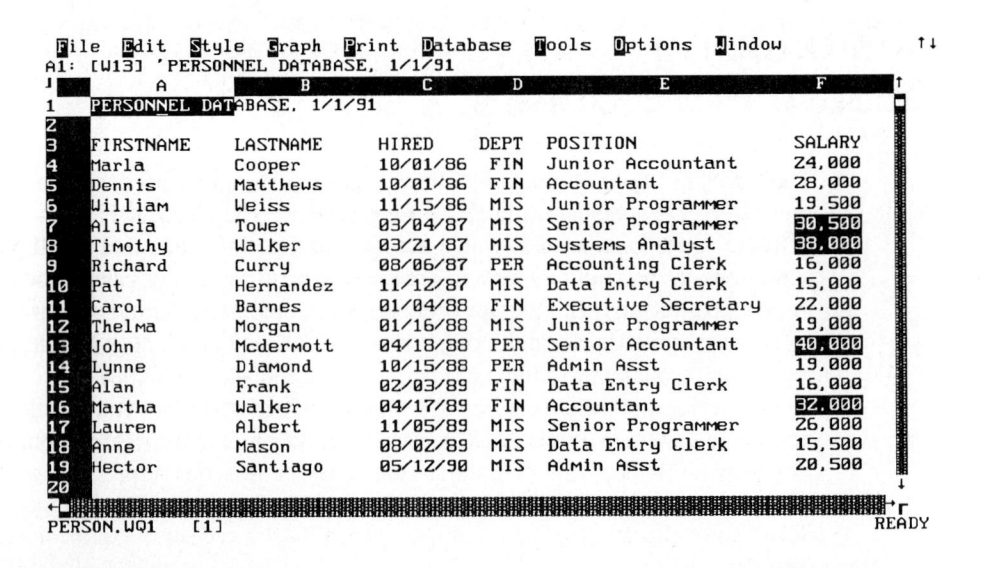

FIGURE 12-1. Using the Greatest Normal Value conditional setting

Conditional colors are specific to the spreadsheet on which they are defined. You cannot save them as system defaults.

REINSTATING DEFAULT COLORS Quattro Pro provides the / Options | Colors | Palettes command for returning all colors to their system default settings. When you issue this command, Quattro Pro displays a menu with the options Color, Monochrome, Black & White, and Quit. To return the colors to normal, select the option appropriate to your screen.

> **Note** Once you have saved a set of colors as system defaults by issuing the / Options | Update command, you can no longer reset them with one of the / Options | Colors | Palettes commands. Instead you need to reset the colors individually and then update the default settings again.

The International Settings

The / Options | International commands allow you to define special symbols or formats for displaying currency, punctuation, dates, and times.

CURRENCY The International Currency option determines the appearance of values displayed in Currency format. The initial default setting is a dollar sign displayed before each formatted value. To display currency types other than dollars, you can select the Currency option on the Options | International menu, press [ESC] or [BACKSPACE] to erase the current default symbol, and enter a new symbol. You can use any symbol(s) you like, including special ASCII characters. (You can enter special characters that do not appear on your keyboard, such as £, by holding down the [ALT] key while typing the ASCII code for the character on the numeric keypad. A list of ASCII codes appears in Appendix G of the *Quattro Pro User's Guide*.)

Once you have entered the new currency symbol, Quattro Pro asks whether this symbol is to be used as a prefix or suffix. Figure 12-2 shows a spreadsheet after the Currency setting has been set to a suffix of £. You can also use a string like "Deutsche Marks" as a currency symbol.

You can use only one currency symbol on any given spreadsheet. For example, you cannot display some values with dollar signs and others with pound signs.

PUNCTUATION The Punctuation setting determines the punctuation characters used to designate a decimal point in numbers; separate arguments in function statements and commands in macros; and separate hundreds from thousands, thousands from millions, and so on in numbers displayed with the , (comma) and Currency

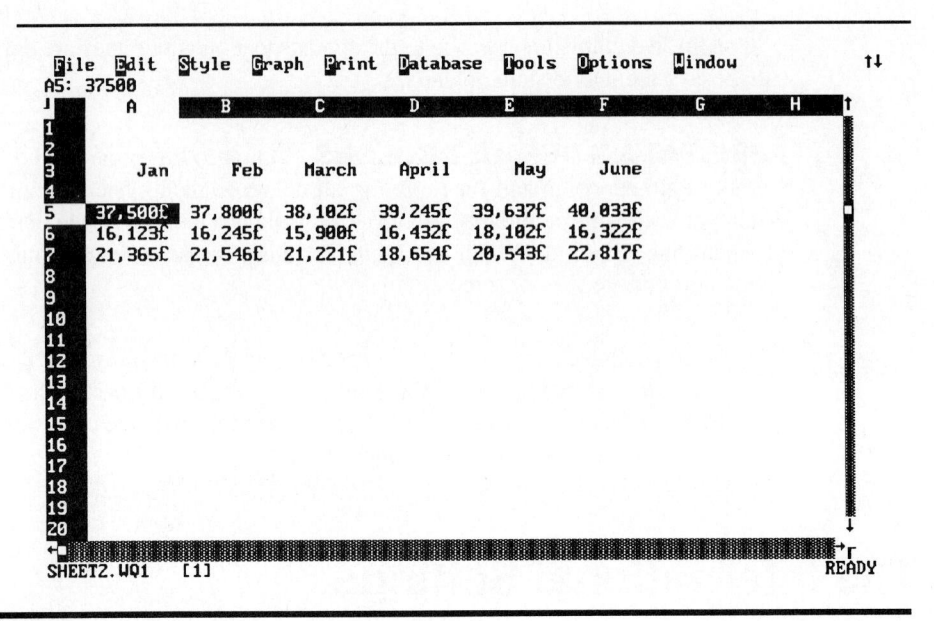

FIGURE 12-2. Changing the Currency setting

formats. When you select the Punctuation option on the International menu, a submenu with the following options appears:

A. 1,234.56 (a1,a2)
B. 1.234,56 (a1.a2)
C. 1,234.56 (a1;a2)
D. 1.234,56 (a1;a2)
E. 1 234.56 (a1,a2)
F. 1 234,56 (a1.a2)
G. 1 234.56 (a1;a2)
H. 1 234,56 (a1;a2)

The character separating a1 from a2 inside the brackets in each of these options indicates the punctuation mark that you can use to separate arguments in functions and macros. The A option, Quattro Pro's initial default, uses periods to mark decimal places and commas to separate thousands. It also uses commas to separate arguments in functions and macros. By choosing one of the other seven options, you can alter this default setting.

DATES AND TIMES As mentioned in Chapter 10, you also can modify the Long and Short International display formats for displaying dates and times. Note that all International Time formats use the 24-hour clock (two o'clock in the afternoon, for example, would be expressed as 14:00 in Short International format A option).

The following are alternative international date formats:

Format	Long Int'l	Example	Short Int'l	Example
A	MM/DD/YY	10/22/88	MM/DD	10/22
B	DD/MM/YY	22/10/88	DD/MM	22/10
C	DD.MM.YY	22.10.88	DD.MM	22.10
D	YY-MM-DD	88-10-22	MM-DD	10-22

The following are alternative international time formats:

Format	Long Int'l	Example	Short Int'l	Example
A	HH:MM:SS	09:43:27	HH:MM	09:43
B	HH.MM.SS	09.43.27	HH.MM	09.43
C	HH,MM,SS	09,43,27	HH,MM	09,43
D	HHhMMmSSs	09h43m27s	HHhMMm	09h43m

In Time Format option D, the lowercase letters are displayed as shown. The time 9:43:10 AM, for example, would be displayed as 09h43m10s in Long International format.

Changing the Display Mode

If you have a monochrome or CGA monitor, you have only one option—80 × 25—which is the initial system default. It means 80 characters per line and 25 lines per screen. Because 5 lines are occupied by the menu bar, input line, spreadsheet area borders, and the status line, 20 lines remain for data.

If you have a high-resolution display (EGA or above), the / Options I Display Mode menu will list a number of additional choices—such as EGA 80 × 43 and VGA 80 × 50. These options allow you to display more rows and columns than you could using the initial system default. The actual choices available depend on your display adapter.

If you have an EGA, VGA, or other high-resolution display, you will also find a Graphics Mode choice on the / Options I Display Mode menu. Several aspects of the Quattro Pro display appear different in Graphics mode:

- If you are using a mouse, Quattro Pro displays the mouse pointer as an arrow rather than as a block.

- If you insert a graph into your spreadsheet, you can see it in detail in the spreadsheet area itself.

- Quattro Pro displays some menus as *galleries* rather than conventional menus. This means that it displays a series of images that represent options in place of the usual option names.

Graphics mode also tends to be slower than Text mode, and you may occasionally have to wait a few seconds for Quattro Pro to refresh the screen image. You may prefer to use Text mode most of the time, but switch to Graphics mode when using embedded graphs.

Defining Startup Settings

The / Options | Startup commands direct Quattro Pro to perform certain operations every time you load the program. These Startup options include:

- **Directory** Defines the default data directory—that is, the directory in which Quattro Pro looks for and stores spreadsheet files unless another directory is specified. You can define a default data directory for the current work session using the / File | Directory command, but that setting (unlike the Options | Startup | Directory setting) is not saved when you issue the / Options | Update command.

- **Autoload File** Designates a spreadsheet file to be loaded automatically whenever you load Quattro Pro.

- **Startup Macro** Specifies a certain macro to be executed automatically every time you retrieve a spreadsheet.

- **Extension** Designates default extensions for spreadsheet files. If you are using the regular Quattro Pro menus, the initial default is WQ1, which you may want to change if you are planning to exchange spreadsheets regularly with other programs.

- **Beep** Sounds the beep when you commit an error.

- **Menu Tree** Displays a menu of options for using the Lotus 123-compatible menu tree or the old Quattro-style menu tree.

Changing the Mouse Palette

If you are using a mouse, the / Options | Mouse Palette command allows you to customize the palette of buttons displayed at the right edge of your screen.

When you issue the / Options | Mouse Palette command, Quattro Pro displays a menu with options for each of the seven buttons. As soon as you select one, it displays a submenu with the options Text, Macro, and Quit.

Use the Text option to define the descriptive text you want displayed on the mouse palette itself. You are limited to three characters, including graphics characters.

To define the function of a button, select Macro and enter a macro command. If you want clicking on a button to be equivalent to pressing a particular key on the keyboard, you must enter the appropriate macro keyboard command. For example, if you want the fifth mouse button to function like the (TAB) key, you select the Text option, enter (TAB), select the Macro option, and then enter the macro keyboard command {TAB}. Macro commands are beyond the scope of this book, but you can research the subject on your own using the Quattro Pro *Functions and Macros* manual. You can also use (SHIFT-F3) (Macros) for a menu of macro command categories and then select the ones you are interested in. Press (F1) (Help) with one of these menus on the screen to display more detailed information.

The "Other" Default Settings

The Options | Others menu contains five options that don't fit into any of the other categories:

- **Undo** Lets you enable or disable Quattro Pro's Undo feature. If Undo is enabled, you can use the / Edit | Undo command or its shortcut (ALT-F5) to undo the effects of many commands.

- **Macro** Lets you specify which sections of the screen you don't want redrawn during macro execution (the less redrawing the faster the macro will execute). Your choices are Panel (menus), Window (including the status line and input line), Both, or None.

- **Expanded Memory** Determines what Quattro Pro stores in expanded memory (if your computer has such memory installed). Your choices are Both, Spreadsheet Data, Format, and None. While using expanded memory (EMS) allows you to work with very large spreadsheets, it can also slow down Quattro Pro's performance. If you generally work with small spreadsheets, tell Quattro Pro to store only formatting codes (Format) or nothing at all (None) in EMS. If you are working with a large spreadsheet and are running out of memory, direct Quattro Pro to store both spreadsheet data and formatting codes in EMS (Both).

- **Clock** Allows you to display the date and time on the status line. When you issue the / Options | Other | Clock command, Quattro Pro displays a menu with three choices. Standard, the default setting, displays the date and time in DD-MMM-YY and HH:MM AM/PM format. Choose International to display the date and time in the current Long International formats. Use the None option (the initial system default) to eliminate the date and time display.

- **Paradox** Allows you to specify several network options if you plan to transfer files between Quattro Pro and Paradox—a database management program distributed by Borland International. When you issue the / Options | Other | Paradox command, Quattro Pro displays a menu with the choices Network Type, Directory, and Retries. Use the Network Type option to specify the type of local area network you are using. Use the Directory option to tell Quattro Pro where to look for the PARADOX.NET file. Use the Retries option to specify the number of seconds that Quattro Pro should wait before making another attempt to open a locked file.

Recalculation Settings

Unlike many other spreadsheet programs, Quattro Pro recalculates only formulas affected by new changes on the spreadsheet, so recalculation time is minimized. The / Options | Recalculation commands let you control the way that spreadsheet formulas are recalculated. When you select this option, Quattro Pro displays a menu with options for Mode, Order, and Iterations.

RECALCULATION MODE If you select Mode, Quattro Pro displays a menu with three choices: Automatic, Manual, and Background. The initial setting is Background, which means that Quattro Pro recalculates formulas between key-strokes, rather than forcing you to wait until recalculation is complete. The Automatic setting directs Quattro Pro to recalculate simultaneously all formulas affected by the most recent change in data, forcing you to wait until the recalculation is complete. The Manual setting directs Quattro Pro to postpone spreadsheet recalculation until you press F9, the Recalculation key. Quattro Pro still recalculates individual formulas as you enter or edit them, but holds off recalculating other formulas that refer to the newly changed cell. Whenever some of the spreadsheet's formulas need recalcuation, a CALC status indicator is displayed at the bottom of the screen.

RECALCULATION ORDER   When you issue the /Options | Recalculation | Order command, Quattro Pro displays a menu with the options Natural, Row-wise, and Column-wise. The Natural setting evaluates every cell in a spreadsheet that is referenced in a formula before calculating the formula itself. In other words, the first formula in any particular chain of formulas is calculated first, and the resulting value is then passed on to all dependent formulas. These dependents are then evaluated, the results are passed on to subsequent dependents, and so on. As a result, each formula is evaluated using current values, ensuring the accuracy of the spreadsheet. Row-wise and Column-wise orders—recalculation orders used in earlier spreadsheet programs—are included in Quattro Pro to allow you to replicate the sometimes-less-than-accurate results obtained by using these methods in other programs. They are also occasionally used in situations involving circular formulas that you want to be recalculated several times in a particular order.

THE NUMBER OF ITERATIONS   Some mathematical equations cannot be solved by entering a simple formula; they must be entered as one or more circular formulas that must be repeatedly recalculated with different values until the result is acceptably accurate. The Iterations option on the Options | Recalculation menu allows you to perform multiple evaluations of such circular formulas. When you issue the command, Quattro Pro prompts for a number of iterations. The number you enter determines how many times Quattro Pro recalculates circular formulas every time it recalculates the spreadsheet. You can specify up to 255 iterations.

THE CIRCULAR CELL INDICATOR   The Options | Recalculation menu also contains one display-only item: Circular Cell. If your spreadsheet currently contains one or more formulas with circular references, Quattro Pro displays the address of one of those cells to the right of the words "Circular Cell."

Updating the System Defaults

The /Options | Update command transforms all the current default settings into system defaults, which are automatically placed in effect every time you enter Quattro Pro. By changing the system defaults you can customize Quattro Pro to your own tastes. For example, if you find that you like a particular set of colors, you can define them as the colors that you start with in every work session. (You can still override these defaults with an /Options | Colors command.)

When you issue the /Options | Update command, every work session default setting currently in effect is saved as a system default. This includes all settings established through each of the first eight options on the Options menu (the options that appear above Update), except the Options | Colors | Conditional settings. If you have issued more than one / Options command in the current work session, you should verify them before you issue the / Options | Update command. You can do this by moving to all the / Options submenus that contain settings you may have changed.

Unlike the equivalent commands in Quattro (Quattro Pro's predecessor) and Lotus 1-2-3, / Options | Update only saves defaults that apply to the program environment as a whole. It does not save print and graph settings, which you save using the / Print | Layout | Update and / Graph | Customize Series | Update command, respectively.

CREATING STYLE SHEETS

The / Options | Update command does not save any of the settings on the / Options | Formats menu. This means that every time you create a new spreadsheet, the default numeric format is General, the default label alignment is Left, and the global column width is 9. You can change these settings with / Options | Formats commands, but you cannot save those new settings as system defaults. You also cannot define defaults for the options on the / Style | Fonts menu. Any fonts you define with the / Style | Fonts | Edit Fonts command are specific to the spreadsheet you are working on at the time. The minute you create a new spreadsheet, the selection of fonts on the Fonts menu reverts to the system defaults.

Although Quattro Pro does not provide a command for saving spreadsheet defaults, there is a way to avoid redefining those settings on every spreadsheet. If you have a particular set of style attributes that you use on many of your spreadsheets, you may want to create a style sheet—a blank spreadsheet with a standard set of default formats and fonts. You can then use this as the starting point for a new spreadsheet—retrieve the style sheet file, save it under another name, and then enter your data.

If you tend to use different sets of style attributes for different types of spreadsheets, you may want to create several specialized style sheets with names that indicate their purposes.

MENU COMMAND SHORTCUTS

As you know, there are preassigned shortcuts for several of the most commonly used Quattro Pro commands (for example, CTRL-W for the / Style | Column Width command). Table 12-1 lists all the preassigned shortcuts. As you work with Quattro Pro regularly, you may find that you repeatedly use commands for which there are no preassigned shortcuts. In such cases, you may want to define your own shortcuts,

Shortcut	Command
CTRL-A	/ Style I Alignment
CTRL-C	/ Edit I Copy
CTRL-D *	Date prefix
CTRL-E	/ Edit I Erase Block
CTRL-F	/ Style I Numeric Format
CTRL-G	/ Graph I Fast Graph
CTRL-I	/ Edit I Insert
CTRL-M	/ Edit I Move
CTRL-N	/ Edit I Search & Replace I Next
CTRL-P	/ Edit I Search & Replace I Previous
CTRL-R	/ Window I Move/Size
CTRL-S	/ File I Save
CTRL-T	/ Window I Tile
CTRL-W	/ Style I Column Width
CTRL-X	/ File I Exit

* Not reassignable

TABLE 12-1. Preassigned Menu Command Shortcuts

abbreviating the keystrokes needed to issue particular commands. You can also change some of the preassigned shortcuts, in case you want to assign one of those key combinations to a different menu command.

To create a shortcut, follow these steps:

1. Highlight the menu option containing the command you want to abbreviate.

2. Hold down CTRL and press ENTER to initiate creation of the shortcut. Quattro Pro displays the message "Hold down the Ctrl key and press any letter, or <DEL>" on the status line at the bottom of the screen.

3. When prompted for a CTRL key, hold down CTRL and press any letter on the keyboard except D (CTRL-D is reserved for entering dates). This combination of CTRL and a second key becomes the key combination that you use to execute the command. If you need to memorize the combinations, you should choose a key that will be easy to associate with the command.

Quattro Pro allows you to assign shortcuts to any piece of a command. For example, you can assign shortcuts to the / **Style** command, the / **Style** | **Block Widths** command, or the / **Style** | **Block Widths** | **Auto Width** command. In each case, using the shortcut has exactly the same effect as highlighting the associated menu option and pressing (ENTER).

Shortcuts are saved the moment you create them. The next time you reload Quattro Pro, the shortcuts in effect when you left the program remain in effect.

This chapter has introduced a wealth of commands for altering the Quattro Pro environment. Though you may use some of these commands only rarely, it is worth becoming familiar with all the available options. As you work with Quattro Pro, you undoubtedly will develop your own preferences in formatting, colors, shortcuts, and so on. As you do you can use the tools introduced in this chapter to fit Quattro Pro to your own informational needs, work style, and aesthetic.

13

CREATING GRAPHS

Choosing a Graph Type
Printing Graphs
Graph Slide Shows
Inserting Graphs in a Spreadsheet

Creating graphs in Quattro Pro is simple. You begin by choosing a graph type, defining the blocks of spreadsheet data (referred to as *series* in the graph commands) that you want to plot, and then selecting the View option from the Graph menu or pressing F10 (Graph). You then modify, embellish, and customize the graph until you achieve the effect you want.

This chapter introduces you to the types of graphs you can create with Quattro Pro and covers the basics of defining and printing graphs. Chapter 14 covers techniques for improving and customizing graphs.

CHOOSING A GRAPH TYPE

Quattro Pro offers 14 types of graphs: line graphs, area graphs, pie graphs, column graphs, XY graphs, high-low graphs, text graphs, three types of bar graphs (regular, rotated, and stacked), and four types of graphs that use three-dimensional perspective. The following sections describe these graphs and the strong points of each.

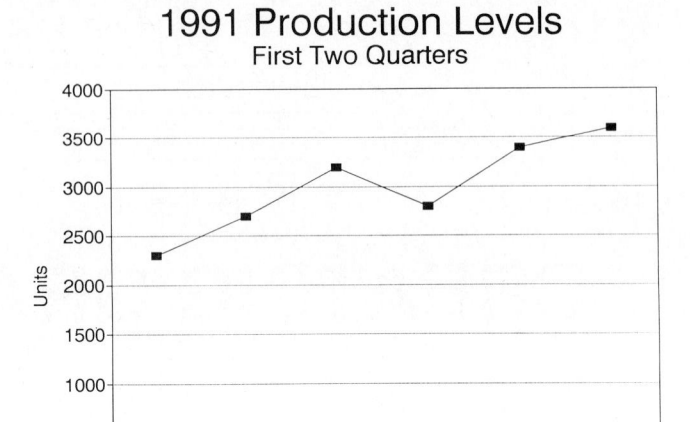

FIGURE 13-1. A line graph

Line Graphs

Line graphs are probably the most commonly used type of graph for business applications. Lines, symbols, or a combination of lines and symbols map anywhere from one to six series of values at a time. If you plot more than one series of values, each series is represented by its own line. Line graphs are best suited to representing trends over time because they make it easy to see increases and decreases in a single series of values. The line graph in Figure 13-1 shows the rise and fall of a company's well production level over a six-month period.

Bar Graphs

Bar graphs are most appropriate for comparing values at one (or more) specific points in time—for example, the sales of five different products in a particular year or the expenses incurred in three different divisions. Quattro Pro offers three types of bar graphs, all of which are similar in form, construction, and capabilities. Although there are some variations in usage—stacked bars are particularly well suited to representing

Divisional Travel Expenses

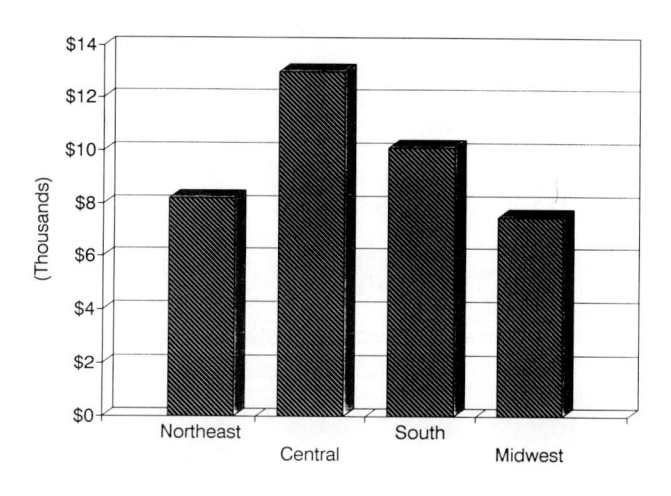

FIGURE 13-2. A bar graph

multiple series of values, and rotated bars are good for representing progress toward a goal—the differences between the bar graph types are primarily aesthetic.

REGULAR BAR GRAPHS   Regular bar graphs are appropriate for comparing the values in one or more series. For example, Figure 13-2 shows a graph of the travel expenses in four divisions. Each value in the series (in this case, each division) is represented by a single vertical bar. When you create a bar graph that plots more than one series of values, Quattro Pro displays the bars for the different series side by side and assigns each series a unique color or *fill pattern,* which is the pattern used to distinguish bars or other segments of a graph when the graph is displayed or printed in black and white.

ROTATED BAR GRAPHS   Rotated bar graphs are similar to regular bar graphs, except the bars extend from the left of the screen or paper rather than the bottom. These graphs can be particularly effective for giving your graphs a more goal-oriented, forward-moving feel. They are often used for profit-and-loss charts, particularly when comparing actual to budgeted profits.

The graph in Figure 13-3 compares year-to-date (Y-T-D) actual sales levels to the targeted sales for four different products. Note that the left-to-right direction of the bars is particularly appropriate for charting progress toward a goal.

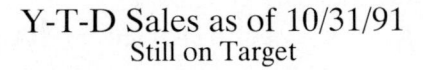

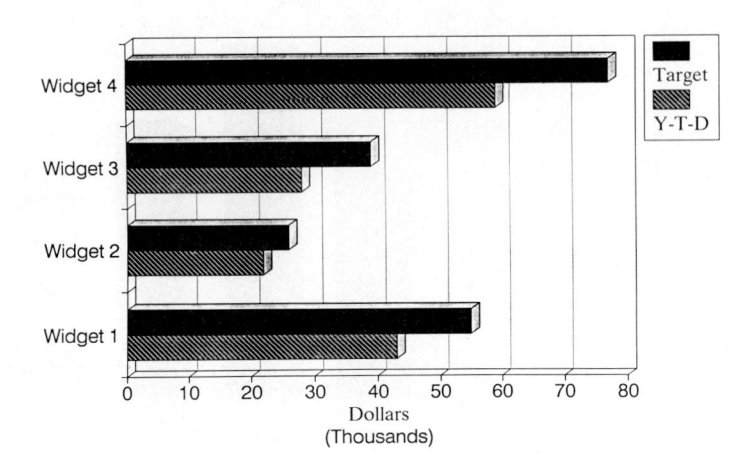

FIGURE 13-3. A rotated bar graph

STACKED BAR GRAPHS Stacked bar graphs use segmented vertical bars to represent multiple series of values, with each segment of the bars representing one value from each series. For example, if you create a stacked bar graph that represents three series, each containing five values, the resulting graph contains five bars of three segments each. The first bar contains segments representing the first value in each of the three series; the second bar contains segments representing the second value in each of the three series, and so on. The height of the bar represents the sum of the values.

The graph in Figure 13-4 shows the sales of four products over a four-year period. Each bar represents the sales for one year. Each segment of each bar represents sales of a particular product within that year. For example, the bottom segment of the first bar represents Widget 1 sales in 1988, the second segment in that bar represents 1988 sales of Widget 2, and so on.

This type of graph gives the reader a sense of each product's relative contribution to the year's total sales while presenting a visual comparison between the total sales levels for each of the four years. It is not particularly good for comparing values within a particular series—determining which was the best year for Widget 3 sales, for example.

Widget Sales Comparison
1988 - 1991

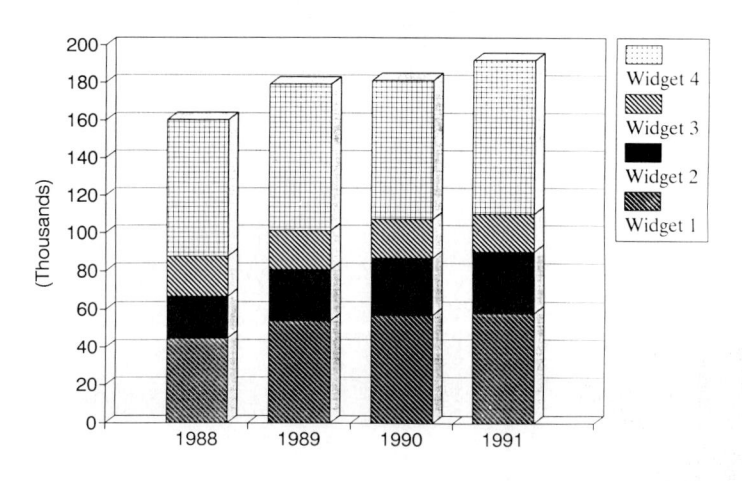

FIGURE 13-4. A stacked bar graph

Area Graphs

Area graphs share characteristics with both line graphs and stacked bar graphs, using both lines and fill patterns to represent multiple series of values. Each series of values in the graph is illustrated by an area filled with a distinctive fill pattern. These areas are layered one on top of another, so the top edge of each area represents the cumulative total of the value series below. Like stacked bar graphs, area graphs are an effective means of showing how various components affect the whole over time. Like line graphs (of the cumulative totals rather than the individual series), they give you a feel for how the totals change over time.

Figure 13-5 shows an area graph that illustrates exactly the same data as that graphed in Figure 13-4—the sales of four products over a four-year period. Note that the graph is most useful for looking at the relative size of the sales level for each product and the rise and fall of the total product sales. It makes a poor and potentially misleading illustration of the increases in sales level of the individual products.

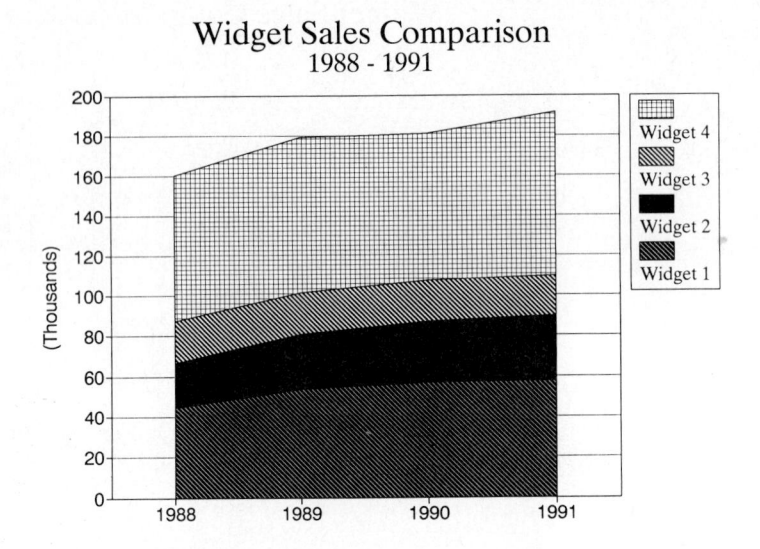

FIGURE 13-5. An area graph

Pie Graphs

Pie graphs use a circle, or pie, to represent a single series of values. Each slice of the pie symbolizes an individual value within the series and is sized according to the percentage it represents out of the total of all values in the series.

Pie graphs are useful for showing the size of different components in relation to the whole. For example, you might use a pie chart to show the portion of total sales represented by each of five product lines or the percentage of total travel expenses incurred by each of four departments. Figure 13-6 shows a graph that illustrates the relative contribution of each of five different financial sources to total fundraising revenues.

Column Graphs

Column graphs are essentially rectangular pie charts. Like pie graphs, they plot a single series of values, representing each value in the series as a percentage of the

Fundraising Revenues

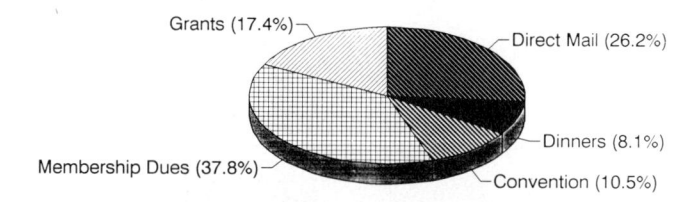

Grants (17.4%)
Direct Mail (26.2%)
Dinners (8.1%)
Convention (10.5%)
Membership Dues (37.8%)

FIGURE 13-6. A pie graph

whole. The only difference between a column graph and a pie graph is that a column graph represents the series values as a vertical column composed of multiple segments rather than as a pie with multiple slices. This layout often affords more room for labeling the individual values in the series. Figure 13-7 shows a column graph that plots the same values as those plotted in the pie graph in Figure 13-6.

XY Graphs

XY graphs are used to show the relationship between two sets of values. They are most useful for showing the effect of one set of values (the *independent variable*) on a second set of values (the *dependent variable*). You can use an XY graph to map the effect of advertising investments or product pricing on sales volume, the impact of income level on the incidence of stress-related illness, or the effect of class size on student test scores. The graph shown in Figure 13-8 traces the correlation between years of post-high-school education and salary among ABC Group employees.

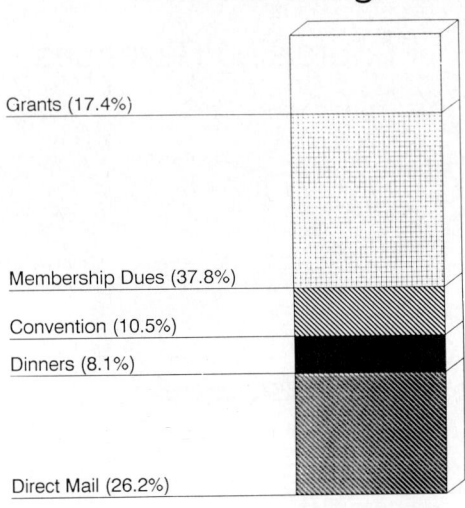

FIGURE 13-7. A column graph

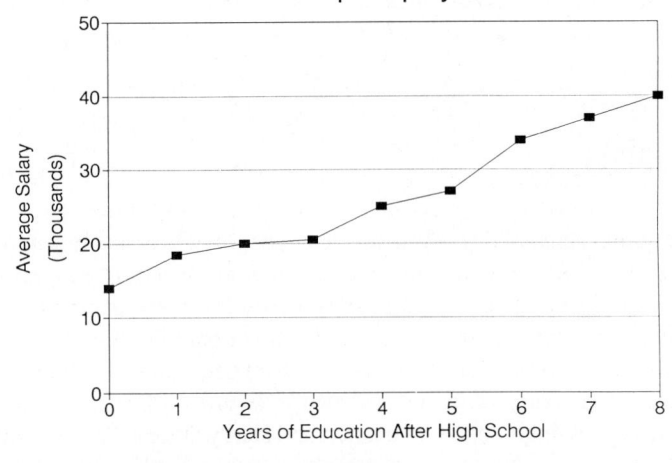

FIGURE 13-8. An XY graph

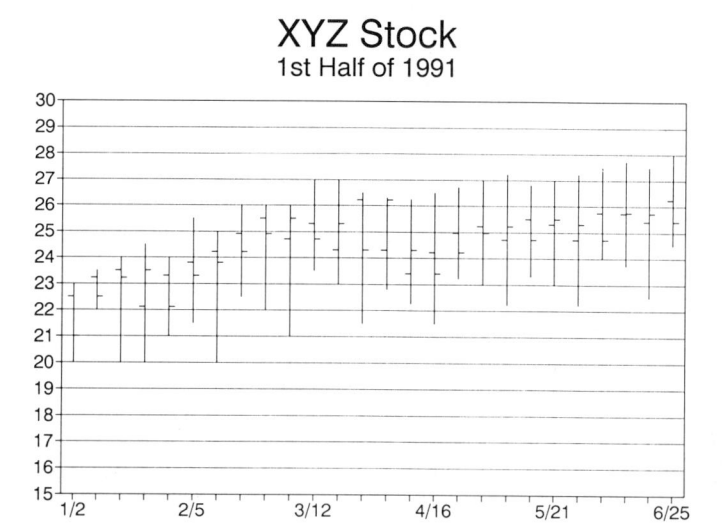

FIGURE 13-9. A high-low graph

High-Low (Open-Close) Graphs

High-low graphs are generally used to plot the daily rise and fall of stock prices, as shown in Figure 13-9. When creating a high-low graph, you define at least two series of values: the highest price each stock reached during the day and the lowest price. The pair of values for each stock on each day is represented by a vertical line. The top of the line represents the highest price, the bottom represents the lowest.

You can also define two additional series that represent the stocks' opening and closing prices. These are represented as tick marks extending from the vertical bars. Lines protruding to the left indicate the opening price (the third series value) and lines protruding right indicate the closing price (the fourth series value).

You can define a fifth and sixth series of values for a high-low graph to represent any additional information you like, such as the daily average price. By default, these last two series are represented as lines with markers. You can eliminate either the lines or markers using the / Graph I Customize Series I Markers and Lines command (discussed in Chapter 14). You can also display these series as bars using the / Graph I Customize Series I Override Type command (also discussed in Chapter 14).

Although high-low graphs are generally used to represent stock prices, they can be used to plot any set of information involving a series of high and low values. If you are running a retail business, you might use high-low graphs to plot retail and wholesale prices or units ordered and units shipped. A scientist might plot high and low temperatures or high and low pollen counts.

Text Graphs

Strictly speaking, text graphs are not graphs at all because they do not involve plotting any data. They are pictures, often containing a large amount of text, that are created using Quattro Pro's Annotator feature. Typical applications include flow charts and organization charts, such as the one shown in Figure 13-10. You might also create text charts to serve as introductions or explanations to graph slide shows.

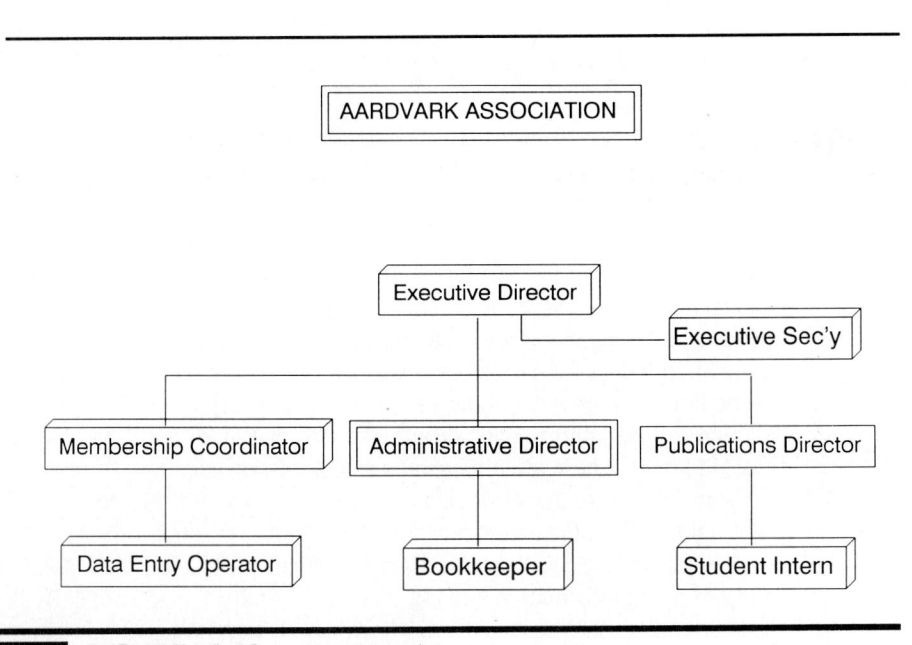

FIGURE 13-10. A text graph

Three-Dimensional Graph Types

Quattro Pro 2 added new "three- dimensional" graph types. Under some circumstances, these are handy for plotting multiple data series. In a 3-D graph, each data series is plotted in front of the previous one. If each series covers a distinct range of values, three-dimensional perspective can make the presentation more dramatic. On the other hand, if all your data series cover approximately the same value range, a 3-D presentation might be harder to understand than a standard 2-D presentation.

The four 3-D graph types are Bar, Ribbon, Step, and Area. To choose one of these types, first select the 3-D Graphs option on the Graph Type menu. Then choose Bar, Ribbon, Step, or Area on the menu that follows.

For more information about 3-D Graphs, as well as examples of how to use them, see the *Quattro Pro User's Guide*.

The Graphing Process

The basic steps involved in creating a graph in Quattro Pro are listed here. The order of these steps is not written in stone (steps 2 and 3 can be reversed, for example, and you can define the graph type at any point prior to viewing), and not every graph requires every step in the process. Nonetheless, this is the basic sequence you should follow and the steps you should at least consider along the way.

1. **Pick the graph type.** Use the Graph Type option on the Graph menu to choose the type most appropriate for conveying the information.

2. **Select the Series option on the Graph menu.** You then define the series of values to be plotted. Because Quattro Pro graphs are based on values stored in the cells of the current spreadsheet, you need to designate sets of adjacent cells on the spreadsheet as series to be plotted.

    Values defined as a graph series must be located in a single block of cells on the spreadsheet. This rule may require that you create a graph section on your spreadsheet, in which you can enter adjacent references to nonadjacent cells located elsewhere on the spreadsheet. For example, if you want to plot the values in cells A10, C10, and D11, you must enter the formulas **+A10**, **+C10**, and **+D11** in three adjacent cells in a separate section of the spreadsheet and then specify those three new values as the series to be plotted.

If you are plotting more than one series of values, and the values for each series are stored in adjacent columns or adjacent rows, you can use the / **Graph** | **Series** | **Group** command to specify several series simultaneously. This command is described shortly.

If you define a series that includes labels or blank cells, Quattro Pro ignores them when plotting the graph.

3. **Define labels for the X-axis**. Use the X-Axis Series option on the **Graph** | **Series** menu. The block of cells that you define as the X- axis series is generally used as a set of labels identifying the different values that are represented on the graph.

The block of values that you specify as the X-axis series can actually contain either values or labels, although Quattro Pro always treats them simply as text unless you are plotting an XY graph. If the X-axis values that you define for an XY graph contain labels or blank cells, Quattro Pro ignores them, just as it does when plotting series values.

4. **View the graph**. The Graph menu contains a View option that allows you to display the currently defined graph on screen. Once you have defined a graph, you can also view it while in either Ready or Menu mode by pressing (F10), Quattro Pro's Graph key. After viewing the graph, you can return to the spreadsheet display by pressing any key except the slash (/), which is used to activate Quattro Pro's Annotator feature.

Once you have defined the essential settings, you should look at your graph (assuming you have a graphics board that allows you to view graphs on screen) to make sure you are getting the results you intended before you add enhancements. In some cases it is obvious that the graph type is not appropriate for the data you are trying to illuminate—either because it does little to dramatize or clarify the information or because it simply looks bad. By viewing the graph early in the design process, you can switch gears before investing too much time in the wrong type of image. You should also view the graph after each of the next three steps to make sure that you are getting the desired results.

5. **Add explanatory text**. Almost all graphs can benefit from explanatory text, including a one or two-line title at the top of the graph and, in some cases, titles for the X-axis and Y-axis. Whenever you plot more than one series of values, you should also add a legend to the graph to identify the symbols, colors, or fill patterns used to represent each series. The / **Graph** | **Text** option contains options for each of these items of text, plus an option for changing the font used for each item.

6. **Customize the graph**. Quattro Pro has many options for refining the graph display, including commands for changing colors, fill patterns, and marker symbols; for mixing and matching graph types; for scaling the axes; and for adding grids and borders to the graph as a whole. These options are covered in Chapter 14.

7. **Annotate the graph.** Quattro Pro has a special feature, known as the Annotator, that allows you to add boxes filled with text, arrows, and a variety of geometric shapes to your graph. The Annotator is covered in Chapter 15.

8. **Print the graph.** The purpose of creating graphs is usually to present information to an audience, so you will almost always want to generate a printed copy of your product. The details of printing are discussed later in this chapter.

9. **Save the graph.** If you intend to create only one graph on a particular spreadsheet, saving the graph is simply a matter of saving the spreadsheet as a whole with the / File | Save or / File | Save As command. To save more than one graph on a spreadsheet, you must assign graph names, as described in the "Naming and Restoring Graphs" section.

Caution If you save your spreadsheet with an extension of .WKQ or .WK1, some characteristics of your graph may be lost. When you use these extensions, Quattro Pro translates your file into formats used by Quattro 1 and 1-2-3 Release 2.01, respectively. Neither of these programs supports the advanced graphics features offered by Quattro Pro.

Whenever you establish graph settings—for graph type, series values, titles, X-axis values, and so on—they remain in effect throughout the current work session unless you change them. If you alter the spreadsheet's data, the settings remain intact; if you change one setting, such as the graph type, the others remain unchanged. This saves you numerous keystrokes if you create several graphs with similar characteristics. It also allows you to experiment with different graph types without redefining all the other settings.

Adding Text to Your Graph

You can add several types of text to a graph. As described in the following sections, you can use the / Graph | Text command to display titles at the top of the graph, a description of the values on the X-axis and Y-axis, and a legend identifying the different series of values. You can also label individual points on the graph using the / Graph | Customize Series | Interior Labels command described in Chapter 14. You also can add text anywhere you like on the graph—with or without a surrounding box—using Quattro Pro's Annotator feature.

TITLES You can add three types of titles to Quattro Pro graphs: a main title to be displayed at the top of the graph, a title for the Y-axis, and a title for the X-axis. The main title generally explains the purpose or main point of the graph. Sometimes this title is objective, describing the content of the graph. In many cases, however, the title is more subjective, telling the reader not only what the graph contains but also placing the data in context.

Each graph title can be up to 39 characters long, and you can enter the text by simply typing it or by referencing a cell on the spreadsheet that contains the desired text. If you choose the latter option, you must precede the cell reference with a backslash, to let Quattro Pro know that you are entering a cell reference rather than text for a title. For example, to use the characters in cell B12 of your current spreadsheet as a graph title, you would select the appropriate title option and enter **\B12**. If you use cell references for graph text, the graph text is updated automatically if you change the referenced cell on the spreadsheet.

Caution Quattro Pro does not update cell references used to display graph text if you use the / Edit | Move, / Edit | Insert | Row, / Edit | Insert | Column, / Edit | Delete | Row, or / Edit | Delete | Column commands to relocate the referenced cell. If you issue a command that causes the text to move on the spreadsheet, you must remember to change the reference yourself.

You can include bullets in all titles except Y-axis titles. Use the \ bullet # \ syntax introduced in Chapter 5. To change the size, typeface, color, or style (underlined, bold, italic, or normal) of a title, use the Font option on the Graph | Text menu and select the appropriate option. This option works exactly like the / Style | Fonts | Edit Fonts command introduced in Chapter 5.

LEGENDS Whenever you plot more than one series of values, you should add a legend to the graph to identify the colors, markers, or fill patterns that are used to represent each series. The Graph | Customize | Legends menu contains options for the first through the sixth series. To add labels to a graph legend, you select the option for the series you want to label and then type in the text that you want displayed. The label can be up to 10 characters long. You can also refer to labels on your spreadsheet by entering a backslash followed by a cell address. You can change the typeface, size, color, or style of the characters used in a legend with the / Graph | Text | Font | Legends command.

The Position option on the Graph | Text | Legends menu lets you specify where you want the legend to appear on the screen, if anywhere. The default setting is Bottom. You can change it to Right to display the legend at the right edge of the screen. Choose the None option to hide the legend temporarily. This option does not actually reset any of the legend series settings. It simply directs Quattro Pro not to display the legend on screen. If you later change the Position setting to Bottom or Right, the legend immediately reappears.

Hands-On Practice

Begin by entering sample data that can be used as the basis for several different types of graphs.

1. If you have anything other than a blank spreadsheet currently on your screen, issue the / File | Erase command. (Save your spreadsheet first, if appropriate.)
2. Enter the following data:

In Cell	Enter
A1	**Five-Year Sales Projection**
A4	**Product 1**
A5	**Product 2**
A6	**Product 3**
A7	**Product 4**
B3	**"1991**
B4	**10000**
B5	**8500**
B6	**13000**
B7	**18000**
C3	**"1992**
C4	**12500**
C5	**9000**
C6	**12000**
C7	**20000**
D3	**"1993**
D4	**14500**
D5	**13000**
D6	**12500**
D7	**23000**
E3	**"1994**
E4	**16000**
E5	**15500**
E6	**12500**

E7	22000
F3	"1995
F4	17500
F5	15500
F6	14000
F7	25000

3. Move to G9 and enter the formula **@SUM(B4..F7)**. The result of this formula should be 304000.

4. Save your work and assign the name GRAPH to the current spreadsheet.

You now have a set of data appropriate for experimenting with most of Quattro Pro's graph types. Start by creating a simple line graph.

1. Type **/G** to display the Graph menu.

2. Select the Graph Type option on this menu and then the Line option on the Graph Type submenu to specify a line graph. (If you are using Graphics display mode, the graph types are displayed as a gallery, as shown in Figure 13-11, rather than as a menu.)

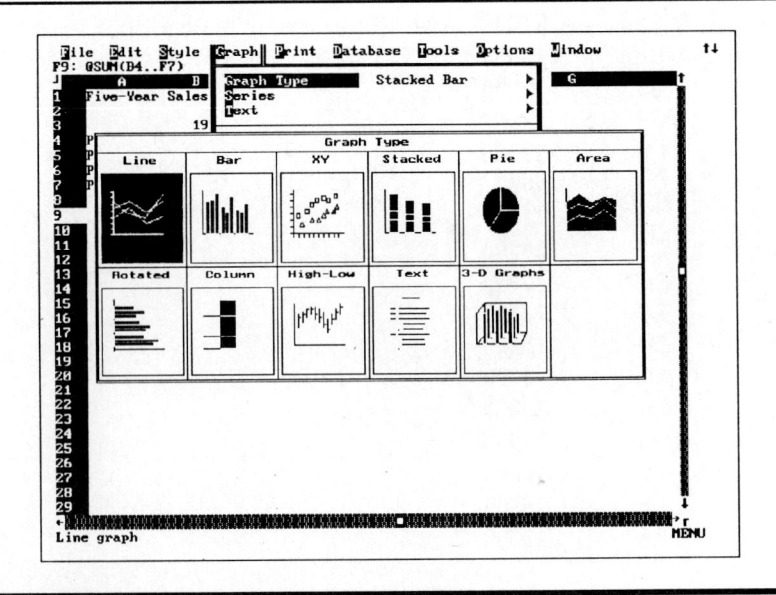

FIGURE 13-11. The gallery of graph types

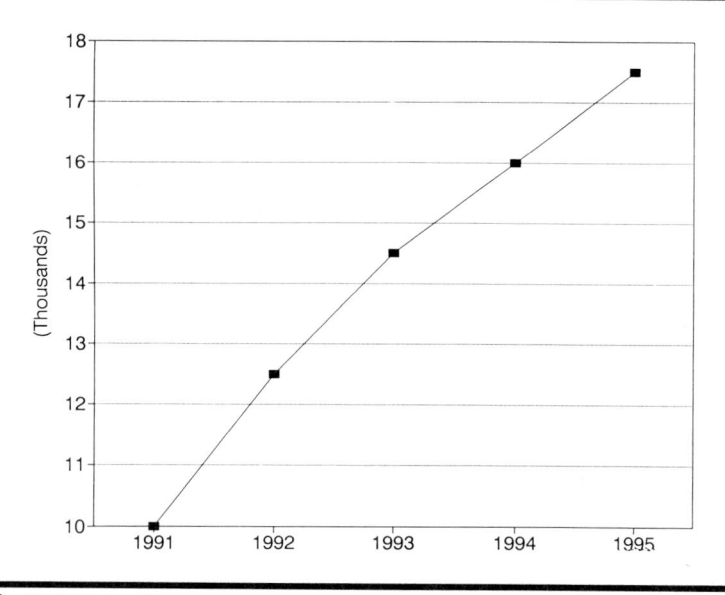

FIGURE 13-12. A line graph of Product 1 sales

3. Select the Series option and then, on the Series menu, select the 1st Series option. Specify B4..F4 (the sales figures for Product 1) as the block to be used for the 1st Series values.

4. Select the X-Axis Series option on the **Graph | Series** menu and specify the block B3..F3 (the numbers 1991 through 1995) as labels to be displayed along the X-axis. Select Quit to return to the Graph menu.

5. Select the View option to see the results: a line graph mapping the progression of Product 1's sales level over the five-year period. The graph should resemble Figure 13-12.

    Quattro Pro automatically scales the Y-axis to accommodate the lowest and highest values in the series and inserts a title at the left edge of the graph to indicate that the numbers are expressed in thousands. You will learn to manually scale axes—that is, changing the starting point, ending point, and the increment—in Chapter 14.

6. Now add a title to the graph. Press (ESC) to return to the spreadsheet display, and select the Text option on the Graph menu. Then select the 1st Line option on the Titles menu and enter \A1 to designate the contents of cell A1 as the title to be displayed on the first line of the graph.

7. Select the 2nd Line option and enter \A4 to designate the contents of cell A4 as the title to be displayed on the second line of the graph.

8. Press (F10) (Graph) to view the results. It may take Quattro Pro a moment to build the necessary text fonts.

9. Press (ESC) twice to return to the Graph menu. Now that you have defined all the elements of the graph, try changing the graph type to see how the same data looks in a different form.

10. Select Graph Type and change the graph type to Bar.

11. Select View to view the results.

Shortcuts for Creating Graphs

Several other sets of values in the current spreadsheet can be graphed; however, rather than specifying them individually, you can save time by designating several graph series with a single command.

FAST GRAPHS   If your data is laid out in the right form, you can use the / Graph | Fast Graph command to create a graph that represents up to six series of values, including both X-axis labels and a legend identifying the values in each series.

The / Graph | Fast Graph command requires that all the data you want to graph be laid out in a single block on the spreadsheet. If the block contains more rows than columns, Quattro Pro treats each column of values as a single series. If the first column in the block contains labels, Quattro Pro uses them as X-axis labels; otherwise it defines them as the first series values. Quattro Pro treats each of the remaining columns as an additional series (up to a maximum of six). If the first row of the fast graph block contains labels, Quattro Pro uses them to create a graph legend. Otherwise Quattro Pro treats the first row entries as part of the values to be plotted.

If the number of columns equals or exceeds the number of rows in the block, Quattro Pro plots the values in each row (up to a maximum of six) as a series. If the block's first row contains labels, Quattro Pro uses them as X-axis labels. If the first column of the block contains labels, Quattro Pro uses them to create a graph legend.

Creating a fast graph involves two steps. First, you issue the / Graph | Graph Type command and select the type of graph you want to create. Second, you issue the / Graph | Fast Graph command. Quattro Pro prompts for a block of data to create. As soon as you specify the block, Quattro Pro displays the graph. Press any key other than / to return to the spreadsheet. You can then use the options on the Graph menu to make additions or adjustments.

The menu command shortcut for the / Graph | Fast Graph command is (CTRL-G).
There are two potential pitfalls when using this command:

- **Using numeric values for the X-axis or legend labels.** If the entries you want to use as X-axis labels or legend text are numeric values, you must either change them to labels, or omit them from the fast graph block and define the X-axis labels and legend text later. Otherwise Quattro Pro treats them as values to be plotted on the graph.

- **Trying to graph a set of values in which the number of series exceeds the number of values in each series.** The / Graph | Fast Graph command works properly only when the number of series you want to plot is smaller than the number of values in each series. If the number of series you want to plot is greater than the number of values in each series, use the / Graph | Series | Groups command.

DEFINING A GROUP OF SERIES When you are plotting several series of values, the values in each series often are arranged in adjacent rows or adjacent columns on the spreadsheet. You can use the / Graph | Series | Group command to define several series at once. This command does less than the / Graph | Fast Graph command; it does not automatically assign X-axis series or legends. However, it affords you more control over the graphing process by letting you tell Quattro Pro how to divide the specified block of values into series.

When you select Group, Quattro Pro displays a submenu with the choices Columns and Rows. Select Columns if the values in each series are stored within one column; select Rows if the values in each series are stored within one row. Next Quattro Pro asks for a block of values. If you have selected Columns, Quattro Pro assigns each column of values in the block to a series. The leftmost column of values becomes series 1, the next column to the right becomes series 2, and so on. If you have selected Rows, Quattro Pro assigns each row of values in the block to a series, starting from the uppermost row in the block.

Try using the two graph shortcuts just discussed to create graphs with multiple series. Start by creating a fast graph for all the data in the spreadsheet. Because the block contains more columns than rows, Quattro Pro plots each of the rows (prod-ucts) as a series.

1. Issue the / Graph | Fast Graph command and, when prompted for a block, enter **A3..F7**. Quattro Pro immediately displays a graph consisting of five groups of bars (representing the five years), each consisting of four bars (representing each of the four products). Quattro Pro uses the four labels at the left edge of the fast graph block (the product names) as legend text and uses the labels in cells B3..F7 (the years 1991 through 1995) as X-axis labels. Note that Quattro Pro also uses the

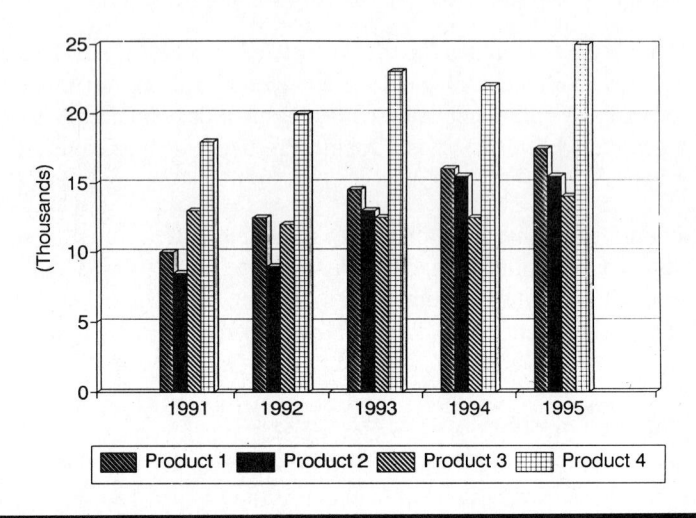

FIGURE 13-13. A fast graph generated for all five years of data

titles from the last graph you displayed because the Fast Graph option does not affect any Text settings.

2. Press any key to return to the Graph menu and select Text. Pick the 2nd Line option, press (ESC) to erase the previous entry, and press (ENTER).

3. Press (F10) (Graph) to view the results. Your graph should now resemble Figure 13-13.

Now try creating a fast graph using the values for years 1991 through 1993 only.

1. Press any key to return to the Text menu and select the 1st Line option. Press (ESC) to erase the previous entry and enter **Three-Year Sales Projection**. Select Quit to return to the Graph menu.

2. Select the Fast Graph option and specify a block of **A3..D7**. The resulting graph should look like Figure 13-14. The specified block contains more rows than columns, so Quattro Pro plots each column (year) as a series rather than treating the products as series as in the last graph.

Three-Year Sales Projection

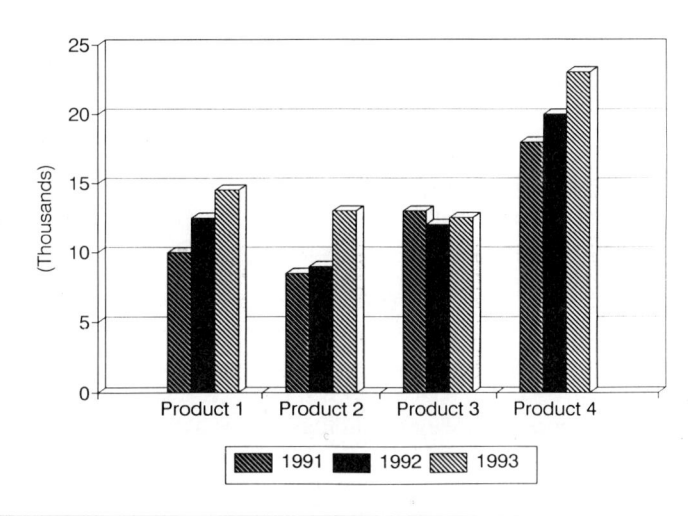

FIGURE 13-14. A fast graph generated for three years of data

The most efficient way to create a graph of this same set of values, treating each product (row) rather than each year (column) as a series, is by using the / **Graph** I **Series** I **Group** I **Rows** command. Try this now.

1. Press any key to return to the Graph menu, and then select Series. Notice that Quattro Pro filled in blocks for the first three series in response to the last / **Graph** I **Fast Graph** command. Select Group from the Series menu, and then choose Rows. Enter a block of **B4..D7**. You should see the settings for the first through fourth series change immediately.

2. Select the X-Axis Series option and enter **B3..D3**. Select Quit to return to the Graph menu.

3. Select the Text option and then select Legends. Enter the following cell references as legend labels. (Use (ESC) to erase settings left over from the last fast graph.)

Option	Enter
Series 1	\A4
Series 2	\A5
Series 3	\A6
Series 4	\A7

3. Press (F10) (Graph) to view the results.
4. Press (ESC) three times to return to the Graph menu.

Now try looking at this graph in several different forms by repeatedly changing the graph type.

1. Select the Graph Type option and choose Stacked Bar. Select View to see the results. Notice that each series is now represented as a single segmented bar rather than as a group of bars. Press any key other than / to return to the Graph menu.

2. Select the Graph Type option and choose Area. Select View or press (F10) (Graph). This time each series is represented as a layer of a single patterned area on the graph, as shown in Figure 13-15. The layers are represented by different fill patterns. The top edge of each layer represents the total of the values in all the series represented below that line. Press any key to return to the Graph menu.

3. Select the Graph Type option and choose Rotated Bar. Note that the graph appears a bit congested in this form. Select View or press (F10) (Graph). The horizontal orientation also does little to clarify the information in this case. Press a key to return to the Graph menu.

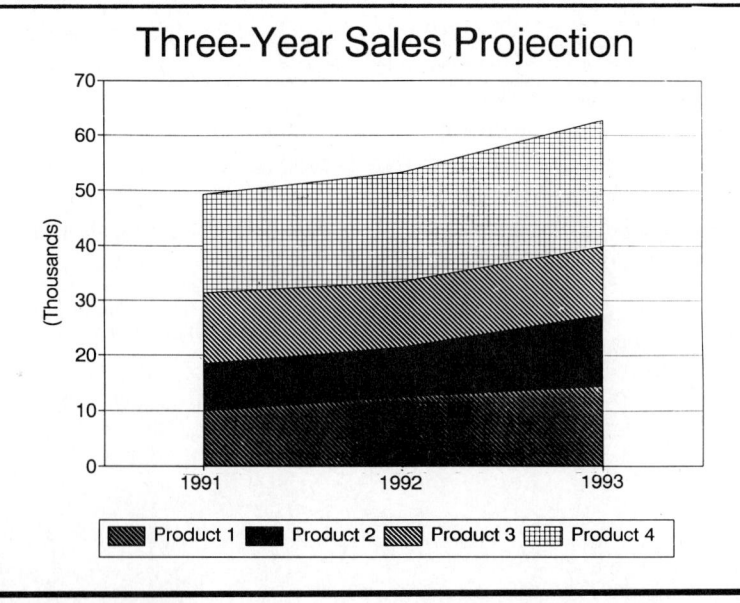

FIGURE 13-15. An area graph for 1991 through 1993

4. Try moving the legend to the right side of the graph by selecting Text, then Legends, then Position, and then Right. Press (F10) (Graph) again to see the results, and then press a key to return to the Graph menu.

5. Select the Graph Type option and choose Line. Select View or press (F10) (Graph). This time each series (product) is represented as a line, and the markers on each line represent the sales figures for particular years. Press any key to return to the Graph menu.

6. Select the Graph Type option one last time and choose Bar to return to your original version of this graph.

Naming and Restoring Graphs

When you create a graph and then save the spreadsheet, the graph settings are saved along with the data. If you change any of the graph settings and resave the spreadsheet, the new graph settings replace the old ones.

You also can save more than one set of graph settings for a particular spreadsheet by assigning names to different groups of graph settings with the / Graph | Name | Create command. This command saves the current graph settings under the name you designate, so that you can recall them later.

The / Graph | Name | Create command directs Quattro Pro to store the settings for the current graph as part of the spreadsheet's data in memory. You still must save the spreadsheet as a whole to disk (with / File | Save or / File | Save As) to preserve those settings for future work sessions. Otherwise the graph settings are lost as soon as you leave the spreadsheet.

When you save a graph by naming it, only the graph settings are saved, not the underlying data. If you modify the data and then recall a saved graph, the old settings are used to graph the new data, resulting in a different graph. However, if you change any of the graph settings—alter a title, for example—you must save the graph again by issuing the / Graph | Name | Create command and specifying the same graph name.

Caution Quattro Pro does not display a warning when you reuse an existing graph name. You should therefore check your list of existing graph names before assigning a name to a new graph.

The command for recalling a stored graph to the screen is / Graph | Name | Display. When you issue this command, Quattro Pro displays the named graph and replaces any graph settings that are currently in effect with the named graph's settings. (If you want to save the current settings, be sure to issue the / Graph | Name | Create command before you display a different graph.) You can eliminate named graphs with / Graph

| Name | Erase, which erases whatever named graph you specify, or with / Graph | Name | Reset, which erases all named graphs for the current spreadsheet.

Resetting Series And Graphs

You can erase any setting except the series values and X-axis values by selecting the related menu option, pressing (ESC) to erase the current setting, and pressing (ENTER). If you try the same procedure with one of the series or X-axis values, however, Quattro Pro simply reinstates the previous setting. The / Graph | Customize Series | Reset command allows you to erase some or all of the series and X-axis values. When you issue this command, Quattro Pro displays a menu with options for all six series and the X-axis. As soon as you select any of these options, Quattro Pro erases the current setting for the related item. The Graph | Customize Series | Reset menu also contains an option called Graph; this option erases all series, the X-axis settings, and all other graph settings so that you can create a new graph from scratch.

You get a chance to name graphs and reset graph settings in the next exercise.

Defining Pie Graphs And Column Graphs

Pie graphs and column graphs show the relative values of the different components of a whole. For these graph types, you need only define values for the first series and, if you like, for the X-axis series. If you define any other series, Quattro Pro simply ignores them.

When you create a pie or column chart, Quattro Pro totals all the values in the first series and calculates the percentage that each value in the series represents of that total. The resulting graph represents the series as a whole, and individual values are portrayed as slices sized according to the percentage they represent of the total. Quattro Pro automatically displays these percentages next to each slice or segment of the pie or column, immediately after the X-axis label (if there is one).

Try saving the settings for the current graph and then resetting all the graph settings. Then create a pie chart from your data.

1. Select the Name option on the Graph menu and then choose Create. Enter the name **BARS**.

2. Select the Customize Series option on the Graph menu, select Reset from the Customize Series menu, and then select Graph from the Reset menu.

3. Select Quit to return to the Graph menu. Note that the Graph Type setting automatically changes back to Stacked Bar, the default. Select the Series option and note that all the series are now undefined.

4. Select 1st Series and enter **B4..B7**.

5. Select X-axis Series and enter **A4..A7**. Select Quit to return to the Graph menu.

6. Select Text and note that all the options on this menu have been reset as well. Select the 1st Line option and enter **1991 Sales**.

7. Select Quit to return to the Graph menu, select the Graph Type option, and choose Pie.

8. Select the View option to see the results. Your screen should now look like Figure 13-16.

9. Press a key to return to the Graph menu, select Name, and then choose Create. Enter the name **PIE**.

10. Select Graph Type and change the type to Column. Press (F10) to view the results.

1991 Sales

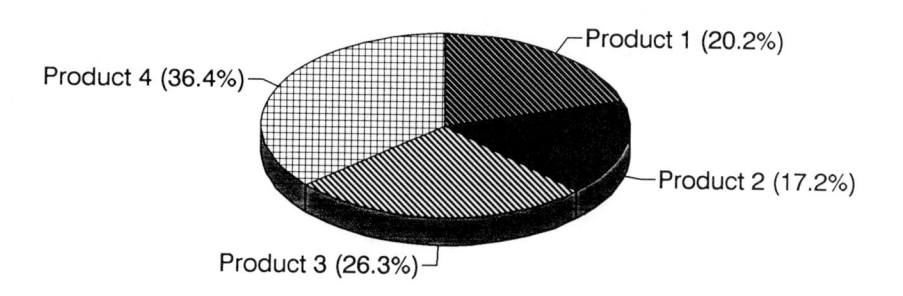

Product 4 (36.4%)
Product 1 (20.2%)
Product 2 (17.2%)
Product 3 (26.3%)

FIGURE 13-16. A pie graph of 1991 sales

11. Press (ESC) to return to the Graph menu. Select Name. Then select Create from the Name menu and enter the name **COLUMN**.

12. Select Name. Then choose Display and enter **BARS** to view the previously named graph. Press any key to return to the Graph menu. Note that the Graph Type setting is now Bar because the BARS graph is now the current graph.

13. Select Quit to return to Ready mode.

Defining XY Graphs

XY graphs differ substantially from most of the other graph types supported by Quattro Pro. In other graphs (except pie graphs) you define one or more series of values to be plotted against the X-axis. The X-axis is simply a baseline, and the only thing you can define about this axis is a series of labels used to identify the plotted values.

In an XY graph you plot the points of intersection between two series. This type of graph maps out the correlation between two variables, charting how the X series of values affects the Y series of values. It is possible to plot several series on an XY graph, but in each case, the values that are plotted are the intersections between X-axis values and the values in one of the series.

XY graphs treat one value series—the X-axis values—as the independent variable against which the other values (the series values) are plotted. In essence, an XY graph answers the question "When the X series is at this level, where is Y?" for every value of X that you specify. For example, the graph shown in Figure 13-8 answers the question "What is the average salary for people with X years of post-high-school education?" for nine different values of X.

Before you try to create an XY graph, you must reset all current graph settings so that you can start your graph definition from scratch. Then you need to enter some additional data on your spreadsheet.

1. Reset all graph settings by issuing the / **Graph** | **Customize Series** | **Reset** | **Graph** command.

2. Widen column A to 11 characters.

3. Enter the following data:

In Cell	Enter
A14	**Unit Price**
B14	**32**
C14	**33**
D14	**34**

E14	**35**
F14	**35.5**
G14	**37**
A15	**Unit Sales**
B15	**480**
C15	**400**
D15	**500**
E15	**550**
F15	**480**
G15	**450**

4. Issue the / **Graph** | **Series** | **1st Series** command, and enter **B15..G15** as the block.

5. Select the X-Axis Series option and enter a block of **B14..G14**.

6. Select Quit to return to the Graph menu and select the Text option. Select the 1st Line option and enter **Effect of Unit Price on Units Sold.**

7. Select the X-Title option on the Text menu and enter **\A14**.

8. Select the Y-Title option and enter **\A15**.

9. Select Quit to return to the Graph menu, choose the Graph Type option, and pick XY.

10. Select the View option. Your screen should now look like the one shown in Figure 13-17.

11. Press a key to return to the Graph menu, select Name, and choose Create. Enter the name **XY**.

12. Select Quit to return to Ready mode.

You have now seen all the Quattro Pro graph types except the Text type, which is covered in Chapter 15.

PRINTING GRAPHS

Printing graphs in Quattro Pro is very similar to printing spreadsheets. The basic steps are as follows:

1. Make sure that the graph you want to print is the current graph. If it is not, use the / **Graph** | **Name** | **Display** command to make it the current graph.

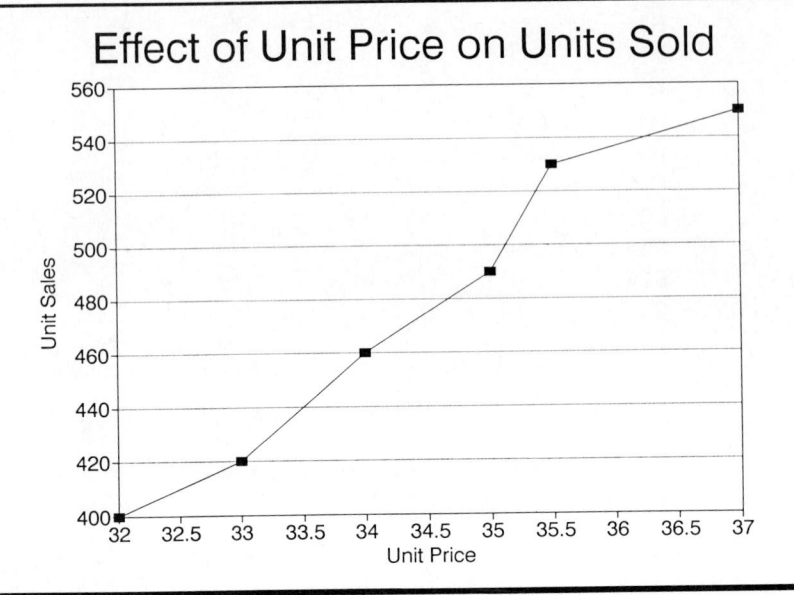

FIGURE 13-17. Creating an XY graph

2. Issue the / **Graph** | **Print Graph** command, and select the Layout option to change any layout options you wish.

3. Make sure the Destination setting on the **Graph** | **Print Graph** menu is set to Graph Printer.

4. Make sure the printer is turned on and the paper properly aligned.

5. Select the Go option on the **Print** | **Graph Print** menu.

If you want to preview the output before printing it, set the **Print** | **Graph Print** | **Destination** setting to Screen Preview. If you want to direct output to a disk file so that you can print it later, set the Destination to File and enter a filename as prompted. If you do not enter an extension, Quattro Pro automatically assigns the **PRN** extension. Then select the Graph Print option, as if you were sending output to your printer. When you are ready to print the file, enter the following command from the DOS prompt (assuming your printer is connected to the LPT1 printer port):

COPY *filename*.PRN /B LPT1:

If your printer is connected to a different port, substitute the appropriate port name, such as COM1, in place of LPT1.

Adjusting Print Speed And Quality

When you first tell Quattro Pro about a printer using the / Options | Hardware | Printer | 1st Printer | Type of Printer or / Options | Hardware | Printer | 2nd Printer | Type of Printer command, Quattro Pro often gives you a choice of print modes. These modes reflect a range of print densities. The higher the print mode, the larger the number of dots per inch and the slower the printer speed.

Autoscaling Fonts

Quattro Pro assigns point sizes for text based on the assumption that you will be producing full-size printouts of your graphs. If you print graphs using dimensions smaller than eight inches by six inches, Quattro Pro automatically adjusts the point sizes, so your output looks like a miniature version of a full-size printout.

If you always print graphs in a particular size (other than full size), you may prefer to manually scale fonts by choosing point sizes appropriate to that graph size. You must issue the / Options | Hardware | Printers | Fonts | Autoscale Fonts command and change the setting to No. This directs Quattro Pro to print text elements in their assigned point sizes, rather than scaling them to fit your graph dimensions. While this affords you slightly more control over the printed text size, it also means that, on screen, the text is scaled differently than the remaining graph elements.

Changing the Graph Print Layout

The / Print | Graph Print | Layout command lets you change the placement, size, and dimensions of a printed graph. When you issue this command, Quattro Pro displays a menu with the following options:

- **Left Edge** specifies the distance between the left edge of the page and the left edge of the graph itself. The default setting is 0 inch. Quattro Pro ignores this setting unless you are printing a graph with dimensions smaller than 8 inches by 6 inches.

- **Top Edge** specifies the distance between the top edge of the page and the top edge of the graph. The default setting is 0 inch. Quattro Pro ignores this setting unless you are printing a graph with dimensions smaller than 8 inches by 6 inches.

- **Height** specifies the length of the graph from top to bottom. If you specify a height of less than 1 inch or more than 10 inches, Quattro Pro prints the graph full size. Because the default setting is 0, leaving the default setting unchanged amounts to directing Quattro Pro to print the graph full size.

- **Width** specifies the width of the graph across the page. The default setting is 0 inch. If you specify a width of less than 1 inch (either by entering a number less than 1 or leaving the default setting of 0) or more than 8 inches, Quattro Pro prints the graph full size.

- **Dimensions** determines whether layout dimensions are expressed in inches or centimeters.

- **Orientation** specifies whether the graph will be printed in portrait or landscape mode. The default setting is Portrait.

- **4:3 Aspect** determines whether Quattro Pro preserves a 4 to 3 width to height ratio when printing graphs or displaying inserted graphs on the screen. If you leave the 4:3 Aspect setting at Yes, Quattro Pro prints the largest graph it can within the height and width you specify while maintaining a 4 to 3 width to height ratio. If you change the 4:3 Aspect setting to No, Quattro Pro stretches the graph to fit whatever height and width you specify.

- **Reset** reinstates the last set of print settings that you saved to disk with the Update option.

- **Update** saves the current print settings to disk. (See the discussion of "Updating Graph Print Options" that follows.)

- **Quit** redisplays the Graph Print menu.

Updating Graph Print Options

The / **Print** | **Graph Print** | **Layout** | **Update** command saves the current graph print settings as permanent defaults, so they are reinstated every time you load Quattro Pro. The settings saved include all the settings on the **Print** | **Graph Print** | **Layout** menu except the 4:3 Aspect setting, which returns to Yes every time you reload Quattro Pro, and is saved with individual files only.

The / **Print** | **Graph Print** | **Layout** | **Update** command also saves any print settings you have established for spreadsheets, as if you had issued the / **Print** | **Layout** | **Update** command. Similarly, the / **Print** | **Layout** | **Update** command saves the settings on the **Print** | **Graph Print** | **Layout** menu as well as those on the **Print** | **Layout** menu.

Although both the **Print** | **Layout** and **Print** | **Graph Print** | **Layout** menus contain Dimensions and Orientation settings, these settings are saved separately. Setting the Orientation option for graphs to Landscape, for example, has no effect on the Orientation setting for spreadsheets.

"Printing" to Disk

As mentioned, you can "print" a graph to disk by changing the Destination setting to File. This allows you to create files that you can later print from DOS.

You can also use the / **Print** | **Graph Print** | **Write Graph File** command to create files for export to other software packages. When you issue this command, Quattro Pro displays a menu with the options EPS File, PIC File, PCX File, and Quit. Select PIC file to create graph files that can be printed through Lotus 1-2-3. Select EPS file to create a PostScript file for use in word processing or desktop publishing programs that support PostScript page description language. Select PCX File to create graph files that can be read by PC Paintbrush, Windows Paintbrush, and other programs that support the PCX file format.

GRAPH SLIDE SHOWS

The / **Graph** | **Name** | **Slide** command allows you to display graph slide shows—a series of named graphs displayed on the screen one after another. To create a slide show, you must first enter two adjacent columns of data in a separate section of the spreadsheet, away from your other data. In the first column enter the names of all the graphs that you want to display. In the second column enter the number of seconds that you want the graph to be displayed, or enter the number 0 if you want Quattro Pro to leave the graph on screen until you press a key. This second column is optional; if you leave it blank, Quattro Pro assumes a value of 0 and therefore displays each graph, waits for you to press a key, displays the next graph, and so on. Even if you enter a number greater than 0 in the second column, Quattro Pro displays the next graph as soon as you press a key. The interval only determines how long the graph stays on screen if you do not press a key.

Once you have entered your one or two columns of data, issue the / **Graph** | **Name** | **Slide** command and, when prompted, specify the block of graph names and their display intervals, if any. Quattro Pro displays each of the graphs in the block and then returns to the Graph menu.

INSERTING GRAPHS IN A SPREADSHEET

The / Graph | Insert command allows you to insert a graph directly into your spreadsheet, so it appears as part of the spreadsheet rather on a screen or printout by itself.

There are three reasons to insert a graph into a spreadsheet:

- To see the graph change as you change data
- To print the graph as part of the spreadsheet when generating reports
- To print multiple graphs on a page

You can view inserted graphs on the screen only if you are using Quattro Pro's Graphics display mode. When Quattro Pro is not in Graphics display mode, an inserted graph simply appears as an empty highlighted block on the screen. This helps prevent you from accidentally entering data in this area.

In Graphics display mode, Quattro Pro redraws inserted graphs whenever the spreadsheet is recalculated. Unless you have set the Recalculation mode to Manual, this means you must wait for Quattro Pro to redraw any inserted graphs that currently appear on your screen every time you enter or change data in any cell of the spreadsheet. If you are making numerous changes to the spreadsheet, you may either want to switch to a Text display mode or set the Recalculation mode to Manual. When the Recalculation mode is Manual, Quattro Pro redraws the graph only when you press (F9) (Calc) or scroll the screen display.

You can insert up to eight graphs in a single spreadsheet. Quattro Pro always displays the name of the graph on the input line whenever you move the cell pointer into the block containing an inserted graph. If your graph contains several inserted graphs, this is the easiest way to determine which one you are looking at.

To display an inserted graph that is not the current graph, move the cell pointer into the graph block and press (F10). If the inserted graph happens to be the current graph, you can display it full-screen by pressing (F10) with the cell pointer anywhere other than the block used for another different inserted graph.

To insert a graph into your spreadsheet, you perform the following steps:

1. If you have an EGA or VGA monitor, make sure that the Options | Display Mode setting is Graphics Mode.

2. Issue the / **Graph** I **Insert** command. Quattro Pro prompts you for a graph to insert and displays a list of named graphs.

3. Choose a graph to insert. To specify the current graph, you can either choose the Current Graph option or the graph name.

4. When Quattro Pro prompts you for a block, specify the block using either the pointing or typing method. If the block you specify contains data, it is not erased by the inserted graph. The data is obscured by the inserted graph, however, and you can view or print it only by removing the graph from the spreadsheet.

An inserted graph may be up to 12 columns by 32 rows. If this isn't large enough for your purposes, you may widen columns to increase width or attach larger fonts in the row to increase row height.

When you first insert a graph, Quattro Pro draws the graph using a 4 to 3 height to width ratio. If the block you specified has different proportions and you would prefer to have the graph stretched to fill the block, issue the / **Print** I **Graph Print** I **Layout** I **4:3 Aspect** I **No** command. Quattro Pro does not actually redisplay the graph until it recalculates the spreadsheet, so you may want to press (F9) (Calc) after changing this setting so you can see the effects.

Printing an Inserted Graph

To print an inserted graph, just include the area that contains the graph in the print block, make sure Destination is set to Graph Printer, and select Spreadsheet Print from the Print menu.

If your print block is too wide to fit on one page, the graph generally breaks at the same column as the rest of the data in the spreadsheet. As a result, part of the graph appears on one page and part on the next. You can fix the problem by moving the graph to a set of columns that fits on one page or, if the graph itself is too wide to fit on a page, by printing in landscape mode.

REMOVING AN INSERTED GRAPH To remove an inserted graph from a spreadsheet, issue the / **Graph** I **Hide** command. Quattro Pro displays a list of graphs—like the one it displays when you insert a graph. Select the graph you want to remove and press (ENTER). Quattro Pro erases the graph from the screen.

The name of this command is a bit confusing. The / **Graph** I **Hide** command does not temporarily conceal an inserted graph; it actually erases it. If you want to see the graph again later, you need to insert it again.

You have now learned all the basics of defining and printing graphs. Chapter 14 builds on this foundation while covering various options for refining and customizing your graphs. If you anticipate using graphs frequently, you might want to experiment on your own with the other graph types, focusing on how series are represented in different graph types and which graphs work best for different types of applications.

14

CUSTOMIZING GRAPHS

Customizing Series
Customizing Pie and Column Graphs
Customizing the Axes
Customizing Graphs as a Whole

Quattro Pro offers numerous commands for customizing and embellishing graphs. This chapter presents only an overview of the possibilities. As you come across options that intrigue you or appear applicable to your work, try experimenting on your own, using the graphs created in the last chapter.

CUSTOMIZING SERIES

When you create a graph, Quattro Pro automatically assigns a different color and, in area and bar graphs, a unique fill pattern to each series that you define. In line graphs it assigns each series a distinct marker type. You can change these and other series attributes using the / Graph | Customize Series command. The options on this menu are discussed in the following sections.

Customizing Colors

If you have a color screen, Quattro Pro displays each series in a graph in a different color. You can change these colors using the / Graph | Customize Series | Colors command. When you issue the command, Quattro Pro displays a menu with options for each of the six possible series. To change the color for a series, select the appropriate option and then select the desired color from the colors list. If you are using Graphics display mode, Quattro Pro displays a gallery of colors rather than a menu.

The series colors are not the only graph colors you can control. To change the color of text, use / Graph | Text | Fonts. To change the colors of the graph's background or the grid lines displayed on the surface of the graph, use the / Graph | Overall | Background Color or / Graph | Overall | Grid command (discussed later in this chapter).

Note: CGA monitors always display graphs in black and white, even though they display spreadsheets in color.

Altering Fill Patterns

The command for customizing the fill patterns to be used in bar graphs and area graphs is / Graph | Customize Series | Fill Patterns. When you issue this command, Quattro Pro displays a menu with the options for each of the six possible series. Once you select a series, Quattro Pro displays a list of 16 fill patterns from which you can choose.

Relationship Between Series And Pie/Column Slices

Quattro Pro uses the same fill patterns and colors for individual slices in pie and column graphs that it uses for different series in other types of graphs. For example, when you change the fill pattern assigned to the third series, the Graph | Customize

Series | Pies | Patterns | 3rd Slice setting changes as well. This change then carries over to any pie or column charts you later create on this spreadsheet.

Changing Lines And Markers

By default, Quattro Pro represents each data point in a line graph with a marker symbol and connects the markers for each series with a line. You may prefer to represent one or more series in a graph with marker symbols only or with lines only. In general, lines are excellent for representing trends over time; markers are preferable for focusing the reader's attention on the individual values. Quattro Pro also allows you to change the line style (solid, dotted, and so on) and marker symbol used for each series.

The command for changing these characteristics of line graphs is / **Graph | Customize Series | Markers & Lines**. When you issue this command, Quattro Pro displays a menu with the options Line Styles, Markers, Formats, and Quit.

Use the Formats option to specify whether you want Quattro Pro to use lines, markers, or a combination of the two to represent each series. When you select this option, Quattro Pro displays a menu with options for the first through the sixth series and a Graph option, in case you want to change the format for the graph as a whole.

When you select one of the options, Quattro Pro displays another menu with the choices Lines, Symbols, Both, and Neither. Choose Lines if you want Quattro Pro to use lines only. Choose Symbols for Symbols only. Select Both (the default setting) if you want to see markers connected by lines. Select Neither if you want Quattro Pro to display neither lines nor markers. You can use this option to temporarily remove a series from a graph without having to redefine the series block later to redisplay it. You might also select Neither if you want to plot a series of values with interior labels rather than lines or markers. In this case, you would, in effect, attach the labels to points on an invisible line. (Interior labels are covered later in this chapter under "Labeling Points on a Graph.")

To specify the type of line or marker symbols used to plot each series, select the Line Styles or Markers options on the **Graph | Customize Series | Markers & Lines | Line Styles** menu. Quattro Pro displays a menu with options for the first through sixth series. Once you select a series to change, Quattro Pro displays a menu of line styles or marker symbols. Choose the one you like and then select Quit to return to the **Graph | Customize Series | Markers & Lines** menu.

You have 8 line styles and 10 marker symbols to choose from.

Changing the Width Of Bars

By default, when Quattro Pro draws a bar graph, it apportions 60% of the amount of space on the X-axis among all the bars on the graph and reserves the remaining 40% of the X-axis for blank space between the bars.

To change the bar widths on a graph, you adjust the percentage of X-axis space that Quattro Pro allocates to bars using / Graph | Customize Series | Bar Width. When you issue this command, Quattro Pro asks you to specify the bar thickness. Enter a number from 20 through 90. The larger the number, the wider the bars will be.

You can also narrow bars slightly by getting rid of the perspective lines at their right edge. See "Eliminating the Three-Dimensional Effect" later in this chapter.

Labeling Points on a Graph

In Chapter 13 you used X-axis labels to identify the values plotted on a graph. You may want to further identify these values by adding labels to the surface of the graph itself. These *interior labels* usually designate the numeric value of each point plotted on the graph. You might use them to indicate the value represented by each bar in a bar graph, as in Figure 14-1, or the value of the points plotted in a line graph. You cannot use interior labels in pie, column, or area graphs.

To define a set of interior labels, you issue / Graph | Customize Series | Interior Labels. Quattro Pro displays a menu with options for series 1 through 6 and, as soon as you pick a series, prompts you for "spreadsheet data to label this series." After you specify a block of cells, Quattro Pro displays a submenu with the options Center, Left, Above, Right, Below, and None, which you use to indicate where you want the labels located in relation to the corresponding values. In the case of bar graphs, you have no choice about the placement of labels; Quattro Pro automatically displays them above the bars in regular or stacked bar graphs and to the right of the bars in rotated bar graphs. You can use the None option on the Interior Labels menu to hide the labels temporarily so you can redisplay them later without having to redefine them.

You can use a block other than the series values block for interior labels. For example, if you are labeling points that are fairly close together and the values themselves are long, you might need to create a second series of values on the spreadsheet (for example, you could divide each value by 100 or 1000) and use those as labels.

Quattro Pro displays interior labels in the same format as the spreadsheet values on which they are based. For example, if a set of interior labels is based on a block of

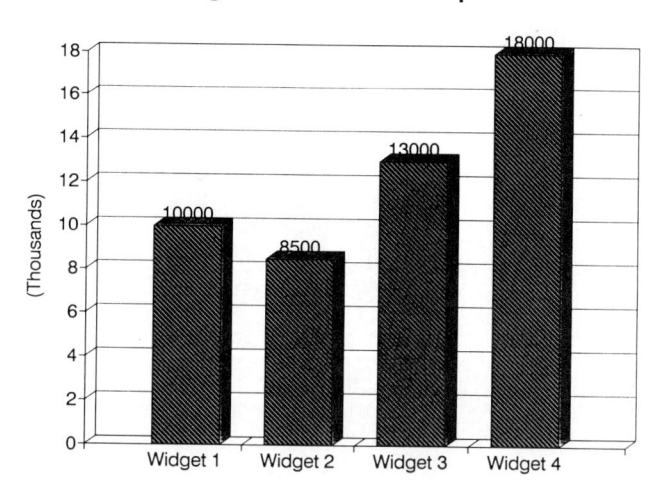

FIGURE 14-1. A bar graph with interior labels

numbers displayed on the spreadsheet in Currency format, the labels also appear on the graph in Currency format.

Once you have defined a set of interior labels, they are not easy to eliminate. You can reset the entire series and thus erase the interior labels along with the series, or you can specify a block of blank cells as labels.

Overriding the Graph Type

The / Graph | Customize Series | Override Type command lets you change the graph type used for one or more series to create graphs that use both lines (with or without markers) and bars. You can override the graph type for a series only if the overall graph type is Bar or Line.

When you issue the / Graph | Customize Series | Override Type command, Quattro Pro displays a menu with options for the first through the sixth series. As soon as you select a series, another menu appears with the options Default (meaning the graph type for the graph as a whole), Bar, and Line. Select the desired option and then select Quit to return to the Customize Series menu.

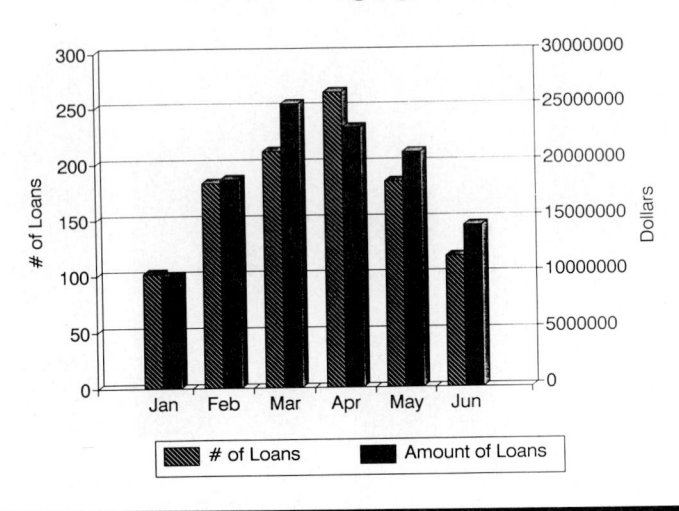

FIGURE 14-2. A graph with two Y-axes

Using a Second Y-Axis

As you have seen, the Y-axis serves as a measuring stick to gauge the value of different data points on a graph. If you are graphing two or more series that differ widely in magnitude, you may want to define a second Y-axis so you can measure and compare two sets of values against two different scales. For example, Figure 14-2 shows a graph that plots two series of values—the number of bank loans made over a six-month period and the amount of those loans—against two different Y-axes. If you plotted both series against a single axis, the Y-axis scale would extend from 0 to 300000 and the bars for the first series' values would be reduced to mere smudges near the bottom of the graph.

To define a second Y-axis, you issue the / **Graph** I **Customize Series** I **Y-Axis** command. Quattro Pro displays a menu with options for each of the six possible series. The first time you open this menu, all the series are set to Primary Y-Axis. To plot a series on a second Y-axis, select the option for that series and change the setting to Secondary Y-Axis. Quattro Pro creates a separate Y-axis at the right edge of the graph and scales this axis on the basis of the range of values in all the series you have assigned it. Once you have defined a second Y-axis, you can use the / **Graph** I **Y-Axis** I **Second Y-Axis** command to customize it.

You can only define a second Y-axis for line, bar, or XY graphs. On other graph types, Quattro Pro plots all the series against a single Y-axis.

Resetting Graph Settings

As you have seen in previous exercises, the graph settings you establish stay in effect even if you change graph types. This allows you to experiment with different graph types without redefining the series, text, and so on. However, it also means that if you create more than one graph on a particular spreadsheet, the graph settings carry over from one graph to the next, which is not always desirable.

The carryover of settings can be particularly problematic if you define one graph with several series and then define another with fewer series. You cannot simply select the appropriate option on the Graph | Series menu and press (ESC) to erase the setting. The only way to eliminate a series is with the / Graph | Customize Series | **Reset** command, introduced in the last chapter. When you issue this command, Quattro Pro displays a menu with options for each of the six possible series, along with options for Graph (to reset all the graph settings).

When you reset a series, Quattro Pro erases the series values setting and the interior labels setting (if any), and sets the color, fill pattern, line style and marker symbol, and override type back to the system default. If you issue the / Graph | Customize Series | **Reset** | Graph command, Quattro Pro resets all the series, changes the graph type to Stacked Bar, and restores the bar width, the axes settings, and the overall settings back to the system defaults.

Updating Graph Settings

As mentioned, resetting a series means returning it to its system defaults. You can change those defaults with the / Graph | Customize Series | Update command. Like other Quattro Pro update commands—such as / Options | Update and / Print | Layout | Update—/ Graph | Customize Series | Update stores a group of settings to disk so they can be recalled and placed into effect in future work sessions. When you issue this command, Quattro Pro saves the current Graph | Overall settings, Graph | X-Axis settings, Graph | Y-Axis settings, and every setting established through the Graph | Customize Series menu except the interior labels block. Once you have changed the graph defaults, Quattro Pro reinstates those settings every time you reload Quattro Pro or issue the / Graph | Customize Series | **Reset** | Graph command.

CUSTOMIZING PIE AND COLUMN GRAPHS

There are two ways to fine-tune the appearance of pie and column charts: by using options on the **Graph | Customize Series | Pies** menu and by defining a second series of values. The attributes you can change include the colors and fill patterns of the pie slices or column segments, the format of the labels used to identify the slices or segments, and, in the case of pie charts, whether or not slices are *exploded* (pulled away) from the rest of the pie.

Changing the Label Format

When you first create a pie or column graph, Quattro Pro displays percentages next to each slice to indicate the percentage that slice represents of the whole pie (or column). If you specify X- axis values for the graph, Quattro Pro displays these next to the X-axis text.

The Label Format option on the **Graph | Customize Series | Pies** menu allows you to specify the information to be displayed next to each slice of the pie or column. If you specify X-axis values for the graph, Quattro Pro displays this information immediately after the X-axis text. You have the following choices:

Value	Displays the series values exactly as they appear on the spreadsheet
%	(The default setting) displays the percentage that each slice represents relative to the whole pie or column
$	Displays the series values displayed in Currency format with zero decimal places
None	Removes all labels from the chart; if you have defined X-axis labels, these are still displayed

If you want to display both the percentages and the spreadsheet values, you can use the same block of data for the X-axis series as you use for series 1 and leave the Label Format option set to %. However, this means that you cannot use the X-axis series to display text that indicates what each slice of the pie or column represents.

The spreadsheet in Figure 14-3 illustrates a trick you can sometimes use to display all three pieces of information—a description, the percentage, and the value itself—next to each slice of the pie or column. As you recall from Chapter 11, the @STRING function converts a numeric value into a character string or label. (The function's first argument designates the value to be converted; the second argument indicates the

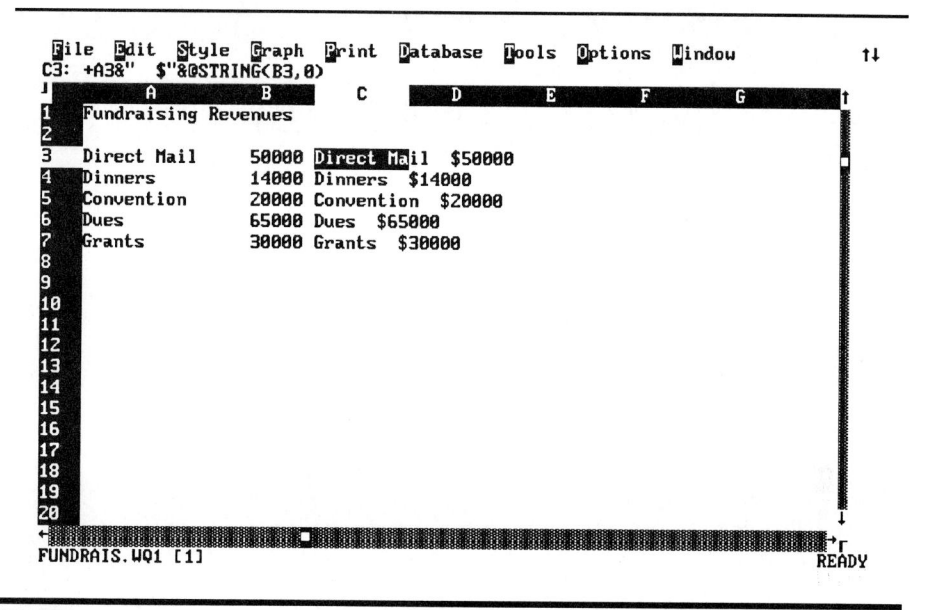

FIGURE 14-3. Creating special labels for a pie graph

number of decimal places to include in the resulting character string.) The & operator can be used to add this converted character string to another label on the spreadsheet.

In the spreadsheet in Figure 14-3, the formula

+A3&" $"&@STRING(B3,0)

was entered into C3 and then copied down column C. This formula creates labels that combine the descriptive labels in column A with the string (text) conversion of the spreadsheet values in column B. The resulting block of labels in column C was then designated as the X-axis series for a pie graph and the **Graph** I **Customize Series** I **Pies** I **Label Format** option was set to %. The resulting graph is shown in Figure 14-4.

Eliminating Tick Marks

By default, Quattro Pro displays lines between each slice in a pie or column graph and its identifying label. *Ticks* or *tick marks* are the short lines displayed and frequently labeled along both axes. If you are plotting only a few values, tick marks may be

Fundraising Revenues

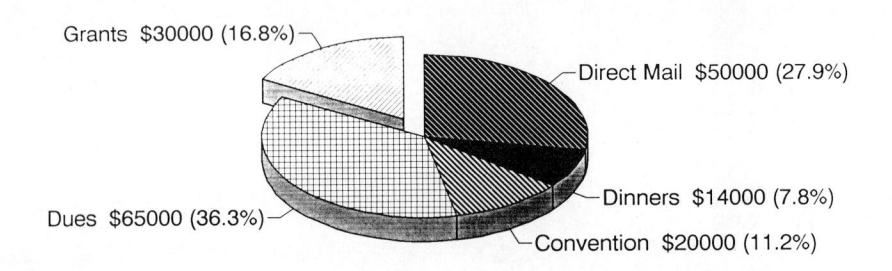

FIGURE 14-4. Exploded pie graph with special labels

unnecessary. You can remove them by issuing the / Graph I Customize Series I Pies I Tick Marks command and changing the setting to No.

Changing Pie or Column Fill Patterns

You can choose fill patterns used for the slices of a pie or column graph in the same way you designate fill patterns for each series in a bar or area graph. When you issue the / Graph I Customize Series I Pies I Patterns command, Quattro Pro displays a menu with options for the first nine pie slices. (The graph slices are numbered beginning at the 12:00 position and proceeding clockwise.) Once you select a slice to customize, Quattro Pro displays a submenu with 12 fill patterns.

If you have more than nine slices in your pie or column, Quattro Pro recycles fill patterns beginning with the tenth slice: Slice 10 is displayed in the pattern that you specified for slice 1, slice 11 is the same pattern as slice 2, and so on.

Altering Colors

The Colors option on the Graph | Customize Series | Pie menu lets you designate colors for the first nine slices of your pie or column graph. When you select this option, Quattro Pro displays a menu with options for the first nine slices and, once you select a slice, displays a menu of colors. If you have more than nine slices in your pie or column, Quattro Pro reuses colors beginning with the tenth slice, so that the tenth slice is the same color as the first, and so on.

Exploding Pie Slices

The **Graph | Customize Series | Pies** menu also contains an option for exploding slices of a pie graph—separating them from the rest of the pie. You use this option to highlight one or more of the values represented in the graph. Figure 14-4 shows a pie graph in which slice 1 has been exploded.

When you select the Explode option, Quattro Pro displays a menu with options for the first nine slices of the graph. Once you select one of the slice options, Quattro Pro displays a menu with the options Don't Explode and Explode. Select Explode to separate a slice from the rest of the pie. Select Don't Explode to return a slice to its original position.

Using a Second Series To Customize Pie and Column Graphs

As mentioned, you can customize pie or column slices using a second series of spreadsheet values rather than issuing the / Graph | Customize Series | Pies command. The attributes you can change using this method include the color and fill pattern and, in the case of pie graphs, whether a slice is exploded.

You enter values from 0 through 8 to specify the color and fill pattern for each slice. These values refer to the settings on the Graph | Customize Series | Pies | Patterns and Graph | Customize Series | Pies | Colors menus, minus one. For example, if you enter **0** to customize a slice, that slice is given the color and pattern currently defined for the first slice on the Graph | Customize Series | Pies | Colors and Graph | Customize Series | Pies | Patterns menus, respectively. If you enter **3** to customize a slice, the slice receives the color and pattern defined for the fourth slice on those two menus.

If you enter values greater than 8, Quattro Pro starts counting from the first slice again. If you enter **9** Quattro Pro uses the color and pattern assigned to the first slice, if you enter **10**, it uses the color and pattern assigned to the second slice, and so on.

To explode a slice on a pie graph, you add 100 to the pattern/color value. For example, you enter **105** to explode a slice and display it in the color and pattern settings currently defined for the sixth slice. If you enter values greater than 108, Quattro Pro starts counting from the first slice again.

Caution If you do not intend to use the second series values to control the display of slices, make sure that there is no second series defined.

CUSTOMIZING THE AXES

The **Graph | X-Axis** and **Graph | Y-Axis** menus each contain a range of options for changing the appearance of the axes of XY graphs, area graphs, and bar graphs of all types. Because the choices on the two menus are almost identical, they are discussed together.

Scaling Axes Manually

When you define a graph, Quattro Pro automatically scales the Y-axis and, in the case of XY graphs, the X-axis, meaning that it determines the starting and ending points for each axis and the intervals between those points. The **Graph | X-Axis** and **Graph | Y-Axis** menus contain options that allow you to adjust these scales manually. They also contain options for changing the display format and layout of the axis values.

On line graphs and XY graphs, the low point on the Y-axis is a round number equal to or slightly less than the lowest value plotted on the graph. The high point is a round number equal to or slightly greater than the highest value on the graph. On bar graphs the low point on the Y-axis is always zero (and cannot be changed), and the high point is equal to or slightly greater than the graph's highest plotted value.

You might occasionally prefer to scale the axes manually for several reasons. Sometimes extending the Y-axis to leave more room at the top of the graph can make the values easier to pinpoint or the axis labels easier to read, can create room for interior labels, or simply can make the graph look better. You may also modify the scaling to dramatize or downplay the differences among plotted values on a line or XY graph. In general, the narrower the range of values on the Y-axis, the more dramatic the differences among values appear. Conversely, the broader the range you use for scaling the axis, the smaller the apparent differences among plotted values.

You can adjust the Y-axis scale on any type of graph, except pie graphs and column graphs, although you can adjust only the upper end on bar graphs. You can adjust the X-axis scale only on XY graphs.

Here are the steps involved in scaling an axis:

1. Issue the / **Graph** | **X**-Axis or / **Graph** | **Y**-Axis command.

2. Select the Scale option and change the setting from Automatic to Manual.

3. Select the Low option and enter the number that you want to appear as the first number on the axis.

4. Select the High option and enter the number that you want to display as the highest number on the axis.

5. Select the Increment option and enter the interval you want between tick marks on the axis. If you leave the Increment setting at 0, Quattro Pro determines the tick marks interval itself.

6. Customize the tick marks, if desired, as described next.

Changing the Tick Marks

You can change the appearance of the axis tick marks using the No. of Minor Ticks and Format of Ticks options on the **Graph** | **X**-Axis and **Graph** | **Y**-Axis menus. Use the Format of Ticks option to change the display format for the numbers displayed along the axis. The default display format for graph tick marks is General.

Use the No. of Minor Ticks option to display ticks between the major (labeled) ticks on the axis. The No. of Minor Ticks setting does not increase the total number of ticks displayed along the axis. Rather, it determines how many of the existing ticks are changed from major (labeled) to minor (unlabeled) ticks. By setting No. of Minor Ticks to 1, you can replace every other label with a tick mark and make the remaining labels easier to read.

You also can alleviate overcrowding among X-axis labels using the Alternate Ticks option (available only on the **Graph** | **X**-Axis menu). If you change the Alternate Ticks setting from No to Yes, Quattro Pro displays the X-axis labels at two alternating levels.

Eliminating
The Scaling Display

When Quattro Pro plots a graph (other than a pie or column graph), it never shows more than three digits to the left of the decimal point along the the graph's Y-axis. If the values to be displayed along this axis exceed 999, Quattro Pro divides them by 10 or 100 or 1000, whatever is necessary to produce a three-digit result, and then adds a scale measurement indicator, such as (Thousands) or (Millions), under the Y-axis title to the left of the axis. The same is true for the X-axis in XY graphs.

If you change the Display Scaling option from Yes to No, Quattro Pro omits these scale measurement labels and displays the full value of the tick marks on the axis. This can be useful if you enter data into your spreadsheet in abbreviated form. When all the numbers in a particular spreadsheet are large, you may occasionally choose to save keystrokes by dividing all values by 1000 as you enter them (for example, entering **200** to mean 200,000 or **330** to mean 330,000). If you graph these numbers and Quattro Pro divides them by 100 when defining the axis labels, the resulting scaling measurement, (Hundreds), would be more confusing than helpful. You would be better off eliminating this scaling label and noting the measurement scale on the axis or main title.

Logarithmic Scaling

When you scale an axis logarithmically, each tick mark represents 10 times the value of the previous tick mark. This type of scaling can be useful for representing a series of values with a wide range of magnitude. Figure 14-5 shows two versions of the same graph: the first has a normally scaled Y-axis and the second has a logarithmically scaled Y-axis. Note the profusion of horizontal grid lines. If you find this confusing, you can eliminate the grid lines using / Graph | Overall | Grid (discussed shortly).

To specify logarithmic scaling, issue the Graph | Y-Axis | Mode or / Graph | X-Axis | Mode command and change the setting from Normal to Log. To return to regular scaling, change the setting back to Normal.

CUSTOMIZING GRAPHS
AS A WHOLE

So far you have learned a variety of commands for customizing individual series on a graph and for adjusting the axes. Quattro Pro also offers several commands for

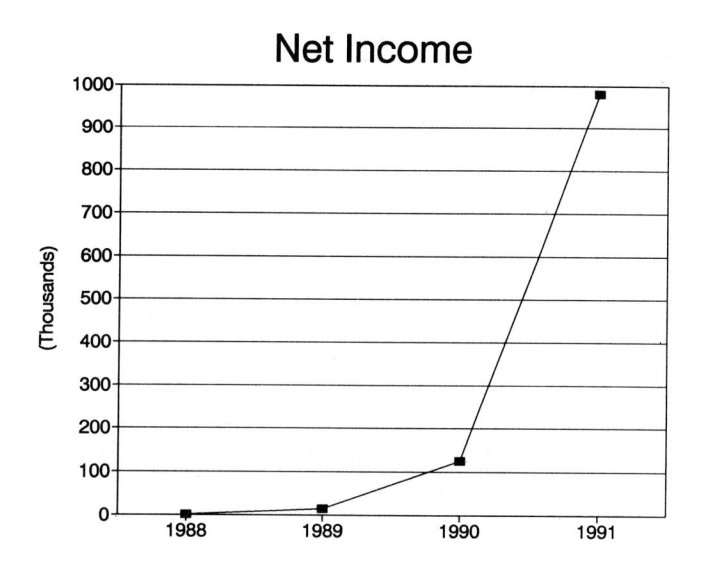

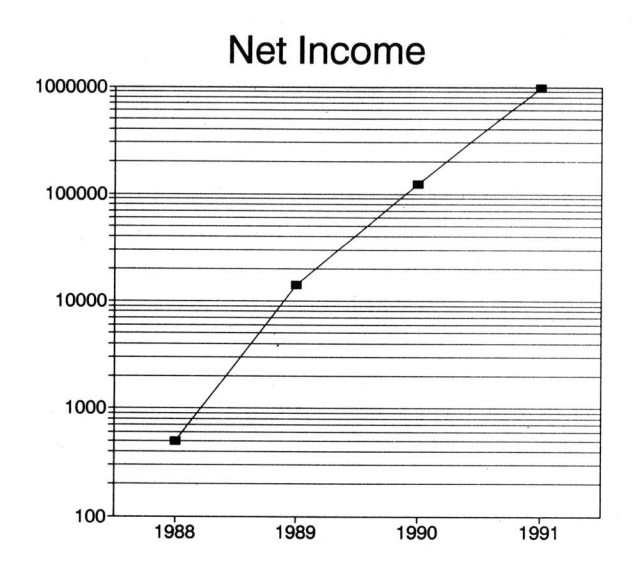

FIGURE 14-5. A graph with and without logarithmic scaling

changing the appearance of the graph as a whole. These commands are located on the Graph | Overall menu. They include commands for changing the grid lines in the interior of the graph, drawing boxes around various graph elements or around the graph as a whole, and eliminating or reinstating the three-dimensional effects from bars, columns, and pies in a graph.

Customizing Grid Lines

When you first create a graph other than a pie, column, or text graph, Quattro Pro displays dotted lines running parallel to the bottom of the graph, perpendicular to the Y-axis. These grid lines can help you pinpoint individual values on a graph by gauging how high they extend on the Y-axis. You can change both the pattern and the color used for these grid lines using the / Graph | Overall | Grid command.

The options on the top half of the Graph | Overall | Grid menu define where the grid lines are displayed. Select the Vertical option to display grid lines that run parallel to the Y-axis. Select Horizontal (the default) to display grid lines running perpendicular to the Y-axis. Select Both if you want to display lines in both directions. Select Clear to eliminate grid lines altogether.

The options on the bottom half of the Graph | Overall | Grid menu control what the grid lines look like. The Grid Color option lets you change the color of the grid lines. The Line Style option lets you choose from the same eight line types you can use in a line graph: Solid, Dotted (the default), Center-line, Dashed, plus heavier versions of those same four styles.

The Fill Color option lets you change the color displayed behind the grid lines, within the area bordered by the X- and Y-axes. (This is different from the graph background color which is the color behind the graph itself—outside the area bordered by the X- and Y-axes.)

Framing the Graph

The Outlines option on the Graph | Overall menu lets you draw or erase boxes around the graph as a whole, the graph titles, and the legend. By default, Quattro Pro draws boxes only around legends. When you issue the / Graph | Overall | Outlines command, Quattro Pro displays a menu with the options Titles, Legend, Graph, and Quit. If you select one of the first three options, Quattro Pro displays a menu of outline types—Box (a single-line box), Double Line, Thick Line, Shadow, 3D, Rnd Rectangle (a rounded rectangle), and None. The default setting for Legend is Box and for Titles and Graph is None. Figure 14-6 shows a graph in which the Outlines setting for Legend is Shadow, and for Graph is Rnd Rectangle.

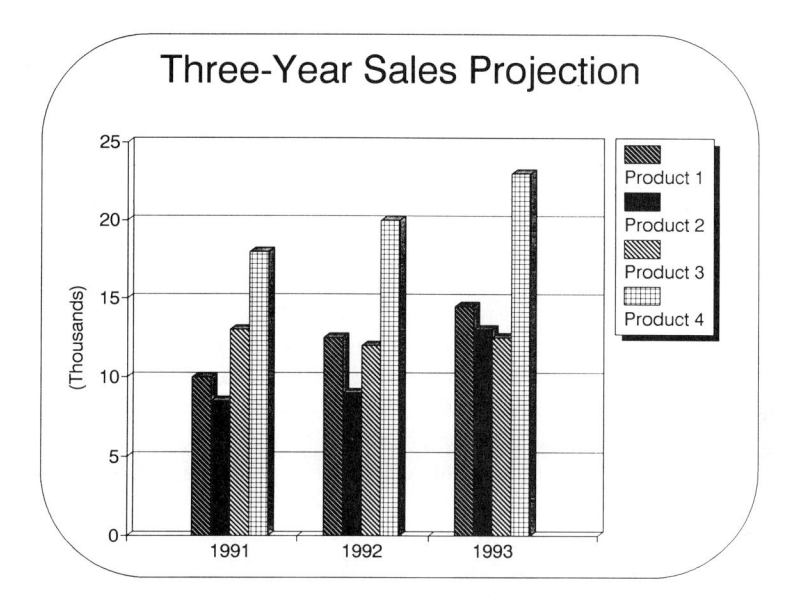

FIGURE 14-6. A graph with title, legend, and graph outlines

Changing The Background Color

The / **Graph** I **Overall** I **Background** Color command allows you to change the background color of a graph—that is, the color that is displayed outside the graph area. If you are using Graphics display mode, Quattro Pro displays a gallery of colors rather than a menu of color names. (To change the background color used inside the graph, issue / **Graph** I **Overall** I **Grid** I **Fill Color**.)

Displaying Graphs In Black and White

The / **Graph** I **Overall** I **Color/B&W** command lets you display graphs in black and white even if you are using a color monitor. You may find this useful if you are planning to print in black and white and want a more realistic preview of your printed graph. Changing the Graph | Overall | Color/B&W setting has no effect if you are using CGA, which always displays graphs in black and white.

Eliminating
The Three-Dimensional Effect

By default, Quattro Pro draws most graphs three-dimensionally—that is, it uses perspective lines to simulate three-dimensions. You can use the / Graph | Overall | Three-D command to add or remove the three-dimensional effect from a graph. In the case of bar graphs, this setting affects the display of perspective lines at the top and right edges of the bars and along the X- and Y-axes.

If your graph plots so many values that it would be unreadable in three-dimensions, Quattro Pro displays it in two-dimensions, regardless of the Three-D setting.

This chapter has covered a wide range of commands that allow you to embellish and fine-tune your graphs. Used judiciously, these commands allow you to create attractive, professional graphs.

15

THE ANNOTATOR

The Annotator Environment
Adding Text and Lines to the Graph
Modifying Graph Elements
Fine-Tuning Text Elements
Drawing Curves
Linking Elements to Points on the Graph
Using the Clipboard

The Annotator is a sophisticated drawing tool for embellishing graphs. You can use it to add text, lines, arrows, and shapes of all types to your graph. You can also use it to rearrange existing elements of the graph—including titles and legends. For example, you can use the Annotator to shift the title to the bottom of the graph or to move the legend a bit closer to the X-axis.

This chapter focuses on the basics—understanding the Annotator environment, creating boxed text and lines, linking design objects to points on a graph, and using clip art. With this foundation you will have enough knowledge to experiment further on your own.

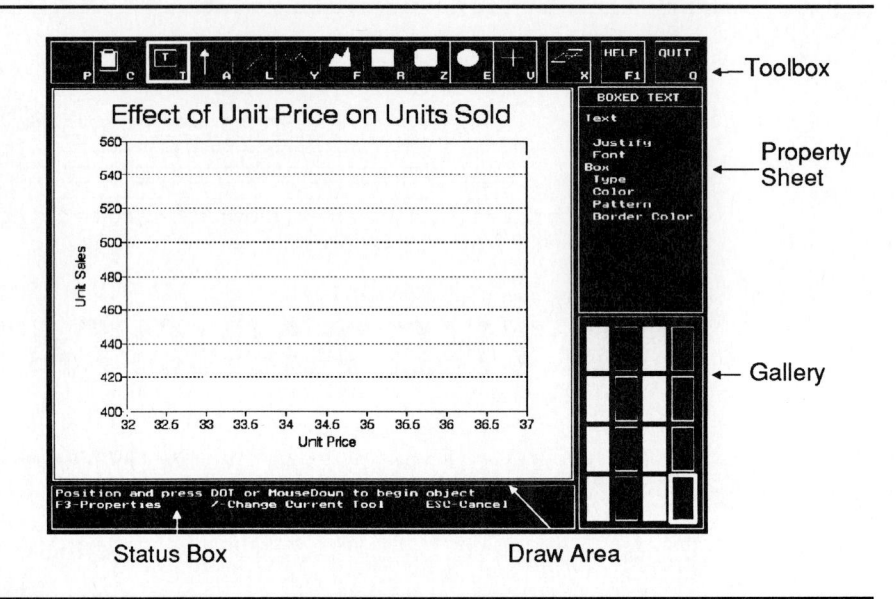

FIGURE 15-1. The Annotator screen

THE ANNOTATOR ENVIRONMENT

The process of annotating a graph involves defining and positioning various design elements—boxed text, lines, and shapes on the surface of a graph. You perform these operations on a separate screen with its own menus and function key assignments. This is the Annotator environment.

The Annotator Screen

You can display the Annotator screen either by issuing the / Graph | Annotate command or by typing / while displaying a full-screen graph.

The Annotator screen consists of five distinct areas, as shown in Figure 15-1.

- **The Toolbox** is the menu of icons (symbols) at the top of the Annotator screen. You use the options on this menu to create design elements, create and use clip art files, and leave the Annotator. To activate the Toolbox, type /. To return to the Draw Area without choosing a command, press `ESC`.

- **The Draw Area** occupies most of the Annotator screen. It contains the graph, titles, and legend. You use this area to create, move, resize, copy, and delete annotation design elements.

- **The Property Sheet** is a menu of the properties that you can adjust for the current design element. For example, when you select a line element in the Draw Area or by highlighting one of the line icons in the Toolbox, the Property Sheet lists Color and Style. You can use the Property Sheet to modify the design element before or after you add the element to the graph. To activate the Property Sheet, you press `F3`. (You must have already chosen a Toolbox option or selected a design element in the Draw Area.) To return to the Draw Area without choosing a property, press `ESC`.

- **The Gallery** displays a menu of options pertaining to the highlighted option on the Property Sheet. For example, if you highlight a Color option on the Property Sheet, the gallery displays all available colors. If you highlight the Box Type property on the Property Sheet, the Gallery displays the available box types. As soon as you choose an option on the Property Sheet, Quattro Pro activates the Gallery so you can choose a new setting for the selected design property.

- **The Status Box** at the bottom of the screen is where Quattro Pro displays instructions, keyboard shortcuts, and command descriptions. This area is essential for finding your way around the Annotator. If you are lost, check the Status Box for directions.

You may find it helpful to think of the Toolbox, Property Sheet, and Gallery as different levels of a single menu system—a menu system primarily used for creating and refining different types of design elements. The main menu is the Toolbox. Once you choose one of the design element options on that menu or select a design element that you previously added to the Draw Area, you can press `F3` to activate a more detailed menu—the Property Sheet. This menu allows you to fine-tune the element's display characteristics. As soon as you select one of the properties on the Property Sheet, Quattro Pro activates the Gallery, where you select the attribute—color, box type, font, and so on—that you want applied to the element.

The function keys have different effects in the Annotator than they do on the spreadsheet screen. The one exception is `F1`, which activates the Help system from either environment. Table 15-1 lists the effect of function keys in the Annotator. These keys are discussed as they become relevant.

Key	Effect
F1	Activates the Help system
F3	Activates the Property Sheet
F7	With a group of elements selected, activates Proportional Resize mode so that you can adjust both the size of the selected elements and the space between them, thus resizing the group of elements as a single image.
SHIFT-F7	Retains the current element selection so you can use TAB or SHIFT-TAB to select additional elements without deselecting the currently selected element.
F10	Redraws the Annotator screen. This is useful when you are annotating a very complex graph (in which case Quattro Pro may only partially redraw the graph to avoid delays).

TABLE 15-1. Effect of Function Keys in the Annotator

The Toolbox

The Toolbox is the Annotator's control center. It allows you to create new elements, copy or move elements from one graph to another (or to or from a clip art file), and provides the only means of leaving the Annotator screen.

There are three ways to select options from the Toolbox: You can highlight an icon and press (ENTER); you can type the letter displayed in the lower-right corner of the icon box; or if you are using a mouse, you can click the icon.

Figure 15-2 shows the Toolbox as it appears if you are using an EGA or VGA graphics adaptor. If you are using a CGA adaptor, the options are displayed slightly differently (although they work the same). In addition, if you are using CGA, Quattro Pro does not display the keys used to select each option. Therefore, to select options from the Toolbox, you must use the point-and-shoot method (highlighting the option and pressing (ENTER)) or refer to this book for the appropriate keys.

The Toolbox options, listed from left to right, are as follows. The keystroke you can use to select each option is shown in parentheses after the option name.

- **The Pick or Edit icon (/P)** looks like an empty arrow. You can think of this icon as a way of deselecting one of the other tools on the keyboard without selecting another design element. It is a means of returning to the Annotator's equivalent of Ready mode.

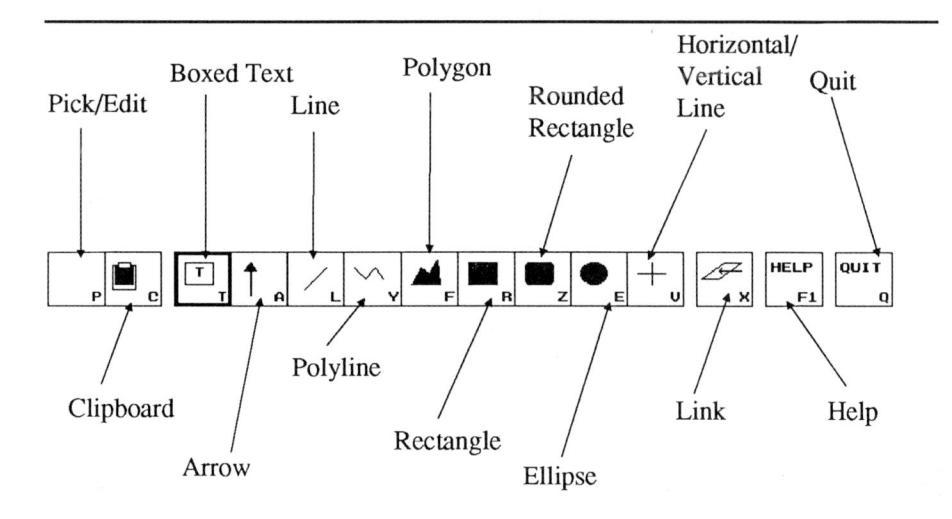

FIGURE 15-2. The Toolbox

- **The Clipboard icon (/C)** allows you to cut and paste elements in and out of a section of memory called the Clipboard or in and out of a disk file. You can also use the Clipboard to move elements in the Draw Area in front of or behind other elements.

- **The design element icons** (the third through eleventh icons in the Toolbox) let you add new design elements to your graph.

    Text (/T) adds a set of characters to the surface of the graph. The text is generally enclosed in a box, and can occupy multiple lines.
    Arrow (/A) draws a line with an arrowhead at one end.
    Line (/L) draws a straight line of any length.
    Polyline or Jointed Line (/Y) creates a straight line that is anchored in more than two places. The resulting element looks like a series of straight lines joined end to end.
    Polygon (/F) creates a multisided object of any size or shape. Unless you have a mouse, each edge of the element is a straight line. If you have a mouse, you can use the polygon icon to draw freehand any shape you like using the Curve Draw mode.
    Rectangle (/R) draws a rectangle of any dimensions.

Round Rectangle (/Z) creates a rectangle with rounded corners.

Ellipse (/E) draws a circle or ellipse of any size.

Horizontal/Vertical Line (/V) draws horizontal or vertical lines parallel or perpendicular to the edges of the graph or screen.

- **The Link option (/X)** lets you connect a design element to a particular point in the graph. If the point changes because you change the underlying value on the spreadsheet, the design element moves along with it.

- **The Help option (/H)** lets you activate the Quattro Pro Help system.

- **The Quit option (/Q)** lets you leave the Annotator and return to the regular spreadsheet or the graph screen.

ADDING TEXT AND LINES TO THE GRAPH

To add a design element to a graph, you activate the Toolbox and then select the appropriate icon. Quattro Pro displays a symbol called the pointer in the middle of the graph. If you are using a mouse, the pointer looks like an arrow; otherwise it looks like a large plus sign. At this point you can type / again to return to the Toolbox without actually adding any new element to the graph.

If you are using a mouse, place the pointer's point in the spot where you want to start drawing the element. Otherwise place the middle of the plus sign in the desired spot.

What you do next depends on the type of element you are adding.

- **To create a box of text**, move the pointer to the spot where you want the upper-left corner of the box located. Type a period or click the mouse to anchor the box in that spot, and start typing text (use the (BACKSPACE) key to erase mistakes, if necessary). The box expands to accommodate the characters you type. You can move to another line by pressing (CTRL-ENTER). You can include bullet characters in text elements using the \bullet #\ syntax described in Chapter 5. When you are done entering text, press (ENTER). Unless you plan to enter other text elements, you can also finish the element by selecting another option from the Toolbox. (See the "Fine-Tuning Text Elements" section to learn how to create text elements without boxes.)

- **To draw lines**, if you are not using a mouse, move the cell pointer to the spot where you want to start the line and type a period. Then use the arrow keys to draw a line extending from that point. Press (ENTER) when you are done.

If you are using a mouse, press the mouse button down in the spot where you want to start the line. Then drag the pointer until you reach where you want the line to stop, and release the button.

- **To draw arrows**, follow the procedure you use for drawing lines, keeping in mind the spot at which you end the line is where the arrowhead appears.

- **To draw horizontal and vertical lines**, follow the procedure for drawing lines. Move the pointer up or down on the screen to create a perfectly vertical line, left or right to create a perfectly horizontal line.

- **To draw rectangles**, if you are using the keyboard, move the cell pointer to one corner of the area where you want the rectangle to appear and type a period. Then move the cell pointer to the diagonally opposite corner of the rectangle and press (ENTER).

   If you are using a mouse, move the cell pointer to one corner. Press the button and hold it down while you drag the pointer to the opposite corner. Then release the button.

- **To draw ellipses**, follow the instructions for drawing rectangles. As soon as you press (ENTER), Quattro Pro draws the largest ellipse that fits in that rectangle and erases the rectangle itself from the screen.

- **To draw polylines and polygons**, if you are using the keyboard, move the pointer to your starting point and type a period. Then drag the pointer until you reach a corner or turning point, and press (ENTER). Next, drag the pointer until you reach the next corner, press (ENTER), and so on. You do not need to draw the last side of a polygon. As soon as you press (ENTER) twice to complete the element, Quattro Pro draws a line from the arrow's current position to the element's starting point. If you are using a mouse, move the pointer to the starting point, press the mouse button and hold it while you draw the first side, and then release the button. You can draw the rest of the lines in the element by moving the pointer where you want the next side of the element to end and clicking the mouse. As soon as you click, Quattro Pro draws a line from the last point in the polygon or polyline to the current position of the pointer. To complete the object, double-click the mouse or select any option from the Toolbox.

You can press (ESC) at any point between the time you start and the time you finish drawing a design element to erase the element from the screen. Then you can either start again or select another option from the Toolbox. Once you press (ENTER), you can erase the element by placing the pointer on the element (if it is not already there) and then pressing (DEL). You can only delete an element in this way until you select another option from the Toolbox. After that, you must select an element before you can delete it. (See "Modifying Graph Elements.")

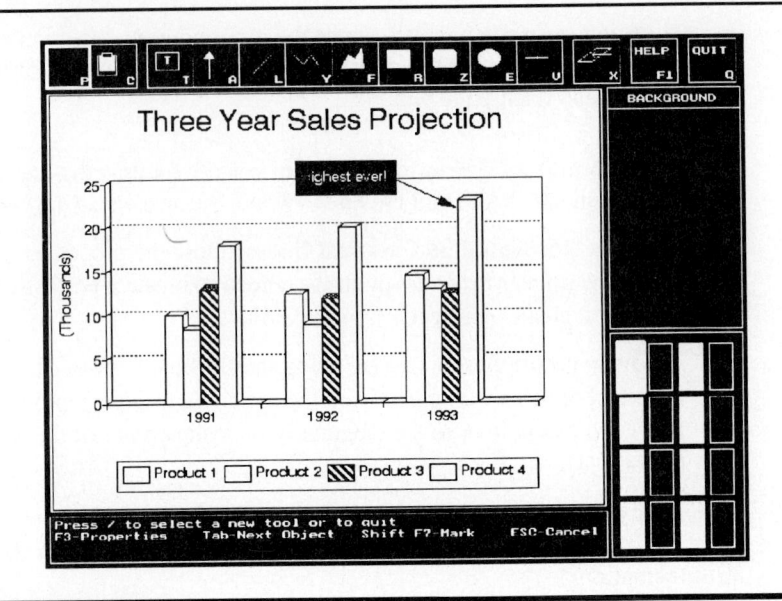

FIGURE 15-3. The BARS graph with box of text and an arrow

When you are finished creating a design element, Quattro Pro leaves the pointer on the screen in case you want to add another element of the same type. If you do want to add another element, follow the same steps. If you want to do something else, select another option from the Toolbox.

Whenever you create a design element, Quattro Pro displays brief instructions in the Status Box at the bottom of the screen. You can press (F1) (Help) to display a help screen with more detailed information on creating design elements.

Quattro Pro treats design elements rather like titles, legends, or any of the graph settings—it carries them over to graphs you subsequently create on the same spreadsheet. If you want to prevent this, issue the / Graph | Customize Series | **R**eset | Graph command before you create a new graph. (Be sure to save your graph using the / Graph | Name | Create command if you want to return to it in the future.)

Hands-on Practice

The following exercise involves adding a box of text to the BARS graph created in Chapter 13 and drawing an arrow from that box to the highest bar on the graph. The result is shown in Figure 15-3.

1. Unless the GRAPH.WQ1 spreadsheet is currently on your screen, save your work if necessary and then retrieve GRAPH.WQ1 using the **/File | Retrieve** command.

2. Issue the **/Graph | Name | Display** command, and select BARS to make that graph the current graph. Press (ESC) to return to the Graph menu.

3. Select the Text option, and then choose Legends. Select Position and change the setting from Right to Bottom. Select Quit twice to return to the Graph menu.

4. Select View to redisplay the graph. Then type / to activate the Annotator.

5. If you are using the keyboard, type / to activate the Toolbox. The Pick option at the left end of the Toolbox should now be highlighted. Press (RIGHT ARROW) twice to move to the Text icon, and press (ENTER). A pointer should now appear in the middle of your graph.
   If you are using a mouse, click on the Text icon.

6. If you are using the keyboard, press (UP ARROW) until the bottom of the pointer is even with the top edge of the graph (the 25000 mark on the Y-axis). Press (LEFT ARROW) until the middle of the pointer is immediately below the left edge of the "S" in the word "Sales" in the graph title. Type a period to anchor the text element. Now you are ready to start entering the text itself.
   If you are using a mouse, move the pointer to a spot about 1/4 inch above the top of the graph and directly below the left edge of the "S" in "Sales." Then click.

7. Type **Highest ever!** and press (ENTER). As you type, Quattro Pro displays the characters on screen, enclosed in a box. When you press (ENTER) the pointer moves to the upper-left corner of the box. At this point, if you want to add another text element, move the pointer to a new spot and start typing. If you are not happy with the box of text, press (DEL) to delete it. The pointer remains in the Draw Area, and you can move it to the desired location and start typing to create another box.

8. Draw a line with an arrowhead at the end from the box of text to the highest bar on the graph (the bar for 1993 sales of Product 4). Select the arrow icon (the fourth option from the left) from the Toolbox.

9. Move the pointer to the middle of the right side of the box of text you just entered. If you are using the keyboard, type a period to anchor the arrow. Press (DOWN ARROW) and (RIGHT ARROW) to move the pointer to the top left corner of the highest bar on the graph. The arrow looks best if you actually point to a spot just below the top edge rather than exactly to the top. Press (ENTER).
   If you are using a mouse, press the mouse button and hold it down while you drag the pointer to the bar. Then release.

10. Select Quit from the Toolbox by typing **/Q** or by clicking the Quit option for a full-screen image of the results. (This only works if you accessed the Annotator from the graph screen. If you displayed the Annotator from the Graph menu,

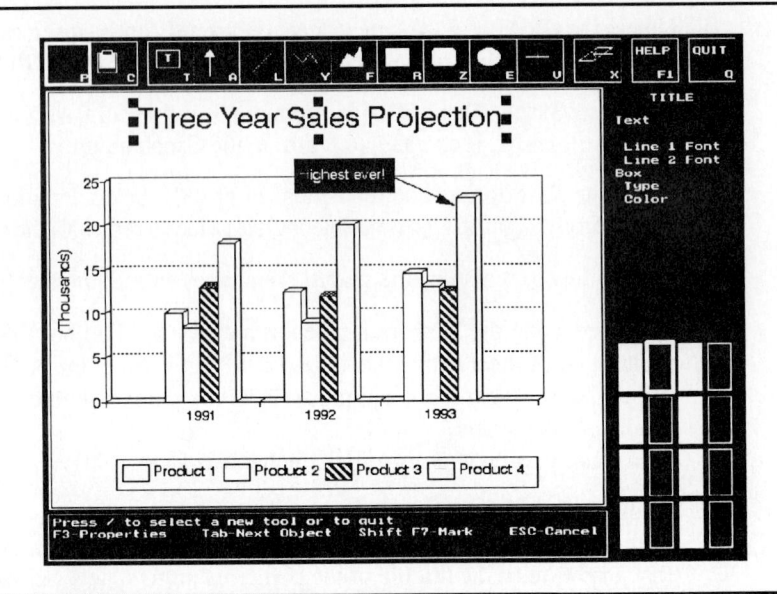

FIGURE 15-4. Selecting an element

Quattro Pro returns you to that menu and you need to select View or press (F10) to display your results on the full screen.)

MODIFYING GRAPH ELEMENTS

The first step in modifying a design element is to select it. To select an element with the keyboard, you press (TAB) to move through all the elements in the Draw Area. As you do, Quattro Pro displays small boxes, called *handles,* around one element at a time to indicate that the element is currently selected, as shown in Figure 15-4. If you keep pressing (TAB), Quattro Pro displays handles around the graph's titles, legend, and the graph itself as well as the design elements you have created through the Annotator. When handles appear around the element you want to change, you are ready to delete, move, or modify it.

If you have several overlapping elements on the screen, you may find it easier to select them using the keyboard. With a mouse it is often hard to determine which element you are clicking. Watch the first line of the Property Sheet (which indicates the selected element's type) to determine when the right element is selected.

To delete a selected element, just press (DEL). To reposition a selected element, use the arrow keys or drag it with the mouse. If you are using a mouse, be sure to place the pointer inside the element rather than on one of the handles. Dragging the handles changes the size of the element rather than its position.

Resizing Elements

The procedure for resizing an element depends on whether you are using the keyboard or mouse. If you are using the keyboard, start by selecting the element you want to resize. Type a period to enter Resize mode. Quattro Pro highlights the lower-right corner of the element, indicating that this is the corner it will use for resizing. If you prefer to resize the element by moving a different corner, keep pressing the period key until the box appears in that corner. Then use the arrow keys to move that corner to a new location. Quattro Pro displays an outline of the element to show you what the element would look like with the corner in each position. Once you press (ENTER) to complete the resize process, Quattro Pro shrinks or expands the element to fill the outline.

If you are using a mouse, select the element you want to resize. Then point to the handle that you want to use to resize the element and drag it to the desired location. With rectangles, use side handles to move one side of the rectangle; use corner handles to move two sides at the same time.

Quattro Pro lets you resize the graph itself as well as any of the design elements you have created through the Annotator. To resize graph text such as titles and legends, however, you must modify the text font using the Property Sheet.

Changing Design Properties

By default, any text elements you create are shown in 18-point Bitstream Swiss font, lines are solid, and two-dimensional shapes are completely filled in. You can change these design properties and others, such as colors and box types, using the Property Sheet at the upper-right of the Annotator screen.

You can change an element's design properties either before or after you add the element to your graph. To define design properties before you create the element, you select the design element from the Toolbox and then activate the Property Sheet by either pressing (F3) or clicking one of the Property Sheet options with the mouse. Next you change any properties you like (as described later) and press (ESC) to return to the Draw Area. Then you proceed to place the element on the graph. To change the design properties of an existing element, you select the element, activate the Property Sheet, make the desired changes, and press (ESC) to deactivate the Property Sheet. Then you can either select other elements or choose another option from the Toolbox.

When you first activate the Annotator, you see the word "Background" at the top of the Property Sheet, which means if you activate the Property Sheet, you can change the display of the spreadsheet's background. As soon as you select an element or choose a design element icon from the Toolbox, the Property Sheet changes to fit that element's type. For example, if you select a text element or select the Text icon from the Toolbox, the Property Sheet title is "Boxed Text," and the options include all the display attributes you can define for text elements.

Once you activate the Property Sheet—by pressing (F3) or clicking with the mouse—Quattro Pro draws a second border around the Property Sheet section of the screen and displays a short description of the currently selected option in the Status Box. To view descriptions of the other options on the Property Sheet, just press (DOWN ARROW) to highlight each option in turn and look at the Status Box descriptions. As you highlight different options on the Property Sheet, you also can see the options in the Gallery change, showing you the range of choices for the currently highlighted property.

You can select an attribute from the Property Sheet by highlighting it and pressing (ENTER) or clicking it with the mouse. In response, Quattro Pro usually activates the gallery, displaying a second border around that portion of the screen, and draws a box around the currently selected option. Use the arrow keys to highlight the option you want, and press (ENTER) or click the option with the mouse.

When you are done changing properties, you must deactivate the Property Sheet by pressing (ESC). The second border disappears from the Property Sheet section. Then you can select an option from the Toolbox or, if you are in the midst of creating an element, continue drawing the element on the graph.

Keep in mind that any settings you define for the various design properties affect all design elements of that type that you create afterward. For example, if you select a particular text element and change the box type to None, all text elements that you subsequently create will be displayed without a box, unless you explicitly assign them a different box type.

Modifying Several Elements at Once

You can perform all the same operations on a group of selected elements that you can perform on just one element, including moving, resizing, deleting, and changing design properties. The first step in modifying a group of elements is to select all of them. The procedure for selecting multiple elements depends on whether you are using the keyboard or a mouse.

If you are using the keyboard, use (TAB) and (SHIFT-TAB) to move through the elements. When you reach one you want to select, press (SHIFT-F7). This retains the current selection and keeps the handles on the element while allowing you to select additional elements. Next, press (TAB) until you reach the next element you want to select. Press (SHIFT-F7) again to retain that selection, use (TAB) to move to the next element you want to select, and so on.

If you are using a mouse, you can select all the elements in a particular section of the Draw Area by dragging from one corner of the area to the opposite corner. This draws a box around the entire area. As soon as you release the mouse button, Quattro Pro displays handles on all the elements in that area. To select several elements in different parts of the Draw Area, hold down the (SHIFT) key while you click each element.

As soon as you select more than one element, the title on the Property Sheet changes to Group, indicating that changes you make will affect a group of design elements.

To deselect a single element, either tab past the element without pressing (SHIFT-F7) or click it again with the mouse. To deselect all currently selected elements, press (ESC) or choose one of the design element icons from the Toolbox.

If you are resizing a group of elements, Quattro Pro by default only resizes the elements themselves. It does not adjust the amount of space between the elements. In other words, Quattro Pro treats each of the selected elements as a distinct entity that you want to shrink or enlarge. It just happens to be shrinking or enlarging several elements at once. This can create problems if you resize a set of elements that form a single image. To resize the space between elements while you resize the elements—so that the elements maintain the same spatial relationship—you must activate Proportional Resize mode. If you are using the keyboard, you can do this by pressing (F7). If you are using the mouse, you can simultaneously select a group of elements and enter Proportional Resize mode by holding down the (ALT) key while you drag to select an area that encloses all the elements that you want to resize. Then release the (ALT) key and drag one of the handles to resize the group.

Modifying Non-Annotator Elements

As mentioned, Quattro Pro allows you to select the graph's titles, legends, and the graph as a whole, as well as any of the elements you create through the Annotator itself. Once you have selected one of these elements, you can move it, change its design properties, or delete it. Any changes you make are recorded on the various Graph menus. For example, if you delete the second line of the Title, Quattro Pro erases the 2nd Line setting on the Graph | Text menu. If you change the font for the legend, Quattro Pro changes the Graph | Text | Font | Legends setting.

FINE-TUNING TEXT ELEMENTS

There are too many design elements, each with too many design properties, to discuss in depth here. This chapter concentrates on text elements, since these are the most commonly used design elements.

Editing Text Elements

To edit the contents of a text element, select the element and press (F2) (Edit). Quattro Pro displays a cursor just after the last character in the text element. Use the arrow keys, (HOME), (END), (BACKSPACE), (DEL), and (INS) just as you would when editing data on the input line. If you want to move the cursor to the next line, press (CTRL-ENTER).

When you are done editing the text, press (ENTER) to save your changes or (ESC) to discard them.

Changing Text Design Properties

You can modify three properties related to the text itself: color, justification, and the font. You can also modify four properties of the box surrounding the text: the box type, interior color, fill pattern, and border color.

By default, the text color is white, the text is left-justified, the text font is 18-point Bitstream Swiss, the box type is single line, the interior color is light blue, the fill pattern is empty, and the border color is blue.

One modification you might make to text elements is changing the box type to None. Quattro Pro eliminates the entire box, fill pattern and all. This allows you to display text directly on the surface of the graph. It is also helpful when you are creating a text graph (as described in the next section) or when you want to place a shape, such as an ellipse, behind the text. The procedure for displaying text on shapes is described under "Using the Clipboard" later in this chapter.

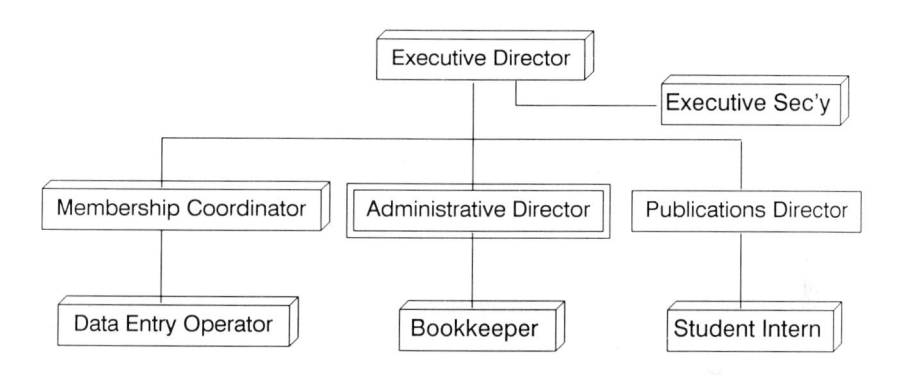

```
                    ┌─────────────────────┐
                    │ AARDVARK ASSOCIATION │
                    └─────────────────────┘


                         ┌───────────────────┐
                         │ Executive Director│
                         └───────────────────┘
                                   └──────────┌────────────────┐
                                              │ Executive Sec'y│
                                              └────────────────┘
         ┌──────────────────────┐  ┌──────────────────────┐  ┌──────────────────────┐
         │ Membership Coordinator│  │ Administrative Director│  │ Publications Director│
         └──────────────────────┘  └──────────────────────┘  └──────────────────────┘
         ┌────────────────────┐    ┌─────────────┐           ┌────────────────┐
         │ Data Entry Operator│    │ Bookkeeper  │           │ Student Intern │
         └────────────────────┘    └─────────────┘           └────────────────┘
```

FIGURE 15-5. An organization text chart

Creating Text Graphs

Text graphs are graphs that consist entirely of elements created through the Annotator. To create a text graph, you can either activate the Annotator when no series are selected or change the graph type to Text before activating the Annotator (in which case, Quattro Pro automatically resets all the series). When Quattro Pro displays the Annotator screen, the Draw Area is completely blank. You can fill it with any design elements you like.

Figure 15-5 shows an organization chart created as a text chart through the Annotator. It was created by setting the graph type to Chart and then adding a text element for each position in the organization. The lines between elements were drawn using the horizontal/vertical lines option.

DRAWING CURVES

If you have a mouse, you can draw curved lines and shapes using Quattro Pro's Curve Draw mode. Start by selecting the proper design element icon from the Toolbox: use Polygon (/ F) if you want to draw a closed shape or Polyline (/ Y) to draw a line. Next, press (SCROLL LOCK) to turn on Curve Draw mode. Then position the pointer, press the mouse button, and drag the mouse. Release the mouse button when you are done. As you drag the mouse, Quattro Pro displays points along the mouse's path; it connects these points with a line when you release the mouse button. The slower you drag the mouse, the more dots Quattro Pro draws.

You can also enter Curve Draw mode by pressing and holding (SHIFT) while you drag. This method is useful when you want to alternate between curves and straight lines. Just press (SHIFT) when you want curves, and release it when you want straight edges.

In Curve Draw mode Quattro Pro does not automatically draw in the last side of a polygon when you double-click or press (ENTER) to complete the object. To close a polygon you can either click the polygon element in the Toolbox or turn off Curve Draw mode (by pressing (SCROLL LOCK) again or releasing (SHIFT)) and then double-click or press (ENTER).

LINKING ELEMENTS TO POINTS ON THE GRAPH

You usually want a design element to maintain its position relative to a particular data point on the graph, even when your data changes. In the case of your BARS graph, for example, you want the arrow to point to the bar for 1993 sales of Product 4, even if you change the underlying value on the spreadsheet. You can accomplish this by linking the design element (the arrow) to the data point (the 1993 sales figure for Product 4).

Linking a design element to a data point on your graph involves the following steps:

1. Select the design element you want to link.

2. Select the Link icon from the Toolbox. Quattro Pro displays a menu of the six graph series in the Property Sheet section of the screen.

3. Tell Quattro Pro which spreadsheet value you want to link the element to. This is a two-step process. You start by selecting a series. Quattro Pro displays a box with the prompt "Enter link index," and you enter a number indicating where the value

occurs within the specified series. For example, if you want to link a design element to the second value in the third series, you would select 3rd Series from the menu and then enter **2** as the link index.

To unlink an element, select the element, choose the Link option from the Toolbox, and choose Unlink.

Practice using this linking feature on the BARS graph. Try raising the amount for Product 4 in 1993 to see what happens when you change data without linking design elements. Then link the two design elements that you created (the text element and the arrow) to the data point, and change the data again.

1. Move to D7 and enter **30000**.

2. Press (F10) to view the graph, and note that the arrow no longer points to the top of the bar.

3. Press (ESC) to return to the spreadsheet display, and enter **23000** so that the arrow now points to the desired spot on the bar.

4. Press (F10) and then type / to activate the Annotator.

5. Select both the arrow and the text elements by pressing (TAB) until handles appear around one of those elements. Then press (SHIFT-F7) to select that element, and press (TAB) until handles appear around the other element. If you are using a mouse, you can simply drag the pointer to draw a rectangle around both elements.

    If you link just the arrow, the arrow moves with the data point but becomes disconnected from the box in the process.

6. Select the Link option from the Toolbox, and then select 4th Series from the Property Box. When prompted for a link index, enter **3**.

7. Press (ESC) to deactivate the Property Sheet.

8. Leave the Annotator by typing **/Q** or clicking the Quit option.

9. Press (ESC) to return to the spreadsheet display.

10. Enter **30000** in D7, and press (F10) to view the results. This time the design elements rise with the associated bar.

11. Issue the **/ Graph | Name | Create** command and enter **BARS2** to save the current graph.

12. Issue the **/ File | Save** command to save the spreadsheet, replacing the previous version.

USING THE CLIPBOARD

The Clipboard option (the second option in the Toolbox) gives you the following capabilities:

- You can cut and paste design elements from one graph to another or to duplicate a design element within a graph.

- You can create and use clip art (design elements saved as disk files). Quattro Pro comes packaged with 35 clip art files (all of which have the extension CLP) with designs ranging from pictures of airplanes, clocks, and computers to maps of the U.S. and the world. You can also use third-party clip art files produced in the CLP file format, such as those produced by Marketing Graphics, Inc. in Glen Allen, VA.

- You can move elements between the foreground and background when two or more elements overlap. This can be particularly useful for displaying text against a shape such as an ellipse.

Each of these operations is described in the following sections.

When you select the Clipboard, Quattro Pro displays and activates a Clipboard menu in the Property Sheet section of the screen. To select an option, highlight it and press (ENTER) or click it with the mouse. To leave the Clipboard, press (ESC).

Cutting and Pasting Graph Elements

You can use the Clipboard as a place to temporarily store design elements. You then can copy or move them from one graph to another or temporarily remove them from a graph and paste them back later. Cutting and pasting is particularly useful when you create a company logo or other shape that you want to reuse.

To cut and paste a graph element, follow these steps:

1. Select the element or elements that you want to cut and paste.

2. Select Clipboard from the Toolbox.

3. Select the Copy option if you want to copy the selected elements from the current graph to the Clipboard. Choose Cut if you want to remove the selected elements from the current graph and transfer them to the Clipboard.

4. If you want to copy the elements to a different graph, choose the Quit icon from the Toolbox. Then do whatever you need to do to display the other graph.

5. Once the graph in which you want to insert the Clipboard contents is displayed, activate the Annotator.

6. Select Clipboard.

7. Choose Paste. Quattro Pro inserts the element exactly where it was positioned in the original graph. The inserted elements remain selected, so you can easily move or resize them.

Cutting and pasting works fine if you want to immediately copy or transfer from one graph to another. If you plan to reuse the element in a future work session, however, you must save it to a clip art file, as described in the next section.

Creating and Using Clip Art Files

A *clip art file* is a graphic image saved in a disk file. Quattro Pro is packaged with a set of clip art files with images ranging from airplanes to world maps.

You can import these images into your own graphs using the Clipboard's Paste from option. As soon as you select the Paste from option, Quattro Pro displays a list of all the clip art files in the default data directory—clip art files that you have created as well as the ones packaged with the Quattro Pro program. As soon as you select a file from the list, Quattro Pro displays the clip art image in the center of the Draw Area (on top of any design elements that are already there).

Most of the Quattro Pro clip art files consist of design elements (some of them contain dozens) that form a single image. When you first insert clip art into your graph, all the design elements in the image are already selected. This makes it easy for you to resize or reposition the image. However, it also makes the image hard to see because of all the handles. If you have a mouse, you can easily reselect all the elements (unless they happen to be on top of other design elements) by dragging the pointer to draw a rectangle around the image. If you do not have a mouse, it may be extremely difficult to reselect all the elements later, particularly in images that consist of many small elements. In this case you must resize or reposition the image when you first copy it into your graph, before you do anything that deselects the elements.

Caution: Be sure to activate Proportional Resize mode by pressing (F7) before resizing an image from one of the Quattro Pro clip art files. Otherwise the individual elements lose their original spatial relationships, and the image may be thoroughly scrambled.

You may want to create your own clip art files to save one or more design elements for future use. Follow these steps to create a clip art file:

1. Select the element or elements that you want to save to the file.
2. Select Clipboard.
3. Choose the Copy to option. Quattro Pro displays a list of clip art files in the current directory. Enter a filename or select one from the list if you want to overwrite an existing clip art file. Do not include a file extension because Quattro Pro automatically assigns the CLP extension.

When you want to retrieve the design elements from the clip art file into a graph, activate the Clipboard, select Paste from, and either enter the name of the clip art file or select it from the files list.

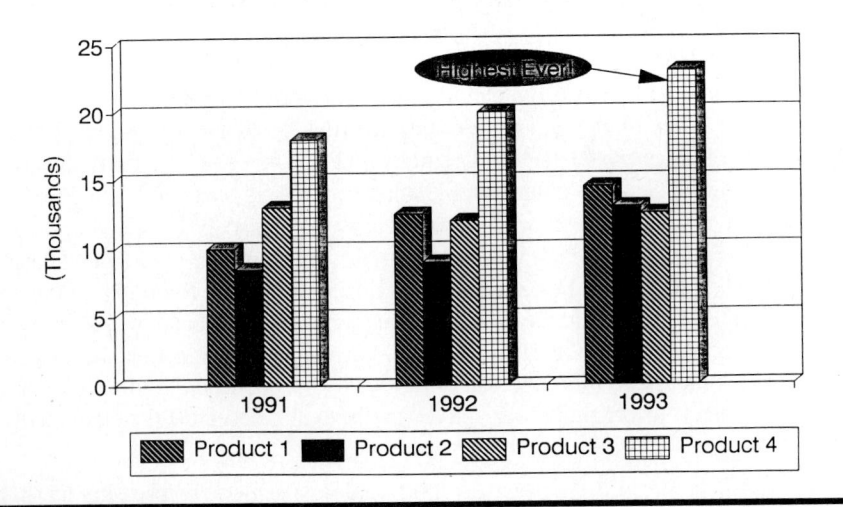

FIGURE 15-6. BARS graph with an ellipse behind the text element

Moving Elements Between Foreground and Background

If two or more design elements on a graph overlap, you can use the Clipboard to determine which element will be placed on top. The To Bottom option moves the currently selected element to the bottom of the stack, and the To Top option places it on top.

These options are particularly useful when you want to display text against a shape such as an ellipse. For example, Figure 15-6 shows a revised version of the graph you have been working on throughout this chapter. It was created by changing the box type for the text element to None, drawing an ellipse over the element, changing the fill pattern of the ellipse to light dots, and moving the ellipse to the background, behind the text element.

This chapter has provided an overview of Quattro Pro's graph Annotator. If you have a need for graphic images and an eye for design, you may want to experiment further, using some of the other design element types and combining design elements into more complex images. The Quattro Pro *User's Guide* provides a few illustrations of the type of images that can be created through the Annotator. If you have the talent and the interest, try creating some of your own.

16

DESIGNING AND BUILDING DATABASES

Database Terminology
Designing a Database
Data Entry Commands
Building a Sample Database
Adding and Deleting Records
Modifying Your Database

    A database is a collection of data that share a common structure. In almost all cases, databases consist of information about a group of related people, things, or events, such as a set of customers, inventory items, or financial transactions. Phone books, customer ledger cards, and card catalogs are all examples of databases. In each case information is maintained about a particular type of entity (people with telephones, customers, library books), and the same items of information (name, address, and phone number in the case of a phone book) are maintained for each person or thing in the group.

    This chapter covers the creation of databases in Quattro Pro—from designing a database to entering and updating the data. In subsequent chapters you learn to manipulate databases, including how to rearrange the data into particular orders, find or extract records that meet specified conditions, and generate database statistics.

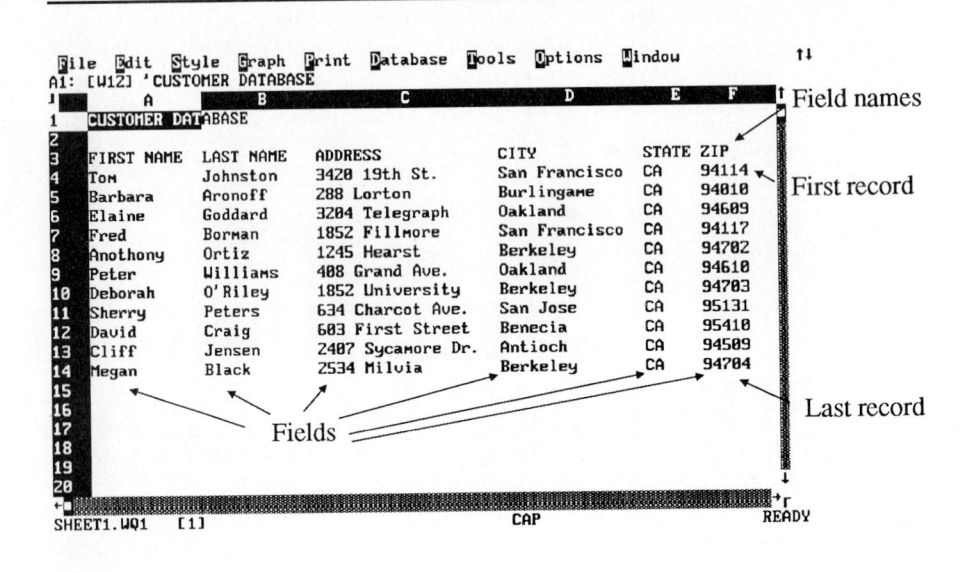

FIGURE 16-1. Database terminology

DATABASE TERMINOLOGY

Figure 16-1 shows a database consisting of customer records. Note that each row contains the same items of information. The customer's first name is in column A, the last name is in column B, the street address is in column C, the city is in column D, the state is in E, and the ZIP code is in F. In database terminology, each logical unit in the database (in this case one customer) is called a *record*. Each item of information in the row is known as a *field*. In Quattro Pro databases, each record occupies a single row and all the fields line up in columns.

At the top of each column is a label indicating the column's contents. Such column headings are known as *field names*. As discussed in Chapter 18, these field names are frequently used to express instructions for locating or extracting selected records from a database.

DESIGNING A DATABASE

Although it is possible to add, delete, or rearrange fields after entering data, you can save a lot of time if you think out your application as carefully as possible beforehand.

In general it is a good idea to begin this design process by considering the type of output—lists, reports, statistics, graphs, and other types of information—that you need to generate. When you have a clear sense of what you want *out* of your database, you have a better idea of what to put *in*. When you know generally what the database will contain, you can begin planning the specifics—deciding what fields you want to include, their data types, and their order. The following sections cover rules and suggestions to keep in mind during this process.

Field Content

The first issue to consider is how to separate your information into individual fields. Start by making a list of the basic categories of information, then go back and refine your list. Generally, you should create a separate field for every item of information you will use for sorting or selecting records. For example, if you plan to arrange all the records in your database alphabetically by last name, you must either place the last name before the first name in the name field or create separate fields for last name and first name.

Values or Labels?

Once you have decided what fields to include, you must determine the type of data you will enter in them. You should always use a consistent data type for each field, so you can easily manipulate the data later.

The primary choice is between values and labels. In general you should enter data as a value if you want to use it in any mathematical calculations or if you want to sort the database into numerical order on the basis of that field.

Another important factor in deciding whether to fill a field with labels or values is the way you want the field to be sorted. When you sort labels that consist entirely of digits, Quattro Pro orders the labels one digit at a time. For example, the label 12 is placed before the label 2 because Quattro Pro compares the first character in each label and finds the first character in 12 (the number 1) to be less than the first character in 2 (the number 2). If you enter the same digits as values, however, and then sort those values, the database is arranged in numerical order and 2 comes before 12.

There is another important difference in how Quattro Pro handles labels and values. If you enter a *leading zero* (a zero entered to the left of any other digits and the decimal point) in a value, that zero is dropped as soon as Quattro Pro stores the value. If you enter **01234**, for example, Quattro Pro records it simply as 1234 (which is disastrous if you are entering ZIP codes). In a label, a leading zero is treated as a distinct character when sorted.

Keep in mind that Quattro Pro treats your entry as a value if it starts with a number or arithmetic operator. This means that when you enter the phone number **555-1234**, Quattro Pro subtracts 1234 from 555 and returns the value -679. You encounter similar problems with social security numbers or any other entries that consist of only numbers and dashes. Until now you have prevented such problems by entering a label prefix character at the beginning of the entry to inform Quattro Pro that you want the data treated as text. You will learn a more efficient means of doing this in the "Data Entry Commands" section later in this chapter.

Field Order and Length

Designing a database also entails deciding on the order of the fields. Your goal should be to arrange fields in a way that makes the data both easy to read and easy to enter. The order of fields should be as intuitive and natural as possible, with related items of data grouped together. If you intend to enter data from a set of input forms that cannot be changed easily, make sure that you arrange the data in similar order in your database. You should always place fields that can be used to identify each record (such as name, account code, or inventory item name) in the leftmost columns so that you can easily freeze these fields at the edge of the screen with the Layout Titles command while you scan the remaining fields in the database. If certain fields will be left blank in many records, try to place these fields on the right side of the database, making it easier to skip over them during input and move on to the next row.

Field Names

Database field names serve a dual purpose: as column headings and as a means of identifying fields in selection criteria (which is covered in Chapter 18). You should follow a few rules when creating field names:

- Make each field name unique.

- Avoid using names that are already used for named blocks.

- Do not use decorative characters, such as dashes or asterisks, between the field names and the first record in the database, even though you may prefer the way they look. They are treated as rows in the database and can cause undesirable results when you try to sort, select, or analyze your data.

Although you can draw a line underneath the field names using the / Style I Line Drawing command, this is not advisable either because it adds line-drawing characters to each field in the first record. If you then change any of the calculated fields in the first record and copy the new formula down the column, you generate unwanted lines throughout your database.

- Do not use more than 15 characters in a field name. As you learn in Chapter 18, the process of selecting records from your database generally involves using the field names as block names, and the maximum length for block names is 15.

- Remember to enter all field names within a single row. If you want to use the field name ACCOUNT NUMBER, for example, enter both words in a single cell (abbreviate them if necessary) rather than entering **ACCOUNT** in one cell and **NUMBER** in the cell below.

Cell Referencing in Databases

Although most databases consist primarily of constants (values and labels entered directly into the spreadsheet), they can also contain formulas. By entering formulas in your spreadsheet, you create *calculated fields*—fields that are computed from other values rather than entered directly.

There are two rules for cell referencing in calculated fields. Unless you follow them carefully, the cell references will not be adjusted properly when you sort the database into a different order, and your formulas will yield incorrect results.

- **Rule 1** Whenever you enter a formula referencing another cell in the same row, make the row reference relative so that it is adjusted as it is copied down the row and refers to the proper cell even if the record's row position changes as a result of sorting. In the database shown in Figure 16-2, cell E11 contains the formula

    @IF(C11=3,D11+364,D11+182)

    which calculates the subscription expiration date based on the rate code (1, 2, or 3) in that record. (Code 3 indicates an annual subscription; the other two codes indicate a semiannual subscription.) If the rate code is 3, then 364 days are added to the subscription date; otherwise 182 days are added to the subscription date. Note that all cell references in this formula are relative. As a result, if the database is sorted into alphabetical order by last name, for example, the cell references are adjusted to refer to the cells in columns C and D of the row to which the record is relocated.

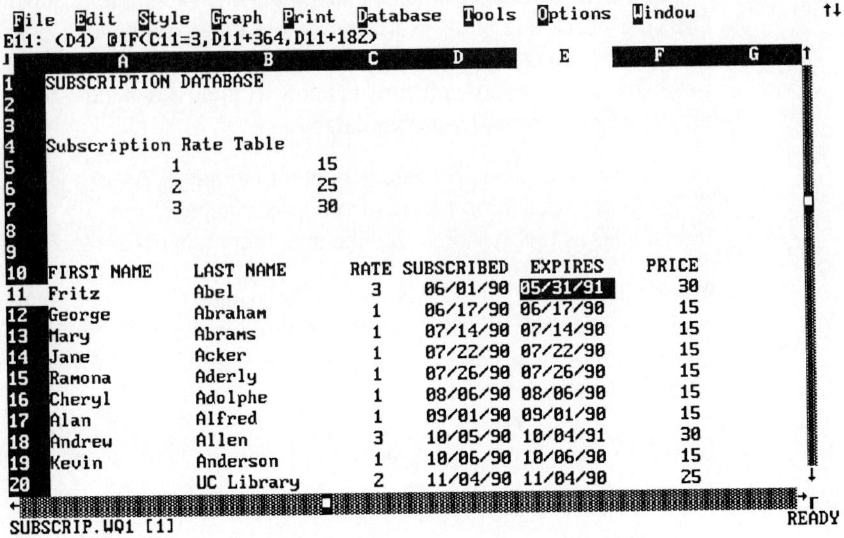

```
File  Edit  Style  Graph  Print  Database  Tools  Options  Window         ↑↓
E11: (D4) @IF(C11=3,D11+364,D11+182)
          A              B          C       D         E          F       G
 1  SUBSCRIPTION DATABASE
 2
 3
 4  Subscription Rate Table
 5              1                   15
 6              2                   25
 7              3                   30
 8
 9
10  FIRST NAME     LAST NAME     RATE  SUBSCRIBED  EXPIRES    PRICE
11  Fritz          Abel           3    06/01/90    05/31/91    30
12  George         Abraham        1    06/17/90    06/17/90    15
13  Mary           Abrams         1    07/14/90    07/14/90    15
14  Jane           Acker          1    07/22/90    07/22/90    15
15  Ramona         Aderly         1    07/26/90    07/26/90    15
16  Cheryl         Adolphe        1    08/06/90    08/06/90    15
17  Alan           Alfred         1    09/01/90    09/01/90    15
18  Andrew         Allen          3    10/05/90    10/04/91    30
19  Kevin          Anderson       1    10/06/90    10/06/90    15
20                 UC Library     2    11/04/90    11/04/90    25

SUBSCRIP.WQ1 [1]                                                    READY
```

FIGURE 16-2. Relative cell referencing in a database

- **Rule 2** Whenever you reference cells outside the database, make the reference absolute so that it will not change as it is copied down columns of the database or when the database is sorted. The subscription database also contains the formula

@VLOOKUP(C11,A5..B7,1)

in cell F11. This formula determines the price of each subscription by looking up the rate (C11) in a lookup table (A5..B7) located outside the database. Because the reference to the lookup table is absolute, it remains unchanged as it is copied down column F and when the records in the database are sorted into a different order.

DATA ENTRY COMMANDS

Quattro Pro offers two commands—/ Database I Data Entry I Labels Only and / Database I Data Entry I Dates Only—that allow you to restrict the type of data entered in a block of cells. The / Database I Data Entry commands are most often used in database applications, where all the entries in an entire column are of the same data type. You can, however, use them in any spreadsheet you like, whenever you want all the entries in a particular block to be either labels or dates. Note that the / Database I Data Entry commands affect only new entries; they have no impact on previously entered data.

You can use / Database I Data Entry I Labels Only to allow only label entries within a specified block. If you then enter a number into one of the cells in that block, Quattro Pro automatically adds the default label prefix character to your entry, thus turning it into a label. This can be extremely useful when you are entering data such as phone numbers, social security numbers, and ZIP codes.

You can use / Database I Data Entry I Dates Only to allow only date entries within a specified block. If you enter characters in any one of Quattro Pro's five Date formats or its four Time formats, Quattro Pro automatically translates your entry into a date serial number, as if you had pressed CTRL-D at the beginning of the entry. If the data you enter are not in one of the allowable formats, Quattro Pro beeps, displays the error message Invalid date or time, and automatically enters Edit mode.

When you issue either the / Database I Data Entry I Labels Only or / Database I Data Entry I Dates Only command, Quattro Pro stores hidden codes in each cell of the specified block. You can always tell whether the current cell has been designated as a label cell or date cell by looking for the word "Label" or "Date" at the beginning of the input line.

If you no longer want to restrict the type of data entered into a cell, you can issue the / Database I Data Entry I General command to remove the dates-only or labels-only designation.

BUILDING A SAMPLE DATABASE

You can practice the various database commands and techniques by constructing a small sample database. This practice application is an order-tracking database for a mail order company that sells discount floppy disks. You will be building, refining, and manipulating this database for the remainder of this chapter as well as in Chapters 17 through 19. The database includes fields for account name, order date, item number, quantity ordered, price, subtotal, tax, total, payment date, payment amount, and amount due. Both the subtotal and total fields are calculated fields. Assume that most but not all the orders are paid for as they are placed and that customers generally order only one type of item at a time. Sales tax is applied only to orders within New York State. Assume that you are going to look up the tax rate for customers in New York as you enter the data.

1. Start with a blank spreadsheet and adjust the column widths as follows:

Column	Number of Characters
A	14
B	11
C	6
D	5
G	7
I	10

   Leave rows E, F, and H set to 9 characters.

2. In cell A1, enter **MAIL ORDERS**.

3. Draw a double line under this title by issuing the / **Style** | **Line Drawing** command, pressing (ENTER) to accept the default block of A1..A1, selecting a Placement of Bottom, and choosing a Line Type of Double. Select Quit to return to Ready mode.

4. Enter the following field names:

In Cell	Enter
A4	**ACCOUNT**
B4	**ORDER DATE**
C4	**ITEM**
D4	**QUANT**
E4	**PRICE**
F4	**SUBTOTAL**
G4	**TAX**
H4	**TOTAL**
I4	**PMT DATE**
J4	**PMT AMT**
K4	**AMT DUE**

5. Right align the last seven field names by issuing the /**Style** | **Alignment** | **Right** command and specifying the block E4..K4.

6. Issue the / **Database** | **Data Entry** | **Labels Only** command and specify a block of C5..C12 (the ITEM field for eight records).

7. Issue the / **Database** | **Data Entry** | **Dates Only** command and specify a block of B5..B12 (the ORDER DATE field for eight records). Issue the same command again and specify a block of I5..I12 (the PMT DATE field for eight records).

8. Enter the first record in your database:

In Cell	Enter
A5	**Arby & Sons**
B5	**8/20/90**
C5	**34-35**
D5	**1**
E5	**19.95**

9. Enter the next seven records. Leave the SUBTOTAL, TOTAL, and AMT DUE fields blank for now; many of the records have other blank fields as well.

In Cell	Enter
A6	**Micro Center**
B6	**9/3/90**
C6	**32-45**
D6	**5**
E6	**22.95**
I6	**9/3/90**
J6	**114.75**
A7	**ABC Group**
B7	**9/3/90**
C7	**32-45**
D7	**2**
E7	**22.95**
I7	**9/3/90**
J7	**45.90**
A8	**CompuSchool**
B8	**9/7/90**
C8	**38-21**
D8	**2**
E8	**20.50**
G8	**3.38**
A9	**XYZ Co.**
B9	**10/10/90**
C9	**34-35**
D9	**3**
E9	**19.95**
I9	**10/10/90**
J9	**59.85**

A10	**Craig Assoc.**
B10	**10/11/90**
C10	**38-21**
D10	**1**
E10	**20.50**
A11	**Jim Stern**
B11	**10/15/90**
C11	**32-45**
D11	**1**
E11	**22.95**
G11	**1.89**
I11	**10/15/90**
J11	**22.95**
A12	**Smith & Co.**
B12	**11/1/90**
C12	**38-21**
D12	**2**
E12	**20.50**
G12	**3.38**
I12	**11/1/90**
J12	**44.38**

10. Move to F5 and enter **+D5∗E5** to calculate the subtotal. Then copy the formula down column F by issuing the / **Edit** I **Copy** command, accepting the default source block F5..F5, and specifying the destination F5..F12.

11. Move to H5 and enter the total formula **+F5+G5**. Copy it down the block H5..H12.

12. Move to K5 and enter **+H5-J5** to calculate the amount due. Copy it down the block K5..K12. (Don't worry about the value in cell K9 for now.)

13. Change the default numeric format for the spreadsheet by issuing the / **Options** I **Formats** I **Numeric** Format command and specifying the , (comma) format with two decimal places. Type **Q** twice to return to Ready mode.

14. Format the values in the QUANT field by issuing the / **Style** I **Numeric Format** command, selecting the Fixed format, and specifying zero decimal places. Enter **D5..D12** as the block to be modified.

15. Save your work by issuing the / **File** I **Save** command and entering the file name **ORDERS**. Your database should now look like the one shown in Figures 16-3 and 16-4.

Cell K9 contains the value (0.00). Before you changed the spreadsheet's numeric format, the value appeared as -7.1E-15, meaning .0000000000000071. This result is due to a slight rounding error generated by the formula in cell F9 (the subtotal column).

Designing and Building Databases   359

```
File  Edit  Style  Graph  Print  Database  Tools  Options  Window        ↑↓
A1: [W14] 'MAIL ORDERS
       A              B           C      D       E       F         G      H
  1  MAIL ORDERS
  2
  3
  4  ACCOUNT       ORDER DATE  ITEM   QUANT   PRICE   SUBTOTAL   TAX    TOTAL
  5  Arby & Sons    08/20/90   34-35    1     19.95    19.95             19.95
  6  Micro Center   09/03/90   32-45    5     22.95   114.75            114.75
  7  ABC Group      09/03/90   32-45    2     22.95    45.90             45.90
  8  CompuSchool    09/07/90   38-21    2     20.50    41.00    3.38     44.38
  9  XYZ Co.        10/10/90   34-35    3     19.95    59.85             59.85
 10  Craig Assoc.   10/11/90   38-21    1     20.50    20.50             20.50
 11  Jim Stern      10/15/90   32-45    1     22.95    22.95    1.89     24.84
 12  Smith & Co.    11/01/90   38-21    2     20.50    41.00    3.38     44.38
 13
 14
 15
 16
 17
 18
 19
ORDERS.WQ1    [1]                                                       READY
```

FIGURE 16-3. The first seven fields of the ORDERS database

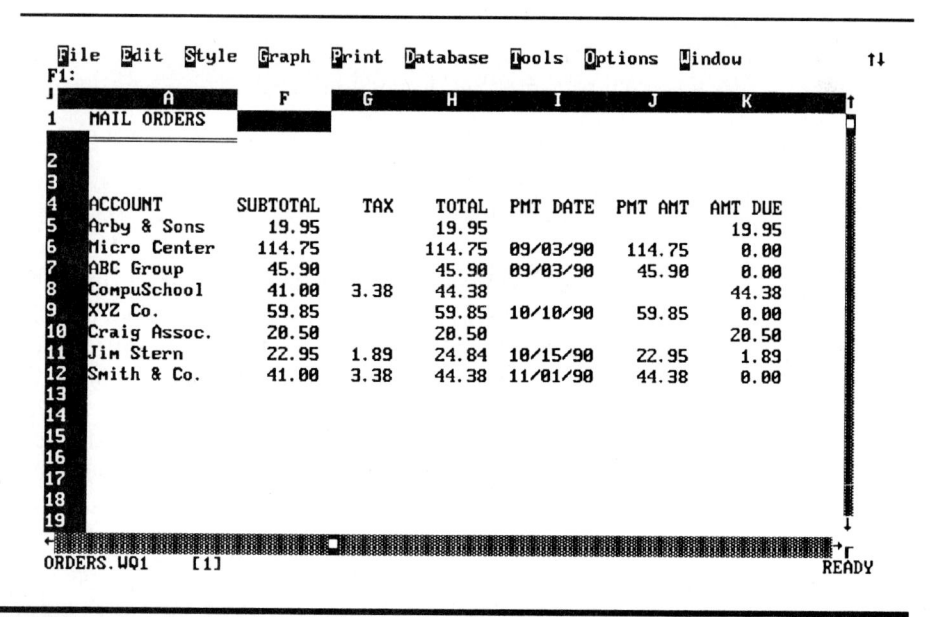

```
File  Edit  Style  Graph  Print  Database  Tools  Options  Window        ↑↓
F1:
       A             F         G       H        I         J         K
  1  MAIL ORDERS
  2
  3
  4  ACCOUNT      SUBTOTAL    TAX     TOTAL   PMT DATE  PMT AMT   AMT DUE
  5  Arby & Sons    19.95             19.95                        19.95
  6  Micro Center  114.75            114.75   09/03/90  114.75      0.00
  7  ABC Group      45.90             45.90   09/03/90   45.90      0.00
  8  CompuSchool    41.00    3.38     44.38                         44.38
  9  XYZ Co.        59.85             59.85   10/10/90   59.85      0.00
 10  Craig Assoc.   20.50             20.50                         20.50
 11  Jim Stern      22.95    1.89     24.84   10/15/90   22.95      1.89
 12  Smith & Co.    41.00    3.38     44.38   11/01/90   44.38      0.00
 13
 14
 15
 16
 17
 18
 19
ORDERS.WQ1    [1]                                                       READY
```

FIGURE 16-4. First field and last six fields of the ORDERS database

When Quattro Pro multiplies the unit price by the quantity, it produces a result slightly lower than 59.85. When you subtract the payment of exactly 59.85 from this value, the result is a number slightly less than zero. Because the default display format is , (comma) with two decimal places, this value is rounded to two decimal places, yielding an apparently negative zero. You can eliminate this problem by including the @ROUND function in the formula in column F, as follows:

1. Move to F5 and change that cell's contents to @ROUND(D5*E5,2).

2. Use the / Edit I Copy command to copy the formula to F5..F12.

ADDING AND DELETING RECORDS

In databases that contain calculated fields or different display formats for different fields, you can save time when you enter a new record by copying an entire adjacent record into the row you intend to use for the new record and then overwriting the data as necessary.

Add a new record to your database now using two different methods.

1. Enter the following data in row 13:

In Cell	Enter
A13	Ace Personnel
B13	11/2/90
C13	34-35
D13	1
E13	19.95

   The results are shown in Figure 16-5. Both the order date and the item number are treated as formulas because this new row was not included in the block for the / Database I Data Entry commands issued earlier. Similarly, the format for the quantity is wrong, because cell D13 was not included in the block for the earlier / Style I Numeric Format command.
   You could solve the problem by reentering the date with the (CTRL-D) prefix, reentering the item number with a label prefix character, and formatting the quantity field with / Style I Numeric Format. Then you must either enter formulas in cells F13, H13, and I13 or copy them from row 12. Instead, try the second method.

2. Copy the block A12..I12 to cell A13.

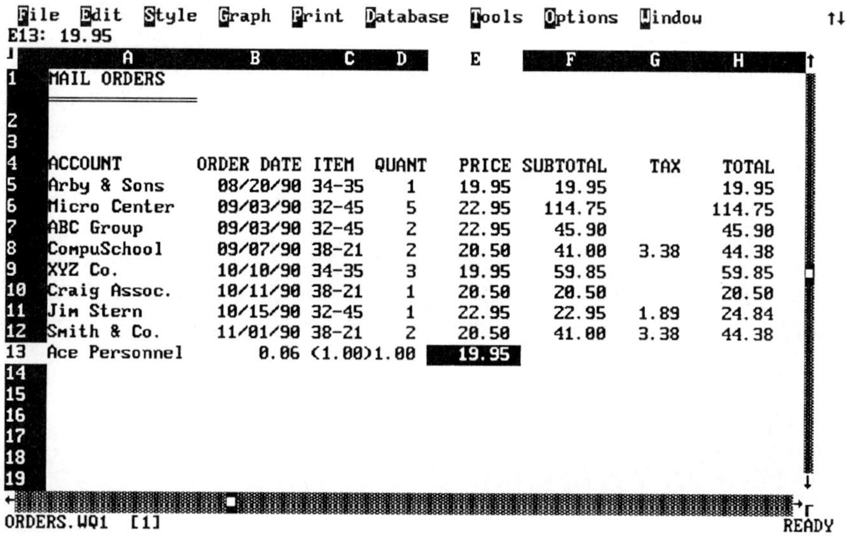

```
File  Edit  Style  Graph  Print  Database  Tools  Options  Window         ↑↓
E13: 19.95
         A            B         C      D       E       F        G       H
 1   MAIL ORDERS
 2
 3
 4   ACCOUNT      ORDER DATE  ITEM   QUANT   PRICE  SUBTOTAL   TAX    TOTAL
 5   Arby & Sons   08/20/90   34-35    1     19.95   19.95            19.95
 6   Micro Center  09/03/90   32-45    5     22.95  114.75           114.75
 7   ABC Group     09/03/90   32-45    2     22.95   45.90            45.90
 8   CompuSchool   09/07/90   38-21    2     20.50   41.00   3.38     44.38
 9   XYZ Co.       10/10/90   34-35    3     19.95   59.85            59.85
10   Craig Assoc.  10/11/90   38-21    1     20.50   20.50            20.50
11   Jim Stern     10/15/90   32-45    1     22.95   22.95   1.89     24.84
12   Smith & Co.   11/01/90   38-21    2     20.50   41.00   3.38     44.38
13   Ace Personnel            0.06 (1.00)1.00  19.95
14
15
16
17
18
19
ORDERS.WQ1  [1]                                                       READY
```

FIGURE 16-5. Attempting to add a new record

3. Replace the data in the following cells:

In Cell	Enter
A13	**Ace Personnel**
B13	**11/2/90**
C13	**34-35**
D13	**1**
E13	**19.95**

   This time the entries in B13, C13, and D13 are properly formatted because the label only, date only, and numeric formatting codes were copied from the preceding row.

4. Use (DEL) to erase the entries in G13, I13, and J13 (the TAX, PMT DATE, and PMT AMT fields left over from row 12.)

The simplest way to add new records is to fill in the next empty row at the bottom of your database. If you add records frequently, however, you may want to try a different approach. Several operations you perform on your database, such as sorting and selecting records and generating database statistics, require specifying the block of cells that contains all the records in your database. If you add new records by entering data in the next available blank row at the bottom of the database, you must constantly adjust the coordinates for these blocks. You can solve this problem by inserting new records within the parameters of the established database coordinates (somewhere below the first record in the database and above the last one). The block coordinates automatically expand to accommodate the new row. If you delete either the first or last row in the database block, you must adjust the coordinates for the sort block and for the database block specified in all database selection criteria.

To delete a record from a database, you simply delete the row in which that data is stored. If you delete either the first or the last record in a database, remember to adjust the coordinates of any blocks that refer to the database as a whole.

MODIFYING YOUR DATABASE

After you enter your initial set of data, you may need to go back and improve the appearance of your database—to change the numeric formats for some of the fields or change field widths. To perform these operations you use the same commands you use on other spreadsheets—such as / Options | Formats commands for changing spreadsheet defaults and / Style | Numeric Format, / Style | Column Width, and / Style | Block Widths commands for changing blocks of data.

You may also decide, after entering some data, that you want to rearrange the order of fields in your database. You can do this by using the same set of cut-and-paste commands you use on other types of spreadsheets. Because it is easy to make a serious and irrevocable mistake in this process, however, you should always save your spreadsheet before repositioning fields. First make room for the field in the desired location with the / Edit | Insert | Columns command. Then use / Edit | Move to move the field to the new location, but be careful to include all the records in the database and the field name. You can then close up the space formerly occupied by this field with / Edit | Delete | Columns. If you want to relocate several fields it is generally safer to move one field at a time. If you simply want to switch the location of two fields, however, you can temporarily move field 1 to another section of the spreadsheet while you move field 2 to the column that field 1 previously occupied. You can then move field 1 to the column vacated by field 2.

Improving the ORDERS Database

So far you have created a simple and fairly standard database. Although it includes a few calculated fields, it does not yet fully exploit Quattro Pro's potential as a database manager. By making two substantial changes to your database, you can let Quattro Pro take over tasks currently performed manually, so it assumes more of the work involved in the order-tracking system.

The first modification involves adding a STATE field to the database, entering the current sales tax rate elsewhere on the spreadsheet (outside the database), and changing the content of the TAX field to a formula. Once you make these changes, Quattro Pro automatically performs sales tax calculations as you enter data into the spreadsheet.

1. Move to B4 and issue the / Edit | Insert | Columns command. Press (ENTER) to accept the default block B4..B4.

2. Narrow the new column to six characters.

3. In the new cell B4, enter the field name **STATE**.

4. Fill in the STATE field for the eight records currently in your database as follows:

In Cell	Enter
B5	CA
B6	MA
B7	OH
B8	NY
B9	TX
B10	NJ
B11	NY
B12	NY
B13	MT

5. Move to A3 and issue the / Edit | Insert | Rows command. When prompted for a block, move the cell pointer down to row 10 (so that A3 through A10 are highlighted) and press (ENTER).

6. In A3, enter **Sales Tax Rate**.

7. Move to C3 and enter **.0825**.

8. Issue the /Style I Numeric Format command, select the Percent format, and specify two decimal places. Press (ENTER) to accept the default block.

9. Issue the /Edit I Names I Create command, specify a block name of TAX RATE, and accept the default block C3.

10. Move to H13 and enter the formula

    @IF(B13="NY",@ROUND(G13*$TAX RATE,2)," ")

    This formula calculates sales tax using the tax rate in cell C3 for those records in which the state field contains the characters NY.

11. Copy this formula to H13..H21. None of the numbers in the database should change since the formula results should be the same as the tax amount you previously entered manually.

12. Save the database.

The second modification of the database entails adding a lookup table for the unit prices and changing the PRICE field to a calculated field employing the @VLOOKUP function. As a result, Quattro Pro assumes the work of looking up the price of each item ordered.

1. Construct a price lookup table by entering the following data in the following cells:

In Cell	Enter
A5	PRICE TABLE
A6	Item No.
B6	Price
A7	'32-45
B7	22.95
A8	'34-35
B8	19.95
A9	'38-21
B9	20.50

2. Draw a line under PRICE TABLE by issuing the /Style I Line Drawing command, specifying a block of A5..A5, a Placement of Bottom, and a Line Type of Single. Select Quit to return to Ready mode.

Designing and Building Databases

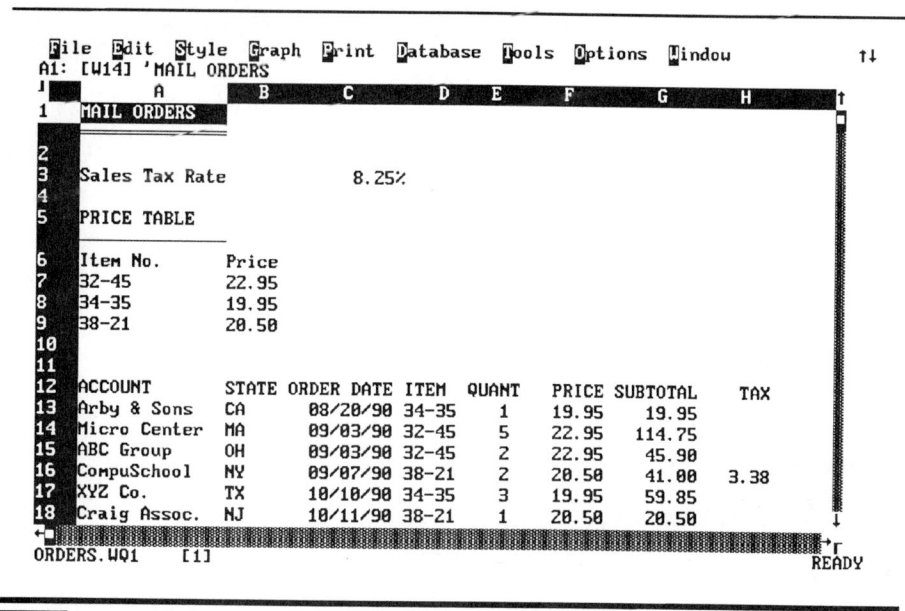

```
  File  Edit  Style  Graph  Print  Database  Tools  Options  Window         ↑↓
A1: [W14] 'MAIL ORDERS
        A            B        C        D      E      F        G        H
 1  MAIL ORDERS
 2
 3  Sales Tax Rate          8.25%
 4
 5  PRICE TABLE
 6  Item No.     Price
 7  32-45        22.95
 8  34-35        19.95
 9  38-21        20.50
10
11
12  ACCOUNT      STATE  ORDER DATE  ITEM   QUANT  PRICE  SUBTOTAL   TAX
13  Arby & Sons   CA    08/20/90   34-35    1    19.95   19.95
14  Micro Center  MA    09/03/90   32-45    5    22.95  114.75
15  ABC Group     OH    09/03/90   32-45    2    22.95   45.90
16  CompuSchool   NY    09/07/90   38-21    2    20.50   41.00    3.38
17  XYZ Co.       TX    10/10/90   34-35    3    19.95   59.85
18  Craig Assoc.  NJ    10/11/90   38-21    1    20.50   20.50

ORDERS.WQ1   [1]                                                     READY
```

FIGURE 16-6. The improved ORDERS database

3. Create a block name for the lookup table by issuing the / Edit | Names | Create command. Enter **PRICE TABLE** and specify a block of A7..B9.

4. Move to F13 and enter the formula

   @VLOOKUP(D13,$PRICE TABLE,1)

   If Quattro Pro returns a value of ERR, the item number in D13 was not found in the price table. Check the item number entries in that cell and the first column of the price table.

5. Copy the formula to F13..F21. Your database should now look like Figure 16-6.

To see the effect of the changes you have just made, try adding a new record to the database.

1. Copy A21..L21 to A22.

2. Make the following changes in row 22:

In Cell	Enter
A22	**AAA Plumbing**
B22	**NY**
C22	**11/7/90**
D22	**38-21**
E22	**3**

The price in F22 and the tax in H22 are calculated automatically.

3. Save the database again.

In this chapter you have learned basic database concepts and terminology and techniques for designing, constructing, and maintaining a database in Quattro Pro. A fairly sophisticated database was used as the sample application in order to acquaint you with the range of calculations possible within Quattro Pro. By using this database in the following three chapters, you will learn how to exploit Quattro Pro's capabilities as a database management program.

17

SORTING YOUR DATABASE

The Sorting Process
Sort Order
Single-Key Sorts
Multiple-Key Sorts
Undoing a Sort
Changing the Sort Rules

Sorting a database means arranging the records in a particular sequence based on the contents of one or more fields. The fields that you specify for this purpose are known as *sort keys* or *key fields*. The main reason for sorting a database is to make it easier to locate records. Sorting also allows you to group related records together so that you can compare, print, or gather statistics on subsets of your database.

THE SORTING PROCESS

The process of sorting a database consists of the following steps:

1. Display the Sort menu by typing **/DS** (for **/ D**atabase **I** **S**ort).
2. Define the block of cells to be sorted. In almost all cases, the sort block consists of all the records in your database. *Be careful not to include the field names in the sort block.* Also be sure to include all the fields in the database; otherwise Quattro Pro rearranges the order of some fields in the database while leaving others in their current positions.
3. Define the sort key by selecting the 1st Key option on the Sort menu.
4. When prompted, indicate whether you want the records arranged in ascending or descending order.
5. If you want to sort on more than one key field, repeat steps C and D to define the additional sort keys. (Multiple-key sorts are explained later.)
6. Select Go to initiate the sort.

It is always a good idea to save your database before sorting, in case you make an error in defining the sort block or keys.

SORT ORDER

Quattro Pro sorts records in a specific but not necessarily intuitive order. As discussed later in this chapter, you can change this order with the **/ D**atabase **I** Sort **I** Sort Rules command, but in most cases you will prefer to use the default order setting. The default sort order for an ascending sort is

- Blank cells
- Labels beginning with numbers, in numerical order
- Labels beginning with letters, in alphabetical order

- Labels beginning with punctuation marks or special nonkeyboard characters, such as in numerical order by ASCII code

- Values, in numerical order

The default sort order for a descending sort is

- Values, in reverse numerical order
- Labels beginning with punctuation marks or special nonkeyboard characters, in numerical order by their ASCII codes
- Labels beginning with letters, in reverse alphabetical order
- Labels beginning with numbers, in reverse numerical order
- Blank cells

Formulas are always sorted by their results rather than by the characters they contain. For example, the formula (3∗25) comes before (2∗50) in an ascending sort, because 75 is less than 100. Dates are always sorted by their serial numbers. For example, 12/31/87 comes before 01/01/88 because the serial number for the former is 32142 and for the latter is 32143. Unless you change the **Database** | **Sort** | **Sort Rules** setting, Quattro Pro ignores capitalization when sorting.

SINGLE-KEY SORTS

The easiest type of sort is a single-key sort. You designate one field as the basis for the sort, and Quattro Pro arranges all the records in the database according to the content of the single field. Try performing a single-key sort now by following these steps:

1. Retrieve the ORDERS.WQ1 database, if necessary, and move to cell A13.

2. Issue the / **Database** | **Sort** | **Block** command. Type a period to anchor the cell pointer, press (END-HOME) to extend the block to A13..L22, and press (ENTER).

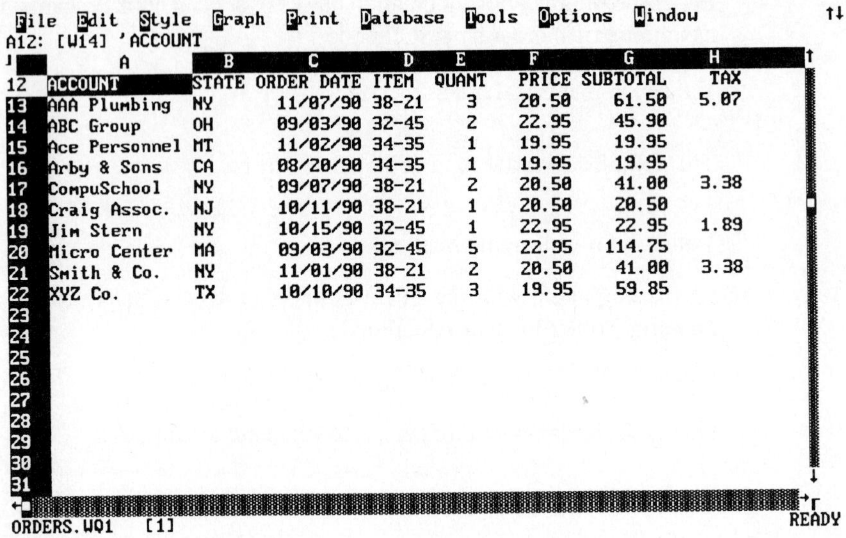

```
   File Edit Style Graph Print Database Tools Options Window        ↑↓
A12: [W14] 'ACCOUNT
          A          B      C      D     E      F       G       H
 12  ACCOUNT      STATE ORDER DATE ITEM  QUANT  PRICE SUBTOTAL   TAX
 13  AAA Plumbing  NY   11/07/90  38-21    3    20.50   61.50   5.07
 14  ABC Group     OH   09/03/90  32-45    2    22.95   45.90
 15  Ace Personnel MT   11/02/90  34-35    1    19.95   19.95
 16  Arby & Sons   CA   08/20/90  34-35    1    19.95   19.95
 17  CompuSchool   NY   09/07/90  38-21    2    20.50   41.00   3.38
 18  Craig Assoc.  NJ   10/11/90  38-21    1    20.50   20.50
 19  Jim Stern     NY   10/15/90  32-45    1    22.95   22.95   1.89
 20  Micro Center  MA   09/03/90  32-45    5    22.95  114.75
 21  Smith & Co.   NY   11/01/90  38-21    2    20.50   41.00   3.38
 22  XYZ Co.       TX   10/10/90  34-35    3    19.95   59.85
 23
 24
 25
 26
 27
 28
 29
 30
 31
ORDERS.WQ1  [1]                                              READY
```

FIGURE 17-1. ORDERS.WQ1 database sorted on the ACCOUNT field

3. Select the 1st Key option, move to any cell in column A, and press (ENTER) to designate the ACCOUNT field as the first sort key.

4. When prompted for the sort order, type **A** to indicate Ascending.

5. Select Go to initiate the sort. Your database should now look like Figure 17-1.

The record for Jim Stern is now ordered by the first name because the name was entered first name first in the ACCOUNT field. To order by last name, you must enter the last name first, as follows:

1. Move to A19 and enter **Stern, Jim** to replace Jim Stern.

2. Issue the / **D**atabase | **S**ort | **G**o command. (Because Quattro Pro remembers the sort block and sort key from the last operation, you can issue the Go command immediately without defining any settings.)

If you have a database that contains a high proportion of individual names, you might want to create separate fields for first and last names and use the last name as the first key. If you have more than one record with the same last name, you can then use the first name field as the second key for the sort to achieve full alphabetical order.

MULTIPLE-KEY SORTS

It is possible to sort on up to five keys at one time. Whenever you sort on more than one key, records are first arranged in order by the contents of the first key field. Then, within each first key field grouping, records are arranged by the contents of the second key field, and within each second key field grouping, they are arranged by the contents of the third key field, and so on.

To perform a multiple-key sort, you simply define additional sort keys by selecting the appropriate key options on the Sort menu and designating the columns containing the fields on which you want the sort to be based.

1. Issue the / Database I Sort I 1st Key command. Move to any cell in column D, and press (ENTER) to designate the ITEM field as the first sort key. When prompted for the sort order, type **A** to specify Ascending.

2. Select the second Key option, move to any cell in column E, and press (ENTER) to designate the QUANT field as the second sort key. When prompted for the sort order, type **D** to specify Descending.

3. Select Go to initiate the search. Your spreadsheet should now look like Figure 17-2.

If you want to erase keys (to change from a five-key to a two-key sort, for example) you must use the Reset option on the Sort menu. This command erases the sort block setting as well as all the key settings so that you can begin defining your sort from scratch. (Sort Rules settings are not affected by the Reset command.)

UNDOING A SORT

Quattro Pro does not have a specific command for undoing a sort, but you can return records to their presort order by adding a field filled with consecutive numbers. Once you have created this field, you can sort on that field whenever you want to restore the records to their original sequence.

The quickest way to add a consecutive-number field to your database is with the / Edit I Fill command (covered in Chapter 9) with a Start value of 1 and a Step value of 1.

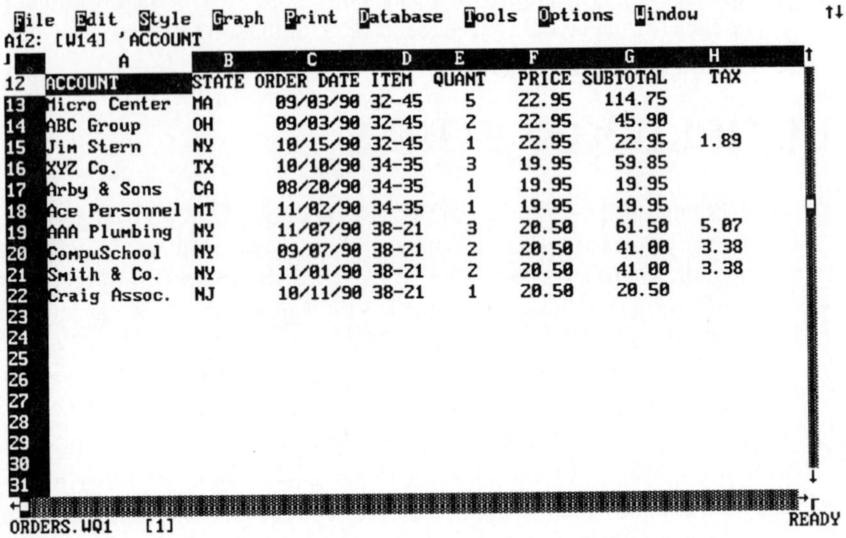

```
File  Edit  Style  Graph  Print  Database  Tools  Options  Window              ↑↓
A12: [W14] 'ACCOUNT
        A              B       C          D      E      F      G        H
12   ACCOUNT         STATE  ORDER DATE  ITEM   QUANT  PRICE  SUBTOTAL  TAX
13   Micro Center    MA     09/03/90    32-45   5     22.95  114.75
14   ABC Group       OH     09/03/90    32-45   2     22.95   45.90
15   Jim Stern       NY     10/15/90    32-45   1     22.95   22.95   1.89
16   XYZ Co.         TX     10/10/90    34-35   3     19.95   59.85
17   Arby & Sons     CA     08/20/90    34-35   1     19.95   19.95
18   Ace Personnel   MT     11/02/90    34-35   1     19.95   19.95
19   AAA Plumbing    NY     11/07/90    38-21   3     20.50   61.50   5.07
20   CompuSchool     NY     09/07/90    38-21   2     20.50   41.00   3.38
21   Smith & Co.     NY     11/01/90    38-21   2     20.50   41.00   3.38
22   Craig Assoc.    NJ     10/11/90    38-21   1     20.50   20.50
23
...
31
ORDERS.WQ1   [1]                                                      READY
```

FIGURE 17-2. ORDERS.WQ1 database sorted on multiple keys

You do not need to create a record number field in the mail order database, because the records were entered by order date. You can, therefore, restore the original order at any point by sorting in ascending order on the ORDER DATE field.

1. Issue the / Database | Sort | Reset command to erase all the current sort settings.

2. Select the Block option and specify the block A13..L22 again.

3. Select the 1st Key option and designate column C as the sort key. Specify Ascending order.

4. Select the Go option to start the sort.

Your database should now be restored to the order it was in at the beginning of this chapter.

CHANGING THE SORT RULES

The / Database I Sort I Sort Rules command allows you to alter the sequence in which Quattro Pro sorts records. When you select this option, Quattro Pro displays a menu with the options Numbers Before Labels and Label Order. If you select Numbers Before Labels, Quattro Pro displays a submenu with the options No (the default setting) and Yes. If you change this setting to Yes, Quattro Pro places values before labels (the order among the labels themselves is unaffected).

The Label Order option allows you to change the way in which labels—as distinct from values—are sorted. When you select this option, Quattro Pro displays a submenu with two options: Dictionary and ASCII. The Dictionary setting (the default) directs Quattro Pro to arrange labels alphabetically, placing those labels that start with punctuation and special nonkeyboard characters at the end. If you change this setting to ASCII, Quattro Pro arranges labels by the ASCII codes of their first characters. This means that control characters (characters generated by holding down CTRL while pressing another key) come first, followed by some punctuation marks, the digits 0 through 9, other punctuation marks, uppercase letters, a few other punctuation marks, lowercase letters, more punctuation marks, and lastly graphics characters, foreign letters, and other nonkeyboard characters. You can refer to Appendix G of the Quattro Pro *User's Guide* for the exact order of ASCII codes. This fairly esoteric option can be used to alphabetize uppercase letters separately from lowercase letters.

This chapter introduced you to the process of sorting the records in your database according to the data contained in one or more fields. Sorting allows you to enter data in the order in which you receive it and later arrange it into a different and more meaningful order. It also allows you to view your records in different sequences for different purposes; for example, arranging your database by ACCOUNT field in order to print a reference list and later by ORDER DATE in order to perform a bank reconciliation.

18

SELECTING RECORDS FROM YOUR DATABASE

Database Query Commands
Criteria Tables
Putting Your Selections to Work
Database Statistical Functions
Using Quattro Pro to Manipulate External Databases

One of the most useful operations you can perform on your databases is searching for and selecting records on the basis of their content. For example, in your mail order database, you might want to extract all records that have a particular item code, order date, or order total. This chapter discusses the rules and techniques for constructing and using database selection criteria to locate, extract, delete, or perform calculations on subsets of your database.

DATABASE QUERY COMMANDS

Quattro Pro's / **Database** I **Query** commands allow you to find and manipulate the records that match a particular set of selection criteria. The criteria you can define range from simple (for example, all records that contain NY in the STATE field) to complex (all records in which the state is NY, the order date is prior to 10/1/88, the item code is either 32-45 or 34-25, and the quantity is greater than one).

Once you have defined your selection criteria, you can direct Quattro Pro to perform any of four operations on the selected records. You can use the Locate option on the **Database | Query** menu to locate the records one at a time, stopping at each record so that you can view and edit the data. Using the Extract option you can extract all the records that match your selection criteria, creating copies of the selected records in a separate section of the spreadsheet. The Unique option allows you to extract unique records or unique portions of records, eliminating duplicates. Lastly, you can delete all the records that match your selection criteria using the Delete option.

Preparing a Query

Before searching for records, you need to take several preparatory steps:

1. **Define the query block.** Before you perform a database query, you must use the / Database | Query | Block command to tell Quattro Pro which block cells to search through. The query block almost always consists of the entire database, including the field names.

2. **Assign names to fields in the first record if you want to reference fields by block name.** Most selection criteria are defined by referring to the fields in the first record on the database. For example, if you want to select ORDERS.WQ1 records in which the SUBTOTAL field contains a value greater than 41, you would specify that the value in cell G13 (the SUBTOTAL field of the first record in the database) must be greater than 41 to be selected. Quattro Pro then applies the same condition to every record in the database.

   The Assign Names option on the **Database | Query** menu facilitates the process of defining selection criteria by automatically assigning block names to each cell in the first row of the database block, using the field name immediately above each cell. This command works almost exactly like / **Edit | Names | Labels**, except it always assigns the labels located in the first row of the database (the field names) to the second row of the database (the first database record).

3. **Set up a criteria table on the spreadsheet.** A *criteria table* is a block of cells on the spreadsheet in which you enter criteria for a database query.

4. **Tell Quattro Pro where the criteria table is.** Before you initiate the query, you must tell Quattro Pro where to find the query criteria. You can do this by issuing the **Database | Query | Criteria Table** command.

5. **If necessary, define an output block.** If you want to copy the records that match your selection criteria to another section of the spreadsheet, you must define an output block in which these records will be copied.

You cannot assign names until you define the query block. Other than that, the order of these preparatory steps does not matter.

Once you have taken these steps, you are ready to tell Quattro Pro what to do with the selected records by choosing the Locate, Extract, Unique, or Delete option on the Database | **Query** menu.

CRITERIA TABLES

A criteria table is a block of cells that contains the criteria for a database query. This block can be located anywhere on the spreadsheet. The block consists of at least two rows; the exact number depends on the complexity of your selection criteria. The first row contains one or more field names from the database. The rows below that contain the selection criteria.

Caution — It is important that you not include any blank rows in the criteria block; if you do, Quattro Pro selects every record in the database.

Exact Matches

Any selection criterion that you can express in the form *Field = Value* can be entered in a criteria table by simply entering *Value* under the appropriate field name. For example, if you want to see all the records in which the STATE field equals CA, you can simply type **CA** below the field name STATE as shown in Figure 18-1. The output block in this figure shows the one record found to match the table's criterion.

You can use this type of *exact match criteria* to search for either values or labels. In either case, Quattro Pro pays attention only to the basic data, not the embellishments. If you are searching for values, for example, Quattro Pro ignores any differences in display format between the criteria you enter and the values for which you are searching. Similarly, if you are searching for labels, Quattro Pro ignores capitalization and label prefixes.

You can also search for the results of formulas using exact match criteria. For example, you can locate records in which the value displayed in the TOTAL field (which contains a formula adding SUBTOTAL to TAX) is 24.84 by entering **24.84** in the criteria table under the field name TOTAL.

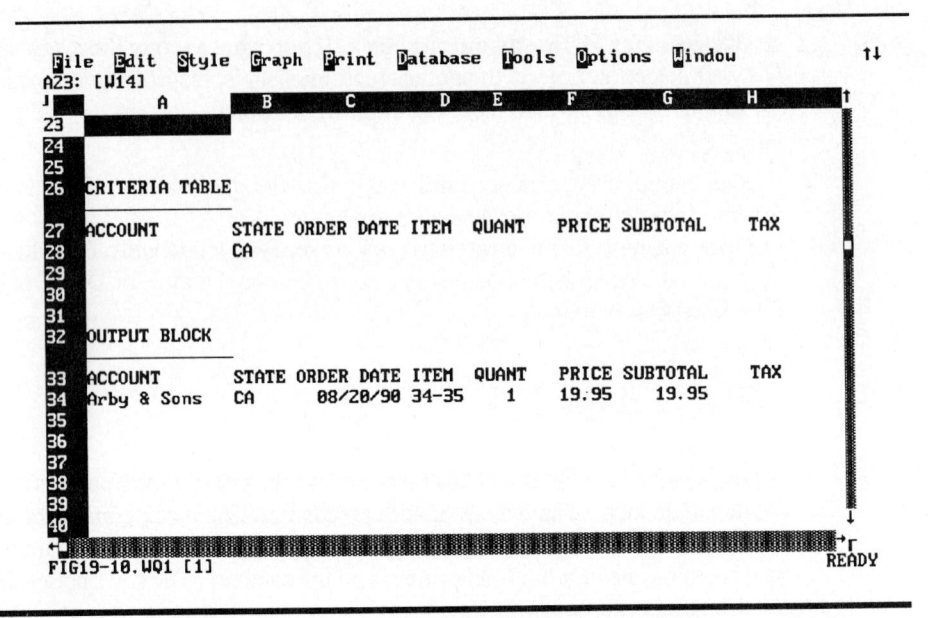

FIGURE 18-1. A query using an exact match criterion

Using Wild Cards

Quattro Pro provides three wild-card characters you can use to define conditions in a criteria table. These characters increase the power of exact match criteria, allowing you to express conditions that may be difficult or impossible to express otherwise.

The ? character can be used to indicate any single character. For example, if you enter the selection criterion **N?** under the field name STATE in your criteria table, Quattro Pro selects all records in which the data in the STATE field consist of two characters starting with N. The criterion ST??? can be used to find stare, store, stair, steel, steer, state, stone, stage, stale, and so on, but not stir, star, or any words that are more or less than five characters and start with anything other than ST.

You can use the * to indicate a series of characters of any length. For example, if you enter the selection criterion **A*** under the field name ACCOUNT in your criteria table, Quattro Pro selects all records in which the ACCOUNT field starts with the letter A.

You can use the ~ (tilde) to locate all records except those that match the selection criteria that you specify. For example, if you enter the selection criterion **~NY** under the field name STATE, Quattro Pro selects all records except those in which the STATE field is NY.

Locating Records One at a Time

When you issue the / Database | Query | Locate command, Quattro Pro highlights the first record in the database that matches your selection criteria. Every time you press (DOWN ARROW), Quattro Pro highlights the next record that matches your criteria. You can can press (ESC) or (ENTER) to return to the / Database | Query menu or the spreadsheet (depending on where you initiated the query)—either after you have viewed all the selected records or at any point before.

During a locate query operation, you can edit any of the records that match your criteria. When Quattro Pro highlights a record that you want to change, use (LEFT ARROW) and (RIGHT ARROW) to move the cursor to the field you want to modify. If you want to replace the field, just type the new entry and press (ENTER). To change the contents of the field, press (F2) (Edit), use any of the usual editing keys to alter the data, and press (ENTER).

The Query Key

You can press (F7) (Query) to repeat the last database query operation that you performed (Locate, Extract, Unique, or Delete) using the current settings for the query block, the criteria table block, and the output block (if any). This key can save you numerous keystrokes, particularly when you want to change the contents of the criteria table and then reexecute a query.

Hands-on Practice

Try creating and using a criteria table by following these steps:

1. Retrieve ORDERS.WQ1 from disk.

2. Move to A26 and enter the label **CRITERIA TABLE**.

3. Issue the / Edit | Copy command. Specify the source block A12..L12 and the destination A27.

4. In A26, issue the / Style | Line Drawing command. When prompted for a block, press (ENTER) to accept the default block of A26..A26. Choose Bottom and then

```
     File Edit Style Graph Print Database Tools Options Window            ↑↓
B28: [W6] 'NY
          A            B       C        D      E       F        G       H
    12  ACCOUNT      STATE  ORDER DATE  ITEM  QUANT  PRICE   SUBTOTAL   TAX
    13  Arby & Sons   CA    08/20/90   34-35    1    19.95    19.95
    14  Micro Center  MA    09/03/90   32-45    5    22.95   114.75
    15  ABC Group     OH    09/03/90   32-45    2    22.95    45.90
    16  CompuSchool   NY    09/07/90   38-21    2    20.50    41.00    3.38
    17  XYZ Co.       TX    10/10/90   34-35    3    19.95    59.85
    18  Craig Assoc.  NJ    10/11/90   38-21    1    20.50    20.50
    19  Jim Stern     NY    10/15/90   32-45    1    22.95    22.95    1.89
    20  Smith & Co.   NY    11/01/90   38-21    2    20.50    41.00    3.38
    21  Ace Personnel MT    11/02/90   34-35    1    19.95    19.95
    22  AAA Plumbing  NY    11/07/90   38-21    3    20.50    61.50    5.07
    23
    24
    25
    26  CRITERIA TABLE
    27  ACCOUNT      STATE  ORDER DATE  ITEM  QUANT  PRICE   SUBTOTAL   TAX
    28                NY
    29
    30
ORDERS.WQ1  [1]                                                        READY
```

FIGURE 18-2. Creating a criteria table

Single to draw a line under the label CRITERIA TABLE. Select Quit to return to Ready mode.

5. In B28 enter the criterion **NY**. Your spreadsheet should now look like Figure 18-2.

In the next few steps you assign names to both the criteria table and the database as a whole.

6. Name the criteria block by issuing the / Edit | Names | Create command. Enter the block name **CRITERIA** and the coordinates **A27..L28**.

7. Name the database (including the field names) by issuing the / Edit | Names | Create command. Enter the block name **DATABASE** and the coordinates **A12..L22**.

8. Issue the / Database | Query | Block command. Press (F3) (Choices), and choose DATABASE from the list of block names.

9. Select the Criteria Table option, press (F3) (Choices), and select CRITERIA from the list.

10. Select the Locate option on the Database | Query menu, and use (DOWN ARROW) to move through all the records for customers in New York State.

11. Press (ENTER) or (ESC) to return to the Database | Query menu, and select the Quit option to return to Ready mode.

12. In B28, press (F2) (Edit), press (LEFT ARROW) twice so the cursor is on the "N" in NY, type ~, and press (ENTER).

13. Press (F7) (Query) to locate the records for all customers in states other than New York.

14. When you reach the last record that matches your criteria, press (ENTER) or (ESC).

Defining Complex Searches In a Criteria Table

You can use the exact match method to express conditions that involve multiple criteria by filling in more than one cell in the criteria table. Quattro Pro responds

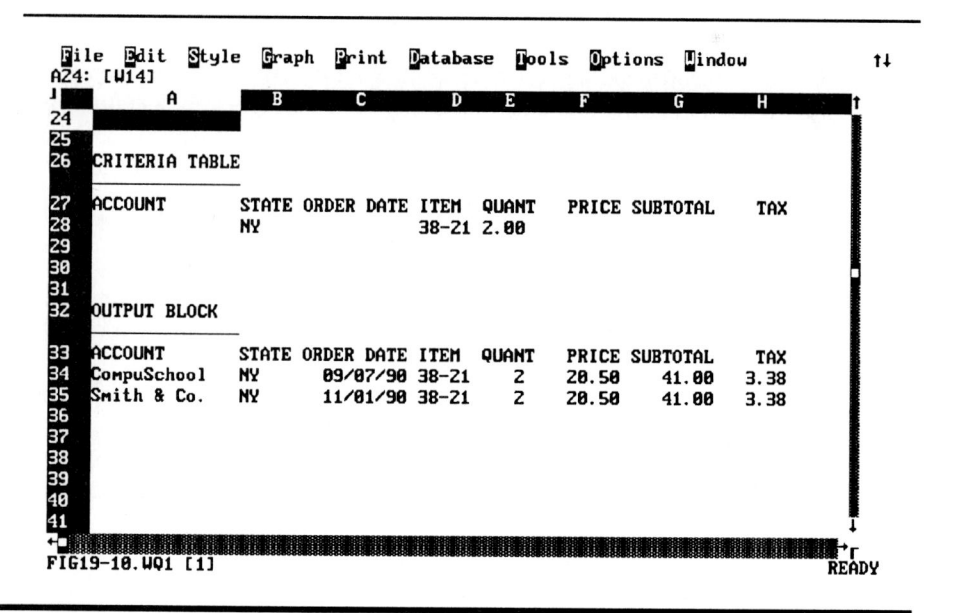

FIGURE 18-3. A criteria table that expresses an #AND# condition

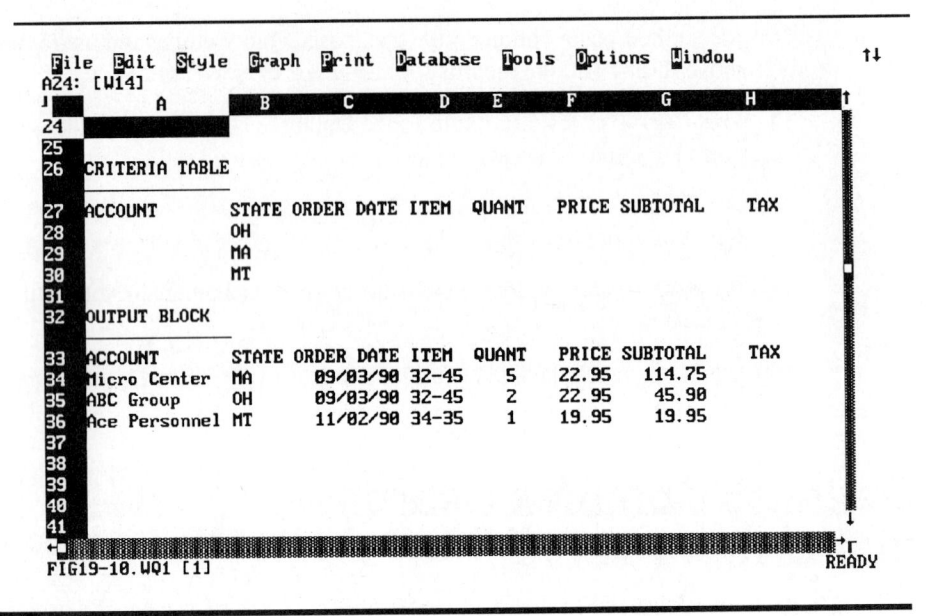

FIGURE 18-4. A criteria table with an #OR# condition

differently depending on whether you enter the criteria in the same or different rows. When you enter more than one criterion in the same row, Quattro Pro selects only those records that fulfill all of the criteria in the row. Figure 18-3 shows a criteria table for selecting records in which the state is NY, the item number is 38-21, and the quantity is 2. Below the table is an output block containing the two records that met these criteria.

When you enter criteria in different rows, Quattro Pro finds records that fulfill the criteria in any one of the rows in the criteria table. This is referred to as an #OR# criterion or #OR# condition. Figure 18-4 shows a criteria table for locating records in which the STATE field contains OH, MA, or MT.

You can also combine #AND# and #OR# conditions within the same criteria table. Again, Quattro Pro selects all the records that meet the criteria in any one row of the table. The criteria table in Figure 18-5 could be used to select those records in which the STATE field contains NY and the ITEM field contains the code 38-21, plus those records in which the state is MA and the item code is 32-45.

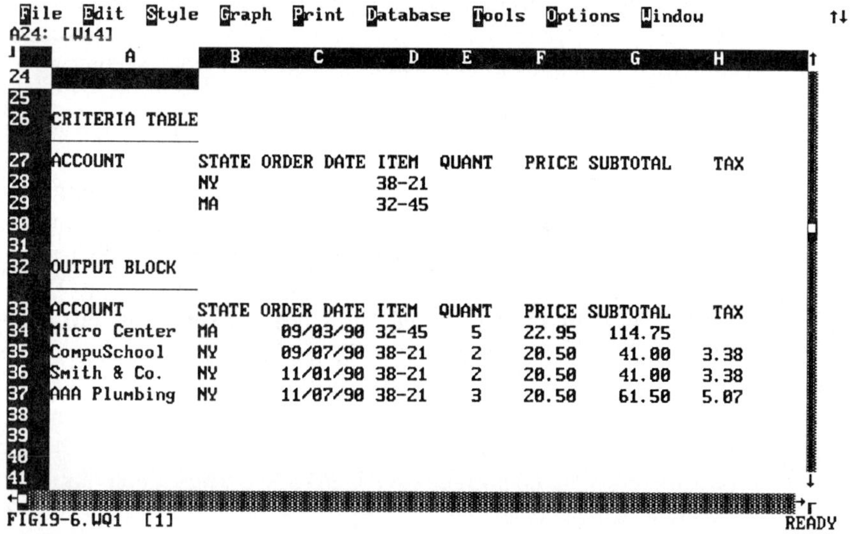

```
      File Edit Style Graph Print Database Tools Options Window        ↑↓
A24: [W14]
         A         B     C          D     E      F      G        H
24
25
26  CRITERIA TABLE
27  ACCOUNT       STATE ORDER DATE ITEM  QUANT  PRICE SUBTOTAL   TAX
28                NY                38-21
29                MA                32-45
30
31
32  OUTPUT BLOCK
33  ACCOUNT       STATE ORDER DATE ITEM  QUANT  PRICE SUBTOTAL   TAX
34  Micro Center  MA    09/03/90   32-45   5    22.95  114.75
35  CompuSchool   NY    09/07/90   38-21   2    20.50   41.00   3.38
36  Smith & Co.   NY    11/01/90   38-21   2    20.50   41.00   3.38
37  AAA Plumbing  NY    11/07/90   38-21   3    20.50   61.50   5.07
38
39
40
41
FIG19-6.WQ1  [1]                                                 READY
```

FIGURE 18-5. Combining #AND# and #OR# conditions

Using Formulas In a Criteria Table

There are many selection criteria that cannot be expressed through exact match criteria, even with the help of wild-card characters. For example, you cannot select records in which the amount in the TOTAL field is greater than 50 by simply entering a value in a criteria table. You also cannot select records in which one field equals another. The only way to express such criteria is by entering a condition in the criteria table, usually using the form +*Field Operator Value*—that is, a cell reference or block name that refers to a field in the first record of the database, followed by a comparison operator (such as < or >=), followed by the number, character string, or expression to which you want the field compared. For example, assuming you have assigned block names to each field in the first record of your database, you could use the condition +AMT DUE>40 to select records in which the value in the amount due field is greater than 40.

Notice that this formula started with a plus sign. As with any other formula that you enter in a spreadsheet, you need to introduce logical formulas with a plus sign, parenthesis, or number to let Quattro Pro know that you are entering a formula rather than a label.

When you enter a condition in a spreadsheet (rather than as an argument to an @IF function, for example), Quattro Pro reads it as a *logical formula*—a formula that evaluates to the value True or False. Accordingly, Quattro Pro immediately performs the specified calculation and displays the result rather than the formula on the spreadsheet. The value False is represented by the number 0, and the value True is represented by the number 1.

You can test this by entering the logical formula 3>4 in any cell of your spreadsheet. Note that Quattro Pro returns the value 0 for False. If you change the formula to 4>3, Quattro Pro returns the value 1. Similarly, if you enter the condition +E13>2 anywhere on your spreadsheet, Quattro Pro looks to see whether the field in the first record in the database is greater than 2. (Once you assign block names to the first record's fields, you can express this condition as +QUANT>2). Because the condition is false, Quattro Pro returns a value of 0.

Figure 18-6 shows a criteria table in which the condition +SUBTOTAL<50 was entered in cell G28. The value 1 appears in that cell because the condition is true for the first record in the database. The output block below the criteria table contains the

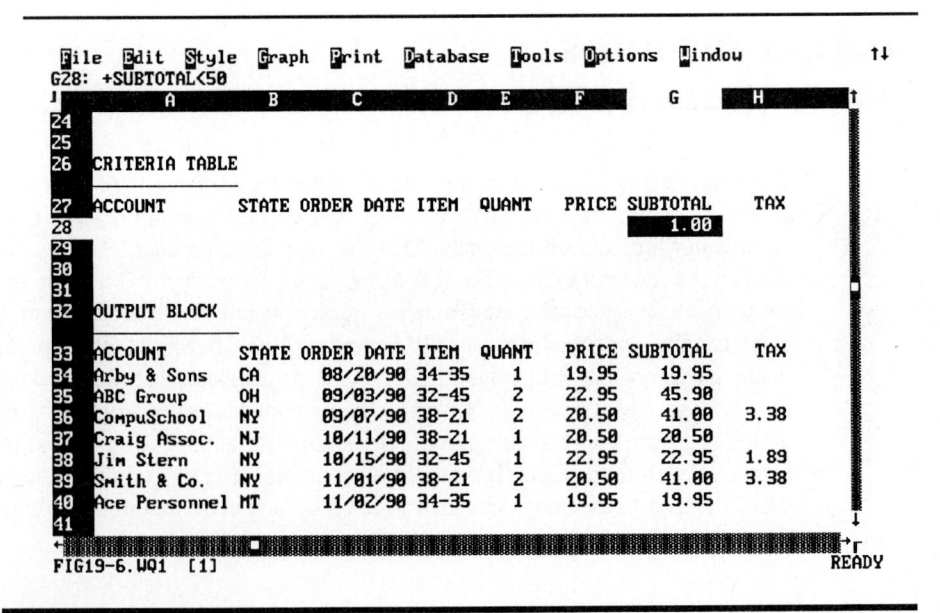

FIGURE 18-6. Extracting data with a logical formula

seven records that meet that criterion. Although the condition has been entered below the field name TOTAL for clarity's sake, it could be entered anywhere in row 28.

Try entering a logical formula in row 28, defining an #AND# condition in the criteria table.

1. Issue the **/ Database | Query | Assign Names** command to assign the field names at the top of the query block to the fields in the first record. This allows you to refer to fields by name when entering logical formulas. Select Quit to return to Ready mode.

2. Leave the criteria ~NY in cell B28. Move to A28 and enter **+TOTAL>=50**. Quattro Pro displays a 0 in the cell because the condition happens to be false for the first record in the database. The two decimal places are displayed because the global numeric format for the spreadsheet is , (comma) with two decimal places.

   Recall that the column in which you enter a logical formula in a criteria table does not matter. The ACCOUNT column is used in this example only because it is adjacent to the STATE column.

3. Press (F7) (Query) to locate the records for customers outside of New York State who placed orders worth $50 or more. You can press (RIGHT ARROW) to scroll fields until the TOTAL field is visible on the screen.

4. Press (ENTER) when you reach the last record that meets your criteria.

There are a few rules to keep in mind when constructing logical formulas. First, you can use any of the comparison operators, including

```
>    >=   <>
<    <=   =
```

Do not enter blank spaces either before or after comparison operators; they can generate syntax errors. Keep in mind that you can use any of the comparison operators to compare character data as well as numeric values. For example, if you want to select all records in which the ACCOUNT field starts with the letter "M" or any letter that comes alphabetically after "M", you can use the formula criterion +ACCOUNT>"M".

Enclose character strings within quotation marks in logical formulas. To select all records in which the STATE field contains CA, for example, you would enter the formula criterion **STATE="CA"**. If you enter **STATE=CA** instead, Quattro Pro assumes that CA, like STATE, refers to a block on the spreadsheet, and returns a syntax error when it does not find a block with this name.

Although most logical formulas take the form of a field name followed by a comparison operator followed by a value, they can take other forms as well. You can compare two fields within the same record using the form *Field 1 Operator Field 2*.

For example, the formula +ORDER DATE=PMT DATE can be used to select all records for orders that were paid on the same day as they were placed. You can also use functions, references to cells outside the database, or any other expressions that evaluate to a value of True or False. The formula +TOTAL*1.15>100 could be used to find all records in which the total order amount exceeds $100 if you were to raise your prices by 15%.

The rule of thumb is that you can use any expression that does not violate rules of syntax and that always returns a value of True or False. You can also include functions in your criteria. For example, you would use a condition such as

+ORDER DATE>@DATE(90,9,30)

to select records for orders placed after September 30, 1990.

Complex Conditions In Logical Formulas

You can define more complex logical formulas using the #AND#, #OR#, and #NOT# operators. For example, to select orders for more than one item that are less than 30 days old, you could enter the formula

+QUANT>1 #AND# @TODAY-ORDER DATE<30

Using More Than One Complex Operator in a Condition

Quattro Pro adheres to an order of calculation among the complex operators similar to the one it uses with mathematical operators: #NOT# operators have top priority and are always interpreted first; #AND# and #OR# operators share the same level of priority and are always evaluated from left to right. Unlike the order used with mathematical operators, however, the order used with complex operators always results in a simple left to right sequence of interpretation. If you want a condition interpreted in another order, you must use parentheses to group those elements of the condition that you want to be interpreted first or arrange the components of the condition in a different order.

PUTTING YOUR SELECTIONS TO WORK

In addition to locating records, you can also use the **Database | Query** commands to extract records to another section of the spreadsheet, create lists of unique values, and delete selected records. These options are discussed next.

Extracting Records

Quattro Pro's **/ Database | Query | Extract** command lets you create more meaningful and manageable subsets of your data by copying selected records (or selected fields within the records) to a new location on the spreadsheet. Using this command you can view all the records that match your criteria as a group. You can also perform all the same operations on this subgroup as you would on any other database, such as sorting, performing calculations, and generating lists, graphs, or reports.

Before you can extract records, you need to define an output block—a section of the spreadsheet to which the selected records will be copied. The usual location is below the database and below the criteria table (if you have one). The output block is structured much like the database: The first row consists of field names and the subsequent rows hold the extracted records. You will probably want to extract all fields for each record in the same order as they appear in the database. However, you can extract only some of the fields by including only selected field names in the first row of your output block. Be careful not to include blank columns in the output block; just enter the names of those fields that you actually want to extract without leaving any empty cells between field names. You can also change the order of fields by entering the field names in a different sequence in the top row of the output block.

Once you have entered or copied the field names to the section of the spreadsheet that you want to use as your output block, you need to select the Output Block option on the **Database | Query** menu and supply Quattro Pro with the block's coordinates. If there are no data located below the output block, you need only specify the first row (the field names) and the extracted data will occupy as much space as necessary. If there is data below the output block, you should specify an output block that is large enough to accommodate the extracted records without encroaching upon the other data. If the block is not large enough to accommodate all the records selected in a particular query, Quattro Pro displays an error message. As soon as you press (ESC), Quattro Pro extracts as many records as fit in the block.

Caution When you reuse an output block for a new query, Quattro Pro erases the entire block before extracting the new set of data. If you have defined a single-row output block, Quattro Pro erases any data below that output block, no matter how far down the spreadsheet that data is located.

Whenever you extract data from a database, Quattro Pro converts any formulas in the extracted data to their results when copying them to the output block. Thus the Extract option functions like a variation of the / Edit | Values command. Once the formulas have been converted to numbers or, more rarely, to labels, they no longer respond to changes in data elsewhere on the spreadsheet.

Extracting Unique Records

The / **Database** | **Query** | **Unique** command works exactly like / **Database** | **Query** | **Extract**, except it automatically eliminates duplicates from the selected records before copying them to the output block.

You can use / **Database** | **Query** | **Unique** to strip duplicate records from the database by specifying selection criteria that will be true for every record in the database (such as including a blank row in the criteria table) or leaving the criteria table empty. You can then erase the original database and use the new one.

You can also use this command to create lists of all the unique entries in a particular field. Leave the criteria table empty, and include only a single field name in your output block. For example, if you leave the criteria table blank, include only the ITEM field in your output block, and select the Unique option, Quattro Pro returns a list of the three item codes that occur throughout the ITEM column of the sample database. Similarly, you can create lists of all the unique combinations of entries in two or more fields by leaving the criteria table empty and including the combination of fields that you want to analyze in the output block. For example, if you include the names of both the ITEM field and the QUANT field in your output block, Quattro Pro generates a list of all the unique combinations of a particular item code with a particular quantity amount.

You can also enter criteria in the criteria table to produce a list of all the unique entries or combinations of entries that occur within the specified subset of records. For example, if you include only the ITEM field name in your output block, enter the criteria **ORDER DATE > @DATE(90,10,1)** in the criteria table or as a formula criterion, and then issue the / Database | Query | Unique command, Quattro Pro returns a list of the unique item codes that occur in all records with an order date after the date of October 1.

Try extracting selected records by following these steps:

1. In row 28, insert a single row by issuing the / **Edit** | **Insert** | **Row** command and pressing (ENTER).

2. Enter **+ORDER DATE<@DATE(90,10,1)** in A28.

3. Move to B29 and press [DEL] to erase ~NY from that cell. Leave the logical formula in A29; this formula and the one you just entered in step 2 are located on two different rows of the criteria table, so Quattro Pro treats them like an #OR# condition, selecting all records that fulfill either criterion.

4. Move to A32 and enter **OUTPUT BLOCK**.

5. Move to A33 and issue the /Edit | Copy command. Specify A27..L27 as the source block and accept the default destination A33.

6. Issue the / **Database** | **Query** | **Output Block** command. Enter the coordinates **A34..L34**. (Because no data is entered below the output block on the spreadsheet, you can simply specify the one row block and let Quattro Pro use as much space as it needs.)

7. Select the Extract option on the Database | Query menu to copy the selected records to the output block.

8. Select the Quit option on the Database | Query menu to return to Ready mode. Your spreadsheet should now look like the one shown in Figure 18-7.

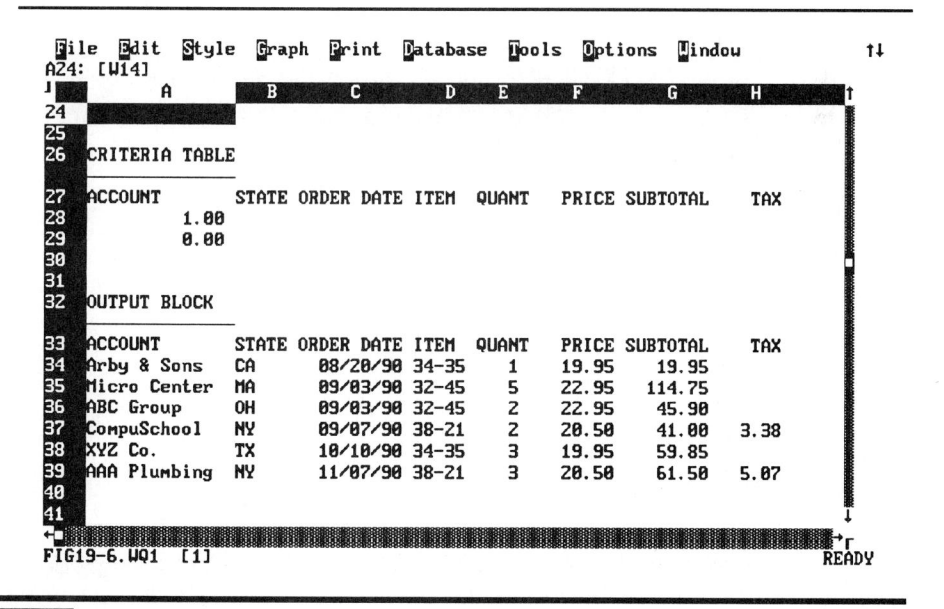

```
File Edit Style Graph Print Database Tools Options Window
A24: [W14]
        A            B    C          D     E      F      G         H
24
25
26  CRITERIA TABLE
27  ACCOUNT       STATE ORDER DATE ITEM  QUANT  PRICE SUBTOTAL    TAX
28          1.00
29          0.00
30
31
32  OUTPUT BLOCK
33  ACCOUNT       STATE ORDER DATE ITEM  QUANT  PRICE SUBTOTAL    TAX
34  Arby & Sons   CA    08/20/90 34-35    1     19.95   19.95
35  Micro Center  MA    09/03/90 32-45    5     22.95  114.75
36  ABC Group     OH    09/03/90 32-45    2     22.95   45.90
37  CompuSchool   NY    09/07/90 38-21    2     20.50   41.00   3.38
38  XYZ Co.       TX    10/10/90 34-35    3     19.95   59.85
39  AAA Plumbing  NY    11/07/90 38-21    3     20.50   61.50   5.07
40
41
FIG19-6.WQ1  [1]                                               READY
```

FIGURE 18-7. Extracting data with an #OR# condition

390　Quattro Pro 2 Made Easy

9. Enter **NY** in both B28 and B29 to limit the records extracted to customers in New York. Note that you have to enter this criterion on both rows of the table in order to limit the query to New York customers. If you enter **NY** in cell B28 only, Quattro Pro extracts records in which the order date is less than 10/1/90 and the state is NY, plus records in which the total is greater than or equal to 50, regardless of the state. If you enter **NY** in cell B29 only, the records extracted would include all orders placed before 10/1/90, regardless of the state.

10. Press (F7) to initiate the query. Quattro Pro extracts only two records this time—the ones for CompuSchool (which matches the criteria in the first row of the criteria table) and AAA Plumbing (which matches the criteria in the second row.) Notice that Quattro Pro automatically erased the output block before extracting the records for this query so that no data is left over from the previous query.

11. Erase all criteria in the criteria table by issuing the / **Edit** | **Erase Block** command and specifying a block of A28..B29.

12. Start creating a second output block by entering **STATE** in A44 and **ITEM** in B44.

13. Issue the / **Database** | **Query** | **Output Block** command and specify A44..B44.

14. Select the Unique option on the **Database** | **Query** menu.

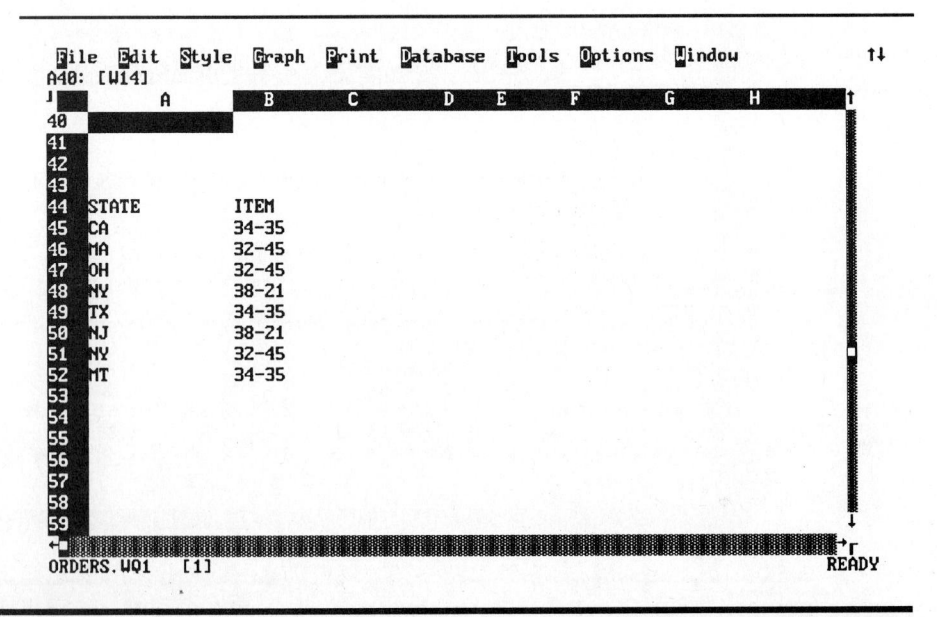

FIGURE 18-8.　Extracting a unique list of state and item combinations

15. Select the Quit option to return to Ready mode. Your spreadsheet should now look like Figure 18-8.

The new output block contains eight unique combinations of state abbreviations and item codes. Because no selection criteria were specified for this query, these represent every combination of state and item codes that occurs in the database.

Deleting Selected Records

The Delete option on the Database | Query menu allows you to delete all the records that match your selection criteria. For example, you could use this command to purge obsolete records by specifying selection criteria for all orders paid in full over six months ago.

When you select the Delete option from the Database | Query menu, Quattro Pro asks for confirmation so you do not delete records accidentally.

The / Database | Query | Delete command functions like a combination of the / Edit | Erase Block and / Edit | Move commands rather than like / Edit | Delete | Rows. Remaining records in the database move up to fill in blank rows, but any data located below the database remains where it is. Data to the right of the database is left intact and in the same location, and display format codes in the erased rows of the database are left as is. If you have created a named block for the database, its coordinates are not changed by the / Database | Query | Delete command, so you will need to adjust them yourself after executing the command. The query block itself is automatically adjusted.

Resetting the Query Settings

If you want to change the parameters of your query, you can erase the Block, Criteria Table, and Output Block settings on the Database | Query menu with / Datatabase | Query | Reset. This command is primarily used when you are querying more than one database on a single spreadsheet.

DATABASE STATISTICAL FUNCTIONS

Seven Quattro Pro functions are designed specifically for use with databases: @DCOUNT, @DSUM, @DAVG, @DMAX, @DMIN, @DSTD, and @DVAR.

These functions share a common syntax:

@Dfunction(Database,Offset,Criteria)

Database refers to the name or cell coordinates of the block containing the database records and field names.

Offset indicates the number of columns to the right of the first column Quattro Pro should move to look for the data to be used in this calculation. If, for example, you want to specify the values in the SUBTOTAL field of your mail order database, the offset value would be 6 because the SUBTOTAL column is located 6 columns to the right of the first column in the database block.

Criteria is the name or coordinates of a criteria table. It is this argument that gives the database functions their power and utility, allowing you to perform calculations on subsets of your database without having to extract the records first.

The @DCOUNT Function

@DCOUNT allows you to count the number of records that satisfy a particular set of selection criteria and that have data in the field specified by the offset value. This is the only database function in which the field specified by the offset value can be filled with labels. You could count the number of orders placed for a particular type of item (item 32-45, for example) by specifying that item code on your criteria table and then entering the function statement

@DCOUNT(DATABASE,3,CRITERIA)

in any blank cell on your spreadsheet (assuming you assigned the block names DATABASE and CRITERIA to your database and criteria table, respectively). The offset value of 3 (the ITEM field) is used so none of the records that match the criteria in the table will be skipped if the field indicated by the offset value is blank. (Any record that matches the criteria will contain data in the ITEM field.)

The @DSUM Function

@DSUM values in a particular field (specified by the offset value) of the records that meet the specified criteria. You could sum the quantity of item 32-45 by using the criterion used in the @DCOUNT example and entering the function statement

@DSUM(DATABASE,4,CRITERIA)

which directs Quattro Pro to sum the values in the QUANT field (four columns to the right of the first field in the database) in all records that match the selection criteria in the designated criteria table.

The @DAVG Function

Like @AVG, @DAVG calculates the average in a group of values. In the case of @DAVG, however, the values averaged are those contained in the field specified by the offset value within those records that meet the specified criteria. Using the same selection criterion, you could calculate the average number of items in each order placed for item 32-45 by entering the function statement

@DAVG(DATABASE,4,CRITERIA)

The @DMAX And @DMIN Functions

@DMAX is similar to the @MAX function in that it returns the highest value in a specified group of values. The values returned by @DMAX are those contained in the field specified by the offset argument in the records that fit the specified criteria. @DMIN works similarly, except that it returns the smallest rather than the largest value in the group.

Try entering several database function statements on the ORDERS.WQ1 database.

1. Contract the criteria table to a single row by moving the cell pointer to row 28, issuing the / Edit l Delete l Rows command, and pressing (ENTER).

2. Move to L28 and enter **0** to select all records in which the order has been paid in full.

3. Move to F43 and enter **STATISTICS**.

4. Move to F44 and enter

   @DCOUNT($DATABASE,10,$CRITERIA)

5. Issue the / Edit l Copy command. Accept the default source block F44..F44, and specify the destination F44..F48.

6. Edit the function statements in cells F45 through F48 so that the first four characters in each cell read

Cell F45: @DSUM
Cell F46: @DAVG
Cell F47: @DMAX
Cell F48: @DMIN

When you are done, the number, total, average, highest, and lowest payment amounts in the database should appear in cells F44..F48. The results are shown in Figure 18-9.

7. Move to L28 and enter **+AMT DUE>0**.

8. Save the spreadsheet again, replacing the previous version of the file.

The values in F44 through F48 change immediately to reflect the change in criteria. (The statistics now represent figures for all the unpaid orders.) Like other formulas (and unlike query output blocks), formulas using database statistical functions are dynamic and change immediately if you change the data in one of their referents.

This chapter has introduced you to Quattro Pro's / **D**atabase | **Q**uery commands and most of its database statistical functions. It also introduced you to the craft of defining selection criteria, which allows you to pinpoint information within a large and otherwise unwieldy mass of data. Using selection criteria correctly allows you to

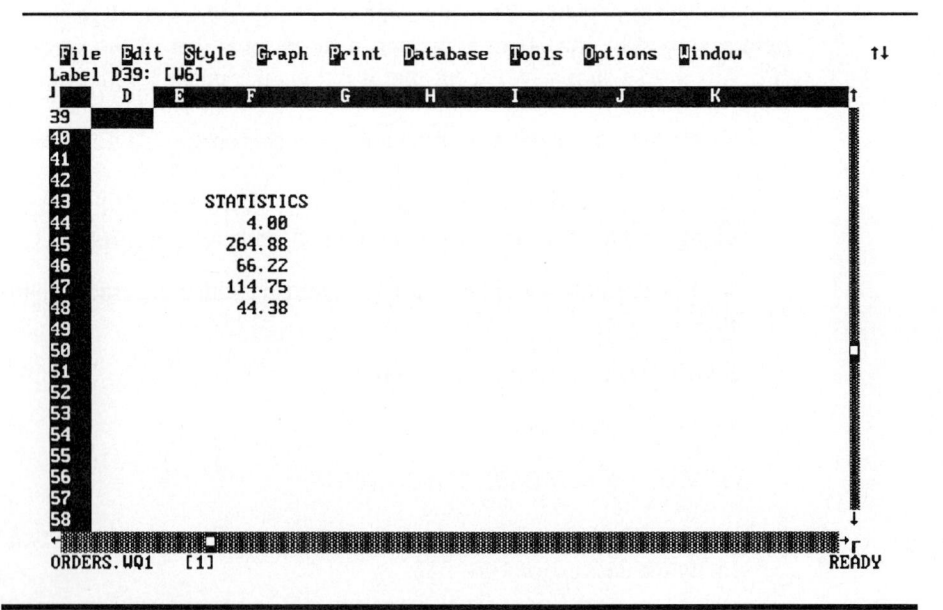

FIGURE 18-9. Generating database statistics

view and extract manageable and useful subsets of your database, focusing on only those records and fields that you want to work with at any given moment.

19

SENSITIVITY TABLES AND DATABASE STATISTICS

Sensitivity Tables
Using Sensitivity Tables With Databases
Creating Frequency Distribution Tables

Your ability to vary key data and see the results quickly makes spreadsheets powerful forecasting and analytic tools. Quattro Pro's set of / Tools | What-If commands are specifically geared toward performing such "what-if" analyses. These commands enable you to create tables that automatically calculate the outcome of a whole range of potential values. For example, rather than viewing the effect on net income of a 5% increase in sales, and then a 6% increase, and then a 7% increase, you can have Quattro Pro automatically calculate and display the effects of all three rates by creating a "what-if" table, or *sensitivity table*. You can also use the / Tools | What-If commands in tandem with database criteria tables and statistical functions to generate database statistics on either an entire database or a specified subset. This chapter also covers the / Tools | Frequency command, which allows you to gather still more database statistics by generating yet another type of table known as a *frequency distribution table*.

SENSITIVITY TABLES

All sensitivity tables consist of at least one formula and one or more sets of variables or input values. One-variable tables allow you to see how changes in a single variable affect the results of one or more formulas. For example, you might want to experiment with a formula that computes sales commissions by multiplying total sales (drawn from a cell elsewhere on your spreadsheet) by a commission rate. You could create a one-variable table with a range of different possible commission rates and direct Quattro Pro to calculate the sales commissions resulting from each. You might also use a one- variable table to chart the effects of different possible growth rates on future sales, gross margin, or net income.

Two-variable tables allow you to see the results of varying two elements within a single formula, drawing values from two different sets of possible values. For example, if you have a formula that computes loan payments based on interest rates and terms of payment, you could use a two-variable table to explore the effects of both different interest rates and different terms.

To create a sensitivity table, you perform the following steps:

1. Create the foundation for the table by entering the input values and formulas on the spreadsheet.

2. Issue the appropriate command: **/ Tools | What-If | 1 Variable** or **/ Tools | What-If | 2 Variable**.

3. When prompted, tell Quattro Pro which block of cells to use as the sensitivity table. (Quattro Pro actually asks for a block of cells to use as a "Data Table.")

4. When prompted, tell Quattro Pro which cells to use as the input cells.

5. Quattro Pro automatically fills in the results, completing the table.

Setting Up
A One-Variable Table

At the core of a one-variable sensitivity table are one or more formulas, known as *table formulas*. These formulas always refer, directly or indirectly, to a cell elsewhere on the spreadsheet known as the *input cell*. This is the cell Quattro Pro uses as a temporary workspace while it computes the values it is going to put in the table. The other major element in the table is a range of input values that are plugged into the table formulas. As soon as you issue the **/ Tools | What-If | 1 Variable** command, Quattro Pro works its way down through the column of input values, replacing the input cell with the current input value, recalculating the table formula, and entering the result in the table.

The tricky part of constructing a sensitivity table is setting up the table properly before you issue the / Tools | What-If command. Both the one-variable and two-variable sensitivity tables have a specific form. The form for a one-variable table is

```
Formula 1 Formula 2 ...
Input Value 1
Input Value 2
Input Value 3
Input Value 4
Input Value 5
...
```

You can use as many input values as you want, as long as you enter them within a single column. The table formulas must be entered horizontally within the row above the first input variable. You can include as many formulas as you like.

Once you have set up a table in this format, you issue the / Tools | What-If | 1 Variable command and specify both the block containing the table and the input cell. The block must be the smallest block that includes all the input variables plus the table

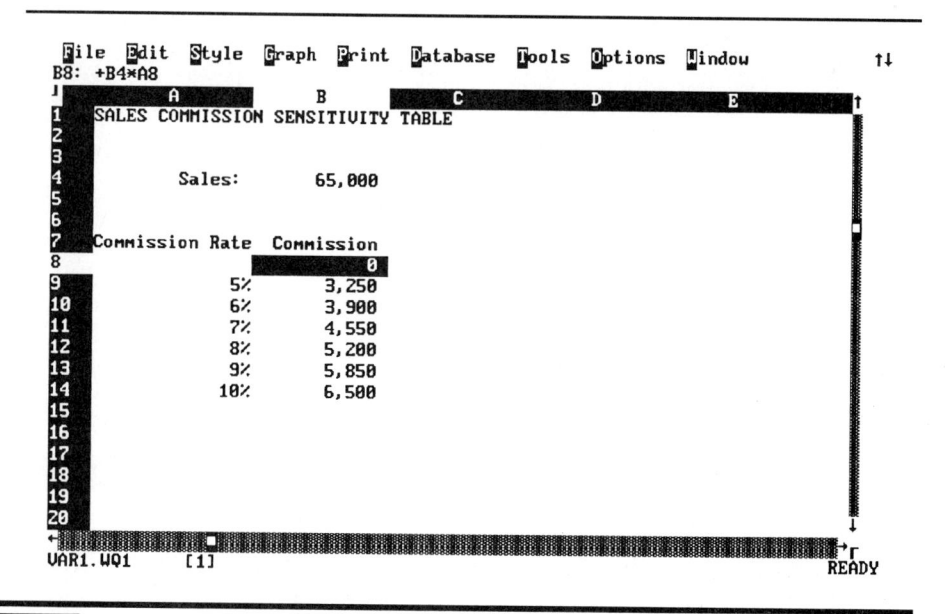

FIGURE 19-1. One-variable sensitivity table for calculating commissions

formulas. The input cell can be anywhere on the spreadsheet, although it is often located in the upper-left corner of the table.

The sensitivity table shown in Figure 19-1 calculates the commissions due on a particular sales amount using different commission rates. The formula +B4*A8 is the core of the table—the mill through which the different commission rates are processed. Cell B4 contains the gross sales amount and cell A8 is the table's input cell. The values in cells A9..A14 are the input values. The values in the block B9..B14 were all calculated by Quattro Pro when the / Tools I What-If I 1 Variable command was issued.

The command works by replacing the input cell A8 with each of the input variables (the commission rates in column A). After each substitution Quattro Pro recalculates the commission rate and enters the result in the column to the right of the input variables.

Figure 19-2 shows a one-variable sensitivity table containing two formulas. Even though this table uses two formulas, it is still a one-variable table: It contains only one set of input values and only one of the values in each formula varies—namely the input cell. This particular table is designed to analyze the potential revenue and expense consequences of a nonprofit organization's upcoming membership drive. The

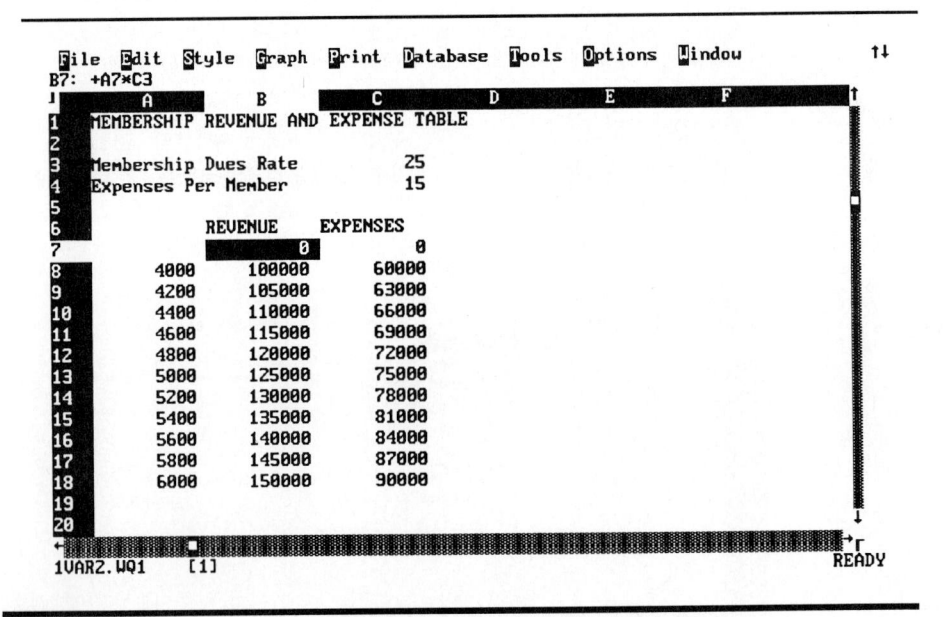

FIGURE 19-2. One-variable table with two formulas

formula in cell B7, +A7*C3, calculates membership revenue by multiplying a range of potential membership levels by the current membership dues rate. The formula in cell C7, +A7*C4, computes membership-related expenses by multiplying the same range of membership levels by the amount of expenses associated with each member.

In each of these examples of one-variable sensitivity tables, the input cell is located in the table's upper-left corner. The input cell can actually be located anywhere on the spreadsheet and at any distance from the table itself.

Try creating your own one-variable sensitivity table to calculate the different net incomes resulting from a range of possible gross sales amounts. This table is based on a formula that calculates net income by taking a gross sales figure and subtracting fixed expenses of $150,000 plus variable expenses calculated at 45% of gross sales.

1. If you have anything other than a new blank spreadsheet on screen, save your work and issue the / File I Erase command.

2. Issue the / Options I Formats I Global Width command, and enter a width of **12**. Select Quit to return to Ready mode.

3. Enter the following data:

In Cell	Enter
A1	**NET INCOME PROJECTION TABLE - SENSITIVITY TABLE**
A2	**@REPEAT("-",@LENGTH(A1))**
A4	**GROSS SALES**
B4	**NET INCOME**
B5	**+A5-(150000+(A5*.45))**

   When you enter the formula in B5, Quattro Pro displays the result -150000. This initial result does not matter, as long as the formula yields a valid result when input values are substituted for the input cell.

4. Issue the / Edit I Fill command. Specify the destination A6..A14, a Start value of 300000, a Step value of 50000, and a Stop value of 700000. You have now finished entering the framework for your table and are ready to fill it in.

5. Issue the / Tools I What-If I **1 Variable** command. At the prompt "Block of Cells to use as Data Table," enter **A5..B14**. When Quattro Pro displays the prompt "Input Cell from Column," enter **A5**. Quattro Pro immediately calculates the table by substituting each of the values in column A for the input cell A5 in the table's formula. The resulting spreadsheet should look like the one shown in Figure 19-3.

6. Issue the / File I Save command and assign the name TABLES to the file.

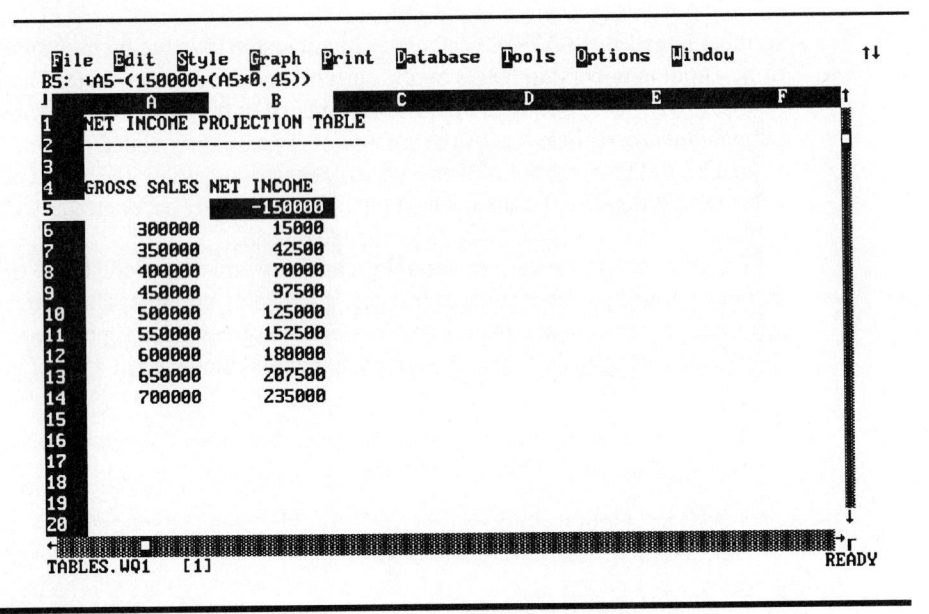

```
      File Edit Style Graph Print Database Tools Options Window
   B5: +A5-(150000+(A5*0.45))
              A           B          C         D          E          F
    1    NET INCOME PROJECTION TABLE
    2    --------------------------
    3
    4    GROSS SALES  NET INCOME
    5                  -150000
    6        300000      15000
    7        350000      42500
    8        400000      70000
    9        450000      97500
   10        500000     125000
   11        550000     152500
   12        600000     180000
   13        650000     207500
   14        700000     235000
   15
   ...
   TABLES.WQ1   [1]                                           READY
```

FIGURE 19-3. One-variable table for projecting net income

Setting Up A Two-Variable Table

The form for a two-variable table is

   Formula Value A Value B Value C Value D
   Value 1
   Value 2
   Value 3
   Value 4

This type of table contains two sets of input values (values 1 through 4 and values A through D in the illustration just given). It also makes use of two different input cells located outside the table itself. As the table is calculated, the first set of input values (values 1 through 4) is substituted into the first input cell, and the second set of input values (values A through D) is substituted into the second input cell.

The table shown in Figure 19-4 is designed to project total sales and to help determine the number of units sold and the prices that are necessary to achieve

```
 File  Edit  Style  Graph  Print  Database  Tools  Options  Window         ↑↓
A5: [W13] +UNITS*PRICE
          A           B        C        D        E        F        G
 1   GROSS SALES SENSITIVITY TABLE
 2
 3   No. of Units          Unit Price
 4
 5              0        200      210      220      230      240      250
 6          2,000    400,000  420,000  440,000  460,000  480,000  500,000
 7          2,200    440,000  462,000  484,000  506,000  528,000  550,000
 8          2,400    480,000  504,000  528,000  552,000  576,000  600,000
 9          2,600    520,000  546,000  572,000  598,000  624,000  650,000
10          2,800    560,000  588,000  616,000  644,000  672,000  700,000
11          3,000    600,000  630,000  660,000  690,000  720,000  750,000
12          3,200    640,000  672,000  704,000  736,000  768,000  800,000
13          3,400    680,000  714,000  748,000  782,000  816,000  850,000
14          3,600    720,000  756,000  792,000  828,000  864,000  900,000
15          3,800    760,000  798,000  836,000  874,000  912,000  950,000
16          4,000    800,000  840,000  880,000  920,000  960,000 1,000,000
17
18
19
20
2VAR.WQ1     [1]                                                       READY
```

FIGURE 19-4. Two-variable table for projecting sales revenue

particular sales levels. At its core is the formula +UNITS*PRICE. UNITS and PRICE are named blocks referring to the two input cells for this table: B4 and D4, respectively.

The table has two sets of input variables. The first set, located in cells A6 through A16, represents the number of units sold. This set of variables corresponds to the first input cell in the table: cell B4, or UNITS. The second set of input values, located in cells B5..G5 represents a range of potential unit prices. These values correspond to the second input cell: cell D4, or PRICE.

When Quattro Pro computes the table, it works its way down column B, substituting each of the input variables in column A for UNITS in the table's formula and substituting the first value in the second set of input variables (200) for PRICE in the formula. Quattro Pro then moves to the second column, again substituting each of the first set of input variables for the UNITS variable in the formula and this time using the second value in the second set of variables (210). Quattro Pro continues across the table in this way, using each PRICE value with each UNITS value, until all the calculations are complete. The result is the set of values in block B6..G16.

Now try constructing your own two-variable table. The formula for this table is similar to the one used in your one-variable table: it calculates net income by subtracting fixed expenses of 150000 and variable expenses from gross sales. In this case, however, you vary the percentage of gross sales used to calculate the variable expenses (variable 2) as well as vary the gross sales amount itself (variable 1).

1. Issue the / Edit | Copy command. Specify a source block of A1..A2 and a destination of A21.

2. Enter the following data:

In Cell	Enter
A24	GROSS SALES
A25	EXPENSE %
B28	GROSS SALES
A29	EXPENSE %
B29	+B24-150000-(B24*B25)

3. Enter the first set of input variables using the / Edit | Fill command. Enter a destination of **B30..B38**, a Start value of **300000**, a Step value of **50000**, and a Stop value of **700000**.

4. Enter the second set of input variables, again using / Edit | Fill. This time specify a destination of C29..F29, a Start value of .35, a Step value of .05, and accept the default stop value of 700000.

5. Issue the / Tools | What-If | 2 Variable command. Specify the block B29..F38. At the prompt "Input Cell from column," enter **B24**. At the prompt "Input Cell from top row," enter **B25**. Quattro Pro immediately generates the table by repeatedly calculating the table's formula, substituting values at the table's left edge for input cell B24 (representing gross sales) and values at the table's top edge for input cell B25 (the percentage used for calculating variable expenses). Select Quit to return to Ready mode.

6. Format the table by issuing the / Style | Numeric Format | Fixed command, specifying zero decimal places and entering a block of **B30..F38**. Your spreadsheet should now look like the one shown in Figure 19-5. Save it again, replacing the old version of the TABLES.WQ1 file.

As with one-variable tables, the input cells can be located anywhere on the spreadsheet, as long as they are referenced in the table's formula (or formulas).

Using F8 to Recalculate Sensitivity Tables

Once you have defined the parameters of a sensitivity table and calculated it once, you can recalculate by pressing F8 (the Table key) to instantly repeat the last / Tools

```
File  Edit  Style  Graph  Print  Database  Tools  Options  Window
B29: +B24-150000-(B24*B25)
         A              B              C          D          E          F
21  NET INCOME PROJECTION TABLE
22  ---------------------------
23
24  GROSS SALES
25  EXPENSE %
26
27
28                 GROSS SALES
29  EXPENSE %       -150000       0.35       0.4       0.45       0.5
30                   300000      45000     30000     15000          0
31                   350000      77500     60000     42500      25000
32                   400000     110000     90000     70000      50000
33                   450000     142500    120000     97500      75000
34                   500000     175000    150000    125000     100000
35                   550000     207500    180000    152500     125000
36                   600000     240000    210000    180000     150000
37                   650000     272500    240000    207500     175000
38                   700000     305000    270000    235000     200000
39
40
TABLES.WQ1   [1]                                              READY
```

FIGURE 19-5. Two-variable table for projecting net income

|What-If command. This allows you to change some or all of your input variables or your formulas and then instantly recalculate the table.

USING SENSITIVITY TABLES WITH DATABASES

So far you have used sensitivity tables to perform "what-if" analyses—to test the effects of a set of arbitrary input values on one or more formulas. You can also use sensitivity tables to gather statistics on databases by using table formulas containing database statistical functions and designating input cells within database criteria tables. In effect the input values serve as different selection criteria, and the resulting table contains statistics for each group of records that match those criteria. Because this use of sensitivity tables is easiest to understand when you see it in action, try building a one-variable sensitivity table that gathers statistics on your mail order database.

1. Issue the / **F**ile | **R**etrieve command and select ORDERS.WQ1 from the file list.

2. Erase the contents of the criteria table by issuing the / **Edit** I **Erase Block** command and specifying a block of A28..L28.

3. Erase the output block, including the field names, by issuing the / **Edit** I **Erase Block** command and specifying the coordinates A32..L48. Eliminate the leftover line-drawing character by moving the cell pointer to row 33, issuing the / **Edit** I **Delete** I **Rows** command, and pressing (ENTER).

4. Enter the following data:

In Cell	Enter
D32	**ITEM**
E32	**QUANT**
F32	**"TOTAL**

   Your next step is to define a database query to extract a unique list of item numbers to use as the input values for the sensitivity table.

5. Issue the / **Database** I **Query** I **Output** command and specify a new output block of D32..D32.

6. Select the Unique option on the **Database** I **Query** menu, generating a list of item codes in cells D33.. D35. Select Quit to return to Ready mode.

7. Move to D33, and insert a row by issuing the / **Edit** I **Insert** I **Row** command and pressing (ENTER).

8. Sort the list of item codes by issuing the / **Database** I **Sort** I **Block** command and entering a block of D34..D36. Select 1st Key and press (ENTER). Type **A** to specify ascending order. Select Go.

9. Issue the / **Style** I **Line Drawing** command and specify a block of D33..F33, a placement of Top, and a line type of Single. Select Quit.

10. Issue the / **Style** I **Numeric Format** I **Fixed** command, specify zero decimal places, and enter a block of E33..E36.

11. Move to E33 and enter

    @DSUM(DATABASE,4,CRITERIA)

    Notice that Quattro Pro immediately returns the value 21, the sum of the QUANT field for all records in the database.

12. Move to F33 and enter

    @DSUM(DATABASE,8,CRITERIA)

Sensitivity Tables and Database Statistics   407

This time Quattro Pro displays the number 461.07, indicating the sum of the TOTAL field for all records in the database.

13. Issue the / **Tools** I **What-If** I **1 Variable**. Specify the block D33..F36 and an input cell of D28. Your spreadsheet should now look like Figure 19-6.

14. Save the spreadsheet using the / **File** I **Save As** command, and enter a new file name, **ORDERS2**.

Notice that the values in cells E34..E36 add up to 21, the total number of items ordered in all records in the database. These three values (8, 5, and 8) represent the distribution of that total among the three item codes. Similarly, the values in F34..F36 add up to the database total of 461.07 in F33.

Now consider how this table works. As with any other one-variable table, Quattro Pro works its way down the column of input variables at the left of the table, moving one input value at a time into the input cell. Because the input cell (D28) is part of the criteria table specified in the table formulas, this amounts to specifying one exact match selection criterion after another. On the first pass, for example, Quattro Pro moves the input value '32-45 into the input cell D28. This is the same as entering the

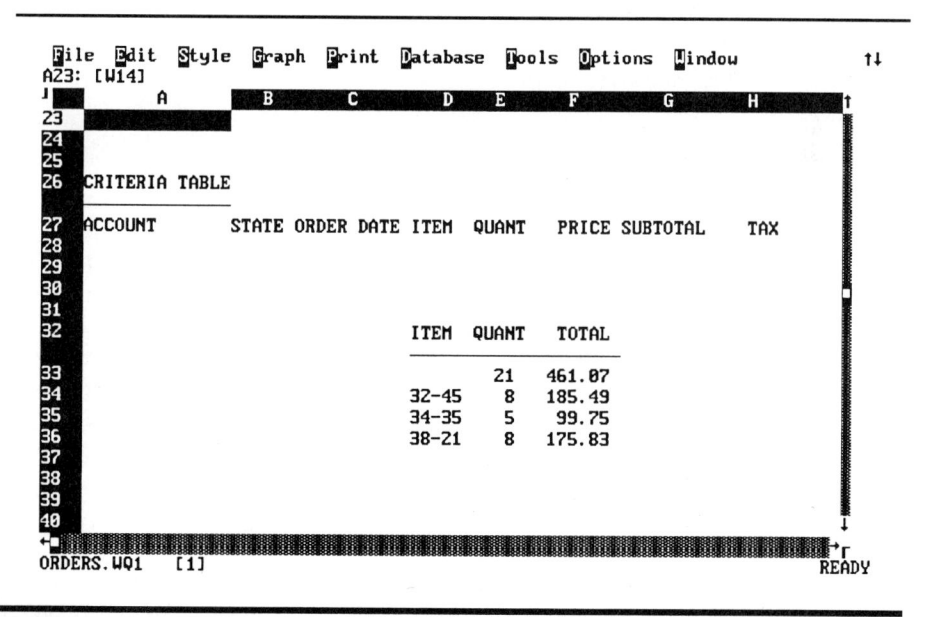

```
 File  Edit  Style  Graph  Print  Database  Tools  Options  Window            ↑↓
A23: [W14]
          A          B       C       D       E       F        G         H
23
24
25
26   CRITERIA TABLE
27   ACCOUNT       STATE  ORDER DATE  ITEM   QUANT   PRICE  SUBTOTAL    TAX
28
29
30
31
32                                   ITEM   QUANT   TOTAL
33                                           21    461.07
34                                   32-45    8    185.49
35                                   34-35    5     99.75
36                                   38-21    8    175.83
37
38
39
40
ORDERS.WQ1   [1]                                                       READY
```

FIGURE 19-6. One-variable table for generating database statistics

value '32-45 into that cell, thereby defining an exact match selection criterion equivalent to ITEM="32-45." Quattro Pro then recalculates the formula

@DCOUNT(DATABASE,4,CRITERIA)

using this selection criteria, enters the result of 8 in cell E34, and moves on to the next input value ('34-35). When Quattro Pro has finished calculating the @DCOUNT formula with each of the three input values, it moves on to calculate the second formula in the table

@DSUM(DATABASE,8,CRITERIA)

using the same set of input values. First it moves the label '32-45 into the input cell D28, recalculates the @DSUM formula, and enters the result of 185.49 in F34. Then it repeats the process with the second input value ('34-35) and then the third ('38-21).

This spreadsheet illustrates that sensitivity table formulas need not refer directly to the table's input cell; instead, the formulas can reference the input cell indirectly by referring to the criteria table that contains the input cell. This indirect reference is perfectly valid because the table formulas are still indirectly dependent on the value of the input cell; that is, they are affected by changes in the input cell's value.

Because the criteria table is currently empty, the statistics you have generated apply to the database as a whole. By entering criteria in the criteria table, you can also generate statistics on subsets of your database.

1. Move to C28 and enter

    @MONTH(ORDER DATE)=10

    Note that the results of the table formulas in E33 and F33 change immediately to reflect the new criterion. The value in E33 changes to 5, the total number of items ordered in October, and the value in F33 changes to 105.19, the total value of those orders. Because these two cells contain formulas, they remain dynamic. The other values on the table—the ones calculated when you issued the / Tools | What-If command—remain unchanged because they are constants rather than formulas. To update these values, you need to reissue the / Tools | What-If command, directing Quattro Pro to perform all the new calculations.

2. Press (F8) (Table) to reissue the last / Tools | What-If command.

Now that you have set up this table, you can continue to enter different criteria in the criteria table and press (F8) to gather statistics on different subsets of your database.

You can also use two-variable sensitivity tables to generate database statistics, defining a range of possible values for one field as the first set of input values and a range of values for another field as the second set of input values. Try this now by creating a two-variable table to calculate the number of items ordered for each item code placed from accounts in each state.

1. Still in C28, press (DEL). Recalculate the table again by pressing (F8).

2. Move to D39 and enter the label **NO. ORDERED**. If you like, underline that label by issuing the / **Style** | **Line Drawing** command, specifying a block of D39..E39, a placement of Bottom, and a line type of Single. Select Quit.

3. Copy the list of item codes to the new table by issuing the / **Edit** | **Copy** command and specifying the source block D34..D36 and the destination D41.

    Now you want to extract a list of all the states represented in the database using / **Database** | **Query** | **Unique**, sort the list using / **Database** | **Sort**, and copy the list from a column to a row using / **Edit** | **Transpose**.

4. Move to B39 and enter **STATE**.

5. Issue the / **Database** | **Query** | **Output Block** command, and specify an output block B39..B39.

6. Select the Unique option on the **Database** | **Query** menu to extract a list of all the state codes that occur within your database.

7. Press (ESC) to return to the Database menu, and select the Sort option. Select the Block option and specify the block B40..B46. Select the 1st Key option and type **B40**. Type **A** to specify ascending order. Select Go. The list of state codes should now appear in alphabetical order.

8. Next copy that list horizontally by issuing the / **Edit** | **Transpose** command and specifying a source block of B40..B46, and a destination of E40.

9. Right justify the list by issuing the / **Style** | **Alignment** | **Right** command and specifying a block of E40..K40.

10. You can now erase the original list of states if you like by issuing the / **Edit** | **Erase Block** command and specifying a block B39..B46.

11. Move to D40 and enter the table formula

    @DSUM(DATABASE,4,CRITERIA)

12. Issue the / **Tools** | **What-If** | **2 Variable** command. Specify the block D40..K43. Designate D28 as the first input cell and B28 as the second. Select Quit to return to Ready mode.

13. Issue the / **Style** | **Numeric Format** | **Fixed** command. Specify zero decimal places and a block of D40..K43. Your spreadsheet should now look like Figure 19-7.

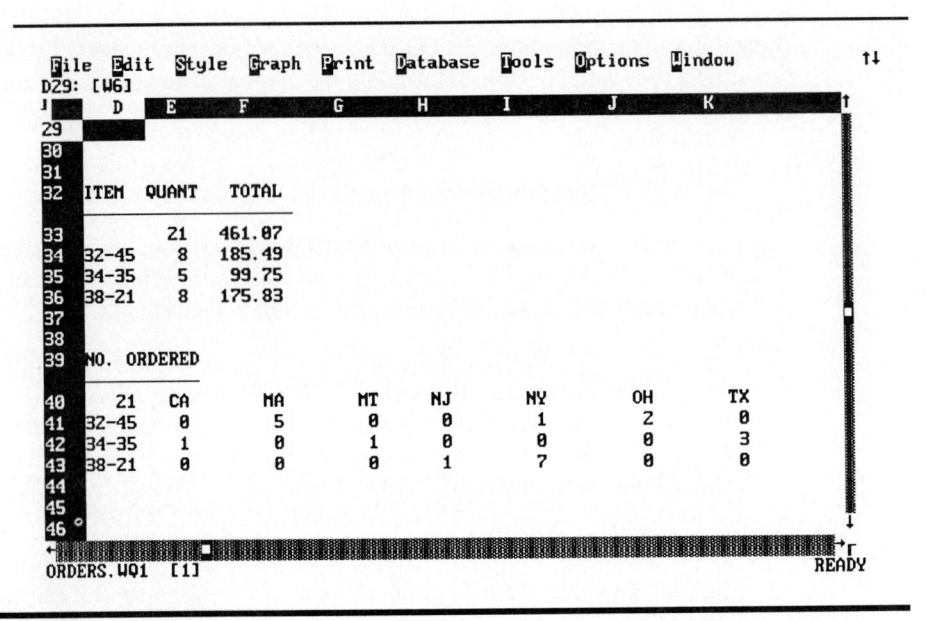

```
File Edit Style Graph Print Database Tools Options Window              ↑↓
D29: [W6]
      D       E       F       G       H       I       J       K
 29
 30
 31
 32  ITEM   QUANT   TOTAL
 33          21    461.07
 34  32-45    8    185.49
 35  34-35    5     99.75
 36  38-21    8    175.83
 37
 38
 39  NO. ORDERED
 40          21    CA      MA      MT      NJ      NY      OH      TX
 41  32-45    0     5       0       0       1       2       0
 42  34-35    1     0       1       0       0       0       3
 43  38-21    0     0       0       1       7       0       0
 44
 45
 46
ORDERS.WQ1  [1]                                                    READY
```

FIGURE 19-7. Two-variable table for generating database statistics

14. Save the spreadsheet again with the / File I Save command, replacing the previous version.

When Quattro Pro constructs this sensitivity table, it moves two sets of input values into the criteria table, generating a table filled with the quantities ordered for each possible combination of item number and state. For example, 5 of item number 32-45 were ordered from accounts in Massachusetts, and 7 of item 38-21 were ordered from accounts in New York.

Note that the total of all the computed values on the table is again 21, the total number of items ordered. You can also cross-check the numbers in each row of that block against the numbers in the previous table. For example, the total of the numbers in row 41 equals the number 8 in cell E34 (the total quantity ordered of item 32-45). The numbers in row 42 add up to the number 5 in E35, and so on.

CREATING FREQUENCY DISTRIBUTION TABLES

The / Tools | Frequency command allows you to generate statistical tables by calculating the number of values that fall within a set of numeric ranges or *bins*. Although this command is most often used to analyze the values that occur within a single field of a database, you can apply it to any series of related values.

The first step in creating a frequency distribution table is to enter the framework for the table on the spreadsheet. You must enter a set of numbers, known as *bin values*, each of which indicates the high end of a numeric range. Then, when you issue the / Tools | Frequency command, Quattro Pro completes the table by calculating the number of values that are less than or equal to each bin value but greater than the previous bin value. At the bottom of the table, Quattro Pro automatically adds an extra bin, which indicates the number of records that contain values higher than the last bin value.

Figure 19-8 shows a frequency distribution table for analyzing a set of quiz scores. This table shows the number of scores that fall in each of five numeric ranges, plus

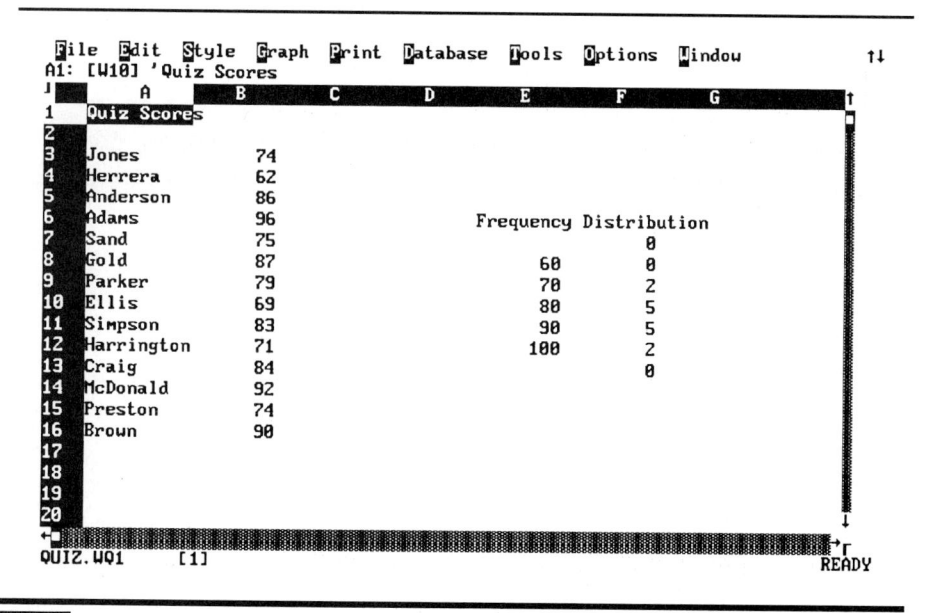

FIGURE 19-8. Frequency distribution table for analyzing quiz scores

the additional bin for the number of values that are greater than the last bin value in the table.

Creating a frequency distribution table in Quattro Pro involves the following steps:

1. Enter a series of bin values in ascending numeric order within a single column of the spreadsheet. You can save time by entering these values with the / Edit | Fill command.

2. Issue the / Tools | Frequency command.

3. When prompted for a values block, specify the block of cells in your database that contains the set of values that you want to evaluate. This block generally consists of a single column or database field.

4. When prompted for a bins block, specify the block containing the bin values that you have entered for this table. When you press (ENTER), Quattro Pro calculates and displays the distribution to the right of this block.

Like sensitivity tables, frequency distribution tables are not updated automatically because the computed values are all constants rather than formulas. If you change any

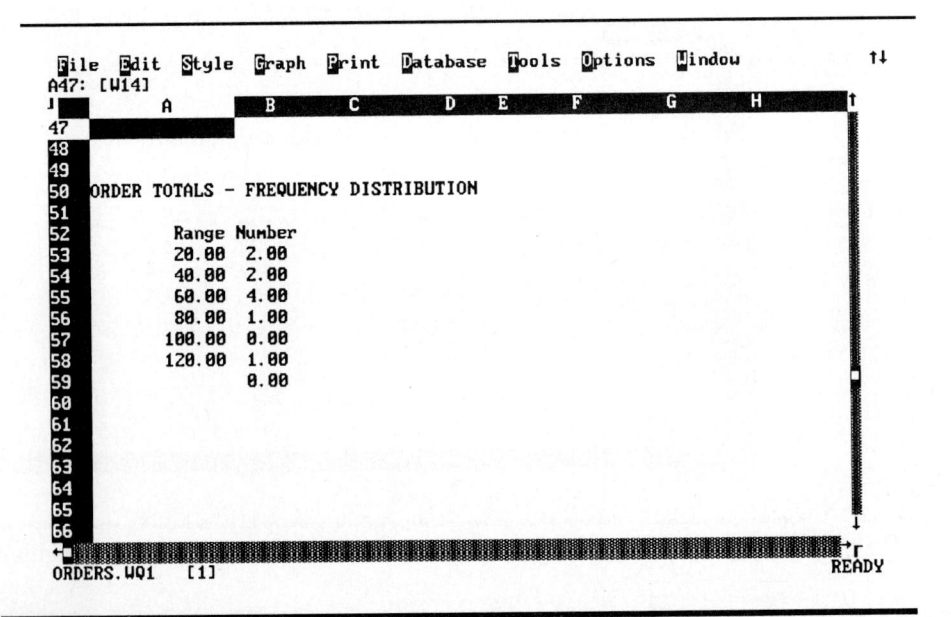

FIGURE 19-9. Frequency distribution table for totals in ORDERS database

of the values in the values block, you must reissue the / Tools | Frequency command to bring the distribution table up-to-date.

Perform the following steps to create a frequency distribution table that shows the distribution of values in the TOTAL field of the ORDERS database spreadsheet.

1. Enter the following labels:

In Cell	Enter
A50	**ORDER TOTALS - FREQUENCY DISTRIBUTION**
A52	**"Range**
B52	**"Number**

2. Fill in the bin range values by issuing the / **Edit** | **Fill** command and specifying a destination of A53..A58, a Start value of 20, a Step value of 20, and a Stop value of 120.

3. Issue the / **Tools** | **Frequency** command. When prompted for a values block, specify I13..I22. When prompted for a bin block, specify A53..A58. Quattro Pro calculates the frequency distribution, indicating the number of orders whose total value falls in each of the bin ranges, and enters the resulting values on the table. Your spreadsheet should now look like Figure 19-9. Save it again.

Using sensitivity tables takes a little practice. Beginners often have trouble learning not only how to create them but, even more, how to apply them to real-world situations. These tables make more sense and spark more ideas for potential applications the more you practice with them.

20

MANAGING YOUR FILES

Using Different Directories
Manipulating File Lists
Shortcuts for Retrieving Files
Using Passwords
Managing Disk Space
Managing Memory
Backing Up Files
Exiting to the Operating System

This chapter covers various aspects of file management: saving and retrieving files, manipulating file lists, protecting files from unauthorized access, using different directories, saving disk space, and managing memory. It also covers accessing the operating system from within Quattro Pro.

USING DIFFERENT DIRECTORIES

If you do not share your computer with other users and use Quattro Pro only occasionally, you will probably do fine storing all your spreadsheets in the Quattro Pro program directory. If you are highly organized, create dozens of spreadsheets a year, or share your computer with others, you will probably prefer to create additional subdirectories for your spreadsheets.

The following sections assume that you know how to create directories and how to move from one directory to another. If you do not, read Appendix B of your *Quattro Pro User's Guide*.

Loading Quattro Pro From Other Directories

When you install the program, Quattro Pro asks whether you want to include the Quattro Pro directory in your DOS search path. If you choose Yes, Quattro Pro creates or modifies a special program file called AUTOEXEC.BAT. This file is stored in the root directory of your hard disk, so the Quattro Pro program directory is included in your DOS search path every time you turn on or reboot your computer. (The DOS search path defines the set of directories in which DOS will look for any program files that it cannot find in the current directory.)

Once the Quattro Pro directory is included in your DOS search path, you can load Quattro Pro from any directory on your hard disk. You can create as many directories as you like for storing Quattro Pro spreadsheets and, when you are ready to work, switch to the appropriate spreadsheet directory and type **Q** to load the program.

If you did not let Quattro Pro change your AUTOEXEC.BAT file, refer to Appendix B of the *Quattro Pro User's Guide* for instructions on creating one yourself. If you already have an AUTOEXEC.BAT file but it does not include the Quattro Pro program directory in the search path, refer to your DOS manual for instructions on modifying the file. If someone else installed Quattro Pro on your computer or you cannot remember whether you allowed the installation program to modify your AUTOEXEC.BAT file, issue the following command from the DOS prompt:

TYPE C:\AUTOEXEC.BAT

If you see the message File not found, you do not have an AUTOEXEC.BAT file. Refer to Appendix B of the *Quattro Pro User's Guide* for instructions on creating one. If you see a list of DOS commands (followed by a blank line and another DOS prompt), check whether the list includes a command that starts with PATH. If so, look for your Quattro Pro program directory—generally C:\QPRO or D:\QPRO in the list of directories that appears to the right of PATH.

Changing the Default Directory

By default, Quattro Pro assumes that you want to store and search for spreadsheet files in the directory from which you loaded the program. If you switch to the SALES directory, and then type **Q** to load Quattro Pro, your computer reads the Quattro Pro program files from the Quattro Pro directory but assumes that you want to work with spreadsheets in the SALES directory. Whenever you issue the / **File** | **Retrieve** or / **File** | **Save** command, Quattro Pro displays the prompt C:\SALES*.W?? followed by a list of files in that directory.

You can use the / **File** | **Directory** command to designate a different default directory. This command is particularly useful when you want to work with several files that are located somewhere other than in your default data directory. For example, if your default directory is C:\QPRO, but you want to work with multiple files on a floppy disk in drive A, typing **A:** to designate the temporary directory can save you the trouble of pressing (ESC) and typing in **A:*.W*** every time you want to retrieve or save a spreadsheet or view a list of spreadsheet files.

To change the default directory more permanently, issue the / **Options** | **Startup** | **Directory** command. (Remember to issue the / **Options** | **Update** command afterward to make this setting permanent.) This command lets you specify a directory to use as the default directory every time you load Quattro Pro, regardless of which directory you are in when you load the program. If you later decide that you do not want any startup directory, issue the / **Options** | **Startup** | **Directory** command again, press (ESC) to erase the setting, and press (ENTER). Then issue the / **Options** | **Update** command to save your change to disk.

Using Subdirectories

Whenever you issue the / **File** | **Retrieve** command, Quattro Pro displays a list of files in the default directory. At the bottom of this file list, it displays the names of any subdirectories of the current directory. (These subdirectory names are always preceded and followed by a \ to distinguish them from file names.) You can display a list of all the files in one of those subdirectories by highlighting the subdirectory name and pressing (ENTER).

If you tend to use files from several different directories in a single work session, you can use the following strategy to take advantage of this subdirectory listing at the bottom of file lists. First, make all your spreadsheet directories subdirectories of the

Quattro Pro program directory itself. This requires switching to the Quattro Pro program directory before you issue the DOS MD (Make Directory) command. Do not store any spreadsheet files in the Quattro Pro program directory itself. When you want to use Quattro Pro, load the program from the Quattro Pro program directory, so that it becomes the default directory. Whenever you retrieve a file or save a new one, Quattro Pro displays a file list consisting solely of subdirectories. Select one of those subdirectories to display a list of the files in that group. Whenever you want to work with files in another subdirectory, just issue the / File | Retrieve command and select a different subdirectory from the list.

MANIPULATING FILE LISTS

Whenever you issue either a / File | Save, / File | Retrieve or / File | Open command, Quattro Pro displays an alphabetical list of all the spreadsheet files in the default data directory. There are several ways of manipulating these lists to display more detailed information, display more file names at once, and display more selective lists.

Displaying More Informative File Lists

You can obtain more information about the files by typing + (plus). Quattro Pro displays a more detailed file list, with each row containing a file name, the date and time the file was last modified, and the size of the file in bytes. The date and time information can help you determine whether a particular file is the most current version of a particular spreadsheet. It can also sometimes provide a hint as to the spreadsheet's contents. If you are saving a file, the size information may help you determine whether a particular spreadsheet fits on a disk. To return to the normal file list display—without the date, time, and file size—type - (minus).

To display more file names at a time, press [F3] (Choices). Quattro Pro expands the file list to fill the screen. The name, date, time, and size of the currently highlighted file appears just above the file list.

Searching Through File Lists

You can also search for files by letter using the (F2) (Edit) key. Whenever you press (F2) (Edit) while viewing a file list, Quattro Pro displays the prompt Search for: * at the bottom of the screen. As soon you type a letter, Quattro Pro displays them before the asterisk in that prompt and then highlights the first file name in the list with a name that matches the currently specified file name pattern. For example, if you type **B**, Quattro Pro displays Search for: B* at the bottom of the screen and highlights the first file name that starts with "B." You can type additional letters to continue honing in on the desired file name. For example, if you type **U** after typing **B**, Quattro Pro changes the prompt at the bottom of the screen to Search for: BU* and highlights the first file that begins with those two letters. If you then type **L**, it highlights the first file name that begins with "BUL," and so on.

If you have a mouse, you have another option for quickly moving through file lists: you can move the scroll box on the scroll bar at the right edge of the file list box. Drag the box to the bottom of the bar to display the bottom of the file list, drag it to the middle of the bar to display the middle of the file list, and so on.

Displaying More Specific File Lists

By default, Quattro Pro file lists include the names of all files in the default data directory that have a file name extension that begins with the letter "W." This is indicated by the file name pattern displayed immediately underneath the prompt "Enter name of file to retrieve." If your default directory is the QPRO directory on drive C, the second line in the box reads

C:\QPRO*.W??

The characters *.W?? indicate that the list includes files with any file name (indicated by the wildcard character *) and an extension that starts with "W" and is followed by any two other characters. This list includes regular Quattro Pro files (extension WQ1), Lotus 1-2-3 files (extension WK1 or WKS), and files created with Quattro 1.0, Quattro Pro's predecessor (extension WKQ).

As you accumulate spreadsheets it can become quite tedious to hunt through a list of every spreadsheet file in the current directory. Quattro Pro therefore allows you to enter a different file name pattern that specifies exactly which files you want to see. For example, if you want to see all the spreadsheet files that begin with the letters "ABC," you can press (ESC) to erase the default file name pattern and then enter **ABC*.W??**. To see Quattro Pro spreadsheet files that begin with the letters "BUDG," you enter **BUDG*.WQ1**. To see a list of files created in Quattro 1.0, you enter ***.WKQ**. You can also use wildcards to list files other than spreadsheet files. For example, entering ***.DB** generates a list of all files in the default directory that have a DB extension.

You can also display lists of files that are stored in other directories by pressing (ESC) twice—once to erase the file name pattern and a second time to erase the directory path—and then entering the full path name of the directory followed by a file name pattern. For example, to list all the spreadsheet files in the SALES directory on drive C, you enter **C:\SALES*.W*** or **C:\SALES*.W??**. To list all the Quattro Pro files on the disk in drive B, you enter **B:*.WQ1**. To display a list of spreadsheet files in the parent directory (the directory one level above the current directory in the directory tree), you can press (BACKSPACE) (rather than pressing (ESC) twice and entering the path and file name pattern). To display a list of spreadsheet files in a subdirectory of the current directory, you can move to the bottom of the file list, highlight the name of the subdirectory, and press (ENTER).

If you press (ESC) twice by accident, erasing both the file name pattern and the directory path from the prompt line, you can press (ENTER) to redisplay the current directory path followed by the file name pattern *.W??.

SHORTCUTS FOR RETRIEVING FILES

If you know which spreadsheet you want to work with when you load Quattro Pro, you can specify the file name when you start the program. For example, if you know that you want to work with LEARN1.WKQ, you can enter **Q LEARN1** at the DOS prompt rather than just **Q**. Once the program is loaded, Quattro Pro retrieves the file automatically. Be sure to leave a space between the Q and the name of the spreadsheet file. If you are using the regular Quattro Pro menus (rather than the 123-style menus or the Quattro menus) and want to load a file with an extension other than WQ1, you must specify the file name extension. (If you are using the 123-style menus, Quattro Pro assumes an extension of WK1; with the Quattro menus, it assumes an extension of WKQ.) To load a file from a directory other than the default directory, include the path name with the file name. For example, to retrieve the SALES90.WQ1 file from the SALES directory on drive C, enter

Q C:\SALES\SALES90

If you continually work with the same spreadsheet file or always begin your work sessions with the same spreadsheet file, you can make it an *autoload file*—a file that is retrieved automatically every time you load Quattro Pro. The default file name for the autoload file is QUATTRO.WQ1. This means that if you ever assign the name QUATTRO to a spreadsheet, Quattro Pro displays that spreadsheet on screen at the beginning of every future work session. To change the name of the autoload file, issue the / Options | Startup | Autoload File command, press (ESC) to erase the current setting, and enter the new file name. Remember to issue the / Options | Update command afterwards to make the change permanent.

USING PASSWORDS

Occasionally you will construct spreadsheets containing sensitive or confidential information that you need to protect from unauthorized access. Quattro Pro allows you to assign passwords to your worksheets simply by typing a space followed by **P** after the file name when you save a file. As soon as you press (ENTER), Quattro Pro prompts you for a password. The password can be up to 16 characters long and can include any characters you like.

As you enter the password, Quattro Pro displays square bullets on the screen in place of the characters you type, in case anyone is looking over your shoulder. If you make a typographical error, use the (BACKSPACE) key to erase characters or press (ESC) to erase the entire password and start again. Once you have entered the password, Quattro Pro asks you to verify the spelling by entering it a second time. If this second set of characters is not identical to the first set you entered, Quattro Pro displays an error message and lets you try again, starting with the entry of the file name.

If you forget a file's password, you cannot access the data, and you have no way to determine the password through either Quattro Pro or any other program. For this reason, it is critical that you record your passwords as you create them, either on paper or in another encrypted file. It is also a good idea to assign passwords sparingly, encrypting only those files that you really need to protect from unauthorized access.

Once you have assigned and verified a password, Quattro Pro encrypts the file so it cannot be retrieved or combined into another file without the password. Whenever you try to retrieve a file that has been encrypted, Quattro Pro prompts you for the password and displays square bullets as you type the password, just as it did when you entered the password originally. If you enter the password incorrectly, Quattro Pro beeps and displays the error message Invalid Password. As soon as you press the spacebar, Quattro Pro returns to Ready mode and you can try again.

If you decide that you no longer want to encrypt a file, issue the / **File** I **Save As** command. Quattro Pro displays [Password protected] after the file name in the dialog box. Press (ESC) once to erase those characters. If you want to save the file under the same name, but without the password protection, just press (ENTER). If you want to change the file name, press (ESC) again to erase the file name and then enter or select a different name.

MANAGING DISK SPACE

As you create more and larger spreadsheets, you may run short of disk space. If you try to save a file that is larger than the amount of available space on your disk, Quattro Pro displays an error message. At this point, you have the following choices:

- You can save the file on a different disk. If you are trying to save the spreadsheet onto a floppy, you can insert a new disk that has more free disk space and issue the save command again. If you are attempting to save the spreadsheet to your hard disk, you can save to a floppy disk instead. Then you can exit from Quattro Pro, delete some disk files to make more room, and copy the spreadsheet file from the floppy disk to your hard disk.

- You can clear space on your disk without leaving Quattro Pro by deleting files through the File Manager (see Chapter 21) or by issuing the / **File** I **Utilities** I **DOS Shell** command (discussed later in this chapter) and then erasing files with DOS commands. Some likely candidates for deletion are files with the FON extension. Quattro Pro creates more as you need them.

- You can try compressing the file by using the SQZ! ("squeeze") feature, which is explained in the next section.

As you accumulate more and more spreadsheet files, you should perform periodic disk "housekeeping," not only to save disk space but to make it easier to find and keep track of your files. If you are using a hard disk, this entails copying old spreadsheet files to floppies and then erasing them from your hard disk. If you are using a floppy-based system, it means keeping only your current spreadsheets on your working data disk and periodically archiving the rest to other floppies, preferably grouping related spreadsheets on the same disks.

Compressing Files

Quattro Pro's SQZ! feature allows you to store files in a compressed form to save disk space. You can use this feature to squeeze a large spreadsheet file onto a floppy disk. It can also save disk space if you find that you frequently run out of room on your hard disk. In fact, if you do not mind the slower speed with which Quattro Pro saves and retrieves compressed files, you might want to use this option for all your files. You can direct Quattro Pro to use this compression feature simply by assigning one of the following special extensions to your file as you save it:

Use Extension	To Compress
WQ!	Quattro Pro spreadsheet files
WKZ	Quattro 1.0 spreadsheet files
WK$	Lotus 1-2-3 WKS files
WK!	Lotus 1-2-3 WK1 files

If you do decide to use the !SQZ feature all the time, you can assign one of these extensions as a default using the / **Options** | **Startup** | **File Extension** command. (Remember to issue the / **Options** | **Update** command afterward.)

A file saved with !SQZ occupies approximately one-third to one-half the space it would normally occupy on disk. As soon as you retrieve a file that has been compressed, Quattro Pro automatically expands it to its original form and size. You can change the exact way in which Quattro Pro performs file compression using the / **File** | **Utilities** | **SQZ!** command. When you issue this command, Quattro Pro displays a menu with the following options:

- **Remove Blanks**   specifies whether to store blank cells. If you change this setting from No to Yes, all numeric formatting codes in cells that are currently blank or that contain labels are deleted as the file is saved.

- **Storage of Values**   lets you specify how formulas are saved. By default, Quattro Pro stores both formulas and their current results with a spreadsheet. If you set Storage of Values to Remove, Quattro Pro erases the current results and saves only the formulas themselves. If you set it to Approximate, Quattro Pro saves the formula results with up to 7 digits of accuracy, rather than the usual 15 digits. If you leave the setting at Exact, Quattro Pro stores the exact formula results, with all 15 digits of accuracy Quattro Pro uses in calculations.

- **Version** specifies which version of SQZ! to use for performing file compression. Select SQZ! Plus for the latest and most efficient version. Use SQZ! if you want to share files with someone who is using Lotus 1-2-3 or Symphony.

- **Quit** returns you to Ready mode.

If you choose an option that changes the data as the file is compressed, the resulting alteration in your data is permanent. You cannot get your formatting codes or extra eight digits of accuracy back after the fact. You are most likely to use these options when you are archiving files that you no longer intend to use or modify extensively in the future.

MANAGING MEMORY

When you work in Quattro Pro, all open spreadsheets must fit into the computer's memory at one time. As a result, both the size of your spreadsheets and the number of spreadsheets you can open at one time are limited by the amount of memory installed in your computer. This limitation may become a concern as you enter substantial databases or build larger and more complex spreadsheets.

How Memory Is Utilized

DOS and Quattro Pro together occupy approximately 270K of memory. This means that if your computer has 640K of memory, by the time you load DOS and Quattro Pro, you will have about 370K available. If you only have 512K of memory, you will have only about 242K available. This amount of available memory determines the largest spreadsheet you can create in Quattro Pro. Every entry you make into Quattro Pro consumes memory. The amount it consumes depends on the type of entry and its length. Formulas occupy more memory than labels or other values. Decimal values occupy more space than integers. Blank cells do not take up memory, but cells that contain formatting codes do. Named graphs and named blocks consume space as well. On a small spreadsheet none of these is enough to cause problems, but on a larger spreadsheet you need to think about memory limitations and how memory-saving techniques can affect the size of your files.

Determining How Much Memory Is Available

There are two ways to determine how much memory you have to work with at any point. The @MEMAVAIL function returns the number of bytes of conventional memory (memory up to 640K) that are available. The @MEMEMSAVAIL function returns the number of bytes of expanded memory (EMS) available. (Expanded memory is discussed later in this chapter.) You also can see both of these figures at one time by displaying the Options I Hardware menu. For example, the menu shown in Figure 20-1 indicates that 379,694 bytes of normal memory and 3,124,992 bytes of expanded memory are currently available.

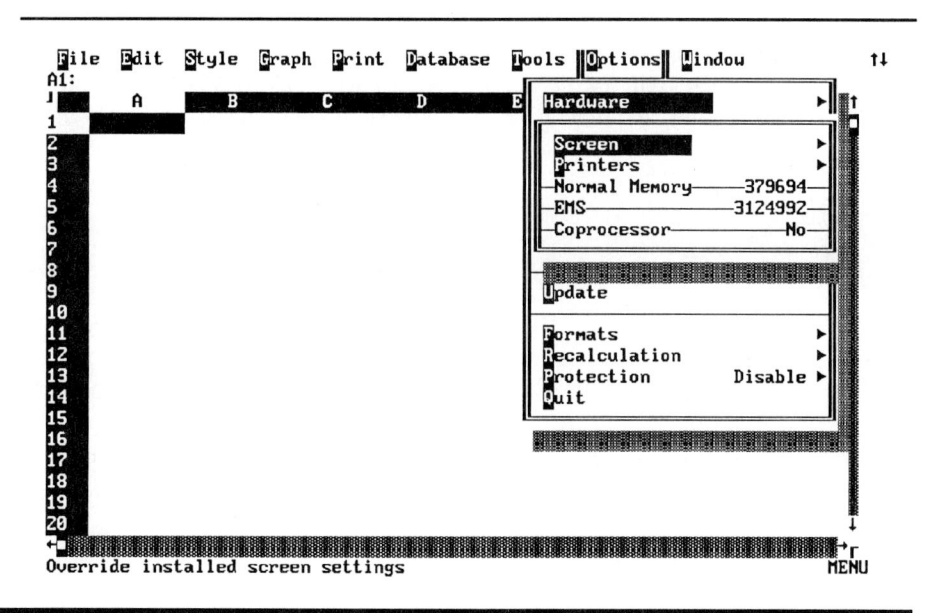

Figure 20-1. The Options I Hardware menu

Estimating How Much Memory You Need

Unfortunately there is no simple way to estimate the amount of memory that is consumed by a particular spreadsheet. You can usually make an educated guess based on the size of other, similarly structured files.

In the case of databases, the best method of estimating future file size is to quickly generate a sample database by entering one sample record and copying it down the number of rows that you anticipate using. If you anticipate entering 1000 records, for example, enter a record in row 1 (forget about field names for now) and then use the / Edit | Copy command, specifying the destination A1..A1000. Remember to include any numeric formatting and column width codes that you plan to use.

You can determine the amount of memory occupied by this sample database by subtracting the amount of memory before entering data from the amount of memory available afterwards. One simple way to do this is to enter the function @MEMAVAIL in a cell or, if you have expanded memory @MEMAVAIL+@MEMEMSAVAIL. Then press (F2) (Edit), (F9) (Calc), and then (ENTER), replacing the formula with its current result. Then go ahead and create the sample database. Finally, enter @MEMAVAIL or @MEMAVAIL+@MEMEMSAVAIL in another cell on the spreadsheet, and then enter a formula subtracting the first memory amount from the second, as shown in Figure 20-2.

Running Out of Memory

If you run out of memory, Quattro Pro beeps and displays an error message. At this point, you can try any or all of the following to free up enough memory to continue your work:

- If you have several open windows, try tiling them so that several unzoomed windows share the screen at once. If you are still short of memory, close some of the windows altogether.

- Unload any memory-resident programs (such as Sidekick or Superkey) that you have loaded.

Note Memory-resident software must be removed from RAM in reverse order to the way you loaded it. For example, if you loaded Sidekick and then Superkey and then Quattro Pro, you need to unload Quattro Pro and then Superkey and then Sidekick to reclaim memory. Do not try to unload memory-resident programs

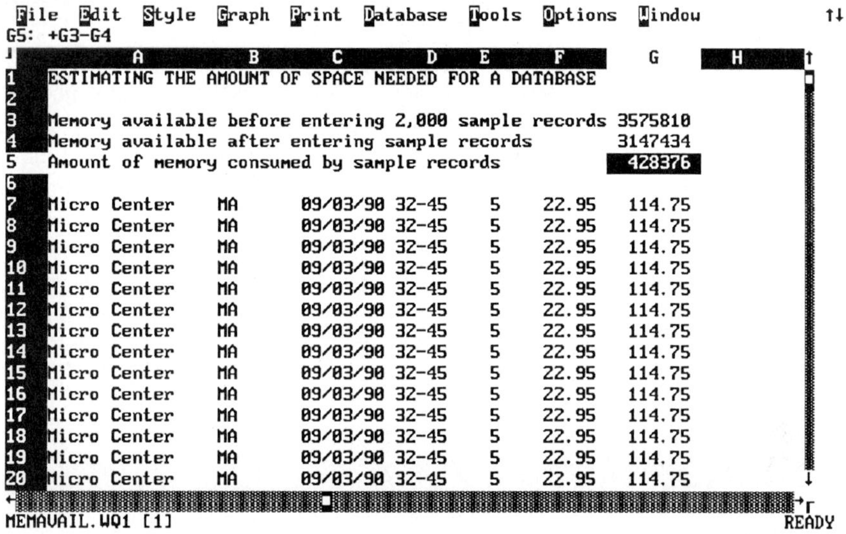

Figure 20-2. Estimating the potential size of a database

while temporarily exiting from Quattro Pro using the / File | Utilities | DOS Shell command; it almost certainly will crash the system.

- If you have expanded memory, change the Options | Other | Expanded Memory setting to Both to utilize more expanded memory. (This may cause a slight decrease in performance.)

- If you are using an 80 X 50 or 80 X 43 display mode, or one of the 132-column display modes offered by Quattro Pro 2.0, change back to 80 X 25.

- If you are trying to print in high-quality mode, try using non-Bitstream fonts. (Quattro Pro needs 125K of free memory to create Bitstream fonts.)

Recovering Memory

The amount of space that a spreadsheet occupies in memory is not just a matter of how much data it contains; it also depends on how many formatting codes and formulas it contains. Often you can help prevent memory shortages by reducing the storage size of your spreadsheets. If you are using a lot of display formats but most of the values on the spreadsheet share the same format, you might try using a default display format or at least resetting the format in all empty cells with the / Style | Numeric Format | **Reset** command. If the spreadsheet contains many formulas, some of which no longer need to be dynamic, you can save space by converting them to values with the / Edit | **Values** command. Sometimes these techniques produce an immediate increase in available memory. More often you will not actually recover additional memory until you save the spreadsheet and then retrieve it.

If your spreadsheet is still too large to fit comfortably into memory, try splitting it into smaller files using the / Tools | **Xtract** command. Then you can create and periodically update links between those files. (Both extracting and linking files are covered in Chapter 22.)

Expanded Memory

The term *expanded memory* refers to an optional computer card that extends the amount of memory installed in your computer. Quattro Pro is designed to take advantage of several standard expanded memory cards. When you add one of these cards, user memory—memory that is available for running programs—is divided into two basic sections: normal or conventional memory of up to 640K, and expanded or upper memory of over 640K.

Quattro Pro supports all LIM 3.2 or 4.0 memory cards, including AST RAMpage, Intel AboveBoard, Quadram Liberty, and STB Memory Champion. If you have a different type of memory card, you may or may not have problems making use of this additional memory. Some 80286- and 80386-based computers have extended as opposed to expanded memory. Quattro Pro does not recognize extended memory. However, there are special software drivers—such as HI386 from RYBS, 386MAX from Qualitas, and QEMM-386 from Quarterdeck—that allow extended memory to emulate expanded memory. Quattro Pro may be able to make use of your system's nonconventional memory if you have such a driver installed.

As discussed in Chapter 12, you can use the / Options | Other | **Expanded Memory** command to change the way that Quattro Pro uses expanded memory. By default, Quattro Pro stores spreadsheet data but not formatting codes in expanded memory. If you store formatting codes in expanded memory, you can create larger spreadsheets or open more spreadsheets at once, but the program slows down slightly.

BACKING UP FILES

All disks are fallible; if you have not already experienced a disk crash, you probably will at some point. You may also accidentally overwrite one of your files, irreversibly replacing the data previously stored under a particular file name.

The only way to protect yourself from such mishaps is to regularly create backup copies of your data. There are several ways to do this. As you know, every time you save a file that has already been saved, Quattro Pro offers you the option of canceling the command, replacing the previous version of the file, or backing up the file. If you select the Backup option, Quattro Pro stores the current spreadsheet to disk with the extension BAK (rather than WQ1). Unless you specify otherwise, these backup files are stored in the same directory as your regular spreadsheet files: the default data directory. If your WQ1 file is damaged—either due to hardware problems or user error—you can simply retrieve the BAK file with the / File | **R**etrieve command and save it with a WQ1 extension, overwriting the damaged version of the spreadsheet.

While creating and storing a backup copy of a spreadsheet in the same directory as the WQ1 file is useful when your spreadsheet file is damaged, it does not protect you against damage to the disk itself. There are three strategies you can use to protect your spreadsheet in the event of disk failure. First, you can store duplicate copies of your spreadsheet on a different disk by issuing the / File | **S**ave As command, pressing (ESC) when the default directory is displayed, and entering the full path name before the file name. If you choose this method, you should save the spreadsheet twice every time you make modifications—once on the default directory disk and the second time on a backup disk.

Alternatively, you can use the DOS COPY or BACKUP commands to copy some or all of your spreadsheet files to other disks at the end of every work session. If you tend to change several spreadsheets in a single work session, using DOS commands with wildcard characters can save you time by allowing you to back up several files—for example, all your spreadsheet files or all the spreadsheet files that start with a particular set of characters—with a single command. In most cases you will store backup copies of your files on floppy disks. If the file or group of files that you are backing up is too large to fit on a single floppy, you need to use the DOS BACKUP command to copy it across two or more disks. Files created with the DOS BACKUP command should only be copied back onto your hard disk using the DOS RESTORE command.

The third alternative for creating backup copies of your files is using Quattro Pro's File Manager utility, which is discussed in the next chapter.

EXITING TO THE OPERATING SYSTEM

The / File | Utilities | DOS Shell command allows you to exit to the operating system without unloading either Quattro Pro or your current spreadsheet from memory. This enables you to leave the program temporarily, execute a few DOS commands, and then get back into Quattro Pro without reloading the program or retrieving your current file. You will find this useful when you are ready to back up your work and discover that you do not have any formatted disks, or when you discover that your system clock is wrong and you want to access DOS to execute a DATE command. If you have a lot of available memory, you may even be able to run small programs, like simple text editors, from within the DOS shell.

When you issue the / File | Utilities | DOS Shell command, the spreadsheet display disappears and you will see the message "Type exit to return to Quattro," followed by the operating system sign-on message and the same DOS prompt that you saw before you loaded Quattro Pro. You can then perform any DOS operation, even loading another program if it fits into system memory. If not enough memory is available, you will see the DOS error message "Program too big to fit in memory." You will see the same error message if you forget that you have only temporarily exited Quattro Pro and try to reload the program by typing **Q**. When you are ready to return to Quattro Pro, you simply type **EXIT**. Your spreadsheet immediately reappears on the screen in the same form it was in when you left it.

If you have only 512K of memory or are using memory-resident programs, you may not have enough memory to issue the / File | Utilities | DOS Shell command.

As you work with Quattro Pro, you will create more and larger spreadsheets, and your ability to manage, protect, and access them will become increasingly important. The problems with disk and memory limitations discussed in this chapter are not unique to Quattro Pro. You will encounter them with almost any program, particularly any spreadsheet program. Learning to deal with these problems is essential to working with Quattro Pro effectively.

21

THE FILE MANAGER UTILITY

The File Manager Window
The Control Pane
The File List Pane
Manipulating Files
Displaying and Using Directory Trees
Other File Manager Options

Quattro Pro's File Manager utility allows you to perform disk housekeeping tasks, such as copying or moving files from one directory to another, renaming or deleting files, and opening several files at once. Using this utility, you can not only manipulate disk files without exiting to DOS, but also perform a few operations that are difficult or impossible to perform from the operating system, such as displaying file lists in alphabetical or date order, determining how much space a given set of files occupies, and displaying a graphic image of the directory structure of a disk.

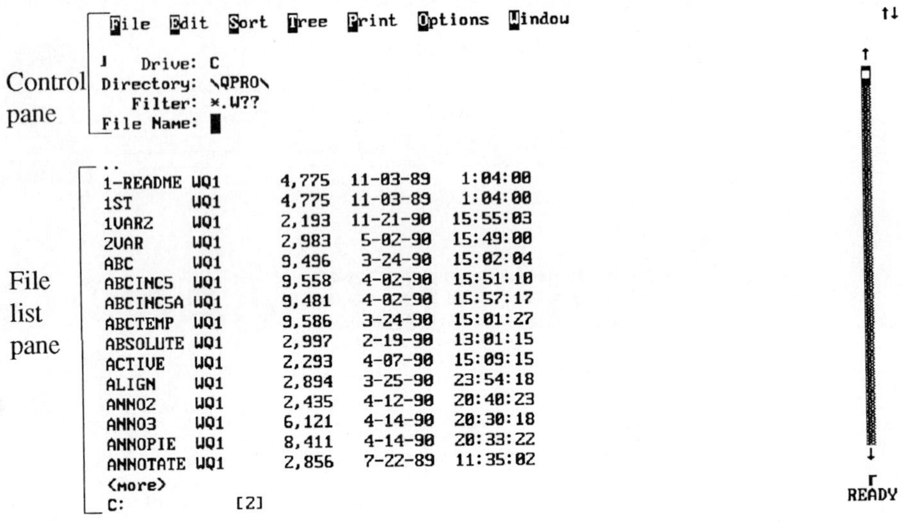

```
         ┌─File Edit Sort Tree Print Options Window              ↑↓
         │     Drive: C
Control  │ Directory: \QPRO\                                      ↑
pane     │    Filter: *.W??                                       ▓
         └─ File Name: █                                          ░
                                                                  ░
              ..                                                  ░
              1-README  WQ1    4,775   11-03-89    1:04:00        ░
              1ST       WQ1    4,775   11-03-89    1:04:00        ░
              1VAR2     WQ1    2,193   11-21-90   15:55:03        ░
              2VAR      WQ1    2,983    5-02-90   15:49:00        ░
              ABC       WQ1    9,496    3-24-90   15:02:04        ░
File          ABCINC5   WQ1    9,558    4-02-90   15:51:10        ░
list          ABCINC5A  WQ1    9,481    4-02-90   15:57:17        ░
pane          ABCTEMP   WQ1    9,586    3-24-90   15:01:27        ░
              ABSOLUTE  WQ1    2,997    2-19-90   13:01:15        ░
              ACTIVE    WQ1    2,293    4-07-90   15:09:15        ░
              ALIGN     WQ1    2,894    3-25-90   23:54:18        ░
              ANNO2     WQ1    2,435    4-12-90   20:40:23        ░
              ANNO3     WQ1    6,121    4-14-90   20:30:18        ░
              ANNOPIE   WQ1    8,411    4-14-90   20:33:22        ░
              ANNOTATE  WQ1    2,856    7-22-89   11:35:02        ░
              <more>                                              ↓
           └─ C:            [2]                               READY
```

Figure 21-1. The File Manager window

THE FILE MANAGER WINDOW

To use the File Manager utility, you issue the / File | Utilities | File Manager command. Quattro Pro displays a File Manager window, as shown in Figure 21-1.

The File Manager window initially contains two sections, or panes. Although there is no dividing line between these sections, as there is between panes in a spreadsheet window, Quattro Pro treats them as distinct areas. Only one pane is active at any time. The upper pane, known as the *control pane,* contains four prompts that let you specify a different disk drive and directory, a filter (filename pattern) that determines which files appear in the window, and the name of a file that you want to open. The *file list pane,* which appears directly below the control pane, contains a list of all the files in the specified directory that match the specified filter, followed by a list of any subdirectories of the specified directory. You can use the / Tree | Open command to activate a third pane called the *tree pane,* which shows a graphic representation of the directory structure on the specified disk drive.

The active File Manager pane is the one that contains the highlight. This highlight appears as a small bright rectangle within the control pane, as a bar highlighting a whole row within the file list pane, or a bar highlighting a directory name within the tree pane.

You must activate a pane before you can use it. You can do this by pressing (F6) (Pane) or (TAB) to activate the next pane in the window. You can use the (UP ARROW) and (DOWN ARROW) keys to move between the control pane and the file list pane. You can also activate the control pane and move the highlight directly to the File Name prompt by pressing (SHIFT-TAB). Finally, you can activate different panes by clicking with the mouse.

You can open two or more File Manager windows at a time to display different groups of files simultaneously. To open a second File Manager window, just issue the / File | Utilities | File Manager command again.

You can move from one File Manager window to another or between File Manager windows and spreadsheet windows using any of the usual window-changing keys or commands. Press (SHIFT-F6) to move to the next open window. Use (SHIFT-F5), (ALT-0), or / Window | Pick to display a list of windows from which to choose. File Manager windows are always represented in these lists by a drive letter rather than a file name. To relocate or resize File Manager windows, use the / Window | Move/Size command. Use either (ALT-F6) (Zoom) or the / Window | Zoom command to zoom windows to full screen. To close an active File Manager window, issue the / File | Close command.

THE CONTROL PANE

The control pane consists of four prompts: Drive, Directory, Filter, and File Name. The first three let you control which files appear in the file list. The File Name prompt allows you to retrieve a particular file.

To change any of the prompts, use the arrow keys to move to the prompt, and press (ESC) to erase the whole prompt or (BACKSPACE) to erase one character at a time. You can also use any of the usual editing keys to change the entry.

Switching Drives Or Directories

To display a list of files on a different disk, move the highlight to the Drive prompt, press (ESC) or (BACKSPACE) to erase the current entry, and enter the desired drive letter. To display files from a different directory, press (ESC) to erase the current entry (or use the (BACKSPACE) key to erase one character at a time) and enter a new directory. Be sure to include \ (backslash) before each directory name.

Selecting Files to Display

The Filter prompt lets you enter a file name pattern to limit the files within the specified drive and directory that are included in the file list. By default, the file name pattern is *.W??, which displays all files in the specified directory that have an extension starting with "W." To see all the files in a directory, change the filter to *.*.

You can express negative filters by enclosing a file name pattern in square brackets. A filter of [*.WQ1] displays a list of all files except those with the WQ1 extension. [SAL*.*] lists all files except those that start with the letters "SAL."

To create more complex filters, combine two or more file name patterns in a single filter expression. For example, the filter expression

.WQ1,[ABC.*]

or

.WQ1,[ABC.WQ1]

displays a list of all files with the WQ1 extension except those that start with "ABC."

The file filter remains in effect until you explicitly change it, even if you switch drives or directories. This makes it easy for you to look for the same types of files in different places. Quattro Pro also carries the file filter over from one File Manager window to the next, even if you open your next File Manager window in another work session.

Opening a File

The control pane's File Name prompt lets you select a spreadsheet file to open. If the file you want to open happens to have the default file extension, you do not need to type it when you enter the file name. If you enter the name of a file other than a spreadsheet file or a database file in one of the formats that Quattro Pro knows how to read (Paradox, dBASE, or Reflex), Quattro Pro displays an error message.

After you enter the file name, Quattro Pro opens a new window and retrieves the specified file.

If you specify a file that does not exist within the current directory, Quattro Pro assumes that you want to create a new file. It therefore opens a new spreadsheet window with a blank spreadsheet and assigns it the specified file name.

Searching for a File

You can also use the File Name prompt in combination with the (F5) (GoTo) key to search for a file anywhere on the specified disk drive. This is extremely useful when you can remember what you called the file but not where you put it. To search a drive for a file, type the name of the file at the File Name prompt and press (F5). Quattro Pro searches through every directory on the currently specified drive. If you happen to have a directory tree pane open, Quattro Pro highlights the directory it is currently searching so you can follow the progress of the search. If Quattro Pro cannot find a file with the specified name, it displays an error message. Otherwise, it changes the Directory prompt to match the directory in which the file was found, adjusts the file list accordingly, and places a check mark next to the file name in the file list pane. If you want to open the file, just press (ENTER). If the current drive includes other files with the specified name, you can press (F5) again to move to the next one.

Changing the Startup Directory

By default, when you first open a File Manager window, Quattro Pro displays a list of files in the default directory. If you prefer, you can direct Quattro Pro to carry over the directory setting from one File Manager window to the next by issuing the / Options I Startup I Directory command and choosing Previous rather than the default setting of Current. Quattro Pro then lists files from the last directory you displayed in a File Manager window.

If you frequently look for specific sets of files in directories other than the default directory, you may find this setting less confusing. As mentioned, Quattro Pro automatically carries over filters from one File Manager window to the next. As a result, if you leave Options I Startup I Directory set to Current, change the directory setting in the control pane, define a file name pattern to list files in that directory, and then open a new File Manager window, Quattro Pro lists any files within the default directory that match that previous filter expression. In contrast, if you change the Options | Startup | Directory setting to Previous, both the directory and the filter carry over from one File Manager window to the next.

THE FILE LIST PANE

The file list pane contains a list of all the files that match the drive, directory, and filter specified in the control pane.

At the bottom of the file list, Quattro Pro displays a status line with information about the number of files in the current list, the total number of files in the current directory, the number of bytes used, and the number of bytes still available on the specified drive. The status line in Figure 21-2 indicates that 149 files meet the filter condition *.WQ1 out of a total of 267 files in the \QPRO directory, that these 149 files occupy 1,745,520 bytes of disk space, and that there are 1,884,160 bytes still free on drive C.

As you move through the file list pane, Quattro Pro displays a check mark to the right of the file name extensions. This check mark indicates your current position within the file list. It is particularly useful if your display uses inverse video to show

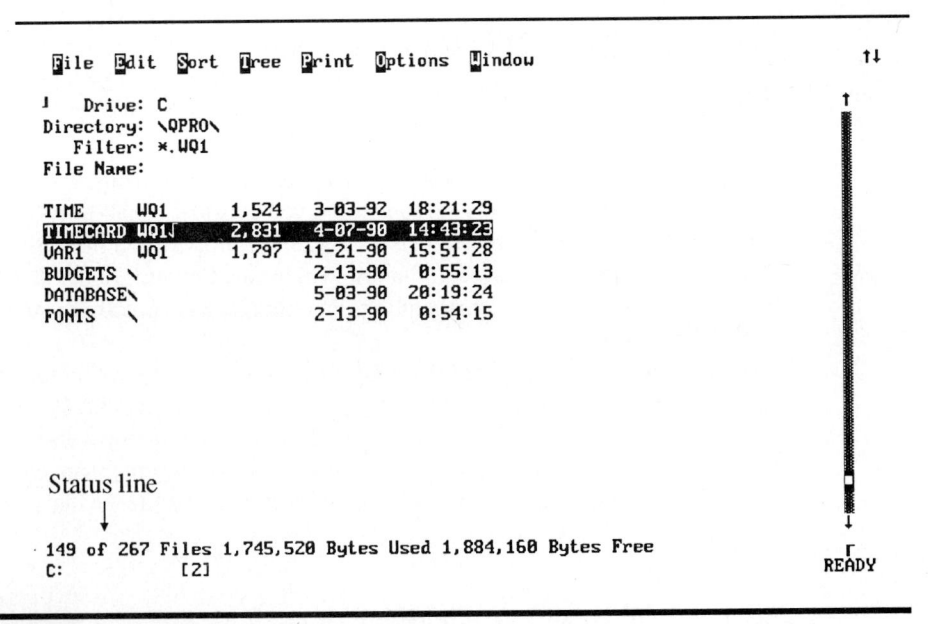

```
 File  Edit  Sort  Tree  Print  Options  Window                          ↑↓

    Drive: C                                                              ↑
 Directory: \QPRO\
     Filter: *.WQ1
 File Name:

     TIME      WQ1     1,524   3-03-92   18:21:29
     TIMECARD  WQ1√    2,831   4-07-90   14:43:23
     VAR1      WQ1     1,797  11-21-90   15:51:28
     BUDGETS   \               2-13-90    0:55:13
     DATABASE\                 5-03-90   20:19:24
     FONTS     \               2-13-90    0:54:15




                                                                          
                                                                          
     Status line
         ↓
     149 of 267 Files  1,745,520 Bytes Used  1,884,160 Bytes Free
     C:           [2]                                               READY
```

Figure 21-2. The File Manager status line

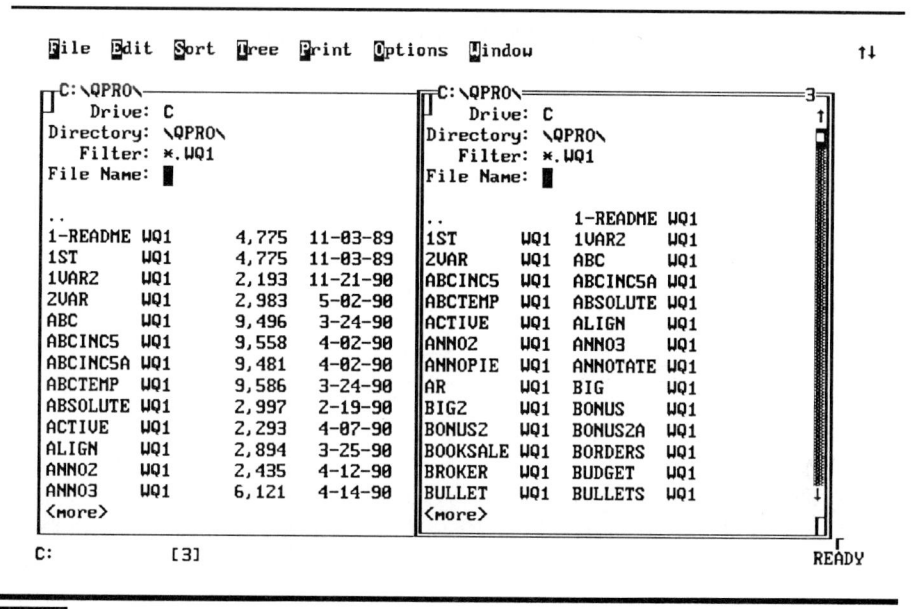

```
┌─C:\QPRO\──────────────────┐┌─C:\QPRO\═══════════════════3═┐
│    Drive: C               ││    Drive: C                  ↑
│Directory: \QPRO\          ││Directory: \QPRO\             ▓
│   Filter: *.WQ1           ││   Filter: *.WQ1              ▓
│File Name: ▌               ││File Name: ▌                  ▓
│                           ││                              ▓
│..                         ││..            1-README WQ1    ▓
│1-README WQ1  4,775 11-03-89││1ST      WQ1  1VAR2    WQ1    ▓
│1ST      WQ1  4,775 11-03-89││2VAR     WQ1  ABC      WQ1    ▓
│1VAR2    WQ1  2,193 11-21-90││ABCINC5  WQ1  ABCINC5A WQ1    ▓
│2VAR     WQ1  2,983  5-02-90││ABCTEMP  WQ1  ABSOLUTE WQ1    ▓
│ABC      WQ1  9,496  3-24-90││ACTIVE   WQ1  ALIGN    WQ1    ▓
│ABCINC5  WQ1  9,558  4-02-90││ANNO2    WQ1  ANNO3    WQ1    ▓
│ABCINC5A WQ1  9,481  4-02-90││ANNOPIE  WQ1  ANNOTATE WQ1    ▓
│ABCTEMP  WQ1  9,586  3-24-90││AR       WQ1  BIG      WQ1    ▓
│ABSOLUTE WQ1  2,997  2-19-90││BIG2     WQ1  BONUS    WQ1    ▓
│ACTIVE   WQ1  2,293  4-07-90││BONUS2   WQ1  BONUS2A  WQ1    ▓
│ALIGN    WQ1  2,894  3-25-90││BOOKSALE WQ1  BORDERS  WQ1    ▓
│ANNO2    WQ1  2,435  4-12-90││BROKER   WQ1  BUDGET   WQ1    ▓
│ANNO3    WQ1  6,121  4-14-90││BULLET   WQ1  BULLETS  WQ1    ↓
│<more>                     ││<more>                        ▓
│                           ││                              ▓
│ C:          [3]           │└──────────────────────────────┘
└───────────────────────────┘                          READY
```

Figure 21-3. File lists in Full View and Wide View

both the highlight bars and the files that have been selected. If you are using the black-and-white palette, this check mark is the only way to determine your place within the file list. When you activate other panes by pressing (F6), the check mark remains in the file list pane and serves as a kind of placeholder or bookmark indicating which file name will be highlighted when you reactivate that pane.

By default, the file list consists of five columns of information: the file's name, the extension, the size of the file in bytes, and the date and time when the file was last altered. This type of file list display is known as the Full View. If you prefer, you can change to a Wide View which lists only the filenames (including extensions), displaying as many columns of names as fit within the pane. Figure 21-3 shows two adjacent File Manager windows. The left window shows the file list in Full View and the right window shows the same list in Wide View. To change from one of these views to the other, issue the / Options | File List command and select either Full View or Wide View.

At the top of every file list, Quattro Pro displays two dots to represent the parent directory—the directory that is one level above the current directory in the directory structure. You can select this symbol to switch to the parent directory. For example, if the current directory is \QPRO\SALES, selecting .. changes the directory prompt to \QPRO and displays a list of all files in that directory that meet the specified filter, followed by a list of that directory's subdirectories. Selecting .. from the \QPRO directory changes the directory prompt to \ and displays a list of files and subdirectories in the root directory. To switch to a subdirectory of the current directory, select one of the subdirectory names at the bottom of the file list. When you select a different directory from the file list pane, Quattro Pro automatically changes the Directory prompt in the control pane and reconstructs the file list to display all files in the new directory that meet the current filter.

Several of the function keys and cursor-movement keys have special meanings within the file list pane. Table 22-1 lists all the special keys that you can use in this environment and notes which of them can be used in the control pane and tree pane as well.

Sorting File Lists

By default, Quattro Pro lists the names of files and subdirectories in alphabetical order. To change this order, issue the / Sort command and choose one of the following options:

- **Name**   This is the default setting. Arranges files and subdirectories alphabetically by name.

- **Timestamp**   Arranges files and subdirectories according to the date and time they were last modified.

- **Extension**   Sorts the file list alphabetically, first by extension and then by the files' first names.

- **Size**   Sorts files and subdirectories by file size, from smallest to largest.

- **DOS Order**   Arranges files and subdirectories in the same order that the DOS command DIR would list them.

MANIPULATING FILES

The main purpose of the File Manager is to let you move, copy, rename, and delete files on your disk without accessing DOS. If you want to manipulate a single file, you can simply highlight that file's name on the file list and then initiate the desired

Key	Action
`F2` (Rename) *	Lets you rename the highlighted file (same as / Edit | Rename).
`SHIFT-F7` (Select) or +	Selects the highlighted file so that you can open, move, copy, or delete it. If the file is already selected, these keys unselect it.
`ALT-F7` (All Select)	Selects all files in the file list in preparation for moving, copying, or deleting. If any files on the list are selected, `ALT-F7` unselects them.
`SHIFT-F8` (Move)	Moves the selected files into the paste buffer (so that you can move them to another directory), removing them from the current file list.
`DEL` **	Deletes the selected file from the disk.
`F9` (Calc) **	Reads the disk and redisplays the file list (same as / File | Read Dir).
`SHIFT-F9` (Copy)	Copies the selected files into the paste buffer (so that you can paste them into another directory) while leaving them on the current list.
`SHIFT-F10` (Paste)	Inserts the file names in the paste buffer into the current file list, and moves or copies the named files into the current directory.
`ESC` **	Unselects any selected files in the file list, activates the control pane, and moves the cursor to the File Name prompt.
`ENTER`	Opens the selected files. If either the .. (parent directory) item or a subdirectory name is highlighted, moves to that directory.
`HOME`	Moves the highlight to the .. (parent directory) item at the top of the file list.
`END`	Moves the highlight to the end of the file list.
`PGUP`	Moves the file list display up one screen.
`PGDN`	Moves the file list down one screen.

* Works in the control pane and the file list pane
** Works in the tree pane and the file list pane

Table 21-1. List of Special Keys for Use in the File List Pane

operation. To open, move, copy, or delete several files at once, however, you must first select all the files that you want to manipulate.

Using the File Manager can be more efficient than managing files in DOS because it gives you the ability to hand pick files to manipulate. In DOS, the only groups of files that you can manipulate are those that you can specify by entering a file name pattern using DOS wild-card characters. In contrast, the File Manager lets you define a filter to narrow your file list so you can hone in on the files that you want to manage. Then it lets you pick exactly those files that you want from the resulting list. Once you have selected all the files that you want to work with, you press the appropriate key or issue the appropriate command to open, move, copy, replicate, rename, or delete them as a group.

Selecting Files

To select files one at a time, highlight the file name and either press (SHIFT-F7) (Select), type + (plus), or issue the / Edit | Select File command. Quattro Pro highlights that file name and keeps it highlighted even as you move to other file names to repeat the same procedure. To unselect a file, just highlight it and again press (SHIFT-F7), type +, or issue the / Edit | Select File command. You can select and unselect files with a mouse by clicking on the file names.

To select all the files in the current file list, press (ALT-F7) (All Select). If you can define an appropriate file name pattern—one that defines all the files that you want to manipulate—you can use the Filter prompt to display those files and then press (ALT-F7) to select them all at once.

If you press (ALT-F7) when any of the files in the current list are selected, Quattro Pro unselects all the files on the list—giving you a clean slate from which you can start reselecting files.

Opening Files

To open a single file, highlight its name on the file list and press (ENTER), or double-click on the file name with the mouse. You can open several files at once—each in its own window—by selecting the files on the file list and then pressing (ENTER) or double-clicking. Quattro Pro asks you to confirm that you want to open those "documents."

Keep in mind that you can also open a single file by entering its name at the File Name prompt in the control panel. This is particularly useful if you want to open a file that is not included in the current file list.

Copying Files

There are four steps involved in copying files to a different directory:

1. Highlight the files that you want to copy.

2. Press (SHIFT-F9) (Copy) or issue the / Edit I Copy command. Quattro Pro displays the selected file names in a different color or intensity and stores those names in a section of memory known as a *paste buffer*.

3. Switch to the directory to which you want to copy the files by either choosing a subdirectory from the bottom of the file list, choosing the .. option at the top of the file list, activating the control pane and entering a new directory name next to the Directory prompt, or moving to a different File Manager window.

4. Press (SHIFT-F10) (Paste) or issue the / Edit I Paste command to paste the file names from the buffer to the current directory. Quattro Pro inserts the selected file names into the current file list, positioning them according to the current sort order, and copies the files themselves into the specified directory. If the files that you copied do not match the filter in the new directory, Quattro Pro automatically changes the filter to accommodate the new files.

When you copy several files at once, Quattro Pro considers the currently highlighted file to be selected, even if you have not explicitly selected it with (SHIFT-F7), +, or / Edit I Select File.

Caution As in DOS, when you copy a file to a directory that already contains a file of that name, Quattro Pro overwrites the existing file without issuing any warnings. (This is also a potential problem when you move files from one directory to another.) The only way to prevent this is to search for the file name in the target directory before you paste the files from the buffer. This is easy to do if you perform the operation using two different File Manager windows. You can simply copy the file names to the paste buffer, open or activate the second File

Manager window, change to the target directory if necessary, define the same filter, and check whether the file names that you are about to copy appear on the list. If they do not, go ahead and paste the file names from the buffer.

Copying a Group of Files To Multiple Disks

Quattro Pro includes an undocumented feature that allows you to copy or move a large group of files to two or more floppy disks with a single paste command. Start by copying or moving the files from the original directory. Then switch to the floppy disk drive and issue the / Edit | Paste command or press (SHIFT-F10). As soon as the disk you are pasting to is full, Quattro Pro displays the name of the first file that did not fit, followed by the message Disk Full. It also presents you with three options: Stop Copying, Try again with another disk, and Ignore this file. You can then insert a new disk and choose the Try again with another disk option to copy the remaining files in the paste buffer onto a second disk.

This feature provides an efficient means of creating backup copies of your spreadsheet files. Unlike the DOS BACKUP command, which also lets you copy a group of files to several floppy disks, pasting from Quattro Pro never splits individual files across multiple disks. As a result you need not use any special commands to copy the files back to the original disk. If you use the DOS BACKUP command, you must use the RESTORE command to restore the files. You cannot copy or read them directly.

Moving Files

The process of moving one or more files to a different directory is very similar to copying them. Once you have highlighted the files that you want to move, you press (SHIFT-F8) (Move) or issue the / Edit | Move command, copying the selected file names to the paste buffer. Then you move to the directory to which you want to transfer the files by choosing .. or a subdirectory or by moving to a different File Manager window. Finally, you press (SHIFT-F10) (Paste) or issue the / Edit | Paste command. Quattro Pro inserts the specified files in the current file list, copies them to the current directory, and then removes them from the original directory.

Deleting Files

To delete files, just highlight their names and either press (DEL) or issue the / Edit | Erase command. When Quattro Pro asks if you are sure you want to "delete this file" or "delete the marked files," type **Y** for Yes (or **N** for No if you want to cancel the operation).

Once you have deleted all the files in a directory, you can also delete the directory itself by highlighting its name at the bottom of the parent directory's file list and pressing (DEL) or issuing the / Edit | Erase command.

Duplicating Files

You can use the / Edit | Duplicate command to create a new copy of a file under a different name. This is the only way you can replicate a file within the same directory (since you cannot have two files in a directory with the same name). You can only duplicate one file at a time. If several files are selected when you issue this command, Quattro Pro ignores all but the currently selected file—that is, the one marked with the check.

To duplicate a file, start by highlighting the file name on the file list. Then issue the / Edit | Duplicate command. When Quattro Pro prompts you for a file name, enter the name of the file. You must include the extension, even if you want to assign the default extension to the file. (If you omit the extension, the new file will have no extension at all.) If you want to store the duplicate in a different directory, include the directory path with the file name. If the name that you assigned to this duplicate file matches the current filter, Quattro Pro adds the file to the file list.

Renaming Files

You can change the name of the current file by issuing the / Edit | Rename command. When Quattro Pro prompts you for a file name, enter the name of the file, including the extension. Quattro Pro removes the old name from the file list and, assuming the new name matches the current filter, displays the new one.

> **Caution** Never change the file name extension when you rename a spreadsheet file. Quattro Pro determines how to interpret the contents of a file from its extension.

For example, Quattro Pro assumes that files with the extension WK1 are Lotus 1-2-3 spreadsheet files, and treats them accordingly. If you change a Quattro Pro spreadsheet file's extension from WQ1 to WK1, Quattro Pro has trouble making sense of the information, particularly if the file includes any desktop publishing features like fonts, shading, and line drawing. If you want to change a Lotus 1-2-3 file to a Quattro Pro file, use the / File | Save As command, which directs Quattro Pro to actually translate the file contents in the format specified by the extension. Then you can use the File Manager to delete the old file from the disk.

DISPLAYING AND USING DIRECTORY TREES

A *directory tree* is a graphic representation of the entire directory structure of a disk, as shown in Figure 21-4. You will want to open a directory tree pane for two reasons: it gives you a clear picture of how your disk is organized, and it makes it easy to switch back and forth among several different directories.

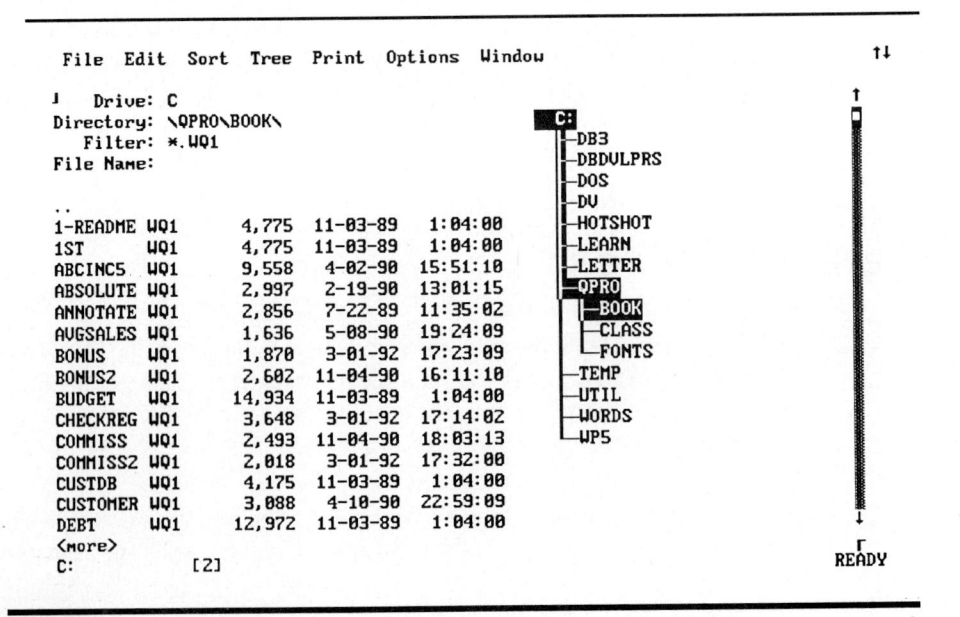

```
File  Edit  Sort  Tree  Print  Options  Window                      ↑↓
   Drive: C
Directory: \QPRO\BOOK\                          C:
   Filter: *.WQ1                                ├─DB3
File Name:                                      ├─DBDULPRS
                                                ├─DOS
..                                              ├─DU
1-README  WQ1    4,775   11-03-89   1:04:00     ├─HOTSHOT
1ST       WQ1    4,775   11-03-89   1:04:00     ├─LEARN
ABCINC5   WQ1    9,558    4-02-90  15:51:10     ├─LETTER
ABSOLUTE  WQ1    2,997    2-19-90  13:01:15     ├─QPRO
ANNOTATE  WQ1    2,856    7-22-89  11:35:02     │  ├─BOOK
AVGSALES  WQ1    1,636    5-08-90  19:24:09     │  ├─CLASS
BONUS     WQ1    1,870    3-01-92  17:23:09     │  └─FONTS
BONUS2    WQ1    2,602   11-04-90  16:11:10     ├─TEMP
BUDGET    WQ1   14,934   11-03-89   1:04:00     ├─UTIL
CHECKREG  WQ1    3,648    3-01-92  17:14:02     ├─WORDS
COMMISS   WQ1    2,493   11-04-90  18:03:13     └─WP5
COMMISS2  WQ1    2,018    3-01-92  17:32:00
CUSTDB    WQ1    4,175   11-03-89   1:04:00
CUSTOMER  WQ1    3,088    4-10-90  22:59:09
DEBT      WQ1   12,972   11-03-89   1:04:00
<more>
C:            [2]                                                 READY
```

Figure 21-4. File Manager window with a directory tree

To display a directory tree, issue the / Tree | Open command. Quattro Pro opens a third pane, known as the tree pane, either below or to the right of the file list pane. If the File Manager window fills the entire screen, the tree pane appears to the right of the file list, as shown in Figure 21-4. Otherwise, the tree appears below the file list pane. You can press (ALT-F6) to zoom the window if you want to move the directory to the right. If you have many different directories on the currently selected disk, it may take a few moments for Quattro Pro to construct the directory tree.

The root directory is represented on the directory tree by the drive letter at the top of the tree. Below and slightly to the right of the drive letter, you can see the first level of directories. If those directories have any subdirectories, they appear below and slightly to the right of their parent directory's name. For example, in the directory tree in Figure 21-4, the names of the QPRO directory's three subdirectories (BOOK, CLASS, and FONTS) appear below and to the right of QPRO.

Use the (LEFT ARROW) and (RIGHT ARROW) keys to move from one level of the directory structure to another. Use the (UP ARROW) and (DOWN ARROW) keys to move up and down within the same directory level. As you move the highlight bar through the directory tree, the Directory setting in the control pane changes to display the name of the highlighted directory, and the file list displays all files in that directory that match the current Filter setting. If your directories contain many files, your progress from one directory to another can be somewhat sluggish. You may find using the control pane's Directory prompt more efficient to move to a directory that is placed far from the current directory on the tree.

By default, Quattro Pro displays the directories on each level in order by name. If you prefer to see the directories in the order DOS uses when you issue a directory command, issue the / Sort | DOS Order command. The / Sort | Timestamp, / Sort | Extension, and / Sort | Size commands have no effect on the directory tree.

Resizing the Directory Tree

When you first display a directory tree, Quattro Pro divides the File Manager window equally between the tree pane and the other two panes in the window—the control pane and file list pane. You can allocate the space differently by issuing the / Tree | Resize command and, at the Relative Tree size prompt, entering a number between 10 and 100. Do not include a percent sign. If you change this setting to 100%, Quattro Pro devotes as much room to the tree pane as it can while still displaying the control pane and a small portion of the file list pane. The default setting is 50%.

You might want to enlarge the tree pane if your directory structure contains many levels of subdirectories or if the tree is displayed below the file list pane. You might shrink the tree pane to display more file names if you are using the Wide View. For example, Figure 21-5 shows a File Manager window with the file list in Wide View

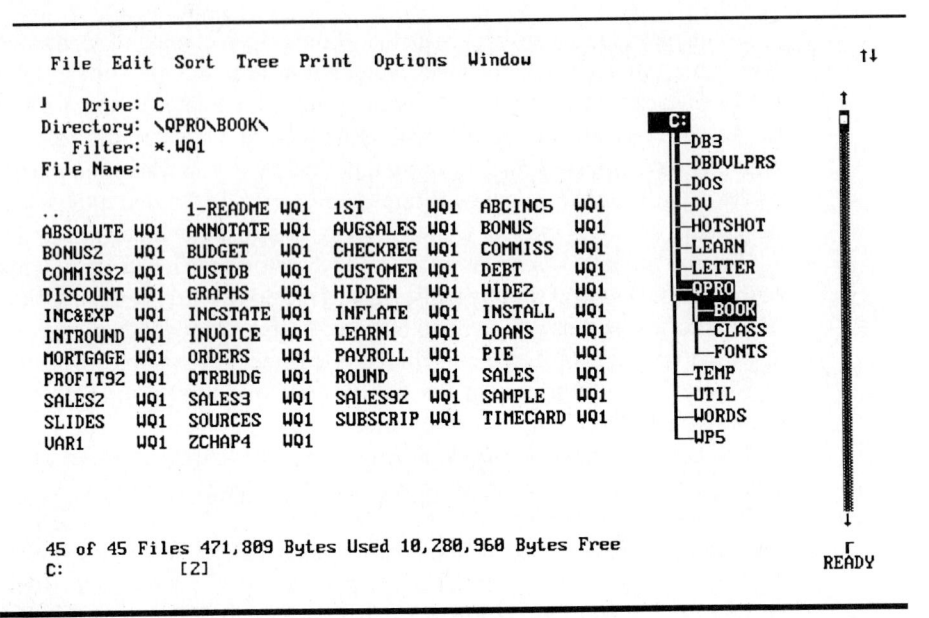

```
  File   Edit   Sort   Tree   Print   Options   Window                              ↑↓
↵   Drive:  C                                                      ┌─C:
Directory:  \QPRO\BOOK\                                            ├─DB3
    Filter:  *.WQ1                                                 ├─DBUULPRS
 File Name:                                                        ├─DOS
                                                                   ├─DU
  ..             1-README  WQ1   1ST       WQ1   ABCINC5   WQ1     ├─HOTSHOT
  ABSOLUTE  WQ1  ANNOTATE  WQ1   AVGSALES  WQ1   BONUS     WQ1     ├─LEARN
  BONUS2    WQ1  BUDGET    WQ1   CHECKREG  WQ1   COMMISS   WQ1     ├─LETTER
  COMMISS2  WQ1  CUSTDB    WQ1   CUSTOMER  WQ1   DEBT      WQ1     ├─QPRO
  DISCOUNT  WQ1  GRAPHS    WQ1   HIDDEN    WQ1   HIDE2     WQ1     │  ├─BOOK
  INC&EXP   WQ1  INCSTATE  WQ1   INFLATE   WQ1   INSTALL   WQ1     │  ├─CLASS
  INTROUND  WQ1  INVOICE   WQ1   LEARN1    WQ1   LOANS     WQ1     │  └─FONTS
  MORTGAGE  WQ1  ORDERS    WQ1   PAYROLL   WQ1   PIE       WQ1     ├─TEMP
  PROFIT92  WQ1  QTRBUDG   WQ1   ROUND     WQ1   SALES     WQ1     ├─UTIL
  SALES2    WQ1  SALES3    WQ1   SALES92   WQ1   SAMPLE    WQ1     ├─WORDS
  SLIDES    WQ1  SOURCES   WQ1   SUBSCRIP  WQ1   TIMECARD  WQ1     └─WP5
  VAR1      WQ1  ZCHAP4    WQ1


 45 of 45 Files 471,809 Bytes Used 10,280,960 Bytes Free
 C:          [2]                                                                READY
```

Figure 21-5. A tree pane resized to 30%

and a tree pane at 30%. If the tree pane in this figure were displayed at 50%, only three columns of file names would be visible.

Quattro Pro remembers any changes that you make to the size of the directory tree. The next time you open a tree pane, it is the size that you last specified. To remove the tree pane from the screen, issue the / **T**ree | Close command. Quattro Pro erases the directory tree and expands the control pane and file list pane to fill its space.

OTHER FILE MANAGER OPTIONS

Most of the remaining options on the File Manager menus are replicates of options on the regular Quattro Pro menu tree. The few other options that are unique to the File Manager or operate slightly differently in this context are described in the following sections.

Rereading the File List

The / File | Read Dir command directs Quattro Pro to reconstruct the current file list by rereading the files on the specified drive. If you are displaying a list of files on a disk in drive A or B, you should use this command whenever you place a new disk in that disk drive. You should also issue the / File | Read Dir command when you are using a local area network and suspect that someone else may have just added files to the specified directory. The (F9) (Calc) key performs exactly the same function as the / File | Read Dir command—it "recalculates" the current file list.

Making Directories

The / File | Make Dir command lets you create new directories on a disk. When you issue this command, Quattro Pro prompts you for a directory name. Enter a name of up to eight characters. Quattro Pro assumes that you want the new directory to be located immediately under the currently selected directory. If you want it placed elsewhere, specify the full directory path when you enter the file name.

Printing the Contents Of a File Manager Window

You can use the File Manager's Print menu to print the information in different File Manager panes. This menu is similar to the regular Print menu, except that the Block option leads to a submenu with the options Files, Tree, or Both. Files, the default option, prints the current file list, Tree prints the directory tree, and Both prints the file list followed by the directory tree.

This chapter has covered the use of Quattro Pro's File Manager utility. If you are already familiar and comfortable with DOS, you may be tempted to ignore the File Manager and just use DOS (via the / File | Utilities | DOS Window command) whenever you want to manipulate files. However, even if you know how to copy, move, rename, and delete files from DOS, the File Manager has some advantages that are worth considering. It gives you more ways to define groups of files to manipulate—both because it lets you define complex filter conditions (including negative filters) and because it lets you hand pick files from the resulting lists. The File Manager also lets you easily display file lists in different orders, which can make it easy to create copies of only your old files or to figure out which files are consuming the most space on your disk. Lastly, the File Manager lets you diagram your disk's directory structure by creating a directory tree.

22

COMBINING, EXTRACTING, AND LINKING FILES

Extracting Files
Combining Files
Linking Spreadsheets

This chapter covers several tools for working with multiple spreadsheet files: extracting a section of an existing spreadsheet to create a new spreadsheet file, combining data from two spreadsheets, and linking spreadsheets by creating formulas that refer to cells in another file.

EXTRACTING FILES

The / Tools | Xtract command lets you copy a block of data from your current spreadsheet to a new file, creating a spreadsheet that consists solely of the extracted block. When you first issue the / Tools | Xtract command, Quattro Pro displays a menu containing options for Formulas and Values. If you use the Formulas option, all values contained in the extracted block are transferred "as is" to the new spreadsheet. If you use the Values option, any formulas contained in the extracted block are converted to their end values when they are copied to the new spreadsheet file.

Whenever you use the / Tools | Xtract | Formulas command, be careful to extract all cells referenced by extracted formulas; otherwise you can generate ERR values or unwanted adjustments in cell references.

Once you choose between the Formulas and Values options, Quattro Pro prompts you for a block of values to extract. As soon as you supply a block name or set of block coordinates, Quattro Pro requests a name for the new spreadsheet file and displays a list of all the spreadsheet files currently in the default data directory. All global formats and all formatting codes within the extract block are copied from the original spreadsheet to the new extracted file.

Copying or Moving Versus Extracting Data

Copying data from one spreadsheet window to another and extracting data to a new file with / Tools | Xtract produce the same results. Each method has its advantages. Copying data between windows allows you to see exactly what you are doing. You can use it to move data into an already existing file, whereas extracting data always creates a new file. However, you can only copy data from one spreadsheet to another if you have enough memory to load the two files at once. It also may be more than you need. If you simply want to extract a section of a spreadsheet to use later, the / Tools | Xtract command is more efficient: rather than opening a new spreadsheet file, copying data from one file to the other, and then saving the new file, you can perform the entire operation with a single command. The / Tools | Xtract command also copies default formats as well as any formatting codes in specific block of cells that you specify. This can save you the trouble of redefining column widths and specifying default numeric formats. In contrast, when you copy data from one spreadsheet to another, only those formats that apply to the particular cells that you copy are transferred to the destination file. Default formats and column widths are left unchanged.

COMBINING FILES

The / Tools | Combine commands allow you to combine data from separate spreadsheet files. There are three options available for combining files:

Copy	Copies all or part of another spreadsheet file, as is, into the current spreadsheet, overwriting the block of cells into which it is copied
Add	Adds the values in all or part of another spreadsheet file to values in the current spreadsheet
Subtract	Subtracts values in all or part of another spreadsheet file from values in the current spreadsheet

Regardless of which option you choose, combining files involves the following steps:

1. Save your current spreadsheet. The / Tools | Combine commands have a dramatic effect on the spreadsheet and are easy to bungle.

2. Move the cell pointer to the cell you want to be the upper-left corner of the incoming block or spreadsheet.

3. Issue the appropriate / Tools | Combine command.

4. Choose either the File or Block option from the displayed submenu. The File option allows you to combine an entire spreadsheet file with the current spreadsheet. The Block option allows you to combine a block of cells in another spreadsheet with the current spreadsheet.

5. If you choose the Block option, specify a set of block coordinates or a block name. Because you have no way of viewing the incoming spreadsheet or of generating a list of available block names on the second spreadsheet, you need to know the name or coordinates of the block you want to import before issuing the / Tools | Combine command. It is a good idea to name the block that you want to import, both because names are easier to remember than cells and because using block names prevents you from importing the wrong data due to errors in entering block coordinates.

6. Supply the name of the file to be combined with the current spreadsheet. If you want to use a file from another directory, press (ESC) twice, type in the name of the directory, and press (ENTER) to display a new file list. To designate a file, either type its name or select it from the file list.

Note: When you issue any of the / Tools | Combine commands, Quattro Pro reads the incoming data from disk. This means that if the source spreadsheet is open in another window, you must save any changes you have made to that file to disk before you issue the / Tools | Combine command to ensure that Quattro Pro uses your current data.

The / Tools | Combine | Copy Command

The / Tools | Combine | Copy command copies all or part of another spreadsheet file into your current spreadsheet. You can use this for operations such as copying a lookup table or a set of column headings from another spreadsheet. When you issue this command, Quattro Pro acts as if you had specified the current location of the cell pointer as the destination for a copy command. It copies the upper-left corner of the incoming data in the current cell and the rest of the data below and/or to the right of that cell. The incoming data occupies as much room as necessary, overwriting any data in its way, and assumes the column widths and display formats of the cells into which it is copied.

Quattro Pro ignores blank cells in the source file when combining files; therefore, cells on the current spreadsheet may be overwritten with values or labels, but they are never replaced with blank cells.

The / Tools | Combine | Add Command

The / Tools | Combine | Add command allows you to add values from the source spreadsheet to values in the current spreadsheet. Labels in the source spreadsheet are ignored in this process; only numeric values are imported. The / Tools | Combine | Add command is extremely useful for combining figures for different corporate divisions or different financial periods to create consolidated or year-to-date financial statements.

When you add data from the source spreadsheet, you must be particularly careful to position the cell pointer correctly before you issue the command, especially in cases where the two spreadsheets have different layouts. You also must be sure that the structure of the incoming block or file is identical to the section of the current spreadsheet so like values are added to like values. If you are off by a single cell, the result can be two different line items added together incorrectly.

Values are added according to the following rules:

- Values in the current spreadsheet are replaced by the sum of the original and the incoming values, except in the case of formulas; formulas in the current spreadsheet always remain unaltered.

- Quattro Pro converts all incoming formulas to their results and interprets all labels and blank cells as zero as it adds the values together.

- Any cells in the current spreadsheet that contain labels, ERR, or NA values are not changed by the incoming data.

The / Tools | Combine | Subtract Command

The / Tools | Combine | Subtract command allows you to subtract source spreadsheet values from current spreadsheet values. It functions according to the same rules as / Tools | Combine | Add, except the incoming values are subtracted from values on the current spreadsheet rather than added to them. This command is often used to break down a spreadsheet in which values have been previously combined with the / Tools | Combine | Add command.

Hands-On Practice

Try the various / Tools | Combine commands by creating and then merging two monthly expense statements. Start by creating an expense statement template that contains the labels and formulas used in both the two monthly spreadsheets and the consolidated spreadsheet.

1. If you have anything other than a blank screen, save your work and erase the screen by issuing the / File | Erase command.

2. Change the width of column A to 17 characters.

3. Enter the following data:

In Cell	Enter
A1	**MONTHLY EXPENSE REPORT --**
A3	**Meals**
A4	**Entertainment**
A5	**^SUBTOTAL**
A7	**Hotel or Motel**
A8	**Transportation**
A9	**Car Rental**
A10	**Car Expenses**
A11	**Parking & Tolls**

A12	**Miles * 22¢** (You can enter the cents symbol by holding down (ALT) and typing **155**, the ASCII code for that symbol.)
A13	**Other**
A14	**^SUBTOTAL**
A16	**TOTAL**
A18	**TOTAL DEDUCTIBLE**
B5	**@SUM(B3..B4)**
B14	**@SUM(B7..B13)**
B15	**+B5+B14**
B18	**(B5*.8)+B14**

The last formula is based on the assumption that only 80% of meals and entertainment expenses are deductible.

4. Issue the / Options | Formats | Numeric Format | Fixed command, and press (ENTER) to specify two decimal places. Select Quit twice to return to Ready mode.

5. Underline the spreadsheet title if you like by issuing the / Style | Line Drawing command, specify a block of A1..C1, a placement of Bottom, and a line type of Single.

6. Create a named block for the section of the spreadsheet that will contain the expense figures by issuing the / Edit | Name | Create command, entering the block name **EXPENSES**, and specifying coordinates of B3..B18.

7. Save this spreadsheet skeleton under the name **EXPTEMP** (for Expense Template).

Now create a January expense report spreadsheet.

1. Enter the following data:

In Cell	Enter
C1	**JAN. 1991**
B3	**400**
B4	**75**
B7	**800**
B8	**300**
B9	**200**
B10	**50**
B11	**15**
B12	**45**
B13	**30**

Your spreadsheet should now look like the one shown in Figure 22-1.

```
File  Edit  Style  Graph  Print  Database  Tools  Options  Window
B18: (B5*0.8)+B14
            A              B        C        D        E        F        G
1   MONTHLY EXPENSE REPORT -- JAN. 1991
2
3   Meals                  400.00
4   Entertainment           75.00
5      SUBTOTAL            475.00
6
7   Hotel or Motel         800.00
8   Transportation         300.00
9   Car Rental             200.00
10  Car Expenses            50.00
11  Parking & Tolls         15.00
12  Miles * 22¢             45.00
13  Other                   30.00
14     SUBTOTAL            1440.00
15
16  TOTAL                  1915.00
17
18  TOTAL DEDUCTIBLE       1820.00
19

JANEXP.WQ1  [1]                                                READY
```

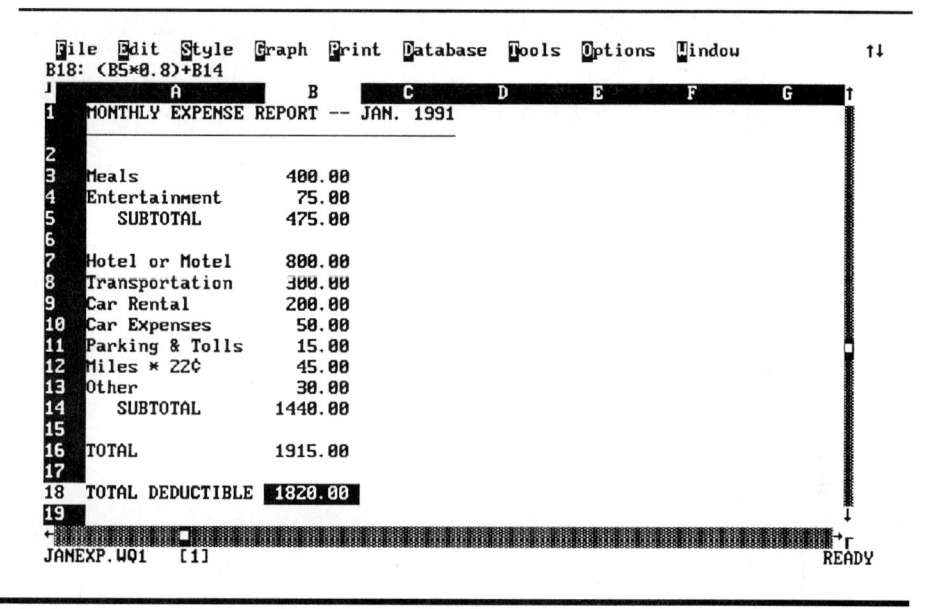

Figure 22-1. The JANEXP spreadsheet

2. Issue the / File | Save As command and assign the name JANEXP to the modified file.

Next, retrieve EXPTEMP and fill in data for February, creating a February expense sheet.

1. Issue the / File | Retrieve command and retrieve EXPTEMP to the screen.

2. Enter the following data:

In Cell	Enter
C1	**FEB. 1991**
B3	**500**
B4	**175**
B7	**600**
B8	**400**
B9	**100**
B10	**20**
B11	**25**
B12	**145**
B13	**60**

456   Quattro Pro 2 Made Easy

```
File  Edit  Style  Graph  Print  Database  Tools  Options  Window        ↑↓
B18: (B5*0.8)+B14
        A              B         C        D        E        F        G
 1  MONTHLY EXPENSE REPORT -- FEB. 1991
 2
 3  Meals            500.00
 4  Entertainment    175.00
 5     SUBTOTAL      675.00
 6
 7  Hotel or Motel   600.00
 8  Transportation   400.00
 9  Car Rental       100.00
10  Car Expenses      20.00
11  Parking & Tolls   25.00
12  Miles * 22¢      145.00
13  Other             60.00
14     SUBTOTAL     1350.00
15
16  TOTAL          2025.00
17
18  TOTAL DEDUCTIBLE  1890.00
19
FEBEXP.WQ1    [1]                                                    READY
```

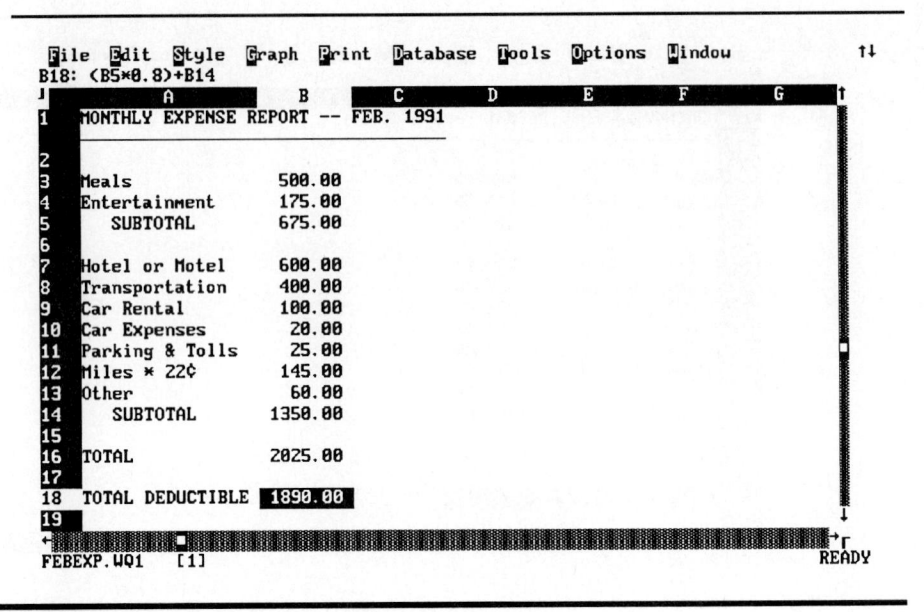

Figure 22-2.   The FEBEXP spreadsheet

Your spreadsheet should now look like the one shown in Figure 22-2.

3. Save the file under a new name by issuing the / **File** I **Save As** command and assigning the name FEBEXP.

Finally, create a consolidated expense spreadsheet.

1. Start by retrieving EXPTEMP again with the / **File** I **Retrieve** command and immediately save it under the name CONSOL using the / **File** I **Save As** command.

2. Move to A1 and enter a new spreadsheet title:

   MONTHLY EXPENSES, JAN - FEB, 1991

3. Still in cell A1, issue the / **Tools** I **Combine** I **Add** I **File** command, and specify the file JANEXP. Because you have used / **Tools** I **Combine** I **Add** rather than / **Tools** I **Combine** I **Copy**, only values are copied from one spreadsheet to the other; the new label in cell A1 is therefore not overwritten.

4. Issue the / **Tools** I **Combine** I **Add** I **File** command again and specify the file FEBEXP. This time Quattro Pro adds all February expenses to the January

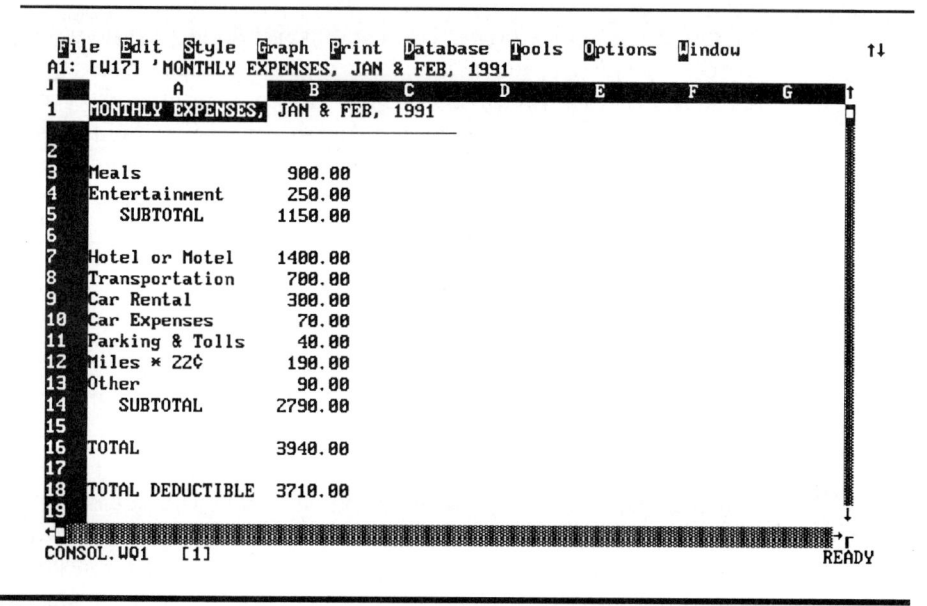

```
      File Edit Style Graph Print Database Tools Options Window         ↑↓
      A1: [W17] 'MONTHLY EXPENSES, JAN & FEB, 1991
              A              B          C       D       E       F       G
       1  MONTHLY EXPENSES, JAN & FEB, 1991
       2
       3  Meals              900.00
       4  Entertainment      250.00
       5     SUBTOTAL       1150.00
       6
       7  Hotel or Motel    1400.00
       8  Transportation     700.00
       9  Car Rental         300.00
      10  Car Expenses        70.00
      11  Parking & Tolls     40.00
      12  Miles * 22¢        190.00
      13  Other               90.00
      14     SUBTOTAL       2790.00
      15
      16  TOTAL             3940.00
      17
      18  TOTAL DEDUCTIBLE  3710.00
      19
      CONSOL.WQ1   [1]                                               READY
```

Figure 22-3. Combining JANEXP and FEBEXP values

expenses, which were previously added to this spreadsheet. Because the layouts of the spreadsheets are identical and you positioned the cell pointer in the home cell before issuing the command, Quattro Pro has no trouble correctly combining the two sets of values.

5. Save the file again, replacing the previous version of CONSOL. Your spreadsheet should now look like Figure 22-3.

LINKING SPREADSHEETS

Two spreadsheets are considered linked when a formula in one refers to a cell or cells in another. The spreadsheet that contains the linking formula is known as the *primary spreadsheet*, the spreadsheet to which the formula refers is called the *supporting spreadsheet*, and the values in the referenced cells are called *supporting values*. Once you have created a link between two spreadsheets, a change in the referenced cells in the supporting spreadsheet is immediately reflected in the primary spreadsheet whenever the two spreadsheets are open.

There are several reasons for linking spreadsheets:

- **To break a complex model into small, specialized, easy-to-manage components.** Linking lets you manage large amounts of data by linking several small spreadsheets (each of which contains data for a discrete piece of a complex problem) rather than by creating a single huge spreadsheet. Splitting a complicated and potentially confusing spreadsheet into manageable sections can decrease mistakes. It also lets you distribute work among several people, each of whom can be charged with maintaining one or more supporting spreadsheets. This can be a particularly effective way to organize work on a local area network.

  Linking also lets you follow the traditional accounting model of primary statements and supporting statements. Figure 22-4 shows a balance sheet and its supporting documents. In Quattro Pro you might create a separate spreadsheet for each of these documents, and then create a balance sheet spreadsheet that draws data from those supporting files.

- **To prevent duplication of data in several spreadsheets.** If you need to use a particular piece of information in several different contexts, linking can save you the trouble and disk space involved in storing the same data in more than one file. By storing tax tables, price tables, and other lookup tables in spreadsheets of their own, you can access the data whenever you need it without copying it to multiple files.

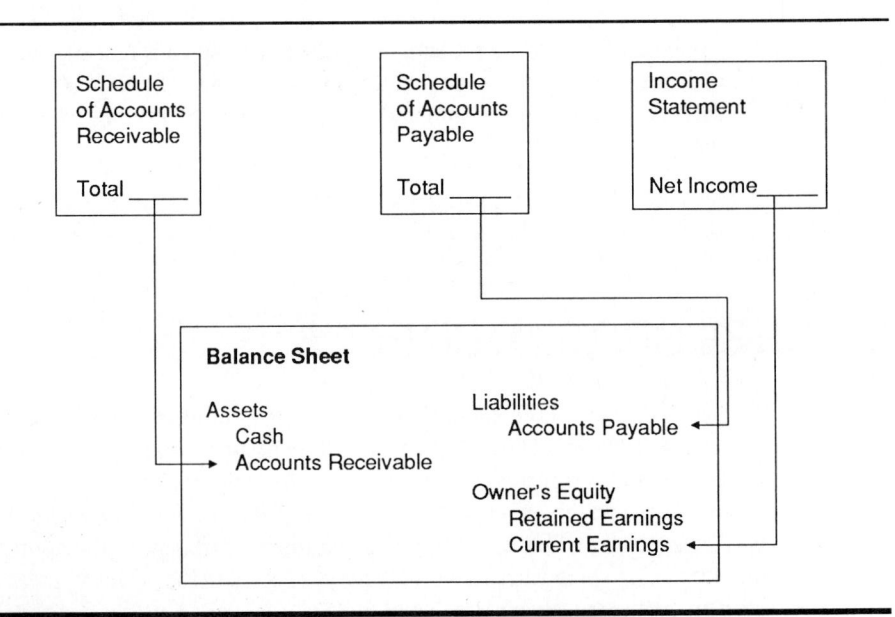

Figure 22-4. A balance sheet and its supporting documents

- **To create models that are too large to fit in memory at one time.** When you load a primary spreadsheet, Quattro Pro lets you look up supporting values without loading the entire supporting spreadsheet into memory. You can build models that exceed the amount of available memory in your computer by splitting an application across several files and loading only the file that you need to view or change at the moment.

- **To access information in an external database file.** Quattro Pro lets you create links to Paradox, Reflex, and dBASE database files in order to perform database queries, generate graphs, or compile database statistics.

Creating Spreadsheet Links

The only difference between a spreadsheet link and a normal cell or block reference is that link references include the name of an external spreadsheet enclosed in square brackets. For example, the reference [ABCINC5.WQ1]A100 means cell A100 in the ABCINC5 spreadsheet, and [ABCINC5]CALCULATIONS means the block named CALCULATIONS in the ABCINC5 spreadsheet.

There are four ways to create a spreadsheet link:

- You can type the link reference while entering a formula.

- You can point to a cell or block in another open spreadsheet while entering a formula.

- You can include an asterisk enclosed in square brackets in a formula. The asterisk serves as a 3-D link character (described under "Creating Links to All Open Spreadsheets") directing Quattro Pro to create links to the specified cell or block within all the open spreadsheets. If you enter the formula **@SUM([*]G10**, for example, Quattro Pro replaces the characters [*]G10 with a list of references to cell G10 in every open spreadsheet (except the current spreadsheet) and displays the resulting total.

- You can move a referenced cell to another spreadsheet without moving all the formulas that refer to it, or move a formula to another spreadsheet without moving all the cells it references.

TYPING LINK REFERENCES To type a link reference, you use the form

[file specification]cell

where *file specification* is the file name, and *cell* is a cell reference, block coordinates, or a block name. If the link reference is the first item in a cell, you must precede it with a plus sign to inform Quattro Pro that you are entering a value rather than a label.

The *file specification* can include from one to four parts. At minimum it must include the file's first name. If the file's extension is not the default extension (generally WQ1 if you are using the regular Quattro Pro menu tree), you must include the extension as well. If you are referring to a file in another directory, you must specify the directory path. For example, to refer to the block named EXPENSES in the INC91.WQ1 file in the current directory, you enter

+[INC91]EXPENSES

To refer to the block F10..F15 in the ABCINC.WK1 file in a directory called \QPRO\SALES, you enter

+[\QPRO\SALES\ABCINC.WK1]F10..F15.

When you type a link reference, the supporting spreadsheet need not be open, but it must exist within the specified directory (or the current directory if no directory was specified). Otherwise Quattro Pro beeps and displays a box with the message "Not found. Change to:" followed by the incorrect reference. You can either edit the reference or press (ESC) to display a list of spreadsheets in the default directory.

The bottom half of Figure 22-5 shows a spreadsheet that contains link references to the two spreadsheets shown in the upper half of the figure. The input line shows the formula in cell B3 of this spreadsheet, which calculates January sales for the two divisions. Both link references refer to single cells.

POINTING TO LINK REFERENCES   Before you can point out link references, you must open the supporting spreadsheet in another window. Then you type a plus sign, a different arithmetic operator, or a function name followed by a parenthesis—some character or set of characters that is appropriate immediately before a cell reference. This allows you to enter Point mode. Next, either press (SHIFT-F6) (Next Window), (ALT-0) or (SHIFT-F5) (Pick Window), or (ALT) plus the appropriate window number to activate the supporting spreadsheet. Move to the cell that you want to reference. If you are referencing a block, type a period to anchor the cell pointer, and move to the opposite corner of the block. Finally, press (ENTER) if the link reference is the last item in your formula or another operator if the formula is not yet complete. Quattro Pro automatically redisplays the primary spreadsheet.

CREATING LINKS TO ALL OPEN SPREADSHEETS   Quattro Pro makes it extremely easy to create links to an entire group of spreadsheets that have the same layout. You will find this feature particularly useful for consolidating a group

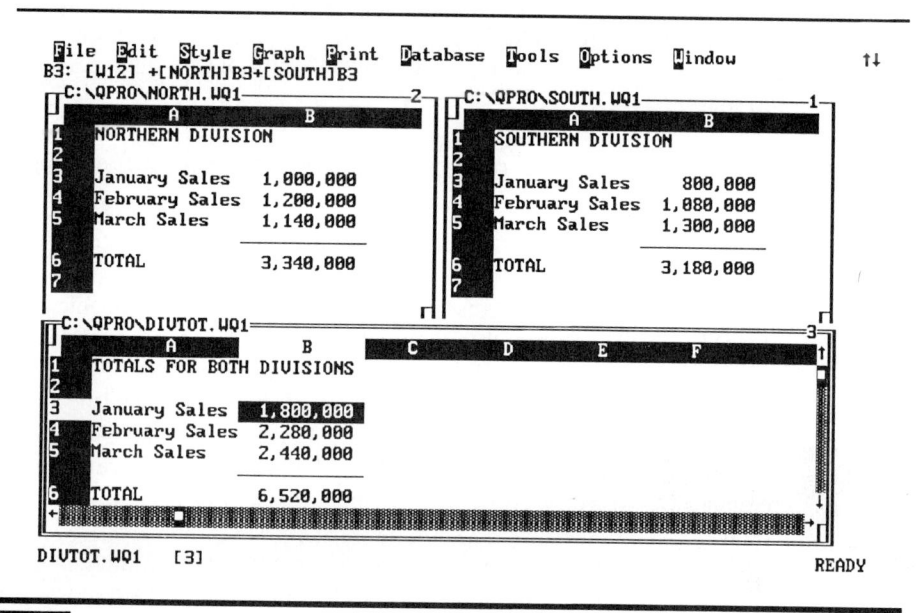

Figure 22-5. A consolidated spreadsheet created through linking

of similar spreadsheets—a set of monthly income statements, for example, or departmental expense reports.

To create links to several spreadsheets at once, start by opening all the spreadsheets that you want to link. Then activate the primary spreadsheet and enter a link reference using the form

@function([*]block)

where *@function* is a statistical function that can be applied to a block of values and *block* is a cell reference, set of block coordinates, or block name. For example, to add the values in cell B4 in all open spreadsheets (except the current spreadsheet), you enter

@SUM([*]B4)

To average the values in the same group of cells, you enter

@AVG([*]B4)

This type of reference is known as a *3-D link reference*. The asterisk serves as a kind of spreadsheet wild-card, signifying all the currently open spreadsheets. As soon as you enter a 3-D reference, Quattro Pro replaces that reference with a set of link references to individual spreadsheets. For example, if you open a set of spreadsheets called DEPT1.WQ1, DEPT2.WQ1, and DEPT3.WQ1, and then create a new spreadsheet and enter the formula **@SUM([*]B4..B10)**, Quattro Pro converts the formula to

@SUM([DEPT1.WQ1]B4..B10,[DEPT2.WQ1]B4..B10,[DEPT3.WQ1]B4..B10)

It is this new version of the formula (rather than the 3-D version that you entered) that is saved with the spreadsheet. This means that if you open one or more additional spreadsheets the next time you open the primary spreadsheet (opening DEPT4.WQ1 along with DEPT1.WQ1, DEPT2,WQ1, and DEPT3.WQ1 for example), Quattro Pro will not automatically extend the link to those additional files.

You can also create links to only some of the open spreadsheets by including wild-card characters in the 3-D reference. For example, the 3-D reference [XY*] generates links to only those spreadsheets that have names starting with "XY." The reference [X*Z] would create links to spreadsheets whose names start with "X" and end with "Z."

If you want to build links to several spreadsheets that have slightly different structures, you can still employ 3-D links by referencing named blocks.

CREATING LINKS BY MOVING CELLS TO A DIFFERENT SPREADSHEET When you move a formula from one spreadsheet to another without moving all the cells that it references, Quattro Pro automatically creates links to the original spreadsheet. Similarly, you can generate links by moving a cell to another spreadsheet without moving all the formulas that reference it. You can try this yourself by moving some of the cells from the LEARN1.WQ1 spreadsheet to a different file. Copying formulas or referenced cells from one spreadsheet to another never generates linking formulas. Even if you copy formulas with absolute references from one spreadsheet to another, Quattro Pro assumes that you want to refer to cells on the current spreadsheet. The implications of moving and copying link references or cells referenced by link formulas are covered later in this chapter.

Hands On Practice

Take a few minutes to practice linking spreadsheets. The following two exercises give you a chance to try two different standard linking scenarios: splitting an existing spreadsheet into two smaller files, and creating a consolidation spreadsheet to total values in other files.

First, try moving all the expense line items from the LEARN1 spreadsheet to a separate spreadsheet. (If you did not create the LEARN1 spreadsheet, refer to Figure 22-6 and read through the following exercise.)

Combining, Extracting and Linking Files 463

```
ABC Group Income Projection          Created:  02/14/92

                               1991      1992
                             Actual       Est   Variance
                             ------------------------------

Sales                       450,000   472,500     22,500
Cost of goods sold          193,500   203,175      9,675
Gross margin                256,500   269,325     12,825

Salaries                     86,000    90,300      4,300
Rent                         42,000    44,100      2,100
Utilities                    15,500    16,275        775
Depreciation                 22,000    22,000          0
Miscellaneous                 8,000     8,400        400
Total operating expenses    173,500   181,075      7,575

Interest expense             10,500    10,500          0

Profit before tax            72,500    77,750      5,250
Income tax                   29,000    31,100      2,100
Net income                   43,500    46,650      3,150
```

Figure 22-6.   The LEARN1 spreadsheet

1. Issue the / **F**ile | **E**rase command to clear the current window in preparation for creating a new spreadsheet.

2. Issue the / **F**ile | **O**pen command and retrieve LEARN1.WQ1 into a new window.

3. Move the individual expenses for 1991 to the new spreadsheet by issuing the / **E**dit | **M**ove command and specifying a source block of A11..B15. When prompted for a destination, press (SHIFT-F6) to display the new spreadsheet, move to A3, and press (ENTER). Quattro Pro redisplays LEARN1.

4. Move to B16 and note the formula

   @SUM([SHEET2]B3..B7

   on the input line. (The reference on your spreadsheet may be to SHEET3 or SHEET4 if you created other spreadsheets earlier in this work session.)

5. Move to C16 and change the formula to (B16*1.05). This produces a slightly different result than the previous formula because it calculates the 1992 expenses by multiplying the sum of the 1991 expenses by 1.05. (The original spreadsheet multiplied all the expense items *except* Depreciation by this growth factor.)

6. Move to row 11 and issue the / **Edit** | **Delete** | **Rows** command. Press (DOWN ARROW) until cells in rows 11 through 15 are highlighted, and press (ENTER) to delete five blank rows.

7. Issue the / **File** | **Save As** command and enter a filename of **LEARN3**.

8. Press (SHIFT-F6) to display the new spreadsheet. Widen column A to 13 characters using the / **Style** | **Column Width** command.

9. Move to A1 and enter the label **ABC Group 1991 Expenses**.

10. Issue the / **File** | **Save** command and enter a filename of **ABCEXP**.

Figure 22-7 shows the ABCEXP and LEARN3 spreadsheets.

In this exercise, you automatically created a link reference by moving the block of cells referenced in an @SUM formula to a different spreadsheet. The resulting link formula referred to the block of cells containing the expense items. This is only one way of splitting LEARN1.WQ1. You might prefer to move the @SUM formula to the new spreadsheet along with the individual expense. Then you could reference that one cell by manually entering the link formula +[ABCEXP]B8 in cell B11 of LEARN3 (assuming the @SUM formula is in cell B8).

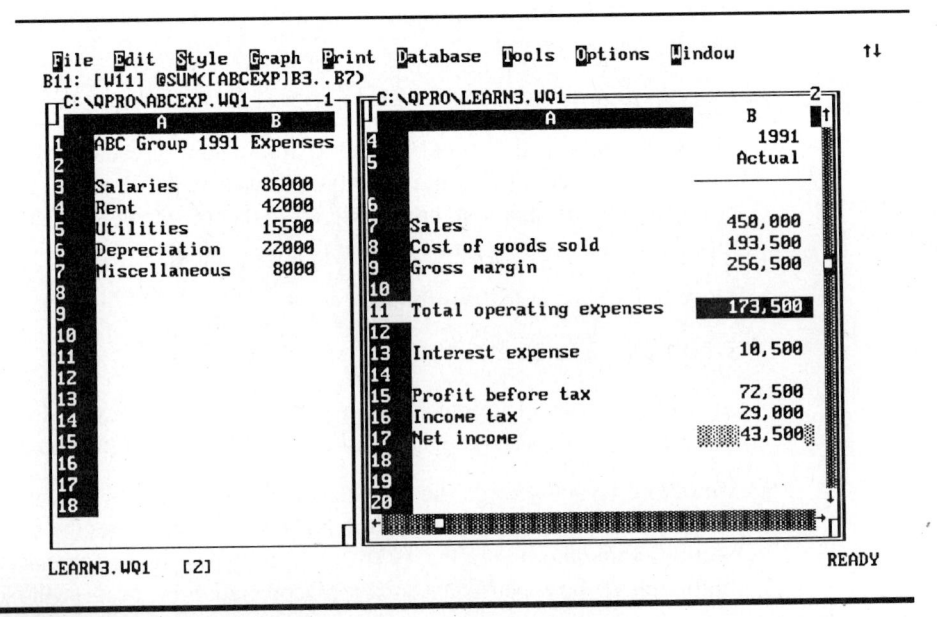

Figure 22-7. Splitting the LEARN1 spreadsheet

Now try creating a consolidated spreadsheet to add up the values in JANEXP.WQ1 and FEBEXP.WQ1. This is an alternative method of performing the type of consolidation that you performed using the / Tools I Combine I Add command earlier in this chapter.

1. Issue the / File I Close All command to close all the open windows.

2. Issue the / File I Open command and open JANEXP.WQ1.

3. Open a second window using the / File I Open command, and open FEBEXP.WQ1.

4. Issue the / File I Open command a third time and open EXPTEMP.WQ1. Assign a new name to this spreadsheet by issuing the / File I Save As command and entering **CONSOL2**.

5. Overwrite the label in A1, entering a spreadsheet title of **Y-T-D Expenses—Jan & Feb, 1991**.

6. Move to B3 and enter the formula **@SUM([∗]B3)**. Quattro Pro should display a result of 900.00. Note that the formula, as displayed on the input line, now reads

    @SUM([JANEXP]B3,[FEBEXP]B3)

    because Quattro Pro has replaced the 3-D link with references to each open spreadsheet other than the current spreadsheet.
    Next, copy this formula to the other expense rows.

7. Issue the / Edit I Copy command, and specify a source block of B3 and a destination of B4.

8. Issue the / Edit I Copy command again, specifying a source block of B3 and a destination of B7..B13. Your spreadsheet should now look like Figure 22-8.

9. Save the spreadsheet and replace the previous version.

There is one problem with the CONSOL2 spreadsheet at this point: It only includes links to JANEXP and FEBEXP spreadsheets. As you create spreadsheets for future months, you will need to modify all the link references to include those new files. One way to prevent this is to create spreadsheets for all twelve months at the beginning of the year by saving EXPTEMP under a different name twelve times or by using the File Manager to duplicate the file. You can link CONSOL2 to all twelve spreadsheets using 3-D references, and then fill in the monthly spreadsheets as the year progresses. As a result the figures in CONSOL2 would always refer to all the year's data, and you would not have to adjust the formulas each month to take a new spreadsheet into account.

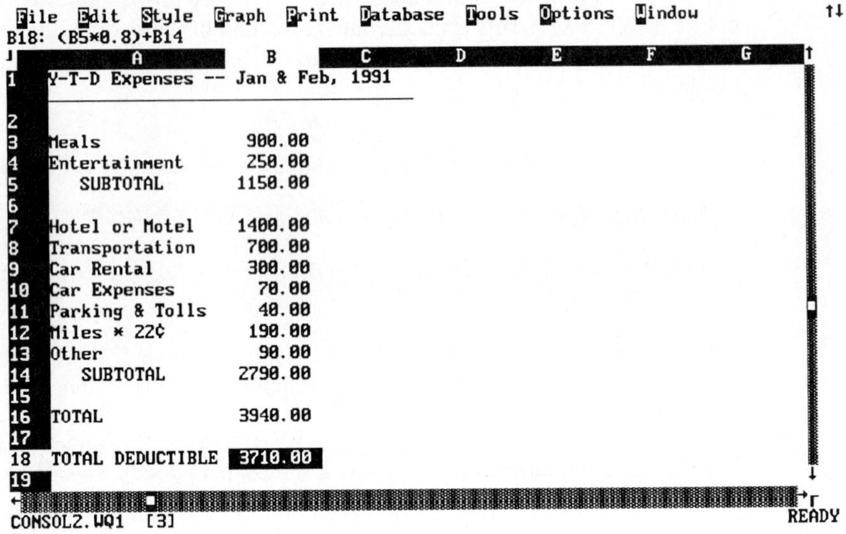

```
    File Edit Style Graph Print Database Tools Options Window        ↑↓
B18: (B5*0.8)+B14
         A              B         C      D      E      F      G
 1  Y-T-D Expenses -- Jan & Feb, 1991
 2
 3  Meals              900.00
 4  Entertainment      250.00
 5     SUBTOTAL       1150.00
 6
 7  Hotel or Motel    1400.00
 8  Transportation     700.00
 9  Car Rental         300.00
10  Car Expenses        70.00
11  Parking & Tolls     40.00
12  Miles * 22¢        190.00
13  Other               90.00
14     SUBTOTAL       2790.00
15
16  TOTAL             3940.00
17
18  TOTAL DEDUCTIBLE  3710.00
19
CONSOL2.WQ1  [3]                                                READY
```

Figure 22-8. Consolidating JANEXP and FEBEXP by linking

Opening Linked Spreadsheets

Whenever you load a spreadsheet that contains linking formulas, Quattro Pro checks whether all its supporting spreadsheets are already open. If not, it displays a Link options menu with the choices Load Supporting, Update Refs, and None.

The Load Supporting option automatically loads each of the supporting spreadsheets into a spreadsheet window. If any of those supporting spreadsheets contain links to other unloaded spreadsheets, Quattro Pro loads those as well, and then loads their supporting spreadsheets, and so on until all spreadsheets referenced on any of the open spreadsheets are loaded. This is actually one of the fastest and easiest ways to open a set of linked spreadsheets—you just open the primary spreadsheet, select Load Supporting, and let Quattro Pro do the rest. Another strategy for opening a set of linked spreadsheets is to open them once, create a workspace file, and then open the workspace file whenever you want to work with that group of spreadsheets. This method of opening linked spreadsheets is particularly useful if you want other users, particularly novice users, to work with this set of files. The user need not choose between the potentially confusing options on the Link options menu.

When all the supporting spreadsheets are open, changes in the supporting values are automatically reflected in the primary spreadsheet (unless you have changed the Recalculation mode to Manual). If you move any of the supporting values, Quattro Pro automatically adjusts the primary spreadsheet's references. The only potential drawback to opening the supporting spreadsheets is that it can consume a lot of memory—possibly more memory than you have available.

The Update Refs option directs Quattro Pro to look up the current value of each of the supporting values in the supporting spreadsheets so that the data displayed is current. This consumes much less memory, but it also means that you cannot view or update the supporting spreadsheets. If you later decide that you want to work with one of those supporting files, use the / Tools | Update Links | Open command, described shortly.

Whenever you load a primary spreadsheet that contains many linking formulas and select either the Load Supporting or Update Refs option, you may have to wait several seconds before the mode indicator changes to READY. Quattro Pro automatically recalculates all the link formulas on the assumption that you may have opened one or more of the supporting spreadsheets and changed the supporting values since the last time you saved the primary spreadsheet.

If you select the third linking option, None, Quattro Pro does not open or read any supporting spreadsheets that are not already open. Instead, it temporarily replaces the links to unopened supporting spreadsheets with the value NA. This method of opening a primary spreadsheet is quite fast because you do not need to wait for Quattro Pro to read the supporting spreadsheets into memory. You can use it to save time whenever you want to quickly scan or edit a large spreadsheet and do not need to see the current values of the link formulas.

Linking Spreadsheets Hierarchically

Just as Quattro Pro allows you to enter circular formulas, even though they can create problems on your spreadsheet, it also allows you to link spreadsheets in a circular fashion. This means, for example, that formulas in spreadsheet A refer to cells in spreadsheet B, formulas in spreadsheet B refer to cells in spreadsheet C, and formulas in spreadsheet C refer back to spreadsheet A, as illustrated in Figure 22-9. You should avoid this type of linking whenever possible. When you create circular links among a group of spreadsheets, Quattro Pro is unable to properly pass updated values from one file to another unless you load all the spreadsheets into memory every time you make changes. If you do link spreadsheets in a circular fashion, be sure to open all the spreadsheets whenever you want fully current results. Better yet, avoid the problem altogether by linking your spreadsheets hierarchically, so the links flow in only one direction. For example, if you have three levels of linked spreadsheets, be sure that

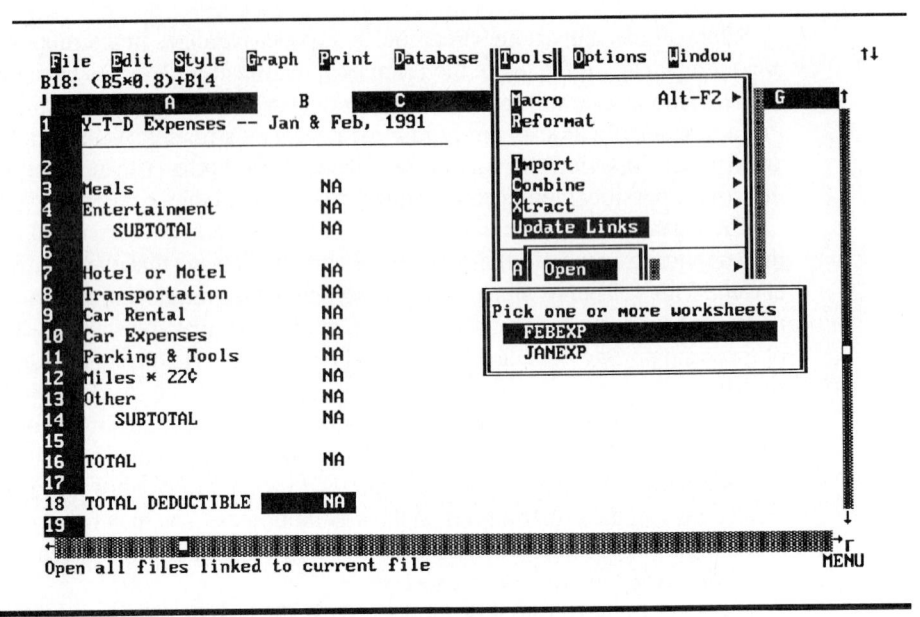

Figure 22-9. Circular versus hierarchical links

the links flow from level 1 to level 2 to level 3 without ever referring back to spreadsheets higher up in the hierarchy. This allows you to update references properly using the Update Refs option, even if some or all of the supporting spreadsheets are closed.

Updating Spreadsheet Links

The / **Tools** | Update Links command displays a menu of options specifically related to spreadsheet linking. These options allow you to open a supporting spreadsheet (the Open option), update data in the current spreadsheet based on unopened supporting spreadsheets (the Refresh option), switch all the links to a particular supporting spreadsheet from one spreadsheet to another (the Change option), and remove all link references to one or more supporting spreadsheets (the Delete option).

OPENING SUPPORTING SPREADSHEETS LATER IN THE WORK SESSION Occasionally you load a spreadsheet without its supporting spreadsheets—choosing the Update Refs or None option when you retrieve the file—and then later decide that you want to work with one or more of the supporting spreadsheets after all. Although you can load the supporting spreadsheets using the / File I Open or / File I Retrieve command, Quattro Pro also provides the / Tools I Update Links I Open command specifically for this purpose.

When you issue the / Tools I Update Links I Open command, Quattro Pro displays a list of the unopened supporting spreadsheets. To open a single spreadsheet on the list, highlight its name and press (ENTER). To open multiple spreadsheets, select each spreadsheet that you want to open by highlighting its name and pressing (SHIFT-F7) (Select), or select all the files on the list by pressing (ALT-F7) (All Select). Then press (ENTER). Quattro Pro opens each selected spreadsheet in a different window.

REFRESHING LINKED FORMULA RESULTS The / Tools I Update Links I Refresh command directs Quattro Pro to read in linked values from one or more unopened spreadsheets. It has exactly the same effect as choosing the Update Refs option when you first open a primary spreadsheet, except that you can use it whenever you like and you can specify exactly which spreadsheets you want to update values from.

There are three reasons to use the / Tools I Update Links I Refresh command:

- If you chose the None option when opening the primary spreadsheet (so that NA values appear on the spreadsheet) and then later decide that you need to use values in some or all of the supporting spreadsheets.

- If you only want to update values based on a few of the supporting spreadsheets. In this case, you would deliberately choose the None option when opening the primary spreadsheet, and then issue the / Tools I Update Links I Refresh command and select only those supporting spreadsheets that contain values that you currently need.

- If you are working on a local area network and updated link references when you first loaded a primary spreadsheet, but believe that someone may have changed one of the supporting spreadsheets since then.

When you issue the / Tools I Update Links I Refresh command, Quattro Pro displays a list of unopened supporting spreadsheets along with the prompt "Pick one or more worksheets." If you only want to update references to a single spreadsheet, just highlight that file name and press (ENTER). Otherwise use (SHIFT-F7) (Select) to select file names one at a time or (ALT-F7) (All Select) to select all the files in the list, and press (ENTER).

If you issue the / Tools I Update Links I Refresh command when all the supporting spreadsheets are already opened or when there are no link formulas in the current spreadsheet, Quattro Pro displays an error message.

SWITCHING LINKS FROM ONE SPREADSHEET TO ANOTHER

You can use the / Tools | Update Links | Change command to transfer links from one spreadsheet to another. You might use this option when you have changed the name of a supporting spreadsheet or if you simply want to reference another spreadsheet with an identical structure. When you issue the / Tools | Update Links | Change command, Quattro Pro displays a list of supporting spreadsheets for the current spreadsheet. Highlight the one containing the links that you want to change and press (ENTER). Quattro Pro prompts you for a spreadsheet name, displaying the selected file's name as a default. Enter the name of the new supporting spreadsheet or press (F2) (Edit) or the (SPACEBAR) to enter Edit mode; then change the default name and press (ENTER).

DELETING LINKS   The / Tools | Update Links | Delete command undoes the links between the current spreadsheet and one or more supporting spreadsheets. When you issue the / Tools | Update Links | Delete command, Quattro Pro displays a list of supporting spreadsheets. To cancel links to a single spreadsheet, just highlight the file name and press (ENTER). To cancel links to multiple spreadsheets, use (SHIFT-F7) (Select) or (ALT-F7) (All Select) to select files, and then press (ENTER). Quattro Pro immediately displays ERR values in each cell that contains one of the canceled link references without removing the formulas themselves from the cells. Your next task is to edit or replace all those formulas with valid references.

You also can unlink spreadsheets by using the / Edit | Values command to replace link formulas with their current results. This method is preferable if you no longer need the values in those cells to respond to changes in other cells. However, if you want the link formulas to remain formulas—referring to cells on the current spreadsheet or a different supporting spreadsheet—use the / Tools | Update Links | Delete command: the ERR values will help you find all the formulas that you need to change.

Copying and Moving Link Formulas

When you copy a link formula to another cell in the same spreadsheet, Quattro Pro adjusts link references in the same way as it adjusts other cell references: Relative references are changed to fit the formula's new position and absolute references are left unchanged.

When you copy link references to a different spreadsheet, Quattro Pro treats them in exactly the same way, adjusting the relative references and leaving the absolute references unchanged. It also leaves the reference to the primary spreadsheet as is, even if you copy the link formula into the file that it references.

When you move a link formula from one cell to another, Quattro Pro leaves the cell references unchanged. If you happen to move the formula into the spreadsheet that it refers to, Quattro Pro removes the file link while leaving the cell references the same. For example, if you move the formula @SUM([ABCEXP]B3..B7) from LEARN3 into any cell in ABCEXP, Quattro Pro changes the formula to read simply @SUM(B3..B7).

You must guard against one potential problem with linked references: If you move a cell (including the corner cell of a block) that is referenced by a link formula, Quattro Pro automatically adjusts the link reference *only if the primary spreadsheet is open at the time*. It does not adjust link references in unopened spreadsheets, even when you open those spreadsheets later. The only way to correct the problem is to edit or reenter the link formulas, specifying the current addresses of the supporting values (that is, the values to which the link formulas refer). You can avoid this problem in one of two ways: You can open the primary spreadsheet every time you modify the supporting spreadsheet, or you can always use named blocks rather than cell addresses in link formulas. Whenever a formula contains a block reference, Quattro Pro will look up the current address of that block whenever you update the spreadsheet links or load the supporting spreadsheets.

For example, if you open ABCEXP without opening LEARN3, and then add an extra row in the middle of the expenses block, the link reference in LEARN3 becomes out-of-date. Even if you open both spreadsheets later, the formula in cell B11 of LEARN3 still refers to block B3..B7 in the ABCEXP spreadsheet, rather than to B3..B8. To prevent this problem you must assign a name (such as 1991 EXP) to the block B3..B8 in ABCEXP.WQ1 and change the formula in cell B11 of LEARN3 to @SUM(1991 EXP). Then, even if you add a row to the expenses block in ABCEXP without opening LEARN3, the link reference is adjusted properly the next time you open the LEARN3 spreadsheet, because Quattro Pro looks up the current location of the named block before recalculating the link formula.

Graphing Linked Spreadsheets

In Quattro Pro you can graph data from one or more subsidiary spreadsheets by using link references when defining series, titles, and other graph settings. By using link references when defining graphs, you can graph data from several different spreadsheets without creating a consolidated spreadsheet as an intermediate step. You

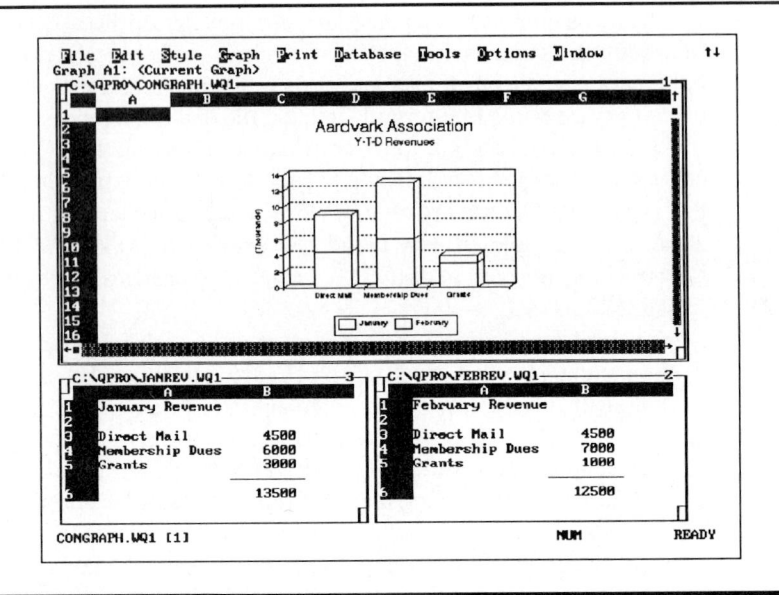

Figure 22-10. A graph based on values in other spreadsheets

will find this ability particularly useful when you want to view consolidated information only in graphic form, rather than as numbers on a spreadsheet.

The window at the top of Figure 22-10 shows an inserted graph based on values drawn from the two spreadsheets in the bottom half of the figure. The Series 1 setting for the graph is [JANREV]B3..B5. The Series 2 setting is [FEBREV]B3..B5. With your workspace organized like this, you can make changes in both of the subsidiary spreadsheets and see them immediately reflected on the graph. You might also create a spreadsheet with one or more graphs and even a graph slide show based on a group of subsidiary spreadsheets. Then, whenever you want to view the updated graphs, you can simply load the graph spreadsheet, select Update Refs to update the graph values, and display your graphs on the full screen.

If you want to use link references for text, such as titles and legends, you must first enter a link reference on the current spreadsheet. For example, if you want to use the label in cell A1 of the JANREV.WQ1 spreadsheet as your first line title, you enter +[JANREV]A1 in a cell of the spreadsheet, issue the / Graph | Text | 1st Line command, and enter a backslash followed by the address of the cell that contains the link reference. You cannot refer to another spreadsheet directly when defining graph text. If you specify a first line title of \[JANREV]A1, for example, Quattro Pro displays \[JANREV]A1 at the top of your graph.

> **Note:** Graphs that draw values from other spreadsheets always use the current values, even if you do not open the supporting spreadsheets and select the None option from the linking options menu when you open the primary spreadsheet.

Linking Versus Combining Files

You have now learned two different methods of consolidating data from different spreadsheets: the / Tools | Combine commands and link formulas. In general, the / Tools | Combine commands are preferable when you have no intention of changing the data that you want to consolidate. For example, if you periodically import summary data from an external database (perhaps downloading it from a mainframe computer) and simply want to combine it with earlier data, / Tools | Combine | Add can save both disk space (you end up with a single spreadsheet filled with numeric constants rather than space-consuming formulas) and time (you issue only one command and need not wait for recalculation every time you load the spreadsheet). On the other hand, you should use linking to consolidate data if you want your totals to remain responsive to changes in the supporting spreadsheets. If there is any chance that you will modify the original data, linking rather than combining spreadsheets will save you the trouble of reconsolidating.

In this chapter you have learned to extract, combine, and link data from different spreadsheets. The / Tools | Xtract command allows you to extract smaller self-contained spreadsheets or the foundations on which to build new spreadsheets. The / Tools | Combine commands give you the ability to combine data from multiple spreadsheets and generate numbers (rather than formulas) that reflect data from more than one file. Lastly, the ability to link spreadsheets lets you dynamically combine data from two or more files, so that changes in one spreadsheet are reflected in another.

23

INTRODUCTION TO MACROS

Creating Macros
Pasting Macros into the Spreadsheet
Interpreting Macros
Editing Macros
Sample Database Macros
Applications for Recorded Macros
Introduction to the Macro Language
Maintaining and Using Macros
Playing Macros Automatically

A *macro* is a recording of a series of actions that can be replayed with a single command. You can use the simplest macros to automate tasks that you would normally perform by pressing keys on your keyboard or by moving and clicking the mouse. These tasks include entering and editing data, moving the cell pointer, and issuing menu commands. Using such simple macros is like speed-dialing on a telephone: You press one or two keys and the machine responds as if you had pressed a series of keys, one after another. The most elaborate macros carry out functions that you cannot perform by pressing keys or using the mouse—functions such as pausing to collect input from the user or making use of programming structures such as loops and subroutines. Using these special commands, expert users can develop customized applications that require little or no knowledge of Quattro Pro to use.

There are two basic reasons for creating and using macros. The first is speed. Quattro Pro can move the cell pointer and execute commands faster than the fastest typist. If you repeatedly perform the same keystrokes, macros can save time and effort, streamlining your work tremendously. The second reason is accuracy. Once your macro works properly, it is reliable and consistent. A macro performs the same steps every time you execute it and so is a much safer method of performing complex and delicate operations—such as combining data from several spreadsheets—that can ruin your spreadsheet if done incorrectly.

This chapter covers only the basic type of macros—those that can be recorded as a series of keystrokes. Even at this level macros are extremely powerful tools for automating and streamlining your work. If you want to go further after mastering the techniques introduced in this chapter, refer to the Quattro Pro *@Functions and Macros* manual.

CREATING MACROS

Quattro Pro offers two ways to create macros:

- You can direct Quattro Pro to record a series of actions as you issue them. This is the simplest and usually the most efficient way.

- You can enter macros directly onto the spreadsheet, typing in the macro commands yourself.

This chapter deals almost exclusively with the process of recording macros—a perfectly adequate method for creating simple macros. At the end of the chapter, you will try entering one macro manually.

All commands related to creating and executing macros are located on the Macro menu. You can access this menu either by issuing the / Tools | Macro command or by pressing (ALT-F2) (Macro Menu).

Recording Macros

Before you start recording a macro, you should always determine exactly what you want the macro to do and which keystrokes will be required. Once you begin to record the macro, every keystroke is recorded, including all your mistakes and typos, plus the keystrokes you use to correct them. These extra actions then become part of your macro and can slow its execution considerably. It is possible to edit keystrokes out of your macro after recording, but it is a delicate operation and can usually be avoided by careful planning.

Once you have thoroughly planned your macro, you can record it with the following steps:

1. Press (ALT-F2) (Macro Menu) and type **R** to select the Record option. Quattro Pro displays REC on the status line at the bottom of the screen, indicating that your actions are now being recorded.

2. Perform all the actions that you want to record. Quattro Pro translates them into macro form and writes them in the cell or block of cells you specified. Avoid using the mouse when recording macros because Quattro Pro will not be able to record the selections that you make on various lists of choices, including lists of named blocks and files as well as some menus and submenus.

3. Press (ALT-F2) (Macro Menu) again, and type either **R** to stop recording and return to Ready mode or **P** for Paste if you want to paste the macro into the spreadsheet (as explained shortly).

Note You can record macros only when the **O**ptions | **R**ecalculation | **M**ode setting is Background. If you have changed the recalculation setting to either Automatic or Manual, none of your keystrokes will be recorded.

Quattro Pro always remembers the last macro that you created and lets you replay it using the Instant Replay option on the Macro menu. As soon as you record a second macro or leave Quattro Pro, however, the old macro is lost unless you already pasted it to the spreadsheet (that is, stored the macro commands in individual cells). You must paste your macro to the spreadsheet to use it in a future work session. You also have to paste macros if you want to use more than one in the current work session. The process of pasting macros is covered shortly.

As mentioned, you can replay the last macro that you recorded by selecting the Instant Replay option on the Macro menu. The steps for playing back a pasted macro depend on the type of name that you assign to the macro (as explained under "Naming Macros.")

As soon as you start playing a macro, the MACRO mode indicator appears on the bottom line of the screen. You can interrupt macro execution at any point by pressing (CTRL-BREAK).

A Macro for Date-Stamping A Spreadsheet

The first macro that you will create records today's date in your spreadsheet using the @TODAY function and the (F9) (Calc) key. Be sure to follow the instructions exactly. For example, do not use arrow keys to select menu options when the instructions specify typing option letters.

1. If you have anything other than a blank spreadsheet on your screen, issue the / File | Erase command.

2. Issue the / Options | Recalculation command, and make sure that the Mode setting on the Options | Recalculation menu is Background. Otherwise, change it to Background so that your keystrokes are recorded properly.

3. With the cell pointer in A1, press (ALT-F2) and type **R** to open the Macro menu and select the Record option.

4. Type **@TODAY**, press (F9) (Calc), and press (ENTER) to enter the calculated value into the current cell.

5. Type **/SND4** to issue the / Style | Numeric Format | Date command and select Date format number 4 (Long International). Press (ENTER) to designate the current cell as the block to be formatted.

6. Press (ALT-F2) and type **R** to open the Macro menu and select Record again. The macro recording is terminated.

7. Move to A3, and replay your macro by pressing (ALT-F2) and typing **I** to open to Macro menu and select the Instant Replay option. Quattro Pro briefly displays MACRO just to the left of the mode indicator on the status line to indicate that it is now playing back a macro, and enters the date into the current cell.

PASTING MACROS INTO THE SPREADSHEET

Pasting macros means directing Quattro Pro to take a series of macro commands that are currently stored in memory and entering them into the spreadsheet as a set of labels stored in adjacent cells within a single column. Pasting a macro involves two steps: First you specify a name for the macro, and then you specify the macro's location.

You can paste a macro into your spreadsheet as the last step in the recording process or sometime after you finish recording. To paste a macro immediately, just select the Paste option from the Macro menu (rather than the Record option) when you are done recording. To paste a macro later, select the Paste option before you either record another macro or leave Quattro Pro.

In general it is easiest and safest to paste the macro as part of the recording process. However, there are two situations in which you might hold off. First, occasionally you may want to test out a macro before committing it to the spreadsheet. Second, you may sometimes create a macro that you intend to use for only a short time. In this case you might forego pasting altogether and just use the Instant Replay option.

Naming Macros

When you name a macro you name the first cell in which Quattro Pro stores the recorded macro commands. Later, when you execute the macro, you supply Quattro Pro with this block name. Quattro Pro then goes to the named cell and moves down that column, executing each macro command it finds. As soon as it encounters either a blank cell or a value, it stops and returns to Ready mode.

The two types of macro names are standard and instant. The type of name that you assign determines which steps you must take to replay the macro. Instant macro names consist of a \ (backslash) followed by a single letter. (It does not matter whether you enter the letter in upper- or lowercase.) To execute instant macros, you simply press (ALT) and type the assigned letter. Because you can only use single letters to name instant macros, you are limited to 26 instant macros per spreadsheet. Standard macro names, like any other block names, can contain up to 15 characters, including letters, digits, punctuation marks, and characters such as $, N, or %. You should avoid using mathematical operators such as +, -, *, or /. To play back a standard macro, you select the Execute option on the Macro menu and then specify the block name—either by entering the name manually or by pressing (F3) (Choices) and selecting from the list of block names. If you have assigned names to cells other than the starting cells of macros, you see those block names on the list as well.

When you name macros try to pick names that are easy to remember and to associate with the macro's function. For example, if you create a macro to sort a database by the ACCOUNT field, you might name it ACCTSORT or SORTACCT. Even when you name instant macros, try to choose names that remind you of the macro's purpose. You might assign the name \P to a macro that prints the spreadsheet.

You cannot assign the same name to a macro and to another block of cells on the same spreadsheet. If you issue the / Edit Names | Create or / Edit | Names | Labels command and enter a name that was previously assigned to a macro, you cannot execute that macro.

Where to Store Your Macros

Quattro Pro allows you to execute macros that are stored either in the current spreadsheet or in another open spreadsheet that you have designated as a macro library. You will learn to create and use macro libraries later in this chapter. For now just be aware that macros need not be specific to one spreadsheet. When you create macros that can be used in several different spreadsheets, you should store them in a macro library so that they can be executed from any other open spreadsheet. However, when you create macros that are specific to one spreadsheet, just store them in that particular spreadsheet file.

Whenever you store macros in a regular spreadsheet (as opposed to a macro library), try to place them in a safe spot. Until you execute it, a macro that has been pasted to a spreadsheet is just a contiguous block of labels and is as vulnerable to damage or deletion as any other set of data. The / **Edit** | **Delete** | **Columns** and / **Edit** | **Delete** | **Rows** commands can be particularly dangerous to macros. / **Edit** | **Insert** | **Rows** can also destroy macros if the inserted row falls in the middle of a macro.

The standard location for macros is well below and to the right of your data, but you can also place them above and to the left if your data is not at the upper-left corner of the database. For extra safety you may want to use Quattro Pro's protection feature to prevent accidental overwriting of data or deletion of columns or rows within the macro section of your spreadsheet.

It is also good practice to place all your macros in the same section of the spreadsheet so you can easily find and compare them. Regardless of the location of your macros, be sure to leave adequate room underneath the starting cell. A lengthy macro can easily consume a dozen or more cells, and Quattro Pro overwrites any data in its path when pasting a macro. You should also leave at least a few empty columns to the right of the starting macro cell so you can read macro labels that are too wide to be displayed in a single cell. Also leave space in the adjacent columns for documenting your macros. (Macro documentation is discussed later in this chapter.) Finally, be sure to leave at least one blank row between the last cell of one macro and the first cell of the next.

Try splitting the current window into two panes and then pasting the macro that you just created into the spreadsheet.

1. Move to A7 and issue the / **Window** | **Options** | **Horizontal** command to split the window horizontally.

2. Issue the / **Window** | **Options** | **Unsync** command so that you can move the cell pointer independently in the two panes.

3. Press (F6) (Pane) to move to the bottom pane. Press (F5) (GoTo) and enter **I50**. Press (F6) again to return to the top pane.

4. Press **ALT-F2** and type **P** to open the Macro menu and select the Paste option. When Quattro Pro prompts you for a block name, enter **\D**. When prompted for a location, enter **I50**. Your spreadsheet should now look like Figure 23-1. The macro commands are explained in the next section.

5. Move to A5 and press **ALT-D** to replay your macro.

Note: If your macro contains the keystrokes /SN in place of the menu-equivalent command {/ Block:Format}, the **Tools | Macro | Macro Recording** setting has been changed from Logical (the initial default) to Keystroke, as explained under "Changing the Macro Recording Method." Change it back to Logical for now by entering **/TMML** (for / Tools | Macro | Macro Recording | Logical). This way your macros match the figures as you perform the exercises in the remainder of this chapter.

INTERPRETING MACROS

When Quattro Pro records a macro, it translates your keystrokes into a special form. Quattro Pro records any characters that you type—aside from those you use to issue commands—as is. In the date macro, for example, the characters @TODAY appear

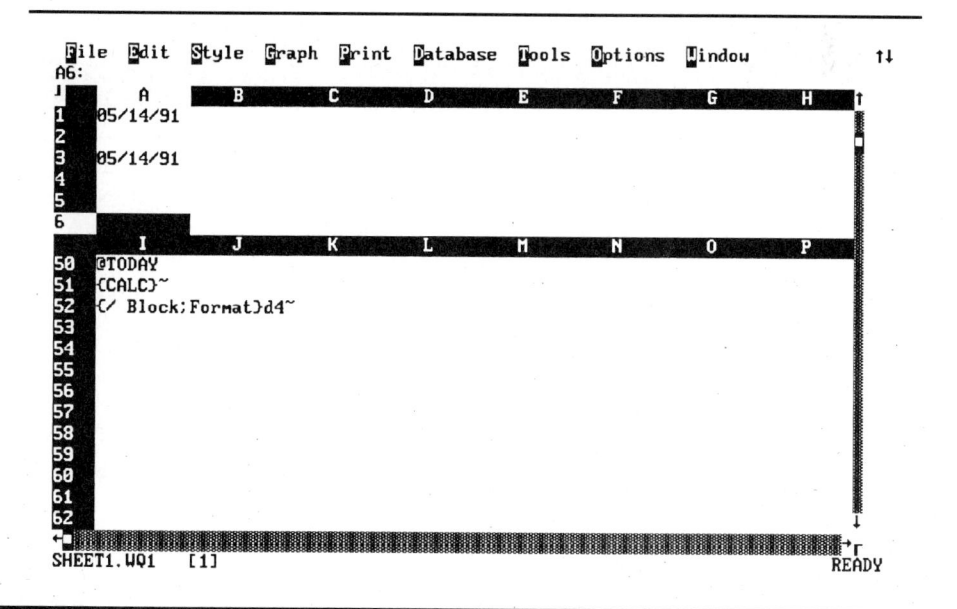

Figure 23-1. Your first practice macro pasted into the spreadsheet

just as you typed them. The only difference is that Quattro Pro added an apostrophe at the beginning to designate the entry as a label. (Otherwise you would see a value in cell I50 rather than the characters @TODAY.) As with any other label prefix character, this apostrophe does not appear in the cell itself; it appears only on the input line when you highlight or edit the cell.

Quattro Pro represents some keys—such as the function keys, the arrow keys, (HOME), and so on—using sets of characters known as *key-equivalent commands*. These sets of characters are called commands not because they are Quattro Pro commands per se, but because they are commands in the macro language. They function as commands during macro execution.

Table 23-1 is a list of all the cursor-movement, editing, and function keys and their macro representations. If you press a particular key several times in a row, Quattro Pro uses a shorthand to record your keystrokes, using {UP 3} rather than {UP}{UP}{UP} to represent pressing (UP ARROW) three times. In the \D macro, {CALC} is the key-equivalent command for the (F9) (Calc) key. The ~ (tilde) character, which appears after {CALC} and again at the end of the macro, is Quattro Pro's symbol for the (ENTER) key.

Quattro Pro also has a special way of recording menu commands in macros, using a set of codes known as *menu-equivalent commands*. Menu-equivalent commands consist of a slash followed by a space followed by two words or, more rarely, a word and a number separated by a semicolon. Like all macro commands they are always enclosed in curly braces. For example, in the \D macro Quattro Pro recorded the / Style | Numeric Format command as

{/ Block;Format}

Rather than having separate menu-equivalent commands for each / Style | Numeric Format command, Quattro Pro has a menu-equivalent command for / Style | Numeric Format and then simply records the keystrokes used to specify different formats. In the case of the \D macro, the characters d4~ that appear after {/ Block;Format} represent the keystrokes you used to specify the Date format, select Date format number 4, and accept the default block by pressing (ENTER).

Sometimes menu equivalent commands contain compound words. For example, the menu-equivalent command

{/ PieExploded;1}

represents the / Graph | Customize Series | Pies | Explode | 1st Slice command. Although the words used in menu-equivalent commands are rarely identical to the menu options they represent, you usually have little trouble deciphering their meaning.

Function Keys:

Command	Key
{ABS}	F4
{CALC}	F9
{CHOOSE}	SHIFT-F5
{COPY}	SHIFT-F9
{EDIT}	F2
{FUNCTIONS}	ALT-F3
{GOTO}	F5
{GRAPH}	F10
{MACROS}	SHIFT-F3
{MARK}	SHIFT-F7
{MARKALL}	ALT-F7
{MOVE}	SHIFT-F8
{NAME}	F3
{NEXTWIN}	SHIFT-F6
{PASTE}	SHIFT-F10
{QUERY}	F7
{TABLE}	F8
{UNDO}	ALT-F5
{WINDOW}	F6
{ZOOM}	ALT-F6

Cursor-Movement Keys:

Command	Key
{LEFT} or {L}	LEFT ARROW
{RIGHT} or {R}	RIGHT ARROW
{UP} or {U}	UP ARROW
{DOWN} or {D}	DOWN ARROW
{PGDN}	PGDN
{PGUP}	PGUP
{TAB}	TAB
{BACKTAB}	SHIFT-TAB
{BIGLEFT}	CTRL-LEFT
{BIGRIGHT}	CTRL-RIGHT
{HOME}	HOME
{END}	END
{WINDOWn}	Selects window n

Table 23-1. Key-Equivalent Commands

Editing Keys and Other Keys£

Command	Key
{BS} or {BACKSPACE}	BACKSPACE
{DEL} or {DELETE}	DEL
{INS} or {INSERT}	INS
{ESC} or {ESCAPE}	ESC
{BREAK}	CTRL-BREAK
{CR} or ~	ENTER
{DATE}	CTRL-D

Table 23-1. Key-Equivalent Commands (*continued*)

Because of the way Quattro Pro records menu selections, you should generally select menu options by typing letters rather than using the arrow keys when you record macros. Otherwise, at least some of your selections will be recorded as cursor movements, which takes up more room, makes the macro harder to read, slows down macro execution, and opens up the possibility of the macro not working if you ever modify the menus. For example, in the previous macro, if you used arrow keys to select all the menu options, Quattro Pro would have recorded the application of the data format to the cell as

{/ Block;Format}
{DOWN 7}~
{DOWN 3}~

meaning / Style I Numeric Format, press DOWN ARROW seven times and press ENTER, press DOWN ARROW three times and press ENTER again. As you can see, it is almost impossible to tell what this macro does without actually performing the keystrokes.

Now try recording a second macro so you can see how Quattro Pro records cursor movements. This macro underlines the characters in the cell above the current cell using equal signs. It uses both the @REPEAT and @LENGTH functions to display as many equal signs as there are characters in the cell above. Before you start recording the macro, enter a label to underline.

1. Move to C1 and enter **This is a test**.

2. Move to C2, and press ALT-F2 and type **R** to start recording the macro.

3. Type **@REPEAT("=",@LENGTH(**.

Introduction to Macros   485

4. Press the (UP ARROW) key to move the cell pointer to C1.

5. Type)) and press (ENTER) to complete the formula and enter it into the cell.

6. Press (ALT-F2) and type **P** to open the Macro menu and select Paste. This terminates the recording and initiates the pasting process. When Quattro Pro prompts you for a macro name, enter **UNDERLINE**. When Quattro Pro prompts you for a block, enter **I54**. Your spreadsheet should now look like Figure 23-2. The key-equivalent command {UP} in cell I55 represents the pressing of (UP ARROW).

7. Move to C4 and enter **Here is a longer label**.

8. Move to C5, press (ALT-F2), and type **E** to execute the macro. Press (F3) (Choices) and select UNDERLINE from the list of block names. Quattro Pro underlines the new label with equal signs.

By pointing to cell C1 rather than typing an explicit cell reference, you made this function generic. You can use it to underline the cell above the current cell in any spot on the spreadsheet. In addition, because the @LENGTH function is used as an argument to the @REPEAT function, the number of equal signs displayed depends on the number of characters in the referenced cell.

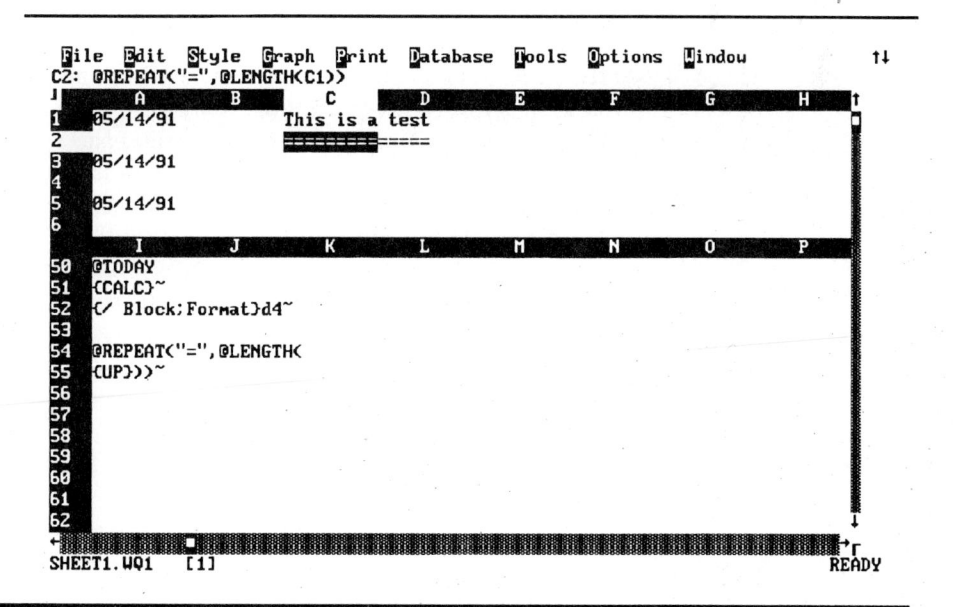

Figure 23-2.   Creating the UNDERLINE macro

In most cases you design your macros so you can use them in the widest possible set of circumstances. How you do this depends on the macro's function and your own work needs. For example, if you create a macro to widen a column by one character, you get a different result if you enter **10** as the width than if you change the width to 10 by pressing the (RIGHT ARROW) key. In the first case, the macro always widens or narrows the column to 10, regardless of its current width. In the second case, the macro widens the column by a single character, and the resulting width depends on how wide the column was when you initiated the macro.

A similar issue arises when you refer to cells or blocks of cells in macros. Using the pointing method to reference cells gives macros tremendous flexibility, allowing you to apply a series of actions to different cells on the spreadsheet. In some cases, however, you want a macro to affect particular cells or blocks of cells, regardless of your current position. You can accomplish this by entering cell references or block names, rather than pointing.

In general block names are the preferable method of referencing cells in a macro, because explicit cell references can produce problems if you later rearrange your spreadsheet. When you use cell references in formulas, print blocks, or sort blocks, and then make changes on your spreadsheet that affect those cell references, Quattro Pro makes all necessary adjustments on the spot. In contrast Quattro Pro does not adjust macro cell references because macros are simply labels on your spreadsheet; they are not dynamic formulas. If you direct Quattro Pro to move to or use a particular cell address within a macro and then subsequently rearrange the spreadsheet, your macro will still contain the original, unadjusted cell references. You can prevent this by using block names rather than specific cell references whenever you direct Quattro Pro to go to or use a particular cell within a macro. That way, when the macro is executed, it uses the current block coordinates, which have been updated automatically as you have made changes on the spreadsheet. Always type block names rather than using the (F3) (Choices) key when recording macros so the name itself rather than a set of cursor movements is recorded. Using block names in macros also allows you to use the same (or similar) macros in different spreadsheets even when those spreadsheets are not identical in structure.

The remaining macro exercises in this chapter are more involved than the ones you have tried so far. If you want to try creating a few more simple macros first, try some or all of the following on your own:

- Create a macro that widens the current column by a character, as just described.

- Create a macro that draws a double line underneath the current cell using the / Style | Line Drawing command.

- Create a macro that sums up all the values in the column immediately above the current cell by entering **@SUM(**, moving up one cell, anchoring the cell pointer, pressing (END-UP ARROW) to move to the top of the block, typing the final parenthesis, and pressing (ENTER).

EDITING MACROS

If you make a mistake while recording a macro, the simplest solution usually is to rerecord it. Start by erasing the cells that contain the faulty macro, in case the new macro is slightly shorter than the old one. Then record the macro again.

In the case of long or complicated macros, you may want to edit the macro rather than record it again, particularly if you have made only a minor mistake. Because a macro is simply a series of labels on your spreadsheet, you can edit it as you would any other label.

You might also edit a macro when you cannot stop recording at exactly the point you would like, because you are not in Ready mode and therefore cannot display the Macro menu. To illustrate this problem, try creating a macro to streamline the process of macro execution. This macro opens the Macro menu, selects the Execute option, and presses (F3) (Choices) to display a list of block names.

1. Move back to A5. Press (ALT-F2) and type **R** to open the Macro menu and start recording.

2. Press (ALT-F2) to reopen the Macro menu and type **E** for Execute.

3. When Quattro Pro prompts for a macro name, press (F3) to display a list of named blocks. This is the point at which the macro should actually stop. However, because you cannot display the Macro menu at the moment, you must continue recording until Quattro Pro is back in Ready mode.

4. Type **\D** and press (ENTER) to select the \D macro from the list, and let Quattro Pro enter today's date into the current cell (overwriting the date that is already there).

5. Press (ALT-F2) and type **P** to stop recording and paste the macro into the spreadsheet. When Quattro Pro prompts for a block name, enter **\M**. When prompted for a block, enter **I57**. Your spreadsheet should now look like Figure 23-3.

488   Quattro Pro 2 Made Easy

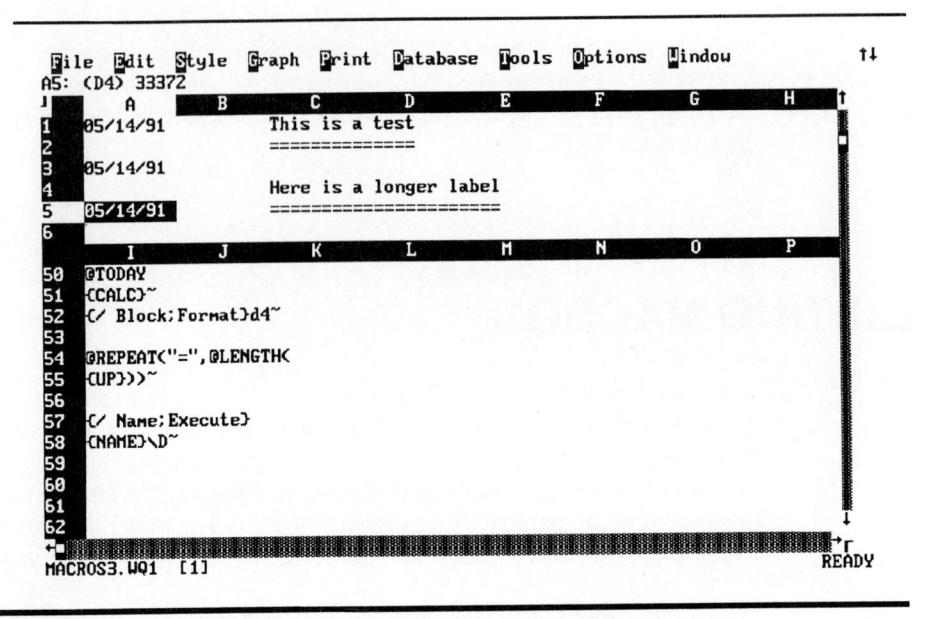

```
 File  Edit  Style  Graph  Print  Database  Tools  Options  Window        ↑↓
A5: (D4) 33372
       A         B         C         D         E         F         G         H
1  05/14/91            This is a test
2                      ==============
3  05/14/91
4                      Here is a longer label
5  05/14/91            ======================
6
       I         J         K         L         M         N         O         P
50 @TODAY
51 {CALC}~
52 {/ Block;Format}d4~
53
54 @REPEAT("=",@LENGTH(
55 {UP}))~
56
57 {/ Name;Execute}
58 {NAME}\D~
59
60
61
62
MACROS3.WQ1  [1]                                                        READY
```

Figure 23-3.   Creating a macro to execute macros

Now you need to manually delete the extra keystrokes from the macro.

1. Press (F6) to switch to the bottom pane of the window, and move to I59. (If you have extra keystrokes in your macro, move the cell pointer to the cell that contains the characters \D~ or, if you selected the macro by using the arrow keys, the characters {RIGHT}~.)

2. Press (DEL) to delete the contents of the cell.

3. Now try playing the macro. Press (F6) (Pane), move to C6, and press (ALT-M). When Quattro Pro displays a list of block names, select UNDERLINE. Your spreadsheet should now resemble Figure 23-4.

4. Issue the / File l Save command and enter a file name of **MACROS**.

SAMPLE DATABASE MACROS

You are now ready to create two more elaborate macros. Both are designed for use with the ORDERS.WQ1 database, but their functions are suitable to any database. If

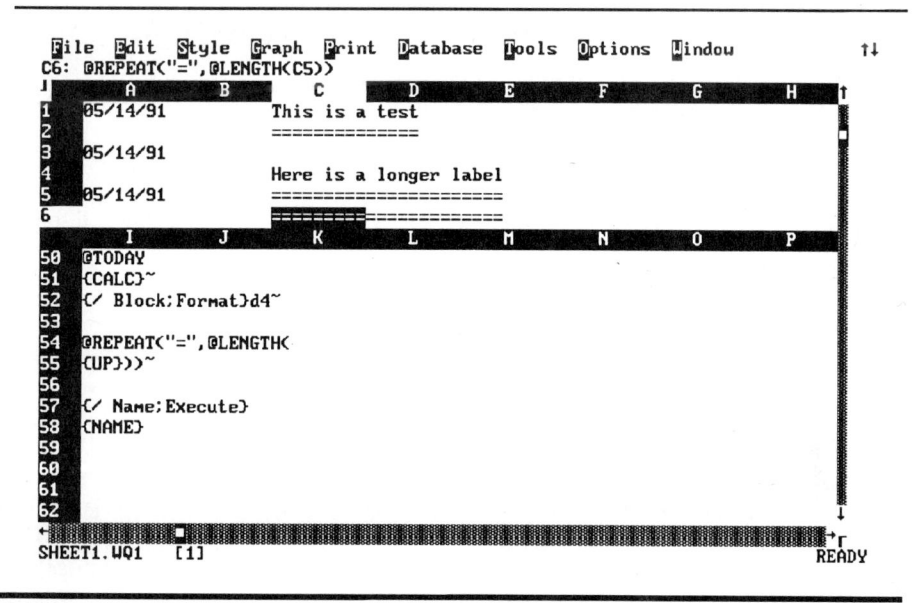

```
 File  Edit  Style  Graph  Print  Database  Tools  Options  Window         ↑↓
C6: @REPEAT("=",@LENGTH(C5))
        A         B         C         D         E         F         G         H
  1  05/14/91              This is a test
  2                        ==============
  3  05/14/91
  4                        Here is a longer label
  5  05/14/91              ======================
  6                        ==============
        I         J         K         L         M         N         O         P
 50  @TODAY
 51  {CALC}~
 52  {/ Block;Format}d4~
 53
 54  @REPEAT("=",@LENGTH(
 55  {UP}))~
 56
 57  {/ Name;Execute}
 58  {NAME}
 59
 60
 61
 62

SHEET1.WQ1   [1]                                                        READY
```

Figure 23-4. The \M macro after editing

you did not create ORDERS.WQ1 in earlier chapters but have another database to work with, read through the instructions first and then try adjusting the keystrokes to fit your own database's structure.

The first macro facilitates the entry of new records in your database. This macro inserts a new row within the current borders of the database, copies an adjacent record into this row, and then erases all the labels and numeric constants in the row, leaving the formatting codes and formulas intact. Because this new row is inserted within the borders of the database, you do not need to adjust the block settings on the **Database I Sort** and **Database I Query** menus or the database argument in statistical functions as you add new records.

Before you start recording this macro, you assign a block name to the column heading for the first field in the database. This named block serves as a starting point when you execute the macro, so the macro always starts from the same spot. From there the macro uses the (END-DOWN ARROW) key combination to move to the first field of what is currently the last row of the database before inserting a new row. Note that (END-DOWN ARROW) works properly only if the first field of every record is filled in, as it is in most databases and should be in this one.

If you make a serious mistake at any point, just press (ESC) to return to Ready mode; then open the Macro menu and select Record to stop recording, and start over again.

1. Retrieve the ORDERS.WQ1 database using the **/ File | Retrieve** command.

2. Issue the **/ Edit | Names | Create** command, enter the block name **FIELD1**, and enter the address **A12**.

3. Press (ALT-F2) and type **R** to start recording a macro.

4. Press (F5) (GoTo) and enter the block name **FIELD1** as the cell to go to.

5. Press (END) and then (DOWN ARROW) to move to the first field in the last record of the database (cell A22 at this point).

6. Type **/EIR** to issue the **/ Edit | Insert | Row** command, and press (ENTER) to insert a new row at row 22.

7. Type **/EC** to issue the **/ Edit | Copy** command. When prompted for a source block, press (ESC) to unanchor the cell pointer, and then press (DOWN ARROW) to move the cell pointer to cell A23. Type a period to anchor the cell pointer. Then press (RIGHT ARROW) 11 times to move the cell pointer to the AMT DUE field (cell L23) and press (ENTER). When prompted for a destination, press (ENTER) to accept the default of A22. Quattro Pro copies the data in row 23 to row 22. (Note that pressing (RIGHT ARROW) 11 times is safer than pressing (END-RIGHT) twice because there is no way to predict which fields in the record are filled and which blank.)

8. Erase all the cells in the row except those that contain formulas by typing **/EE** to issue the **/ Edit | Erase Block** command, pressing (RIGHT ARROW) four times to extend the block to A22..E22, and pressing (ENTER). This erases any data that may have been copied to the ACCOUNT, STATE, ORDER DATE, ITEM, and QUANT fields.

9. Type **/EE** to issue the **/ Edit | Erase** command again. Press (ESC) to unanchor the cell pointer, press (RIGHT ARROW) nine times to move to column J, and type a period to anchor it again. Press (RIGHT ARROW) to extend the block to J22..K22, and press (ENTER), erasing any data that may have been copied to the PMT DATE and PMT AMT fields.

10. Press (ALT-F2) and type **P** to stop recording and paste the new macro into the spreadsheet. When prompted for a name, enter **\A**. When prompted for a location, enter **Q100**.

11. Delete row 22 by issuing the **/ Edit | Delete | Rows** command and pressing (ENTER). This eliminates the row that you created while recording the macro.

12. Press (HOME) to move to A1 so that you can prove to yourself that the macro will work from anywhere.

13. Now test the macro by holding down (ALT) and typing **A**.

14. Fill in the new record with the following data.

In Cell	Enter
A22	N.L.G.
B22	NY
C22	12/1/90
D22	32-45
E22	3

Your spreadsheet should now look like Figure 23-5. If it does not, try again from step 1.

The entries in C22 and D22 are automatically formatted as a date and a label respectively due to the date-only and label-only codes that were copied from the existing record. Similarly, because of the F0 formatting code in the cell, Quattro Pro displays the entry in cell E22 without decimal places, even though the global numeric format is the comma format with two decimals.

15. Press (F5) (GoTo) and enter \A. Your spreadsheet should now look something like Figure 23-6. Don't worry about an extra keystroke or two, as long as the macro works.

16. Issue the / File | Save command to replace the previous version of the spreadsheet.

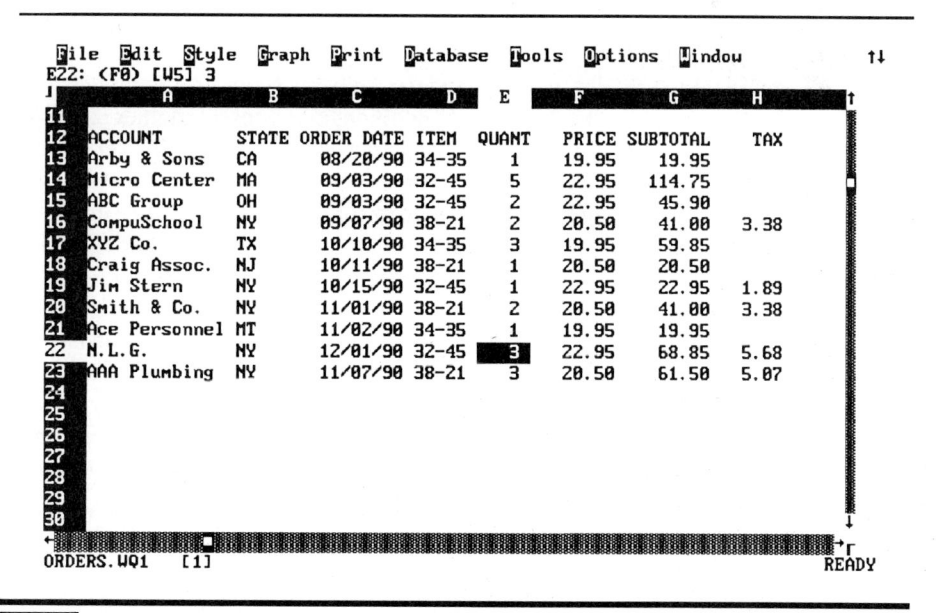

Figure 23-5. Using the \A macro to add a new record to the database

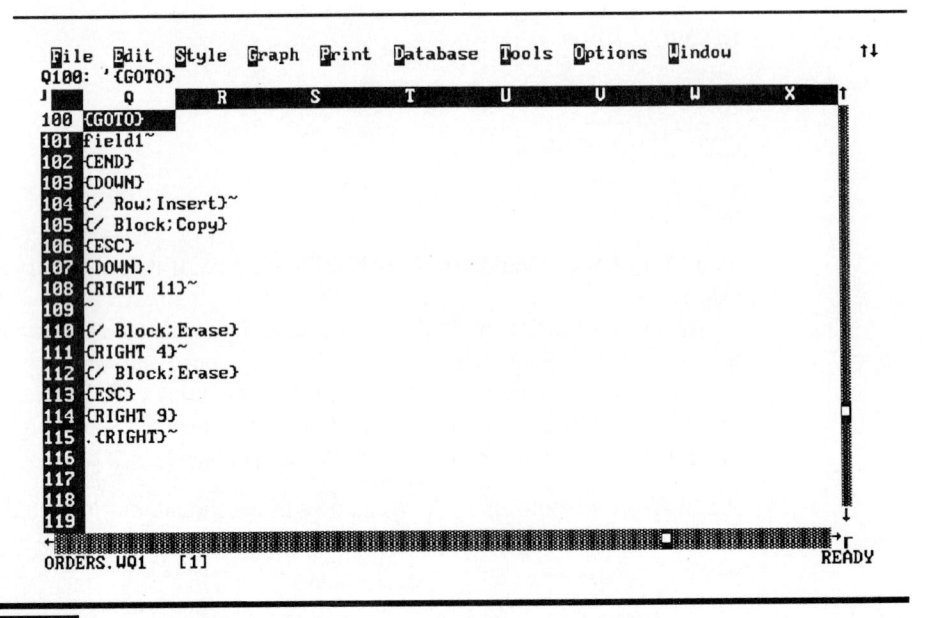

```
       File  Edit  Style  Graph  Print  Database  Tools  Options  Window
Q100: '{GOTO}
       Q         R         S         T         U         V         W         X
100 {GOTO}
101 field1~
102 {END}
103 {DOWN}
104 {/ Row;Insert}~
105 {/ Block;Copy}
106 {ESC}
107 {DOWN}.
108 {RIGHT 11}~
109 ~
110 {/ Block;Erase}
111 {RIGHT 4}~
112 {/ Block;Erase}
113 {ESC}
114 {RIGHT 9}
115 .{RIGHT}~
116
117
118
119
ORDERS.WQ1   [1]                                                    READY
```

Figure 23-6. The \A macro for adding new records

You could have used the named block ACCOUNT (referring to the ACCOUNT field in the first record) rather than FIELD1 as the starting position for this macro. The reference to FIELD1 is safer, however, because it continues to work even if you delete the first record in the database. In addition, if you insert another column to the left of ACCOUNT, you only need to change the coordinates of FIELD1 rather than editing the macro to enter the new field name.

Now try creating another macro to restore the database to date order after you insert new records. Before recording this macro, you must create a new block name for the block of records to be sorted (the entire database minus the field names). Whenever you add records using the \A macro, the coordinates of the named block change to include the new data, because the \A macro inserts new rows within the block's current borders. Then, whenever you execute the sort macro, Quattro Pro looks up the current coordinates of the named block and sorts all the records currently in the database. In contrast, if you define the sort block in this macro in terms of specific cell references, those references are not updated as the database changes, and you cannot rely on the macro to sort all the records.

1. Press (F5) (GoTo) and enter **FIELD1**, moving the cell pointer to the top of the database.

2. Issue the / Edit | Names | Create command, and specify the block name SORT and the coordinates A13..L23.

3. Press (ALT-F2) and type **R** to start recording the macro.

4. Type **/DSB** to issue the / Database | Sort | Block command. When prompted for a block, enter **SORT**.

5. Type **1** to select the 1st Key option. When prompted for a "Column to be used as first sort key," enter **C1** to specify the date field. (It would be preferable to enter a block name, but Quattro Pro cannot accept one in this context.) When the Order submenu is displayed, type **A** and press (ENTER) to select Ascending order.

6. Type **G** to select the Go option.

7. When the sort is completed, press (ALT-F2) and type **P** to stop recording and paste the macro. Enter **\S** as the macro name and **Q125** as its location.

8. To try your macro, change the ORDER DATE for Smith & Co. to 9/20/90 and then press (ALT-S) to resort the database. (If the database is not resorted properly, retrieve ORDERS.WQ1 from disk and start again from step 1 of this exercise.)

9. Press (F5) and enter \S to move the cell pointer to the new macro. Your spreadsheet should now look like Figure 23-7.

10. Issue the / File | Save command to replace the previous version of the spreadsheet.

APPLICATIONS FOR RECORDED MACROS

Any time you find yourself repeating the same keystrokes over and over, try automating them with a macro. Whenever you want to ensure that a particularly delicate operation is performed correctly, record it in a macro to ensure accuracy and consistency. These are just a few of the operations that you might want to automate with macros:

- Entering a set of standard column or row headings, such as the names of all twelve months or the days of the week

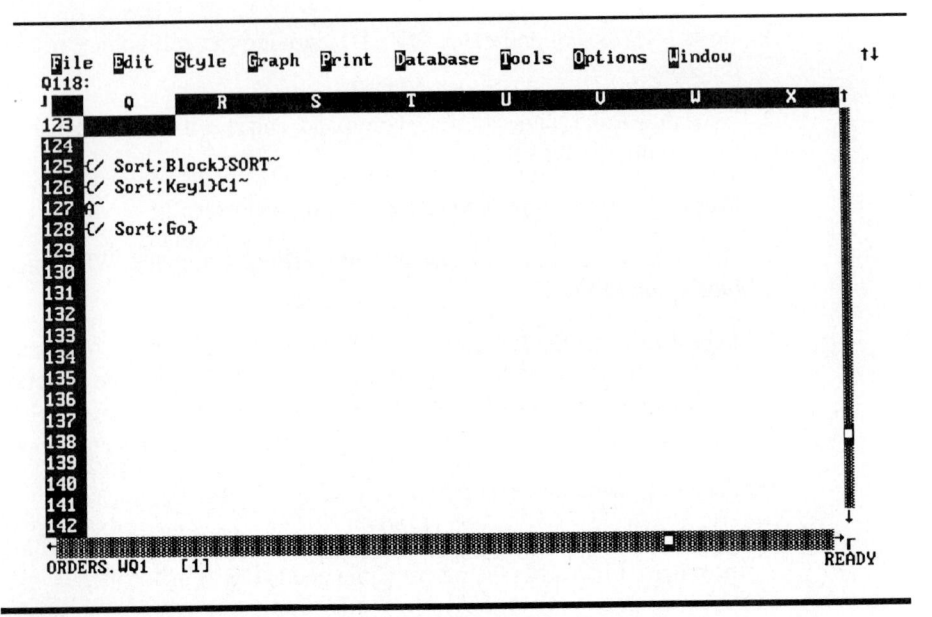

Figure 23-7. The \S macro for sorting the database

- Erasing data from an assumptions or starting-data block or a criteria table that you reuse frequently

- Printing a series of reports, including performing such preparatory steps as hiding or moving columns, inserting extra rows, and defining print ranges, set-up characters, and print layout

- Printing a series of graphs

- Consolidating spreadsheets using the / **Tools** | **Combine** | **Add** command

You undoubtedly will think of many more as you continue to work with the program.

INTRODUCTION TO THE MACRO LANGUAGE

You now have a good sense of what you can accomplish by recording macros. As you have seen, when you record and then paste a macro, Quattro Pro stores a record of your actions in the spreadsheet using a special macro language. This language also includes several categories of commands which you cannot record, including interactive commands (which pause for user input or activate custom menus) and screen commands (which control the screen display during macro execution). If you want to use one of these commands, you must either insert them into a macro that you previously pasted to the spreadsheet or enter the entire macro manually.

Advanced users and programmers often use the macro language to create elaborate and highly customized macros, including macros that present the user with custom menus. This level of macro usage is far beyond the scope of this book. If you are interested in exploring more advanced macros, try reading Chapter 16 of the *Quattro Pro User's Guide* and the macro chapters in *Using Quattro Pro* by Stephen Cobb (Osborne/McGraw-Hill, Berkeley, 1990).

MAINTAINING AND USING MACROS

As you accumulate macros you must think about organizing and manipulating them, performing the macro equivalent of file management. This involves documenting your macros (entering descriptions on the spreadsheet to remind you of the macro's function), renaming them, deleting them, and copying them from one file to another.

Documenting Your Macros

If you use instant macros, create several macros on a spreadsheet, or use a spreadsheet infrequently, it is easy to forget what your macros do. You can eliminate the need to

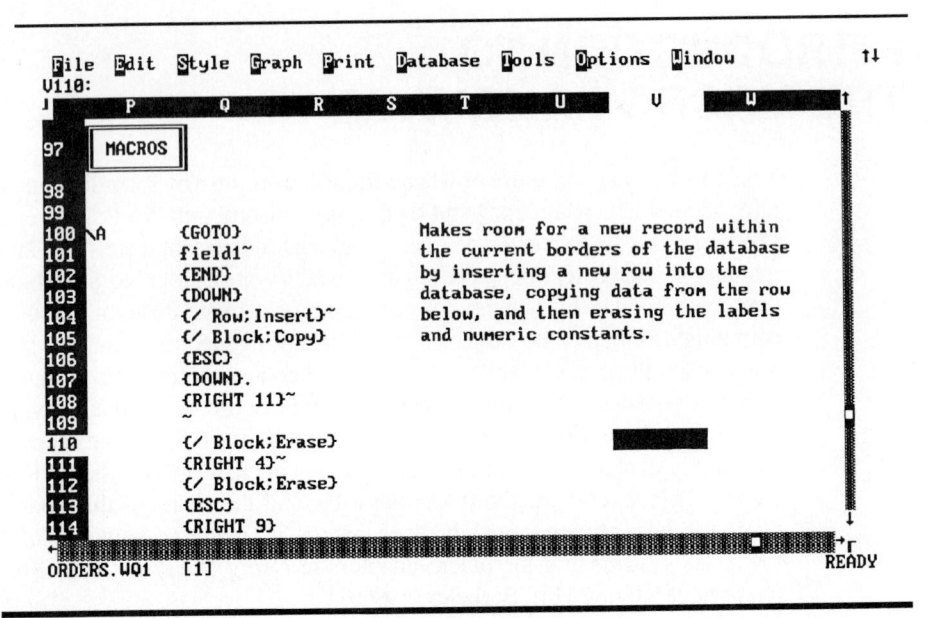

```
    File  Edit  Style  Graph  Print  Database  Tools  Options  Window         ↑↓
V110:
        P         Q            R      S       T         U         W
 97          MACROS
 98
 99
100   \A      {GOTO}                 Makes room for a new record within
101           field1~                the current borders of the database
102           {END}                  by inserting a new row into the
103           {DOWN}                 database, copying data from the row
104           {/ Row;Insert}~        below, and then erasing the labels
105           {/ Block;Copy}         and numeric constants.
106           {ESC}
107           {DOWN}.
108           {RIGHT 11}~
109           ~
110           {/ Block;Erase}
111           {RIGHT 4}~
112           {/ Block;Erase}
113           {ESC}
114           {RIGHT 9}
ORDERS.WQ1  [1]                                                          READY
```

Figure 23-8. A well-documented macro

decipher macros later by entering brief descriptions of their functions as you create them. These descriptions need not be long or elaborate; in most cases a few words or a sentence will suffice. Figure 23-8 shows the documentation for the first macro in the ORDERS.WQ1 spreadsheet. Note that the macro name was entered to the left of the macro and a description to its right. You can use any layout you like, as long as you include both the macro name and a description. (As described shortly, placing the macro names in a single column makes it easy to name macros after copying them to another spreadsheet.)

Renaming And Deleting Macros

Renaming a macro is a two-step process. First you delete the old name by selecting the Name option on the Macro menu and choosing Delete. When Quattro Pro displays a list of block names, either enter a macro name or select one from the list. Quattro Pro does not ask for confirmation as it does when you delete a file; it simply deletes the macro name. The macro itself—the actual labels containing the representations of cursor movements, keystrokes, and commands—remains on the spreadsheet (just as Quattro Pro leaves a block's data intact when you delete a block name). If you want to erase the labels containing the macro from the spreadsheet, use the / Edit | Erase Block command.

You assign a new name to a macro by selecting the Name option on the Macro menu and choosing Create. When Quattro Pro displays a list of block names, enter the name that you wish to assign. (The only time you would choose an existing block name is if you want to recycle that name, removing it from one block and assigning it to another.) Then specify the coordinates of the first cell of your macro by either entering the address or pointing to the cell.

Copying Macros To Another Spreadsheet

When you copy macros from one spreadsheet to another, remember that the block names are not copied. You therefore need to name the macros again. If you enter the macro names in a single column to the left of the macros, you can name a group of macros simultaneously using the / Edit | Names | Labels | Right command. Just specify the block of cells that contains the macro names as the label block.

Using Macro Libraries

A *macro library* is a spreadsheet that contains macros that you can execute from other open spreadsheets. You can designate a spreadsheet as a macro library by choosing the Library option on the Macro menu and changing the setting to Yes. Once you have marked a spreadsheet as a macro library, that designation remains with the spreadsheet permanently, unless you explicitly change it by selecting the Library option on the Macro menu and changing the setting to No.

Whenever a macro library is open, Quattro Pro allows you to execute macros from that file. When you invoke either an instant or a standard macro, Quattro Pro looks for the macro on the current spreadsheet. If it does not find it there, it searches through every open macro library until it finds the macro and then executes it.

You should start building a macro library as soon as you start creating macros. Whenever you prepare to create a macro, consider whether the macro may have applications beyond the current spreadsheet. Many macros, such as the date-stamping and underlining macros created near the beginning of this chapter, are completely generic (or can be made so) and can be applied to any spreadsheet file. You should store all such macros in a macro library for the following reasons:

- You need not waste time and disk space copying macros to several different spreadsheets
- You do not have to worry about damaging macros while modifying the rest of your spreadsheet
- You know where to look for macros when you want to use them in the future
- You only have to edit a single spreadsheet if you decide to change one of them

Other macros are specific to individual spreadsheets but general in their basic function; they can be modified to work in other contexts but cannot be made completely context-free. The first database macro that you created falls into this category. Some of the individual keystrokes are specific to the structure of the ORDERS.WQ1 spreadsheet, but you can use a similar macro to add records to other databases. You may also want to store this type of macro in a library to make it easy to copy into new spreadsheets (before modifying the macro instructions to fit the new data). This spares you the task of tracking down the macro in a spreadsheet file.

There are a few practices that can help you use macro libraries effectively. If your macro library contains more macros than fit on a single screen, you can enter a table of contents at the top of the macro library spreadsheet. This makes it easy to determine the names and purposes of all the macros stored in a particular library. You will find this particularly helpful when you are having trouble remembering a particular macro name. Figure 23-9 shows a sample table of contents for a macro library.

If you create dozens of macros, you may want to develop specialized macro libraries—for example, one library of editing and formatting macros and another for database macros. Although you can open more than one macro library at a time, you should do so with care. If two open libraries contain a macro with the same name, it is difficult to predict which one will execute when you invoke the macro from a third spreadsheet. To avoid this problem either open only one library at a time or choose unique names for all your macros, regardless of where you store them.

You also encounter problems if your spreadsheet contains a macro or any other named block with the same name as a macro in an open spreadsheet library. Whenever you issue the / Tools I Macro I Execute command or press (ALT) and a letter for an instant macro, Quattro Pro always looks on the current spreadsheet for a block with the specified name. Only if it cannot find one does Quattro Pro continue its search in any open macro libraries. For example, suppose you issue the / Tools I Macros I Execute command and enter **PERCENT** in an attempt to execute the PERCENT macro in an open macro library. If the current spreadsheet contains a named block named PERCENT, Quattro Pro attempts to execute it as a macro, even if that block is simply a collection of cells that you happened to assign that name.

If you use macro libraries extensively, you may want to develop a naming scheme to help avoid such problems. For example, you could decide that the names of all

```
    File Edit Style Graph Print Database Tools Options Window              ↑↓
A20: [W12]
         A            B         C         D         E         F         G
  1   ALL-PURPOSE MACRO LIBRARY
  2
  3
  4   Macro Name    Location  Purpose
  5   ----------    --------  ----------------------------------------------
  6
  7   DATE          B50       Enters today's date into the current cell and
  8                           formats it as a date.
  9
 10   UNDERLINE     B60       Draws a line of equals signs to underline
 11                           data in the cell above the current cell.
 12
 13   COMMA2        B70       Changes the global numeric format for the
 14                           current spreadsheet to comma format with 2
 15                           decimal places.
 16
 17   %             B80       Formats the current cell with the Percent
 18                           format with 0 decimal places.
 19
 20
MACLIB.WQ1    [1]                                                       READY
```

Figure 23-9. Table of contents for a macro library

macros in macro libraries will start with either a backslash (for instant macros), the letters ML (for macro library), or a special character such as an asterisk. You can then simply avoid those characters at the beginning of regular block names or macros that you create on regular (nonlibrary) spreadsheets.

Changing the Macro Recording Method

By default, the Macro Recording option on the Macro menu is set to Logical. This means that Quattro Pro records menu selections as macro-equivalent commands rather than as a series of keystrokes. If you change this setting to Keystroke, Quattro Pro records commands in terms of the individual keystrokes that you use to issue those commands. Figure 23-10 shows two versions of the same macro—a macro that assigns the Percent format with no decimals to the current cell, using the / Style | Numeric Format command. The first macro was recorded with the Logical recording method. The second was recorded with the Keystroke recording method.

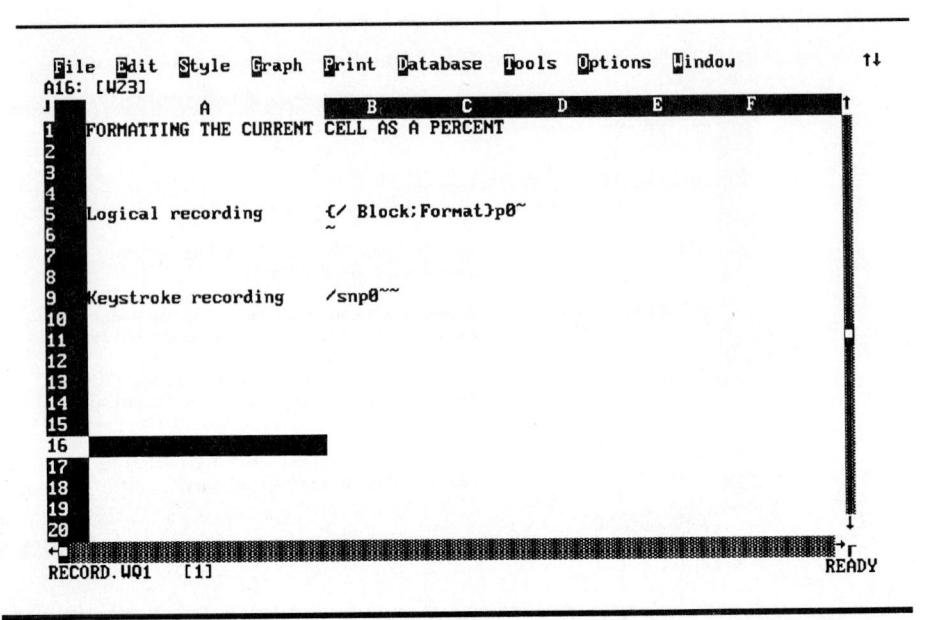

Figure 23-10. Logical versus keystroke recordings

You should change to the Keystroke recording method only if you must be able to import your spreadsheet into Lotus 1-2-3, because Lotus does not recognize Quattro Pro's menu-equivalent commands. You should switch to the 123-compatible menu tree within Quattro Pro so the menus are similar to those found in the Lotus 1-2-3 program. Then set the macro recording method to Keystroke. Be sure to select menu options by typing letters rather than by using the arrow keys. Because Quattro Pro's 123-compatible menus contain some options that you do not find in Lotus 1-2-3 itself, you cannot rely on the menu options being in exactly the same spot in both programs' menus.

If you use the 123-compatible menus but do not need to actually work with your spreadsheets within the Lotus 1-2-3 program, leave the recording method set to Logical. Then your macros will work if you later change to the Quattro Pro menu tree.

PLAYING MACROS AUTOMATICALLY

There are several ways to automate the execution of a macro, so it is replayed as soon as you load the spreadsheet or as soon as you load Quattro Pro.

Startup Macros

You can use the / Options | Startup | Startup Macro command to assign a particular name to a macro that you want to invoke automatically when you load a spreadsheet. For example, if you create a spreadsheet specifically for displaying a graphics slide show, you might create an instant macro to initiate the slide show as soon as you retrieve the file. The initial setting for the startup macro name is \0, but you can change it by entering a new name and selecting the Update option to save the new default. You are restricted to one startup macro per spreadsheet.

If you no longer want a macro to be invoked automatically when you retrieve the spreadsheet, you can either change its name, delete it with the / Tools | Macro Name | Delete command, or change the Startup Macro name. Keep in mind that changing the Startup Macro name affects every spreadsheet that contains a startup macro, not just the current spreadsheet. If you have created macros with the old Startup Macro name on other spreadsheets, they are affected as well.

Autoloading Macros

Quattro Pro offers two ways to execute a particular macro as soon as you load Quattro Pro. First, you can create a startup macro on an autoload spreadsheet. An autoload spreadsheet is a spreadsheet that is loaded immediately whenever you load the Quattro Pro program. If you define a startup macro on this spreadsheet (as described in the previous section), every time you load Quattro Pro, the autoload file is retrieved and the startup macro executed.

You can also initiate a macro from the DOS command line by typing the macro name after the Quattro Pro load command and the name of the file that contains the macro. For example, to load a macro called \A on the ORDERS spreadsheet, you type **Q ORDERS \A**. This command loads the Quattro Pro program, retrieves the ORDERS.WQ1 spreadsheet, and invokes the \A macro.

As you work with any program, you inevitably find yourself repeating particular sequences of keystrokes. Macros allow you to save time and minimize mistakes by automating such keystroke sequences and letting Quattro Pro do more of your work for you. This chapter has barely scratched the surface of what you can accomplish with macros. Once you have mastered the techniques introduced here and have created new macros on your own, you may want to explore further. As mentioned, you can start with Chapter 16 of the Quattro Pro User's Guide and with Stephen Cobb's *Using Quattro Pro*. You may also get some help from reading material on Lotus 1-2-3 macros: although there are differences between the Lotus and Quattro Pro macro commands (Lotus does not use menu-equivalent commands, for example), most of the advanced commands are the same.

24

EXCHANGING DATA WITH OTHER PROGRAMS

Exchanging Data with Lotus 1-2-3 and Symphony
Trading Data with Paradox, dBASE, and Reflex
Exporting Data to Word Processing Software
Exporting Data to Other Types of Software
Importing Data into Quattro Pro
Parsing ASCII Text Files

Quattro Pro offers several different methods for importing and exporting data, depending on the type of data and the type of program with which you are exchanging data. Although this chapter covers the range of possibilities, it cannot, of course, cover every program. It is designed to point out potential problems and offer general solutions rather than to provide step-by-step instructions on each situation. Therefore, you may need to experiment the first time you trade data with another software package before you achieve the desired results.

EXCHANGING DATA WITH LOTUS 1-2-3 AND SYMPHONY

Quattro Pro can read any spreadsheet created in 1-2-3 Release 1A or Release 2. Whenever you retrieve a spreadsheet file that has the extension WKS or WK1, Quattro Pro translates the data into Quattro Pro format. This translation process is automatic; you will not even know it is happening.

Saving your Quattro Pro spreadsheets in Lotus-compatible form is simply a matter of using a 1-2-3 file name extension when you issue the File Save command. If you want all your files to be Lotus-compatible, you can define one of the 1-2-3 file extensions as the default extension (in place of Quattro Pro's own WQ1 extension) with the / Options | Startup | File Extension command or, if you are using the 1-2-3-compatible menu tree, with the / Install | Startup | Extension command.

To translate a Quattro Pro spreadsheet into a form usable by Symphony, you need only save it with an extension of WRK (for version 1.2) or WR1 (for version 2.0). Quattro Pro can also read Symphony files, provided you either turn off all windows before saving the file in Symphony or save it as a 1-2-3 spreadsheet.

Trading Macros with Lotus 1-2-3

To run macros created in Lotus 1-2-3, you need to load the 1-2-3-compatible menu tree. If you want to record a macro in Quattro Pro and be able to run it in 1-2-3, you need to perform two steps. First, switch the macro recording method from Logical to Keystroke using the / Worksheet | Macro | Macro Recording | Keystroke command on the 1-2-3-compatible menu tree or the / Tools | Macro | Macro Recording | Keystroke command on the Quattro Pro menu tree. Second, use the 1-2-3-compatible menus while recording the macro.

You cannot run Symphony macros in Quattro Pro or Quattro Pro macros in Symphony.

Trading Data with Other Spreadsheet Programs

Many spreadsheet programs other than Lotus 1-2-3 (including Excel) can read and write files in Lotus format. As a result, you can use the Lotus format as a middle ground between these programs and Quattro Pro. To import an Excel file into Quattro Pro, for example, use Excel to save the file in Lotus 1-2-3 format. Then include the WK1 extension when retrieving the file in Quattro Pro. If you plan to transfer the data back to Excel, use the WK1 extension whenever you save the file. Otherwise, you may want to change the extension to WQ1 so that you can make use of Quattro Pro's desktop publishing and linking features.

Quattro Pro can also read and write files in Surpass format: Just include the WKP extension when you save or retrieve the file.

The "Desktop Settings Are Removed" Message

Whenever you save a Quattro Pro spreadsheet in an external file format, Quattro Pro automatically replaces link formulas with their current results and removes all codes related to desktop publishing features that are not supported by other programs. The codes that are removed include those related to line drawing, shading, fonts, data entry restrictions (label-only or date-only designations), and alignment of numbers. Quattro Pro warns you of this removal of codes by displaying the message "Desktop settings are removed" when you issue the / File | Save or / File | Save As command.

TRADING DATA WITH PARADOX, dBASE, AND REFLEX

Quattro Pro excels at exchanging data with three major dedicated database management programs: Paradox, Reflex, and dBASE. Quattro Pro can read and write dBASE II, dBASE III, dBASE IV, and Paradox files with such ease and speed that you can use any of these programs as an adjunct or "sister program" to Quattro Pro. Assuming your file is small enough to load into Quattro Pro, you may want to use Quattro Pro as an extension of your database program when performing extensive database management. Alternatively, if your database requires calculated fields or intensive computations, you may want to do most of your work in Quattro Pro and then switch programs to perform operations that your database management program is better equipped to handle.

Reading Paradox, Reflex, And dBASE Files

To import a Paradox, Reflex, or dBASE file into Quattro Pro, simply retrieve it using / File | Retrieve or / File | Open. You can also use the / Tools | Combine | Copy command to copy Paradox or dBASE data directly into an existing spreadsheet.

Quattro Pro's Paradox, Reflex, and dBASE translation skills are excellent. Whenever possible, Quattro Pro retains the data types and even the display formats used in the other program. It correctly reads date fields as dates (translating them into date serial values displayed in the Long International Date format). In the case of Paradox files, it automatically translates dollar fields into values displayed in Currency format. If you retrieve a dBASE file with a numeric field containing three decimal places, Quattro Pro displays it in Fixed format, 3 decimal places. As discussed later in the chapter, Quattro Pro can even translate dBASE memo fields into labels. In short, Quattro Pro does everything you could hope for to maintain the content and appearance of the database while translating the data to its own format. It even assigns block names to the fields in the first record, using the field names at the top of the file, just as if you had issued the / Database | Query | Assign Names command. This allows you to use field names when entering logical formulas in criteria tables, without any prior preparation.

MEMORY CONSTRAINTS When you use a database program such as dBASE III, dBASE IV, Paradox, or Reflex, the size of your database is limited only by the amount of available disk space that you have, not by the amount of available memory. This is because these programs only read data into memory as needed, rather than reading in the whole database at once. In contrast, when you retrieve a database in Quattro Pro, the entire file must be able to fit into memory at the same time. If your computer only has 640K of installed memory, this can place severe limitations on the size of the database that you can manipulate in Quattro Pro. If you try to retrieve a database that is too large to fit in available memory, Quattro Pro displays the error message "Not enough memory for that operation" and then loads as much of the data as it can. In this case, be sure not to save the file (unless you change the file name); otherwise, the new, partially retrieved file will replace the old, complete file on disk. If you receive a "Not enough memory for that operation" message and you have an expanded memory card in your computer, you might try changing the Options | Other | Expanded Memory setting to Both (so that more data is stored in expanded memory) and then retrieve the file again.

A NOTE ON DELETED RECORDS IN dBASE FILES When you delete a record in dBASE the record is not physically removed from the database file. Instead, it is simply marked for deletion at a later time. When you retrieve a dBASE file into Quattro Pro, these deletion-marked records are automatically omitted—as if you had issued a SET DELETED ON command in dBASE to screen them out. If you then modify the data in Quattro Pro and save it again, overwriting the original file, the deletion-marked records are permanently erased.

Writing Paradox, Reflex, And dBASE Files

Just as Quattro Pro translates Paradox, Reflex, and dBASE data into Quattro Pro format when you retrieve files, it can also translate it back into the external format if you save a file with a Paradox, Reflex, or dBASE extension. The extension tells Quattro Pro to save the file using the appropriate external file format. If you intend to pass data to and from dBASE, Paradox, or Reflex regularly, you will probably want to store the data with the database extension. If you intend to do most of your future work with a particular file from within Quattro Pro, however, you can save time by storing the data with a WQ1 extension until you need to use it in your database program. This way Quattro Pro will not need to translate each time you save or retrieve the spreadsheet.

You can save Quattro Pro databases as Paradox, Reflex, or dBASE files using either the / File l Save or / File l Save As command, or the / Tools l Xtract l Values command. If your spreadsheet contains data other than the database, use / Tools l Xtract. Otherwise, you will, at best, wind up with useless extra "records" containing the non-database data. At worst, the database file structure will not properly match the database. When you use the / Tools l Xtract command to extract a database in an external format, be sure to select the Values option. Quattro Pro always converts formulas to values anyway when you extract a file with a DB, RXD, R2D, DBF, or DB2 extension, but it will run into problems if any of the calculated fields refer to cells outside the block you are extracting, that is, outside the database. Also be sure to include the field names in your extract block.

To save or extract a file for use in Paradox, assign the extension DB; for use in Reflex, assign the extension RXD for version 1 or R2D for version 2. When saving or extracting a file for use in dBASE III, dBASE III PLUS, or dBASE IV, assign the extension DBF; for use in dBASE II, use the extension DB2. The DB2 extension for dBASE II files (rather than the standard DBF extension used in the program itself) is necessary to inform Quattro Pro that you will be using the earlier version of dBASE. You can then either rename the file in DOS, changing the extension to DBF, or else specify the DB2 extension whenever you open the file in dBASE II.

The process of saving data in Paradox, Reflex, or dBASE format is the same whether you entered the data in Quattro Pro or retrieved it from disk after entering it in the external database program. Each time you save a file with a Paradox, Reflex, or dBASE extension, Quattro Pro displays a File Save submenu with the choices View

Structure, Write, and Quit. Choose the View Structure option to see and, if necessary modify, the names, data types, and lengths that Quattro Pro intends to assign to each field. Once you are satisfied with the file structure, press (ESC) to return to the File Save submenu and select the Write option.

When you save a file with a Paradox, Reflex, or dBASE extension, Quattro Pro automatically makes use of whatever text, number, date, and currency field types are available in the external program when designing the initial file structure. Quattro Pro also allows you to change fields to still other field types; specifically, the logical type in dBASE and the short number type in Paradox. The only field type that Quattro Pro cannot write is the dBASE memo type. It is always a good idea to view Quattro Pro's proposed file structure before actually writing the file for the first time and before saving a file after making changes that might affect the structure.

All formulas in your database are translated to their results when you save in dBASE, Reflex, or Paradox format. If you want to save your formulas, be sure to save your file with a WQ1 extension.

Modifying the File Structure

To change a file's structure before saving, select the View Structure option on the File Save submenu. Quattro Pro displays a picture of your file structure. To delete a field from the structure so it is omitted from the new file altogether, highlight the field and press (DEL). To change a field's attributes, highlight the field and press (ENTER). When Quattro Pro displays a submenu with the options Name and Type, choose the attribute that you wish to change and enter a new setting. If you select the Type option, Quattro Pro displays another submenu with the available field type options. Once you select a type, Quattro Pro prompts you for the field length, if applicable (some field types have a fixed length that cannot be changed). This is the only way to change the length of a field; if you want to change a field's length but not its type, select Type anyway, select the same type, and then specify the desired field length. When you have completed your modifications, press (ESC) to return to the File Save submenu and select the Write File option to save the data using the newly modified structure.

When you alter a field type, do not expect this change to be remembered in future sessions. In most cases, when your choice of field type differs from Quattro Pro's, you must tell Quattro Pro to use this alternate field type every time you save or extract the database. You are most likely to encounter this problem when saving dBASE logical fields or Paradox short number fields. Although Quattro Pro can write these field types, it never chooses them as defaults; if your file contains these field types, you must modify the file structure and adjust those field types every time you issue the / File | Save, / File | Save As, or / Tools | Xtract command.

> **Caution:** If you back out of saving a dBASE, Paradox, or Reflex file by pressing (ESC) or (CTRL-BREAK) to return to Ready mode without selecting the Write File option, Quattro Pro displays the message "Warning. File has been erased. Please try again." This means that the file has been erased from the disk, but not from memory. Unless you save the data by issuing a / File | Save or / File | Save As command before you issue the / File | Erase, / File | Retrieve, or / File | Exit command, you will not be able to retrieve it again later.

dBASE Memo Fields

The good news about Quattro Pro's handling of dBASE memo fields is that it can translate memo field data into labels. This means you can actually use Quattro Pro to perform character-string manipulation on dBASE memo field data—such as searching for particular words or modifying the text with the use of string functions—that you cannot perform in dBASE. For example, you can extract a list of records that have memo fields containing the name Anne Woods by entering the exact match criterion *** Anne Woods *** underneath the name of the memo field in a criteria table.

The bad news is twofold. First, because the maximum length of a label in Quattro Pro is 254 characters, any memo field data beyond this limit will be lost in the translation. Second, Quattro Pro cannot write memo fields. Therefore, you cannot create a file in Quattro Pro and then save it with memo fields. In addition, if you retrieve a file created with memo fields in dBASE, the memo field data is immediately converted into labels (and data beyond the 254th character is truncated). If you then resave the data as a DBF file, it will be saved in exactly this form. You cannot recover the truncated text or change the field type to memo. If you try to change the structure, the memo field type is not even on the list of options. This means, in effect, that you cannot easily pass a dBASE file containing memo fields back and forth with Quattro Pro. You can load such a file into Quattro Pro to perform specific types of calculations if you like, but you cannot pass the results back to dBASE without losing the memo field type.

Because of the potential loss of memo field data, if you retrieve a dBASE file that contains memo fields, Quattro Pro prevents you from overwriting the original file when you save the database. If you attempt to do so, Quattro Pro displays the error message "Cannot save without destroying family files." This message refers to the fact that dBASE stores memo field text in a separate file, apart from the other fields in the database. This file has the same first name as the database file and an extension of DBT rather than DBF. When Quattro Pro says that it "cannot save without destroying family files," it means that saving the database under its original name would destroy the link between the DBF file and the DBT file so that you could no longer access the memo field data as a memo field within dBASE.

Quattro Pro will allow you to save the file in dBASE format provided you supply a different file name. If your memo field data is short and was therefore not truncated when you retrieved the file into Quattro Pro, you may want to save the file as is. Otherwise, you may prefer to remove the memo field from the file structure before saving.

Potential Problems In Exchanging Data With Database Programs

There are several potential problems that can occur when you retrieve external database files in Quattro Pro, modify them within Quattro Pro, and then save them again for use in the external database program. Although none of these problems is insurmountable, you need to be aware of them and take steps to ensure that your data is usable in the external program.

Most external database programs maintain index files that allow you to locate particular records quickly. If you retrieve a database into Quattro Pro, modify the data, and then save it in the external file format, you may create a discrepancy between the index file and the database file itself. To be safe, rebuild your indexes in the database program.

When you retrieve an external database file, Quattro Pro bases the width of each column on the length of the field in the external database. This means that if the field is narrow, you may not be able to read the entire field name (column heading) without widening the column. Also, if the data in a particular field is as wide as the field itself, there may be no spaces separating the data in that field from the data in the next field to the right. For these reasons, you will often alter column widths as soon as you retrieve an external database to make the data easier to read. If you save the file in this format, you will inadvertently modify the structure of your external database. To avoid this, write down the original column widths before you make your adjustments and reinstate them before you save the file.

Another potential problem relates specifically to saving and retrieving dBASE files. As mentioned, whenever you retrieve a dBASE file in Quattro Pro, Quattro Pro only retrieves records that have not been marked for deletion. If you then save the file under the same file name, the deletion-marked records will be permanently lost (as if you had performed a PACK operation in dBASE). If this is acceptable, just be sure to rebuild all your dBASE index files so that they will match the newly trimmed database. If you are not willing to part with the deletion-marked records, you can copy them to a separate file in dBASE before you retrieve the data in Quattro Pro. Then, after you save the database in Quattro Pro, you must reload dBASE and append data from that second file. Then rebuild your indexes.

Linking to External Databases

You can query and generate database statistics on dBASE, Reflex, and Paradox database files without retrieving those files into Quattro Pro. To do this, you simply create a spreadsheet with a criteria table containing link references to the external database.

Even though you don't need to load a dBASE, Paradox, or Reflex database into Quattro Pro to access its data, Quattro Pro acts as if you had. That is, it acts as if the database starts in cell A1, and each record occupies one row and each field one column. You therefore refer to the first field of the database as column A, the second field as column B, and so on. Quattro Pro also acts as if the first row of this database contains the field names rather than the first record. If you have a database of 100 records and 10 fields, its coordinates (as far as Quattro Pro is concerned) would therefore be A1..J101. The block A1..J1 would be considered to contain field names. The coordinates of the first record would be A2..J2.

When you define a database query that refers to an external database file, you do not actually need to worry about the database coordinates. You can simply enter a query block setting that uses the form

[*database file name*]A1..A2

and let Quattro Pro determine the number of fields and records (columns and rows) in the database. This block reference only works in queries, however. If you enter database statistical formulas that refer to external databases, the first argument in the function statement (the database block) must refer to all the records and fields that you want included in the calculation.

When you query an external database file, Quattro Pro also lets you refer to the fields within the first record by field name—as if you had issued the / Database | Query | Assign Names command. This allows you to use field names when entering logical formulas in a criteria table.

Figures 24-1 and 24-2 show a spreadsheet designed to perform queries and generate statistics on a dBASE database called MEMBERS.DBF which is stored in the DBASE directory. This database, which contains 1,475 records, contains information on members of a national membership organization.

Figure 24-1 shows the names of members in the MEMBERS.DBF database who joined within the last month. This list was created by first entering the logical formula @TODAY-[C:\DBASE\MEMBERS.DBF]JOINED<=31 in cell A4. This formula tests whether the difference between today's date and the date stored in the JOINED field of the MEMBERS database is less than or equal to 31 days— that is, whether the date in the JOINED field falls within the last month. Next, the block

512   Quattro Pro 2 Made Easy

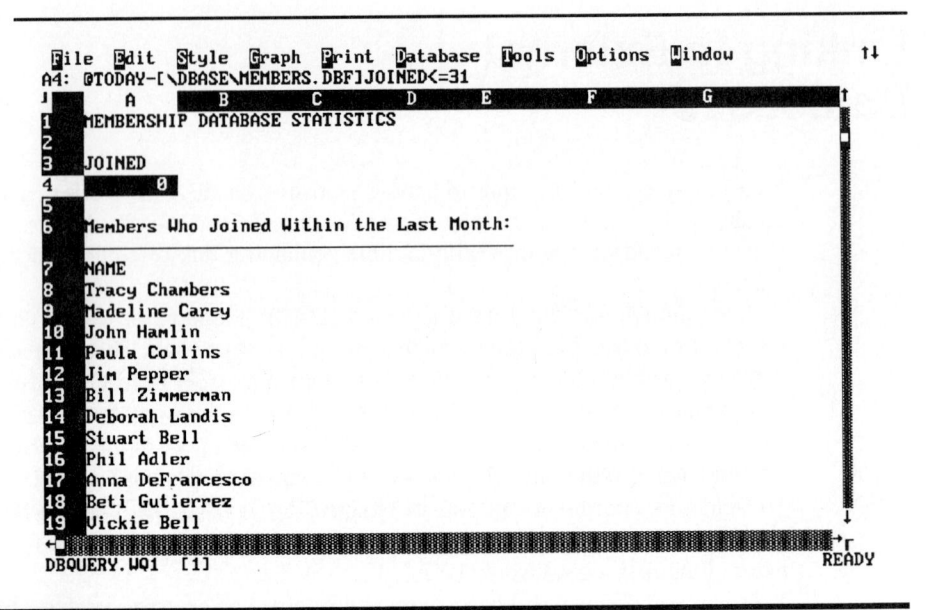

```
 File  Edit  Style  Graph  Print  Database  Tools  Options  Window          ↑↓
A4: @TODAY-[\DBASE\MEMBERS.DBF]JOINED<=31
      A         B         C         D         E         F         G
 1  MEMBERSHIP DATABASE STATISTICS
 2
 3  JOINED
 4         0
 5
 6  Members Who Joined Within the Last Month:
 7  NAME
 8  Tracy Chambers
 9  Madeline Carey
10  John Hamlin
11  Paula Collins
12  Jim Pepper
13  Bill Zimmerman
14  Deborah Landis
15  Stuart Bell
16  Phil Adler
17  Anna DeFrancesco
18  Beti Gutierrez
19  Vickie Bell
DBQUERY.WQ1   [1]                                                        READY
```

Figure 24-1.   Querying an external database

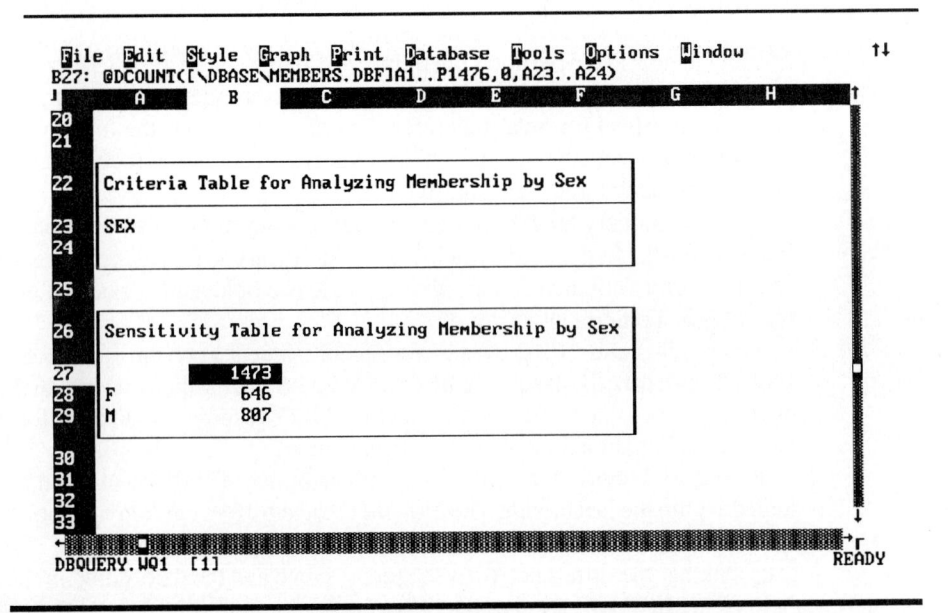

```
 File  Edit  Style  Graph  Print  Database  Tools  Options  Window          ↑↓
B27: @DCOUNT([\DBASE\MEMBERS.DBF]A1..P1476,0,A23..A24)
      A         B         C         D         E         F         G         H
20
21
22  Criteria Table for Analyzing Membership by Sex
23  SEX
24
25
26  Sensitivity Table for Analyzing Membership by Sex
27         1473
28  F       646
29  M       807
30
31
32
33
DBQUERY.WQ1   [1]                                                        READY
```

Figure 24-2.   Gathering statistics from an external database

[\DBASE\MEMBERS.DBF]A1..A2 was specified as the Block setting on the Database | Query menu. (The block coordinates could also have been entered as A1..P1476.) Next, the block A3..A4 was specified as the Criteria Table, and A7 (the label NAME) was designated as the Output Block. Finally, the Extract option on the Database | Query menu was selected.

Figure 24-2 shows a one-variable table for calculating the number of men and women in the database. The table formula in cell B27 is

@DCOUNT([DBASE\MEMBERS.DBF]A1..P1476,0,A23..A24)

The first argument in this statement is a block that includes all the records in the external database plus the field names. The last row referenced is 1476 because there are 1475 records and the first row is reserved for field names. The second argument is 0, indicating an offset of one. This directs Quattro Pro to examine the first field of the database (an account number field) when counting records. The third argument is a block reference to the criteria table. The input cell is A24, the cell immediately below the field name SEX in the criteria table.

Every time you open a spreadsheet that contains link references to an external database file, Quattro Pro displays an Open Links menu with the options Load Supporting, Update Refs, or None, just as it does when you load other primary spreadsheets. If you choose Update Refs or Load Supporting and your database is large, it may take several minutes for Quattro Pro to recalculate the formulas. For this reason, you may want to print your spreadsheet every time you use it. If your data has not changed, it will be far more efficient to view the printout than to load the primary spreadsheet and wait for Quattro Pro to recalculate the link formulas.

Note When you link a spreadsheet to an external database file, you are bound by the same memory constraints that you face when you retrieve databases: there must be room for the entire file to fit in memory at once.

EXPORTING DATA TO WORD PROCESSING SOFTWARE

Exporting Quattro Pro data to word processing software is as simple as printing a spreadsheet. Using the same Quattro Pro print commands covered in Chapter 6, you can send any Quattro Pro report to a disk file rather than to your printer. The resulting file is a straight ASCII text file, a set of text data written in a format that can be interpreted by most standard software packages, including almost all word processing programs.

In most cases, you can obtain better results by handling all report formatting options such as margins, headers, footers, page breaks, and titles from within your word processing program rather than including them in your file when you "print" to disk. This means that you should set the left, top, and bottom margins to zero (using the / Print | Layout | Margins command) before "printing" to a file. You should also make sure that the right margin of the report is no wider than the page width set in your word processor. Set the Print | Layout | Break Pages setting to No so that the file contains one long "page" without any pages breaks, headers, footers, or headings. You should also erase all setup codes before sending reports to disk because they can cause unpredictable results in several word processing programs.

When you have defined your page layout, change the Destination setting on the Print menu to File. When prompted, enter a name for the text file "report." Unless you specify a different extension for the file, Quattro Pro automatically assigns the extension PRN. Then select Spreadsheet Print to "print" the data to a disk file. You can output different sections of the spreadsheet to the same file by simply changing the print block and reselecting the Spreadsheet Print option.

You can also print several different spreadsheets to the same text file, appending new reports to the end of the existing text. Whenever you set the Print | Destination setting to File and specify a name that is already assigned to a disk file, Quattro Pro warns you that a file with that name already exists, just as it does when you try to save a file under an already existing file name. In this case, however, Quattro Pro gives you the option of appending data to the existing file, in addition to the usual options for canceling the command, replacing the old version of the file, or creating a backup file. Select the Append option to add your new report onto the old one.

Once you have printed your data to disk, you are ready to import it into your word processing program. If your word processor has an option for translating ASCII files or DOS text files, you should try using that option first. If it does not have an option for translating ASCII files, try retrieving the report file as is. At worst, you are likely to find carriage returns placed a few characters to the right of where you would like them or experience minor problems with line breaks, which you can repair without much trouble. If you do experience such problems, try experimenting with different margin settings, both before creating the file in Quattro Pro and after retrieving it in your word processing program.

EXPORTING DATA TO OTHER TYPES OF SOFTWARE

Exporting data from Quattro Pro to other types of programs, such as database management programs other than Paradox and dBASE or mainframe computer software, is similar to the process described in the previous section. You create an

ASCII text file by "printing" a report to a disk and then using your other program's facility for importing or processing an ASCII file or DOS text file.

You must observe two rules when creating the ASCII file. First, you should always include just plain data in the file, without any embellishments. This entails setting the top, left, and bottom margins to 0, changing the **Page** I **Layout** I **Break Pages** setting to No, and making sure that no headers, footers, titles, or setup codes are included in your output. In exporting a database, be sure to write only your database records, not the field names, to disk. Second, you must match the structure of the file into which you will be importing data so that the other program will be able to read your file properly.

When you create an ASCII file from Quattro Pro by printing a report to disk, you create a fixed-length file, in which all blank spaces between characters are stored to disk along with the characters themselves. For example, if you have an ACCOUNT field in your database that is ten characters wide and you only fill in six characters, four blank spaces are included before the next field's data. When the data is read into another program, the only way the program "knows" when one field ends and the next begins is by counting characters: The first x characters are the ACCOUNT field, the next x characters are the STATE field, and so on. Therefore, whenever you export Quattro Pro data to a database program other than dBASE or Paradox, the order and widths of the columns (or fields) in the target database file must match those in your Quattro Pro spreadsheet. If they do not, you can make the necessary adjustments at either end of the data transfer process: adjusting the Quattro Pro column widths to match the new database or spreadsheet structure, or arranging your new file in exactly the same format as your Quattro Pro data.

You should also set your right margin to accommodate one entire row of data (and no more) per line because most translation programs interpret a carriage return as an end-of-record marker. For example, if you are exporting a database that is 125 characters wide (consisting of one 25-character column and ten 10-character columns), you would set the left margin to 0 and the right margin to 125.

In general, database programs for mainframe computers do not expect carriage return and line feed characters at the end of each record. You must therefore tell the program that such characters are included in the file.

IMPORTING DATA INTO QUATTRO PRO

You can import data into Quattro Pro by issuing the / **Tools** I **Import** command. This command is similar to the / **Tools** I **Combine** I **Copy** command in that it copies incoming data onto the current spreadsheet, potentially overwriting data. If you do, in fact, want to add the imported data into your current spreadsheet, just move the cell pointer to an empty section of the spreadsheet before issuing the command. Otherwise, be sure to issue the / File I Erase command before importing. Quattro Pro expects you to import files that have PRN extensions, so when you issue the / Tools I Import I ASCII command, Quattro Pro displays a list of all PRN files in the current directory. You can retrieve files with other extensions by entering the file name including the extension.

When you issue the / Tools I Import command, Quattro Pro displays a submenu with the options ASCII Text File, Comma and "" Delimited File, and Only Commas. Most word processing, database, and spreadsheet programs are capable of creating files in at least one of these formats. As discussed next, Quattro Pro handles ASCII text files and delimited files quite differently.

Importing Delimited Files

A Comma and "" Delimited file contains individual items of data separated by commas and character strings enclosed in quotation marks (see Figure 24-3). WordStar MailMerge and some other programs use this format. When you import a delimited file, Quattro Pro places each item of data in a separate column, reading every set of characters enclosed in quotation marks as a label and every other set of characters as

```
C:\QPRO>type delimit.txt
"Robert Bagley","5842 Geary Blvd.","San Francisco","CA","94121",500.00
"Ann McAndrews","420 California Street","San Francisco","CA","94102",2200.00
"Elliot Dryden","25 California Street","San Francisco","CA","94111",3000.00
"Joseph Christian","80 Fremont Street","San Francisco","CA","94105",4500.00
"Anne Webster","530 California Street","San Francisco","CA","94104",2450.00
"Patick Young","800 Montgomery Street","San Francisco","CA","94111",1600.00
"Samuel Levy","100 Bush Street","San Francisco","CA","94111",500.00
"Susan Walton","745 Front Street","San Francisco","CA","94111",1000.00
"Jeffrey Alsop","1240 Ashmont Avenue","Oakland","CA","94610",750.00
"Douglas O'Donnell","450 Pacific Avenue","San Francisco","CA","94133",1000.00

C:\QPRO>
```

Figure 24-3. A comma and quote delimited file

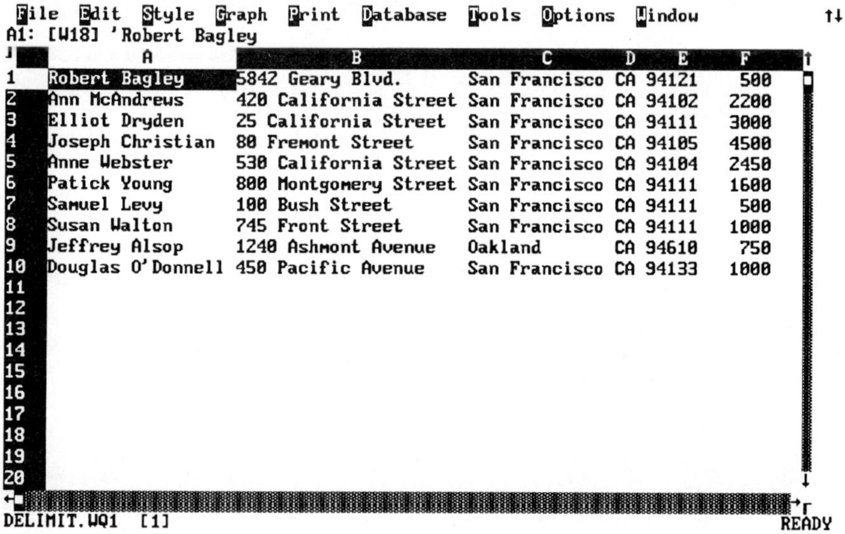

```
File  Edit  Style  Graph  Print  Database  Tools  Options  Window           ↑↓
A1: [W18] 'Robert Bagley
            A                 B                 C         D    E       F
1    Robert Bagley      5842 Geary Blvd.    San Francisco CA 94121     500
2    Ann McAndrews      420 California Street San Francisco CA 94102  2200
3    Elliot Dryden      25 California Street San Francisco CA 94111   3000
4    Joseph Christian   80 Fremont Street   San Francisco CA 94105    4500
5    Anne Webster       530 California Street San Francisco CA 94104  2450
6    Patick Young       800 Montgomery Street San Francisco CA 94111  1600
7    Samuel Levy        100 Bush Street     San Francisco CA 94111     500
8    Susan Walton       745 Front Street    San Francisco CA 94111    1000
9    Jeffrey Alsop      1240 Ashmont Avenue Oakland       CA 94610     750
10   Douglas O'Donnell  450 Pacific Avenue  San Francisco CA 94133    1000
11
...
20
DELIMIT.WQ1  [1]                                                    READY
```

Figure 24-4. Delimited file imported into Quattro Pro

a value. Figure 24-4 shows the same data after importing with the / Tools | Import | Comma and "" Delimited File command and adjusting column widths.

An Only Commas delimited file is just like the Comma and "" Delimited file, except it generally doesn't include quotation marks around character fields. Quotation marks are only used to demarcate a field that happens to contain a comma.

When you create a Comma and " Delimited file, numeric data that includes formatting such as commas or dollar signs is usually written to the delimited file as a character string and, therefore, translated as labels when imported into Quattro Pro. When you import an Only Commas delimited file, Quattro Pro determines field types by examining the first character in that field in the first row of data. If the first character is a dollar sign, the data will be treated as a label. In both cases, the easiest solution is to eliminate these extraneous characters before exporting. Otherwise, you must use Quattro Pro string functions to delete these characters and convert the results to values.

PARSING ASCII TEXT FILES

When you first import an ASCII text file, the data in each row consists of a single long label. Figure 24-5 shows a file created with a word processing program (WordPerfect) and then exported in ASCII format. As you can see on the input line, all of the data in

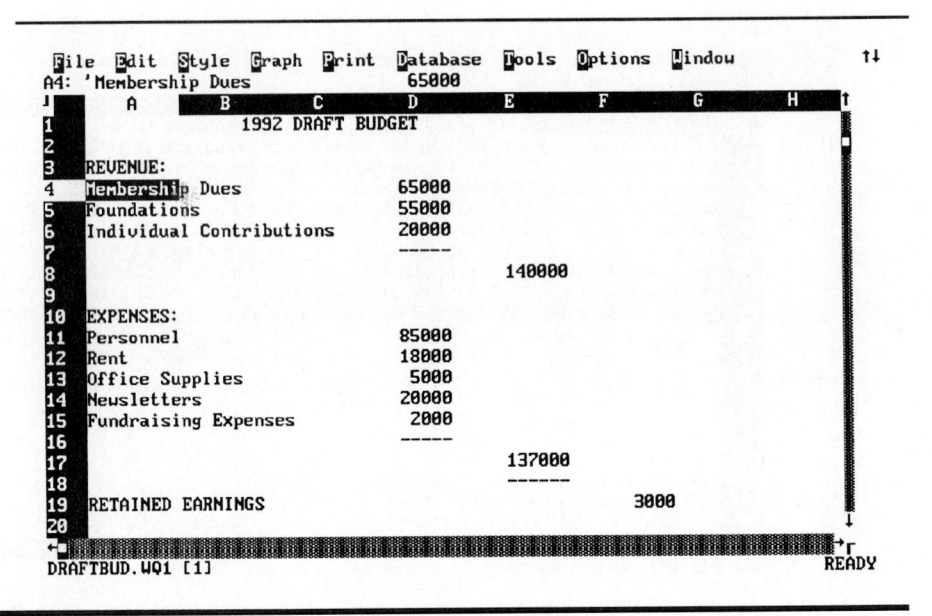

```
    File  Edit  Style  Graph  Print  Database  Tools  Options  Window        ↑↓
A4: 'Membership Dues              65000
        A         B         C         D         E         F         G         H
1                           1992 DRAFT BUDGET
2
3    REVENUE:
4    Membership Dues                65000
5    Foundations                    55000
6    Individual Contributions       20000
7                                   -----
8                                              140000
9
10   EXPENSES:
11   Personnel                      85000
12   Rent                           18000
13   Office Supplies                 5000
14   Newsletters                    20000
15   Fundraising Expenses            2000
16                                  -----
17                                             137000
18                                             ------
19   RETAINED EARNINGS                                       3000
20
DRAFTBUD.WQ1 [1]                                                          READY
```

Figure 24-5. An ASCII text file imported into Quattro Pro

row 4 is stored as a single label in cell A4 even though it spills into adjacent columns on the spreadsheet display. The data in every other row in the file is stored as single labels in column A as well. Before you can effectively use this data in Quattro Pro, you need to divide these long labels by placing each item of data in a separate cell. This process is known as parsing, and consists of the following five steps:

1. Create format lines to guide Quattro Pro in dividing the data into columns by selecting the Create option on the File Parse menu.

2. Edit the format lines as necessary.

3. Define the input block containing the labels to be parsed.

4. Define the output block where you want Quattro Pro to write the newly parsed data.

5. Select the Go option on the File Parse menu to initiate the parse.

All of these steps are simple and straightforward except for the second one, editing the format lines, which can be a little tricky. If the file you are parsing is large, you should save your file with a WQ1 extension before you begin the parsing process.

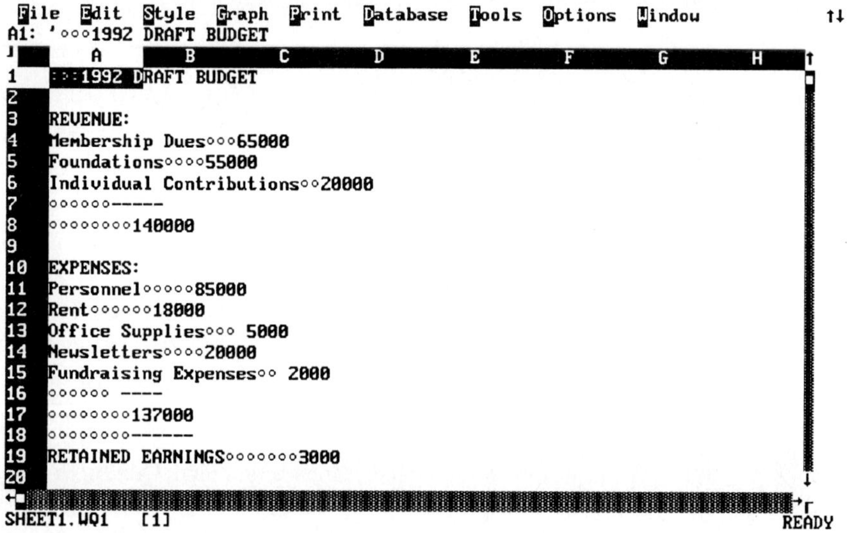

Figure 24-6. An ASCII text file with tab characters

This way, if you need to start over because of an error in parsing, you can save time by retrieving the spreadsheet file rather than importing again, which is a slower operation.

> **Note:** If you use tabs when creating a document in a word processing program and then import that document into Quattro Pro as an ASCII file, the tabs will often show up as ° characters in your spreadsheet, as shown in Figure 24-6. There is no way to eliminate these characters in Quattro Pro shy of manually deleting them. If at all possible, try replacing the tabs with blank spaces in your word processing program before importing the data into Quattro Pro.

Creating Format Lines

The / **Tools** | **Parse** | **Create** command inserts a new row above the current position of the cell pointer. This row, known as a format line, contains symbols indicating how Quattro Pro intends to parse the labels below.

The following seven symbols are used in format lines:

L   Beginning of label block
V   Beginning of value block
D   Beginning of date block
T   Beginning of time block
S   Beginning of skip block
\>   Additional character in block
*   Blank space between blocks

When Quattro Pro initially creates format lines it never uses the S symbol, but you can insert this symbol yourself if you want to exclude a certain section of the data from the output block. Format lines always begin with a | (vertical bar), which is the character that Quattro Pro always uses as a prefix for special codes (such as printing and page break codes).

When you issue the /Tools | Parse | Create command, Quattro Pro displays a format line containing its "best guess" as to how the labels should be split. It uses the data in the row immediately below the format line (the row in which the cell pointer was located when you issued the command) to gauge the column breaks and data types to use for the entire input block. In many cases, you must generate multiple parse format lines because the layout of data is not consistent throughout the spreadsheet. Figure 24-7, for example, contains an imported database with two format lines: one in row 1, which is used as a guide to dividing the field names in row 2, and a second in row 4, which guides the division of database records into individual fields.

To format data correctly, you must use a different format line every time you have a long label directly underneath a format line and then shorter entries that you want to place in separate fields underneath. You also need a new format line every time the type of data changes as you move down one or more columns. In Figure 24-7, for example, a new format line is required immediately above the database records because all the field names need to be entered as labels and the database records include date and numeric data.

As you can see, Quattro Pro does a fairly good job of "guessing" how the labels should be divided. The format line in row 1, for example, correctly breaks the first five field names into individual labels. The only adjustment that must be made is in the PMT DATE field name, which Quattro Pro proposes to split into two fields. In the second format line (row 3 in Figure 24-7), both the name and the address field must be adjusted. The format line indicates a column break after the third character in the first column (the first blank space in the row below the format line) and considers the first three characters in the address field as a value field because they consist of digits in the row below. Note that Quattro Pro has correctly formatted the last field as a date field (that is, as a numeric value displayed in date format). Quattro Pro guesses that a set of characters is a date provided they are entered in any one of Quattro Pro's five date formats. It also properly recognizes times entered in any of Quattro Pro's four time formats. Although the V indicating the start of the ORDERS column is one

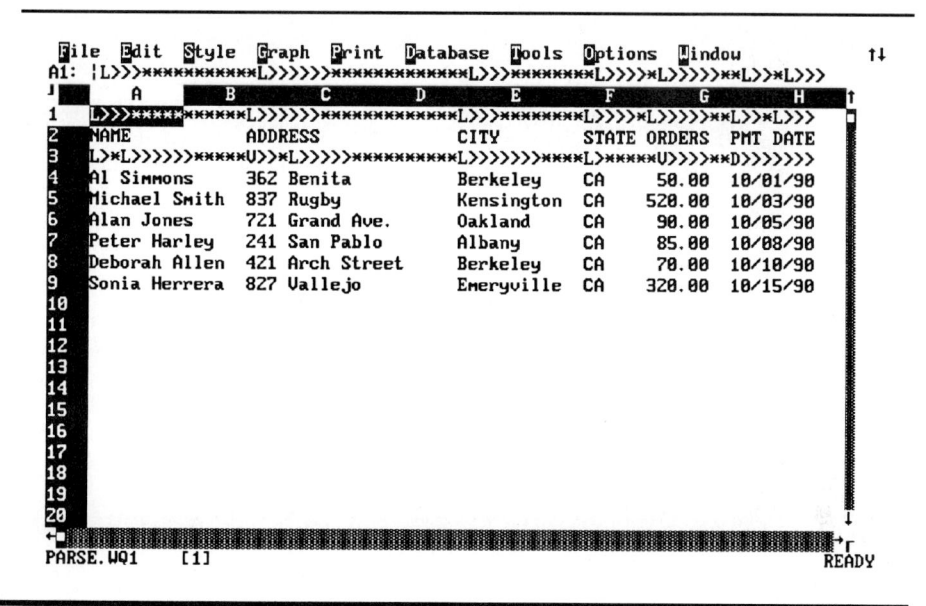

Figure 24-7. ASCII text file with unadjusted format lines

character to the right of the first digit in the column, this will not create a problem when parsing.

Block A12..H18 of Figure 24-8 shows the output produced if you simply accept the format lines created by Quattro Pro without any adjustment. (The column widths have been modified so that you can see all the data.) When you first select the Go option, Quattro Pro simply uses the column widths of the spreadsheet. In many cases, this means that your data will appear to be truncated, and your first task should be to adjust the column widths as necessary so that you can see all the data in each column.

Editing Format Lines

To modify format lines, move the cell pointer to the row containing the format line that you wish to change and issue the / **Tools** | **Parse** | **Edit** command. You can then edit the line— deleting characters and inserting or overwriting characters using one of the seven valid format line symbols—and press (ENTER) when you are done. The usual cursor movement techniques apply: the (END) key takes you to the end of the format line, (HOME) takes you to the beginning, and (TAB) moves the cursor five spaces to the right. If you press (DOWN ARROW), the lines of data underneath the format line

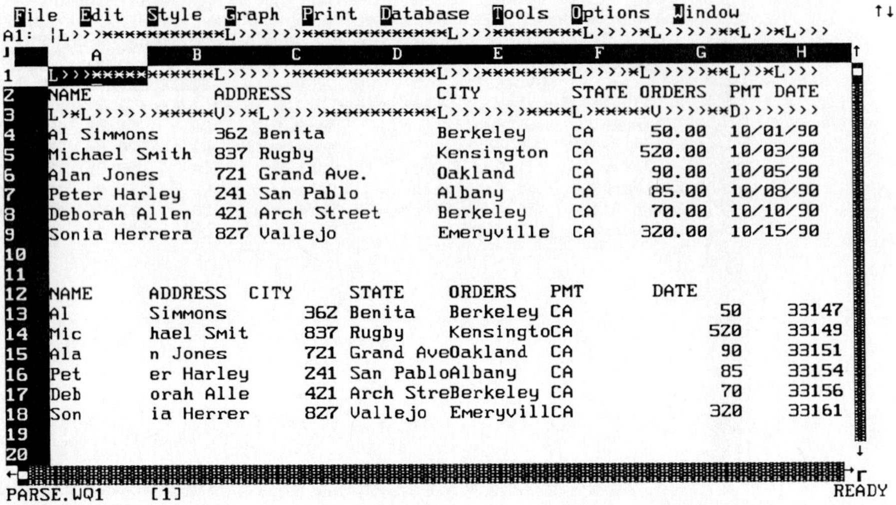

```
     File  Edit  Style  Graph  Print  Database  Tools  Options  Window              ↑↓
A1:    |L>>>********L>>>>>*********L>>>********L>>>*L>>>>**L>>*L>>>
         A           B           C              D         E      F        G       H
  1    L>>>****************L>>>>>**************L>>>>>****L>******U>>>>**D>>>>>>>
  2    NAME        ADDRESS                    CITY       STATE  ORDERS   PMT DATE
  3    L>*L>>>>>>****U>>*L>>>>*************L>>>>>>****L>*****U>>>>**D>>>>>>
  4    Al Simmons      362 Benita            Berkeley    CA      50.00   10/01/90
  5    Michael Smith   837 Rugby             Kensington  CA     520.00   10/03/90
  6    Alan Jones      721 Grand Ave.        Oakland     CA      90.00   10/05/90
  7    Peter Harley    241 San Pablo         Albany      CA      85.00   10/08/90
  8    Deborah Allen   421 Arch Street       Berkeley    CA      70.00   10/10/90
  9    Sonia Herrera   827 Vallejo           Emeryville  CA     320.00   10/15/90
 10
 11
 12    NAME       ADDRESS    CITY      STATE    ORDERS    PMT     DATE
 13    Al         Simmons    362 Benita    Berkeley CA             50     33147
 14    Mic        hael Smit  837 Rugby     KensingtoCA             520    33149
 15    Ala        n Jones    721 Grand AveOakland  CA              90     33151
 16    Pet        er Harley  241 San PabloAlbany   CA              85     33154
 17    Deb        orah Alle  421 Arch StreBerkeley CA              70     33156
 18    Son        ia Herrer  827 Vallejo   EmeryvillCA             320    33161
 19
 20
PARSE.WQ1     [1]                                                         READY
```

Figure 24-8. ASCII text file after parsing

move up on the screen so that you can see how data "lines up" with the format line. You can move the lines back down to their original position by pressing (UP ARROW), or they will move back automatically when you press (ENTER) to finish editing.

You should watch for two potential problems when editing format lines. First, because Quattro Pro uses the row immediately under the format line as a model, each set of characters in that row that is surrounded by blank spaces is interpreted as a separate item of data. This often results in the creation of extra, unintended columns or fields, as shown in column A of the spreadsheet in Figure 24-8. You can correct the problem by extending the > symbol as far as the last character in the column that you want included in the field.

Second, watch for incorrect data types. Specifically, Quattro Pro assumes that blocks of characters consisting entirely of digits, such as Zip codes, should be translated as values. Be sure to change the starting symbol for these blocks from V to L if you want them to be treated as labels.

Figure 24-9 shows the properly edited format lines and the output produced by parsing with those adjusted lines after adjusting column widths. Note that this time Quattro Pro has properly distributed the data across the columns.

Parsing does not affect the column widths. Extending the > symbol beyond the last character of data in a column does not make the column any wider, and you will almost

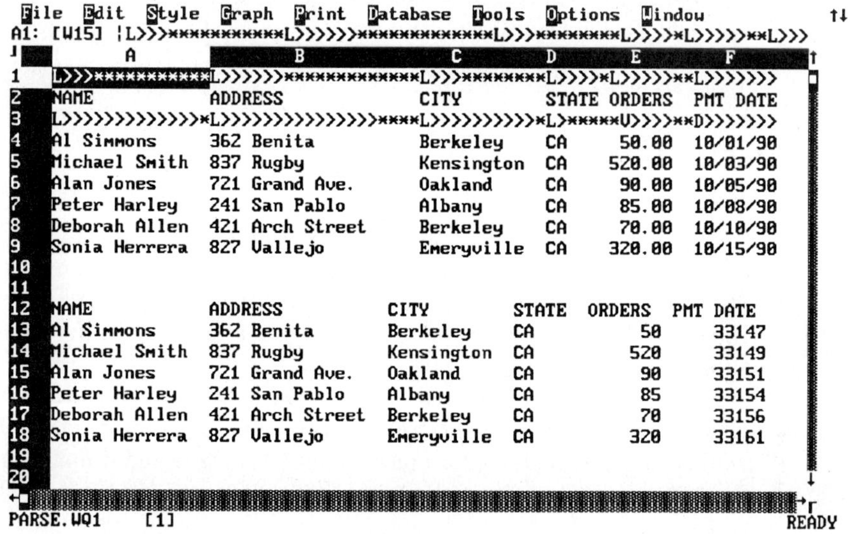

Figure 24-9. ASCII text file after adjusting format lines and parsing

always need to adjust column widths either before or, more commonly, after parsing labels. The / Style | Block Widths | Auto Width command is a great tool for doing this.

Defining Input And Output Blocks

The input block for a file parse should consist of the single-column block containing the labels to be parsed and all the format lines. (Remember that the unparsed labels are displayed across several columns of the spreadsheet, but they are actually stored within a single column.) The output block can consist of either a block of cells, or more commonly, the cell in the upper-left corner of the area where you want Quattro Pro to place the newly parsed data. Although Quattro Pro allows you to overwrite the input block by specifying a cell at the upper-left corner of the unparsed labels, this can be dangerous. If you overwrite the unparsed labels and then discover that you have made a mistake in parsing, you can use / Edit | Undo to undo the operation, provided that you notice the mistake right away and have previously enabled the Undo feature.

Otherwise, you will need to import your ASCII text file again, or if you have already saved the data in Quattro Pro, retrieve your spreadsheet and start over.

Initiating the Parse

Once you have created and edited your format lines and defined the input and output block for a parse, select Go on the Tools | Parse menu to initiate the parse. Quattro Pro will divide up the labels according to your specifications, delete any blank rows, and delete the format lines. In most cases, you will still need to make at least a few adjustments to the data.

This chapter has introduced commands and strategies for exchanging data with other software packages. These techniques enable you to use Quattro Pro in concert with other types of software. You can translate data to and from Quattro Pro format on a one-time basis or regularly, using different types of software to perform the types of work for which they are best suited. You can, for example, use your word processing program to enhance Quattro Pro's report printing capabilities or use Quattro Pro to perform periodic statistical analysis of your dBASE database. Rarely can a single software package meet all your informational and reporting needs. The more you learn to integrate various software packages, the more computing power and flexibility you will have at your disposal.

A

NEW FEATURES IN QUATTRO PRO 2

Solve For
New Display Options
Paradox Access
Improved LaserJet Printing
Support for the Lotus 1-2-3 Release 2.2 File Format
Three-Dimensional Graph Types
Graph Buttons
Copying Graphs
Saving Graphs in Slide EPS and PCX Formats
Importing CGM Clip Art

Quattro Pro 2 was announced just as this book was on its way to the printer. This appendix summarizes the most important new features and provides a few notes on how to use them.

SOLVE FOR

The /Tools | Solve For command makes it possible for Quattro Pro 2 to find the value of a cell that will produce a desired target value in another cell. For example, suppose you want to know what size of 30-year fixed mortgage you can afford, given an interest rate of 9.25 percent and maximum monthly payments of $5,000. To solve this problem with / Tools | Solve For, you could proceed as follows:

1. In B2, enter a hypothetical principal amount—say, **$750,000**.
2. Enter **+9.25%/12** in B3.
3. Enter **360** in B4.
4. Enter **@PMT(B2,B3,B4)** in B5.

The formula in B5 now returns approximately $6,170, which means the hypothetical loan amount is too high. To find out what amount you can afford, continue as follows:

5. Issue the **/T**ools | Solve For command.
6. Choose Formula Cell and enter **B5**.
7. Choose Target Value and enter **5000**.
8. Choose Variable Cell and enter **B2**.
9. Choose Go.

Quattro Pro 2 puts the appropriate value, 607773, in cell B2.

NEW DISPLAY OPTIONS

The /Options | Display Mode command now includes many more options. Depending on your video hardware, you may be able to see as many as 132 columns of data on screen at once. To see what choices are available, issue the /**O**ptions | Display Mode command and scroll through the list box.

If you accidentally select a display option that your hardware does not support, your screen may become scrambled. If that happens, you can restore the normal display by following these steps:

1. Press <kbd>CTRL-BREAK</kbd>.
2. Issue the /Options | Display Mode command and select the 80x25 text display mode.

PARADOX ACCESS

If you have Paradox version 3.5 or later and at least 2 MB of memory, you can take advantage of Quattro Pro 2's Paradox Access feature. This allows you to start Paradox and then run Quattro Pro 2 without quitting Paradox. Once you're in Quattro Pro 2, you can load a Paradox table, work with the table, and then return to Paradox with a single keystroke.

With Borland's SQL Link (a separate product available for version 3.5 or later of Paradox), you can also use Paradox Access to retrieve information stored in a remote SQL database and work with that information in Quattro Pro 2.

IMPROVED LASERJET PRINTING

Quattro Pro 2 offers faster printing to Hewlett-Packard LaserJet and compatible printers. The new version also supports the 25-in-One printer cartridges from Pacific Data Products.

SUPPORT FOR THE LOTUS 1-2-3 RELEASE 2.2 FILE FORMAT

Lotus 1-2-3 Release 2.2 uses a slightly different syntax to record file-linking formulas (formulas that reference cells in another file) than Quattro Pro 2. Quattro Pro 2 can translate the Lotus syntax into Quattro Pro 2's syntax and vice versa.

When you use /File | Retrieve to load a WK1 file, Quattro Pro 2 automatically converts any Release 2.2 file-linking formulas to Quattro Pro 2's syntax. When you use /File | Save to save a file with the WK1 extension, if that file contains file-linking formulas, Quattro Pro 2 will display a warning message and give you three choices:

- If you choose No, Quattro Pro 2 aborts the save.

- If you choose Yes, Quattro Pro 2 converts all file-linking formulas to their current values (removing the formulas) and saves the file in Lotus format. This option allows you to reuse the file in 1-2-3 Release 2.01.

- If you choose Use 2.2 Syntax, Quattro Pro 2 converts the file-linking formulas to Release 2.2's syntax. Because 1-2-3 Release 2.2 formulas can reference only single cells (not ranges) in external worksheets, Quattro Pro 2 changes any external range references so that they reference the first value in the range.

Caution: If you choose No, the original WK1 file is removed from disk. If you want to use this worksheet again, be sure to save it as a WQ1 (Quattro Pro 2) file.

THREE-DIMENSIONAL GRAPH TYPES

The /Graph | Graph.Type menu has a new option, called 3-D Graphs. Choosing this option presents a submenu with four additional graph types: Bar, Ribbon, Step, and Area. You'll find these new graph types invaluable for charting multiple data series.

GRAPH BUTTONS

Using the Annotator in Quattro Pro 2, you can add "buttons" to graphs. A button is a special kind of "active" text field, linked either to another graph or to a macro. When you click the mouse on a button, the display switches to the linked graph, or the associated macro runs.

To create a graph button, follow these steps:

1. Display the graph.

2. Press / to activate the Annotator.

3. Choose the text icon to create a text box.

4. Type what you want the button to say.

5. Press [ENTER].

6. Use the pointer tool to position and size the button as desired.

7. Choose Graph Button on the Boxed Text menu. The Annotator prompts for a name. If you want the button linked to another graph, type the name of that graph. If you want the button linked to a macro, type the name of your macro (or type the actual macro commands).

8. Choose Quit to leave the Annotator.

9. Use the /Graph | Name | Create command to save your graph.

The button will be active whenever your graph is displayed in full screen. It is not active when you're working in the Annotator or when the graph is displayed on the worksheet.

You can put as many buttons as you like on a graph.

COPYING GRAPHS

In Quattro Pro 2, you can copy graphs from one spreadsheet to another. Follow these steps:

1. Name the graph with /Graph | Name | Create.

2. Open the spreadsheet to which you want to copy the graph (if it's not already in memory). This is the target worksheet.

3. Return to the source worksheet (the one in which you created the graph), and issue the /Graph | Name | Graph Copy command.

4. Move to the target worksheet and press (ENTER).

SAVING GRAPHS IN SLIDE EPS AND PCX FORMATS

The /Print | Graph Print menu has two additional options in Quattro Pro 2. To save a graph in a format suitable for generating a 35mm slide, choose Slide EPS. To save a graph in the PCX format (so you can import it into another program that supports PCX files), choose PCX File.

IMPORTING CGM CLIP ART

The Annotator in Quattro Pro 2 allows you to import clip-art images stored in the CGM (Computer Graphics Metafile) format. To do so, just follow the same procedure you would use to import a CLP file. From the Clipboard menu, choose Paste From. Then specify the name of your CGM file.

INDEX

A

Absolute cell references, 87
Accounts receivable, schedule of, (illus., 226)
Align option, 128, 132
Alignment
    changing default label, 110-112
    default, 96
    default label, 112
    label, 36-38, 110-112
    of blocks, 110-112
    of numeric values, 112
Alignment character, 141
Alignment code, hidden, 112
Annotator, 7, 327-347
    activating property sheet in, 337-338
    defined, 327, 328
    environment, 328-332
    functions keys, 329
    menus, 329
    organized text chart in, (illus., 341)
    screen, 328-330, (illus., 328)
    selecting an element in, (illus., 336)
    toolbox for, 330-332
Area graph, 279, 296, (illus., 280)
Argument
    block, 157
    character string, 157
    numeric, 157
Arithmetic formulas, 51
    contents, 52
    length, 52
Arithmetic operators, 52, (list, 52), (exercise, 52)
Arrow keys, 10, 11, 14
    in macro recording, 484
    moving cell pointer with, 14

Arrow keys, *continued*
    used in Help, 22
Art, importing clip, 530
ASCII codes, 134, 176
ASCII files, creating, 515
ASCII text file, 516
    after format lines and parsing, (illus., 523)
    after parsing, (illus., 522)
    imported into Quatro Pro, (illus., 519)
    parsing, 517-524
    with tab characters, (illus., 519)
    with unadjusted format lines, (illus., 521)
Asterisks, 39
    in column width, 106
Attributes, changing font, 144
AUTOEXEC.BAT, 416
Autoload file, 421
Autoloading macros, 501-502
Automatic line feed option, 126-127
Automatic recalculation, 4, 55-57, (illus., 57), (exercise, 56-57)
Autoscale fonts, 126, 303
AVG function, 160, 162

B

Backslash, 38
Backup files, storing, 429
Balance sheet, (illus., 458)
Bar graphs, 276-279, (illus., 277, 313)
    regular, 277
    rotated, 277, (illus., 278)
    stacked, 278, (illus., 279)
    translating numbers into, 102
    with an ellipse, (illus., 346)
    with text and arrow, (illus., 334)

Baud rate, 125
Bin values, 411
Bins, 411
Bitstream fonts, 142-143. *See also* Fonts, bitstream.
Block
    destination, 77
    source, 77
    source and destination in copying, 80
Block coordinates
    pointing out, 62
    typing, 61-62
Block corners, "remembering," 78
Block names
    changing, 190
    choices list and, 186, 187
    create command and, 187
    creating a table of, 191-192
    deleting, 190
    dollar sign and, 186-187
    formulas and, 186
    in a formula, (illus., 189)
    length of, 188
    restoring deleted, 190
    using in macros, 486
Blocks, 60-61
    advantages of named, 185-186
    cautions on moving and copying, 87-88
    copying, 76
    copying and moving, (illus., 92, 93), (exercise, 90-94)
    defined, 60
    defining in Point mode, 76-80
    defining input and output, 523-524
    designating, 61-62
    erasing, 90
    filled with values, 204-206
    inserted row effect on referenced, (illus., 73)
    listed with choices key, 188
    manipulating, 75-90
    moving corner cells of, 186
    named with adjacent labels, 190-191
    naming, 187
    options for defining, 76
    overwriting named, 186

Blocks, *continued*
    pointing out in advance of manipulating, 79
    referencing cell, 60-62
    table of named, (illus., 193)
    transposing, 209-211
    using named, 185-192
Boldface type, 134
Borders, drawing, 38
Box, drawing around title, 117-118
Boxes, drawing, 115
Break Pages setting, 135
Budget, (illus., 5)
Building Font message, 142
Bullets, adding, 153-154
Buttons
    graph, 528
    mouse palette, 24-25

C

Calculation, order of with arithmetic operators, 59-60, (illus., 59)
Calculations, performed by Quattro Pro, 4
Calculator, contrasted with Quattro Pro, 4
Capitalization, importance of in setup strings, 134
Case Sensitive option, 203
Cell address, 31
Cell blocks, copying multiple, 82-84
Cell pointer, 10, 30
    in defining blocks, 76-77
    moving, 88, 89
    moving with mouse, 24
Cell references, 53-55, (illus., 54), (exercises, 182-184)
    absolute, 87, 180-184, (illus., 180, 182, 185)
    after naming blocks, (illus., 192)
    coordinates of, 181
    including in a formula, 58
    mixed, 184
    relative, 86-87, 180-184, (illus., 184)
    within a formula, 53, (exercise, 54-55)
Cells
    copying, 80-84, (illus., 81)
    determining address of, 10, (illus., 11)

Cells, *continued*
    duplicate, 239
    in spreadsheet area, 10
    locked, 239, (illus., 242)
    modifying, 214
    naming, (exercise, 188-189)
    protecting, (exercise, 215)
    referencing blocks of, 60-62
    removing duplicate, 239
    reprotecting, 215
    shading, 119-122, (illus., 120, 121)
    unhiding, 103
    unprotecting, 214
Centering, columns, 111-112, (illus., 111)
CGA monitor, 267
CGM (Computer Graphics Metafile) format, 530
Change directory (CD) command, 7
CHAR function, 176
Choices key ((F3)), 185-186, 188, 479
CIRC error message, 65
Circular cell references, 63-65
    using recalculation menu to find, 65, (illus., 65)
Click, 23
Clip art
    creating files of, 345-346
    importing, 530
    proportional resize mode for, 345-346
Clipboard, 344
Clock display, changing, 18, 19, (illus., 19)
Codes, removed by Quattro Pro, 505
Color (printer) option, 144
Color settings, conditional, 264-265
Colors
    defined for labels, 264
    designating, 264
    emphasizing data with, 264-265
    for unprotected cells, 264
    reinstating default, 265
    selection on Screen Previewer, 149
Column and row borders, eliminating, 243
Column graphs, 280-281, (illus., 282)
    defining, 298-300
Column heading, entry of numeric, 37-38
Column width codes, eliminating, 97

Column widths
    adjusting, 96-97
    changing, 34-36
    changing several, 98-99
    default, 35, 96
    increasing by macro, 486
    measuring, 147
Columns
    concealing, 211
    copying multiple-cell blocks down, 82-84
    deleting, 75
    hiding, 211-213, (illus., 212), (exercise, 212-213)
    inserting, 75, (exercise, 191)
    labels transposed to, (illus., 210)
    leaving blank space at beginning of, 99
    separating, 112
    transposing two, (illus., 211)
    undoing hide command, 213
Comma format, 102, (illus., 104), (exercise, 104)
Command keys, Screen Previewer, (table, 151)
Command shortcuts, 91, (exercise, 273-274)
    menu, (table, 273)
Commands, sequence of, 19
Comparison operators, 167
Compound words, in menu-equivalent commands, 482
Concatenation, 174
Conditional setting, (illus., 264)
Constants, distinguished from formulas, 57
Control-Break, 20
Control buttons, 21
Control character, 134
Coordinates cell, 10
Copying
    cells, 80-84
    data, 450
    files, 441
    formatted cells, 107
    formulas, 84-87
    multiple-cell blocks across rows or down columns, 82-84
    single cell across a block, 81-82, (illus., 82)

Corrections, 41-42. *See also* Editing.
COUNT function, 160
CTRL-F numeric format command
    shortcut, 105
Currency format, 102
Currency setting, changing the,
    (illus., 266)
Current cell, 10, 11
Cursor movement keys, 14
    in data editing, 42
    in data entry, 30
    in macro recording, 484,
        (table, 483)
Curves, drawing, 342
Custom menus, creating, 495
Cutting and pasting. *See also* Copying.
    graph elements, 344-345

D

Dashes, 38-39, (illus., 39)
    substituting for lines, 147
Data
    default label prefix for, 355
    editing, 41-44
    exchange with other programs,
        503-504
    exchanging with Lotus 1-2-3 and
        Symphony, 504-505
    exporting to other software, 514-515
    exporting to word processing,
        513-514
    extracting, 450
    extracting combinations of,
        (illus., 390)
    extracting from a logical formula,
        (illus., 384)
    importing to Quattro Pro, 515-517
    problems in exchanging, 510
    restricting the type of, 354-355
    trading with Paradox, dBASE and
        Reflex, 505-513
    translating into external format, 507
    types, 31-33
    values, 351
Data blocks, aligning, 110-112
Data entry, 30, 31
    commands, 354-355

Data field names, 352-353
    entering, 353
    number of characters in, 353
Data fields
    freezing, 352
    location of, 352
Data type codes for map view, 246
Database fields, 350
    assigning names to, 385
    key fields as, 367
    sort keys as, 367
Database files, generating statistics on, 511
Database formulas, 353-354, 513
Database functions, entering, 393-395
Database logical formulas, 386
Database macros, 488-493
Database management, 6, 505
Database program memory, 506
Database query, 376-377
    assigning field names to, 376
    commands, 375-377
    complex searches in a criteria table,
        381-383
    criteria, 377-379
    criteria table, 377-386, (illus., 380),
        (exercise, 379-381)
    defining, 376
    defining an output block for, 376
    formulas for criteria table, 383-386
    options for, 376
    resetting, 391
    using exact match criteria in, (illus.,
        378)
Database records, 350. *See also* Databases.
    adding new, 360-362, (illus., 361)
    defining output blocks of, 387
    deleting, 360-362, 391
    eliminating duplicate, 388
    extracting, 387-388
    extracting unique, 388-391
Database statistical functions, 391-395
Database statistics, generating, 405-407,
    409-410, (illus., 394)
Database terminology, 350, (illus., 350)
Databases, 5-7, 349-366
    adding records to with macros,
        488-493, (illus., 491, 492)
    ascending default sort in, 368-369

Databases, *continued*
 building sample, 355-360
 calculated fields in, 353
 cell referencing in, 353-354
 changing numeric formats in, 362
 changing order of labels in, 373
 changing sort rules in, 373
 characteristics of, 5
 comparison operators in, 385
 complex conditions in logical formulas in, 386
 creating, 349-366
 deleting records from, 362
 descending default sort in, 369
 designing, 350-354
 displaying sort menu in, 368
 estimating size of, (illus., 427)
 fields in, 351-353, (illus., 359)
 inserting new records in, 362
 label order option in, 373
 labels in ASCII codes in, 369
 linking external, 511
 logical formulas in, 384-386
 modifying, 362-366
 multiple-key sorts in, 371
 querying external, (illus., 512)
 rearranging field order in, 362
 records, 520
 relative cell referencing in, (illus., 354)
 retrieving external, 510
 searching values and labels in, 377
 selecting records from, 375-395
 sensitivity tables used with, 405-410
 single-key sorts in, 369-371
 sort order in, 368-369
 sorting, 367-373, (exercise, 368)
 sorting with macro, (illus., 494)
 statistics from external, (illus., 512)
 undoing a sort in, 371-372
 values and labels in, 351-352
Date and time, inserted with NOW function, 232-233
Date arithmetic, 220-221, (exercise, 220)
Date codes, elimination of, 219
Date formats, 103, 219, (exercise, 219-220)
Date formulas, (illus., 229)

Date functions, 221-228, 230, (illus., 227, 229), (exercise, 228)
Date macro, 481-482
Date serial number, 218
Date-stamping, macro for, 478
Dates, 217-230
 displaying, 18, (illus., 19)
 entering with functions, 225-228
 entering as a label, 41
 entering as a value, 41, (illus., 42)
 extracting part of, 221-222
 for column headings, (illus., 230)
 formats for, 218
 formatting numbers as, 219
 International options for, 219
 printing current, 132
 with missing day or year, 218
DAVG function, 393
DAY function, 221, 222
Day of week, determining, 223-224
dBASE
 saving a file for, 507, 508, 509-510
 trading data with, 505-513
dBASE files
 deleted records in, 506-507
 reading, 506-507
 saving and retrieving, 510
 writing, 507-508
dBASE memo fields, 509-510
DCOUNT function, 392
Decimal places, 162-163
 functions for, 162-163
 in default format display, 100
Default directory
 changing the, 417-418
 displaying files in a, 417
Default format setting, 99-100
Default formats, 96
 changing, 103
Default settings, 261-272
 clock, 270
 colors, 263-265
 expanded memory, 269-270
 international, 265-267
 macro, 269
 paradox, 270
 recalculation, 270-271

536 Quattro Pro 2 Made Easy

Default settings, *continued*
    spreadsheet, 262
    updating the system, 271-272
Deletion
    block names, 190
    effect on formatting code of, 105
    effective on label alignments, 110
Destination option, 129
Directories, 415-418. *See also* Directory.
    loading Quattro Pro from, 416
    making, 447
    ordered by name, 445
Directory
    changing the default, 417
    deleting the, 443
    parent, 437
    permanent change of default, 417
    temporary, 417
Directory tree pane
    enlarging the, 445, (illus., 446)
Directory trees, 444-446
    resizing, 445-446
    root directory on, 445
Directory structures, moving between, 445
Discount payment date formula, 220
Discounts, calculating with arithmetic, (illus., 221)
Disk, saving to, 45-47
Disk space
    exceeding, 422
    managing, 422
    saving, 422
    saving a file too large for the, 422
Display, 8-12
    sections, 8, (illus., 9)
DMAX function, 393-395
DMIN functions, 393-395
Draft-quality printing, 130-132
Drag, (definition), 23-24
DSUM function, 392-393

E

Edit Fonts option, 143-144
Edit mode, 42
    entering with a mouse, 44
Editing, data, 41-44
    title, (illus., 43), (exercise, 43-44)

Editing commands, advanced, 197-215
Editing keys, (table, 44)
    macro, (table, 484)
EGA monitor, 267
Elements, moving, 347. *See also* Blocks.
(END) key
    combinations with, 88-89,
        (exercise, 89-90)
    defining large blocks with, 88-90
    moving about with, 94
Epson printers, code for, 134
Erasing, 30, 42
    blocks, 90
    entire cell contents, 31
    graphs, 298
ERR message, in row deletion, 74
ERR value, 66-67
Error messages, 88
    in formula entry, 62-63, (listed, 63)
Errors, typographical, 63
(ESC) key, 15, 20
Escape sequence, 134
Excel file, imported into Quattro Pro, 505
Execute option, in macro menu, 479
Exit, 27-28, 48
Expanded memory, 428
Exponential notation, display in, 102
Extension, file, 48, 49

F

Field length, changing, 508
Field type, altering a, 508
File compression, menu for, 423-424
File format, external, 507
File list pane, 432, 436-438. *See also* File manager.
    check marks in, 436
    extensions in, 436
    special keys in, (table, 439)
File lists, 418, (illus., 437)
    manipulating, 418-421
    obtaining information with plus sign, 418
    rereading, 447
    searching, 419
    sorted, 438
    specific, 419-420

Index

File manager, 431-448
    activating panes, 433
    changing start-up directory in, 435-436
    control pane, 432-436
    opening files, 434-435
    options, 446-448
    printing contents of window of, 447-448
    searching for files, 435
    selecting files to display, 434
    sorting file lists, 438
    status line, (illus., 436)
    switching directories, 433
    window, 432-433, (illus., 432)
    window with directory tree, (illus., 444)
File menu
    opening, 18, (illus., 17)
File name, 46
    caution in changing extension in, 443-444
File not found message, 416
File overwriting, 441
File retrieval, 45
File structure, modifying, 508-509
Files
    backing up, 429
    combining, 450-457, (exercises, 453-457)
    command for adding values in, 452-453
    command for copying, 452
    command for subtracting values in, 453
    compressing, 423-424
    copying, 441-442
    deleting, 443
    delimited, (illus., 516)
    directions for displaying, 420
    duplicating, 443
    encrypted, 421
    erasing, 509
    extensions for compressing, 423
    extract command, 449
    extracting, 449-450
    importing delimited, 516-517, (illus., 517)

Files, *continued*
    linking distinguished from combining, 473
    managing, 415-430
    manipulating, 438-444
    moving, 442
    opening, 440-441
    options for combining, 450-451
    renaming, 443-444
    resaving, 47-48, (illus., 47)
    retrieving, 48-50, (illus., 49), (exercise, 50)
    saving for first time, 45-46, (illus., 46)
    saving on a different disk, 422
    selecting, 440
    shortcut for reviewing, 420-421
    stored in compressed form, 423
Fixed format, 102
Font, default, 143
Font code, eliminating, 143
Fonts, 130, (exercise, 145-146)
    autoscaling, 126, 303
    Bitstream, 141, 144, 149, (illus., 146)
    Hershey, 141, 144
    option, 126
    printer-specific, 141, 144
    problems with, 146-149
    proportional, 147
    saving, 144
    using, 141
Footers, adding, 132
Footnotes, printing, 134
Form Feed option, 128
Format, moving with cell, 106-107
Format lines
    creating, 519-521
    editing, 521-523
    symbols for, 520
Formats, default, 96, 113-122
    advantages, 114
Formats, display, 99-109, (table, 101), (listed, 105)
Formatted cells, formatting, 107
Formatting, 95-122
    commands, 197-215, (table, 97)
    data, 520
    general rules for, 122

Formulas, 51-68, 179-195
    absolute cell references in, 180-184
    adjusted during moving of blocks, 79
    and named blocks, 185-192
    beginning characters in, 55
    circular references in, 64-65, (illus., 64)
    converted to their values, 192-195
    copying, 84-87, (illus., 85, 86), (exercise, 84)
    effect of copying, 86
    error messages in entry of, 62-63, (listed, 63)
    freezing, 192
    mistakes, 62-65
    mixed cell references in, 184
    overwriting, 57
    printing, 153
    recalculating, 87
    recalculating in database, 408
    referencing other, (illus., 56)
    relative cell references in, 180-184
    showing with text format, 108-109, (illus., 109)
    spreadsheet, 4
    transposing, 211
Frequency distribution table, 397, (illus., 411, 412)
    creating, 411-413
Function arguments, 161
Function formula, 157
Function keys, 15-16
    coded colors for, 15
    macro, (table, 483)
    template, 15
Function statements, constructing, 158
Functions, 155-177
    arguments for, 157
    AVG, 160
    basic statistical, 159-162
    blank cells and labels in, 161-162
    CHAR, 176
    complex operator, 168-170
    constructing SUM function, 158
    COUNT, 160
    date and time, 156
    database statistical, 156
    dropping decimal, 162-168

Functions, *continued*
    financial, 156
    formula, 157
    help with, 176-177
    HLOOKUP, 170-173
    INT, 163
    key, 158
    logical, 156
    lookup, 156
    mathematical, 156
    MAX and MIN, 161
    miscellaneous, 157
    nesting, 158
    REPEAT, 175-176
    ROUND, 163-166
    statement, 157
    statistical, (illus., 159)
    string, 156, 174-176
    SUM, 159-160
    syntax, 157-158
    system, 156-157
    types of, 156-157
    VLOOKUP, 170-173

G

General format, 99-100, 102
    characteristics of, 99-100
Global column width setting, overriding, 97
Global option settings, 262
GoTo key ([F5]), 16
Graph axes, customizing, 320-322
    logarithmic scaling for, 322
    manual scaling of, 320-321
    scaling display for, 322
    scaling steps for, 321
    tick marks for, 321
Graph colors, customizing, 310
Graph design element icons, 331-332
Graph elements
    changing design properties of, 337-338
    cutting and pasting, 344-345
    linking points to, (exercise, 342-344)
    modifying, 336-339
    modifying non-Annotator, 339
    resizing, 337

Index

Graph fill patterns, altering, 310
Graph handles, 336
Graph key ([F10]), warning about, 16
Graph name, reusing a, 297
Graph points, linking elements to, 342-344
Graph print layout, 304
Graph print options, updating, 304-305
Graph series
    customizing, 309
    defining a group of, 293-297
    eliminating, 315
    erasing, 298
    pie/column slices, 310-311
Graph settings
    resetting, 315
    updating, 315
Graph slide show, 305-306
Graph text
    changing the color of, 310
    legends, 288-289
    titles, 287-288
Graph titles, 287-288
    bullets in, 288
    character length for, 288
    referencing a cell with, 288
Graph types
    number of, 275
    overriding, 313
Graph x-axis, erasing, 298
Graphics, 7
Graphics mode, mouse in, 23
Graphing process, 285-287
    annotating, 287
    printing, 287
    saving, 287
Graphs, 279-284
    adding text and lines to, 332-336
    adding text to, 287
    adjusting print speed for, 303
    adjusting quality for, 303
    area, 279
    autoscaling fonts for, 303
    bar, 276-277
    changing lines and markers of, 311
    changing print layout for, 303-304
    changing width of bar, 312
    choosing, 275-301
    clipboard for, 344

Graphs, *continued*
    copying, 529
    column, 280-281
    creating, 275-308, (exercise, 289-292)
    creating text in, 332
    customized as a whole, 322-326
    customizing, 309-326
    customizing grid lines of, 324
    defining pie and column, 298-300
    defining XY, 300-301
    displaying in black and white, 325-326
    drawing arrows in, 333
    drawing curves in, 342
    drawing ellipses in, 333
    drawing horizontal and vertical lines in, 333
    drawing polylines and polygons, 333
    drawing rectangles, 333
    eliminating 3-D in, 326
    fast, 292-293, (illus., 294, 295)
    fill patterns for, 277
    framing, 324
    gallery of, (illus., 290)
    high-low, 283-284
    inserted in a spreadsheet, 268, 306-308
    interior labels in, 312-313
    labeling points on, 312-313
    line, 276
    location of labels in, 312
    naming, 297-298
    numeric values, 293
    pie, 280
    presentation-quality, (illus., 8)
    printing, 301-305, 307-308
    printing to disks, 305
    regular bar, 277
    relocating the referenced cell for, 288
    removing inserted, 307
    resetting series and, 298
    restoring, 297-298
    rotated bar, 277
    saving in slide EPS and PCX formats, 529
    shortcuts in creating, 292-297
    stacked, 278
    texts in, 284, (exercise, 334-336)

Graphs, *continued*
    three-dimensional, 285-289, 528
    types, 7
    with a second Y-axis, 314-315
    with title, legend and outlines,
        (illus., 324)
    with two Y-axes, (illus., 314)
    without logarithmic scaling, (illus.,
        323)
    XY, 281
Gridlines, 115, 118 119, (illus., 118, 119)

H

Headers, adding, 132
Help, 20-22
    keywords, 21
Help display, on Screen Previewer, 149
Help icon, 24
Help Topics screen, 21, (illus., 22)
Hidden alignment code, 112
    eliminating, 112
Hidden format, 103
High-low graphs, 283-284, (illus., 283)
HLOOKUP function, 170-173, (illus., 174)
Home cell, 10
(HOME) key, 14
HP LaserJet printer, 120. *See also* LaserJet
    printer.

I

IBM graphics printers, code for, 134
IF argument condition, 166-168
IF function, 166, (illus., 168, 170)
Income statement, building a, (exercise, 67-68)
Input cell, 398, 401, 402-403
Input line, 8, 10-11
    information in cell distinguished form,
        35
    pointer method help from, 77
Input values
    in one-variable table, 398
    in two-variable table, 402
Input variables, 403
Insert mode, 42
Installing Quattro Pro, 7, 416

Instant Replay option, in macro menu, 477
INT function, 166
    difference with ROUND function,
        166
Interactive commands, in macro creation, 495
International settings
    currency, 265
    dates and times, 267
    punctuation, 265-266

K

Keyboard, 12-16
    layout, (illus., 13)
Key-equivalent commands, 482, (table,
    483-484)
Keypad, numeric, 14
Keys
    movement, 14-15
    nonalphanumeric, (listed, 12-13)
Keystrokes
    in macro creation, 476-477
    recording, 481
    recording method (macro), 499-500

L

Label alignment, 36-38
    comparing, 37
Label prefix character, 36, 37, 38
Labels, 31
    aligning, 96, 110-112
    entering, 32-33, (illus., 33)
    length limitation of, 39
    overlapping number, 34, (illus., 34)
Landscape mode, printing in, 135-136
LaserJet printer, 128, 133, 135, 142, 527. *See
    also* HP LaserJet.
    fonts for, 142
Layout options, 136-137. *See also* Page layout.
Legends, 288-289
    for graph text, 288-289
LENGTH function, 175, 484, 485
Libraries, macro. *See* Macro libraries.
Library option, 497
Line drawing feature, 147
Line graphs, 276, (illus., 276, 291)

Line length, 148
Line Types menu, 115
Lines
    drawing, 114-119
    drawing between cells, 115
Logical expression, 166
Logical formulas, 51
Logical recording method, in macro, 499-500, (illus., 500)
Look In option, 201-202
Lookup table, character string in a, (illus., 172)
Lookups, executing numeric, 172
Lotus 1-2-3, 500, 502, 527
    exchanging data with, 504-505
    extensions, 48
    format, 504
    menus, 9
    trading macros with, 504

M

Macro language, 495
Macro libraries, 497-499, (illus., 499)
Macro library, 480
Macros, 475-502
    applications for recorded, 493-494
    autoloading, 501-502
    changing recording method, 499-500
    copying, 497
    creating, 5, 476-478
    creating macro to execute, 487-488, (illus., 488)
    dangers to, 480
    database, 488-493
    date-stamping, 478
    deleting, 496-497
    documenting, 495-496, (illus., 496)
    editing, 487-488
    ending sessions with [CTRL-BREAK], 477
    errors in creating, 487
    in Lotus 1-2-3, 504
    in mouse palette, 25
    in Quattro Pro and Symphony, 504
    interpreting, 481-487
    naming, 479

Macros, *continued*
    pasting to spreadsheets, 477, 478-481, (illus., 481)
    reasons for, 476
    recording, 476-477
    renaming, 496-497
    replaying, 477
    startup, 501
    storing, 480-481, 497-498
Main menu bar, 8
    options, 9
Map view, 246-247, (illus., 247)
    uses of, 247
Margins
    changing for landscape mode, 135
    setting, 132-133
Match option, 202-203
MAX function, 161
Memo field data
    losing, 509
    translated into labels, 509
Memory
    availability of, 425
    computer, 45
    displaying, 425
    estimating amount of, 426-428
    expanded, 428
    freeing up, 426
    managing, 424
    recovering, 427-428
    running out of, 426-427
    utilizing, 424
Memory-resident software, removing, 426-427
Menu bar, 16
Menu command shortcuts, 272-274
Menu options, 16
Menu system, 16-20
    activating, 17
Menu-equivalent commands, (defined, 482)
Menus, pull-down, 17
MIN function, 161
MOD function, 223-224
    formula for, 223
Mode indicator, 12
Modes, 12
Monitor, color, 121-122

MONTH function, 221, 222
Month headings, creating, 228-230,
 (exercise, 228-229)
Months and days, displaying names of,
 224-225, (illus., 224)
Mouse, 9, 23-27, (exercise, 26-27)
 avoiding in macro creation, 477
 changing column width with, 36
 icons, (illus., 26)
 in data entry, 30
 palette, 9, 24-25, (illus., 25)
 pointer, 23
 pointing out blocks with, 80
 techniques, 23-24
Movement keys, 14-15
Moving data, 450
Moving files, with a paste command, 442

N

Names
 instant macro, 479
 standard macro, 479
Net income, calculating, 401, (illus., 402)
 two-variable table, 404, (illus., 405)
NOW function, 232-233, (exercise, 233)
NUM LOCK key, 14
Numbers, entering, 39-50, (exercise, 40)
 rules for, 39-40
Numeric data, formatting, 99-109
Numeric format
 changing for block, 105-108,
  (exercise, 105-106)
 changing the, 103-104
 of a block, 105-108
 trying another, (illus., 107)
Numeric values, aligning, 112

O

One-variable table, 398-401, (illus., 399,
 400, 402)
 form, 399
 setting up, 398-401
 uses of, 398

One-variable table, *continued*
 with databases, 405-407, (illus., 407)
 with two formulas, 400
Open-close graphs, 283-284
Operating system, exiting to, 430
Operators, 168-169
 complex, 168-170
 concatenation, 174
Options Reset, 203-204
Options/Hardware menu, (illus., 425)
Overwrite mode, 42
Overwrite protection, macro, 480
Overwriting, cell, 87, 88
 formulas, 87

P

Page breaks
 code for hard, 140
 codes, 140-141
 inserting, 139-141
 manual, 141
Page guide, 150
Page layout, 132-137
Page length, setting, 128, 132-133
Page numbering, 132
Pane key, 244
Panes
 synchronizing, 245-246
 unsynchronized, 245
Paper sizes, printing on different, 133
Paradox
 saving a file for, 507, 508
 trading data with, 505-513
Paradox access feature, 527
Paradox files, 506-508
 retrieving, 506
Parentheses, in changing calculation
 precedence, 60
Parity option, 125
Parsing
 ASCII text files, 517-524
 data, 518
 initiating the, 524
Passwords, 421-422
 assigning, 421

Passwords, *continued*
    erasing, 421
    invalid, 422
Paste
    macros to spreadsheets, 477, 478-481, (illus., 481)
    option, 479
PATH command, 416
Payroll, calculating, (illus., 235)
PCX format, 529
Percent format, 103
(PGDN) key, 14
(PGUP) key, 14
Pie and column graphs
    colors for, 319
    customizing, 316-320
    exploding pie slices in, 319
    fill patterns for, 318
    label format for, 316-317
    percentages in, 316
    second series for, 319-320
    tick marks for, 317-318
Pie graphs, 280, 298-300, (illus., 281, 299)
    exploded, (illus., 318)
    special labels for, (illus., 317)
Pie slices
    exploding options for, 319
    recycling excess, 318
Placement menu, 115
    options, 115
Plotter speed option, 126
Plus/minus format, 102
Point (mouse movement), 23
Point mode, in entering SUM function, 62
Point size, 143
Pointing method, 17
    in defining a block, 76-80
    in macros, 486
    including cell references with, 58-59
PostScript printer, 135, 143
Print layout, changing the graph, 303-304
Print options, 153-154
    updating graphs, 304-305
Printer codes, 134
Printer graphics, installing, 124
Printer specifications, saving, 127

Printers
    daisy wheel, 124
    dot matrix, 124
    laser, 120, 124
    selecting, 124-127
    serial, 125-126
    switching between, 126
Printing
    contents of a file manager window, 447-448
    draft-quality distinguished from high quality, 130-132, (illus., 131)
    graph to disk, 305
    graphs, 301-305
    inserted graphs, 307-308
    interrupting, 128
    large spreadsheets, 137-139
    spreadsheets, 123-154
    wide spreadsheets, 137-139, (illus., 138)
PROPER function, 175
Pull-down menu, 17

Q

Quattro Pro default, 326
Quattro Pro Users' Guide, 347

R

Recalculation
    automatic, 55-57, (illus., 57)
    circular cell indicator in, 271
    number of iterations in, 271
    order, 271
Recalculation mode, 270
Record option, 477
Recycling spreadsheets with automatic recalculation, 56
References, circular cell, 63-65
Reflex files, 506-508
    trading data with, 505-513
Reformatted text, 206-209, (illus., 207, 209)
Relative cell references, 86-87
REPEAT function, 175
    in macro recording, 485

Replace. *See also* Search.
    string, 198, 199
Resize box, 25
ROUND function, 163-166, (illus., 165)
Rounding
    errors, (illus., 164)
    number in default format, 100
Rows
    copying multiple-cell blocks across, 82-84, (illus., 83)
    deleting, 74-75
    inserting, 71-72, (illus., 72)
    within a block, 72-74
Ruler, in Screen Previewer, 150
Ruler option, in line adjustments, 149

S

Scientific format, 102
Scientific notation, 39
Screen commands, in macro language, 495
Screen Preview option, 128
    in column selection, 149
Screen Previewer, 149-152
    command keys for, (table, 151)
Screen type, 263
Scroll bars, 25
Scrolling, spreadsheet, 25
Search, 200-201
    block, 199
    by column, 200
    by row, 199-200
    direction, 199-200
    error message, 200
    for exact matches, 203
    for ranges of values, 202
    menu option for, 200
    prompt, 419
    simple, 198-199
    string, 198, 199, 201-203
    with the Next option, 199
    within spreadsheets, 201
Search and replace, (exercise, 200-201, 203-204)
    numeric digits, 204
    options, 201-204, (illus., 202)

Select function key, 79
Sensitivity tables, 397-413
Scientific format, 102
Scientific notation, 39
Screen commands, in macro language, 495
Screen Preview option, 128
    in column selection, 149
Screen Previewer, 149-152
    command keys for, (table, 151)
Screen type, 263
Scroll bars, 25
Scrolling, spreadsheet, 25
Search, 200-201
    block, 199
    by column, 200
    by row, 199-200
    direction, 199-200
    error message, 200
    for exact matches, 203
    for ranges of values, 202
    menu option for, 200
    prompt, 419
    simple, 198-199
    string, 198, 199, 201-203
    with the Next option, 199
    within spreadsheets, 201
Search and replace, (exercise, 200-201, 203-204)
    numeric digits, 204
    options, 201-204, (illus., 202)
Select function key, 79
Sensitivity tables, 397-413
    calculating, 404-405
    contents of, 398
    creating, 398
    using with databases, 405-410
Serial port, 125
Series. *See also* Graph series.
Settings, standard, 127-130
Setup strings
    embedded, 134-135
    using, 133-135
Shading, 114, 147
    effect of delete on, 121
    of cells, 119-122, (illus., 120, 121)
Shortcut key combination, 27

Shortcuts, command, (listed, 91)
Shortcuts, menu command, 36
Single sheet option, 127
Slide EPS format, 529
Solve For command, 526
Spreadsheet area, 8, 10
    dimensions of, 10
    splitting into sections, 10
Spreadsheet files
    alphabetical list of, 418
Spreadsheet linking, (illus., 466)
Spreadsheet links
    circular and heirarchical, (illus., 468)
    creating, 459-462, (exercise, 462-465)
    pointing to link references in, 460
    typing link references in, 459-460
    updating, 468-470
Spreadsheet Print option, 128
Spreadsheet programs, trading data with, 504-505
Spreadsheets, 4-5, (illus., 241, 455, 456, 463)
    accessing information in, 459
    adding values to, 452-453
    breaking complex models into small components in, 458
    circular links in, 467
    combining data from multiple, 473
    combining values, (illus., 457)
    copying link formulas in, 470-471
    creating links to all open, 460-462
    creating through linking, (illus., 461)
    defaults, 262
    deleting links in, 470
    graph values in other, (illus., 472)
    graphing linked, 471-473
    hierarchical linking of, 467-468
    inserting graphs in a, 306-308
    link references in unopened, 471
    linking, 5, 258, 457-473
    loading supporting, 466
    models too large for memory in, 459
    moving cells to different, 462
    moving formulas among, 471
    moving link formulas in, 470-471
    opening linked, 466-467

Spreadsheets, *continued*
    opening supporting, 468-469
    pointing to link references in, 460
    preventing duplicate data in, 458
    primary, 457
    protecting from disk failure, 429
    rearranging, 69-94
    refreshing linked formula in, 469
    saving and retrieving, 45-50
    subtracting values from, 453
    supporting, 457
    switching links between, 470
    typing link references for, 459-460
    update refs option in, 467
    with enabling protection, 214
SQL Link, 527
Startup, 7
    autoload file, 268
    directory, 268
    extension, 268
    macro, 268
    settings, 268
Status line, 9, 11-12
    divisions of, 11
Stop bits option, 125
STRING function, 239
String functions, 174-176
Style option, 144
Style sheets, creating, 272
Subdirectories, using, 417-418
SUM block, new rows in, 162
SUM chart, 160
SUM formula
    copying, (illus., 85)
    effect of move on, 77-78, (illus., 78)
SUM function, 61, 159-160
    inserting new cells in block with, 72-74
    pointing, 62
    typing a formula containing, 61-62
SYMBOL function, 132
Symphony, exchanging data with, 504-505

T

Table formulas, 398, 407

Table key (F8), 404-405
Tables, sensitivity, 397-413. *See also* Sensitivity tables.
Text design properties, changing, 340
Text elements
    editing, 340
    fine-tuning, 340-341
Text entry, 29-50
Text format, 103, 108-109, (illus., 109)
    problems with, 109
Text formulas, 51
Text graphs, 284, (illus., 284)
    creating, 341
Three-dimensional graphs, 285
Three-dimensional types, 285
Tick mark, 317
Time, 231-236
    displaying, 18, (illus., 19)
    entering, 232
Time arithmetic, 234-236
Time display formats, 233
Time formats, 103
TIME function, 231
TIMEVALUE function, 234, (exercise, 234)
Title, spreadsheet, (illus., 32)
Titles, for graph text, 287-288
TODAY function, 478
Toolbox, 330-332, (illus., 331)
    options, 330-332
    with EGA graphics adaptor, 330
    with VGA graphics adaptor, 330
Top Heading option, 137
Tree command, changing, 9
Two-variable tables, 398, 402-404, (illus., 403)
    building, 403-404
    form, 402
    generating database statistics with, 409-410, (illus., 410)
    setting up, 402-404
Type, condensed, 133
Typeface option, 143
Typing method, 17
    in defining a block, 76

U

UNDERLINE macro, 485, (illus., 485)
Undo feature, 69-71, (exercise, 70-71)
    enabling, 70
    operations, (listed, 70)
    precedence of, 70
    row deletion and, 75
Unzoom, 151
Update option, 127
UPPER function, 175

V

Value, 31
VLOOKUP function, 170-173, (illus., 171)
    syntax for, 170-171

W

What-if analyses, 397, 405. *See also* Sensitivity table.
Width
    adjusting column, 96-97
    changing for several columns, 98-99
Window commands, 238
Window, file manager, 432-433, 447-448
Windows, 237-260. *See also* Panes.
    activating, (exercise, 249)
    active, 249
    arranging, (exercise, 254-256)
    Both option for, 239
    closing, 249
    copying, (exercise, 259)
    copying and moving data between, 257-260
    customizing individual, 238-243
    entering data, 240-241, (exercise, 240-241)
    horizontal option for, 239
    horizontal panes for, (exercise, 245-246)
    horizontal split of, 243-244, (illus., 244, 245)

Windows, *continued*
    layered, 251
    locking, (exercise, 241-243)
    macros and, 480-481
    moving, 252, (illus., 253)
    moving around, 249
    moving and repositioning keys, 253
    moving and resizing, 252-254
    moving with a mouse, 253
    multiple, 254-256
    number of, 249
    opening, 248
    opening additional, 248
    opening and closing, 248-249
    panes, 243
    positioning the pointer to split, 243
    rearranging, (illus., 256)
    rearranging and resizing, 250-254
    rearranging open, 250
    saving, 254
    saving workspace for, 256-257
    shrink, 252
    split in two, 243-244
    stacked, (illus., 250)
    tiled, (illus., 251, 255)
    tiling and stacking, 250-251
    titles with, 238-243

Windows, *continued*
    vertical option for, 239
    vertical split of, 243
    zooming, 252
Workspace, saving and restoring a, 257
Wrap-around, formula, 88

X

XY graphs, 281, 300-301, (illus., 282, 302)
    dependent variable in, 281
    independent variable in, 281

Y

YEAR function, 222, (illus., 223)
    formula using, 222

Z

Zero
    attempting to divide by, 66-67, 90
    hiding, 114
Zoom, 149, 150, 151, 252
    box, 150
    icon, 24, 25

COMMAND CARD

EDITING KEYS

Key	Function
ESC	Discards changes and exits EDIT mode
LEFT ARROW	Moves cursor one space to the left
RIGHT ARROW	Moves cursor one space to the right
BACKSPACE	Deletes character to the left of the cursor
CTRL-BACKSPACE	Erases entry from the input line in EDIT mode
INS	Toggles between INSERT and OVERWRITE modes
DEL	Deletes character above cursor
TAB or CTRL-RIGHT	Moves cursor five spaces to the right
SHIFT-TAB or CTRL-LEFT	Moves cursor five spaces to the left
HOME	Moves cursor to first character in the entry
END	Moves cursor to last character in the entry
UP ARROW	Enters data, exits EDIT mode, and moves down one cell; if cursor is located after an operator, enters POINT mode
DOWN ARROW	Enters data, exits EDIT mode, and moves down one cell; if cursor is located after an operator, enters POINT mode
PGDN	Enters data, exits EDIT mode, and moves cell pointer down 20 lines; if cursor is located after an operator, enters POINT mode
PGUP	Enters data, exits EDIT mode, and moves cell pointer up 20 lines; if cursor is located after an operator, enters POINT mode

PREASSIGNED SHORTCUTS

Key Combinations	Menu Equivalents
CTRL-A	/Style l Alignment
CTRL-C	/Edit l Copy
CTRL-D	Date prefix (not reassignable)
CTRL-E	/Edit l Erase Block
CTRL-F	/Style l Numeric Format
CTRL-G	/Graph l Fast Graph
CTRL-I	/Edit l Insert
CTRL-M	/Edit l Move
CTRL-N	/Edit l Search & Replace l Next
CTRL-P	/Edit l Search & Replace l Previous
CTRL-R	/Window l Move/Size
CTRL-S	/File l Save
CTRL-T	/Window l Tile
CTRL-W	/Style l Column Width
CTRL-X	/File l Exit

©1990 Osborne/McGraw-Hill

Quatro Pro 2 Made Easy

FUNCTION KEYS

Key	Name	Description
F1	Help	Displays information about highlighted menu option or active function
F2	Edit	Enters EDIT mode; if in EDIT mode, returns to VALUE or LABEL mode
SHIFT-F2	Debug	Enters DEBUG mode, so you can execute a macro one step at a time
ALT-F2	Macro Menu	Displays the Macro menu
F3	Choices	Displays a list of existing block names for the current worksheet; press PLUS to display block coordinates
SHIFT-F3	Functions	Displays a list of Quattro Pro 2's functions; press PLUS to see function syntax
ALT-F3	Macros	Displays a list of macro commands
F4	Abs	In EDIT mode, makes the cell address to the left of the cursor absolute
F5	Goto	Moves the cell selector to a specified address or block name
SHIFT-F5	Pick Window	Displays a list of open windows
ALT-F5	Undo	If enabled, reverses last undoable action
F6	Pane	Moves the cell selector to the inactive window pane when the window is split into two panes
SHIFT-F6	Next Window	Displays the next open window

Key	Name	Description
ALT-F6	Zoom	Expands the active window so that it fills the screen; if active window is already zoomed, returns it to previous size
F7	Query	Repeats the last Query command
SHIFT-F7	Select	Allows you to select a block of cells in EXT mode
ALT-F7	All Select	Selects all files in the active File Manager file list
F8	Table	Repeats the last What-If command
SHIFT-F8	Move	Removes the files marked in the active File Manager file list and stores them in temporary memory so you can insert them somewhere else
F9	Calc	In READY mode, calculates any formulas that have been entered or changed since you turned off automatic recalculation; in VALUE or EDIT mode, converts the formula on the input line to its end result
SHIFT-F9	Copy	Copies the files marked on the active File Manager file list into temporary memory so you can insert them somewhere else
F10	Graph	Displays the current graph
SHIFT-F10	Paste	Inserts any files stored in temporary memory into the directory displayed in the active File Manager file list